ACKLAM CROSS

SEAHORSES OF THE TEES

Fig. 1 Lingdale *assisted by other units of the fleet taking control of* London Victory *after her launch from the Furness Shipyard, September, 1951.*

Seahorses of the Tees

The story of Tees Towing Company Limited

by
John H. Proud

John H. Proud

Tees Towing Company Limited 1985

The Author

Born within sight of the sea at Seaton Carew, County Durham (now Cleveland), John Proud has every excuse to have had over forty years' interest in matters maritime. However his interest in tugs stems from 1941 when he started his first job at a factory which overlooked the River Tees estuary and gave him the opportunity to observe the tugs of Tees Towing Company in action.

Later he spent over thirty years with Imperial Chemical Industries initially as a mechanical engineer working on the design, construction and maintenance of a great variety of chemical plants and in later years concerned with commercial and financial aspects of plant operation.

Now living in Middlesbrough, an early retirement gave him the opportunity to fulfil a desire to record the story of the foundation and development of Tees Towing Company and its tugs. This book is the result of that desire.

He is currently Chairman of the Teesside Branch of the World Ship Society.

Bert Spaldin whose contributions are incorporated in this book is a Hartlepool Pilot.

Cover Design: The specially-commissioned cover design for this book has been reproduced from an original painting by Barrie Wright of Kirkby-in-Cleveland. The design incorporates the outlines of the three tugs *Acklam Cross* of 1933, *Lingdale* of 1882 and *Greatham Cross* of 1976, seemingly viewed through a ship's port.

Front end paper shows: *Acklam Cross* in Middlesbrough Dock in September 1933 when newly-arrived from her builders in Aberdeen. From left to right on the monkey island, Captain Charlie Rounce and Cecil Crosthwaite; second from the left on the main deck, George Albert Robinson. In the background, a busy dock with Brocklebank and British India vessels in evidence.
(Stewart Bale)

Back end paper shows: *Temple Cross,* later to be the last steam tug in the Tees Towing fleet, towing the Ellerman liner *Andalusian* out of Middlesbrough Dock into the Dock Cut and thence to sea in 1949. On the bridge, Joe Purvis; third and fourth from the right on the deck George Robinson and N. Scott.
(W. Haig Parry)

First published in 1985 by Tees Towing Company Limited, Reg. Office: Cleveland Buildings, Queens Square, Middlesbrough, Cleveland TS2 1NX. From whom copies of this book may be obtained.

ISBN 0 9510232 0 9 (Hardback); 0 9510232 1 7 (Paperback).

Typeset in Baskerville and printed by Lithography by Studio Print, Admiral Chaloner House, Belmangate, Guisborough, Cleveland TS14 7AD, England.

Contents

Foreword

There are many reasons for a company deciding to have its history written. More often than not a centenary provides a convenient excuse and in our case the excuse is there if only because the history was started on the one hundredth anniversary of our founder's birth.

But the real reason is that four years ago John Proud – having taken early retirement from ICI – found that he had time to indulge a lifelong passion for tugs and decided to pay our company a visit. This history is the result of that visit.

This book is more than a history of the company: it is the story of a man, of a family, of the men who built up the company, and of every tug we ever operated. To tie it all together John Proud decided that my grandfather should occupy centre stage. Although he died sixteen years ago his impact is still felt especially in this year (1984) which is the fiftieth anniversary of the British Tugowners Association and the twenty-first anniversary of the European Tugowners Association – the two tug organisations which he founded.

Like all leaders his main contribution was to inspire others to give substance to his ideas. If a history like this sometimes gives the impression that leadership is everything it needs to be borne in mind that without the loyalty and hard work of hundreds of men nothing of any substance would have been achieved.

June 1984 — Richard Crosthwaite

Acknowledgements

My first acknowledgement must be to the Chairman and Directors of Tees Towing Co. Ltd. for their encouragement and assistance in enabling me to write this history. In particular to Richard Crosthwaite and Arthur Greenwell for their help in indicating where useful information could be found, for making available the company's photographic collection and latterly for reading and commenting upon the final text. Without their help the story in its present form could not have been written. In addition Arthur Greenwell allowed me to quote from his valuable record of towage activities related to the invasion of Normandy in 1944. Finally Richard Crosthwaite has written the Foreword to this volume. All of this help has been very much appreciated.

To my World Ship Society colleague Bert Spaldin I give my sincere thanks for the considerable contribution he has made to this book. Whilst the text has been written by me a large number of his contributions have been incorporated into the final result. His searches for elusive photographs and missing items from the Tug Histories section have proved invaluable. In particular he has provided information regarding the tug machinery throughout the period of this history and has prepared the Appendix regarding Funnel and Flag colours.

Without exception all of the employees of Tees Towing Company have been helpful in the extreme. I am most grateful to them all for the information they have provided. A most pleasant outcome has been that many of them I now count as being new found friends. Invidious though it may be it is necessary to mention a number of them by name but this is not to detract from the help given by them all. Bill Scrafton's assistance has been particularly valuable in searching for historical documents and photographs in the company records, without his help my task would have been impossible; Brian James, Bill Robinson, Vic Johnson, Ian Gardiner, Arthur Azemar, Bob Briggs, Ted Carr, Bob Fulton and Dennis Furnass and many others have always made me feel so welcome when pestering them with questions.

Not to be overlooked are the retired employees who kindly gave of their time to afford me long interviews with them. The information they gave was very valuable and in a number of cases has been tape recorded. My thanks go to them all; in particular to Brigadier and Mrs. Fairweather, Charles M. Duncan, Captain R. Harrison, Captain E. Watson Jnr. and Dick Hutchinson.

A great many individuals, societies and organisations have helped in the supply of information; I am most grateful to them. Particularly I must single out Mr. Bruce and his staff at the Middlesbrough Central Reference Library and the staff of the Middlesbrough Custom House for their considerable help, the former over a lengthy period of time. My thanks also go to B.V. Andrew; the County Archives Departments at Middlesbrough and Newcastle-upon-Tyne; Jim Barnett for information about the Duncan family; Tom Brown for heraldic details of the crest of Sir William Crosthwaite; Ian Brodie regarding *Electric Arc;* the Cleveland Scientific Institute; the Custom House at Glasgow; Soc. Esercizio Rimorchi E. Salvattaggi, Ravenna and Fremantle Tug Operators, Western Australia. Also to Dennis Gunn for details of the Crosthwaite memorial chair in St. Barnabas' Church; D.S. Hellier, author of "The History of the Tees Pilots"; Graham E. Langmuir for photographs; Jim Layton and other members of the

Teesside Branch of the World Ship Society; Lloyds Register of Shipping; Marine Survey Office of the D of T & I; Jack Marriott; the Mitchell Library, Glasgow; the Museum of Science & Engineering, Newcastle-upon-Tyne; Charles G. Robinson; Mr. and Mrs. Blackwell; Mr. and Mrs. Jim Rounce; Mr. and Mrs. Rounce, Australia. Similarly to Smith's Dock Company Ltd.; Stockton-on-Tees Reference Library; Straits Engineers Contracting Pte. Ltd., Singapore; South Shields Library Local History Room; The Tees and Hartlepool Port Authority and in particular Peter Quorn who set up their Study Centre during the period of the writing of this history.

I am indebted to those who carried out the typing of the early drafts of the manuscript, Irene Taylor, Sheila Vickers, Bert Spaldin and Ernest Wright all have my sincere thanks. As well as typing a large part of the drafts Sandra Whiteland of Tees Towing Company has produced the final typescript of the book; this she has done willingly and uncomplainingly despite the many minor alterations introduced at a late stage. I am very grateful to her for this important contribution.

Credits for the photographs are given along with the appropriate captions where the photographer or the owner of the copyright is known. Where none is given then the origin of the photograph is not known and it has usually come from the Company achives. Wherever possible an attempt has been made to obtain permission to reproduce photographs and to give due credit. If this has not been done in any particular instance then it is due to the fact that information as to the original photographer is not available. It is, therefore, inevitable, particularly with the older photographs, that some credits may have been omitted unintentionally. If this is so then I offer my apologies.

Finally my thanks must go to my wife Win for her unfailing support during the compilation of this book, for missing out on many hours of my company without complaint and for her practical help in reading, criticising and checking the manuscript.

Middlesbrough, 1984. John H. Proud

Abbreviations

AC	Alternating current.
BHP	Brake horse power.
BMMIA	British Marine Mutual Insurance Association Ltd.
DEMS	Defensively Equipped Merchant Ships.
DL	Deputy Lieutenant.
FCIS	Fellow of the Chartered Institute of Secretaries.
grt	Gross registered tonnage.
HP	Horsepower.
HWOST	High Water Ordinary Spring Tides.
ICI	Imperial Chemical Industries.
IHP	Indicated horsepower.
JP	Justice of the Peace.
LC	Lifting Craft.
LCT	Landing Craft Tank.
LNER	London and North Eastern Railway.
LST	Landing Ship Tank.
LWOST	Low Water Ordinary Spring Tides.
MA	Master of Arts.
MBE	Member of the Most Excellent Order of the British Empire.
MMS	Motor Minesweeper
ms	Motor Ship
OBE	Officer of the Most Excellent Order of the British Empire.
p.t.	per ton
p.g.	per gallon
QEII Jetty	Queen Elizabeth II Jetty.
RNR	Royal Naval Reserve.
rpm	Revolutions per minute.
SNO	Senior Naval Officer.
ss	Steamship.
TA	Territorial Army.
T & HPA	Tees and Hartlepool Port Authority.
TCC	Tees Conservancy Commissioners.
TD	Territorial Decoration.
VE Day	Victory in Europe Day.
VJ Day	Victory over Japan Day.

Introduction

My interest in ships, and particularly in tugs, stems from the time when, in 1941, I was working at a factory overlooking the then un-developed Teesmouth estuary and Seal Sands area. Although at that time the activities of the tug fleet of Tees Towing Company Limited were of prime interest to me it was not until about forty years later that I felt the desire to compile a history of the Company and its tugs. An approach to the management of Tees Towing obtained their approval and encouragement in the Autumn of 1981 and this present volume is the result.

An early decision had to be made as to just what this history should cover – and just as important, what it should not include – since the nineteenth-century story of towage on the River Tees is complicated and little documented. A satisfactory solution seemed to be to describe the period of existence of Tees Towing and its forbears throughout the lifetime of Sir William Crosthwaite and his descendants. Since Tees Towing is essentially a family firm this approach allowed the story of the family and the companies to be told in parallel throughout the period 1880 to 1983.

The history has been interspersed with local, national and occasionally international events so that the company story can be located in the time-scale of contemporary happenings. This procedure is useful for another reason in that the Crosthwaite family have been closely connected with a great many civic and other voluntary activities; thus their extra-business affairs can, for example, be linked into the growth and development of the town of Middlesbrough.

Part I details the Company history. The many inovatory developments introduced by Tees Towing are given special emphasis, although it is hoped, in not too technical a manner to discourage the general reader. All of the tugs and associated vessels owned or managed are referred to; where figures in brackets thus, (87/1884), follow a vessel name they refer respectively to the gross tonnage and the year of build; where the figures in brackets thus (1) or (2) appear after a name then these indicate that the vessel was the first (or the second) of that name in the fleet. Where the size of a vessel is of interest to the context then the dimensions in feet are the length x beam. Over the years the tugs have taken part in a great many salvage events. Brief descriptions of only a few of these are given and these are either taken from contemporary accounts or compiled from personal reminiscences.

A large number of people are mentioned by name in this history. Similarly many who could have been included have not been, primarily due to space limitations. My apologies in advance to those who may feel they have been overlooked. The illustrations in Part I have been largely chosen to illustrate the text and where this is so are cross-referred by Fig. No.

Part II gives the full technical details and the origins, histories and fates of almost all the eighty vessels owned to the end of 1983. About three-quarters of these histories are accompanied by a photograph which is intended to give the general appearance and outline of the particular tug. Photographs of all tugs acquired since 1933 have been found but, as one would expect, some of the earlier ones have proved elusive. If the reader can provide any of the missing photographs this would be appreciated.

Various Appendices complete the book giving supplementary information on vessel names, shipbuilders, engine builders, funnel and flag colours, the Seahorse insignia and ownership evolution and chronology.

'To the friends which the river has given me.'

PART I

THE COMPANY HISTORY

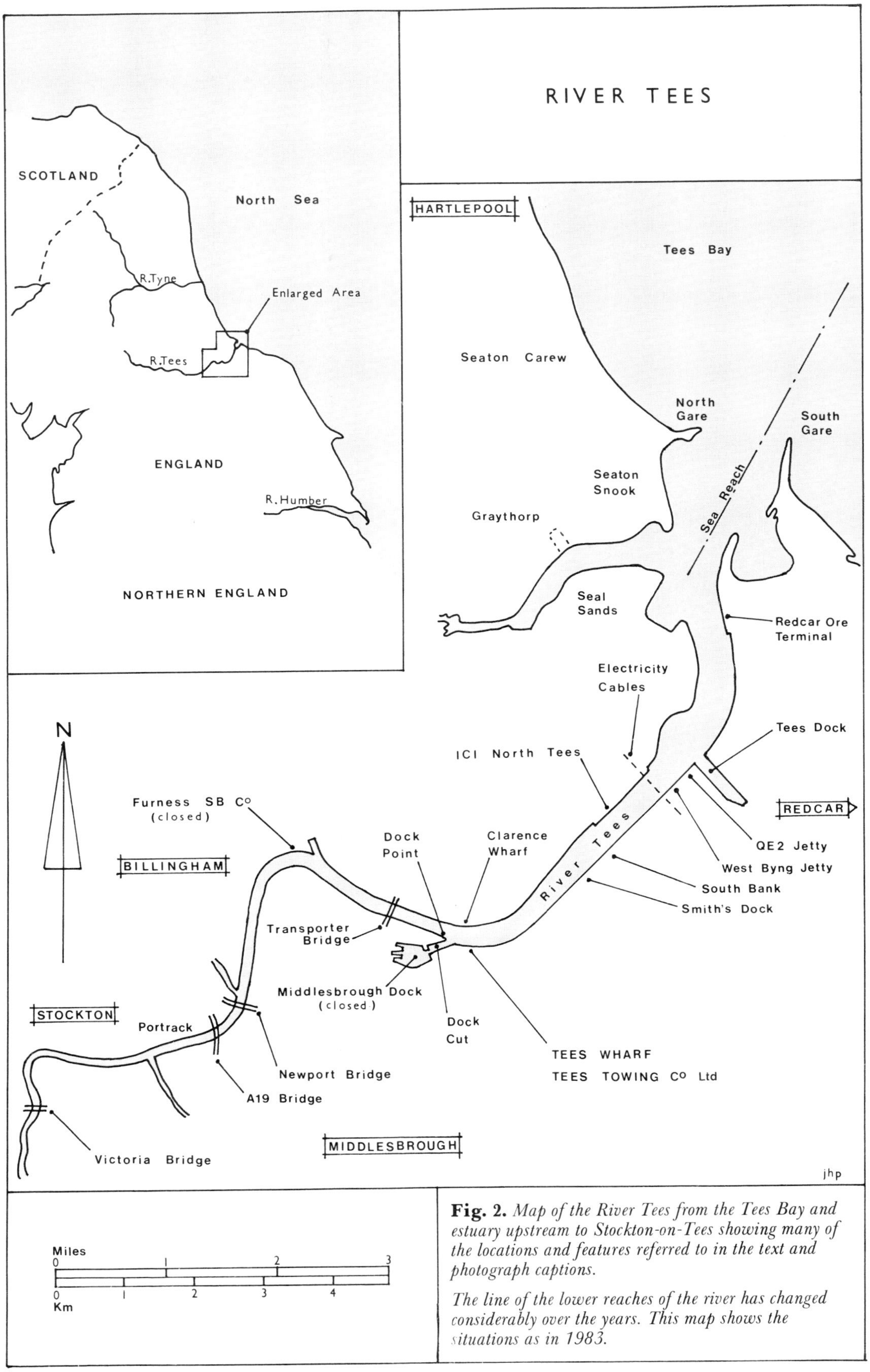

Fig. 2. *Map of the River Tees from the Tees Bay and estuary upstream to Stockton-on-Tees showing many of the locations and features referred to in the text and photograph captions.*

The line of the lower reaches of the river has changed considerably over the years. This map shows the situations as in 1983.

Chapter One

Tees Towing Company Limited

When the First World War ended in November 1918 it was a time when those who had survived looked forward to years of peace and prosperity. Forward also to a time when there would be a surfeit of work, business and trade whilst the deprivations and shortages of war were remedied.

It was in this period that the owners of the two major tug companies then operating on the River Tees in north-east England decided that they could operate more economically by amalgamating. It was thus that, in 1920 about one and a half years after the war had ended, Tees Towing Company Limited came into being by virtue of the combination of The Robinson Tug Company Limited and The Tees Tug Company Limited. Tees Towing Company Limited is the firm which exists today, sixty-four years on, as the sole tug operator based on the River Tees.

The period after the First World War turned out, however, to be far from producing the trade boom that had been expected and the infant company had to weather many years of recession and strife before it could be considered to be on a safe footing. Looking back it is perhaps surprising that it managed to survive at all; that it did so was no doubt due to the sound management of, initially, Charles William Robinson and William Henry Crosthwaite and later the latter on his own.

So the new company got off to a rough start; with its large fleet of twenty steam tugs it obviously had plenty on its hands. Before looking at the fortunes of Tees Towing Company in detail, it is necessary to go back in time not only to the early years of the twentieth century to review the formation and progress of its constituent companies but also back into the previous century to the time of the birth of William Crosthwaite.

In developing this story, as explained in the introduction, the lives of William Crosthwaite and his descendants have been taken as the central theme around which will be woven the histories of the companies with which they from time to time were associated.

So now to step back in time some forty years before the formation of Tees Towing, to the year 1880.

Fig. 3 *Thomas and Jane Crosthwaite and their family about the year 1900. Their six children are, left to right, back row; Frederick, John Thomas, Laura May, William Henry; front row; Elsie Charlotte and Frank.*
(Fairclough).

Chapter Two

William Henry Crosthwaite – His Early Life and First Excursions into Tug Ownership 1880-1908

William Henry Crosthwaite was born in Middlesbrough at 6 Elder Street on 1st July 1880. He was the eldest child of Thomas Crosthwaite, born in 1857 at Threlkeld in the English Lake District, and Jane Crosthwaite, born 1861 at the Yorkshire town of Tadcaster. What brought his parents to Middlesbrough from, what were in those days in terms of time, widely separated places is not known.

Thomas was working as a rolleyman (or, as we would call him today, a haulier). Crosthwaite seems to have been a rare surname for at that time no other families so-named appeared in the Middlesbrough directories and this is still so today.

Perhaps significantly William Henry was born only a few hundred yards away from the municipal and commercial centre of Middlesbrough, in which he was to contribute so much later on in his life. By 1895 William was to be joined by three brothers and two sisters; John Thomas, Frederick, Laura-May, Elsie Charlotte and Frank. (Fig. 3).

The house at Elder Street has been demolished in relatively recent times but the family's next home at 33 Montrose Street, Middlesbrough, where they were living by 1887, is still in existence and the whole street has recently been attractively renovated by the Endeavour Housing Association.

When William entered this world in 1880 he, like Tees Towing Company in 1920, arrived at a time of severe trade depression which on this occasion lasted from 1875 to 1888. As will be seen he was to experience several such periods of slack trading conditions during his long business career.

Middlesbrough was a town only 50 years old having sprung up in 1830 when the Stockton and Darlington Railway was extended from Stockton to Middlesbrough. Whilst the population in 1830 was negligible, occupying just a collection of farms and scattered cottages, by 1880 it was supporting 55,000 inhabitants.

Thus the town had reached its 50th Anniversary in the year William was born – but that event was not celebrated until October 1881 because of the trade depression. During his boyhood he attended the large Southend School in Boundary Road and he would no doubt have been aware in 1889 of the opening of the new Town Hall near his home by Their Royal Highnesses The Prince and Princess of Wales (later King Edward VII and Queen Alexandra). On this occasion the Princess started the Town Hall clock on the new building and although William would not know it at the time this small ceremony was to be of poignant significance to him and his future wife as far ahead as 1943. Also in 1889 he would have been old enough to notice that Middlesbrough, having been a Borough since 1853, because of its increasing size and with a population of then about 70,000 had been designated a County Borough.

Of major importance to the future prosperity of the River Tees, and of course to the business in which he was to become so deeply involved, was the completion of both the North and South Gare breakwaters (Fig. 2) at the entrance to the river by the time of his eleventh birthday. These erections were to give the much needed protection from the sometimes vicious North Sea so that deeper, well-defined channels and safe berths and anchorages could be provided for larger ships inside the estuary. Even so over 5,300 vessels were cleared on the river in the previous year albeit only small ones when compared to those of the present day.

On leaving school at 12 years of age William Crosthwaite was apprenticed, on the 15th September 1892, to James Harris, Ship Chandler, sail and nautical instrument maker. James Harris was at various times the Pilot Master, Collector of the Pilotage Dues and Secretary of the Tees Pilotage Commission and employed, as the manager of his ship chandlery, John Wesley Brown who was to become a lifelong associate of William Crosthwaite in business, municipal and political affairs.

Several sources state that William went to sea and served before the mast in sailing vessels and had voyaged round Cape Horn. Unfortunately no details have been left as to the shipping companies or the names of the ships with which or on which he served. The period when he was thus employed would have been approximately from 1897 to 1903.

On returning to Middlesbrough he would have observed some quite dramatic changes to his home town. In particular, Middlesbrough had expanded rapidly, the population now being over 90,000. Electric tramways had displaced the earlier horse drawn vehicles in 1898 and electric lighting was beginning to be publicly available. Ayresome Park football ground had been opened but there was still no crossing of the River Tees, other than by ferry, below the Victoria Bridge at Stockton-on-Tees 12 miles from the mouth of the river and 5 miles upstream from Middlesbrough. Nationally the country had been saddened by the death of Queen Victoria in 1901 after having so happily celebrated her Diamond Jubilee four years earlier. Edward VII had been crowned King in 1902. Internationally, the Wright Brothers had made the first sustained aeroplane flight in December 1903 at Kitty Hawk in the U.S.A. The rate of industrial development was clearly on the increase presenting a challenging prospect to anyone about to embark on a business career.

So it was that William Crosthwaite returned from his voyages and settled down to, as he was to describe it over 60 years later, a lifetime of work on and about the River Tees. He would naturally have had continuous acquaintance with the shipping, tugs and river craft in and around Middlesbrough Dock and the adjacent reaches of the river during his apprenticeship at the ship chandlery. For his work on behalf of his employer James Harris, when he left to go to sea, he was made a gift of a share in a tug; probably one sixty-fourth. No doubt it was this kindness which sparked off his interest in the towage business and that his aims for the future matured in his mind during the period he was away from home. In 1903 the towage business was highly competitive, there being at least seven companies in operation whose work ranged from the towage of barges to the handling of the largest ships then visiting Middlesbrough Dock. They were:

1. Florence Tugboat and Salvage Company Limited
2. North Eastern Railway Company
3. George Robinson
4. George Petrie

5. C.W. Duncan & Company
6. Charles Robinson
7. Tees Conservancy Commissioners

Some of the tugs of these companies would also at times carry out coastal towage to and from nearby ports and would need to go outside the river entrance and along the coast "seeking" their tows of incoming vessels.

The river at this time was, and of course still is, a major waterway that then formed the boundary between the North Riding of the County of Yorkshire and County Durham having risen high in the Pennines near Cross Fell. In its course of some 100 miles it passed over spectacular waterfalls and tortuously traversed the beautiful northern countryside ever widening as it is fed by its many tributaries. The river after having passed through the town of Barnard Castle, skirted Darlington, and almost encircled the one time port of Yarm, reached the industrial towns of Stockton-on-Tees and Middlesbrough having in its progress been transformed into a wide navigable highway for ships of many types and nations carrying their diverse cargoes. (Fig. 2)

But it was not always so. Before the Tees Conservancy Commissioners (TCC) took it in hand in 1852 and subsequently built many miles of half-tide training walls through its lower reaches seawards of Middlesbrough it broadened out into a wide estuary with several alternative channels and many shifting sandbanks. Navigation was then slow and costly and at times highly dangerous. However the work done by the TCC in confining the course of the lower river to a clearly defined, well buoyed and lighted channel coupled with its maintenance by dredging had made a dramatic difference. But it had taken a long time since controlling the forces of nature is never an easy task.

In the latter part of 1904 William Crosthwaite took his first step into tugownery (a contemporary description) when with his partners James Blumer and John Graham he bought the iron screw tug *Primrose,* (126/1883), then owned by the Florence Tugboat & Salvage Co. Ltd. She had a two-cylinder compound steam engine and had originally been the Aberdeen trawler *North Star.* Little is known of this and several other early tugs and no photograph of this vessel has been traced. The buyers of the *Primrose* let her remain as part of the Florence Company thus becoming, in effect, shareholders in the firm. This purchase was soon followed by the acquisition of the iron paddle tug *Challenger* (1),(104/1881), from J.G. Everson of South Shields. Like the *Primrose* the *Challenger* (1) was transferred to the Florence Company and it was thus that William Crosthwaite became the largest shareholder in the company. How he was able to finance his entry into tug ownership at the age of twenty-four has not been discovered.

The Florence Company had been incorporated in December 1902 with a capital of £5,000, its first directors being B.O. Davies and William Slater (Managing), and its initial shareholders were the directors together with Hariette Annie Harrison, Wm. Harrison, John Bryden, Wm. Stephenson Slater and Tom Slater. The company was formed to operate the tug *Florence,* (117/1879), which William Slater had recently purchased from T. Devlin, Jnr., of Edinburgh and of course the new firm had been named after the tug. She was paddle driven and constructed of iron and when newly built had worked at Maryport for over 20 years; she was destined to stay with the Crosthwaite companies for much longer than either the *Primrose* or *Challenger* (1). The offices of the company were at 7 Dock Street, Middlesbrough overlooking Middlesbrough Dock.

In early 1904 the double-engined iron paddle tug *Charles Dickens,* (121/1872), owned by the TCC since 1880 was purchased by the Florence Company. She was, however, sold again within a few months to one of the ironworks on the river. For the first eight years of her life she had worked on the Thames and was to be of service on the Tyne until 1915 when she was broken-up.

At the time that William had made his initial investment in the Florence Company that firm had owned five vessels one of which had subsequently been lost and one of which was in the process of being sold. There was, therefore, an active fleet of three tugs at the beginning of 1905; *Florence, Primrose* and *Challenger* (1) with an average age of 23½ years. William Crosthwaite was 24½ years old!

1904 had been an important year for William in another quite different respect for on the 27th July he married Ada Mary Elliott the eldest daughter of Captain George Elliott; they were to enjoy over 50 years of happy married life together.

By January 1906 the Florence Company, after having three managers in four years was found to be insolvent. Obviously the competition for business on the river was severe. William Crosthwaite took the company over on terms and became its manager and secretary though not a director. The directors were B.O. Davies, J. Blumer and J. Graham. At about this time the offices of the company were moved a short distance round the corner to 85, Lower Commercial Street, Middlesbrough (Fig. 7).

When the *Florence* came to the River Tees she already carried a carved symbol of the Seahorse (Hippocampus) and the motto "Facta non Verba" (Deeds not words) on the paddle boxes. When the *Florence* came under William Crosthwaite's management he adopted the symbol and the motto as his own and they both have been used by his companies to this day. (See Appendix E).

On 15th December 1906 William Crosthwaite's first child, a daughter, Alice Mary was born. Together with J. Blumer and J. Graham, William purchased the iron screw tug *Clarissa,* (92/1883), from the Cardiff owner W. Lee. They launched a new company named the Clarissa Tug Company c. 1907, to deal with its management. It is an interesting thought that W. Lee at Cardiff owned vessels named *Kings Cross* and *Charing Cross* and it might just be that during the transaction, William got the seed of an idea that stayed with him until eventually all his tugs bore ". . . . . *Cross*" names. For a small vessel only 86 feet long she had had her exciting moments – two substantial salvage awards and a collision in the Cardiff/Bristol Channel area – and more salvage awards were to come her way.

On the morning of 31st January 1907 occurred one of the worst shipping tragedies in and around the River Tees with the stranding of the outward bound *ss Clavering* (3328/1907, 325' x 46') on the North Gare sands. In the face of the NNE gale which was blowing right into the river entrance the Seaton Carew lifeboat found it difficult to approach the stricken vessel in the high seas. However with the help of the Robinson tugs *Hero* and *Glen Rosa* forty-two members of the crew were rescued by the late afternoon. Both of these tugs were, before long, to become part of William Crosthwaite's growing fleet. Charles Rounce and Wallace Robinson, respectively skippers of the *Hero* and the *Glen Rosa,* were later to become prominent figures in the Tees Towing Company organisation. The *Clavering* was not salvaged.

July of the same year saw the paddle tug *Challenger* (1) sold to Pounder of

West Hartlepool presumably for breaking up since her single–cylinder lever engine would have made her manoeuvring very difficult. However she was not scrapped but converted into a lighter and re-appears in our story again as late as 1929! She was replaced in the Florence Company's fleet by the London steel screw tug *Empress of India,* (138/1898).

Thus from mid 1907 through to the Spring of 1909 William Crosthwaite was managing a fleet of four tugs; three for the Florence Company and one for the Clarissa Company, one of the former being paddle-driven.

About this time the Tees pilots resorted to the use of chartered tugs as pilot cutters during periods of bad weather when their cobles could not venture outside of the river. Some of the Crosthwaite's tugs are likely to have been used for this purpose. This practice was to continue until 1914 when the Admiralty requisitioned the TCC tug *Joseph Constantine* as an examination vessel/pilot cutter and stationed her off the mouth of the Tees. Later, under another name, she was to become part of the Tees Towing Company's fleet in 1934.

Smith's Dock Company, during 1907, purchased a site at South Bank for the construction of a shipbuilding and ship repair yard. This was about two miles down-stream from Middlesbrough and was the beginning of the eastwards industrialisation of the riverside following the confining of the river by the construction of the training walls previously mentioned.

By 1908 William Crosthwaite had established his home at his newly-built house at 34, Newlands Road, Middlesbrough.

FLORENCE

The Tees Tug Company, Ltd.

IN WHICH IS INCORPORATED

WATKINS PETRIE, LIMITED.

W. H. CROSTHWAITE - Managing Director.

Owners of the Largest, most Powerful and best equipped Fleet of Tugs on the North-East Coast.

SCREW TUGS:

Empress of India, Liberia, Glen Rosa, Vixen, Knight of St. George, Primrose, Clarissa, Hero.

DOUBLE-ENGINED PADDLE TUGS:

Challenger, Champion, Florence, Triumph, Hibernia, Scotia.

National Telephone (all hours) - No. 357.

Telegraphic Address - "Tug, Middlesbrough."

15 DOCK STREET, MIDDLESBRO'.

Fig. 4 *An advertisement of the Tees Tug Co. Ltd. placed in the brochure "Ports of Middlesbrough and Stockton Annual" in 1913. As the advertisement indicates this was the time when the Watkins Petrie Company was absorbed.*

Chapter Three

The Constituent Companies 1909-1919

The year 1909 was the first important milestone in the process of integration of the individual towage companies on the River Tees culminating in the formation of Tees Towing Company Limited in 1920.

One of the significant competitors of Crosthwaite's Florence and Clarissa Companies was the firm of George Robinson and Company, who, in January 1909, owned six tugs. The Robinson Company had been in existence for about ten years and was owned originally by George Robinson, he later being joined by his three sons Charles William, Wallace Sinclair and George Albert. All of these sons were to figure prominently in the later parts of this story.

An important common denominator within the Florence, Clarissa and Robinson Companies was that one person, namely John Graham, was a director of them all. It is not, therefore, surprising that in his managerial role William Crosthwaite could see that a larger and more varied fleet would give him improved economy and flexibility of operation. No doubt John Graham played an important part in smoothing the way for the amalgamation which was about to take place. In this re-organisation the Florence and Clarissa Companies moved back around the corner once again to take over Robinson's offices at 15 Dock Street, whilst the Robinson's were shunted further along to 30a Dock Street! Thus it came about that a new company The Tees Tug Company Limited was incorporated on 24th May, 1909 to take over the Florence Tugboat and Salvage Company Limited with its three tugs, the Clarissa Tug Company with its single tug and five of the six tugs owned by George Robinson & Company, hence forming a combined fleet of nine tugs; three paddle and six screw. The company's initial capital was £45,000. The first directors of the Tees Tug Company were James Blumer, John Graham and William Robinson Lister but not William Crosthwaite who, although a substantial shareholder, preferred to remain as Manager and Secretary. As well as the tugs *Florence, Primrose, Empress of India* and *Clarissa* which William Crosthwaite already managed he now took control of *Glen Rosa,* (110/1895), *Champion,* (124/1876), *Challenger* (2), (153/1873), *Hero,* (66/1892), and *Vixen,* (119/1896), which previously had been part of the Robinson fleet. This fleet of nine vessels was still fairly elderly; the average age being 23 years.

Reference to the Block Diagram at Appendix F will assist the reader to understand the many transfers, purchases and sales of tugs during this complicated event.

All this reorganisation did not mean that the Robinson Company was to disappear from the scene; far from it. Although, after the transfer, they had only one remaining tug, *Nunthorpe*, they too formed a new company in 1909 with a capital of £10,000, namely The Robinson Tug Company Limited, and were soon, by purchases, to develop into the owners of a sizeable fleet again. The first manager of this company was George Albert Robinson but he soon gave way to Charles William Robinson, both of them being sons of George Robinson.

All of these changes would appear to have taken place in an atmosphere of friendly co-operation and no doubt were made in furtherance of operating economies and efficient operation of a more balanced fleet. Therefore, operating side by side on the river with offices very near to each other they were to continue in friendly competition for another eleven years before further amalgamation took place.

This must have been an exciting and exacting year for William Crosthwaite because it is likely that most of the work of re-organisation would have fallen on his shoulders. Further excitement, outside of his business life, was the birth of his son Cecil who was later to succeed him in his tug ownership business.

Smith's Dock had, by now, begun building and repairing ships at their new yard at South Bank. Here, therefore, was a potential for more work for tugs. The future must have looked rosy for the 29 years old William Crosthwaite at the end of 1909.

But there were still problems too; and rules to be worked to even in the early days of the century. Just prior to the *Hero* being transferred to The Tees Tug Company from George Robinson her skipper was fined £2.14s.6d. (£2.725) for depositing Night Soil from a barge only one mile off the South Gare whereas he should have been at least three miles out to sea! At that time there was a considerable amount of barge and lighter traffic around the river and some of this involved the dumping at sea of domestic and industrial waste. Still it all provided work!

After all the activity of 1909 there was, not surprisingly, a period of relative quiet as the tugs of the newly-formed companies went about their normal business of manoeuvring ships and barges to and from their river or dock-side berths and standing by to assist vessels to their fitting-out quays following a launch from one of the several shipyards. As regards towage of incoming ships there was still a considerable element of luck as to which company's tug was able to hail the new arrival first and thus obtain the job. Tugs would need to go "seeking" by steaming up or down the coast in the hope of meeting a ship which was intending to enter the Tees. Once away from base the only means of communication would be by visual signals.

In 1910, King Edward VII died and King George V became King, William Crosthwaite was 30 years old and managing The Tees Tug Company, with his now well known drive and energy. Competition on the river was still strong; as well as the friendly co-existence with The Robinson Tug Company there were notably the companies of George Petrie and C.W. Duncan both with sizeable fleets of tugs. Still the volume of traffic on the river had, if anything, increased although most of the ships were still quite small.

In later years William Crosthwaite, when he became deeply involved in municipal affairs, was a strong advocate of the amalgamation of all the local authorities which surrounded the lower reaches of the River Tees. This integration actually took place in 1968, with the formation of the County Borough of Teesside. It is interesting to note that in 1910 William Crosthwaite made a speech which sparked off a discussion regarding formation of a greater Teesside. This subject appears at regular intervals in the local press over more than fifty years, so there can be no doubt of his persistence in pursuing this question.

On the international scene there was already much uncertainty and real fears of a war developing in Europe. On the local front Middlesbrough was still expanding and several significant events took place during 1911. The town had now a population of approximately 105,000 and was steadily spreading southwards through the villages of Ayresome and Linthorpe. On the river there had long been a need for a road crossing between the Yorkshire and the Durham sides below the Victoria Bridge at Stockton-on-Tees. This was met by the opening of the famous Transporter Bridge between Middlesbrough and Port Clarence which on a suspended moving platform carried both foot and vehiclar traffic. (Fig. 2). The bridge was opened by Prince Arthur of Connaught on the 17th October 1911 and with its coming into operation the existing ferries were displaced. The bridge which operates to this day is 5 miles from the mouth of the river and gives 160 feet clearance to shipping at high water. Plenty of headroom for the local tug fleets!

Due to the scouring effects caused by the erection of training walls in the lower reaches of the river the depth of water on the bar had increased from only 3½ feet to 20 feet at L W O S T and to 37 feet at H W O S T; thus there was now the facility to encourage the use of the river by deeper draught ships thereby increasing the tonnage throughput. The largest vessel to have visited to river by 1911 was the *Kamo Maru* (8524/1908, 473' x 54').

No less than one hundred new ships were built on the River Tees in 1911 but fifty-five of these were small vessels of the trawler or whale-catcher type, built by the recently opened Smith's Dock at South Bank.

On the 15th November 1911 William Crosthwaite's wife gave birth to their third child – a second daughter who was christened Dorothy Elliott.

In 1912 William Crosthwaite was elected an Associate of the Chartered Institute of Secretaries, and had moved house further along Newlands Road to No. 56. He would have seen the town's new Public Library opened. No changes had taken place in the tug fleets under his management since the formation of The Tees Tug Company Ltd. in 1909.

Watkins Petrie Limited had been formed in 1911 when the Tees based company of George Petrie amalgamated with the Thames tug company of William Watkins Limited who wished to expand their activities to other parts of the British Isles. George Petrie had inherited his company from his uncle Alex Petrie who had died c. 1895. To build up the combined fleet Watkins had moved some of their Thames tugs to the Tees to work alongside those owned by Petrie. However the venture was short lived as Watkins found that having their attention divided between the two rivers did not work out in practice. So it came about on the 1st January 1913 that The Tees Tug Company absorbed the Watkins Petrie concern. Some of the tugs involved in this transfer namely *Knight of St. George,* (129/1885), *Hibernia,* (237/1874) and *Scotia,* (263/1874), were quickly scrapped and did not actually enter the service of The Tees Tug Company but those that did were the *Liberia,* (128/1905), a steel screw tug with a triple expansion steam engine, the first to be so equipped under William Crosthwaite's management and the *Triumph,* (76/1875), an iron-hulled paddle tug. (Fig. 4). The Petrie organisation had been called the Red Star Line Steamboats each of their paddle tugs sporting a red star on the forward and aft faces of the paddle boxes.

In this year, 1913, William Crosthwaite became Managing Director of The Tees Tug Company. By the middle of the year he had decided to sell the screw tug *Empress of India* to the Anglo Persian Oil Co. Ltd. by whom she was renamed *Sirdar-I-Naphte.* After alterations on the Tyne she sailed out to Persia (now Iran). Unfortunately she did not last very long in her new owner's hands since she foundered in the Persian Gulf in 1915.

At the end of 1913 Tees Tug's fleet had grown to 10 vessels with an average age of 28 years; four paddlers and six screw driven. Middlesbrough town had also continued to grow, its population was now 122,000 and with an eye to the future the North Eastern Railway had purchased 1000 acres of the Wilton Estate on the south bank of the river for dock construction. This area, however, was never developed by the railway companies and it was to be 50 years later in 1963 that a new dock was opened on the same site by the TCC. Some wheels certainly grind slowly!

The River Tees had handled 5.8 million tons of cargo and cleared 5,644 ships in the year.

During 1914 the tugs *Glen Rosa* and *Liberia* went to the River Thames on charter to William Watkins Ltd. the latter vessel thus going back temporarily into the hands of her earlier owners.

At home the tendency was for vessels visiting the port to become larger. The record for size was now held by the *Llandovery Castle*, (11,423/1914, 500' x 63'), which sailed in January on her maiden voyage to East Africa via the Suez Canal. When a hospital ship, late in the forthcoming war, she was torpedoed without warning and sank with large loss of life, the occurrence becoming one of the worst episodes of the First World War at sea. The handling of such large vessels through the narrow 80ft. entrance to Middlesbrough Dock would be quite a problem for the tugs which were fitted with engines of from only 220 to 450 indicated horsepower. Strangely it was the two tugs at the top end of this power range which were sent away to the Thames.

The company of Charles Duncan & Sons Ltd. was incorporated on the 28th May 1914 for the purchase of the tugs *Ida Duncan*, (139/1891), and *Frank*, (76/1896), – the latter for £2,300 – from C.W. Duncan & Company. This latter company which had been formed c. 1900 then went into liquidation. The directors of the new company were Charles William Duncan, Charles William Robinson and William Henry Crosthwaite who together with The Tees Tug Co. Ltd. held the company capital of £10,000 represented by £4,000 in preference shares and £6,000 in ordinary shares. It was in this way that Charles Duncan & Sons Ltd. became an associate company of The Tees Tug Co. Ltd. C.W. Duncan remained as the nominated manager of the Duncan side of the business. Thus was forged a link with the past for the Duncan family had been associated with pilotage, ferry operation and tug ownership on the River Tees for many years. Indeed Charles William's father Charles Chrystal Duncan had also been a tug owner on the Tees. Charles William Duncan worked as skipper towing barges and lighters over virtually the whole length of the English and Scottish east coasts. It is on record that few men in those days knew the east and north-east coast ports of England as he did. One of the tugs which he owned for a while was the gloriously named paddle vessel *Citie of the Tribes*, (117/1872), so named after the Irish town of Galway from whence she came. However she had left the fleet to be broken up by the time that the Duncan Company joined forces with The Tees Tug concern.

It is interesting to note that the Duncan, Robinson and Crosthwaite families at one time serious competitors, had now come together for the first time as directors of the newly formed firm of Charles Duncan & Sons. The Duncan and The Tees Tug Companies shared an address at Dock Chambers, Dock Street which may have been the same accommodation at 15, Dock Street previously occupied by The Tees Tug Company.

At this time too, The Robinson Tug Company had moved to the other side of the railway line at 5, Exchange Place hard by the Albert Bridge.

Whatever else happened in 1914 it must have been overshadowed in August by the outbreak of the war with Germany. Apart from the personal worries of the time many would have wondered what would happen to the trade of the River Tees with, as it were, the North Sea being the no-mans-land between the warring countries. Would there be less traffic? Would there be more traffic? Would there be naval (or even air) attacks on the area? Nobody knew for sure but what they did know was that any change at all in the type or pattern of traffic would most certainly affect the operations of the towage companies. Time only would tell.

In November 1914 The Tees Tug Company purchased from the Dover Harbour Board the iron paddle tug *Lady Vita*. Renamed *Lingdale*, (174/1882), before the end of the year, she was to become the most familiar and best-loved tug on the River Tees. Often referred to as the 'Old Lady' as reference to her original name she was to be seen on the river until 1954 when almost 72 years old she went to the breakers at Gateshead on the Tyne. Her striking appearance with two upright funnels arranged athwartship made her unmistakeable. She is to be seen in several photographs at the stern of many a trading vessel or manoeuvring a newly launched ship to her berth. Her long life is reputed to have been due to the fact that not only was she built of iron but she was built of Lowmoor Iron which was of very high purity and quality made by Lowmoor Best Yorkshire Iron Ltd. of Bradford. *Lingdale* had a two-cylinder side-lever disconnecting engine and would be ideally manoeuvrable for work at the stern of a towed vessel. (Fig. 5). She was, however, to leave the River Tees temporarily when requisitioned by the Admiralty for work in the Grand Harbour, Malta where she remained from 1916 to 1919.

Also in November 1914, the screw tug *Vixen* was renamed *Archdale*. Why this change took place and why this particular name was chosen has not been discovered. *Archdale* was requisitioned by the Admiralty for a time during the First World War and it may be it was they who insisted on a name change to avoid

Fig. 5 Lingdale *in the River Tees proceeding up river opposite Clarence Wharf, c.1915, shortly after her purchase by The Tees Tug Co. Ltd.*

confusion with existing naval ships. A second possibility is that William Crosthwaite desired to create a fleet having "....... *Dale*" names, since there were to be four vessels with names on this theme. If he did then it was only a passing thought for no such names were introduced after 1925.

On the 16th December 1914 people in the area of the Tees Bay were awakened by the noise of heavy gunfire which put feelings of fear and dread into them. It was the bombardment of Hartlepool and West Hartlepool by a German fleet which they were hearing. Many believed that the shelling was the precursor to an invasion and departed from the towns on foot into the surrounding countryside. The Middlesbrough area was not attacked although its densely packed industry along the banks of the river would have made an easy target. Whitby and Scarborough were bombarded on the same day.

At the end of the year the iron screw tug *Primrose* was broken up when 31 years old, her last eleven years having been spent on the River Tees. With the year's other changes The Tees Tug and Duncan Companies now had between them the significant fleet of twelve vessels.

Since 1909, when the Robinson Company was severely depleted due to the transfer of most of its vessels to The Tees Tug Company it had not stood still for it had or was to have no less than eight tugs added to its fleet most of which came from outside of the Tees river. They were *Athlete,* (119/1893), (Fig. 6.), *George Robinson,* (95/1896), *Adonis,* (80/1875), *Pendennis,* (73/1863), *Samphire Batts* (174/1893), *Cleveland,* (172/1881), *Privateer,* (117/1883) and *George Peabody,* (115/1867) in the order of acquisition. *Athlete, George Robinson* and *Samphire Batts* were screw tugs and the others were paddle tugs. There was, therefore, all told a very considerable fleet of tugs available to work about thirteen miles of river; attend to the continuing launches; deal with whichever of the 5,000 vessels trading to the river needed towage and cover the demand of local coastal barge and ship traffic.

In the years ahead several of the persons involved in the management of the tug companies which appear in this history became immersed in municipal affairs and public service in one way or another. The first to do so was John Graham, a director of The Tees Tug Company, who was elected to Middlesbrough Town Council in 1915, serving until his death in 1927.

February 1915 saw Charles Duncan & Sons purchasing the trawler *Lionel* for £975 from North Shields and converting her for towage purposes. Within a few months she was renamed *Dora Duncan,* (126/1891), and was soon requisitioned for work with the Admiralty for most of the remainder of the war. Her master was Lionel Duncan one of the sons of Charles William Duncan. Before she went away on war service she was to hit the headlines in the local press when one of her crew, L. Robinson, assisted by George Alder saved three boys from drowning in the river near Dock Point. For a while she was liberty ship for the naval submarine depot ships stationed at Teesport.

More tugs did not necessarily mean more business on the river for the end of 1915 found the number of ships cleared on the River Tees down to only just over 3,000. Obviously the level of trade on the east coast of England was being much affected by the war. Perhaps, though, the increase in naval traffic went some way in recompense. At about the time of the Battle of Jutland, which both sides claimed as a victory, the *Lingdale* was on her way to Malta under Admiralty orders. B.O. Davies, previously a director of the Florence Company when William Crosthwaite first became involved in tug operation was elected a Tees

Conservancy Commissioner representing Middlesbrough shipowners.

Their majesties King George V and Queen Mary visited the shipyard of William Harkess and Son Ltd. on the 14th June 1917. This yard was quite near to the offices and centre of tug operations so that, no doubt, William Crosthwaite and his employees would have been cheered by the visit during the dark days of war. Another shipyard on the river was in its embryo stages since the Furness Shipbuilding Company had purchased a site on the north bank at Haverton Hill. In the years to come this yard was to provide much work for the tug companies at launches and ship trial trips. The Furness yard was to produce the largest ships built on the river.

If these were some of the high spots of the year 1917 there were however tragedies too. On the 31st January *Ida Duncan* struck a mine a half mile east of the South Gare lighthouse and sank with the loss of all hands. She had innocently been towing some barges of rubbish to sea for dumping and had no defence whatever against such a devastating explosion. Charles William Duncan lost his two sons Charles Chrystal and Lionel in this disaster; the former aged 30 being the engineer and the latter at 28 being the skipper. The death of Charles Chrystal Duncan was all the more tragic since he was not a member of the crew but was merely standing-in for someone whilst home on leave from the Merchant Navy. His son Charles Marshall Duncan was later to become the Marine

Fig. 6 Athlete *aground in the River Tees, c.1912 when in the ownership of The Robinson Tug Co. Ltd. Note the Robinson funnel markings. (Thirlwell & Co.)*

Superintendent of Tees Towing Company. The others in the crew, all lost, were Harry Scott and T. Walker both firemen; R. Tinmouth, deckhand and James Gibson, cabin boy. No less than sixty-five years later in 1982 the Teesmouth Sub-Aqua Club divers found, in almost undamaged condition, the bridge telegraph and steam whistle from what is almost certainly the wreck of the *Ida Duncan.*

Just two months later a very similar tragedy was to be enacted off the entrance to Sunderland harbour when the *Hero*, a small tug only 78 feet in length, struck a mine and sank. In this incident the master lost his life but the remainder of the crew were saved. The names of those involved are, in this instance, not known. So after 2½ years of war with no losses The Tees Tug and Duncan fleets had each suddenly suffered a severe blow.

Another casualty occurred on the 26th October 1917 when the Robinson paddle tug *Cleveland* sank at the foot of the training wall at the south side of Sea Reach and she remained there for some months. The reason for this episode seems not to have been recorded. The Robinson Tug Company had bought *Cleveland* from the North Eastern Railway in January 1914 when the railway company minuted the transaction as follows:-

> "*Cleveland* sold to the Robinson Tug Company of Middlesbrough for £2,700 (at short notice because the price was felt to be a favourable offer considering the tug's condition)."

Notwithstanding this comment she was not re-boilered until 1924 and remained in service on the River Tees for another 33 years before being broken up!

During February of 1917 Charles Duncan & Sons bought the paddle tugs *Privateer,* (117/1883), and *Adonis*, (80/1875), for £1,450 and £100 respectively from The Robinson Tug Company; the latter had a wooden hull. Presumably they were acquired quickly to make up for the loss of the *Ida Duncan.* Both had only single side-lever engines and therefore could not have been very manoeuvrable as tugs. *Privateer* had started her career in 1883 as a passenger pleasure vessel in the south-west of England as the illustration in Part II of this volume shows.

At about the same time Duncans purchased the *Fifeshire*, (146/1887), for £1300 from Kirkcaldy owners. She also was a single-engined paddle tug and had originally been the *Flying Swallow* of the Clyde Shipping Company when built. *Fifeshire* was not to stay in the fleet for long since by 1919 she had gone back to Scotland to work in the Firth of Forth.

The Tees Tug Company also needed to replace their loss of the *Hero*. This they did by purchasing the *Marie* from Kings Lynn. She was an iron paddle tug already 42 years old and was soon renamed *Monsdale*, (77/1875), by her new owners and nicknamed "Mongoose" by her crew.

At the end of 1917 William Crosthwaite would have seen that the combined fleets of The Tees Tug and Duncan Companies, with which he was involved, had increased in number to fourteen vessels and that their average age had leaped up to 33 years. This would today be an unbelievable age for a fleet but was no doubt due to the longevity of iron hulls and steam operated machinery which was simple and usually very reliable. Of the fourteen tugs, one had a hull of wood, nine were made of iron and four were constructed in steel. The oldest tug was *Challenger* (2), built no less than forty years previously and the newest was *Liberia* just twelve years old; all fourteen had of course been second-hand purchases.

When the first World War came to an end in November 1918 there were quite naturally, hopes of a quick return to normality and for the trade of the River Tees to expand to new levels of activity. But it was not to be that easy.

About the time of the Armistice a rather unusual event occurred involving the paddle tug *Triumph* whose skipper was Charlie Rounce. He had come upon the semi-submerged remains of a seaplane not far from the Eston (Teesport) submarine base with the pilot still clinging to the wreckage. The pilot was taken aboard the *Triumph*, dried out, and taken back to the seaplane base at Seaton Snook (near the present day nuclear power station). Such an event would no doubt have broken the normal routine of towing duties when one remembers that only fifteen years had passed since the Wright Brothers had made the first flight in an aeroplane.

On the river generally the Furness Shipbuilding Company launched their first ship and it is likely that at least one of William Crosthwaite's tugs would have been in attendance. Much nearer the mouth of the river, off Greatham Creek, and near to the seaplane base William Gray & Company began developing a drydock and ship repair yard at Graythorp. Since the approach to this yard was both narrow and twisting it was obvious that more work for tugs would result from this development.

During 1918 there was no change to The Tees Tug Co. fleet but Charles Duncan & Sons, firstly in August, purchased the small barge-tug/ communications launch *Lily* from John Thomas Mitford of Middlesbrough. This vessel, built as early as 1866, had passed through several owners' hands and been subject to much modification after starting life as a sailing trawler. Nevertheless she was, by 1919, rebuilt again by Teesbank Engineering Company, Middlesbrough, a firm engaged in ship repair and general engineering and owned by William Crosthwaite and John Wesley Brown. Later, in October 1919 she was renamed *Lily Duncan*, (28/1866). There is no doubt that a vessel of this kind used for communication between the tug office, pilots, dock master and the tugs could be very valuable when one remembers how rudimentary were the means of contacting tugs at work in the river from Stockton-on-Tees to the South Gare.

Secondly, in October, Duncans purchased a vessel named *Comet* which was to be used in a similar way to the *Lily Duncan*. She too had had a chequered career having suffered a boiler explosion on the Tyne in 1890. No doubt she had also been rebuilt. Charles Duncan & Sons renamed her *Betsy Duncan*, (29/1889).

It will be remembered at the beginning of this story that Tees Towing Company was formed by amalgamation in 1920. Having now related the events that led up to the arrangements of that year the reader will note that as well as following the Crosthwaite line of interest the narrative has, from time to time, kept abreast of what was happening to The Robinson Tug Company. This has been done so that when the fleets combined in 1920 it would readily be seen that the Robinson Company was making a full contribution to the merger. In 1919 Charles William Robinson entered the fishing business and became a trawler as well as a tug owner. He formed the Ebor Fishing Co. Ltd. when he purchased the trawlers *Nellie Dodds* and *Grannweal* which were promptly renamed *Ebor Abbey*, (220/1911), and *Ebor Belle*, (174/1909), respectively. Three other newly built vessels *Ebor Court*, (276/1919), *Ebor Downs*, (275/1919), and *Ebor Elect*, (275/ 1919), were also taken into the fleet. It is interesting to note the alphabetical sequence A to E of the naming of these trawlers. The fishing business was operated from the small tidal Corporation Dock on the south side of the river just upstream of the Transporter Bridge and from Aberdeen. Although the fishing business was not to be very long-lived William Crosthwaite became involved with it due to the 1920 amalgamation – perhaps involuntarily.

A few days after the end of the war the screw tug *Archdale* was sold. She was soon however replaced by the *Lingdale* on her return from war service at Malta.

At this time the tug moorings were normally on the North Wharf of the Dock Cut which was the channel leading from the river to the lock gates of Middlesbrough Dock. The Company had a small cabin there from which the tugs would be controlled and from which minor repair and servicing could be carried out. Coaling facilities were available further along North Wharf towards Middlesbrough Dock and just around the Dock Point corner on the south bank of the river proper.

The trade of the river had dropped steadily throughout the war and during 1919 only about 2,100 ships had been cleared. It was to be a long time before the numbers of ships reached pre-war figures again.

As the decade ended John Wesley Brown was elected a Middlesbrough Town Councillor. He continued in this public service, later as an Alderman, until his death in 1944.

Fig. 7 *Letterheads of some of the companies referred to in this history. That of the Florence Company was in use about 1908, that of the Duncan Company about 1922 and the Tees Towing heading is of the present day.*

Chapter Four

Amalgamation – The Early Years of Tees Towing Company Limited 1920 - 1925

It is clear that William Crosthwaite now 39 years of age had for quite a long time been logically working forward to the day when the tugs on the River Tees would be combined into one large fleet. It would seem likely that he had had this plan in his mind since The Tees Tug Company was formed in 1909 and that with persistence he was, piece by piece, slowly achieving his objective. As well as part of the Robinson fleet, Watkins Petrie and Duncans there had been other minor acquisitions from Thomas Eason and William Lennard where the vessels were either broken up or disposed of immediately.

Tees Towing Company Limited was formed to acquire the assets of The Tees Tug Company Limited and The Robinson Tug Company Limited both of which had themselves been formed in 1909 as previously related. The new company was officially incorporated on 9th April 1920 and this date represents the second important milestone in this history. Once again it will help the reader to follow the changes of ownership of the vessels by making reference to Appendix F.

The fleets thus drawn together by the amalgamation were:-

		Book valuation at Transfer
Tugs ex The Tees Tug Co. Ltd.		
Steam paddle tug	*Florence*, (117/1879).	£1,972
Steam screw tug	*Clarissa*, (92/1883).	2,543
Steam screw tug	*Glen Rosa*, (110/1895).	3,600
Steam paddle tug	*Challenger*, (2) (153/1873).	1,900
Steam screw tug	*Liberia*, (128/1905).	8,091
Steam paddle tug	*Triumph*, (76/1875).	1,150
Steam paddle tug	*Lingdale*, (174/1882).	4,090
Steam paddle tug	*Monsdale*, (77/1875).	1,055
		£24,401
Tugs ex The Robinson Tug Co. Ltd.		
Steam paddle tug	*Nunthorpe*, (122/1876).	£ 5,000
Steam screw tug	*Athlete*, (119/1893).	4,750
Steam screw tug	*George Robinson*, (95/1896).	6,000
Steam paddle tug	*Pendennis*, (73/1863).	2,500
Steam screw tug	*Samphire Batts*, (174/1893).	7,250
Steam paddle tug	*Cleveland*, (172/1881).	5,000
Steam paddle tug	*George Peabody*, (115/1867).	668
		£31,168
	Total	**£55,569**

A total of nine paddle and six screw tugs; these were actually taken over by the new company on the 24th March 1920.

The authorised share capital of Tees Towing Company was initially £100,000, a figure which was not to be varied until 1962. The Tees Tug Company and The Robinson Tug Company were liquidated at the time of the merger.

The managing owners of Tees Towing Company were Charles William Robinson and William Henry Crosthwaite in partnership and usually simply styled "Robinson and Crosthwaite". The first directors were William Henry Crosthwaite, John Wesley Brown, John Graham, George Albert Robinson and Charles William Robinson and the secretary was John Adams. The initial subscribers to the company were Charles William Robinson, William Henry Crosthwaite, John Graham, George Albert Robinson, Wallace Sinclair Robinson, Charles Edward Robinson and John Adams.

Wallace Sinclair Robinson was appointed Marine Superintendent and Salvage Officer and George Albert Robinson became Engineering Superintendent, positions they were both to hold for many years to come. The company office was set up at 8 Exchange Place, Middlesbrough which although having a roadway frontage was set at a level below that of the North Eastern Railway Company's Middlesbrough Station adjacent to the Albert Bridge; here they were to stay until 1952.

At the time of the amalgamation Tees Towing Company acquired the shares in Charles Duncan & Sons already held by The Tees Tug Company and also purchased additional shares thus becoming the majority shareholder in the Duncan Company. This latter company thus became an associate company of Tees Towing and shared the same offices (Fig. 7). They of course had a fleet of tugs and supporting craft which at the 24th March 1920 comprised:-

Charles Duncan & Sons Ltd.

Steam screw tug	*Frank*, (76/1896).
Steam screw tug	*Dora Duncan*, (126/1891).
Steam paddle tug	*Adonis*, (80/1875).
Steam launch	*Lily Duncan*, (28/1866).
Steam launch	*Betsy Duncan*, (29/1889).

However, this group of vessels was soon to change since *Betsy Duncan* was sold to South Shields on the 30th April and about this time *Adonis* also was disposed of, more than likely to be broken up. These disposals were counterbalanced by the transfer of *Clarissa* from Tees Towing – she ran under the Duncan colours from the end of September 1920 – and the purchase of *Lord Warden* (118/1868) from Sunderland.

Almost as soon as Tees Towing Company was formed they made alterations to their fleet also. The paddle tug *Champion* was converted to a hulk, ultimately coming into the hands of George Alder Limited who along with the North Eastern Railway was a competitor of Tees Towing. *George Peabody* was broken up in October 1920. Balancing these changes they purchased the *Powerful*, (182/1878), for £1,150 from Liverpool. She had originally been the *Flying Huntress* of the Clyde Shipping Company and was larger than any other paddle tug previously owned by the companies covered by this history but had the serious handicap of having only a single-cylinder side-lever engine.

Also purchased for the fleet in September was the strangely named iron paddle tug *Borwick Rails*, (136/1871). She cost the company £1,250 and was to work on the Tees for over a year before being named *Ironopolis*. Her original name has perhaps caused more puzzlement than the names of any other of the eighty vessels covered by this narrative. In truth the answer is simple and straight forward – she was named after the quay Borwick Rails, near Millom in Cumbria where she was first put to work towing vessels which came there to load ironstone from the local mines.

The war to end all wars was over, Tees Towing Company had been formed and had re-arranged its fleet and no doubt William Crosthwaite and Charles Robinson were looking forward to a peaceful and prosperous time to come with the volume of trade on the river increasing again to a more normal level and then expanding beyond that. But all was not well for Europe was in disarray; the peace treaty and reparations had not been settled; there was civil strife in Ireland and there was industrial unrest at home. And so, just as the last changes in the fleet were being completed, the tug crews went on strike on the 13th October 1920 for more money and better conditions and the stoppage was to last until 24th January 1921. Some of the argument between the men and the management (in this case W.H. Crosthwaite) took place via the media in letters to the local newspapers. Hard words were said publicly on both sides – the men claimed that their working conditions were probably the worst in the country and William Crosthwaite wrote (referring to the engineers) that since they were only "drivers" they did not deserve any higher pay. Both sides of course strongly refuted what the other said. The union involved at that time was the Tyne Steam Packet Provident Society.

Payment was on a rate per day for a standard working week of 56 hours plus overtime. Reference is made to an actual average working week of 90 hours! Over and above these payments there was a bonus scheme which the press did not detail.

The rates were:-

Captain	£1 per day	+ 1/3 (6.25p) per hour overtime
Engineer	17/6 (87.5p) per day	+ 1/- (5p) per hour overtime
Mates & Firemen	12/6 (62.5p) per day	+ 9d (3.75p) per hour overtime
Boys	5/- (25p) per day	+ 5d (2.1p) per hour overtime

all plus an unspecified bonus scheme

What was wanted by the men was to increase the above standard rates by between 5% and 30% and for overtime to be paid at one and a quarter times normal rate but for the bonus scheme to be dropped.

The strike must have affected all the tugs on the Tees since William Crosthwaite was writing on behalf of the Tees Tug Owners Association of which he was Chairman. His main argument was that tugmen on the Tees had earnings some 20% higher than at other north-east coast ports. About 200 men in all were involved in the strike and by the time it was settled in January 1921 – how is not stated – only 50 of them were able to return to work because of the lack of towage jobs; so many of the trading ships had been diverted elsewhere that there were only 3,175 clearances on the river during 1920. So quite clearly the new combined company had got off to a poor start in its very first year due to the damaging effects of this fifteen weeks' long strike.

Fig. 8 Athlete *and* George Robinson *assisting the* Berlin *which in 1920 was the largest vessel to have visited Middlesbrough Dock.* Athlete, *at this time, had not received her new Tees Towing funnel colours. (Courtesy, B.V. Andrew).*

Robinson and Crosthwaite became the joint managing owners of the Ebor Fishing Company whose fleet has already been described. They were now to increase the size of this operation by the purchase of the trawlers *Lynmouth*, (140/1892), and *Brisbane*, (139/1894). The venture was short-lived since in 1923 the whole of the "Ebor" fleet was to be either sold or scrapped.

Riverside development was still continuing; the TCC had obtained their Act of Parliament to permit reclamation of the Seal Sands area on the north side of the Tees estuary. This was an extensive project and the reclaimed land did not support new industry until well after the Second World War. Middlesbrough Dock continued to handle larger ships; the record in 1920 now being held by the *Berlin*, (17,324/1908, 590' x 69'), which was an ex North German Lloyd vessel. (Fig. 8). She had been in for a post-war refit by Smith's Dock Company.

William Crosthwaite, who had celebrated his fortieth birthday in July, had moved the family home to 5, Thornfield Road, Middlesbrough, once again to the perimeter of the still growing town. Nevertheless he was even then only just over two miles from his offices, Middlesbrough Dock and the river. Charles Robinson and John Adams were at that time living at the seaside town of Redcar.

Quite clearly 1920 had been an exciting year of change, but it had also been a frustrating one because the post-war level of business was not improving as had been expected and some of the work which could have been available had been lost due to the strike. No doubt all concerned were looking forward to better things in 1921 and beyond. However they were to be disappointed for there were to be difficulties for some years ahead.

The year 1921 was to see the peak number of vessels in Tees Towing's and its associates' fleets at twenty-two in all, a figure which was to be maintained for only two years. The small screw tug *Frank* was sold to W.J. Guy of Cardiff by the

Duncan Company whilst Tees Towing purchased the *Granite City*, (113/1882), a wooden-hulled paddle steamer from Aberdeen, the similar *William Findley*, (87/1884), from the same source and the *United*. This latter vessel was probably a trawler, though whether intended for fishing or towing operations is not known. At the end of the year as previously mentioned the *Borwick Rails* was renamed *Ironopolis* – a reference to the major industrial base of the Middlesbrough area in the previous century.

The town continued to grow, its population had risen to 131,000 and William Crosthwaite had been elected to the Town Council representing the Grove Hill ward. He was to remain a councillor until 1948 when he was appointed an Alderman. John Wesley Brown, a director of Tees Towing, became a Tees Commissioner representing Middlesbrough Council at the Tees Conservancy Commissioners' meetings. Quite clearly William Crosthwaite and his colleagues were beginning to give their time and services to the town and other controlling bodies to a considerable degree. Ultimately they were to hold positions of great influence in local society.

William Crosthwaite's Teesbank Engineering Company whose ownership he shared with members of his family and John Wesley Brown, was located at 7, North Street, Middlesbrough. Not a great deal has been discovered about this company's operations but it carried out ship repair work in and around the Tees and no doubt did general engineering jobs where metal working was involved.

The number of ship clearances on the River Tees in the year 1921 was only 2,328 no doubt severely influenced by the 1920/21 strike which had driven trade away from the river. Over 7 million tons of shipping had been built to Lloyds classification in the past two years but notwithstanding this there began a serious recession in trade.

As well as owning the record number of 22 tugs at the year end the companies now had the unenviable record of possessing tugs whose average age was 39 years. Unbelievably an even higher average age was to be achieved later on. These average ages are not quoted as criticism of the companies but to illustrate the quality of the vessels with which they had to work. If a vessel had a sound hull then no doubt the simple steam machinery was easy and inexpensive to repair. There was of course little standardisation and the large number of engine builders involved with the fleet over the years will be noted from the vessel individual histories. (See Appendix C). It will also be seen that, to date, no new vessel had been bought by Tees Towing Company or Charles Duncan & Sons but the time was approaching when they would do so.

In 1922 when William Crosthwaite became a member of the Tees Port Health Authority, John Wesley Brown was elected Member of Parliament for the constituency of Middlesbrough East, a responsibility he was to hold for only one year. At the end of May the Tees Pilotage Commission was superseded by the Tees Pilotage Authority and John Wesley Brown became a member of the new organisation having been appointed to represent the Tees Conservancy Commissioners. So once again the management and directors of Tees Towing were widening their sphere of influence in local affairs; and quite rapidly too. This must have been a reflection on the high standing of their company in business circles generally and in particular in matters concerning shipping and the River Tees.

In the 1920's accidents, breakdowns and strandings of vessels were commonplace compared with the present day in consequence of which the local tug fleets were able, by their adeptness, to pick up salvage awards when they were successful in assisting ships in difficulties. The awards, when made, were shared between owners, skipper and crew. A typical example of such an event occurred on 12th May 1922 when the tugs *Dora Duncan* and *Nunthorpe* re-moored the steamship *Sixty-Four*, (2,428/1907, 295' x 43'), after she had broken her stern moorings at No. 4 Buoys. The £130 salvage was awarded to *Nunthorpe* only, she presumably having been judged the tug which had given the essential assistance. One wonders what the crew of the *Dora Duncan* had to say about the decision.

The local press at this time carried reports of shipowners complaints as to the high towage charges on the River Tees. William Crosthwaite replied, also in the newspapers, claiming that the charges were reasonable and totally refuting the idea that there was a price ring amongst tug owners. George Alder even had a court case to defend over similar claims. Results of these arguments are not recorded but it seems likely that the shipowners, due to the serious recession, were looking for someone to attack with the object of cutting some of their costs. The tug operators would, therefore, be near-at-hand and a ready target.

In March 1922 *William Findley* was lost. Although an insurance payment is recorded as having been received against the loss no details of what happened to her have been discovered. In the same month *Granite City* was sold to Aberdeen with the expectation that she was to be broken up but in fact she remained in service until 1927 when she foundered at Blaydon buoys on the River Tyne. Both the *William Findley* and *Granite City* were close on forty years old and had wooden hulls and single cylinder engines. Their usefulness would be very limited and it is difficult now to understand why they had been purchased at all. One employee of the company still remembers how it was possible to see daylight through the gaps in the hull planking of *Granite City!*

Another trawler was purchased in June 1922 jointly by William Crosthwaite and Charles William Robinson and after conversion to a salvage vessel she was transferred to the ownership of Tees Towing. She was the *Laceby*, (118/1892), and had, as the *Toni*, been captured from the Germans by British Naval Forces in 1916. She was not to stay long on the Tees.

In September 1922, Tees Towing decided that they had need of a launch for communication purposes and for transference of personnel in and around the river. They purchased from Aberdeen the Glasgow registered *Electric Arc* (24/1911), which as such could easily be passed over as an ordinary launch of little significant interest. But *Electric Arc* was no ordinary 50-foot launch. As her name suggests she was something special. She was an experimental vessel built by McLaren Bros. Ltd. at Dumbarton for the electrical engineering firm of Mavor & Coulson Ltd. of Glasgow who provided her propulsion machinery. This was a 45 BHP Wolsley 6-cylinder petrol engine driving an AC Dynamo/Exciter which supplied 3 phase current to an electric motor. This latter drove the propeller. *Electric Arc* is believed to be the first electrically propelled vessel in the world and was certainly a novelty even eleven years after she had been built. William Crosthwaite, although he had no part in the inception of this vessel, must have noted some of its important features; in particular perhaps the direct control of the engine and propeller by the helmsman and its ready availability from a cold start. In the years to come these features would no doubt exercise his mind regarding inovatory ideas in relation to tug propulsion and control systems. But all that was more than ten years in the future. This interesting vessel was to stay on the Tees for less than three years, going to Jersey in 1925 into the ownership of shipowner

John Milburn by whom she was renamed *Olive*. Her ultimate fate is not known.

The grouping of the main-line railways on the 1st January 1923 saw the absorption of the owners of Middlesbrough Dock, the North Eastern Railway Company, into the London and North Eastern Railway Company (LNER). The railway company, under its various titles, had operated tugs on the River Tees to assist vessels in and out of their dock, though not to the exclusion of the tugs of other companies. The LNER were to continue operating thus for about another eight years albeit it is believed with a single tug which was then transferred to Hartlepool Docks across the Tees Bay. This would then leave only George Alder Ltd. as effective competition for towage business on the river although of course the Tees Conservancy Commission operated tugs for their own use.

Work on tugs had never been a sinecure and at times could be hard, frustrating, risky and dangerous. A very special breed of tough men always capable of dealing with the unexpected and working long hours had developed over the years. Different generations of several local families continually appear in the crew lists of the tugs suggesting that there is some hereditary fascination for the kind of life involved.

Fig. 9 Coalopolis *was, in 1923, the first tug in the Tees Towing fleet to be purchased new. Here she is seen on one of her first jobs towing the three-masted sailing vessel* Garthneill *to sea on the 10th April.* Garthneill *had been built in 1895. (W. Haig Parry)*

Life on the tugs in 1923 was no different as the following extract from the press of the time illustrated:–

> "From the smoke and grit-laden atmosphere of the steel plants, furnaces and mills on the river bank it seems that the lives of tugboatmen are cast in pleasant places. Towing the world's-end steamers down a placid stream to the sea, or towing the slag hoppers to the tipping limit beyond the buoys, on a warm sunny summer morning, however, is only the pleasant side of a job which has its full share of discomforts and dangers. The time of year to appreciate the disadvantages of the riverman's calling is winter, when the chill nor'easter howls across the waters and there are jobs to be done beyond the breakwaters. Only a fatuous optimist can see anything attractive in little ship handling and navigation in the wintry North Sea, but the tugs and their crews are required to undertake long risky trips, on occasions as part of the day's work — and there is no definite "knocking off" time. Before one envies the tugboatman of his easy and pleasant job, he would do well to consider the ordeal of the Middlesbrough tugs *Athlete, Liberia* and *Dora Duncan* recently, and when in a howling gale and heavy sea, they hunted for a ship which drifted from her wirelessed positions, like a will-o'-the-wisp. They couldn't steer head to sea for fear of swamping and despite the most cautious handling took sufficient green water aboard to necessitate pumping out at Bridlington so that the hunt could be continued. After enduring 48 hours of sleepless peril, only for other tugs to secure the prize, one might agree that a shore berth is best".

This little contemporary account says it all and needs no benefit of hindsight.

Several changes were now to take place in the Tees Towing and Duncan fleets, most notable being the purchase of their first newly-built tug the *Coalopolis*, (175/1923) (Fig. 9). She was completed in March 1923 for Tees Towing Company by A. Hall & Co. Ltd. at Aberdeen her screw being powered by a 500 IHP triple-expansion steam engine. New though the vessel was her engine and boilers were second-hand having come from a wrecked trawler. Her master was J.C. (Charlie) Rounce and the mate was J.W. (Micky) Spink. Her life on the Tees was surprisingly short. Only two years later she was sold to Canada for £9,000; first at Halifax N.S. eventually becoming the *Bansurf* and later at Toronto as the *Shawanaga*. People who remember her on the Tees have suggested that she was sold so quickly because of her high coal consumption. This seems unlikely since she worked in Canada until she was broken up in 1971, 48 years after she was built. More likely her disposal was occasioned by the depressed state of trade and the financial constraints ensuing therefrom. When *Coalopolis* sailed to Canada her deck was loaded to maximum capacity with coal. Her route was by way of the Pentland Firth, Loch Eriboll and Bantry Bay where she took on board further coal. Her skipper on this voyage was Gus Anderson Snr. and the voyage to Halifax took altogether 10 weeks; part of this time being taken up whilst she was weather-bound in the north of Scotland.

On the 16th March 1923 the *William Fallows*, (122/1888), a double-engined iron paddle tug belonging to the TCC was purchased by Tees Towing but in just over seven months was disposed of to the Ridley Steam Tug Co. Ltd.

on the Tyne for £1,800. The short period of ownership may be explained by the fact that she was employed to lay a telegraph cable across the River Severn when her skipper was Ernie Watson Snr. Possibly *William Fallows* was bought specifically for this job and then sold as soon as it was completed. Charles Duncan & Sons acquired the *Presto*, another twin-funnelled iron paddle tug, from Ellerman's Wilson Line Ltd. at Hull. She cost them £800 and was renamed *Beattie Duncan*, (155/1893), early in 1924. Later she was to be the last tug carrying the Duncan funnel colours. An ex-Tyne ferry boat was brought to the Tees by Tees Towing at the end of the year. She was the *C.M. Palmer*, (95/1884), and was bought from Tyne General Ferry Co. for £350. If she was employed on the Tees as a tug then it was only for a short while for the *C.M. Palmer* was soon converted to a lighter.

To complete the fleet changes Tees Towing disposed of *Monsdale, United, Pendennis* and *Powerful* for breaking up and *Triumph* for further service on the Tyne realising £100, £80, £150, £180 and £325 respectively. At about the same time *Nunthorpe* and *Cleveland* were fitted with fire pumps so that they could be of assistance in the event of ship or riverside fires.

On the river the improved navigation lighting provided by the TCC was in operation and in the industrial sphere Synthetic Ammonia and Nitrates Ltd. had opened their chemical and fertiliser factory on the north bank of the river at Billingham. Later, as Imperial Chemical Industries Ltd. this huge works was to provide much trade for the river and work for the tugs. There were already hopeful signs that the level of business was picking up since 3,513 ships were cleared on the river in the year.

But there was sadness too for Charles William Robinson died on the penultimate day of 1923 leaving William Crosthwaite as the sole proprietor who decided to retain the name of Robinson and Crosthwaite for the managers of the Tees Towing Company. This was to remain so for the next 25 years. It was a nice tribute to his recent partner and also no doubt maintained the now familiar name with his customers, the shipowners and shipping agents. So it was at the beginning of 1924 that William Crosthwaite became, for the first time, the sole managing director of his firm. He was also chairman of the board of directors.

The employment position locally was not good, 7,400 men were unemployed in Middlesbrough in January. Bad though the situation was, it was nevertheless to get worse in the years to come.

Charles Duncan & Sons sold their paddle tug *Lord Warden* at the beginning of the year to be broken-up. She was replaced in March, by the *Vigilant*, (44/1906), a small compound-engined screw tug which had been built in Holland at Hendrik-Ido-Ambacht. She was to be used mainly for the towage of barge traffic within the river and out to the dumping grounds in Tees Bay.

At the 31st March 1925 Tees Towing were reporting a monetary loss on the past year's operations due to the shortage of work and noting that there were fewer tugs at work on the river than in the last 20 years. Presumably, with diversification in mind, William Crosthwaite set up the Crosthwaite Steamship Company Limited which was officially incorporated on the 21st May 1925 with a capital of £1,000. The intention was for this new company to operate summer-time excursion trips out of Scarborough forty miles down the coast from the Tees, and for this purpose the paddle steamer *Lord Roberts* was purchased from the Furness Shipbuilding Company for £825. She was immediately renamed *Bilsdale*, (199/1900), and painted white overall apart from the black top to her funnel (Fig. 10). She was to become very well known in Scarborough – and Whitby too – over the next ten summers. Her Captain was Charles William Duncan who became popularly known as the "singing Captain" due to his habit of joining in with the musical entertainment provided for the excursionists. (Fig. 11). Her sailing master was Frank Verril of Staithes. In the winter the *Bilsdale* was usually laid up at the buoys near the Transporter Bridge. The Board of Trade Certificate issued to the vessel was for the carriage of 386 passengers, no mean number for North Sea coastal operations in a ship only 135 feet long. The initial subscribers to the Crosthwaite Steamship Company were William Crosthwaite, Tugowner, and his son Cecil Crosthwaite, student, both of 5, Thornfield Road, Middlesbrough.

More changes were about to occur in an attempt to reduce the size of the Tees Towing fleet. In April 1925 *Challenger* (2) was sold for breaking up after 18 years' service on the Tees and the *Electric Arc* went to Jersey. During August *C.M. Palmer* was scrapped, realising £105 and *Coalopolis* began her adventurous journey to Canada. There was, however, in April an addition to the fleet in that *Conqueror* was purchased from the Firth of Forth. She was a large, unwieldly, paddle steamer with two funnels fore and aft and had been used latterly as an excursion steamer. She cost £1850. Whether Tees Towing intended to use her also as an excursion vessel, perhaps in conjunction with *Bilsdale*, is not known but it appears that she was used as a tug notwithstanding her rather lengthy hull. She was quickly renamed *Hurworth*, (199/1897), and just over two years later she was renamed again becoming the *Hutton Cross* (1).

As a replacement for the *Electric Arc* Tees Towing acquired the launch *Arandsea* for communications purposes. No details whatever of this vessel have been discovered but her name is of interest since it is a phonetical play on the initial letters of Robinson and Crosthwaite (R & C). The company also used the word "Arandsea" for their telegraphic address at this time. The *Arandsea* was disposed of after only a few months of ownership.

For many years Tees Towing Company and Robinson & Crosthwaite used in their advertising, the slogan "Tow Anything Anywhere" (Fig. 15). It seems that this originated in the mid 1920's and although never literally accurate was quite acceptable in the so-called "good-old-days". Present day trade description legislation would of course not allow it; a pity since surely this catch phrase never misled anybody. It seems to have been dropped from the company advertising about 1967. Charles Duncan & Sons in the mid 1920's maintained their separate identity by having their own advertisements (Fig. 14).

Another important event in William Crosthwaite's career was his appointment in 1925 as the 67th Mayor of Middlesbrough. To have been so chosen after only four years as a councillor was unprecedented and is an indication of his high standing in the eyes of his fellow aldermen and councillors and also the Conservative Party of which he was a member (Figs. 12, 13 and 17). During his year of office he provided, for the annual carnival parade, a lorry made up to look like one of his tugs. Fortunately this display was photographed in Exchange Place, Middlesbrough in front of the company's office together with William Crosthwaite, Charles Duncan and many other employees of the company. The delightful group is reproduced here at Fig. 16.

Fig. 10 *The excursion vessel* Bilsdale *fully loaded with holidaymakers from Scarborough c.1930.* *(H. Hudson)*

Fig. 11 *The crew of the Crosthwaite Steamship Company's* Bilsdale *in 1925. They are, left to right; back row, Clinton Aydon, William Crosthwaite, W. Knowles, H. Butter, F. Ranson; centre row, E. Carr, Mrs. Williams, ?, Mrs. Dunning; front row, Captain Charles William Duncan, O. Fulton, W. Warren, G. Scarlet, F. Thompson, John Robinson.* *(R.C. Clifford)*

Fig. 12 *Councillor William Henry Crosthwaite wearing his mayoral robes and chain of office when Mayor of Middlesbrough in 1925. (M. Wright)*

Fig. 13 *Mrs. Ada Mary Crosthwaite wearing her chain of office when Mayoress of Middlesbrough in 1925. (M. Wright)*

At the end of 1925 the combined fleet of 18 vessels were made up as follows:–

Tees Towing Co. Ltd.

Steam paddle tug	*Florence*
Steam screw tug	*Glen Rosa*
Steam screw tug	*Liberia*
Steam paddle tug	*Lingdale*
Steam screw tug	*Athlete*
Steam paddle tug	*Cleveland*
Steam screw tug	*George Robinson*
Steam paddle tug	*Nunthorpe*
Steam screw tug	*Samphire Batts*
Steam paddle tug	*Ironopolis*
Steam salvage vessel	*Laceby*
Steam paddle tug	*Hurworth*

Charles Duncan & Sons Ltd.

Steam screw tug	*Clarissa*
Steam screw tug	*Dora Duncan*
Steam launch	*Lily Duncan*
Steam paddle tug	*Beattie Duncan*
Steam screw tug	*Vigilant*

Crosthwaite Steamship Co. Ltd.

Steam passenger vessel	*Bilsdale*

The average age of the fleet was still very high at 37 years.

Fig. 14 *An advertisement placed by Charles Duncan and Sons Limited in a port handbook of 1926. Compare the claim of longevity with that in the Robinson & Crosthwaite advertisement in* **Fig. 19.**

Fig. 15 *An advertisement placed in the handbook "Middlesbrough, Pictorial and Industrial" in 1926 by the management partnership Robinson and Crosthwaite.*

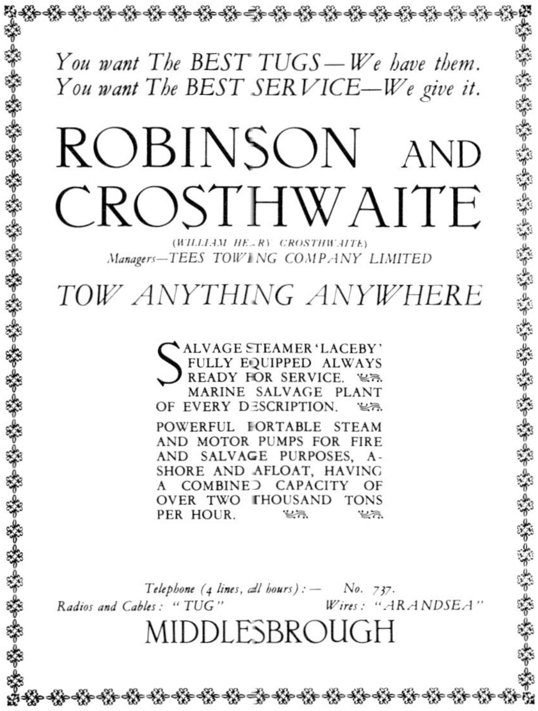

Fig. 16 *The lorry, camouflaged as a tug, makes an excellent entry for the Middlesbrough Carnival procession in 1925. It is photographed in Exchange Place outside of the Tees Towing Company's office, the entrance to which is just behind the funnel of the tug. Middlesbrough railway station is in the background. Of the many people in the photograph those identifiable are George Robinson, Wallace Robinson, William Crosthwaite, John Adams and John Robinson (in centre of gateway).* *(R.C. Clifford)*

Fig. 17 *A family group taken in 1925 to commemorate the first mayoralty of Middlesbrough for Councillor William Crosthwaite. With him from left to right are; back row, Cecil Crosthwaite (16), Captain George Elliott, Thomas Crosthwaite; front row, Mrs. Elliott, Dorothy Elliott Crosthwaite (14), The Mayoress, Mrs. Ada Crosthwaite, Alice Mary Crosthwaite (19) and Mrs. Jane Crosthwaite.*

Chapter Five

Difficult Times 1926-1931

It was quite clear that, for the amount of work available, there were too many tugs on the River Tees and it therefore comes as no surprise to find that in 1926 the fleet was reduced in size by the disposal of three vessels. The *Nunthorpe,* the *Glen Rosa* and the *Laceby* were broken-up by Hughes Bolckow Ltd. at Blyth.

Struggling against the effects of the low level of business the tug companies were soon to be hit by a much worse situation. The whole country was brought to a standstill by a General Strike on 4th May 1926 and although that was to last only for about a week the miners chose to remain on strike for approximately seven months. Although the tugmen's strike had ended after nearly a month, by the 7th June, only four tugs were able to recommence working because of the effects of the coal strike. These arrangements were on a week to week basis only. During the tug strike the management and staff are known to have operated at least one tug, perhaps for emergency needs, and the photograph of *Beattie Duncan* reproduced as Fig. 18. shows her manned with such a crew. By September, the local press was reporting that "most Teesside works were in a state of complete idleness because of the coal dispute."

Whilst in his mayoral year William Crosthwaite took his fellow councillors, aldermen and officials of the council on a tour of the river in his vessel *Bilsdale.* This was done when most of the local works were idle so the passengers would not have seen a very typical view of the riverside scene. William Crosthwaite's son Cecil, writing in later years, noted that he had joined Tees Towing in 1926, when aged 17, after having been educated at Uppingham School and commented that the fifteen tugs then in the fleet were "highly valued and underpowered". Quite clearly a pertinent observation.

Another of the first directors of Tees Towing Company, John Graham, died in April 1927. He had been engaged in the towage business in co-operation with William Crosthwaite since the early years of the century, beginning with their involvement in the Florence Tugboat and Salvage Company Limited. Five months later the company secretary, John Adams, was appointed a Director in succession to John Graham.

William Crosthwaite, as a member of the Teesside Chamber of Commerce was asked to represent the local organisation at the International Chamber of Commerce in Cape Town. Coupled with this representation he no doubt would be able to see and discuss tug ownership and operation in that part of the world and possibly also at ports of call on the way there. It was from this type of experience and from other similar visits overseas in later years that he was able to obtain his very wide knowledge of what was happening in the towage business in many parts of the world.

In 1927 there was to be a net reduction of three in the size of the combined fleets as the management attempted to match their facilities to the level of demand. February saw the 36 year old screw tug *Dora Duncan* taken a few miles up river to be broken up at Stockton-on-Tees and the launch *Lily Duncan* followed her to the same scrapyard five months later. Next to go in August was the *Ironopolis* an iron paddle tug built in 1871. She was sold to Thomas and McGregor for £375 for breaking up at Bo'ness and was towed there by *Athlete.* Finally in

1927, the *Florence* was sold to C.W. Dorkin & Co. at Sunderland also for breaking-up. No doubt William Crosthwaite would be sad to see her go since she was one of the first tugs with which he had been involved. She was not modern by any standards, nor apparently had she been much modernised, since there was no bridge/engine room telegraph on board. Communication between the skipper, in his pulpit, and the engine room was as follows:–

> To start, the skipper stamped once on the deck.
> To stop, the skipper stamped twice on the deck.
> To go astern, the skipper stamped thrice on the deck.
> All orders for manoeuvring were shouted through a
> cracked, battered and almost useless voice tube.

However, she was 48 years old and had given nearly 25 years service to Tees Towing and its forbears when she sailed to the breakers. One must admit, that communications have changed for the better since 1927.

Fig. 18 *On board the* Beattie Duncan *during the General Strike in 1926 are, left to right, on the bridge deck William Chrystal Duncan, George Robinson, William Crosthwaite and Charles William Duncan; on the main deck, Wallace Robinson, ?, Norman Thompson and George Mayhew. (W. Haig Parry)*

In March 1927 William Crosthwaite went to Fishguard to inspect the paddle tug *Pen Cw* (sic) then owned by the Great Western Railway Company and his very detailed report on the condition of the vessel makes interesting reading. Despite the fact that the *Pen Cw* "had no forward hook, but good anchorage for one; not easy to pass rope forward to aft; and had no mast-lights on funnel" he must have been adequately impressed because he purchased her in July for £1,750. He may have been satisfied with his purchase but it is interesting to note that the tug skippers of the time, had affectionately christened her "all smoke and backwash". The photograph in Part II rather suggests that their description was justified. She was renamed *Ingleby Cross* (1), (168/1912), on the 24th August 1927 to become the first vessel in Tees Towing's fleet to bear the now familiar "*Cross*" appendage to her name. What a happy choice it was for William Crosthwaite to have made, for the same naming system is in use today and remains just as appropriate as it was 57 years ago. A few days later, as already mentioned, the *Hurworth* was renamed *Hutton Cross* (1). Thus *Ingleby Cross* (1) and *Hutton Cross* (1) together made the beginning of a fleet which in the years to come was to be referred to in company advertising as "Cross Line Tugs".

The fleet reduction and rationalisation programme continued into 1928. Two more vessels were sold; one a small compound-engined barge tug, and the other a large paddle tug both belonging to Charles Duncan & Sons. In March the *Vigilant* was sold to Canada. She was carried as deck cargo on the forward hatch covers of the Great Lakes steamer *Aycliffe Hall* on her maiden voyage following construction at Smith's Dock, South Bank shipyard. (See Part II, Ship History No. 43). The second tug to be sold was the *Beattie Duncan*, 25 years old but having been on the Tees for only 4½ years. She went to the Aberdeen Steam Tug Co. Ltd. with whom she was to continue working until 1933.

In an attempt to diversify still further in the face of the poor state of business on the River Tees, William Crosthwaite decided that he would enter the sea towage business in addition to dealing with river and coastal tows. This was a business in which for some time the Dutch had held a predominant position and it was clearly a courageous decision to take in the light of the low level of trade at home. Nevertheless this was probably as good a time as any for the venture since his fleet had been reduced in size over the last year or two and the dead wood was being cut out. There was, of course, no vessel in the present fleet suitable for sea towage and one had to be found on the market. It so happened that the Aberdeen Steam Tug Co. Ltd. to whom the *Beattie Duncan* was being sold wished to dipose of the *Audax II* which had been built in 1918 for Bureau Wijsmuller of Ijmuiden as the *Gelderland* and for whom she had made many long distance tows. *Audax II* was immediately renamed *Kings Cross* (1), (282/1918), on arrival in the Tees. This vessel was something quite different to the tugs which had been owned to date: her triple-expansion engine produced 600 IHP, she was very sturdily built, was only 10 years old, was fitted with wireless apparatus, and had cost the enormous amount of £8,000. It is not surprising therefore, that the *Beattie Duncan* was "traded in" in part exchange.

Within two months of her acquisition by Tees Towing, *Kings Cross* (1) had hit the headlines. Together with *Samphire Batts* she was scheduled to tow *H.M.S. Colossus*, the last of the Dreadnought class battleships, from Devonport to the scrapyard at Charlestown near Rosyth on the Firth of Forth. This tow which took from the 25th August to the 5th September 1928 was considered, at the time, to be a considerable achievement since the battleship displaced over 20,000 tons

ROBINSON & CROSTHWAITE

(WILLIAM HENRY CROSTHWAITE)
MANAGERS
TEES TOWING COMPANY LTD.

FOUNDED IN 1835

The OLDEST ESTABLISHED BUSINESS IN MIDDLESBROUGH

UNDER FOUR REIGNS

WILLIAM IV

VICTORIA

H.M.S. "COLOSSUS" IN TOW OF TUGS "KINGS CROSS" & "SAMPHIRE BATTS"
FROM DEVONPORT TO ROSYTH, AUGUST 1928

EDWARD VII

TOW ANYTHING ANYWHERE

WE HAVE BEEN TOWING ON THE RIVER TEES AND ROUND THE COASTS OF GREAT BRITAIN FOR 95 YEARS & ARE STILL DOING IT.

RADIOS, CABLES, & WIRES: "TUG"

MIDDLESBROUGH
ON-TEES

HOOD DESIGNERS M'BRO'

GEORGE V

and measured 546 feet x 86 feet and the contract had been won against stiff continental competition. Quite naturally Tees Towing made as much publicity out of the event as possible and as well as obtaining widespread newspaper coverage they produced, in 1930 a most striking advertisement which is illustrated here as Fig. 19. In this advertisement, the reference back to the founding of the business in 1835 relates of course to the line of descent through the acquired Robinson and Duncan Companies. The former having been the descendant owners of the William Fallows, Middlesbrough-on-Tees Steam Tug Company of 1839 which had incorporated tugs owned by Fallows since 1835. Tees Towing Company still have in their possession the original indenture document dated 25th November 1839. The Duncan companies also had their roots in ferry boats and tugs at about this same time or even slightly earlier. Tees Towing Company and Robinson & Crosthwaite had, as will have been seen, come into being only in 1920.

On the river two large vessels newly-built by Furness Shipbuilding Company were taken down river on their trial trips and delivery voyages using the company's tugs in conjunction with the shipyard tug *Dragon*. These were the passenger vessels *Santa Maria* and *Santa Barbara* each of 8,153 gross tons and with dimensions 466' x 64' (Fig. 20). In May *Athlete* was badly damaged by heavy seas whilst assisting the engineless, newly-built, steamer *Llanfair*, (4,960/1928, 400' x 53') into the river. The incident occurred near the South Gare and *Athlete* had to be towed back into the river and put into the graving dock for repairs. Two salvage events during the year brought tugs into the news. First, in the summer, *Lingdale* refloated the Middlesbrough built and owned s.s. *Trentwood*, (791/1912, 195' x 30'), from off the south training wall and in December *Ingleby Cross* (1) assisted at the refloating of the tanker *British Thrift*, (707/1928), just inside the river mouth.

William Crosthwaite who always took a firm line when dealing with any differences of opinion with his work force nevertheless appears always to have applied a fatherly attitude to them in other ways. This was never more so than at Christmas time when for example in the late 1920's all the children of the company's employees who went to the office in Exchange Place received a new half crown piece and a bag of fruit and were treated to a Christmas Party at the Holy Cross Mission in Cannon Street (now demolished). The tug skippers had a turkey sent to their homes.

Once again a ship was in trouble when the Duncan Company's tug *Clarissa* and Tees Towing's *Ingleby Cross* (1) salved the s.s. *Thala*, (4,399/1928, 370'x 52'), which had run aground on the Gare Sands during May 1929. They and the company shared a salvage award of £950.

In the same month an agreement was drawn up for the purchase of the fleet and other assets of the towage firm of George Alder Ltd. which was then in liquidation. Although the purchase was formally in the name of William Crosthwaite's daughter Alice Mary in effect he would have been responsible for the arrangements of the transfer. The vessels taken over were:–

Steam screw tug	*Graythorpe*	Lighter	*Champion*
Steam screw tug	*Garnet*	Lighter	*Challenger* (1)
Steam screw tug	*No. 6.*	Lighter	*Eddystone*
Steam paddle tug	*Glenthorpe*	Water boat	*Victory*
Steam paddle tug	*Prince of Wales*	Keel	*Agnes*

Plus all tackle etc., office furniture and the goodwill of the company. All this was

Fig. 19 *This attractive advertisement of 1930 appeared under the heading of the managing partnership Robinson and Crosthwaite. It is so full of information that it speaks for itself without any further explanation.*

obtained for a modest £2,800.

The actual transfer of ownership did not occur until January 1930 when *Glenthorpe*, (149/1892), and *Graythorpe*, (119/1881), were absorbed into a new company entitled the Middlesbrough Towage Company Limited (not to be confused with the Middlesbrough-on-Tees Steam Tug Co. of 90 years earlier). J.W. Nellist, who had been manager for George Alder, was appointed Manager. The paddle tug *Prince of Wales* and the lighter *Challenger* (1) were immediately broken up but the fate of the other six vessels has not been established. It seems likely that they also would have been scrapped. Just what William Crosthwaite's stake was in the Middlesbrough Towage Company is not clear but it seems that he must have held, at least within a year or so, the controlling interest. The company had its offices at Court Chambers, 17 Albert Road, Middlesbrough, not far away from Exchange Place. The operating base was at Corporation Dock hard by the Transporter Bridge.

Whilst making arrangements for the new company, William Crosthwaite celebrated his silver wedding anniversary on the 27th July 1929. He and his family could be well satisfied with the progress he had made in the past 25 years both in his sphere of business and in public life. On the 9th July 1930 William Crosthwaite's daughter Alice Mary married Claude Cyril Fairweather the son of Nicholas Fairweather a Middlesbrough stevedore. In later years Claude Fairweather will be seen to figure prominently in the affairs of Tees Towing Company and also to achieve high rank and recognition for his services in the Second World War. William himself celebrated his fiftieth birthday and his son Cecil now 21 years of age was appointed a director of Tees Towing at the 1930 A.G.M. To commemorate his silver wedding he and his wife presented gowns and

Fig. 20 Santa Maria *being towed downstream from her builders, Furness Shipbuilding Co. by the tugs* Athlete, Dragon *and* Cleveland *in 1928. Seen passing under the Middlesbrough Transporter Bridge.*
(W. Haig Parry)

cocked hats to the Middlesbrough councillors. He was now senior vice-president of Teesside Chamber of Commerce and had for some time been Deputy Chairman of Middlesbrough Conservative Association. Fellow director John Wesley Brown was Chairman of the latter organisation

In March 1930 the Tees District Development Board was formed with the intention of attracting new businesses to the whole Teesside area and attempting to move away from the near total reliance on heavy industry. William Crosthwaite was Chairman of this Board. Further, he was appointed to the Tees Conservancy Commission to represent Middlesbrough Council, presumably taking over these duties from John Wesley Brown. The Tyne Shipowners were complaining in 1930 about the high towage costs on the River Tees. These objections were clearly aimed at William Crosthwaite who, as has been related, was now effectively in charge of all the commercial towage on the river. Whether as a result of the complaints or not is not known but over a year later the towage rates on cargo liners were reduced.

Whilst 1929 had seen no changes in the tug fleet 1930 returned to the more normal pattern of disposals and acquisitions. Firstly the iron paddler *Glenthorpe* went to the breakers after only four months in the fleet of Middlesbrough Towage Company; she had a single-cylinder side-lever engine and therefore would have had rather restricted manoeuvrability. Next Tees Towing's *Liberia* was sold to the Newport Screw Towing Co. Ltd. at Newport (Monmouth) where she was to give another seven years' service before being scrapped. Last to go in the year was *Clarrisa* of Charles Duncan & Sons; she too was dismantled.

To balance these disposals Middlesbrough Towage purchased the paddle tug *Troon*, (130/1902), from the London, Midland and Scottish Railway Co. Ltd. for whom she had worked in the Clyde area and Charles Duncan & Sons took over the *Amore* from the Johnston Line Ltd. of Liverpool for the price of £1250. This latter vessel was a relatively high-powered screw tug with a triple-expansion steam engine developing 520 IHP. She was soon renamed *Steelopolis*, (155/1896), on arrival in the Tees and even at 34 years of age would no doubt have proved a very useful vessel.

At the end of 1930 the combined fleet of twelve vessels was made up as follows:–

Tees Towing Co. Ltd.

Steam paddle tug	*Lingdale*
Steam screw tug	*Athlete*
Steam paddle tug	*Cleveland*
Steam screw tug	*George Robinson*
Steam screw tug	*Samphire Batts*
Steam paddle tug	*Hutton Cross* (1)
Steam paddle tug	*Ingleby Cross* (1)
Steam screw tug	*Kings Cross* (1)

Charles Duncan & Sons Ltd.

Steam screw tug	*Steelopolis*

Middlesbrough Towage Co. Ltd.

Steam screw tug	*Graythorpe*
Steam paddle tug	*Troon*

Crosthwaite Steamship Co. Ltd.

Steam passenger vessel	*Bilsdale*

Their average age was 35 years; still a very high figure which had not changed significantly since Tees Towing had been formed 10 years ago.

The trade depression continued, the annual number of ships cleared on the river was soon to be below three thousand again and the 1931 annual report of Tees Towing noted that three of their eight tugs were laid-up for want of work. William Crosthwaite was, however, looking to the future and had his sights fixed on the need for more economical, better controlled and more manoeuvrable tugs for his fleet. The idea of utilising the internal combustion engine for tug propulsion particularly interested him and he specifically wanted to know more about the merits of diesel-electric drive. As noted earlier, the launch *Electric Arc* may have sown the seeds of interest in his mind when she was in his ownership between 1922 and 1925. Diesel-electric drives were already established in tugs in the United States of America and it was to that country that William Crosthwaite went on the 28th April 1931 to find out about the experiences of tug owners over there. He was away from Middlesbrough until 7th July and whilst in the U.S.A. he once more represented the Teesside Chamber of Commerce, of which for two years he was now President, at the International Chambers of Commerce in Washington.

On his return he was able to join in the celebration of the Centenary of Middlesbrough which took place from 5th to 12th July 1931 – one year late, as its 50th anniversary celebrations had been in 1881! Middlesbrough was still expanding in spite of the depression; the population by now being 139,000.

Although not strictly to do with the tug history it is interesting to note that Mrs. Fairweather (William Crosthwaite's daughter) bought the motor sand barges *Sweep*, (116/1910), and *Leeds Sun*, (44/1910), and with them formed the Tees Sand and Gravel Co. Ltd. This occurred in April 1931 and it is perhaps significant that they both had paraffin-fuelled engines.

Whilst William Crosthwaite was away in America he had missed the pleasant sight of seeing the famous full-rigged sailing ship *Grace Harwar*, (1,816/1889, 266' x 39') in the River Tees. She was towed in by the Middlesbrough Towage Company's *Graythorpe* and had come to load sulphate-of-ammonia at Billingham. When passing the Transporter Bridge there was only 1'6" clearance above her masts.

The venture into longer distance sea towage seemed to be going well. Details have survived of one typical example, in October 1931, of how tough and dangerous a job this work could be – the article, reproduced below, is entitled "Night of Terror in Pentland Firth".

> "The tug *Kings Cross* (1) was towing the s.s. *Athendale*, (3,130/1905, 331' x 48'), from the Tees to the Clyde, to be broken up at Lithgows yard, Port Glasgow when she ran into mountainous seas in the Pentland Firth with *Athendale* tossing about like a cork. Things were so bad that the tug and tow had to run for shelter in Loch Eriboll where they stayed for over six days whilst the weather moderated somewhat. No sooner had they set sail again than they were assailed by even worse storms and the inevitable happened, the towing hawser snapped. The *Athendale*, though not under power had a rigging crew of five under Captain Ransom, all from Middlesbrough. The steamer quickly drifted ashore within a few feet of the towering rocky cliffs. The tug by this time had assumed that all were lost from the *Athendale* and went off to escort the Thurso lifeboat to the scene where, next day, they were able to rescue all the crew. Two days later *Kings Cross* (1) returned and was able to pull the

stranded vessel off the shore after which the voyage to the Clyde passed off "quite calmly". The report ends "we were glad when we saw the end of our voyage in sight"."

This account illustrates the persistence inherent in seamen generally, and particularly in tug crews, that enables them to overcome frightening obstacles – natural or man-made – whilst going about their daily tasks.

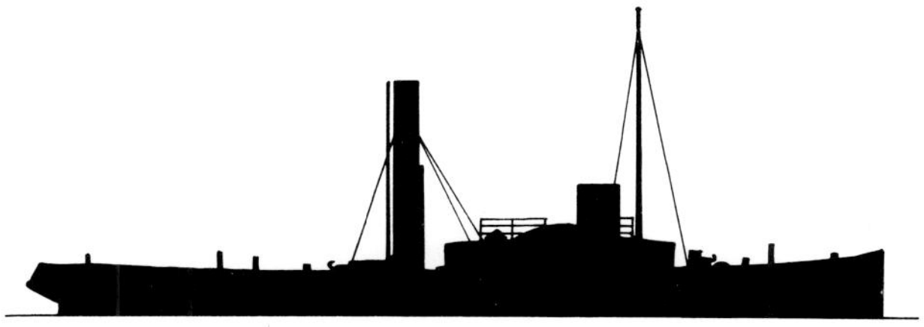

LINGDALE

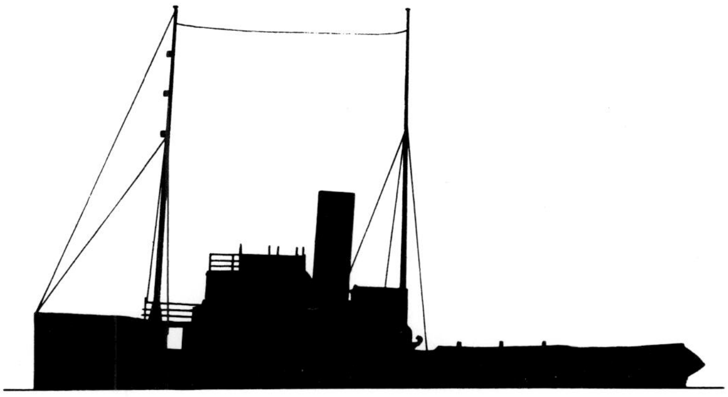

KINGS CROSS (1)

Fig. 21 *The paddle tug* Cleveland *towing the* Winterhude *upstream to Corporation Quay, Stockton past the construction site of the partly-built Newport vertical lift bridge in June 1932. The damage to the top of the mainmast of the* Winterhude *was caused when she collided with the span of the Transporter Bridge on her way up river.*
(Cleveland County Council)

Fig. 22 *Captain J.C. (Charlie) Rounce at the wheel of* Acklam Cross *shortly after her delivery in 1933.*
(Northern Echo)

Chapter Six

A First Experiment in Diesel Propulsion 1932-1939

By 1932 the lack of trade had caused four of the eight tugs of Tees Towing to be laid up and their crews put out of work. Children of the unemployed were being supplied with free milk and meals by the authorities in an attempt to alleviate the suffering which prolonged lack of wages could bring. Whilst Dorman Long & Co. Ltd. had completed their massive bridge over Sydney Harbour they had started erection of the somewhat smaller but no less important vertical lift bridge over the River Tees at Newport (Fig. 21). The erection of this bridge was to be very important for Teesside communications positioned as it was about half way between the existing Transporter Bridge at Middlesbrough and the Victoria Bridge at Stockton. John Wesley Brown had followed in William Crosthwaite's footsteps when he became the 74th Mayor of Middlesbrough; his sister was the Mayoress.

During the year another visit was paid to the United States by William Crosthwaite to study further the use of diesel propulsion in tugs. This experience would have been of help to him in deciding the specification he was going to lay down for the new, unconventional tug which he was about to order for delivery in mid 1933. This was a brave step which he was contemplating since his European contemporaries in tug ownership were quite happy to continue with conventional compound or triple-expansion steam machinery. Depression or no he obviously had his sights on a future when business would pick up again.

The year 1933 was to be a stimulating one for Tees Towing Company for after two years when there had been no changes in the fleet very significant re-arrangements were to take place. For some time a second tug, able to pair up with *Kings Cross* (1), for sea towage had been required. Now one had been found when in July the *Vlaanderen* was purchased for £2,500 from N.V. Bureau Wijsmuller Maatschappij who had also been the original owners of the *Kings Cross* (1). Why there should be such a large difference in price between *Vlaanderen* and *Kings Cross* (1) is difficult to understand since their details show they were very similar.

Presumably *Vlaanderen* was not in very good condition for after purchase a considerable amount of work was carried out on her at Baird Bros., North Shields. Whilst still on the Tyne she was renamed *Queens Cross,* (286/1921), by William Crosthwaite's daughter Dorothy Elliott. Whilst in Dutch ownership the *Queens Cross* had made journeys to the Far East and Australia. Among her feats were the towing of a floating dock from the Tyne to the Persian Gulf and the towing of the liner *City of Singapore,* (6,555/1923, 433' x 57'), from Australia to Holland. At Bairds, she had been fitted with the latest Marconi wireless telephone equipment and direction finders. All-in-all she was a very suitable vessel to partner *Kings Cross* (1). These two vessels were the first British tugs to take advantage of wireless telephone facilities offered by Post Office coast stations. Within two months of her arrival on the Tees *Queens Cross* had been involved in a salvage operation when in a very severe gale she towed the Italian s.s. *Comitas,* (5,245/1919, 377' x 51'), from off Saltburn to the Humber.

On the 22nd June 1933 the keenly awaited diesel-electric tug *Acklam Cross,* (150/1933), was launched by Mrs. Ada Mary Crosthwaite at the shipyard of Hall, Russell & Co. Ltd. at Aberdeen to the order of Tees Towing Co. Ltd. She made her trial trip on the 31st August 1933 from Aberdeen and eleven days later was at work on the River Tees.

Acklam Cross was innovatory in many respects and raised some eyebrows amongst British tugowners of the day who in general were very conservative when it came to tug design. What, then, were these novel features? :–

1. She was the first British built diesel-electric tug.
2. She had direct control of her engines from the bridge.
3. She was the first tug to have a clear after deck with no towing bows.
4. She had no chains or rods to her steering gear.
5. Her engines were electrically started.
6. Her engines ran at a constant speed of 900 RPM.

The *Acklam Cross* was fitted with two 6-cylinder Brotherhood-Ricardo diesel engines each developing 300 BHP. The 500 HP direct current electric propulsion motor and the generators were supplied by the General Electric Co. Ltd. William Crosthwaite was rightly proud of his new tug and defended its relatively high cost on the grounds of improved economy of operation, (largely due to a crew of only four being required) its excellent manoeuvrability and its rapid start-up from rest. An unusual feature of the building of this ship was that the hull, engines and electrical gear were all the subject of separate contracts between the suppliers and the owners. She had cost the Company £30,000.

Fig. 23 Queens Cross *and* Hutton Cross *(1) manoeuvring the Ellerman liner* City of Glasgow *into position to pass through the 80 feet wide exit channel from Middlesbrough Dock in 1933.*
(W. Haig Parry)

Fig. 24 Kings Cross *(1) towing the Finnish four-masted* Passat *to sea from the River Tees c.1933. Note the radio aerials fitted to the tug and also to the sailing vessel. (W. Haig Parry)*

Acklam Cross was to stay in Tees Towing's ownership until 1964 and her skipper, until he retired in 1950, was Charlie Rounce. (Fig. 22). She made her debut on the Tees on the 11th September 1933 by sharing the towage of the British India Steam Navigation Co.'s *Malda,* (8,965/1922, 465' x 58'), to Billingham Reach Wharf with *Kings Cross* (1) and *Lingdale.*

Having made two very important additions to their fleet Tees Towing not surprisingly felt it necessary to dispose of some of their older units. First to go in October was *Samphire Batts;* although a powerful tug she was forty years old and her work would now be able to be carried out by *Queens Cross.* When first built she had been employed as a fish carrier taking the trawlers' catches in the North Sea to Billingsgate fish market in London. In the First World War she had spent some years at Scapa Flow towing coal barges to bunker the warships anchored there. Her end came when she went to Clayton & Davie Ltd. at Dunston-on-Tyne for breaking up. The following month *Ingleby Cross* (1) was sold for further service to Grangemouth and Forth Towing Co. Ltd. with whom as the *Elie* she was to work until 1962. When scrapped in 1963 she was just over 50 years of age.

A further pleasure for the Crosthwaite family was when on the 21st November 1933, Cecil Crosthwaite married Nora Mahoney Bowden. They went to live at 17, Cornfield Road, Linthorpe, Middlesbrough.

In the October severe gale, which lasted for several days, whilst *Queens Cross* was rescuing the s.s. *Comitas* off Saltburn as previously mentioned, the Ropner vessel s.s. *Boulderpool,* (4,805/1928, 405' x 53'), got into trouble inside the river on her way to Smith's Dock where she had been built. She was refloated by *Athlete* after a hard struggle against the elements.

The level of unemployment in Middlesbrough had now reached its peak of

18,000 "on the dole". One of the activities of the townsfolk on a fine Sunday afternoon was to stroll down to Dock Point to watch the movements of shipping up and down the river and in and out of the LNER Middlesbrough Dock. It was common for quite a large crowd to gather. The point where they congregated was of course near to the tug berths and the activities of the tugs engaged no small part of their interest. (Figs. 23 & 24 illustrate the scenes of the times that they would be able to observe). It is sad that today this general interest in the port is missing partly brought about by the lack of suitable public access to points on the river banks where activity can be seen.

In the midst of the excitement of accepting the *Acklam Cross* William Crosthwaite would have been saddened by a fatal accident to one of his Teesbank Engineering Company's employees. John Pearson, aged 15, was drowned when thrown into the river from a launch which was struck by the Hartlepool-built Spanish steamer *Urkiola Mendi,* (3,552/1902, 340' x 47'), whilst that vessel was being fumigated in mid-river. It would seem that the vessel had moved unexpectedly. All activities connected with the sea and ships entail some risk and sadly accidents occurred from time to time.

The year 1934 saw a further reduction in the size of the tug fleets but at the same time their capabilities were strengthened by the addition of another vessel capable of carrying out sea towage. The TCC had in February advertised for sale their tug *Joseph Constantine.* Tees Towing purchased her in May for £1,500 and renamed her *Charing Cross,* (153/1913), a name she was to retain for 23 years whilst in the company's ownership. *Charing Cross* was rapidly brought into operation for by early June, with *Kings Cross* (1), she was towing an Admiralty floating dock from Scapa Flow to Rosyth for demolition.

On the debit side the large paddle tug *Hutton Cross* (1) was sold in August 1934 to Clayton & Davie Ltd. for breaking up on the Tyne and in the same month *Graythorpe* of the Middlesbrough Towage Company was also dismantled. By October *Troon,* also of the latter company, had been sold to J.H. Lamey Ltd. of Liverpool where she remained in service until 1948 even though already 32 years old when she left the Tees. At about the same time the Duncan Company disposed of the *Steelopolis* to the Commonwealth Steam Tug Company at Avonmouth for £2,050. She was 38 years old when she arrived in the Severn estuary but nevertheless had another 15 years of life left in her.

So it was, therefore, that these changes maintained Tees Towing's fleet at eight vessels whilst both Charles Duncan & Sons and Middlesbrough Towage Company now had no tugs in their ownership. For Duncans this was to be only briefly so; but the latter company, although not formally wound up until 1956, was not thereafter to own any more vessels. Whilst the Middlesbrough Towage Company was being denuded of its tugs the Tees Sand & Gravel Company together withs its motor barges *Sweep* and *Leeds Sun,* was sold to its manager J.W. Nellist to form the Middlesbrough Sand & Gravel Company. Thus it was that the former George Alder interests moved outside of the control of William Crosthwaite.

In February 1934 William Crosthwaite was appointed a director of the steelmaking firm of Dorman Long & Co. Ltd. for the next three years to represent the interests of the debenture holders' association. On the 28th of the month that company's Newport vertical lift bridge was opened by the Duke and Duchess of York. Its purpose was to improve communication between Middlesbrough and Billingham and indeed between the whole of the South and North banks of the lower reaches of the river. When raised the bridge gave 120 feet clearance at high water; *Acklam Cross* had the honour of being the first vessel to pass beneath the bridge after the official opening. In its first year of operation the bridge was raised no less than 1,500 times to permit the passage of ships to and from Stockton.

On the 15th September 1934 Cecil Crosthwaite's son Richard was born whilst the family were living at 17 Cornfield Road, Middlesbrough. There were now four generations of the Crosthwaite family, Thomas 75, William 54, Cecil 25 and the newly born Richard the latter three of whom were, or would be, Chairman of the Tees Towing Co. Ltd. During the year William's son-in-law Claude Fairweather was to join the company from ICI Ltd. at Billingham.

William Crosthwaite for some time had realised that there was a need for an association of tugowners in the British Isles so that they could discuss formally matters of common interest relative to the running of their various companies. He convened a special meeting of representatives of the British companies out of which was soon formed the Tugowners' Institute a name later changed to the British Tugowners' Association. From its inception in 1934 to the present day William, his son Cecil and his grandson Richard have played a leading roll in the running and development of this association.

In 1935, again following in William Crosthwaite's footsteps, John Wesley Brown was elected President of the Teesside Chamber of Commerce. Both of them in their civic capacity as councillors would have been very much involved in the town's celebration of the Silver Jubilee of King George V and Queen Mary.

To compensate for the sale of *Steelopolis* in the previous year Tees Towing transferred the paddle tug *Cleveland* from their ownership to that of Charles Duncan & Sons in April 1935. The transfer value was £3,500. One month later the Crosthwaite Steamship Company sold their *Bilsdale,* at the age of 35, for breaking-up. Once again it was Clayton & Davie Ltd. on the Tyne who took her. She had been 10 years with the Crosthwaite Steamship Company spending the summer months running her very popular excursions on the Yorkshire coast and it would appear to have been a successful enterprise for all concerned.

It has been mentioned earlier how Tees Towing in the face of lack of work on the River Tees had diversified into sea towage by the purchase of larger more powerful tugs suited to that purpose. A record still exists of the estimated and achieved costs of the towage of a sailing ship from the Thames to Charlestown on the Firth of Forth for breaking up. The subject of the tow was no ordinary sailing ship for she was the famous three-masted square-rigged *Grace Harwar* which has already been noted as having been in the Tees in 1931. She had been the last full-rigged ship in commercial operation, having been built on the Clyde in 1889 and latterly owned by Gustaf Erikson of Mariehamn. She had arrived in England from Australia less than a month previously and was now being sold for scrapping.

Queens Cross took the job in hand from 14th to 20th July 1935; the record of the times taken and the costs involved given below make interesting reading and are therefore reproduced in full overleaf.

QUEENS CROSS/GRACE HAWAR
14th to 20th July 1935
7 days' voyage

Estimate

Tees to London	300 at 8	= 37½*	
London to Charlestown	420 at 4½	= 93½	
Charlestown to Tees	160 at 8	= 20	
			£151. 0.0
Stern Tug (Thames)			£ 10. 0.0
Commission (Clarksons)			£ 8.15.0
			£169.15.0

Quoted £175

*300 nautical miles at 8 knots = 37½ hours.
Then charged £1 per hour.

Actual Costs

Wages			
Queens Cross			
Wages		£40.17.1	
Food		£ 7.16.7½	
State Insurance		19.0	£49.12.8½
Coal and Stores			
Coal	37 tons at 16/– p.t.	£30. 0.0	
Lub. Oil	15 galls at 1/6 p.g.	£ 1. 2.6.	
Stores	7 days at 10/–	£ 3.10.0.	
			£34.12.6
Disbursements			
Stern tug (Etheridge)			£ 9. 0.0
Commission etc.			
Clarkson & Co. 5%		£ 8.15.0	
Office Expenses		£ 2. 0.0	
Wireless Traffic		5.0	
			£11. 0.0
			£104.5.2½

Balance on the operation £70.14.9½**

(**Whilst the balance on the operation seems high (68% of the costs) it should be remembered that this is not profit since many other costs have to be paid for from the accumulation of such balances. Today the balance would probably be called an operating margin.)

The crew of *Queens Cross* at this time consisted of Master, mate, deckhand, engineer, cook, boy and two firemen.

At the end of 1935 the tug fleet had reduced to eight vessels owned as follows:–

Tees Towing Co. Ltd.

Steam paddle tug	*Lingdale*
Steam screw tug	*Athlete*
Steam screw tug	*George Robinson*
Steam screw tug	*Kings Cross* (1)
Steam screw tug	*Queens Cross*
Diesel-electric screw tug	*Acklam Cross*
Steam screw tug	*Charing Cross*

Charles Duncan & Sons Ltd.

Steam paddle tug	*Cleveland*

The Crosthwaite Steamship Co. Ltd. and the Middlesbrough Towage Co. Ltd. although still in existence did not own any tugs. The fleet still included two paddle tugs both over 50 years of age; these were needed to work at the stern of a vessel under tow. William Crosthwaite had attended George Baird's lecture given to the North East Coast Institution of Engineers and Shipbuilders and entitled "Notes on the Development of Tug Boat Machinery during the past forty-six years", after which he had contributed the following comment.

> "Paddle tugs have many advantages – For taking the way off a ship or stopping her altogether there is nothing better that has such control over a hull as twin side-lever engines."

In January 1936 the whole country mourned the death of King George V who was succeeded by his son King Edward VIII who however abdicated before the year was out in favour of his brother King George VI. The Spanish Civil War had commenced with all the ominous signs of coming unrest throughout Europe.

Also in January 1936 *Queens Cross, Athlete* and *Lingdale* towed the United States ship *West Hika,* (5,372/1919, 410' x 54'), into the Tees after she had run aground three miles south of Seaham Harbour. (Fig. 25).

In Middlesbrough, the unemployment figures had fallen to just below 10,000 for the first time since the 1920's. Nevertheless, the effects of the depression were still very serious in the town and a deputation headed by Councillor Crosthwaite as chairman of the Tees District Development Board tried without success to persuade the Ministry of Labour to include Teesside amongst the newly designated Special Areas. William Crosthwaite, obviously doing all he could to help the desperate situation, was appointed by Lord Rushcliffe as chairman of the Advisory Committee of the Middlesbrough District of the Unemployed Assistance Board. As if he had not enough on his hands we find William Crosthwaite off on his travels again at the end of July 1936 for a two months' tour of North America, starting in Quebec, to enable him to keep abreast of the latest developments in tug design and operation.

Communication between vessels in the River Tees and from ship to shore were still difficult. This applied particularly to tugs which for example could be delayed at the mouth of the river awaiting a due vessel not knowing exactly when she might arrive. Charles. M. Duncan retired Marine Superintendent of Tees Towing, remembers well, as a boy, being sent about four miles down river and then out on a mile-long jetty to deliver a message to a waiting tug – by bicycle! It must have taken about half a day to complete such an errand. It is, therefore, of interest to note that a "Tees Speedo Service" was inaugurated in October 1936 whereby a motor launch service would be run from Acklam Corner to Redcar Wharf stopping anywhere required (including ships) by request. It sounds a fine idea but no details have come to light regarding who was running it or how long it lasted. Its flashy title is more suggestive of the 1960's than 1936.

William Crosthwaite took on even more responsibilities outside of his own towage business. On the 1st January 1937 he was appointed French Consular Agent for Teesside and later in the year he became a Board Member of the Tees Pilotage Authority a post he was to hold until 1946. In his public life he was elected chairman of the Middlesbrough General Purposes and Parliamentary Committee. John Wesley Brown became an Alderman and was soon to be Chairman of the Education Committee and both he and William Crosthwaite were by this time Justices of the Peace.

During the year many salvage services were rendered, the highlight being the efforts by *Lingdale* and *Kings Cross* (1) to refloat the large steamer *Athina Livanos,* (4,824/1936, 419' x 56'), aground at Redcar for some time. As the volume of trade on the river began to pick up again, 4,222 ships were cleared on the river in 1937.

By 1938 the clouds of war were gathering on the European horizon and any ideas that William Crosthwaite had of further modernisation of his fleet, following on the now almost five years of successful experience with *Acklam Cross* had to be weighed very carefully. Prudence suggested that he should wait until he saw how things were going to develop. As it turned out it was to be several years before further development could take place.

Fig. 25 Queens Cross, Athlete *and* Lingdale *towing the disabled United States vessel* West Hika *into the River Tees, in January 1936. She had stranded near Seaham Harbour and was subsequently broken-up. (W. Haig Parry)*

The re-arrangement of the various companies and the changes in the vessel ownership which have occurred through the progress of this story are, to say the least, somewhat involved and probably a little confusing. It might, therefore, be useful to review the situation as it stood in March 1938.

Tees Towing Co. Ltd., owners of one paddle and six screw tugs, owned the Crosthwaite Steamship Co. Ltd. and the Middlesbrough Towage Co. Ltd. both of which companies owned no vessels nor were to do so again. The Crosthwaite Steamship Co. Ltd. in turn owned all the ordinary shares of Charles Duncan & Sons Ltd. who operated one paddle tug. The tug operations were managed by the firm of Robinson and Crosthwaite, the sole partner of whom (since Charles Robinson died in 1923) being William Crosthwaite.

At the end of March 1938 a new tug capable of co-operating with *Kings Cross* (1), *Queens Cross* and *Charing Cross* in sea towage work was purchased by Tees Towing. She was the *Protea* which had been owned briefly on the Thames but had spent most of her time, since being built in 1924, working at Port Elizabeth in South Africa. She cost the company £10,000, no less, and was renamed *Euston Cross,* (226/1924), on arrival in the Tees. She was to give long and valuable service to the company (and to her country too) in the years to come. *Kings Cross* (1) had been put to a use which curiously did not involve towing anything. Because of her wireless telephone equipment she was contracted out for the calibration of Wick and Portpatrick Radio Stations in Scotland.

William Crosthwaite had taken on yet more public duties; he was now a member of the Tees (Newport) Bridge Joint Committee which had control of the finances and operation of the Newport vertical lift bridge and became chairman of the newly-formed Middlesbrough Air Raid Precautions Committee. In the New Year's Honours List it was announced that William Henry Crosthwaite had been honoured for his public services by being made a Knight Bachelor. He was the first Middlesbrough-born man to be so honoured. Naturally his family, his employees, his colleagues in public life and the townsfolk in general were delighed to learn of his well-earned recognition. His coat of arms is illustrated at Fig. 26.

Sailing ships were still trading during this time but were not to do so for much longer. In July 1939 the *Penang,* (1,997/1905, 285' x 40'), was in the Tees and had been towed by *Kings Cross* (1) and *Cleveland.* On the 23rd June *Kings Cross* (1) had been involved in the towing off of the *Ernrix,* (692/1921, 175' x 29'), aground on the North Yorkshire coast, the tug's skipper at the time being Joseph (Joe) Harrison. This rescue nearly had serious consequences for the hull of the *Ernrix* split due to expansion of her cargo and threw into the sea two of the crew of *Kings Cross* (1), Alex Duncan the mate and Gordon Munchin the engineer. Happily they were rescued in the nick of time without sustaining injury. (Fig. 27).

ACKLAM CROSS

Fig. 26 *The Coat of Arms of Sir William Crosthwaite. The motto "Tenax-Animo" translates as "steadfast".*

Fig. 27 *Captain Joe Harrison, skipper of* Kings Cross *(1) pictured with two members of his crew Alex Duncan (left) and Gordon Munchin (right) in June 1939 on their return from the salvage of the* Ernrix. *The two latter had been rescued from the sea when the* Ernrix *foundered. (By courtesy of The Evening Gazette, Cleveland.)*

Chapter Seven

The Second World War 1939–1945

The threat of hostilities with Germany had been present for some time now so that when after many months of fruitless discussions war was declared on 3rd September 1939 everyone was sad and worried but not perhaps greatly surprised. Shortly after the outbreak of war Sir William became the 81st Mayor of Middlesbrough, a position he was to hold for four years until 1943. He was also to remain chairman of the Emergency Committee throughout the war until September 1945 and was thus in a post of great responsibility at a critical time.

Sir William's father Thomas Crosthwaite died during 1939 and his son Cecil who was a Major in 23 Division Signals Regiment (TA) went off at the age of 30 to serve as a Signals Staff Officer at Northern Command and later at the War Office. His son-in-law Claude Fairweather also with the rank of Major went away to serve his country. Fig. 28 shows a family group taken on Christmas Day.

Fig. 28 *A family group taken on Christmas Day 1939 when Councillor Sir William Crosthwaite had been appointed Mayor of Middlesbrough for the second time. With him, in the garden of his home at Thornfield Road, Middlesbrough are from left to right; back row, Lawrence Richmond-Smith, Major Claude Fairweather, Captain Cecil Crosthwaite; front row, Mrs. Dorothy Richmond-Smith and her son, Mrs. Alice Fairweather with her daughter and son, the Mayoress Lady Ada Crosthwaite and Mrs. Mahoney Crosthwaite with sons Richard and John.*
(W. Haig Parry)

The first four months of the war brought eight salvage jobs for the Tees Towing and Duncan tugs. They were all tough assignments and called for great persistence and endurance on the part of the tug crews involved. Whilst space does not permit of inclusion here of all the salvage jobs it is right that a selection of them should be given in some detail through the period of the war to illustrate just how valuable these tugmen were.

Salvage of CAPE COMORIN, (504/1936, 167' x 28').

"*Athlete* and *Lingdale* left Middlesbrough for Whitby at 8 a.m. on 11th December 1939. They towed at the vessel – without success – on the p.m. tide. Both tugs put into Whitby and were ordered to Middlesbrough at 2 p.m. on the 12th arriving at 6 p.m.

On the 13th an agent phoned at noon for tugs to be sent at once. The *Athlete* and *Lingdale* left Middlesbrough at 12.30 p.m. They towed the vessel off on the p.m. tide and berthed her safely in Whitby, finishing at 8 p.m. Both tugs left Whitby at 7 a.m. on the 14th, arriving in the Tees at noon.

Athlete proceeded to Whitby at noon on the 10th January 1940 to commence towage of the vessel to Hartlepool early the following morning. *Athlete* towed at the vessel on the a.m. tide of the 11th but was unable to get her off the ground. On the p.m. tide *Athlete* towed the vessel off and placed her at the quay ready for sailing the following morning. *Athlete* left Whitby with the vessel at 5 a.m. on the 12th arrived at Hartlepool at 10.30 a.m. and Middlesbrough at noon."

Athlete	**Lingdale**
J.W. Spink (Skipper)	E. Watson (Skipper)
H. Scott	A. Appleton
E. Carr	J. Lilley
J. Appleton	H. Lee
R. Insall	A. Hutchinson
D. Williams	J. Watts

Salvage award £400 less expenses £100 = £300 shared on the basis of approximately 25% to the crew and 75% to the company.

Athlete £44 *Lingdale* £31

During the early part of the war three of Tees Towing's fleet were requisitioned by the then Ministry of Shipping. They were the *Kings Cross* (1), *Queens Cross* and *Charing Cross*. *Kings Cross* (1) was away soon after the commencement of the war and *Queens Cross* went in March 1940. Both were away from the Tees for the remainder of the war and did not return until 1946. *Kings Cross* (1) worked initially at Kirkwall until 1941 and then at Loch Ewe. Whilst away, both of these tugs were managed by the United Towing Co. Ltd. of Hull. *Charing Cross* also worked at Kirkwall but returned to the Tees late in 1940; management in her case was retained by Robinson & Crosthwaite. Whilst at Scapa Flow, on one occasion it is said that her master and her crew were awakened at 2 a.m. and ordered by a senior naval officer to take a bouquet of flowers to a nurse on a hospital ship moored some 22 miles away. Perhaps the purveyor of this information had better remain anonymous since he considered that *Charing Cross* was just a "dogsbody" for the SNO Tugs at Scapa, and wasn't doing anything particularly useful.

Depleted as their fleet was by these requisitions Tees Towing was able to cope on its home river since the traffic, as in the First World War, was very much reduced. The recorded clearances on the river in 1940 amounted only to 1,884 ships. It must, however, be remembered that there were many naval movements in and about the Tees which would in reality swell the officially recorded numbers.

On the 1st April 1940 the young Arthur Greenwell joined Tees Towing as office boy in the Exchange Place premises. After having served on tugs during the war he was to rise through the company to be its Secretary and later still its Commercial Director. These posts he still holds.

The war came a lot nearer when, in May 1940, the first German bombs fell on Middlesbrough and surrounding towns and the British population in general were brought face to face with the realities of war with the evacuation of Dunkirk and the fall of France. Invasion of the British Isles now appeared a probability.

A typical salvage job of 1940 involving war damage to a Royal Navy minesweeping sloop was reported at the time as follows.

Salvage of Minesweeping Sloop H.M.S. HALCYON

"Shortly after this vessel had put to sea from the River Tees on the 27th September 1940, she suffered damage as a result of a mine exploding close by, and was without her main engines and down by the stern. The tug *Acklam Cross* was despatched to assist the vessel. Meanwhile the ship had been picked up by the Tees Examination Vessel at about 7 p.m. The ship was later taken over by the Hartlepool tug *N E R No. 6* which commenced towing towards the River Tees. The *Acklam Cross* connected about 7.45 p.m. Together the two tugs towed the ship into the river at 8.00 p.m. The tug *Cleveland* accompanied the ship into the river and connected to her in the vicinity of No. 3 Black Buoy. *NER No. 6* cast off just above the Ninth Buoy. The ship was berthed alongside Smith's Quay about 9 p.m. Both tugs were ordered to stand by, and were further required at 10.45 p.m., in an attempt to drydock the ship but owing to the ship's stern being so low in the water she could not be completely docked. Both tugs let go at 11.15 p.m. and were again ordered to stand by, at 3.40 a.m. both tugs were released, arriving back at their Dock Point base at 4 a.m."

Acklam Cross	**Cleveland**
J.C. Rounce	E. Anderson
A. Appleton	C. Duncan
W. Carr	W. Pennick
A. Azemar	W. Appleton
W. Leddy	R. Anderson
	E. Appleton

Salvage award £900 (paid almost two years later) less £100 expenses.

Acklam Cross £125 *Cleveland* £75

This episode was only one of twenty-four such events in 1940 many due to enemy action but also several due to severe weather.

It was in 1941 that the writer, on leaving school, took up a job at a factory which overlooked the River Tees estuary. It was in this situation that he became interested in ships in general and tugs in particular. Almost every day it was possible to observe the Tees Towing and Duncan tugs in operation. One particular memory from those days is of being able to hear the whine of the electric generator and motor of the *Acklam Cross* coming across the Seal Sands area from anything up to a mile and a half away. She could never have done anything surreptitiously! Curiously those who worked on board had no complaint about any excessive noise.

In June 1941 King George VI and Queen Elizabeth visited Middlesbrough, without advance publicity of course, and Sir William, as Mayor of the town, had the honour and responsibility of greeting the Royal Visitors on arrival and conducting them on their tour (Fig. 29). The sight of their Majesties in the North East was a big morale booster to the populace.

The centenary of the opening of the LNER Middlesbrough Dock was marked on 19th May, 1942. Although modified in size several times in its earlier years it had barely been improved since 1898. Most of the larger general cargo ships visiting the river would use the enclosed dock. However its shape did not help towards efficient berthing of vessels; often it was necessary to move a ship already there to let in a new arrival to its required berth. All useful work for the tugs, but not conducive to quick turn around at a critical time of the war. Quayside access was at that time almost wholly by rail, road access being very difficult indeed.

On the 13th January 1942 the s.s. *Empire Masefield,* (7,050/1941, 433' x 56'), was in trouble. The following is a contemporary report of the event.

Salvage of the EMPIRE MASEFIELD

"This steamer, in the course of putting into the River Tees after being bombed and damaged, stranded on the North Gare very near to the wreck of *Cargo Fleet Steam Hopper.* The bombs had exploded in the tween decks and there was a hole in the steamer's port side giving 2'9" freeboard. The tugs *Euston Cross, Lingdale* and *Acklam Cross* towed at the steamer on the a.m. tide of the 14th January and additionally *George Robinson* and *Athlete* on the p.m. tide; the same five tugs on the a.m. tide of 15th January, and the steamer was refloated and towed up to Middlesbrough Dock on the p.m. tide of that day by the same five tugs. After the tugs *Euston Cross* and *Acklam Cross* had cast off from the steamer on the a.m. tide of the 14th they both stranded on the North Gare sands. The *Acklam Cross* was refloated with the assistance of *Lingdale* and the *Euston Cross* refloated without assistance.

The *George Robinson* backed into and damaged the bow of the salvage tender *T.H. Tilly* (The Hartlepool Pilot Cutter). The lighters *Sweep* and *Leeds Sun* with stevedores and discharging equipment were supplied at the request of the master of the steamer but were not made use of."

Acklam Cross	**Athlete**	**Euston Cross**
J.C. Rounce	J. Harrison	H. Page
C. Hutchinson	A.C. Duncan	H. Scott
W.A. Carr	E. Carr	H. Hutchinson
A.E. Azemar	G. Finley	A. Hudson
J.R. Miller	R. Anderson	J. Purvis
	T.A. Johnson	E. Johnson

George Robinson	Lingdale
G. Boalch	E. Watson Snr.
H. Hudson	R. Walker
G. Scarlett	J. Lilley
N. Lee	E. Robinson
J. Scott	L. Scott
P. Finley	K. Marsden

Salvage award £3,540 less £536 expenses = £3,004 shared amongst the five tugs and the company.

Fig. 29 *Visit of Their Majesties King George VI and Queen Elizabeth to Middlesbrough on the 19th August 1941. They are seen here in Albert Park inspecting the local Civil Defence Services and accompanied by the Mayor and Mayoress of Middlesbrough Councillor Sir William and Lady Crosthwaite.*

Salvage work was still keeping the tugs busy; there had been twenty-six such occasions in 1941 and there were to be a further nine in 1942 following the event just described.

On the 17th April 1942 Sir William Crosthwaite was appointed Deputy Chairman of the Tees Conservancy Commissioners and in that position had a considerable influence on the activities concerning the maintenance and development of the river. By November of the same year he had become the sixth Chairman of the Commissioners a position he was to hold until 1945. During the year he relinquished his chairmanship of the British Tugowners Association, presumably because of his many local commitments throughout the most difficult period of the war. At this time his son Cecil had been honoured by being awarded the Territorial Army Decoration (TD) for his work in the Royal Signals prior to the war.

With *Kings Cross* (1) and *Queens Cross* still away from the River Tees there was a need for an additional tug to cope with the jobs in hand. Obviously in the midst of the war there would not be very many vessels which were not sorely needed where they were already working. However, there was a pilot cutter available in South Wales, which had at one time been employed as a tug by Alexandra Towing Co. Ltd. She was the *Lady Howard Stepney*, (93/1906), and was currently owned by the Llanelly Pilots. She was purchased by Tees Towing for £1,300 in July 1942 and brought to the Tees where she was to work until 1948. This small tug with the large name was the first addition to be made to the fleet since 1938; because of the wartime situation however, she was not renamed although she was re-registered at Middlesbrough.

On August Bank Holiday Monday of 1942 Middlesbrough Railway Station was severely damaged during a daylight bombing raid. Tees Towing's offices at 8, Exchange Place which were in the same block of buildings as the station received a severe shaking, and as was to be expected, most of their windows were shattered. It was fortunate that, being a public holiday, the offices were not occupied at the time. The same area had also suffered badly in raids only a few nights previously but, nevertheless, as everywhere when this happened it was "business as usual" no matter what the difficulties may have been.

All through the six years of war the Tees Towing and Duncan tugs were busily occupied in dealing with vessels of the Royal and Allied Navies from large destroyers to the smallest landing craft which were either new buildings or in the river for replenishment or repair. The variety of ships was truly amazing. None more so than the many types of landing craft built at Stockton, Haverton Hill, Middlesbrough and South Bank. These craft were predominently in evidence during 1943 and 1944 as the build-up for the invasion of Normandy gained momentum and it was with these vessels that the tugs spent a lot of their time whilst the landing craft were on trials or compass adjusting between Redcar Wharf and the Fifth Buoy Light. The tug would typically be made fast amidships and the two would swing together until satisfied with the compass setting. Some idea of the volume of work involved can be judged when it is realised that no fewer than sixty ships and two hundred and ninety-seven large Landing Craft were built on the river for the Royal Navy during the Second World War.

Sir William Crosthwaite was made an Alderman of Middlesbrough during 1943. By this time the threat of a German invasion of the British Isles had receded far enough to allow the use again of church bells and the chimes of public clocks. (Since 1940 they had been banned for normal use and were intended to be rung only as a warning of imminent invasion from the air). So it came about that in September the Mayoress, Lady Crosthwaite, formally restarted the striking and chiming apparatus of the Middlesbrough Town Hall clock after over three years of silence. This may seem of small note now but its significance to the population in 1943 must have meant a great deal. Additionally, it reminds us of the early part of this story when in 1889 Princess Alexandra had started the same clock at the opening of the newly-built Town Hall. With an eye to the future of the river after the war was over the TCC set up their Development Committee of which Sir William was a member. It was chaired by George West Byng and was to consider the post-war requirements having regard to the expected expansion of Teesside and the need for up-to-date shipping facilities.

The year 1944 was to be one of momentous occurrences; in particular the invasion of the Normandy coast of France by Allied forces and the assembly of the

"Mulberry" harbour there to permit unloading of a massive quantity of men, stores, equipment and vehicles. The strange components of this harbour were built at many locations around the coast of Britain and of course these included the River Tees. Two of the concrete caissons, code named "Phoenix" were built in the Graythorp drydock of William Gray. These were taken south to their assembly point by ocean-going Royal Navy and Dutch tugs but were handled out of their building dock by the local tugs, the first being dealt with by *Acklam Cross, Cleveland* and a railway company tug from Hartlepool (Fig. 30).

For the work of towing the unwieldy units from their assembly anchorages on the south and south-east coasts of England and for the varied towing requirements associated with the invasion operation a great many tugs were to be needed. Not surprisingly there were insufficient tugs available. Many more had to be requisitioned by the Ministry of War Transport and temporarily removed from their normal commercial spheres of work. On the Tees it fell to *Euston Cross* and *Charing Cross* to join the armada which eventually totalled 132 tugs based in the Solent on the accommodation ship *Aorangi,* (17,486/1924). *Charing Cross,* with skipper Micky Spink and her local crew augmented by DEMS gunners sailed for the South Coast in early May 1944. Later during this duty George Spencer became her skipper.

Fig. 30 Acklam Cross, NER No. 6 *and* Cleveland *manoeuvring the first of the "Phoenix" concrete caissons out of Wm. Gray's drydock at Graythorp in 1944. These units were towed south to form part of the "Mulberry" harbour built off the coast of Normandy following the landing of allied forces there in June 1944. (W. Haig Parry)*

We are fortunate in having a diary of the movements of *Euston Cross* from the time she left Middlesbrough on the 23rd May, 1944, under the command of Harry Page and with a crew of seventeen, until the 22nd Sepember 1944. The diarist was Arthur Greenwell, then wireless operator, and now the Company's Commercial Director. His notes give a clear indication of how dangerous, hard and at times frustrating a job it was that faced them. When they set off they did not know their ultimate destination or for what purpose the units they were towing were to be used. The *Euston Cross* was to be away from her home river for nine months in all. The "log" records briefly the 80 hour-long gale from the 19th to 22nd June which is referred to as "heavy sea" and "heavy swell" when in fact it was the worst summer-time storm in the Channel for forty years! It was so severe that the American artificial harbour was completely wrecked and so much damage was caused to the British harbour that the entire operation "Overlord" was threatened with disaster. Skipper Harry Page was not to remain with the vessel throughout the invasion duties as he had the misfortune to fall and injure his leg. His place was taken by Tommy Hutchinson.

The assembly points for the individual harbour units were the River Thames, off Dungeness and off Selsey for the concrete "Phoenix" units forming the breakwaters and off Dungeness and in the Solent for the "Whale" units which made-up the floating piers and roadways. *Euston Cross* was involved in all of these areas as were *Charing Cross, Kings Cross* (1) and *Queens Cross.* The large crew of the *Euston Cross* will have been noted. Extra accommodation had been provided – in the rope locker aft! Included amongst the augmented crew were an additional wireless operator, a naval signaller and two DEMS gunners. These latter were to man the Oerlikon gun on the foredeck and also the Lewis gun. Rifles were also provided and the ship was fitted with anti-aircraft wire rope projectiles and bridge protective plating. Her appearance and trim had altered materially.

Let now the following extracts from the diary speak for themselves and, in doing so, pay tribute to all the tugmen who took part in this gigantic operation.

Extracts from the Log of the Movements of EUSTON CROSS 23rd May to 22nd September, 1944

1944

23rd May	Left Tees with *Empire Sara,* 7.45 a.m., towing "Donald Duck". (A concrete "Phoenix" unit.)
25th	Anchored Southend, 10 a.m.
26th	Still anchored in the Warp. Towed in by *Sun VIII* and beached at Southend. Rope in propeller.
27th	Propeller clear. Rejoined *Empire Sara* at Warp.
	Arrived Dungeness, 6.00 a.m. Left "Donald Duck", sailed for Portsmouth, arrived 6.30 p.m., turned round laid in Stokes Bay.
30th May	Laid alongside ss *Spanker* (1,875/1917), Stokes Bay.
1st June	Coaled. Watered at ms *Karabagh,* (6,590/1932). To Lee-on-Solent.
6th	Lee-on-Solent. Invasion started. Picked up the bridge links. ("Whales").

7th June	12.30 p.m., sailed in convoy for France with bridge links.
8th	Cast bridge links adrift. Arrived off Caen 7 a.m. Anchored 2 miles from coast. Weighed anchor 9.35 p.m. Warship bombardment 7 to 7.30 p.m. Bayeaux captured, 6½ miles from where we anchored. 11.45 p.m. ship shelled and sunk; believe it to be one of four enemy destroyers.
9th	Dropped anchor 12.30 a.m. Weighed anchor 6 a.m. Picked up bridge link off Nab and towed to lee-on-Solent. Anchored 11.10 p.m.
10th	Watered and coaled. On board ms *Aorangi* for an hour. Port hole repaired.
11th	Sailed 5.50 a.m. for France with *Dundas* towing pontoon bridge.
12th	Arrived off Isigny 6 p.m. ¼ mile off-shore Grandchamp. Set off 8.30 p.m. 11.45 p.m. stopped by shot across bows from Torpedo Boats.
13th	Anchored 1.30 a.m. Under weigh 6 a.m. Arrived Lee-on-Solent 5.15 p.m. Watered at ms *British Faith,* (6,977/1928). Anchored near *Aorangi.*
17th	Watered at *Karabagh.* Picked pontoon float up at St. Helen's towed to Peel Bank.
18th	Coaled at ss *Sherbrooke,* (1,979/1922). Anchored.
19th	Moved *Thames III* to *British Faith.* Sailed light 2.30 p.m. for France. Heavy sea.
20th	Arrived 1 a.m. Heavy swell. Grounded whilst trying to connect to American ship. Damaged rudder. Taken in tow at 11 a.m. by *Empire Rupert.* Heavy sea still running.
21st	Passed Spithead Gateway 10.30 a.m. To Lee-on-Solent.
26th June	Left Lee-on-Solent in tow of *HMS Resolve* at 11 a.m. Anchored at St. Helen's Bay at noon. Under weigh 2 p.m. bound for Southend.
3rd July	Left Southend 6.30 a.m. in tow of *Empire Belle* for Grimsby. 7 p.m. moored at Yarmouth.
6th July – 18th Aug.	Repairing at Grimsby.
21st Aug.	Left Southend 6.30 a.m. escorting two U.S.A. tugs towing crane. Arrived Folkestone 4 p.m.
22nd	Towed *ss Empire Lough* (2,824/1940, 310' x 44') with *Empire Betsy* from pier to beach.
25th	Left St. Helen's Bay 7.45 p.m. for France.
26th	Anchored 2 a.m. in thick fog. Weighed anchor 6.30 a.m. Arrived Arromanches 8 p.m. Anchored in Mulberry Harbour 9.30 p.m.
27th	Left Arromanches 7.30 a.m. Arrived Lee-on-Solent.
31st Aug.	Laid Dover. Shelling.
9th Sept.	Went to Cowes, I.O.W., 4.15 p.m. and assisted *Empire John* with pontoon outside harbour. Anchored Lee-on-Solent 6.20 p.m.

10th Sept.	Left Lee-on-Solent 10 a.m. for Southampton. Left Marchwood buoys 12 noon towing LC1 to Selsey. Arrived 4.30 p.m. Left 5.30 p.m. towing LC3 for Lee-on-Solent.
17th	Left Portland 12.30 p.m. towing MMS 75 to Southampton. Anchored Netley 8 p.m.
18th	Under weigh 8.45 a.m. Towed MMS 75 to Southampton. Left 10 a.m. for Yarmouth, I.O.W. Left Yarmouth roads 1 p.m. towing two barges. Arrived Peel Bank 4.10 p.m. Anchored Lee-on-Solent 6.15 p.m.
21st	Arrived Netley 2 p.m. Towed LCT 2302 to Gilkicker. Arrived 4.45 p.m.
22nd Sept.	Weighed anchor 12 noon for Ryde. Arrived Ryde but not required for beaching L.S.T. Proceeded to Lee-on-Solent. Left Lee 2.45 p.m. Towed LCT 2302 from Gilkicker to Portsmouth.
	Anchored Lee 5.45 p.m.

Additional information regarding the tugs mentioned in the log.

Empire Rupert *Empire John*	c.480 grt. Built 1943 Deep-sea type	Ministry of War Transport
Empire Sara *Empire Belle* *Empire Betsy*	c. 275grt. Built 1943/44 Coastwise type	Ministry of War Transport

Sun VIII	196 grt. Built 1919. W.H.J. Alexander Ltd.
Dundas	254 grt. Built 1919. Grangemouth & Forth Towing Co. Ltd.
Resolve	Built 1918. Royal Navy.

Euston Cross after completing her D-Day tasks, undertook many tows in the English Channel and to Le Havre and later was based at Ostend serving the Antwerp approaches as a rescue tug until February 1945. Whilst *Euston Cross* and *Charing Cross* were away a tug came to the Tees on charter to help fill in for them. She was the paddle tug *Corsair,* (153/1892), from France Fenwick Tyne & Wear Co. Ltd.

John Wesley Brown who had been a director of Tees Towing since its inception in 1920 and had known Sir William Crosthwaite since the latter had first started work in 1892 had died on the 8th November 1944. Honours had come the way of Sir William's son and son-in-law. Cecil Crosthwaite was made a Member of the Most Excellent Order of the British Empire (MBE) after having served in the Royal Corps of Signals in which he had been active, as a Territorial Officer, in peacetime. During the latter part of the war he held an important position in the War Office as a GSO2 in the branch of the Signals Directorate which dealt with the organisation and equipment of Signals units throughout the Army. In this capacity he was responsible for the construction and planning of the War Establishments of Signals formations all over the world, and obtaining approval to their implementation through the machinery of the War Establishment Committee. Claude Fairweather, now a Colonel in the Royal Signals, was made an Officer of the Most Excellent Order of the British Empire (OBE), in recognition of his service as Chief Signals Officer on the "Wingate" Expedition in Burma and awarded the Territorial Army Decoration.

Whilst four of Tees Towing's tugs were "away to the war" those at home still had plenty to do whilst rescuing ships from awkward predicaments. For example the destroyer *HMS Wizard* was towed into the Tees and the frigate *HMS Cam,* which was under tow to Hartlepool, broke adrift in Tees Bay where she was assisted into the river by *Athlete, Lady Howard Stepney, Cleveland* and *George Robinson.* However running with a strong wind and tide *HMS Cam* ran aground at the foot of the front leading light when inside the river. She was refloated later and berthed at Smith's Dock. And then again early in January 1945 the ss *Empire Prospero,* (6,766/1943, 417' x 57'), ran aground on the North Gare at the entrance to the river. She lost her rudder and propeller and the after part of the ship was flooded. *Athlete, Acklam Cross, Cleveland* and *George Robinson* eventually managed to refloat her. The net salvage award was £3,940 shared amongst the company and the crews of the four tugs.

In 1945, at the age of sixty-five Sir William Crosthwaite decided that he should retire from public life as an Alderman but regarding his own business he had no such thoughts; in fact quite the contrary. He retired also from the Chairmanship of the Tees Conservancy Commissioners a position he had held since 1942. During the year the tugs chartered for work in connection with invasion of France in June 1944 had returned to the river to work on their normal duties of towage of commercial traffic. Both of the requisitioned vessels were, however, still away and did not return until 1946.

The news of the end of the war in Europe came on 8th May 1945 (VE Day) and was shortly followed by the collapse of the enemy in the Far East and the end of that part of the war too. This was on 15th August 1945 (VJ Day). With the end of hostilities it was now possible for Sir William Crosthwaite to re-apply his mind to the modernisation of his tug fleet that had been abruptly interrupted in 1939. Because of the restrictions on the supply of materials and shortages of almost all commodities the improvements were not to follow as quickly as he would have hoped.

In contrast to the losses suffered in the First World War, when two tugs were mined and sunk, the companies had survived the Second World War, most surprisingly, without any losses at all. They must have thought themselves extremely fortunate.

The fleets at the end of 1945 were:–

Tees Towing Co. Ltd

Steam paddle tug	*Lingdale*	
Steam screw tug	*Athlete*	
Steam screw tug	*George Robinson*	
Steam screw tug	*Kings Cross* (1)	Requisitioned
Steam screw tug	*Queens Cross*	Requisitioned
Diesel-electric screw tug	*Acklam Cross*	
Steam screw tug	*Charing Cross*	
Steam screw tug	*Euston Cross*	
Steam screw tug	*Lady Howard Stepney*	

Charles Duncan & Sons Ltd

Steam paddle tug	*Cleveland*

Ten tugs in all but a venerable fleet. The average age was 39 years!

The Directors of Tees Towing Co. Ltd. were:–

Sir William H. Crosthwaite, J.P., (Chairman & Managing Director).
Major Cecil Crosthwaite, M.B.E., T.D.
George A. Robinson.
John Adams, (Secretary).

and the directors of the Crosthwaite Steamship Co. Ltd. were:–

Sir William H. Crosthwaite, J.P. (Chairman & Managing Director)
Major Cecil Crosthwaite, M.B.E., T.D.
John Adams, (Secretary).

Wallace S. Robinson and George A. Robinson were Marine and Engineering Superintendents respectively of both companies.

EUSTON CROSS

Fig. 31 *A group of Tees Towing's tug crews gathered on board* Charing Cross *in March 1947. They are from left to right: Captain E. Watson Snr., retired 1953; Captain H. Scott, retired 1970; J. Lillie, died 1962; R. Sutherland, retired 1973; E. Watson Jnr., retired 1974; E. Silcox; R. Anderson, retired 1973; Captain J. Purvis, retired 1978; J. Jackson, died 1957; ? Hutchinson; T. Hood, ?; ?; ?; Captain R. Harrison, retired 1978; L. Scott Snr., retired 1974 and ? Chester.*

Chapter Eight

From Steam to Diesel 1946–1962

Saturday the 9th February 1946 was a tragic day in the Company's history. The *George Robinson* was head tug towing the ss *Imperial Valley,* (4,701/1924, 402' x 54'), up river from Smith's Dry Dock to Middlesbrough Dock when, approaching the Dock Cut, the steamer over-ran and collided with the tug rolling her over and sinking her within a few seconds. So quickly had the incident occurred that only one of the crew managed to get clear of the *George Robinson* to be picked up by the stern tug *Cleveland;* he was the boy Harold Thompson aged 16. Those who were lost when the tug foundered were:–

George Boalch,	65	Skipper
Edward Davies,	32	Mate
William Hutchinson,	63	Engineer
Norman Lee,	43	Leading hand
John Scott,	56	Fireman

George Boalch had worked on tugs on the Tees for over 40 years and had been away in *Kings Cross* (1) for part of her wartime requisition period.

The *George Robinson* had sunk in mid stream leaving her masts showing at high water. Before long she was raised, refurbished and returned to service on the Tees where she was to work until being scrapped in 1950. Whilst it is well known that it is easy enough for a tug to find herself in the inextricable position that befell the *George Robinson* it is worthy of note that this was the first time that such an accident had occured in the Company's history and neither has there been a similar happening since. There have, however, been some near escapes. When she went back into service, amongst her crew was Richard Hutchinson, son of William Hutchinson who had been drowned when she sank – an action of some courage.

During 1946 the tugs under requisition had returned to the company and, therefore, except for the *George Robinson* temporarily under repair, the whole fleet was once again at the disposal of the managers, Robinson & Crosthwaite. One unenviable record achieved at the end of the year was that the average age of their tugs had now reached its peak of 40 years!

In 1946 the Tees Conservancy Commissioners obtained their Act of Parliament which gave them general powers as the Harbour Authority and gave sanction to the Commissioners proposals for the building, owning and operating of docks, oil berths, road, railways and other works at Teesport. This Act was to lead ultimately to the construction of Teesport oil jetties, Tees Dock at Lackenby and further seawards reclamation of land for industrial development. The volume of commercial traffic on the river was beginning to improve again after the much reduced figures of the war years; 1946 saw 2,310 ships cleared on the river, by no means a good figure but an improving situation was indicated.

In 1947 George Albert Robinson retired from the Board of Tees Towing and also from his position as Engineering Superintendent. He had been in the service of the company and its forbears for 60 years, thirty-one of which had been as Superintendent Engineer. His abilities are clearly indicated by the fact that the company was able to run an efficient service with, on the whole, quite aged vessels. Old though they were G.A. Robinson was able to keep them working long after their normal time for retirement – as he had done with himself too! Because of this he was retained as Consulting Engineer. His successor as Engineer Superintendent was Wilfred Carr who had latterly been engineeer on *Acklam Cross*.

Cecil Crosthwaite who had now returned from his war service was appointed Deputy Chairman of Tees Towing Co. Ltd. and from this time gradually took over the running of the company from his father, Sir William, who was now 67 years of age. Claude Fairweather who had also returned from the war, now with the rank of Brigadier after onerous service in Burma, was appointed a director of the company as was Lawrence Richmond-Smith, the solicitor husband of Dorothy Elliott, Sir William's second daughter. Long service seemed to be the norm at this time; there were five families who for four generations had served the company or its predecessors – the Duncans, Robinsons, Hutchinsons, Waltons and Wells. Another long-serving employee George Finley, Snr., who was fireman in the *Lady Howard Stepney* had started work in 1895.

Whilst, following the ravages of the war, there was a pressing need to modernise the ageing fleet this was to prove impossible for some time because of restrictions, shortages of materials and the high prices which they caused. Also it is likely that every tugowner in the land wished to do the same thing. So Tees Towing had to make do with what second-hand tonnage they could obtain. *Marple,* (123/1888), *Central No 1* and *Central No. 2* were purchased from the LNER on the 21st March 1947; all screw tugs, the last two so named because they had at one time been owned by the Great Central Railway and had worked at Grimsby.

Fig. 32 *An example of the floating docks built by the Furness Shipbuilding Co.; on this occasion, in 1948, being towed by the tugs* Euston Cross, Charing Cross, Lingdale *and* Cleveland *on the first leg of its journey to Sweden.*
(W. Haig Parry)

One could be forgiven for wondering why such an old vessel as *Marple* had been purchased. The reason was that the LNER insisted in selling all three as a job lot, so that if Tees Towing were keen on the other two – which they were – then they had to buy *Marple* as well. She cost them £500 but was sent immediately to the breakers Clayton and Davie at Dunston who paid £160 for her! The other two vessels, which were to give good service, cost the company £2,750 each and were renamed *Silver Cross,* (136/1910), and *Temple Cross,* (137/1912), respectively. They were identical vessels and had 750 IHP compound steam engines. Before entering service on the Tees they were both re-furbished at Smith's Dock, North Shields.

At the beginning of May 1947 Charles Duncan & Sons purchased the *Flying Fish,* (169/1882), a paddle tug very similar to *Cleveland* which a few days later was sent up river to be broken up at Stockton-on-Tees. A most surprising exchange – a sixty-five year old for a sixty-six year old. *Cleveland,* needing new boilers, was beyond economical repair and there was need to replace her with another vessel equally suited to stern work and therefore this did not leave much choice. When one remembers what the North Eastern Railway thought about *Cleveland* in 1914 it is remarkable how much service was obtained from her in the following thirty-three years! *Flying Fish* had in earlier years been used as an excursion vessel on the Firth of Forth and at some period of her life was on a charter that saw her running excursion trips in the Whitby area.

During the Second World War many tugs were built to the order of the Ministry of War Transport. These were in clearly defined groups although all vessels within one group were not precisely the same. One such tug purchased by Tees Towing was the *Empire Mustang* which was classified as a "Coastwise Tug" by the Ministry and was one of over a hundred similar vessels built during the war. She was a strongly built ship with a triple-expansion steam engine giving 1000 IHP; the most powerful vessel owned by the Company to date. She cost £16,250 and was renamed *Dundas Cross,* (242/1943), in August 1947.

The final fleet change of 1947 was when in December *Athlete* was sold to J.H. Lamey Ltd. of Liverpool for work on the River Mersey. She had in her earlier days on the River Thames had plenty of excitement having suffered several collisions and been involved in a number of profitable salvage operations. Although quite a powerful tug for her size her skippers on the Tees apparently considered her to be a poor seaboat. Anyhow she was not to be broken up until 1955 when 62 years old. She sailed from the Tees on 6th January 1948.

Changes to the fleet continued into 1948 when the *Lady Howard Stepney* was sold in April of that year for breaking up at Stockton Shipping and Salvage Co. Ltd. She was not completely scrapped, however, because by 1950 she was reported as "converted into a club house without means of propulsion and to be permanently moored in the River Tees". Her ultimate fate has not been discovered. In September 1948 *Kings Cross* (1) and *Queens Cross,* the two tugs originally bought for sea towage work, were sold to NV Nederland Indische Steenkolen Handelmaatschappij for service in Java. They were renamed *Adrian* and *Goos* by their new owners. Their subsequent fate is not known; they disappeared from Lloyds Register in the late 1950's. Temporarily, the *William Ryan,* (102/1928), came from the Thames on charter for a short period. Whilst on the river her skipper was Harry Page.

The screw tug *New Storm Cock* belonging to the Ocean Salvage and Towage Co. Ltd., London was bought by Tees Towing on the 10th November 1948 for

£12,850 and three months later was renamed *Kings Cross* (2). This was the first time (but not the last) that a fleet name was repeated. This is apt to be confusing for historians now, just as it probably was at the time, since only five months separated the existence of the two vessels with the same name. This was another tug not greatly liked by the skippers; she has been variously condemned as "having very poor steering, having poor steaming qualities, needing a tug to turn her round and being a bad seaboat!" Be that as it may, she nevertheless had a life of thirty-six years.

Salvage jobs were becoming fewer than of late; a steady decline that has continued right through to the present day. A typical occurrence in December 1948 was when the ss. *Brika,* (4,504/1929, 371' x 52'), loaded with 6,600 tons of iron ore stranded in fog on the North Gare. She was refloated next day by *Acklam Cross, Dundas Cross* and *Silver Cross* whose skippers were J.C. Rounce, J.W. Spink and H. Hudson. The gross salvage award for the job was £1,135.

Middlesbrough Dock, following nationalisation of the main line railways, and now operated by the British Transport Commission, reported brisk trade throughout the year. The hoped-for increase in the numbers of vessels using the river as a whole was taking place – 2,936 ships cleared on the river in 1947 and 3,284 in 1948. Post-war improvements were beginning to materialise in the Tees Towing fleet; VHF radio telephone communication was established between the riverside office at Dock Point and the individual tugs. This was a huge step forward towards more economical deployment of the tugs and cut out a lot of the time wasted whilst waiting for ships to arrive. Definitive information could be passed from the office when the exact whereabouts of incoming ships were known from telephone reports from the river mouth or coastal reporting stations.

Fig. 33 Dundas Cross, *(Skipper, J.W. (Micky) Spink) taking the Harrison liner* Trader *out of Middlesbrough Dock, c.1949. (W. Haig Parry)*

At the end of 1948 John Adams the company secretary retired due to ill health after 40 years service with Tees Towing and its forbears. Brigadier Claude Fairweather took his place as company secretary from the 1st January 1949. He was thus only the second person to hold this office in over 28 years of the company's existence. Also at this time Arthur Greenwell was appointed Assistant Secretary. In 1949 William Chrystal Duncan was elected to the Board of Tees Towing but unfortunately within a very short time he died on the 27th May at the age of 58. He, like John Adams, had served the company and its associates for forty years. Earlier in the same month William Chrystal Duncan's father Charles William Duncan had died at Scarborough at the age of 82. It will be remembered that he was the popular captain of the *Bilsdale* which ran summer-time excursions from Scarborough from 1925 until 1934.

On taking his son Cecil into partnership in 1949 Sir William Crosthwaite decided that it was time to rename the managing firm which had retained the title of Robinson & Crosthwaite since its inception in 1920 notwithstanding that Charles Robinson had soon died. The new title for the Managers was William Crosthwaite & Son. After the changes of 1949 the management of Tees Towing Co. Ltd. was constituted as follows:–

Directors:	Sir William Henry Crosthwaite, J.P., Chairman and Managing Director. Major Cecil Crosthwaite, M.B.E., T.D., Deputy Chairman. Brigadier Claude Cyril Fairweather, O.B.E., T.D., Secretary Lawrence Richmond-Smith, M.A.
Managers:	William Crosthwaite & Son
Asst. Secretary:	Arthur Greenwell
Marine Superintendent:	Wallace Robinson
Engineering Superintendent:	Wilfred Carr
Town Office:	8 Exchange Place, Middlesbrough

Business was still improving and in 1949 over 4,000 ships were reported as having been cleared on the river but, although the average size of vessel was increasing, not all of these required towage. A typical scene of the time in Middlesbrough Dock can be seen at Fig. 33. One satisfactory contract which had been obtained over the last few years was the towage to the River Thames of over three hundred sugar, coal and oil dumb barges which had been built by local engineering firms. This traffic commenced in 1946 using *Kings Cross* (1) and *Queens Cross* following their reconditioning on return from war service. River improvements such as the construction of new ore unloaders at South Bank Wharf would, it was expected, encourage the use of larger ships and thus increase the need for towage.

In May 1950 the screw tug *George Robinson* was sold to Clayton and Davie Ltd. at Dunston to be broken up after having spent forty of her fifty-four years on the River Tees. Her departure raised sad memories of her foundering four years earlier with the loss of five members of her crew. In the following month, the company purchased another of the wartime-built "Coastwise" tugs. She was the *Metinda II* (ex *Empire Nan*) owned by Metal Industries Ltd. and was similar to the *Dundas Cross* bought in 1947 though the price paid was startlingly different. She cost £47,000, nearly three times as much as the *Dundas Cross*. Immediately on purchase she was renamed *Banbury Cross* (1), (258/1945). Although steam driven she was oil fired and this may have had some bearing on the price paid. As mentioned earlier these wartime-built tugs were not to an absolutely standard design and one finds slight variations of scantlings from one shipbuilder to another. *Banbury Cross* (1) which had been built by Scott & Sons, Bowling had a particularly strongly constructed hull which would be the basis for her ultimate longevity. It is significant that in the years to come Tees Towing were to build nine new tugs at Scott & Sons perhaps because of the good impression gained from *Banbury Cross* (1). This tug was soon in action and notably in the autumn of 1950, with the apparently ever-lasting *Lingdale,* berthed the ms *British Drummer,* (3,758/1945, 344' x 48') with the first oil cargo for the new Teesport No. 1 Oil Jetty. (Fig. 35). She also towed the newly built tanker ms *Limatula,* (6,476/1950, 430' x 54') from Smith's Dock, South Bank to the River Tyne for the fitting of the latter's engines.

The veteran tug skipper John Charles Rounce retired on the 30th September 1950, at the age of 71. He had been skipper of the *Acklam Cross* since he brought her, newly built, from Aberdeen in 1933. In virtually all the photographs that there are of this vessel Charles Rounce's distinctive silhouette is to be seen at the wheel on the monkey island. He had been the skipper of the brig *Pearl* of Dundee at the early age of twenty-one in 1900 and by 1906 was employed in tugs as the skipper of the *Hero* on board which he met the lady who later became his wife.

Sir William Crosthwaite was now 70 years of age and was largely leaving the running of the Company to Cecil Crosthwaite, the Deputy Chairman. Sir William's grandson, Richard, was at this time at Uppingham School.

Fig. 34 Dundas Cross *mooring the* London Pride *at the fitting-out quay after her launch at Furness Shipbuilding Co. on 30th June 1950. Skipper, Micky Spink; Fireman, J. Walton; Boy, K. Townsend. (W. Haig Parry)*

Fig. 35 Banbury Cross *(1) and* Lingdale *berthing the tanker* British Drummer *at the Teesport No. 1 Oil Berth (later named Queen Elizabeth II Jetty) on 2nd October 1950. She was the first vessel to unload a cargo there and the event marked the first step towards the huge traffic of oil-related cargoes which now enter and leave the River Tees.*
(W. Haig Parry)

The composition of the fleets at the end of 1950 was:–

Tees Towing Co. Ltd.

Steam paddle tug	*Lingdale*
Diesel-electric screw tug	*Acklam Cross*
Steam screw tug	*Charing Cross*
Steam screw tug	*Euston Cross*
Steam screw tug	*Dundas Cross*
Steam screw tug	*Silver Cross*
Steam screw tug	*Temple Cross*
Steam screw tug	*Kings Cross* (2)
Steam screw tug	*Banbury Cross* (1)

Charles Duncan and Sons Ltd

Steam paddle tug	*Flying Fish*

Their average age, now 34 years, was starting to reduce, albeit slowly, as post war modernisation began to be possible notwithstanding the many government restrictions still in force.

In the first month of 1951 Charles Duncan and Sons disposed of their only tug, *Flying Fish*, to breakers J.J. King on the Tyne. Here again was another of the iron-hulled paddle tugs which had given such wonderfully long service to their owners. *Flying Fish* when she went to the scrapyard was no less than sixty-eight years old. However, not all the equipment aboard her was original and perhaps little but the hull was so, for she had been re-engined and re-boilered in 1907. Charles Duncan & Sons Ltd. having lost in 1949 those who had been most closely connected with their origin in 1914, namely Charles William Duncan and William Chrystal Duncan, and having disposed of their last tug, were voluntarily wound up. Prior to liquidation all of the company's voting shares had been owned by the Crosthwaite Steamship Co. Ltd.

Fig. 36 Temple Cross *and* Banbury Cross *(1) experiencing difficult conditions after the launch of* Fragum *from Smith's Dock, South Bank in a strong wind in November 1951.*
(W. Haig Parry)

On the river the volume of traffic improvement seen in 1949 and 1950 had not been maintained in 1951 having fallen by about 10% relative to the previous year and was to fall back still further in 1952. Even so in March 1951 the extension to Stockton Quay was opened indicating that the TCC had faith in the future volume of business. At Haverton Hill the Furness Shipbuilding Co. Ltd. had been taken over by Sears (Holdings) Ltd. and was continuing to build five or six ships per year of steadily increasing size. Smith's Dock Ltd., too, were building ships at a steady rate. (Fig. 36).

Salvage jobs were now averaging about eight per year and continued to do so for the next five years. One such episode worthy of note is that concerning the ss *Gripfast,* (2,866/1941, 311' x 44'), which as the *Empire Brook* had been built at Hartlepool by William Gray & Co. Ltd.

> "A message was received on the 22nd October, 1951 stating that the ss *Pandora,* (203/1893, 127' x 23'), was in distress off Cowbar Nab near Staithes and subsequent information said that she had foundered with the loss of six lives. In going to the *Pandora's* assistance the *Gripfast* had also got into difficulty and required tug assistance herself. *Banbury Cross* (1), in extremely bad weather, left the Tees and arrived on the scene about noon. The *Gripfast* had damaged her propeller and was laid with two anchors down about ½ mile off Runswick Bay (Fig. 37). After several attempts the tug succeeded in connecting to the ship at about 1600 hours, and then towed her to Hartlepool escorted by the *Euston Cross.* The ship was safely berthed by the tugs *Euston Cross* and *Temple Cross* at about 2130 hours."

A brief description of what was no doubt a hard day's work. An award of £6,500 net was made for the recovery of the *Gripfast,* the *Banbury Cross* (1) naturally getting the greater share amongst the tug crews.

Fig. 37 Banbury Cross *(1) going to the assistance of the* Gripfast *off Runswick Bay, 22nd October 1951. (Yorkshire Evening Post)*

The crews involved were–

	Banbury Cross (1)	**Euston Cross**	**Temple Cross**
Skipper	J.W. Spink	R. Harrison	G. Anderson
Mate	D. Williams	H. Robinson Snr.	E. Grayson
Engineman	W.G. Scarlett	W. Walton Snr.	G. Robinson
Fireman	H. Ditchburn	A. Crosby	C. Coleman
Fireman	J. Burr	G. Farquharson	W. Walton Jnr.
Boy	G. Richards	S. Larkman	D. Walton

In 1952 the Board of Tees Towing decided that it was time to improve their town office accommodation. They had been in their rather strangely-arranged and cramped offices at 8 Exchange Place, Middlesbrough since 1920 so clearly they were entitled to a change for the better. They moved a very short distance, to the north side of the railway, to the elegant Cleveland Buildings, Queens Square, Middlesbrough into accommodation which they still occupy today (Fig. 38). They did not need the whole of the building so a part of it has been let to various other firms. The building itself is of considerable interest having been built in 1835 as a pair of houses in which from 1841 to 1860 lived the two founders of the Middlesbrough iron trade John Vaughan and Henry Bolckow. A plaque on the building commemorates this fact. Cleveland Buildings is now a Grade II Listed Building having been so designated in 1968.

On the 6th February 1952 King George VI died suddenly and for the fourth time within the period of this history the country mourned the loss of its monarch. King George was succeeded by his daughter Queen Elizabeth II.

Fig. 38 *Cleveland Buildings, the headquarters of the Tees Towing Co. Ltd., Queens Square, Middlesbrough originally the homes of Bolckow and Vaughan. July 1982. (Richard Crosthwaite)*

Fig. 39 *The Tees Towing Operations & Maintenance Centre at Tees Wharf. Due to be superseded by a new nearby building in 1984. (Richard Crosthwaite)*

In the same month George Albert Robinson died after nearly five years of retirement. His notable service to the company had been remarked upon at the time of his retirement. At this time Charles Marshall Duncan, whose father Charles Chrystal Duncan had been lost when the *Ida Duncan* was mined in 1917, took over as Marine Superintendent at the age of thirty-seven from Wallace Robinson, the latter having held the position since the inception of Tees Towing in 1920. C.M. Duncan had started as a boy in the *Athlete* in June 1933 after finding that three years spent in a shipbroker's office was not to his liking. He was soon promoted to Assistant Towage Superintendent and when the war started in 1939 he found himself at Kirkwall supervising the work of *Kings Cross* (1) which had been requisitioned. Shortly after he returned to the Tees in 1941, he was promoted Towage Superintendent a post he retained until the retirement of Wallace Robinson.

The year 1952 was the Centenary of the setting up of the Tees Conservancy Commission which body had over that period been responsible for the steady but slow improvement and development of the river. In December, Tees Towing made the second of its moves of establishment when, following the setting up of their town office in Cleveland Buildings, they moved their riverside tug berth to new quarters at Tees Wharf. This Wharf and its immediate hinterland, which had earlier been the site of an ironworks, lay on the south side of the river a short distance seaward of the Middlesbrough Dock cut. (Figs. 39 & 40). The buildings which were erected on this site at the time of the move have remained the Company's riverside headquarters to the present day but, as will be noted later, are in 1984 being superseded by new construction containing more appropriate facilities.

On the 2nd February 1953 Arthur Greenwell took over as the third company secretary, a position which he holds today. Brigadier Claude Fairweather who had been company secretary since 1949, took over the job of Operations Director at the riverside office. This was a new position which brought

Fig. 40 *A view of Tees Wharf showing the whole of the operations and maintenance buildings with part of the tug fleet alongside c.1962. (Mather's of Middlesbrough)*

Fig. 41 Euston Cross *and* Banbury Cross *(1) towing* Suhail *to sea from the Furness Shipbuildng Yard at Haverton-Hill, April 1952. (W. Haig Parry)*

the management of the marine and engineering sides of the tug operations together so that any actions taken would be to the benefit of the overall needs of the business. In September there retired surely the doyen of all the tug masters employed by Tees Towing. To say this does no injustice to any of the other skippers. He was Ernest Watson Snr., who at sixty-nine years of age, had been a tug skipper for an incredible forty-five years, fifteen of them in his beloved paddle tug *Lingdale.* (Fig. 42). In the company salvage reports from 1939 onwards every time, bar one, that this tug was involved the skipper was E. Watson whereas for all the other tugs their masters change due no doubt to the intervention of days off etc. One gets the impression that Ernie Watson was always on duty and was so proud of his ship that he would not let anyone else get their hands on her! It would be nice to think so. The affinity between the skipper and his ship could have been heightened by the fact that there was only two years' difference in their ages. Thus it was that the "Old Man" left the "Old Lady". He would however still hear about her regularly since his son Ernest Watson Jnr. became her skipper for the few remaining years of the vessel's life. During the severe East Coast floods of 1953 the *Lingdale* was in considerable danger when with an extremely high water level in the river she floated over the wharf but apparently without serious damage. A model of the *Lingdale* was one of several tugs on show on the Tees Towing stand at the Exhibition held in Middlesbrough Town Hall in April 1953 to commemorate the Centenary of the Charter of Incorporation of the Borough which had been granted in 1853. The model is currently on display at Teesside Airport.

Fig. 42 *Captain Ernie Watson Snr., aged 69, shortly before his retirement in September 1953. (By courtesy of The Evening Gazette, Cleveland)*

Ever since the introduction of the *Acklam Cross* into the fleet in 1933 Sir William and later Cecil Crosthwaite had had the intention of continuing with their ideas of converting the fleet to diesel propulsion. They obviously needed time to evaluate the properties of diesel-electric transmission and by 1938/39 would have been, but for the intervention of the Second World War, in a position to progress further. Once the war was over this did not mean that new construction could go ahead immediately. As has already been mentioned government restrictions, steel control and the fact that all companies were looking for new tonnage at the same time meant a period of further delay. In the circumstances it was 1952 before Tees Towing could place an order for a new vessel. As with *Acklam Cross* they were to make another pioneering decision when they decided to purchase a tug with direct geared diesel drive. One might have thought that the company would have continued with the diesel-electric drive arrangement but largely because of the initial high cost of this type of machinery it had not become as popular in Europe as it was in America.

The new tug, built by Scott & Sons, Bowling and engined by Crossley Brothers Ltd., Manchester was launched and christened *Caedmon Cross,* (132/1953), by Mrs. Mahoney Crosthwaite. The vessel was delivered to the River Tees in November 1953. Although, up to this time, there had been sixty-four tugs covered by this history she was only the third tug newly-built for the Company; thereafter, however, no more second-hand tonnage was to be purchased. The *Caedmon Cross* was the first tug for a British owner to have geared diesel propulsion. Her two-stroke four-cylinder Crossley diesel engine of 750 BHP running at 320 RPM drove through a Hindmarch Modern Wheel Drive Ltd., 2:1 ratio, reverse reduction gearbox to a conventional single screw. She was to attract much attention from other tug owning companies who at first believed that Tees Towing had made an unwise move. *Caedmon Cross* was quite a short tug at just over 80 feet long and this was deliberately arranged to permit easy manoeuvrability particularly in the lock entrance to Middlesbrough Dock. By present day standards her power output was quite small. After six months' service, the Tees Towing management were so delighted with *Caedmon Cross* that in placing a further order for similar vessels Major Cecil Crosthwaite had this to say:–

> "We are thoroughly satisfied with the remarkable performance of *Caedmon Cross* during the first six months of her life. The absence of teething troubles have given us reason to believe she will be an economical vessel to maintain.
>
> We spent a long time in evolving the prototype and deciding on the main propulsion machinery from the bewildering variety offered by manufacturers today. We have not been disappointed in our choice and have been able to say, rather sooner than we anticipated, 'the same again please – twice'. Is there any need to say more?"

The River Tees traffic at 4,324 ships cleared on the river and more than six million tons of cargo handled in 1953 was rising again and was to continue to do so for the next four years.

Sir William and Lady Crosthwaite celebrated their Golden Wedding on the 27th July 1954, their son Cecil had taken up residence at Langbaurgh Hall, Great Ayton and their grandson Richard was 20 years old in September of that year. On the business side Sir William's vision of the early 1930's of a motor-driven fleet of tugs was beginning to become a reality even though it had taken much longer than he could have ever guessed. He must have been a happy man. (Fig. 43).

In May 1954 *Lingdale* was sold to J.J. King & Co. Ltd. for breaking up at Gateshead on the River Tyne. It must have been a sad sight to see her go, but she was not quite to disappear for ever since her mast was used in the refit of the

Fig. 43 *Sir William and Lady Crosthwaite on the occasion of their Golden Wedding 27th July 1954.*
(By courtesy of The Evening Gazette, Cleveland)

Ridley Steam Tug Co. Ltd.'s tug *Momentum* and more importantly her port side-lever engine was preserved and can now be seen at the Newcastle-on-Tyne Museum of Engineering and Science. *Lingdale* came to the end of her run at 72 years of age after having served 39½ years with The Tees Tug and Tees Towing Companies. Could anything more be asked of her? – certainly not!

During the summer, permission had been granted for the go ahead of the construction of a new tidal dock at Lackenby for the TCC. Some time would elapse before this was in operation but it was good news for the towage business since it was expected that the existence of this dock would encourage larger ships to trade to the Tees.

Towage did not always conform to the expected pattern since in 1954 an out-of-the-ordinary contract was obtained which involved carrying out towage work for a film company during the making of "Moby Dick" starring Gregory Peck and Leo Genn. The tug chosen for the job was *Kings Cross* (2), then already 33 years old, skippered by Alex Duncan. They were to be away from the Tees for four months and their job was to tow the sailing vessel *Pequod* and two artificial whales as and where required by the film-makers. (Fig. 44).

Fig. 44 Kings Cross *(2) arriving at Youghal, Eire in 1954 with the sailing vessel* Pequod *during the making of the film "Moby Dick".*

Fig. 45 *The crew of* Kings Cross *(2) on their return to the Tees on 11th November 1954 from assisting in the filming of "Moby Dick". They look very pleased with themselves! They are from left to right; George Robinson, Edward Carr Jnr., Robert Briggs, Captain Alex Duncan, M. McQuinlan, J. Ash and Jack Walton. (By courtesy of The Evening Gazette, Cleveland)*

Initially the tug and *Pequod* were working out of Youghal in Eire but their main operational base was at Fishguard, Pembrokeshire from where the filming took place in St. George's Channel off the Welsh and Irish coasts. The *Pequod* had formerly been the *Hispaniola* and was well known to Scarborough holiday-makers of that time. The whales turned out to be something of a problem to the crew, they being seventy-five feet long and very difficult to handle. On one occasion when a whale broke loose they spent seven hours searching for it without any success only later to find it washed ashore in a nearby cove. A second whale was lost completely. At the end of October the filming was only partly complete and work was broken off for the winter. After a farewell dinner, at which all the tug's complement were presented with momentoes, and after leaving *Pequod* at Cardiff *Kings Cross* (2) returned to the Tees on 11th November 1954. The photograph reproduced as Fig. 45 shows the crew beside their vessel on home ground again looking as though they had had a very good time of it! The two youngest in the photograph are still working with the company, Ted Carr then the fireman is now Chief Engineer on *Ralph Cross* and Bob Briggs then the boy is now skipper of *Coatham Cross.* They both still remember the event well though it happened all of 30 years ago.

Banbury Cross (1) was sold to the Adelaide Steamship Co. Ltd. and Swan River Shipping Co. Ltd. Fremantle, Australia in April 1955 after just five years on the River Tees. Surprisingly she is still in service with World Dredging Ltd., Singapore after several changes of ownership, re-engining with a General Motors Vee-16 diesel and much alteration to her upper works. In Australia she was renamed *Wilga* an aboriginal name meaning teeth and the *W-----a* representing *W*estern *A*ustralia; she still carries this name today.

In July and October the second and third of the Crossley-engined tugs identical to *Caedmon Cross* were delivered (Fig. 46). They were named *Golden Cross,* (132/1955), and *Ingleby Cross* (2), (132/1955), having been christened respectively by Mrs. Alice Fairweather and Mrs. Dorothy Richmond-Smith. The reader will have noticed that once the paddle tugs *Flying Fish* and *Lingdale* had gone in 1951 and 1954 the fleet did not include a tug which was specifically designed for stern work and for quickly taking the way off a ship when manoeuvring in confined spaces. In the meantime Tees Towing had to make do with the screw tugs then available. This problem was exercising the minds of the management at this time but as will be seen was not to be solved until 1958.

Wallace Sinclair Robinson, who had retired from Tees Towing as Marine Superintendent some three years previously, died during 1955. He had a very

Fig. 46 *The first geared-diesel tugs in the Tees Towing fleet.* Caedmon Cross *and* Golden Cross *towing* President Kruger *on trials from Furness Shipbuilding Yard, 12th September 1955.*

long working life on and about the river, most of it in connection with tugs, having started about 1895 in his father's towage business. His son C.G. Robinson has in 1984 just retired as a Tees Pilot. Expansion of the river facilities was continuing; the second oil jetty, a short distance upstream of the first, was opened during the year. It was later to be named the West Byng Jetty in tribute to Mr. George West Byng, Chairman of the Development Committee and Chairman of the TCC Board from 1945 to 1951.

At the end of 1955 the tug fleet was beginning to take on a modern look and the average age had dropped dramatically to 24 years. The fleet comprised the following tugs all of which were screw-driven.

Tees Towing Co. Ltd.

Diesel-electric tug	*Acklam Cross*
Steam tug	*Charing Cross*
Steam tug	*Euston Cross*
Steam tug	*Dundas Cross*
Steam tug	*Silver Cross*
Steam tug	*Temple Cross*
Steam tug	*Kings Cross* (2)
Geared diesel tug	*Caedmon Cross*
Geared diesel tug	*Golden Cross*
Geared diesel tug	*Ingleby Cross* (2)

Fig. 47 Fiery Cross *showing details of her Kort Rudder.*
(W. Ralston Ltd.)

The Middlesbrough Towage Co. Ltd. a subsidiary of Tees Towing Co. Ltd., which was formed in 1930 but had not owned any tugs since the autumn of 1934, was liquidated during the year ended 31st March 1956. This company had originally been owned by the Crosthwaite Steamship Co. Ltd. but latterly the ownership had been transferred to Tees Towing.

Her Majesty Queen Elizabeth II and H.R.H. The Duke of Edinburgh visited the Teesside area on the 4th June 1956 and ended their stay by sailing from the No. 1 Teesport Oil Berth to Sweden in *HMY Britannia*. Tees Towing had the honour of towing the Royal Yacht with their newest diesel tugs *Golden Cross* and *Ingleby Cross* (2).

After the pleasure of the Royal visit came the sadness of the announcement of the death of Lady Crosthwaite on the 20th October 1956. She and Sir William had enjoyed fifty-two years of married life together. Whilst she was not involved in Sir William's business life she had shared with him the responsibilities of public life particularly during the five years of his mayoralty. Later Sir William was to place in their parish church of St. Barnabas, Linthorpe, Middlesbrough a Bishop's Chair as a memorial to his wife. The chair is on the north side of the sanctuary and has on its back the full arms of Sir William Henry Crosthwaite and is inscribed as follows:–

IN MEMORIAM
ADA MARY LADY CROSTHWAITE
OF THIS PARISH

Coat of Arms

Argent a castle enflamed proper on a chief
Gules three 3-masted ships in full sail Or,
Crest upon a mural crown Or charged with three
anchors Sable a cock trimmed and heeled for the pit proper, Knights helmet

FIVE TIMES MAYORESS OF MIDDLESBROUGH

1879 – 1956
"TENAX ANIMO"
(Steadfast)

In March 1957 *Kings Cross* (2) was sold to C.W. Dorkin & Co. at Gateshead for breaking-up having been in the fleet a little over eight years. *Charing Cross* had been with the company for very much longer, in fact since 1934; a very good £1,500's worth! However she was not scrapped, even now at forty-four years of age, for she went to the Tyne to sail under Lawson-Batey Tugs Ltd. colours as the *Westsider.* She lasted for another 2½ years before also being broken-up at Gateshead but on this occasion by J.J. King & Co. Ltd.

Fiery Cross, (192/1957), was the next tug to be built for Tees Towing. She was christened by Mrs. Mahoney Crosthwaite and was a larger vessel, some 18 feet longer, than the "Caedmon Cross" class, and intended for river and coastal towage work. She was built by Scott & Sons and had a Crossley diesel engine of the same type as previously but its power rating was increased to 1125 BHP by the addition of two extra cylinders. The drive was again via a Hindmarch Modern Wheel Drive reverse reduction gearbox. Her general appearance was that of a scaled-up version of the "Caedmon Cross" class but the major technical improvement was the utilisation of a Kort Propulsion Co. Ltd. rudder to enhance her bollard pull to about 18 tons (Fig. 47). A Kort rudder comprises an annular ring, in this case about 11 feet diameter and 7 feet long, which surrounds a conventional stern mounted propeller and has a rudder blade rigidly mounted on its aft end. The annular ring and the rudder blade are pivoted in the stern of the tug and together respond to the steering controls just as would a normal rudder. This arrangement enables the flow of water from the propeller to be concentrated into a smaller area thus increasing the thrust available and improves manoeuvrability. Additionally the tug is able to travel astern in a straight line. Once again Tees Towing was in the forefront of technical development in tugs. *Fiery Cross* was the first tug in England to utilise a moveable Kort rudder and was the first tug built in the United Kingdom with this type of steering gear. *Fiery Cross* was delivered in May 1957 and again, as with their previous diesel powered tugs, Tees Towing were very satisfied with her. Sir William Crosthwaite was soon writing to the ship and engine builders to say:–

> "We are glad to be able to inform you that the vessel is behaving in an exemplary manner and that we are highly satisfied with her performance".

The volume of traffic on the River Tees reached 7 million tons of cargo in 1957 this representing the clearance of 4,818 ships a figure which was not to be bettered for more than ten years.

In 1958 two steam tugs were sold and two new diesel tugs entered service. First to go, in January, was the *Dundas Cross* which was sold to Newport Screw Towing Co. Ltd. by whom she was re-named *Duneagle.* Like her counterpart *Banbury Cross* (1) she was to have a long life for a wartime-built ship, eventually going to Greece where she worked as the *Nisos Syros* until surrendering to the breakers in 1976. Secondly, in March, *Silver Cross* was sold, at the age of 48, for further service in the fleet of J.H. Pigott & Son Ltd. of Grimsby who renamed her *Lady Joan.* She lasted with them until 1964 when she was dismantled at Inverkeithing.

As mentioned earlier, there had been a need, since the demise of the paddle tugs, for a design of tug which was really suited to stern work where steerability

Fig. 48 *Presentation of a bouquet to Mrs. Dorothy Richmond-Smith by a shipyard apprentice at the launch of* Banbury Cross *(2) at Dartmouth in 1958. Others in the family group are from left to right, Mrs. Alice Fairweather, Sir William Crosthwaite, Major Cecil Crosthwaite, Mrs. Mahoney Crosthwaite, Brigadier Claude Fairweather and Mr. Lawrence Richmond-Smith.*
(Nicholas Horne Ltd.)

Fig. 49 *The diesel tug* Hutton Cross *(2), newly arrived from her builders, alongside* Silver Cross *at Tees Wharf on 24th March 1958.* Silver Cross, *the penultimate steam tug in the fleet, was about to depart to her new owners at Grimsby. (By courtesy of The Evening Gazette, Cleveland)*

and the capability of taking the way off a ship were of prime importance. For some time Sir William and Cecil Crosthwaite had been trying to meet this need with a propulsion system completely new to British tugs. Thus it was that two tractor tugs were delivered in 1958; they were the *Hutton Cross* (2), (105/1958), and the *Banbury Cross* (2), (106/1958), which came into service in March and May respectively. The former was built by Scott and Sons, Bowling, having been christened by Mrs. Alice Fairweather, and the latter at Philip and Son Ltd., Dartmouth where she was named by Mrs. Dorothy Richmond-Smith. (Fig. 48). Both to the same design they had Crossley 750 BHP engines identical to those of the "Caedmon Cross" class. Their hulls were very similar in size to those in that class too. (Fig. 49). There the comparison ends since their propulsion unit was mounted about one third of the vessel's length aft from the bow and the towing hook was mounted only a few feet from the stern. Hence the term "tractor tug" which indicates that the propulsion unit is pulling the load on the hook as compared with the conventional arrangement of a stern-mounted screw and amidships hook where the screw in effect pushes the load on the hook. This type of tug, with towing hook aft, had a very important operating advantage in that it was impossible for the vessel to be "girted" – that is pulled over sideways by a tow attached to an amidships-mounted hook.

Fundamentally different though the tractor layout was, there was an equally innovatory feature in the propulsion unit itself. This was a single Voith-Schneider propeller which simultaneously, but independently, propels and steers the vessel, the propulsive thrust being adjustable to any direction in the horizontal plane. There is no conventional rudder but there is a docking skeg constructed aft. The propeller consists of a rotating plate, more than 12 feet in diameter, mounted on a vertical axis, flush with the bottom of the hull on to which are mounted six vertical propelling blades the pitch of which is adjustable about a vertical axis. The pitch is varied throughout each revolution of the plate and additionally the point at which maximum thrust is achieved is variable so that simultaneously control of speed and direction of the tug is achieved. The propeller runs in one direction only and at a constant speed. (Fig. 50.) Voith-Schneider propellers were not new in 1958; they had been known in Europe since about 1930 but had been used mainly in barge and other inland waterway

Fig. 50 *A view of the six-bladed Voith-Schneider propulsion unit of* Hutton Cross *(2) when dry docked in Glasgow. The surrounding protective baseplate and frames can also be seen.* *(A.T. Kelly & Co. Ltd.)*

vessels. The application of Voith-Schneider units in tugs in the United Kingdom was another first for Tees Towing. These highly manoeuvrable, handy-sized, safe-in-operation tugs, therefore, looked set to fill a need which had existed since 1954.

Fig. 51 *Models of* Caedmon Cross, Fiery Cross *and* Hutton Cross *(2). These models show respectively the progression from conventional screw and rudder, through Kort rudder to Voith-Schneider propulsion systems.* *(A.T. Kelly & Co. Ltd.)*

Hutton Cross (2) and *Banbury Cross* (2) did not have davit mounted lifeboats as had been usual practice in the tugs to date. Instead they were fitted with an inflatable life raft and dinghy which could be rapidly and more easily handled in an emergency. At about this time the older river tugs in the fleet had their lifeboats removed and replaced by rafts and/or dinghys. These two tugs differed from the "Caedmon Cross" class in one other respect in that they did not have an enclosed wheelhouse whereas the earlier vessels had a wheelhouse, over which was the usual monkey island. (Fig. 51). Tees Towing Company now owned one of the most modern and efficient fleets of tugs in the British Isles. The change which had been achieved since the commissioning of *Caedmon Cross* in 1953 was quite remarkable. Crossley engines had been installed in all six vessels delivered since that time.

During 1958 Sir William Crosthwaite was elected President of the British Tugowners Association a position he was to hold until 1968. It will be remembered that he had been responsible for setting up the Association in November 1934. No doubt his colleagues in the Association would have been following his pioneering efforts in the field of tug design with very close interest. For some of them it was still to be quite a long time before they would accept the move from steam to diesel and the use of modern propulsion systems.

In May 1959 Tees Towing, in conjunction with I.C.I. Ltd., carried out trials on a system of transporting bulk chemicals by sea in a flexible tubular bag. The "sausage" 100 feet long x 5 feet diameter was intended to be towed by tug and the trial tow of the "Dracone", as it was christened, was from the Tees to Flushing and back with *Fiery Cross* in charge. Although successful the idea has not caught on but a similar scheme for the disposal of effluent from the Northumbrian Water Authority has again been under recent consideration. At long last the construction of No. 1 Quay at the new Tees Dock at Lackenby was begun. One says "at last" because this need had been talked about since the early 1920's due to the inadequacies of Middlesbrough Dock.

After a year without changes to the tug fleet 1960 was to see yet another diesel for steam exchange. After having been christened by Mrs. Mahoney Crosthwaite the *Erimus Cross,* (192/1960), was completed on the 5th February by Scott & Sons (Bowling) Ltd. on the Clyde. She was powered by the 6-cylinder version of the Crossley CGL diesel engine and was a repeat of the design of the *Fiery Cross.* There was now, therefore, in the fleet two identical tugs capable of performing coastal towage work and handling the largest vessels in the river. On the 15th July another of the steam tugs was sold out of the fleet. *Euston Cross* although thirty-six years old and after 22 years service with Tees Towing was purchased by Loucas Matsas & Sons of Piraeus who at first renamed her *Thiseus* then later *Ioannis Matsas* and *Thiseus* once again. She was broken up in 1981 when fifty-seven years old after having given remarkable service to all of her four owners. Her services during the invasion of Normandy in 1944 as described earlier will be long remembered.

Just before the *Euston Cross* left the Tees the tugmen went on strike over the rates of overtime pay. To keep the tugs working, and fulfilling their commitments, four of the fleet were manned by the captains, management and staff. The strike however was short lived and was settled by negotiations with the Transport and General Workers Union. One story of the time is of a crew finishing a job late at night and deciding to have a cup of tea before knocking-off. On investigation it was found that tea could not be had because the b....... "boy" had let the fire go out. The "boy" was Sir William Crosthwaite!

The population of Middlesbrough was now 155,000 a growth of no less than 100,000 during Sir William Crosthwaite's eighty years. Being on the south bank of a river its expansion had all been concentrated into a sector of the compass from south-east to south-west particularly into the surrounding villages of Ormesby, Marton, Nunthorpe and Acklam all of which were swallowed up by the growing town. In September the River Tees was reported as being "crammed with ships – 46 in the river and dock, of which 37 were trading, 4 were new and 5 under repair". It is difficult to assess the level of activity from these figures since the number of vessels in port at any one time depends, not only on the number of arrivals but, on how long they have to stay to be unloaded and/or loaded. Thus high numbers in the river might just mean poor efficiency in working the ships. 4,070 ships were cleared on the river in 1960 carrying, in and out, a total of 7.6 million tons of cargo. Richard Crosthwaite, at this time, obtained his M.A. degree and his father Cecil had been appointed Chairman of the British Tugowners Association. Of the nine tugs in the fleet at the end of 1960 there was now only one that was steam powered, namely *Temple Cross.*

John Charles Rounce who had retired in 1950 as skipper of the *Acklam Cross* died on the 18th February 1961. He, like Ernest Watson Snr., was another of the long serving tug skippers who had virtually given all of their waking hours in the service of their company. His tug was to outlast him by three years as far as its presence on the Tees was concerned. On the 3rd April 1961 Richard Crosthwaite married Barbara Judith Miller Nairn and about this time took up his first full-time job with Tees Towing as assistant to the engineer superintendent. Prior to this appointment he had spent three years' apprenticeship working on tugs at Rotterdam and on the Thames and Clyde, in the drawing office of Scott & Sons, Bowling and with the gearbox manufacturers Modern Wheel Drive at Slough.

Whilst Sir William and Cecil Crosthwaite were respectively Honorary President and Chairman of the British Tugowners Association they tabled the idea that an International Association of Tugowners should be formed. After discussion the proposal was adopted in a somewhat restricted form when the European Tugowners Association was established in 1963. Sir William was to become Chairman for the first three years of its existence.

On the 4th August 1961 a new diesel tug *Danby Cross,* (114/1961), was delivered, again with a 750 BHP Crossley engine but this time built by J. Pollock,

Sons & Co. Ltd. of Faversham, where she had been christened by Mrs. Dorothy Richmond-Smith. Although slightly longer she had the same general appearance as *Hutton Cross* (2) and *Banbury Cross* (2). Her propulsion system however reverted to that installed in the "Caedmon Cross" class but with the inclusion of a Kort rudder instead of a conventional rudder. This gave her an improved pull for the same horsepower engine. *Temple Cross* was towed to the breakers yard at Hendrik-Ido-Ambacht, near Rotterdam by her consort *Erimus Cross* leaving the Tees on the 27th April 1962. This was the end of an era for she was the last steam tug in the ownership of Tees Towing. All the fleet were now diesel powered – it had been a long road from the purchase of the first diesel in 1933, 29 years in fact.

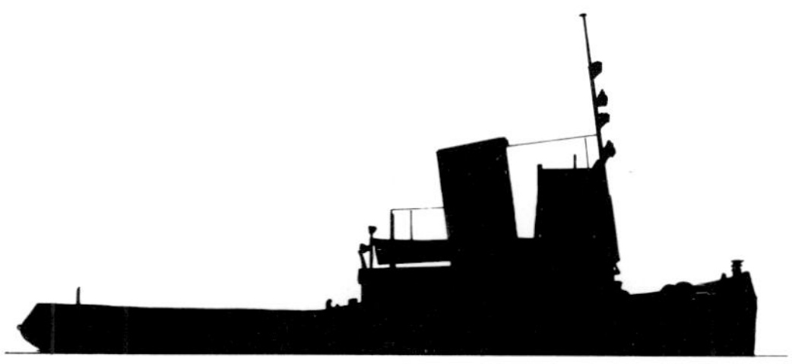

CAEDMON CROSS

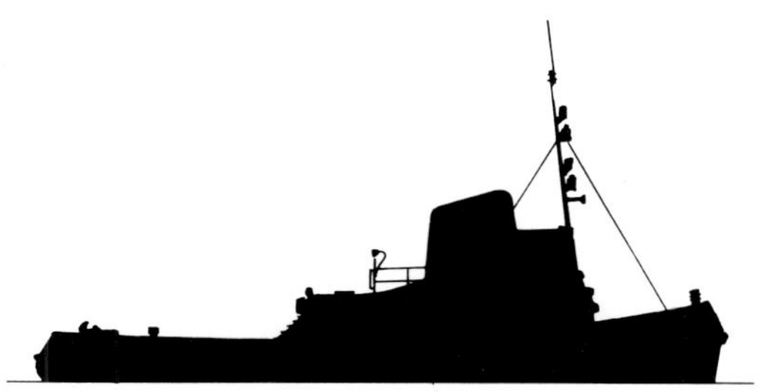

HUTTON CROSS (2)

Fig. 52 *The complete Tees Towing fleet c.1965. From left to right;* Caedmon Cross, Ingleby Cross *(2),* Golden Cross, Banbury Cross *(2),* Hutton Cross *(2),* Danby Cross, Marton Cross, Fiery Cross *and* Erimus Cross.

Chapter Nine
Building on Experience
– The Demand for Increased Power
1962–1975

With the departure of *Temple Cross* it is interesting to note that the nine remaining tugs were named in an alphabetical sequence A to I thus:–

Acklam, Banbury, Caedmon, Danby,
Erimus, Fiery, Golden, Hutton & Ingleby

This was done deliberately so that, in internal communications, a form of shorthand reference could be used to identify a particular tug viz: AX, BX, CX etc. The policy of not having two tugs with the same initial letter has been followed to the present day but a complete alphabetical sequence has not occurred again. At about this time a fibre-glass casting of a seahorse began to be affixed to the centre-line of the bridge bulwark of each tug as will be seen on many photographs. Later, some tugs were to have the company shield in colour on the point of the bow. Whereas the former has been retained to the present day the latter has not.

Adjustments to the issued share capital of the companies were made in 1962. On the 26th November that of the Crosthwaite Steamship Co. Ltd. was increased to £100,000 and on the 19th December that of Tees Towing Co. Ltd. to £500,000. On the 15th September 1962 Sir William Crosthwaite, at the age of 82, celebrated 70 years of active life on and about the river.

Apart from the normal day to day towage of ships about the river and dock there was still the occasional emergency to attend. One such event, in January 1962, involved the stranding of the inward bound British India ss *Pinjarra* (9,888/1944, 475' x 64'), on the north bank of the river opposite Tees Dock. It took almost twenty-four hours of towing effort by *Banbury Cross* (2), *Danby Cross, Erimus Cross, Fiery Cross, Golden Cross and Ingleby Cross* (2) to refloat her but not before *Erimus Cross* had spent the night aground alongside the *Pinjarra*. A net salvage award of £6,400 was made. Even orthodox jobs were not without hazard. On the 20th April 1962 *Erimus Cross* and *Ingleby Cross* (2) towed to the Tyne the mid-body section of the tanker *Fernmount* which had been launched the previous day at Smith's Dock, South Bank. At the launch the hull section collided with *Fiery Cross* causing considerable damage to her frames and plates in way of the engine room resulting in the need for her to be drydocked and repaired at Smith's.

A year later a new tug was delivered. She came from Richard Dunston (Hessle) Ltd., Hessle and at her launching by Mrs. Alice Fairweather was named *Marton Cross,* (133/1963). Her power was provided by a six-cylinder Crossley diesel engine driving a single screw via a two-speed reverse reduction gearbox which could provide either a 2 to 1 or 4 to 1 ratio. Thus at a maximum engine speed of 320 RPM the propeller would revolve at 160 or 80 RPM respectively. The static bollard pull was 17 tons ahead and 6¼ tons astern.

In April 1963 the new deep water tidal Tees Dock at Lackenby on the south side of the river had been opened to traffic. It was 3 miles from the mouth of the river. It's formal opening was performed by Sir William Worsley, Bt. the Lord Lieutenant of the North Riding of Yorkshire and took place on the 4th October.

Initially only the western side (No. 1 Quay) had been constructed; work was continuing, however, on the opposite side. (No. 2 Quay). Since 1946 the tug fleet had been controlled locally by the use of VHF radio. In October 1963 a comprehensive VHF radio telephone system was inaugurated covering Port Operation, Pilotage, etc. into which the tug system was integrated. This made for much easier management of tug schedules and improved communication between tugs and pilot when working ships.

March 1964 was to see Tees Towing's historic diesel-electric tug depart for Malta after being in their fleet for over thirty years. When he purchased her Sir William Crosthwaite was taking a step into the unknown with his choice of machinery but his judgement must have been sound for her to have lasted so long on the Tees. As far as is known this tug gave little trouble and had functioned very well after some initial bothers with her silencers and engine cooling system. Even though her electric motor final drive had not been repeated in the fleet she gave the lead at a very early period to the ultimate displacement of steam by diesel machinery. She was purchased by the Mediterranean Salvage and Towage Co. Ltd. of Malta G.C., who within a year had re-fitted her with two Lister Blackstone diesel engines driving the propeller via an orthodox gearbox and renamed her *Fox Terrier.* After working at Malta for five years she broke adrift and vanished whilst being towed from Valetta to Zueitina, Libya in 1969 – a sad ending for a pioneer vessel.

Also, in March 1964 the Scindia Steam Navigation's *Jalamanjari,* (4,510/ 1956, 438' x 56'), went hard aground inside the Heugh breakwater at Hartlepool during a very severe S.E. gale. She was eventually towed off by *Erimus Cross* (skipper R. Harrison), *Fiery Cross* (L. Miller) and *Marton Cross* (J.W. Spink) ultimately sharing, with the company, a net award of nearly £11,000.

In 1965 Lawrence Richmond-Smith retired from the Tees Towing Board on which he had served since 1947. In the Autumn of 1965 Brigadier Claude Fairweather, who had been further honoured when he became a Commander of the Most Excellent Order of the British Empire, retired as Operations Director at the Riverside Office, Tees Wharf and resigned his directorship of Tees Towing. At the age of 31, Richard Crosthwaite succeeded his uncle as Operations Manager after having understudied him for the previous two years. The modern fleet, all diesel powered under his command at the time was:–

Tees Towing Co. Ltd.

Caedmon Cross	*Banbury Cross* (2)
Golden Cross	*Erimus Cross*
Ingleby Cross (2)	*Danby Cross*
Fiery Cross	*Marton Cross*
Hutton Cross (2)	

having an average age of now only 8 years (Fig. 52).

The whole of this fleet was soon to be involved in a dramatic and dangerous salvage operation which took place within the lower reaches of the River Tees.

Smith's Dock at South Bank were completing the fitting-out of the oil drilling platform *Ocean Prince* when, at 0300 hours on the 1st November 1965 with thirty men on board, she broke free from her moorings in an 85 mph gale. She careered down river for about two miles following a zig-zag path from one side of the channel to the other and finally grounding on the south side some half a mile seawards of Tees Dock. During this journey she had brought down overhead high-voltage power cables which were approximately 200 feet above the water and collided with the Liberian tanker *World Continental* moored at the ICI North Tees No. 2 jetty.

As soon as the Tees Towing night duty operator received the news all crews were alerted and the whole fleet despatched as soon as the tugs could be manned. *Fiery Cross* and *Danby Cross* were the first to locate the rig and were able to make fast at about 0500 but only with difficulty and no little hazard since the rig was not yet fitted with mooring bollards. By about 0600 *Marton Cross, Hutton Cross* (2), *Banbury Cross* (2) and *Caedmon Cross* had also made fast and an attempt was made to tow the rig upstream into the wind and to moor her at the Queen Elizabeth II Jetty. However, during this operation the elements gained the upper hand and the rig was blown downstream again to just below the entrance to Tees Dock. *Ingleby Cross* (2), Golden Cross and *Erimus Cross* were now attached. The whole fleet of nine tugs was thus striving to control the unwieldy unit and managed by about 0840 to get a number of shore wires on to the QE II Jetty.

The weather then took a turn for the worse, all moorings were carried away and the towing wires of three of the tugs parted leaving only six tugs connected such that they were unable to control the rig in the violent conditions. She was blown across to the north side of the river colliding with the dredger *Port Harcourt* and back again to the south side where she came into contact with the rock breaker *Sea Cow II* which had explosives on board. After six hours of effort the rig was now back where she had first been found at 0400.

A third attempt was made, by eight tugs, to get the rig to the QE II Jetty but this failed when two of the tugs soon broke loose. The attempt was abandoned and the platform allowed to fall back onto the soft mud bank on the south side of the river (Fig. 53) with eight tugs towing at half power to ride out the gale. At 1300 the number of tugs attached was again increased to nine. By 2030 the gale eased a

Fig. 53 *The drilling platform* Ocean Prince *being held against the gale on the morning of 1st November 1965 after having broken loose from her moorings at Smith's Dock in the middle of the previous night and careered down river out of control. The whole Tees Towing fleet was involved in the fight against the elements but only* Banbury Cross *(2) and* Danby Cross *can be seen in this particular photograph. (By courtesy of The Evening Gazette, Cleveland)*

Fig. 54 *Marton Cross seen in the background of this composite advertisement was provided by Sir William Crosthwaite in 1965. Here, in 1978 is seen His Royal Highness the Prince of Wales in earnest conversation with Cecil Crosthwaite in the uniform of Lord Lieutenant of Cleveland. Second to the left of the cross is Brigadier Claude Fairweather. The lower part of the panel illustrates another* Marton Cross – *this time the tug of that name. (Cleveland County Council/ Richard Crosthwaite)*

little and it was possible to make some headway and the tugs eventually succeeded in mooring the rig at the QE II Jetty by 2200 though they still had to tow to windward to ease the load on the moorings.

The next morning, the 2nd November 1965, the wind having eased to Force 4/5, it was found possible to move the rig back to Smith's Dock where she was safely moored at 1300 hours. Thus thirty-four hours of gruelling and dangerous work by the whole fleet of nine tugs had achieved the successful conclusion it deserved. It is no surprise that this salvage episode in their own river is still fresh in the minds of those who were involved.

In 1965 Sir William Crosthwaite, for eminent services rendered to France during two World Wars and his long service as French Consular Agent for Middlesbrough and West Hartlepool, was awarded the Cross of Chevalier de la Légion d'Honneur. Sir William at 85, had now spent no less than 60 years in the business of towage on the River Tees – a great achievement by any standards. In a radio interview he had said that he didn't know what growing old was and that he had no intention of retiring from business. At the third general meeting of the European Tugowners Association he was appointed President d'Honneur, a well deserved recognition of his major contribution to tug development and management.

In the Spring of 1965 Sir William Crosthwaite expressed a desire to present a Sanctuary Cross for erection on the Garden of Remembrance at Marton-in-Cleveland on the southern outskirts of Middlesbrough. The cross of Springwell sandstone and standing 15'6" high was unveiled on the 15th November 1965 (Fig. 54).

With the retirement of Brigadier Fairweather there were now only two directors of Tees Towing Co. Ltd., that is until Richard Crosthwaite was appointed to the board on the 15th September 1966 which was appropriately his birthday. At this time Richard Crosthwaite was also appointed a Justice of the Peace on the Middlesbrough (later Teesside) bench and also to the Police Committee. He was Vice-Chairman of the Teesside Council for Voluntary Service.

Early in 1966 there occurred an interesting salvage job in that once again the whole Tees Towing fleet was involved. It is worth quoting the brief report in full:–

> **"OCEANIC LIBERTY,** (12,482/1952, 562' x 73')
>
> This tanker, bound for the Tees with 17,000 tons of low flash point crude oil, ran ashore approximately 6 cables ESE of the South Gare Breakwater at 0100 hours on 16th February. Three tugs towed at the vessel, which was leaking oil, until 0345. On the following two tides eight tugs failed to refloat the vessel but the ship was refloated by nine tugs at 1355 hours on 17th February, and safely berthed at North Tees Oil Jetty."

The award was over £19,000 and was shared between *Caedmon Cross, Golden Cross, Ingleby Cross* (2), *Fiery Cross, Hutton Cross* (2), *Banbury Cross* (2), *Erimus Cross, Danby Cross* and *Marton Cross.*

Phillips Imperial Petroleum Ltd. commenced production at their North Tees Refinery in 1966. This enterprise was to bring much additional liquid cargo to the river (a lot of it of a hazardous nature) although the expected oil throughput did not live up to initial predictions. As the size of tankers rapidly increased there was a need for the services of tugs with much higher power. Two such vessels were now on order.

The first of the geared-diesel tugs *Caedmon Cross* was sold to the Alexandra Towing Co. Ltd. for operation at Swansea and left the Tees for that port on 17th April 1966. At Swansea she was renamed *Margam* and worked there for four years before going, as the *Rilland,* to Willem Muller at Terneuzen where she is still in service.

On the 1st January 1967 the Tees and Hartlepool Port Authority (T&HPA) was established. They took over the management and conservation of the tidal reaches of the River Tees together with the railway company's Middlesbrough Dock whilst the Tees Conservancy Commission was dissolved. Similarly at Hartlepool the railway-owned docks were included in the jurisdiction of the new Port Authority. The two tugs stationed at Hartlepool became the property of the T&HPA and normally were able to cope with the traffic of that port. As previously Tees Towing's tugs continued to work there occasionally as demand required and still do so today. One of the first actions of the newly constituted authority was to commission the port surveillance radar which covered the River Tees, the Tees Bay and the approaches to Hartlepool Docks. This equipment was to increase the safety of ship working in the area and to allow operations to proceed under conditions of reduced visibility which would previously have stopped all movements.

Yet another drilling platform was in trouble in the River Tees. This time on the 28th February 1967 it was the *Staflo* which had broken loose from her berth at the Furness Shipbuilding Company's fitting-out quay and drifted down river for three-quarters of a mile almost to the Transporter Bridge. The rig came very near to colliding with vessels moored at Tyne-Tees and Dent's Wharves but was prevented from doing so in the nick-of-time by the intervention of several tugs of the Tees Towing fleet. They soon took *Staflo* under control and returned her to the shipyard (Fig. 55).

The two tugs needed for handling the large tankers and bulk carriers now visiting the river were delivered in June and October 1967. They were named *Ayton Cross,* (214/1967), and *Ormesby Cross,* (214/1967), and were powered by 1,800 BHP engines supplied by Crossley Premier Engines Ltd. These engines were somewhat different from those previously supplied by Crossleys since they had nine cylinders with smaller bore and stroke but running at 600 rpm; nearly

Fig. 55 *The partly built drilling platform* Staflo *being towed back to the Furness Shipbuilding Co. basin after breaking loose from her berth in February 1967. She had drifted downstream almost as far as the Transporter Bridge and was about to collide with ships berthed at Dent's and Tyne Tees' wharves. Prompt action by several of the Tees Towing tugs prevented this happening. Seen here are* Fiery Cross, Banbury Cross *(2) and* Danby Cross *with everything firmly under control.*

Fig. 56 Ormesby Cross *and* Ayton Cross *alongside Tees Wharf showing clearly the Seahorse motif mounted on the bridge front and on the latter vessel the company badge on the bow.*
(C.E. Jackson)

twice the speed of the earlier type. Both vessels had conventional single screws fitted with Kort rudders (Fig. 56). *Ayton Cross* and *Ormesby Cross* had both been christened at the Haven Shipyard, Hessle by respectively Mrs. Mahoney Crosthwaite and Mrs. Alice Fairweather (Fig. 57).

At a ceremony to commemorate his 75 years of work and life on the river Sir William Crosthwaite was presented by the Mayor of Middlesbrough with a gold seahorse, the emblem of the company. His son Cecil had at the same time completed 40 years service with the company. Yet another of the long-serving tug skippers retired in 1967. He was J.W. (Micky) Spink, aged 69, latterly master of *Banbury Cross* (1), *Golden Cross, Fiery Cross* and *Marton Cross.* He had started work with Tees Towing in 1922 on their launch *Electric Arc.* After serving as mate of the *Coalopolis* he obtained his first command in the *Clarissa* in 1926. It is said of him (like Ernie Watson and Charlie Rounce) that he was never happier than when towing a vessel under difficult circumstances. It would appear that he really could "tow anything anywhere". A tribute by a friend made at the time of his retirement is worth quoting in full:–

> "He was endowed with a combination of judgement, thoroughness and dedication which made the most complicated situations and manoeuvres appear easy and effortless. His mastery of the skills necessary in this exacting and at times hazardous work is a unique example for those who follow his calling. His exploits both in harbour and at sea are legion and his superb performance along with his crew on the occasion of the loss of the *Pandora* and the stranding of the *Gripfast* under storm conditions will long remain in the memories of those involved. His exit from the arena of tugboat operations which consumed his whole life is a loss which though incredible is unlikely to be equalled in the modern conception of individuality. Captain Spink we salute you."

Two years into his retirement Brigadier Fairweather was honoured, in recognition of his public services, by his being appointed a Companion of the Most Honourable Order of the Bath. In addition to those awards and appointments already mentioned he was:–

A Commander of the Most Venerable Order of the Hospital of St. John of Jerusalem.

A Justice of the Peace (since 1963).

One of Her Majesty's Deputy Lieutenants in the North Riding of the County of Yorkshire.

Fig. 57 *The platform party at the launch of* Ormesby Cross *at Hessle in 1967. Including from left to right: Mr. Richard Crosthwaite, Mrs. Judy Crosthwaite, Sir William Crosthwaite, Mrs. Alice Fairweather and Brigadier Claude Fairweather. (Walter Fussey & Son)*

Richard Crosthwaite who when at Cambridge had been commissioned in 50(N) Divisional Signals Regiment (TA) was appointed Major in 34 Signals Regiment (AVR). On the 15th July 1967 his son Adam Jonathan was born – there were now, therefore, four generations of the Crosthwaite family living. (Fig. 58).

On the 1st April 1968 the County Borough, Borough and District Councils bordering the lower reaches of the River Tees combined to form the Teesside County Borough. Not before time in the eyes of Sir William Crosthwaite who is on record as having seen the advantages of, and having advocated, such a move as early as 1911 and on many occasions since that date. So pleased was he that the amalgamation had taken place at last that he presented the new County Borough with its first insignia – a mace.

Changes on the riverside continued. The ship repairing yard at Graythorp on the north side of the Tees estuary ceased work but a new refinery belonging to the Shell company opened on the south bank of the river just seawards of Tees

Fig. 58 *An informal group of four generations of the Crosthwaite family in 1968. Richard (33), Sir William (87), Cecil (59) and Adam Jonathan (9 months). The photograph was taken shortly before the death of Sir William.*
(Richard Crosthwaite)

Fig. 59 *The complete Tees Towing fleet proceeding down river to the Sea Reach to scatter the ashes of Sir William and Lady Crosthwaite on the waters of the Tees, 23rd May 1968.*

Dock. This latter, together with the ICI/Phillips development already mentioned at North Tees was to attract tankers of up to 135,000 tons deadweight and over 900 feet long to this part of the river each often needing four tugs for turning and manoeuvring.

Quite suddenly, after feeling unwell for only a very short time, Sir William Henry Crosthwaite died in Hemlington Hospital, Middlesbrough on the 13th May, 1968 at the age of 87. Only the previous day he had attended a launching ceremony at the Furness Shipyard, Haverton Hill and the day before that he had watched the Middlesbrough v Bristol football match at Ayresome Park. Prior to a commemorative service at St. Barnabas' Church, Linthorpe on the 23rd May the ashes of Sir William and Lady Crosthwaite were scattered in Sea Reach from the stern of *Ayton Cross* with all the other tugs of the fleet in attendance; seahorse emblems prominent on the bridge bulwarks and their house flags and ensigns at half mast the tugs gave their final salute to the River's Great Son when *Marton Cross* sounded "I wish you a safe voyage". (Fig. 59). Before the scattering of the ashes a brief family service had been conducted on board *Ayton Cross* by the Port Chaplain the Rev. D.J. Rowlands. The service in St. Barnabas' Church was conducted by the Bishop of Whitby the Rt. Rev. George Snow and the Rural Dean of Middlesbrough, Canon H.A Wareham. Sir William's death was a loss not only to his family and his company but to the community as a whole. He had been connected at one time or another with almost every social and cultural service in the town – either as President, Chairman, founder or committee member. He had been five times Mayor of Middlesbrough, oddly enough each occasion being during difficult times. He was well known for his stamina and personality and led an unusually full and active life; indeed he was still working daily at his desk until just before his death. Sir William would be sadly missed but also happily remembered for what he had done for the town of Middlesbrough and all of the businesses on and about the river. After the death of his wife in 1956 Sir William had lived for a while with his son-in-law and daughter Brigadier and Mrs. C.C. Fairweather but for the last few years of his life he had occupied a self-contained

Fig. 60 *Major Cecil Crosthwaite M.B.E., K.St. J., T.D., J.P., son of Sir William Crosthwaite (Baron Studios)*

flat alongside Tees Towing's office at Cleveland Buildings.

On the death of his father Cecil Crosthwaite surrendered the agreement which they jointly held for the management of Tees Towing Co. Ltd. Cecil Crosthwaite was then appointed Chairman and Managing Director of Tees Towing. (Fig. 60). It was about this time too that the use of the description "Cross Line Tugs" fell into disuse. It had been used since shortly after the Second World War in advertisements and when describing the tug fleet collectively.

Just two days after Sir William's death the 5th General Meeting of the European Tugowners' Association was held in Copenhagen. As honorary President his loss to the Association would be keenly felt. The results of his efforts since 1934 to bring together the tugowners of Europe in useful discussion could be seen in the Association's complement of 100 companies from 11 countries who owned 900 tugs in 86 European Ports.

During the summer of 1968 two more of the post-war diesel tugs left the company. First *Ingleby Cross* (2) was sold for further service to Fowey Harbour Commissioners and renamed *Gribbin Head;* then *Golden Cross,* renamed *Dunheron,* went to the Newport Screw Towing Company Ltd., Newport. Both of these tugs are still in service.

From January 1969, at the request of the Oil and Chemical industry on the river and the Teesside Fire Brigade Authority it was agreed that Tees Towing would provide fire-fighting cover on the river by the provision of suitable equipment on one of their tugs. Because of the increasing size of tankers now visiting the river it was important that high-mounted monitors should be available and it was for this reason that late in 1968 the appropriately named *Fiery Cross* was modified to incorporate fire pumps and monitors. (Fig. 61). Later, when she was delivered in 1971 *Leven Cross* was to be similarly fitted out.

The Crosthwaite Steamship Co. Ltd. which was incorporated in 1925, with a share capital of £1,000 to operate the excursion vessel *Bilsdale,* was retitled Seahorse Securities Ltd. in October 1969. This was thought to be a more

Fig. 61 Fiery Cross *demonstrating her fire fighting capabilities near the entrance to Tees Dock.* *(Richard Crosthwaite)*

appropriate title since it was now an investment company which had not owned any ships of its own after 1935 when the *Bilsdale* was scrapped. At the beginning of 1969 Michael Edmund Lyon, J.P. was elected a non-executive director of Tees Towing and shortly afterwards the issued share capital of the company was increased to £600,000. Cecil Crosthwaite, now 60 years of age, had by this time taken over the appointment of French Consular Agent, a post which his father had held for 31 years before him. He was also appointed deputy chairman of the T&HPA. Together with his son Richard who was its Honorary Secretary and co-founder he also became Chairman of the Teesside (later Cleveland) Institute of Directors. Richard Crosthwaite was a member of the Tees Liaison Panel which comprised representatives of the T&HPA, tugs, pilots, agents and foyboatmen operating on the Tees, at which they were able to discuss matters of common interest and to deal with any interface problems. He was also Chairman and co-founder of the Teesside (later Cleveland) Consumer Group a position he held until 1970 when he became the group's Vice-President.

In 1969 the Furness Shipyard at Haverton Hill was saved from threatened closure by being taken over by the Tyne-based firm of Swan Hunter (Shipbuilders) Ltd. Tees Towing's tugs were to continue to attend the launches there; though fewer in number nevertheless the vessels were of increased size. They built several standard bulk carriers of 169,000 tons deadweight but the shipbuilding yard could not be kept going for very long and finally closed in 1979.

Due particularly to the opening of the new oil refineries and expansion of the petro-chemicals industry the volume of cargo handled on the River Tees had leapt up to 23 million tons in the year ended 31st December 1970 and had been carried in no less than 6,052 ships. Most of this increased activity was taking place in the lower four miles of the river from about Smith's Dock seawards. Whereas in earlier years the "centre of gravity" of operations had been around the Transporter Bridge at Middlesbrough it was now around the new Tees Dock area.

This progression seawards of the focal point of the shipping activity was of course nothing new. Ever since the 18th century when the village of Worsall, some 25 miles upstream, was a port there has been a steady move eastwards in the search for more room and deeper water. Worsall – Yarm – Stockton – Portrack – Middlesbrough – Lackenby (Teesport) – where next?

On the 11th August 1970 *Hutton Cross* (2) left the Tees having been sold to Willem Muller at Terneuzen who renamed her *Kamperland.* It will be remembered that she was the company's first Voith-Schneider tug when completed in 1958. Although in the fleet for only twelve years, and of particular use as a stern tug, she had proved to be less economical than the Kort rudder/conventional screw propeller type of tug. This was due to the fact that the engine ran continuously at one speed even when no thrust was required from the vertical propeller blades which were, as it might be said, in neutral. Mullers must have been quite satisfied with her for she remained in service with them for thirteen years.

At the year end the Tees Towing fleet consisted of seven vessels, the lowest number it was to reach within the scope of this history.

In 1970 Cecil Crosthwaite became the Chairman of British Marine Mutual Insurance Association Ltd. (BMMIA). Ernest Watson Snr. died in April 1971 at the age of 86 after having enjoyed over 17 years of retirement. During 1971 Dent's and Tyne-Tees' Wharves which were located just upstream of the Transporter Bridge on the Middlesbrough side of the river were closed for trading. They were eventually to become the T & HPA's Craft Depot for their dredging and river maintenance fleet.

Leven Cross, (141/1971), a single screw Kort-rudder tug, built by Fairmile Construction Co. Ltd., Berwick and christened there by Mrs. Hilary McKnight was delivered in May 1971. She had a 6-cylinder Crossley engine similar to that fitted to *Fiery, Erimus* and *Marton Cross* but developing the slightly increased horsepower of 1,235 BHP whilst running at the higher speed of 345 RPM. She had a static bollard pull of 18½ tonnes and as previously recounted she was fitted out as a fire fighting tug. (Fig. 62). In September 1971 *Banbury Cross* (2) was sold out of the fleet. She went to Società Esercizio Rimorchi & Salvataggi S.p.A. at Ravenna, Italy where she was renamed *Gatto.* In 1981 her engines and auxiliaries were replaced and it is likely that her propulsion system was changed; she was still in service in 1982 but her ultimate fate is not known.

Fig. 62 *This view of* Leven Cross *hurrying upstream on the River Tees in 1982 shows her fire-fighting monitors mounted on a special platform high above her bridge.* *(A. Sparrow)*

Fig. 63 *Mr. Arthur Greenwell, FCIS, Commercial Director of Tees Towing Company Limited. (Studio Tristan)*

The Board of Tees Towing was strengthened by the appointment, on 20th October 1972, of Arthur Greenwell, (Fig. 63), the company secretary since 1953, as Commercial Director and Jeremy Pemberton as a non-executive director. A month later the capital of the company was further increased to £800,000.

The discovery of oil in the North Sea had resulted in a great demand for the construction of production platform jackets – huge tubular steel structures which would be towed out to the wells, upended and sunk over the well head. Several construction yards were set up and one of these, in 1972, was the Laing Offshore fabrication yard at the ex-William Gray shipyard at Graythorp on the north bank of the Tees estuary. This yard and its unusual fabrications was to be a new source of work for the tugs but only for a limited period. In the following year the construction of a storage and treatment plant for North Sea oil was started on the newly-reclaimed Seal Sands area in the Tees estuary. The oil was to be pumped through a 34" diameter, 220 miles long, undersea pipe line from the Ekofisk oil field to the huge Phillips storage tanks, from where, after treatment it would be distributed worldwide by large oil tankers. Again more work for the tugs. On the opposite side of the river the new Redcar Ore Terminal came into operation. Large bulk carriers would unload their iron ore cargoes here for use in the new British Steel Corporation's integrated works at Redcar.

In 1973 the company suffered one of its rare tragic accidents, when, whilst towing near the Dogger Bank, three of the crew were swept off the after deck of the *Erimus Cross* by an unexpected swing of the tow rope. The three men were Clive Pickering, Edward Charville and David Featherstone. Sadly all attempts by the tug at the time, and by aircraft of the Royal Air Force later, failed to find any trace of the men.

Richard Crosthwaite continued to expand his out-of-business activities. He became Chairman of the Cleveland Youth Association, Chairman (and later

President) of the Teesside/Redcar Conservative Association and a member of the South Teesside Hospital Management Committee. During 1974 at the age of 40 he was appointed an Associate of the Royal Institute of Naval Architects.

On the 1st April 1974 the short-lived Teesside County Borough ceased to exist and was replaced by a two-tier system of local government. It thus came about that Middlesbrough was designated a District of the new County of Cleveland along with Langbaurgh, Stockton-on-Tees and Hartlepool. On the re-organisation Cecil Crosthwaite was appointed Lord Lieutenant (and Keeper of the Rolls) of the County of Cleveland having since 1963 been Deputy Lieutenant of the North Riding of Yorkshire. At this time he also was appointed a Knight of St. John.

Ernest Watson Jnr. retired in August 1974 after 48 years service with the company. He had followed in his father's footsteps and had skippered many of the tugs since 1953. William Robinson, who had latterly been skipper of the *Ayton Cross* became the Assistant Marine Superintendent with special responsibilities for the training of crews.

A further new tug of much increased power suitable for coastal and North Sea towage was delivered in February 1974 after earlier having been christened by Mrs Judy Crosthwaite (Figs. 64 & 65). She was the *Ralph Cross,* (244/1974); her single screw with Kort rudder being driven by a vee 12-cylinder Ruston Paxman four-stroke diesel engine giving 2,640 BHP when running at 900 rpm. This was the first change of engine manufacturer since 1953 when *Caedmon Cross* was commissioned with a Crossley two-stroke diesel engine. Since then Crossleys had engined twelve of the fleet's tugs. *Ralph Cross* was built at Yarmouth by Richards (Shipbuilders) Ltd.

In November 1974 *Danby Cross* after having been away to Felixstowe on charter to Gaselee Ltd. was put up for sale and by June of the followng year had been sold to Willem Muller and renamed *Finland.* She is still in service with the Muller company at Terneuzen.

Fig. 64 *Mrs. Judy Crosthwaite about to launch the* Ralph Cross *at Richards (Shipbuilders) Ltd., Yarmouth in 1973.* *(Brian Ollington)*

Fig. 65 *Ready for the launch of* Ralph Cross *at Yarmouth in 1973 are three generations of the Crosthwaite family; from left to right, Mrs. Mahoney Crosthwaite, Mr. Richard Crosthwaite, Philippa Crosthwaite, Major Cecil Crosthwaite, Belinda Crosthwaite and Mrs. Judy Crosthwaite.* *(Brian Ollington)*

The first huge, 20,000 ton, 400 feet high steel jacket structure and its 11,000 ton flotation pontoon for the North Sea B.P. Forties Field oil production platforms departed from Graythorp in late June 1974 creating much local and national interest. Several of Tees Towing's tugs were in attendance whilst the structure was towed to sea after which she was taken to her operating position by large foreign tugs much more powerful than any that could be provided locally. (Fig. 66). Similarly in 1975 the second of the oil rig jackets left Graythorp yard for the B.P. Forties oil field. From about this time the modules for placing on the legs of the jacket units began to be fabricated at various sites on the banks of the Tees. These were transported to their site in the North Sea on pontoon barges, usually about 90m long x 30m beam, and which had often had their sea fastenings fitted at Hartlepool. There was thus much new work for the tugs in holding these in position whilst they were loaded and moved in and out of the river and across Tees Bay to Hartlepool. In conjunction with this pontoon traffic there was also the movement of the crane barges which were needed to lift the modules into position in the North Sea. These too required tugs when in the river for a lifting operation or maintenance. This line of business was most welcome and it is illustrative of the speed of change of present day technology in that only a few years previously the movement of such large and heavy loads could not have been contemplated.

Fig. 66 *The 11,000 ton flotation tank which had been used to carry the Graythorp 1 jacket structure to the B.P. Forties Field being returned to the Tees in 1974 by Tees Towing's tugs* Leven Cross, Ralph Cross, Ayton Cross *and* Fiery Cross.

On the 17th October 1975 the first oil via the underwater pipeline from the Ekofisk oilfield was received at the Phillips storage tanks near Graythorp. Nine days later the first tanker load was shipped from one of the new jetties which had been specially constructed for the purpose. More large tankers were, therefore, to be handled by the tugs, this time to and from the berths nearest to the river entrance.

Cecil Crosthwaite was appointed Vice-President of the British Tugowners' Association and Chairman of the European Tugowners' Association. Richard Crosthwaite had locally taken on a further interest in accepting a directorship of the commercial broadcasting station "Radio Tees".

Despite all the new developments the annual volume of traffic in and out of the Tees had fallen a little to 20 million tons carried in 4,800 ships.

At the end of 1975 Tees Towing owned the following seven tugs with an average age of eleven years.

Tees Towing Co. Ltd

Fiery Cross	1,125 BHP	*Ormesby Cross*	1,800 BHP
Erimus Cross	1,125 BHP	*Leven Cross*	1,235 BHP
Marton Cross	1,125 BHP	*Ralph Cross*	2,640 BHP
Ayton Cross	1,800 BHP		

AYTON CROSS

RALPH CROSS

Fig. 67 *The Royal Yacht* Brittania *arriving in the River Tees on the 14th July 1977 bringing H.M. The Queen and H.R.H. The Duke of Edinburgh for their Jubilee visit to Cleveland. In the Sea Reach* Greatham Cross *is shaping to make fast at the head of the vessel.*
(Richard Crosthwaite)

Chapter Ten

Power with Manoeuvrability – The Modern Fleet in Being 1976–1983

As the reader will have noticed the company's fleet had once again passed through a period when it did not possess tugs specifically designed for stern work. However the situation was not so bad as that during the period immediately after the paddle tugs had departed; the introduction of the Kort rudder had improved significantly the tugs manoeuvrability. Nevertheless since *Banbury Cross* (2) was sold in 1971 the company, and in particular Richard Crosthwaite, had been comparing and considering possible successors to the Voith-Schneider tugs. Increases in bollard pull were also being sought, though not at the expense of having a large unwieldy tug. These considerations naturally took a long time from the technical point of view and care had to be taken over cost since the purchase price was to be much more than anything paid previously. In 1976, therefore, there appeared on the river the first two tugs of a very interesting design indeed. The first, after being christened by Mrs. Joan Greenwell, *Greatham Cross*, (193/1976) was delivered on 16th March and then *Skelton Cross,* (193/1976) followed on the 22nd June to be christened later at Middlesbrough by Mrs. Jane Usher. They had both been built at Scott & Sons (Bowling) Ltd. on the Clyde and were each powered by two four-stroke, six-cylinder diesel engines manufactured by Ruston Paxman Diesels Ltd. of Newton-Le-Willows and rated at 1100 BHP (i.e. 2,200 BHP total) when running at 900 rpm. As described earlier in relation to the Voith-Schneider tugs of 1958 these two new vessels were also tractor tugs. Each engine drives, through the bottom of the hull, two rudder-propellers mounted side by side across the beam of the vessel. These rudder-propellers, which independently are capable of working through 360°, are mounted approximately one quarter of the length of the hull aft from the bow. Each of the propellers is fitted with a Kort Nozzle so that the propeller/nozzle units were both propulsion and steering combined; there being no conventional rudder at the stern. These propulsion units were provided by Schottel-Werft, Spay, West Germany and were controlled from the bridge, not by a steering wheel but by a small lever for each engine, the angular movement of which in the vertical plane controlled engine speed and rotational position dictated the direction of thrust from the propeller. With such a system the tugs were manoeuvrable to an extreme degree being able to move forwards, astern or broadside either way and rotate on the spot if the Schottel units are set to thrust at right angles to the centre-line of the vessel (Fig. 68). The towing hook is fully aft and there is a protective frame around the propeller units and a docking skeg aft. The totally enclosed bridge on these tugs is set higher than the twin funnels and gives a perfect all round view for the skipper.

At the risk of sounding monotonous it is necessary to say that this was another first for Tees Towing in that *Greatham Cross* was the first rudder-propeller tug in the United Kingdom. Again there was some scepticism, outside of the company, but events have proved that the choice of this type of vessel for work on the River Tees was well judged, so much so that similar vessels were to follow. Technical achievement apart these vessels must be arguably the most attractive and photogenic tugs in the business. This is to some extent brought about by the use of the striking red and white colour scheme for funnel and upper superstructure set off against the black hull.

In between the delivery of these fine new tugs the *Erimus Cross* was sold to Howard Doris Ltd. for work at Loch Kishorn on the west coast of Scotland. Prior to the sale she had been, for a few months, on charter to that company who on purchase renamed her *Mairi of Kishorn.* She had been in the fleet of Tees Towing for over 16 years.

The new rudder-propeller type of tug had arrived just at the time when the trade of the Tees had made a 60% leap upwards mainly due to the commencement of the North Sea oil traffic. In 1976 the cargo handled had reached 32 million tons carried in 5,745 ships.

Fig. 68 Skelton Cross *in Smith's drydock at South Bank, September 1976. This shows the twin Schottel rudder-propeller propulsion units as viewed from the bow of the tug.*

In 1976 Brian James had joined the Company as Engineering Superintendent at the Riverside Wharf. Cecil Crosthwaite had been elected Vice-President of the European Tugowners' Association and Richard Crosthwaite had joined the Executive Committee of its British counterpart and was to become Chairman in 1978 for two years. The share capital of Tees Towing Co. Ltd. had been revised upward once more, this time on the 22nd November 1976, to £1,250,000.

In 1977 the Silver Jubilee of Her Majesty Queen Elizabeth II was celebrated and in that year she undertook a tour of many cities and towns throughout the British Isles. One of these visits was to the Cleveland area on the 14th July when Her Majesty the Queen arrived in the Royal Yacht *Britannia* at Tees Dock where she was welcomed to the County by the Lord Lieutenant of

Fig. 69 H.M.Y. Britannia *having arrived in Tees Dock is being berthed at the No. 2 Quay by* Ralph Cross *and* Greatham Cross *on 14th July 1977.*

Cleveland, Major Cecil Crosthwaite, MBE, K.St.J., TD, JP. When *HMY Britannia* arrived in the Tees she was assisted to her berth by *Ralph Cross, Greatham Cross* and *Skelton Cross* (Figs. 67, 69 & 70).

During 1977 Richard Crosthwaite was appointed joint managing director of Tees Towing Co. Ltd. sharing the position with his father but beginning to take over the lead in managing the company. The Teesside and District Chamber of Commerce and Industry elected him to be their president for the year 1977-78. He also was Trustee and co-founder of Yarm School for Boys.

Robert Harrison one of the long-serving tug skippers retired in 1978. His working life was perhaps typical of his breed and is therefore worth outlining. Born in 1915 he had started work with Tees Towing in 1929 as boy in the *Lingdale* but because of the depression and part-time working he went away to sea with the British India Steam Navigation Co. from 1932 to 1936 during which time he joined the RNR. In 1938 he well remembers going to Southampton to collect the *Euston Cross* on which occasion the deckhands were Cecil Crosthwaite and Claude Fairweather. He was called up for naval service on the outbreak of war in 1939 and was away until 1946 during which time no less than three of his ships were lost due to bombing, mining and torpedoing! On his return he was given command of *Athlete* after a short time as her mate and subsequently skippered many tugs of the fleet, finally retiring when in command of *Ormesby Cross.* Like his father before him, who had been skipper of *Kings Cross* (1) in the 1930's and 1940's, he had given sterling service to the company.

On Christmas Day 1978 the sad news was announced of the death of Cecil Crosthwaite at the age of 69. Ever since he returned home after the Second World War he had worked, along with his father Sir William, in the modernisation of their tug fleet particularly with regard to the introduction of diesel powered tugs and their further development. Then in his last years he had been able to work

Fig. 70 *Major Cecil and Mrs. Mahoney Crosthwaite with Her Majesty the Queen and H.R.H. The Duke of Edinburgh on their arrival, in the Royal Yacht* Britannia, *at Tees Dock for their Jubilee visit to Cleveland, 14th July 1977.*
(By courtesy of The Evening Gazette, Cleveland)

with his son Richard on the design of the latest sophisticated Schottel tugs. At home he was never happier than when he was spending long hours in his garden at Langbaurgh Hall, Great Ayton. The ashes of Cecil Crosthwaite were scattered in Sea Reach on 3rd January 1979, as had been those of Sir William and Lady Crosthwaite in 1968. The whole tug fleet circled the wreath which was committed to the waters after the scattering of the ashes (Fig. 71).

Only two years after its previous adjustment the share capital of Tees Towing Co. Ltd. was raised to £2,500,000 in 1978. That year also Richard Crosthwaite was appointed Deputy Lieutenant of the County of Cleveland and a member of the Small Firms Council of the Confederation of British Industry. Brigadier Claude Fairweather who had retired in 1965 was appointed Vice Lord Lieutenant of the County of Cleveland.

On the death of his father Richard Crosthwaite was appointed Chairman and Managing Director of Tees Towing Co. Ltd. and took over the responsibility of French Consular Agent for the Teesside area. (Fig. 72). On his assuming the chairmanship he had naturally relinquished the job of Operations Manager which post was taken over by Brian James, who as has been seen, had joined the Company in 1976. William Robinson who had recently been appointed Marine Superintendent on the retirement of Charles Marshal Duncan was joined by Ian Gardiner as Engineering Superintendent. Thus the whole of the Operations Management was in effect a new team although some of its members had for a while been understudying their new jobs. Arthur Greenwell was appointed a director of the BMMIA.

The third rudder-propeller tug *Yarm Cross,* (185/1979), was delivered in August 1979, later being named by Miss Philippa Crosthwaite at Tees Wharf.

Although outwardly similar to the previous two vessels she had her engine power output uprated to 1,320 BHP from each unit, ie 2,640 BHP total. (Fig. 73). The increased power gave her a static bollard pull of 35 tonnes as against 32 tonnes for *Greatham Cross* and *Skelton Cross*.

On the river the volume of traffic had reached the annual figure of 39 million tons in 1979 and the port was rated, on that basis, the third busiest in the United Kingdom. Unfortunately shipbuilding ceased at this time at the Furness Shipbuilding Co. Ltd. at Haverton Hill though the yard was to be used for other purposes at a later date. A further closure occurred in 1980 when Middlesbrough Dock ceased to be used by trading vessels when the Tees and Hartlepool Port Authority judged that the necessary capital expenditure required to keep it in operation could not be justified. It had been in existence since 1842 albeit modified a number of times, but now Tees Dock was able to cope with the dry cargo traffic and with much larger and deeper draught vessels (Fig. 75). Also Tees Dock is an open tidal dock whereas Middlesbrough Dock was enclosed by a restrictive lock entrance.

In the face of the severe industrial depression and high unemployment which resulted from it, the volume of traffic handled on the river, had in 1980, been maintained at 39 million tons and although it fell away in the years following to approximately 35 million tons this was a creditable achievement in the circumstances. Thus when things might have been otherwise the tugs of Tees Towing have been kept busy enough on the river. Salvage jobs were now few and far between and the competition for coastal and sea towage work was and still is fierce. It was because of this steadily maintained level of business that the company were able to continue with their tug replacement programme when they ordered their fourth rudder-propeller tug for delivery late in 1981. A tug of this

Fig. 71 *The complete Tees Towing fleet proceeding down river to the Sea Reach to scatter the ashes of Cecil Crosthwaite on the waters of the Tees, 3rd January 1979.*

Fig. 72 *Richard Crosthwaite, M.A., J.P., D.L., Chairman and Managing Director of Tees Towing Company Limited since 1979. (Studio Tristan)*

nature was now costing some £1.4 million – a far cry from the days when a second-hand tug could be obtained for a few hundred pounds.

In anticipation of the delivery of their new tug *Fiery Cross* and *Marton Cross* were sold to Willem Muller in Holland where they were renamed *Waterland* and *Waasland* respectively. They had served Tees Towing for 24 and 18 years. The Muller company had now taken a total of five tugs from the Tees between 1970 and 1981 and all but one of these vessels were still in service at the end of 1983.

Coatham Cross, (186/1981), was launched on the 16th September 1981 and delivered to the Tees in November of that year (Fig. 77). She was in all important respects similar to *Yarm Cross* which had by now been in operation just over two years. She was christened by Mrs. Mahoney Crosthwaite, wife of the late Major Cecil Crosthwaite at a ceremony at Tees Wharf on the 6th May 1982. By the spring, *Ayton Cross,* although available for service if the need should arise, was not normally kept manned and the fleet was operated with the remaining seven tugs.

The rarity of salvage jobs was an indication of how modern aids had made seafaring a much safer occupation than formerly. However, one job in April 1982 involved the salvage of the tug *Goliath,* (296/1946), ex *Eminent,* ex *Empire Tessa* which found herself in difficulties off Whitby. She was taken in tow by *Ralph Cross* and after a tow of over six hours *Goliath* was berthed at Tees Wharf alongside the Tees Towing fleet. She made an interesting comparison with the modern vessels because she was steam powered and of the same vintage as *Dundas Cross* and *Banbury Cross* (1) which had left the Tees no less than 24 and 27 years previously!

Fig. 73 Yarm Cross *shows her paces whilst on trials from Richard Dunston's shipyard at Hessle. This view illustrates the position of the towing hook near the stern in tractor tugs. The fine all-round visibility from the wheelhouse is also apparent.*
(Walter Fussey & Son)

Early in 1983 a decision was taken to replace the riverside headquarters with a new, purpose-built, building slightly to the west of the existing structures. The old, partly timber, buildings had been in use since the site was first taken over in 1952 and were clearly due for renewal. To enable the construction of the new architect-designed building to proceed five acres of adjacent land were acquired from George Cohen, Sons & Co. Ltd. Accommodation is being provided for operations control, maintenance workshops and stores. The new headquarters is expected to be completed in the autumn of 1984 (Fig. 76).

Also under construction is the fifth rudder-propeller tug, due to be named *Norton Cross,* and similar to *Coatham Cross* but having a different supplier of the propulsion unit. She is being built by Richard Dunston (Hessle) Ltd. and is due to enter service in the Spring of 1984. (Fig. 78).

Following Her Majesty the Queen's Jubilee in 1977 Richard Crosthwaite was appointed a member of the Administrative Council of the Royal Jubilee Trusts in London and was also the Queen's representative of the Trusts in Cleveland. In March of 1983 he was sworn in as the year's High Sheriff for the County of Cleveland.

As this history draws to its conclusion it will be appropriate to review briefly the progress and achievements of the Crosthwaite family and Tees Towing. It will be remembered that Tees Towing Co. Ltd. was formed by the amalgamation in 1920 of the two largest towage companies on the River Tees; The Tees Tug Co. Ltd. and The Robinson Tug Co. Ltd., the latter having the largest share in the combined company at its formation. Due to the death of Charles Robinson soon afterwards, the controlling interest passed into the hands of William Crosthwaite and his family. That may seem all very simple and easily achieved but William Crosthwaite had had a hard struggle to keep his companies going ever since 1906. There had been the need to exist with old second-hand tonnage, there had been the effects of the First World War, the costs of the amalgamation, the strikes of 1920 and 1926 and the severe industrial depression of the late 1920's and early 1930's. It is surprising that the company was able to survive at all. Not until 1923 was it possible to purchase a newly-built tug and then it had to be sold after only a very short period of service on the Tees, presumably because of financial considerations. With all of these difficulties only just beginning to recede it was an act of courage and faith in the future to have built the diesel-electric *Acklam Cross* in 1933. Because of the need of time to gain experience from her, and then the effect of the Second World War, it was, however, to be another 20 years before a further new tug could be commissioned. It will readily be seen that only the forward looking persistence of William Crosthwaite and his son Cecil had kept the fleet in existence through almost thirty years of difficult conditions. Throughout this period too, William Crosthwaite had been dedicated to his work for the town resulting in him having been elected Mayor of Middlesbrough on no less than five occasions. This, and his work for so many other public bodies, as well as for his business acumen led to him being Knighted in 1939. This was an honour for both him and the town of Middlesbrough which had grown up alongside him.

With Cecil Crosthwaite taking an increasingly larger part in the running of the business he introduced the geared diesel tug in 1953 as the beginning of the changeover from steam to diesel power. An all-diesel fleet was achieved by 1962 when the company then possessed, for the first time, a fleet, the individual vessels of which, had all been built to the company's specific requirements. This was a significant point in the company's development and must have been Sir William's

Fig. 74 *This mural appears on the rear wall of the Tees Towing headquarters and it will be noted includes the Union Jack (with Lord Lieutenant's insignia), French Tricolour (French Consulate), the Middlesbrough Town Hall and Transporter Bridge as well as a number of tugs. It was painted by Michael Smith in 1979 when he was a student at the Middlesbrough College of Art. (Richard Crosthwaite)*

Fig. 75 *The vehicle carrier* Pearl Ace *berthing in Tees Dock with the assistance of two of the "Schottel" tugs* Skelton Cross *and* Yarm Cross. (A. Sparrow)

target ever since the amalgamation of 1920. Only his tenacity through the 1920's and 1930's had made it achievable. Having a wholly modern fleet it would have been easy to sit back and retain the type of units they now had. Not so however, the improvements of Kort rudders and Voith-Schneider propellers were introduced, and eventually the revolutionary rudder-propellers were installed in the latest tugs for river operation. These latter were introduced under the guidance of Richard Crosthwaite and it will have been seen through this history how the handover of responsibilities, with suitable overlap, had occurred through three generations of the Crosthwaite family. By this means continuity of thought and application has been achieved over almost 64 years. Ever since its inception the introduction of new ideas has always been in the forefront of the minds of those responsible for the management of Tees Towing Co. Ltd.

Fig. 76 *Artists impression of the new operations centre being built at Tees Wharf and due for completion during 1984. (Dennis Wompra)*

The major achievements over the years have been:

1. 1933 First diesel-electric tug for ship handling in Europe.
2. 1933 First tug with direct bridge control of the engines.
3. 1933 First tug with clear after deck.
4. 1933 First tug with hydraulic steering gear.
5. 1934 British Tugowners' Association founded by Sir William Crosthwaite.
6. 1953 First tug for a British owner with geared diesel propulsion.
7. 1957 First tug built in the U.K. to utilise a Kort rudder.
8. 1958 First tug in the U.K. to utilise Voith-Schneider propulsion.
9. 1963 European Tugowners' Association founded by Sir William Crosthwaite.
10. 1976 First rudder-propeller tug in the U.K.

At the end of 1983 the two private limited companies are managed as follows:–

Seahorse Securities Ltd.

Richard Crosthwaite, M.A., J.P., D.L.	Chairman
Arthur Greenwell, F.C.I.S.	Director and Secretary
Jeremy Pemberton, M.A.	Director

Tees Towing Co. Ltd.

Richard Crosthwaite, M.A., J.P., D.L.	Chairman and Managing Director
Arthur Greenwell, F.C.I.S.	Commercial Director and Secretary
Michael Edmund Lyon, J.P.	Non-Executive Director
Jeremy Pemberton, M.A.	Non-Executive Director
Brian James	Operations Manager
William Robinson	Marine Superintendent
Ian Gardiner	Engineering Superintendent
Victor Johnston	Towage Superintendent

The tug fleet at 31st December 1983 is:–

Ayton Cross	1,800 BHP	—
Ormesby Cross	1,800 BHP	Capt. Derek Parker
Leven Cross	1,235 BHP	Capt. Arthur Azemar
Ralph Cross	2,640 BHP	Capt. Luke Miller
Greatham Cross	2,200 BHP	Capt. Kenneth Townsend
Skelton Cross	2,200 BHP	Capt. Peter Anderson
Yarm Cross	2,640 BHP	Capt. Michael Ferst.
Coatham Cross	2,640 BHP	Capt. Robert Briggs

and ex Tees Towing vessels still in operation with other companies at 31st December 1983 are:

Wilga	ex *Banbury Cross* (1)	*Waterland*	ex *Fiery Cross*
Rilland	ex *Caedmon Cross*	*Mairi of Kishorn*	ex *Erimus Cross*
Dunheron	ex *Golden Cross*	*Finland*	ex *Danby Cross*
Gribbin Head	ex *Ingleby Cross* (2)	*Waasland*	ex *Marton Cross*

Working conditions for the crews in the present day tugs are infinitely better than they used to be but the men still have to work long unpredictable hours in order that the needs of shipping may be met. Whilst tug requirements are normally booked some hours ahead this is not always possible and the tug fleet must be able to respond to urgent demands at any hour of the day or night whether due to weather conditions, loading or discharging problems or just simply change of mind or orders. To maintain their undeniably good reputation the tugs must, therefore, be able to turn out whenever required. The crews normal working week is 0800 – 1700 Mondays to Fridays and 0800 – 1230 Saturdays, any extra to this being paid for on an overtime basis. Each man, by rota, gets two days off per week; the skipper when off is normally replaced by the mate of his particular tug. It will thus be seen that a crew who have worked through one "normal" day could, depending on the demand for tugs, work through the night period and then be required to work their "normal" day shift the following day, hence the long hours which can be clocked-up. However, unlike most industrial work, "working" does not mean being occupied every minute of the overtime period and time can be spent eating, relaxing or sleeping in the very comfortable facilities provided aboard a modern tug. Sickness and holiday periods are covered by a pool of "spare men". The total number of men involved in manning the present seven operating tugs is 57, including the reliefs.

There then is the story of a thriving, efficient and dynamic company, which to quote two very minor, but revealing facts, has held its 35th Christmas Party and issued its 86th annual diary. To listen to the tug skippers seemingly lighthearted and brief responses to a ship's captain's or pilot's commands is misleading. It can give, to the uninitiated, the impression that they are tackling the job in hand in rather a casual manner whereas in truth they know the job so well and are so skilled at nudging ships into tight spaces in a dock or holding them

Fig. 77 Coatham Cross *ready for launching at Richard Dunston's shipyard at Hessle, 16th September 1981.*

NORTON CROSS

steady in a high wind that their efficient performance needs no outward show or histrionics. They are undoubtedly a special breed of men dedicated to providing a first-class service to the shipowners whose vessels visit the Tees.

So much for the past and the present – what of the future? A glance through this history will have shown that through all periods change has been taking place. What is different today is that the rate of change is so much greater than it has ever been before. Consequently a view of the future cannot be expected to see very far with any certainty. However, it is likely, in view of the ability of the river Tees to hold its volume of traffic at about 90% of the peak figure during the recent and current trade depression, that the future prospects are reasonable. Trade dependent on North Sea oil production, after being thought to be in decline, now appears likely to stay steady for at least a few years whilst iron ore imports and steel exports depend on the success or otherwise of the rationalisation of steel production in the United Kingdom.

It will be apparent, that as far as work on the river is concerned, a towage company can do little to influence the amount of business coming its way. Its most effective weapon in this battle, along with all other organisations servicing the vessels using the river, is to keep its costs and therefore its charges as low as possible consistent with adequate profitability and an ability to maintain a modern tug fleet. By so doing Tees Towing Co. Ltd. will in the future be able to continue to offer an efficient, satisfactorily priced service given by modern highly manoeuvrable and powerful tugs; if at the same time the tugs look attractive then so much the better.

Finally there would appear to be no reason why Tees Towing Co. Ltd. should not be able to continue in the years ahead much as they are now with modern rudder-propeller vessels, manned by keen expert crews, backed up by a new riverside operational headquarters. Any idea of what the situation will be in say ten years time is difficult, if not impossible, to predict. Needless to say, whatever the future may bring under the Crosthwaite family ownership it is certain to be as exciting and eventful and changing for Richard Crosthwaite as it had been for his father Cecil and his grandfather William before him.

— Success to the Seahorses of the Tees —

Fig. 78 Norton Cross *in the William Wright drydock at Hull, April 1984, before delivery by her builders Richard Dunston (Hessle) Ltd. to Tees Towing Co. Ltd. (A. Sparrow)*

PART II

TUG DETAILS AND HISTORIES

Tug Details and Histories

Notes

The notation (1) or (2) in brackets after a ship's name indicates that she is the first or the second ship of that name in the fleet.

The dates in brackets following the name are the years of entering and leaving the fleet.

On the first line below the name is given the ship's Official Number (O.N.) in the British Registry followed by her tonnage, gross (g), and net (n) and her dimensions. Dimensions given are registered length x breadth x depth in feet and tenths of a foot for vessels numbered 1 to 64, overall length x extreme breadth x summer draught in feet and inches for vessels numbered 65 to 76 and metres for vessels numbered 77 to 80. To the right of the dimensions is given the material of construction of the hull viz: wood, iron or steel.

On the next line is given the type and size of engines, their power output and the method of propulsion. Below this is given the name of the engine builder. The following abbreviations are used for engine types:–

Steam	S	= simple-expansion engine
	C	= compound-expansion engine
	T	= triple-expansion engine
	B	= beam engine
	L	= lever engine
	D	= diagonal engine
Motor	SA	= single acting } prefixed by 2 for two-stroke or 4
	DA	= double acting } for four-stroke.
All	Cy	= cylinders – prefixed by 1,2,3 etc. for the number of cylinders.
	NE	= new engines } followed by date
	NB	= new boilers } followed by date
	NHP	= Nominal } horsepower
	IHP	= Indicated } horsepower
	BHP	= Brake } horsepower

Next follows the ports of registry (P.O.R.) with the relevant dates.

Finally are given the shipbuilders, owners, change(s) of name and fate details as appropriate. YN = Yard number.

Vessels numbered 58 onwards all have steel hulls and are screw propelled.

FLORENCE in Middlesbrough Dock Cut, c. 1926.

1. FLORENCE (1902 - 1927)

O.N. 76145 | 117 g, 26n; | 94.6 x 18.7 x 9.5 feet | Iron

L. 2Cy. 31" x 48", 70 NHP. Paddle (Engines made 1859). NB, 1896.
J.P. Almond, North Shields.

P.O.R. 1879, Maryport. 1900, Leith. 1902, Middlesbrough.

1879 : Completed by T. Williamson, Harrington for Maryport Steamship Co.
1900 : Sold to T. Devlin jnr, Edinburgh.
13.12.1902 : Sold to W. Slater, Middlesbrough.
16.12.1902 : Transferred to Florence Tugboat & Salvage Co. Ltd. (B.O. Davies, Mgr)
1906 : Manager W.H. Crosthwaite.
30. 6.1909 : Purchased by The Tees Tug Co. Ltd, (W.H. Crosthwaite, Mgr)
30. 7.1920 : Purchased by Tees Towing Company Ltd., (Robinson & Crosthwaite, Mgrs).
31. 8.1927 : Sold to C.W. Dorkin & Co., Sunderland for breaking-up.

2. PRIMROSE (1903 - 1914)

O.N. 88851 | 126 g, 29 n; | 101.5 x 19.0 x 10.2 feet | Iron

C.2Cy. 19" & 38" x 27", 62 NHP. Screw.
Hall Russell & Co., Aberdeen.

P.O.R. 1883, Aberdeen. 1903, Cardiff. 1903, Middlesbrough.

8.1883 : Completed by J. Duthie, Sons & Co., Aberdeen (YN 170) for W. Pyper & Co., Aberdeen as *North Star*.
1901 : Sold to North Line Steam Fishing Co. Ltd. (J.A. Harrow, Mgr.), Aberdeen.
1903 : Sold to W.J. Guy, Aberdeen and renamed *Primrose*.
1903 : Purchased by The Florence Tugboat & Salvage Co. Ltd. (B.O. Davies, Mgr.)
1906 : Manager W.H. Crosthwaite.
30. 6.1909 : Purchased by The Tees Tug Co. Ltd. (W.H. Crosthwaite, Mgr.)
31.12.1914 : Sold for breaking-up.

3. CHARLES DICKENS (1904)

O.N. 65662 | 121 g, 17 n; | 103.2 x 18.3 x 10.1 feet | Iron

L.2Cy. 28" x 48", 55NHP. Paddle.
Readhead, Softley & Co., South Shields.

P.O.R. 1872, London. 1880, Stockton-on-Tees.

1872 : Completed by Readhead, Softley & Co., South Shields for J. Martin, London.
23. 6.1880 : Sold to Tees Conservancy Commissioners (J. Forster, Mgr.)
1888 : Manager now J.H. Amos.
1904 : Purchased by The Florence Tugboat & Salvage Co. Ltd. (B.O. Davies, Mgr.)
1904 : Sold to Linthorpe Dinsdale Smelting Co., Middlesbrough.
1905 : Sold to J. Batey & Son, Newcastle.
1915 : Broken-up on River Tyne.

4. **CHALLENGER (1)** (1905 - 1907)

O.N. 84995 | 104 g, 23 n; | 100.7 x 18.0 x 9.0 feet | Iron

L.1Cy. 36" x 56", 50 NHP. Paddle.
Hepple & Co., South Shields.

P.O.R. 1882, Sunderland. 1905, South Shields. 1906, Middlesbrough.

1881 : Completed by J.T. Eltringham & Co., South Shields (YN 94) for Martha Nicholson, Sunderland.
1886 : Sold to I. Hodgson, Sunderland.
1905 : Sold to J.G. Everson, South Shields.
1905 : Purchased by The Florence Tugboat & Salvage Co. Ltd. (J. Blumer, Mgr.)
12. 7.1907 : Sold to J.H. Pounder, West Hartlepool.
24. 8.1908 : Converted to sailing lighter.
27. 1.1923 : Sold to G. Alder Ltd., Middlesbrough.
9. 5.1929 : Purchased by Alice M. Crosthwaite.
7. 8.1929 : Sold for breaking-up.

CLARISSA opposite Clarence Wharf, c. 1928.
(W. Haig Parry)

5. **CLARISSA** (1907 - 1930)

O.N. 87845 | 92 g, Nil n; | 86.2 x 18.1 x 9.6 feet | Iron

C.2Cy. 18" & 34" x 21", 65 NHP. Screw.
Edward Foden, Sandbach.

P.O.R. 1883, Liverpool. 1920, Middlesbrough.

2.1883 : Completed by Richard Clark, Weston Point for J. Dutton, Cardiff.
1886 : Sold to R. Lee, Cardiff.
1888 : Sold to J. Dutton, Cardiff.
1890 : Sold to W. Lee, Cardiff.
1907 : Purchased by Clarissa Tug Co., Middlesbrough.
1909 : Purchased by The Tees Tug Co. Ltd., (W.H. Crosthwaite, Mgr.)
30. 7.1920 : Purchased by Tees Towing Co. Ltd. (Robinson & Crosthwaite, Mgrs.)
30. 9.1920 : Transferred to Charles Duncan & Sons Ltd. (C.W. Duncan, Mgr.) for £4,000.
25. 8.1930 : Sold for breaking-up.

EMPRESS OF INDIA towing sailing ship out of the River Tees, c. 1910.

(R.C. Clifford)

6. **EMPRESS OF INDIA** (1907 - 1913)

O.N. 109958 | 138g, 6n; | 94.2 x 21.1 x 11.6 feet | Steel

C.2Cy. 19" & 42" x 24", 98 NHP, 530 IHP. Screw. NB 1900.
J.G. Kincaid & Co., Greenock.

P.O.R. 1898, London. 1909, Middlesbrough.

8.1898 : Completed by Carmichael MacLean & Co., Greenock for J. Constant, London.
1903 : Sold to Sir John Jackson Ltd., London.
1907 : Purchased by The Florence Tugboat & Salvage Co. Ltd., (W.H. Crosthwaite, Mgr.)
30. 6.1909 : Purchased by The Tees Tug Co. Ltd., (W.H. Crosthwaite, Mgr.)
8.7. 1913 : Sold to Anglo-Persian Oil Co. Ltd., (J. Hamilton, Glasgow, Mgr.) renamed *Sirdar-I-Naphte.*
19. 3.1915 : Foundered in the Persian Gulf.

GLEN ROSA towing British India liner into Middlesbrough Dock Cut.

7. **GLEN ROSA** (1909 - 1926)

O.N. 105174 | 110g, 2n; | 96.0 x 18.5 x 9.7 feet | Steel

C.2Cy. 19" & 38" x 24", 95 NHP, 400 IHP. Screw.
Muir & Houston, Glasgow.

P.O.R. 1895, Cardiff. 1896, Cardiff. 1913, Middlesbrough.

7.1895 : Completed by J. Shearer & Son, Glasgow for Guthrie, Heywood & Co., Cardiff.
1896 : Sold to J. Guthrie, Penarth. (Lengthened).
1901 : Sold to Cardiff Steam Towing Co.
1904 : Sold to G. Robinson, Middlesbrough.
1908 : Owners redesignated G. Robinson & Co.
5.1909 : Purchased by The Tees Tug Co. Ltd. (W.H. Crosthwaite, Mgr.)
30. 7.1920 : Purchased by Tees Towing Co. Ltd. (Robinson & Crosthwaite, Mgrs.)
22. 4.1926 : Sold to Hughes Bolckow Shipbreaking Ltd. for breaking-up at Blyth.
30. 4.1926 : Sailed from River Tees to Blyth.

HERO.
(P.N. Thomas)

8. HERO (1909 - 1917)

O.N. 101894 66g, 12n; 78.0 x 16.0 x 8.7 feet Iron/Steel

C.2Cy. 16" & 31" x 20", 60 NHP, 300 IHP. Screw.
Vosper & Co., Portsmouth.

P.O.R. 1892, London. 1892, Llanelly. 1913, Middlesbrough.

6.1892 : Completed by Edwards & Symes, Millwall for Burry Steam Tug Co., Llanelly.
1908 : Sold to G. Robinson & Co., Middlesbrough.
5.1909 : Purchased by The Tees Tug Co. Ltd. (W.H. Crosthwaite, Mgr.)
28. 3.1917 : Sunk by mine off Sunderland.

ARCHDALE
during the First World War.

9. VIXEN/ARCHDALE (1909 - 1919)

O.N. 105277 119g, Nil n; 95.8 x 18.2 x 10.1 feet Steel

C.2Cy. $17^1/_2$" & $35^1/_4$" x 24", 60 NHP, 320 IHP. Screw.
W. Allsup & Sons, Preston.

P.O.R. 1896, Plymouth. 1913, Middlesbrough. 1920, South Shields.

1896 : Completed by Allsup & Co. Ltd., Preston for T.W. Fox, Plymouth as *Vixen.*
1908 : Sold to G. Robinson & Co., Middlesbrough.
5.1909 : Purchased by The Tees Tug Co. Ltd. (W.H. Crosthwaite, Mgr.)
23.11.1914 : Renamed *Archdale.*
18. 3.1919 : Sold to Dept. of Director-General of Movements & Railways,
1920 : Sold to Coulson Tug Co. Ltd., South Shields (J.G. Coulson, Mgr.), renamed *John Coulson.*
1929 : Sold to Jane E. Strong.
1937 : Sold for breaking-up.

10. **CHAMPION** (1909 - 1920)

O.N. 76666 124g, 29n; 102.6 x 19.3 x 10.0 feet Iron

L.2Cy. 27" x 50", 80 NHP. Paddle.
J.P. Rennoldson, South Shields.

P.O.R. 1876, Grimsby. 1913, Middlesbrough.

1876 : Completed by J.T. Eltringham, South Shields (YN 57) for S. Oates, Grimsby.
1883 : Owners T. & S. Oates.
1901 : Owner A.D. Oates.
1902 : Sold to G. Robinson, Middlesbrough.
1908 : Owners redesignated G. Robinson & Co.
1909 : Purchased by The Tees Tug Co. Ltd. (W.H. Crosthwaite, Mgr.)
9. 9.1920 : Sold to G. Alder Ltd. Converted to a hulk.
9. 5.1929 : Purchased by Alice M. Crosthwaite.
1929 : Sold for breaking-up.

CHALLENGER (2).

11. **CHALLENGER (2)** (1909 - 1925)

O.N. 68508 153g, 14n; 113.5 x 19.2 x 9.6 feet Iron

L.2Cy. $29\frac{1}{2}$" x 54", 98 NHP. Paddle.
J. Readhead & Co., South Shields.

P.O.R. 1874, London. 1893, South Shields. 1908, Middlesbrough

1873 : Completed by J. Readhead & Co., South Shields (YN 97) for T.W. Elliott, London.
1882 : Sold to W. Sandford, Gravesend.
1893 : Sold to C.E. Walton (R.B. Stewart, Mgr.)
1893 : Sold to R. Stewart, South Shields.
1907 : Sold to G. Robinson, Middlesbrough.
1908 : Owner redesignated G. Robinson & Co.
1909 : Purchased by The Tees Tug Co. Ltd. (W.H. Crosthwaite, Mgr.)
30. 7.1920 : Purchased by Tees Towing Co. Ltd. (Robinson & Crosthwaite, Mgrs.)
21. 4.1925 : Sold for breaking-up.

LIBERIA off Clarence Wharf, c. 1928.
(W. Haig Parry)

12. LIBERIA (1913 - 1930)

O.N. 120612 | 128g, 6n; | 94.0 x 19.6 x 10.9 feet | Steel

T.3Cy. 13", 21" & 34" x 24", 99 NHP, 450 IHP. Screw.
G.T. Grey, South Shields.

P.O.R. 1905, London. 1914, Middlesbrough. 1930, Newport.

10.1905 : Completed by Cochrane & Sons, Selby (YN 354) for W. Watkins, London.
1911 : Transferred to Watkins Petrie & Co., Middlesbrough.
1.1913 : Purchased by The Tees Tug Co. Ltd (W.H. Crosthwaite, Mgr.)
30. 7.1920 : Purchased by Tees Towing Co. Ltd. (Robinson & Crosthwaite, Mgrs.)
25. 6.1930 : Sold to The Newport Screw Towing Co. Ltd., Newport (Mon) (J.A.H. Dunn, Mgr.)
1937 : Broken-up.

13. TRIUMPH (1913 - 1923)

O.N. 70726 | 76g, 18n; | 82.0 x 16.6 x 8.9 feet | Iron

L.2Cy. 22½" x 45", 45 NHP. Paddle.
G. Butchard, Milton Ironworks, Gravesend.

P.O.R. 1875, London. 1889, Plymouth. 1914, Middlesbrough.

1875 : Completed by G. Butchard, Milton Ironworks, Gravesend for J. Williams, Gravesend.
1889 : Owned at Plymouth.
1900 : Sold to G. Petrie, Middlesbrough.
1.1911 : Transferred to Watkins Petrie & Co., Middlesbrough.
1.1913 : Purchased by The Tees Tug Co. Ltd. (W.H. Crosthwaite, Mgr.)
30. 7.1920 : Purchased by Tees Towing Co. Ltd. (Robinson & Crosthwaite, Mgrs.)
21. 6.1923 : Sold to S.E. Simpson (Tug Co.) Ltd., Newcastle-upon-Tyne. (S.E. Simpson, Mgr.) for £325.
31. 3.1926 : Broken-up.

14. IDA DUNCAN (1914 - 1917)

O.N.98291 | 139g, 45n; | 95.0 x 20.3 x 10.6 feet | Iron

C.2Cy. 16⅛" & 32¼" x 21", 40 NHP, 240 IHP. Screw.
J.P. Rennoldson & Sons, South Shields.

P.O.R. 1891, Boston. 1914, Middlesbrough.

1891 : Completed by J.P. Rennoldson & Sons, South Shields for Steam Trawling Co., Boston as *Sturgeon.*
1897 : Sold to Boston Deep Sea Fishing & Ice Co. (D. Walker, Mgr. from 1911).
26. 6.1913 : Sold to Wm Chrystal Duncan (Chas. Wm Duncan, Mgr.) for £775
2.12.1913 : Renamed *Ida Duncan*
8. 7.1914 : Purchased by Charles Duncan & Sons Ltd. (Chas. Wm Duncan, Mgr.)
31. 1.1917 : Sunk by mine off entrance to River Tees with the loss of six lives.

LINGDALE, c. 1928. (W. Haig Parry)

15. LINGDALE (1914 - 1954)

O.N. 79377 174g, 11n; 107.7 x 20.1 x 10.4 feet. Iron

L. 2Cy. 31" x 57", 75NHP. Paddle. NB1907. NB1935.
J. Stewart & Sons Ltd, Blackwall.

P.O.R. 1883, Dover. 1914, Middlesbrough.

10.1882 : Completed by Westwood Baillie & Co., Poplar for Dover Harbour Board as *Lady Vita.*
1914 : Sold to J.P. Rennoldson & Sons Ltd., South Shields.
2.11.1914 : Purchased by The Tees Tug Co. Ltd. (W.H. Crosthwaite, Mgr.)
16.12.1914 : Renamed *Lingdale.*
20. 7.1920 : Purchased by Tees Towing Co. Ltd., (Robinson & Crosthwaite, Mgrs.)
1949 : Managers Wm. Crosthwaite & Son.
5. 5.1954 : Sold to J.J. King & Co. Ltd., Gateshead for breaking-up.

FRANK near the Middlesbrough Transporter Bridge, c. 1920.

16. FRANK (1915 - 1921)

O.N. 108184 76g 3n; 74.5 x 17.7 x 9.0 feet Steel

C.2Cy. 14" & 30" x 22", 65 NHP. Screw.
J. Stewart & Sons Ltd., Blackwall.

P.O.R. 1897, London.

12.1896 : Completed by R. Craggs & Sons, Middlesbrough for J Constant, London as *Looker.*
1896 : Renamed *Frank.*
1897 : Sold to H. Reep, London.
1903 : Sold to J.A. Thompson, Cardiff.
1906 : Sold to C.W. Duncan & Co., Middlesbrough.
26. 1.1915 : Purchased by Charles Duncan & Sons Ltd. for £2,300.
1921 : Sold to W.J. Guy, Cardiff.
Subsequent history not known.

17. DORA DUNCAN (1915 - 1927)

O.N. 96523 126g, 23n; 97.0 x 19.3 x 10.6 feet Iron

C.2Cy. 17" & 34" x 24", 46 NHP, 250 IHP. Screw.
Baird & Barnsley, North Shields.

P.O.R. 1891, North Shields. 1915, Middlesbrough.

1891 : Completed by J.T. Eltringham & Co., South Shields (YN 160) for J.S. Doeg, North Shields as *Lionel*.
19. 2.1915 : Purchased by Charles Duncan & Sons Ltd., (C.W. Duncan, Mgr.) for £975.
21 6.1915 : Renamed *Dora Duncan*.
10. 2.1927 : Broken-up at Stockton-on-Tees.

18. ADONIS (1917 - ?)

O.N. 70396 80g, 8n; 85.4 x 17.9 x 9.2 feet Wood

L.1Cy. 31" x 48", 32 NHP. Paddle.
T.R. Scott & Co., North Shields.

P.O.R. 1875, North Shields. 1898, Blyth.

1875 : Completed by Wouldhave & Johnson, North Shields for W. Stephenson, North Shields.
21. 7.1885 : Sold to J. Reed, North Shields.
1892 : Sold to J. Dent, Newcastle-upon-Tyne.
1898 : Sold to R.L. Manners, Blyth.
c.1911 : Sold to J. Manners, Blyth.
c.1913 : Sold to The Robinson Tug Co. Ltd.
5. 2.1917 : Purchased by Charles Duncan & Sons Ltd. for £100. Subsequent history not known.

FIFESHIRE as FLYING SWALLOW at Kirkcaldy, c. 1905.

19. FIFESHIRE (1917 - 1919)

O.N. 93386 146g, 20n; 108.0 x 18.6 x 9.8 feet Iron

L.1Cy. 36" x 54", 80 NHP. Paddle.
J.P. Rennoldson & Sons, South Shields.

P.O.R. 1887, ? . 1905, Kirkcaldy. 1919, Leith.

1887 : Completed by J.T. Eltringham & Co., South Shields for Clyde Shipping Co. as *Flying Swallow*.
5. 5.1905 : Sold to Kirkcaldy Towing Co., renamed *Fifeshire*.
15. 2.1917 : Purchased by Charles Duncan & Sons Ltd. for £1300
1919 : Sold to Leith Salvage & Towage Co. Ltd. (J. Little & Co. Ltd., Mgrs.)
1924 : Broken-up.

MONSDALE as MARIE at Kings Lynn, c. 1913.

20. MONSDALE (1917 - 1923)

O.N. 73650 — 77g, 10n; — 82.0 x 16.6 x 8.9 feet — Iron

L.2Cy. 22" x 45", 30 NHP. Paddle
G. Butchard, Milton, nr. Gravesend.

P.O.R. 1876, London. 1880, Kings Lynn. 1917, Middlesbrough.

1875 : Completed by G. Butchard, Milton, nr Gravesend as *Marie*
1880 : Sold to Kings Lynn Steam Tug Co.
15. 2.1917 : Purchased by The Tees Tug Co. Ltd. (W.H. Crosthwaite, Mgr.) Renamed *Monsdale.*
30. 7.1920 : Purchased by Tees Towing Co. Ltd. (Robinson & Crosthwaite, Mgrs.)
1923 : Sold to Pounder for £100 for breaking-up.

PRIVATEER at Bideford when employed as an excursion vessel. (North Devon Museum Trust)

21. PRIVATEER (1917)

O.N. 78447 — 117g, 1n; — 96.5 x 18.3 x 9.2 feet — Iron

L.1Cy. 35" x 54", 65 NHP. Paddle.
G.P. Mepple, North Shields.

P.O.R. 1883, Swansea. 1895, Boston. 1915, Middlesbrough.

1883 : Completed by T & W Toward, Newcastle-upon-Tyne for W.P. Ching, Swansea.
1890 : Sold to J.M. Thomas, Swansea.
1895 : Sold to Boston Steam Tug Co. Ltd., (A.H. Read, Mgr.)
1914 : Sold to F. Palmer, Boston.
1915 : Sold to The Robinson Tug Co. Ltd., (C.W. Robinson, Mgr.), Middlesbrough.
15. 2.1917 : Purchased by Charles Duncan & Sons Ltd., (C.W. Duncan, Mgr.) for £1450.
14.12.1917 : Sold to The Lawson Steam Tugboat Co. Ltd., South Shields, (J. Lawson, Mgr.)
23.12.1918 : Vessel total loss. Ashore Equitien, nr. Boulogne on voyage Le Tréport to Boulogne.

22. **LILY/LILY DUNCAN** (1918-1927)

O.N. 55226* 28g, Nil n; 56.5 x 13.8 x 6.0 feet Iron & Steel

S.2Cy. 14" x 18", 50 IHP. Screw. (Originally unpowered. Engine fitted 1879).
Scott, Inverkeithing.

P.O.R. 1866, Liverpool. 1884, Runcorn. 1887, Beaumaris. 1919, Middlesbrough.

1866 : Completed by Bewley & Webb, Dublin for J. Newton, Liverpool as *Herring*.
1879 : Sold to J. Douglas, Belfast, Renamed *Belfast*.
1879 : Lengthened by Harland & Wolff, Belfast.
1887 : Sold to T. Roberts, Conway.
1892 : Sold to Liverpool Screw Towing Co. Ltd., Liverpool renamed *Moorcock*.
1898 : Sold to J.L. Gordon, Liverpool.
13. 4.1905 : Sold to J.T. Mitford, Middlesbrough, renamed *Lily*.
8.1918 : Purchased by Charles Duncan & Sons Ltd., (C.W. Duncan, Mgr.)
1919 : Rebuilt by Teesbank Engineering Co., Middlesbrough. Renamed *Lily Duncan*.
2. 7.1927 : Sold for breaking-up at Stockton-on-Tees.

23. **BETSY DUNCAN** (1918 - 1920)

O.N. 97950 29g, 5n; 60.2 x 14.1 x 7.0 feet Steel

S.2Cy. 12" x 12", 18 NHP. (Engine built 1882). Screw.
Vosper Clark, Portsmouth.

P.O.R. 1890, Newcastle. 1919, Middlesbrough.

1889 : Completed by W. Cook, Middlesbrough for A. Brown Ltd. as *Comet*.
3.12.1890 : Boiler exploded at Quayside, Newcastle-on-Tyne.
4.11.1897 : Sold to owners at Blakeney, Norfolk.
1897 : Sold to E.C. Turner, Holt, Norfolk.
? : Sold to William Chrystal Duncan.
23.10.1918 : Purchased by Charles Duncan & Sons Ltd., (C.W. Duncan, Mgr.) for £980.
2. 1.1919 : Renamed *Betsy Duncan*.
30. 4.1920 : Sold to G. Wardle & T. Mowat, South Shields.
25.11.1920 : Sold to J.G. Potts, Sunderland.
27. 3.1922 : Sank in South Dock, Sunderland.
1922 : Dismantled.

POWERFUL on the River Clyde. (G.E. Langmuir)

24. **POWERFUL** (1920 - 1923)

O.N. 78628 182g, 3n; 122.5 x 20.2 x 10.6 feet Iron

L.1Cy. 41" x 60", 98 NHP. Paddle. NB 1903.
J.P. Rennoldson & Sons, South Shields.

P.O.R. 1878, Glasgow. 1900, Greenock. 1921, Middlesbrough.

1878 : Completed by J.T. Eltringham & Co., South Shields for Clyde Shipping Co. Ltd. as *Flying Huntress*.
1900 : Sold to D. Mackellar, Greenock, (Greenock Towing Co.), renamed *Powerful*.
27. 9.1917 : Sold to British Franco Shipping Co., Newcastle-upon-Tyne.
1918 : Sold to D.L. Griffiths, Liverpool.
1920 : Purchased by Tees Towing Co. Ltd. (Robinson & Crosthwaite, Mgrs.) for £1,150.
24. 7.1923 : Sold for £180 for breaking-up.

ATHLETE
in the River Tees,
c. 1921.

25. ATHLETE (1920 - 1947)

O.N. 101992 | 119g, 2n; | 92.5 x 19.6 x 10.5 feet | Steel

T.3Cy. 13", 21" & 34" x 24", 150 NHP, 500 IHP. Screw. NB 1920
J. Stewart & Sons, Blackwall.

P.O.R. 1893, London. 1920, Middlesbrough. 1948, Liverpool.

4.1893 : Completed by J. Stewart & Sons Ltd., Blackwall for Matthew Brownfield, Poplar.
1908 : Sold to Miss E. Brownfield, London.
10. 6.1909 : Sold to The Robinson Tug Co. Ltd., (C.W. Robinson, Mgr.), Middlesbrough.
30. 7.1920 : Purchased by Tees Towing Co. Ltd. (Robinson & Crosthwaite, Mgrs.)
16.12.1947 : Sold to J.H. Lamey Ltd., (W.H. Lamey, Mgr.), Liverpool.
1955 : Sold to T.W. Ward Ltd, Preston for breaking-up.

CLEVELAND
in Middlesbrough Dock during
the First World War with The
Robinson Tug Co. Ltd. funnel
markings.
(R.C. Clifford)

26. CLEVELAND (1920 - 1947)

O.N. 82753 | 172g, 58n; | 120.0 x 20.6 x 10.6 feet | Iron

L.2Cy. 32" x 54", 95 NHP. Paddle. NB 1888 and 1924.
J.P. Rennoldson & Sons, South Shields.

P.O.R. 1881, Middlesbrough.

1881 : Completed by J.T. Eltringham & Co., South Shields for
The North Eastern Railway Co., (W. Bulmer, Mgr.).
29. 1.1914 : Sold to The Robinson Tug Co. Ltd., (C.W. Robinson, Mgr.), Middlesbrough
for £2,700.
30. 7.1920 : Purchased by Tees Towing Co. Ltd. (Robinson & Crosthwaite, Mgrs.)
5. 4.1935 : Transferred to Charles Duncan & Sons Ltd. for £3,500.
6. 5.1947 : Broken-up at Stockton-on-Tees.

27. GEORGE PEABODY (1920)

O.N. 56905 · 115g, 22n; 100.4 x 18.3 x 9.9 feet Iron

L.2Cy. $27\frac{1}{2}$" x 48", 55 NHP. Paddle. NB 1892.
Readhead, Softley & Co., South Shields.

P.O.R. 1868, London. 1887, Llanelly. 1897, Blyth. 1907, Middlesbrough.

12.1867 : Completed by Readhead, Softley & Co., South Shields for J. Martin, Gravesend.
1879 : Sold to T.A.F. Banks, Gravesend.
1886 : Sold to W. Bowen Jr., Llanelly
1894 : Sold to Blyth Steam Tug Co., (G. Dinsdale, Mgr.)
22. 5.1907 : Sold to W. Slater & J. Robson, (W. Slater, Mgr.)
13.10.1908 : Owned by W. Slater only.
18. 1.1916 : Sold to The Robinson Tug Co. Ltd., (C.W. Robinson, Mgr.)
30. 7.1920 : Purchased by Tees Towing Co. Ltd., (Robinson & Crosthwaite, Mgrs.)
8.10.1920 : Vessel broken-up.

GEORGE ROBINSON in the River Tees c. 1928.
(W. Haig Parry)

28. GEORGE ROBINSON (1920 - 1950)

O.N. 102492 95g, 4n; 87.1 x 18.0 x 9.6 feet Steel

T.3Cy. $12\frac{3}{4}$", 20" & 32" x 22", 52 NHP, 400 IHP. Screw. NB.1914.
Earles Shipbuilding & Engineering Co. Ltd., Hull.

P.O.R. 1896, Bristol. 1900, (Belgium.) 1910, Middlesbrough.

2.1896 : Completed by Earles Shipbuilding & Engineering Co. Ltd., Hull, (YN 404), for Bristol Screw Towage Co. as *Kestrel.*
1900 : Sold to L. Coiseau & J. Cousin, Zeebrugge renamed *Amédée Visart.*
6. 6.1910 : Sold to The Robinson Tug Co. Ltd. (G. Robinson, Mgr.), renamed *George Robinson.*
7. 8.1918 : Manager C.W. Robinson.
30. 7.1920 : Purchased by Tees Towing Co. Ltd., (Robinson & Crosthwaite, Mgrs.)
9. 2.1946 : Sank in River Tees. Later refloated and returned to service.
1949 : Managers Wm. Crosthwaite & Son.
23. 5.1950 : Sold to Clayton & Davie Ltd., Dunston for breaking-up.

NUNTHORPE
in Middlesbrough Dock Cut,
c. 1926.

29. NUNTHORPE (1920 - 1926)

O.N. 76117 122g, 11n; 105.4 x 18.7 x 9.7 feet Iron

1876. L.2Cy. 28" x 51", 52 NHP.
T.R. Scott & Co., North Shields.

1884. L.2Cy. 28" x 50", 50 NHP. Paddle.
J.P. Rennoldson & Sons, South Shields. NB 1884.

P.O.R. 1876, Middlesbrough.

1876 : Completed by J.T. Eltringham, South Shields, (YN 55), for the North Eastern Railway Co., (W. Bulmer, Mgr.).
22. 4.1896 : Manager A.E. Ballan.
21. 8.1897 : Manager T. Pickering.
3.12.1898 : Manager T. Chalt.
1.12.1908 : Sold to G. Robinson & Co., (C.W. Robinson, Mgr.)
4.1909 : Sold to The Robinson Tug Co. Ltd. (C.W. Robinson, Mgr.)
7.1920 : Purchased by Tees Towing Co. Ltd., (Robinson & Crosthwaite, Mgrs.)
24. 3.1926 : Sold to Hughes Bolckow Shipbreaking Co. Ltd. for breaking-up at Blyth.

30. PENDENNIS (1920 - 1923)

O.N. 45230 73g, 20n; 79.4 x 16.9 x 8.9 feet Iron

S.2Cy. 25" x 42", 40 NHP, 50 IHP. Paddle.
Westgarth English & Co., Middlesbrough.

P.O.R. 1863, Falmouth, 1877, Wisbech. 1908, Lowestoft. 1920, Midd esbrough.

1863 : Completed by J. Ash & Co., Cubitt Town, London for R. Taylor, Falmouth.
1876 : Sold to P. Thomas, Falmouth.
1877 : Sold to H.H. English, Peterborough.
1877 : Sold to Pendennis Co. Ltd., Wisbech.
1908 : Sold to W.R. Fasey, Lowestoft.
1913 : Sold to The Robinson Tug Co. Ltd., (C.W. Robinson, Mgr.)
30. 7.1920 : Purchased by Tees Towing Co. Ltd., (Robinson & Crosthwaite, Mgrs.)
1923 : Sold to Slater & Co. for £150.
24. 7.1923 : Vessel broken-up.

SAMPHIRE BATTS in Tees Bay, c. 1928.

31. SAMPHIRE BATTS (1920 - 1933)

O.N. 99241 | 174g, 11n; | 112.0 x 21.1 x 10.1 feet | Steel

T.3Cy. 14", 23" & 36" x 27", 75 NHP, 630 IHP. Screw.
Muir & Houston, Glasgow.

P.O.R. 1893, Leith. 1913, Middlesbrough.

1893 : Completed by Cumming & Ellis, Inverkeithing (Y.N. 6) for Mackay & Co., Leith as *Sea King*.
1899 : Sold to A. Kay.
c.1911 : Sold to National Bank of Scotland (J. Cormack, Jnr., Mgr.)
5.1913 : Sold to The Robinson Tug Co. Ltd., (G. Robinson, Mgr.) renamed *Samphire Batts*.
30. 7.1920 : Purchased by Tees Towing Co. Ltd., (Robinson & Crosthwaite, Mgrs.)
17.10.1933 : Sold to Clayton & Davie Ltd., Dunston for breaking-up.

IRONOPOLIS as BORWICK RAILS before coming to the River Tees.

32. BORWICK RAILS/IRONOPOLIS (1920 - 1927)

O.N. 65924 | 136g, 48n; | 102.6 x 19.1 x 9.6 feet | Iron

D.2Cy. 30" x 36", 70 NHP. Paddle. NB 1900.
G. Forrester & Co., Liverpool.

P.O.R. 1872, Liverpool. 1902, Whitehaven. 1921, Middlesbrough.

1871 : Completed by Liverpool Shipbuilding Co. Ltd., Liverpool for Nathaniel Cane, Liverpool as *Borwick Rails*.
7. 1.1886 : Sold to W.I. Barratt, Hodbarrow for 1/4d.
11.10.1901 : Sold to W.H. Thompson, Millom.
21.10.1901 : Sold to Whitehaven Harbour Commissioners for £530.
27. 8.1918 : Sold to J. Prendiville & Co., (D.L. Griffiths, Mgr.), Liverpool.
26. 9.1920 : Purchased by Tees Towing Co. Ltd., (Robinson & Crosthwaite, Mgrs.) for £1250.
8.11.1921 : Renamed *Ironopolis*.
3. 8.1927 : Sold to Thomas & McGregor for £375 for breaking-up at Bo'ness.

33. LORD WARDEN (1920 - 1924)

O.N. 60856 118g, 6n; 100.4 x 18.3 x 10.1 feet Iron

L.2Cy. 28" x 48", 55 NHP. Paddle. NB 1890.
Readhead, Softley & Co., South Shields.

P.O.R. 1868, London. 1895, North Shields. 1920, Middlesbrough.

1868 : Completed by Readhead, Softley & Co., South Shields for J. Martin, Gravesend.
1874 : Sold to W.J. Homeward, London.
1879 : Sold to T.A.F. Banks, Gravesend.
1886 : Sold to F. Pattison, Gravesend.
2.1895 : Sold to J.T. Eltringham, South Shields.
1895 : Sold to J. Anderson, North Shields.
25. 5.1903 : Sold to Anchor Steam Tug Co. Ltd., Sunderland, (A.B. Atkinson, Mgr.)
1913 : Manager now R. Chater.
27. 7.1920 : Sold to France Fenwick Tyne & Wear Co. Ltd., Newcastle, (C.E. Dawson, Mgr.)
16. 9.1920 : Sold to C.W. Robinson, Middlesbrough.
29. 9.1920 : Purchased by Charles Duncan & Sons Ltd. (C.W. Duncan, Mgr.).
16. 1.1924 : Sold for breaking-up.

GRANITE CITY at Aberdeen, c. 1915.

34. GRANITE CITY (1921 - 1922)

O.N. 84369 113g, 8n; 95.5 x 18.7 x 10.4 feet Wood

S.1Cy. 34¼" x 52", 40 NHP. Paddle.
R.B. Findley & Son, North Shields.

P.O.R. 1882, Aberdeen.

11.1882 : Completed by Wouldhave & Johnson, North Shields for J.N. Newton, Aberdeen.
1914 : Sold to R. Taylor, Aberdeen.
2.1921 : Sold to C.W. Robinson, Middlesbrough.
1921 : Purchased by Tees Towing Co. Ltd., (Robinson & Crosthwaite, Mgrs.).
3.1922 : Sold to Kirton & Foster, Aberdeen for breaking-up but was in fact put to further use.
13. 8.1927 : Foundered at Blaydon Buoys, River Tyne.

35. UNITED (1921 - 1923)

O.N. g, n; x x

P.O.R.

1921 : Sold to C.W. Robinson, Middlesbrough.
2.1921 : Purchased by Tees Towing Co. Ltd., (Robinson & Crosthwaite, Mgrs.)
11.1923 : Sold for breaking-up for £80.

[No further details discovered]

36. **WILLIAM FINDLEY** (1921 - 1922)

O.N. 89800 87g, 3n; 90.0 x 17.9 x 9.5 feet Wood

B.1Cy. 31½" x 48", 32 NHP. Paddle.
R.B. Findley & Son, North Shields.

P.O.R. 1884, North Shields. 1895, Aberdeen.

1884 : Completed by Wouldhave & Johnson, North Shields for W. Osten Jr., North Shields.
4.1895 : Sold to J.N. Newton, Aberdeen.
1916 : Sold to R. Taylor, Aberdeen.
1921 : Sold to C.W. Robinson, Middlesbrough.
2.1921 : Purchased by Tees Towing Co. Ltd., (Robinson & Crosthwaite, Mgrs.).
3.1922 : Vessel lost. No details known.

37. **LACEBY** (1922 - 1926)

O.N. 140812 118g, 41n; 103.8 x 20.6 x 9.6 feet Steel

C.2Cy. 17¾" & 32¾" x 22", 42 NHP. Screw.
J.C. Tecklenbörg, Geestemünde.

P.O.R. 1920, Grimsby. 1922, Middlesbrough.

1892 : Completed by J.C. Tecklenbörg, Geestemünde for C. Kampf, Geestemünde as *Toni*.
1916 : Captured by British forces.
15.10.1920 : Sold to Keelby Steam Fishing Co., (J.R.E. Mordaunt, Mgr.) renamed *Laceby*.
21. 6.1922 : Purchased by W.H. Crosthwaite & C.W. Robinson.
19. 3.1923 : Transfered to Tees Towing Co. Ltd. (Robinson & Crosthwaite, Mgrs.)
29. 3.1926 : Sold to Hughes Bolckow, Blyth for breaking-up.

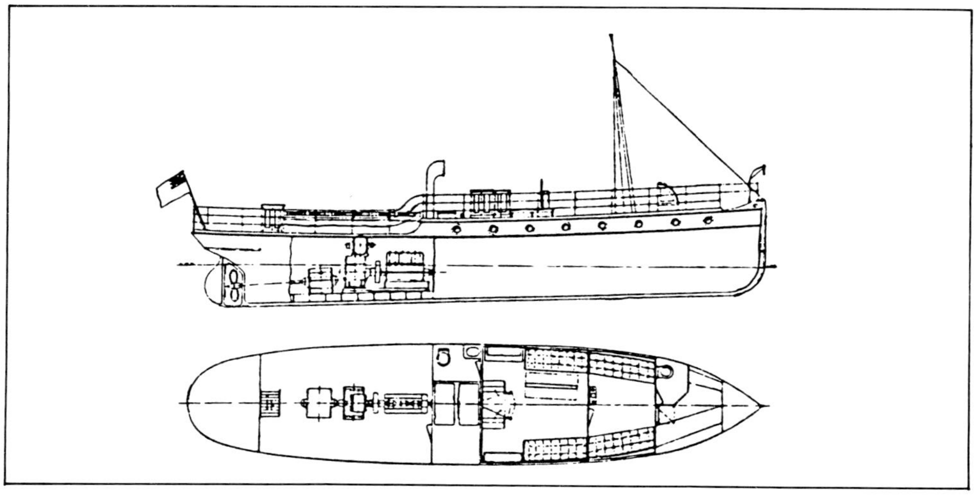

ELECTRIC ARC.
A drawing made at the time of her building, 1911.
("The Shipbuilder")

38. **ELECTRIC ARC** (1922 - 1925)

O.N. 129567 24g, 16n; 51.1 x 11.6 x 5.3 feet Steel

Petrol. 6Cy. 45 BHP. Wolsley. Screw.
A.C. Dynamo/Exciter driving 3ph A.C. motor by Mavor & Coulson Ltd., Glasgow.

P.O.R. 1911, Glasgow. 1925, Jersey.

1911 : Completed by McLaren Bros. Ltd., Dumbarton for themselves and Mavor & Coulson Ltd., Glasgow.
c1916 : Requisitioned by Admiralty for duties at Rosyth.
6.1918 : Sold to S.M. Cannon and J. Grove, Aberdeen.
9.1922 : Purchased by Tees Towing Co. Ltd., (Robinson & Crosthwaite, Mgrs.)
4.1925 : Sold to J.A. Thornton, Middlesbrough.
7.1925 : Sold to J. Milburn, St. Helier, Jersey and renamed *Olive*.
Further details not known after 1932.

39. WILLIAM FALLOWS (1923)

O.N. 95921 | 122g, 34n; | 101.0 x 19.0 x 9.6 feet | Iron

L.2Cy. 25" x 48", 45 NHP. Paddle.
Hepple. & Co., North Shields.

P.O.R. 1889, Stockton. 1923, Middlesbrough. 1928, Newcastle.

1888 : Completed by Hepple & Co., North Shields for the Tees Conservancy Commissioners.
16. 3.1923 : Purchased by Tees Towing Co. Ltd, (Robinson & Crosthwaite, Mgrs.)
31.10.1923 : Sold to Ridley Steam Tug Co. Ltd. (R. Ridley, Mgr.) for £1800.
1933 : Sold to Rolmac Ltd.
1935 : Vessel broken-up.

COALOPOLIS. 1923.

40. COALOPOLIS (1923 - 1925)

O.N. 144964 | 175g, 3n; | 94.7 x 23.1 x 9.2 feet | Steel

T.3Cy. 12", 20" & 34" x 24", 78 NHP, 500 IHP. (Engine made 1919).
Hall Russell & Co. Ltd., Aberdeen.

P.O.R. 1923, Middlesbrough. 1926, Halifax, N.S. 1951, Toronto, Ontario.

3.1923 : Completed by A. Hall & Co. Ltd., Aberdeen (YN 578) for Tees Towing Co. Ltd. (Robinson & Crosthwaite, Mgrs.)
25. 8.1925 : Sold to Halifax Tow Boat Co. Ltd. (G.S. Campbell & Co., Mgrs.) for £9,000.
1931 : Managers now R.A. Corbett & Co. Ltd.
1934 : Sold to Coalopolis Co. Ltd. (R.A. Corbett & Co. Ltd., Mgrs.)
1936 : Sold to Maritime Towage & Salvage Co. Ltd., Halifax, N.S., renamed *Bansurf.*
1947 : Sold to Canadian Dredge & Dock Co. Ltd., Toronto.
1948 : Renamed *Shawanaga.*
1971 : Broken-up at Hamilton, Ontario.

41. C.M. PALMER (1923 - 1925)

O.N. 88805 | 95g, 43n; | 85.3 x 21.0 x 7.1 feet | Steel

B.2Cy, 21" x 42", 30 NHP. Paddle.
Wapping Engine Works Co.

P.O.R. 1885, South Shields.

11.1884 : Completed by H.S. Edwards & Sons, Howden for the Mayor, Alderman and Burgesses of Jarrow.
7. 8.1900 : Sold to Tyne General Ferry Co.
1923 : Sold to C.W. Robinson, Middlesbrough.
1923 : Purchased by Tees Towing Co. Ltd., (Robinson & Crosthwaite, Mgrs.) for £350.
18. 8.1925 : Sold for breaking-up for £105.

BEATTIE DUNCAN as PRESTO.

(World Ship Photo Library)

42. BEATTIE DUNCAN (1923 - 1928)

O.N. 102033 155g, 59n; 107.0 x 19.6 x 10.0 feet Iron

L.2Cy. 28½" x 50", 60 NHP, 200 IHP. Paddle. NB 1910.
Baird & Barnsley, North Shields.

P.O.R. 1893, North Shields. 1894, Hull. 1924, Middlesbrough. 1928, Aberdeen.

1893 : Completed by J.T. Eltringham & Co., South Shields (YN 170) for Baird & Barnsley, North Shields as *Triumph.*
1894 : Sold to T. Wilson, Sons & Co. Ltd., Hull, renamed *Presto.*
1916 : Sold to Ellerman's Wilson Line Ltd.
14.11.1923 : Purchased by Charles Duncan & Sons Ltd. for £800, renamed *Beattie Duncan.*
30. 6.1928 : Sold to Aberdeen Steam Tug Co. Ltd. (W.J.H. Dickson, Mgr.)
c1934 : Broken-up.

VIGILANT en route to Canada as deck cargo on the "Aycliffe Hall" in 1938.

(Smith's Dock Co. Ltd.)

43. VIGILANT (1924 - 1928)

O.N. 123656 44g, 10n; 65.5 x 15.1 x 7.7 feet Steel

C.2Cy. 14" & 28" x 14", 35 NHP, 175 IHP. Screw.
Plenty & Son, Newbury.

P.O.R. 1908, London.

1906 : Completed by Jonker & Stans, Hendrik-Ido-Ambacht, Holland.
c1908 : Sold to Topham, Jones & Railton Ltd., London.
25. 3.1924 : Purchased by Charles Duncan & Sons Ltd., for £900.
1. 3.1928 : Sold to Canada.

HUTTON CROSS (1) off Clarence Wharf, c. 1928.
(W. Haig Parry)

44. HURWORTH/HUTTON CROSS (1) (1925 - 1934)

O.N. 108177 | 199g, 79n; | 131.0 x 21.7 x 10.0 feet | Iron

L.2Cy. 31¼" x 58", 150 NHP, 750 IHP.
Hepple & Co., South Shields.

P.O.R. 1897, London. 1919, Jersey. 1922, Kirkcaldy. 1925, Middlesbrough.

1897 : Completed by J.T. Eltringham & Co., South Shields (YN 188) for T.G. Sandford, Gravesend as *Conqueror.*
c1903 : Sold to Dick & Page, London.
c1919 : Sold to Jersey Steam Shipping Co. Ltd., (J.K. Morris)
1922 : Sold to Kirk Deas & Co., Leith.
1924 : Sold to Stanley Butler Steamship Co. Ltd., Kirkcaldy.
1925 : Sold to John Fenton, Edinburgh, (A. Walker, Kirkcaldy, Mgr.)
28. 4.1925 : Purchased by Tees Towing Co. Ltd., (Robinson & Crosthwaite, Mgrs.) for £1850, renamed *Hurworth.*
30. 8.1927 : Renamed *Hutton Cross* (1).
8.1934 : Sold to Clayton & Davie Ltd., Dunston for breaking-up.

BILSDALE, c. 1927.

45. BILSDALE (1925 - 1935)

O.N. 111060 | 199g, 69n; | 135.0 x 21.4 x 9.7 feet | Steel

D.2Cy. 30" x 48", 65 NHP, 450 IHP. Paddle. (Engines made 1887).
W. Allsup & Sons, Preston.

P.O.R. 1900, Yarmouth. 1925, Middlesbrough.

1900 : Completed by Allsup & Co. Ltd., Preston for Great Yarmouth. Steam Tug Co. Ltd. (G.W. Owen, Mgr.) as *Lord Roberts.*
c1917 : Sold to F.R. Aldred.
c1919 : Sold to Furness shipbuilding Co., (J. McGowan, Mgr.), Haverton Hill.
11. 5.1925 : Purchased by W.H. Crosthwaite for £825, renamed *Bilsdale.*
17. 6.1925 : Transfered to Crosthwaite Steamship Co. Ltd., (W.H. Crosthwaite, Mgr.)
7. 5.1935 : Sold to Clayton & Davie, Dunston for breaking-up.

INGLEBY CROSS (1).
(P.N. Thomas)

46. INGLEBY CROSS (1) (1927 - 1933)

O.N. 135172 168g, 69n; 105.1 x 21.1 x 9.5 feet Steel

D.2Cy. 28" x 48", 68 NHP, 400 IHP. Paddle.
Baird Bros, North Shields.

P.O.R. 1912, London. 1927, Middlesbrough. 1933, Grangemouth.

12.1912 : Completed by J.T. Eltringham & Co., South Shields (YN 291) for the Great Western Railway Co. as *Pen Cw.*
1 7.1927 : Purchased by Tees Towing Co. Ltd., (Robinson & Crosthwaite, Mgrs.) for £1750, renamed *Ingleby Cross* (1).
29.11.1933 : Sold to Grangemouth & Forth Towing Co. Ltd., renamed *Elie.*
12.1962 : Delivered to J.A. White & Co., St. Davids-on-Forth for breaking-up.

KINGS CROSS (1) in the River Tees, 1934.
(W. Haig Parry)

47. KINGS CROSS (1) (1928 - 1948)

O.N. 144826 282g, 60n; 115.6 x 25.1 x 12.7 feet Steel

T.3Cy. 15", 24" & $40^{1}/_{8}$" x 24", 87 NHP, 600 IHP. Screw. (Engine made 1916.)
N.V. Machinefabriek Bolnes, Bolnes.

P.O.R. 1918, . 1920, Le Havre. 1925, Aberdeen. 1928, Middlesbrough. 1948, Amsterdam.

1918 : Completed by Gebroeders Jonker, Kinderdijk, Holland (YN 405) for Bureau Wijsmuller, Ijmuiden as *Gelderland.*
1920 : Sold to Soc. Maritime Nationale, Le Havre, renamed *Audax II.*
1925 : Sold to Aberdeen Steam Tug Co. Ltd.
28. 6.1928 : Purchased by Tees Towing Co. Ltd., (Robinson & Crosthwaite, Mgrs.) for £8,000, renamed *Kings Cross* (1).
3. 9.1948 : Sold to N.V. Nederland Indische Steenkolen Handel Maatschappij, renamed *Adrian.*
1955 : Owners restyled N.V. Nederland Indonesië Steenkolen Handel Maatschappij.
1956 : Not in Lloyds Register. Fate unkown.

48. GLENTHORPE (1930)

O.N. 99858 149g, 16n; 108.0 x 18.6 x 9.7 feet Iron

L.1Cy. 36" x 54", 80 NHP, 325 IHP. Paddle. NB 1912.
J.P. Rennoldson, South Shields.

P.O.R. 1892, Glasgow. 1920, Middlesbrough.

1892 : Completed by J.P. Rennoldson & Sons, South Shields for Clyde Shipping Co. Ltd. (J. Cuthbert, Mgr.) as *Flying Mist.*
13. 9.1920 : Sold to G. Alder, Middlesbrough, renamed *Glenthorpe.*
18. 1.1930 : Purchased by A.M. Crosthwaite and transfered to Middlesbrough Towage Co. Ltd., (J.W. Nellist, Mgr.)
26. 5.1930 : Sold for breaking-up.

49. GRAYTHORPE (1930 - 1934)

O.N. 134960 119g, 2n; 90.6 x 18.3 x 11.8 feet Iron

1881. C.2Cy. 20" & 35" x 22", 54 NHP, 350 IHP. Screw. NB1905
L. Tilkin & Co., Liége.

1923. C.2Cy. 18" & 36" x 22", 74NHP, 450 IHP.
Richardson, Westgarth & Co. Ltd., Middlesbrough.

P.O.R. 1881, , 1914, South Shields. 1919, Middlesbrough.

1881 : Completed by L. Tilkin & Co., Liege for Soc. Anon. de Remorquage Helice, Antwerp as *Samson.*
1914 : Sold to L. Brown, South Shields, renamed *Symbol.*
1915 : Sold to Sunderland Towage Co., (J.E. Dawson, Mgr.)
3.12.1919 : Sold to G. Alder, Middlesbrough.
4. 6.1923 : Renamed *Graythorpe.*
18. 1.1930 : Purchased by A.M. Crosthwaite and transfered to Middlesbrough Towage Co. Ltd., (J.W. Nellist, Mgr.)
24. 8.1934 : Sold for breaking-up.

50. TROON (1930 - 1934)

O.N. 115733 130g, 19n; 100.0 x 19.1 x 9.6 feet Iron

L.2Cy. 28" x 50", 70 NHP, 450 IHP. Paddle.
J.P. Rennoldson & Sons, South Shields.

P.O.R. 1902, Glasgow.

1902 : Completed by J.P. Rennoldson & Sons, South Shields (YN 220) for the Glasgow and South Western Railway Co. Ltd.
1923 : Transfered to the London, Midland & Scottish Railway Co. Ltd.
1930 : Purchased by Middlesbrough Towage Co. Ltd., (J.W. Nellist, Mgr.)
9.10.1934 : Sold to J.H. Lamey Ltd., Liverpool, (W.H. Lamey, Mgr.)
1948 : Broken-up at Tranmere.

51. STEELOPOLIS (1930 - 1934)

O.N. 105393 155g, 11n; 96.8 x 20.6 x 10.9 feet Steel

T.3Cy. 14", 23" & 35" x 24", 90 NHP, 520 IHP. Screw. NB 1916.
Bow, McLachlan & Co., Paisley.

P.O.R. 1896, Liverpool. 1930, Middlesbrough.

5.1896 : Completed by A.W. Robertson & Co., Canning Town, London for Johnston Line Ltd. (Furness Withy & Co. Ltd., Mgrs.) as *Amore.*
12. 5.1930 : Purchased by Charles Duncan & Sons Ltd for £1,250, renamed *Steelopolis.*
26.10.1934 : Sold to S.C. Roberts, Avonmouth, (Commonwealth Steam Tug Co.) for £2,050.
3. 4.1939 : Sold to Fairplay Towage & Shipping Co. Ltd. (Lucy Borchardt, Mgr.).
21. 6.1949 : Broken-up.

QUEENS CROSS
in the River Tees,
1934.
(W. Haig Parry)

52. QUEENS CROSS (1933 - 1948)

O.N. 160740 | 286g, 45n; | 116.2 x 25.1 x 11.8 feet | Steel

T.3Cy. 13$\frac{3}{4}$", 22$\frac{1}{4}$" & 36" x 25", 65 NHP, 550 IHP. Screw.
Machinefabriek Avontuur, Dordrecht.

P.O.R. 1921, Rotterdam. , Ijmuiden. 1933, Middlesbrough. 1948, Amsterdam.

1921 : Completed by N.V. Schps. Nimmerzust, Lekkerkerk (YN 83) for N.V. Bureau Wijsmuller Maatschappij as *Vlaanderen.*
20. 7.1933 : Purchased by Tees Towing Co. Ltd. (Robinson & Crosthwaite, Mgrs.) for £2,500, renamed *Queens Cross.*
9. 9.1948 : Sold to N.V. Nederland Indische Steenkolen Handel Maatschappij renamed *Goos.*
1955 : Owners restyled N.V. Nederland Indonesië Steenkolen Handel Maatschappij.
: Fate unknown.

ACKLAM CROSS
with Captain Charlie Rounce at the wheel,
1934.
(W. Haig Parry)

53. ACKLAM CROSS (1933 - 1964)

O.N. 160739 | 150g, 6n; | 90.5 x 22.1 x 10.6 feet | Steel

1933.Two – 4SA Oil, 6Cy., 7$\frac{1}{2}$" x 12", 300 BHP each, 600 BHP total, with GEC electric motor. Screw. Peter Brotherhood Ltd., Peterborough.

1965.Two – 4SA Oil, 6Cy, 8$\frac{3}{4}$" x 11$\frac{1}{2}$", Lister Blackstone, Stamford.

P.O.R. 1933, Middlesbrough. 1964, (Malta).

8.1933 : Completed by Hall Russell & Co. Ltd., Aberdeen (YN 728) for Tees Towing Co. Ltd. (Robinson & Crosthwaite, Mgrs.)
1949 : Managers Wm. Crosthwaite & Son.
22. 2.1964 : Sold to Mediterranean Salvage & Towage Co. Ltd., Malta G.C. renamed *Fox Terrier.*
18. 2.1969 : Broke adrift and vanished in 32.20 N, 18.31 E whilst being towed by 'Maltese Terrier' from Valetta to Zueitina, Libya.

CHARING CROSS in the River Tees, 1934.
(W. Haig Parry)

54. **CHARING CROSS** (1934 - 1957)

O.N. 128826 | 153g, 67n; | 100.2 x 22.1 x 10.9 feet | Steel

C.2Cy., 20" & 42" x 27", 90 NHP, 700 IHP. Screw.
J.P. Rennoldson & Sons, South Shields.

P.O.R. 1913, Middlesbrough. 1957, Newcastle.

3.1913 : Completed by J.P. Rennoldson & Sons, South Shields (YN 282) for Tees Conservancy Commissioners as *Joseph Constantine.*
24. 5.1934 : Purchased by Tees Towing Co. Ltd. (Robinson & Crosthwaite, Mgrs.) for £1.500, renamed *Charing Cross.*
1949 : Managers Wm. Crosthwaite & Son.
22. 8.1957 : Sold to Lawson-Batey Tugs Ltd., (J.F. Batey, Mgr.), renamed *Westsider.*
1.1960 : Delivered to J.J. King & Co. Ltd., Gateshead for breaking-up.

EUSTON CROSS after structural alterations 1951.
(W. Haig Parry)

55. **EUSTON CROSS** (1938 - 1960)

O.N. 115060 | 226g, 3n; | 100.0 x 24.1 x 12.6 feet | Steel

T.3Cy. 13½", 22" & 35" x 27", 92 NHP, 600 IHP. Screw. NB 1938.
J.I. Thorneycroft & Co. Ltd., Southampton.

P.O.R. 1924, Port Elizabeth. 1937, Cape Town. 1937, London. 1938, Middlesbrough. 1960, Piraeus.

11.1924 : Completed by J.I. Thorneycroft & Co. Ltd, Southampton, (YN 1039), for Union Government of South Africa (Railways & Harbours Administration, Port Elizabeth) as *Sir William Macintosh.*
1938 : Sold to James Dredging, Towage & Transport Co. Ltd., London (R.E.V. James, Mgr.), renamed *Protea.*
30. 3.1938 : Purchased by Tees Towing Co. Ltd. (Robinson & Crosthwaite, Mgrs.) for £10,000, renamed *Euston Cross.*
1949 : Managers Wm. Crosthwaite & Son.
15. 7.1960 : Sold to Loucas Matsas & Sons, Piraeus, renamed *Thiseus.*
1972 : Renamed *Ioannis Matsas.*
1978 : Renamed *Thiseus.*
1981 : Broken-up.

LADY HOWARD STEPNEY as LADY EVELINE, when a Port Talbot pilot cutter.

(P.N. Thomas)

56. LADY HOWARD STEPNEY (1942 - 1948)

O.N. 107005 93g, 3n; 90.4 x 18.0 x 8.2 feet Steel

Two-C.2Cy. 11" & 22" x 15", 47 NHP, 300 IHP. Twin Screw.
Cox & Co. Falmouth.

P.O.R. 1935, Llanelly. 1942, Middlesbrough.

1906 : Completed by Cox & Co., Falmouth for Dundalk Pilotage Service as *The Liberator.*
1920 : Sold to Alexandra Towing Co. Ltd., renamed *Salthouse.*
1928 : Sold to Port Talbot Pilots, renamed *Lady Eveline.*
1932 : Sold to Llanelly Pilots (Wm. Hughes, MBE, Cosmo Wm Darling and Evan Oswin Roberts of Llanelly; Wm. Hy. Mathias and Stanley Reginald Talbot Wilcox of Burry Port), renamed *Lady Howard Stepney.*
9. 7.1942 : Purchased by Tees Towing Co. Ltd., (Robinson & Crosthwaite, Mgrs.) for £1,300.
14. 4.1948 : Sold to Stockton Shipping & Salvage Co. Ltd., Thornaby for breaking-up.
1. 5.1950 : Registry closed. Vessel converted into a club house without means of propulsion and to be permanently moored in the River Tees. Ultimate fate unknown.

FLYING FISH outward bound from Whitby on an excursion trip.

(Langbaurgh Borough)

57. FLYING FISH (1947 - 1951)

O.N. 85014 169g 71n; 116.0 x 19.6 x 10.3 feet Iron

1882. L.1Cy. 38" x 56", 75 NHP. Paddle.
J.P. Rennoldson & Sons, South Shields.

1907. L.2Cy. 30" x 54", 76 NHP, 400 IHP. NB 1907.
Hepple & Co. Ltd., South Shields.

P.O.R. 1882, Sunderland. 1906, Bo'ness. 1919, Leith. 1947, Middlesbrough.

1882 : Completed by J.T. Eltringham & Co., South Shields (YN 100) for J. Siddell, Sunderland.
1887 : Sold to F. Downs, Sunderland.
1894 : Sold to S. Chisholm, Sunderland.
1900 : Sold to T.L. Devlin, Granton.
10.10.1906 : Sold to J.S. Wilson, Bo'ness.
30. 9.1919 : Sold to Leith Salvage & Towage Co. Ltd., (C. Black, Mgr.)
1920 : Managers J. Little & Co. Ltd.
1947 : Purchased by Charles Duncan & Sons Ltd.
22. 1.1951 : Registry closed. Vessel broken-up at J.J. King & Co. Ltd., Gateshead.

DUNDAS CROSS after structural alterations 1952.
(W. Haig Parry)

58. DUNDAS CROSS (1947 - 1958)

O.N. 169308 242g Nil n; 106.7 x 26.7 x 11.6 feet

T.3Cy. 16", 26" & 43" x 30", 1000 IHP.
C.D. Holmes & Co. Ltd., Hull.

P.O.R. 1943, Hull. 1947, Middlesbrough. 1958, Newport, Mon.

8.1943 : Completed by J.S. Watson (Gainsborough) Ltd., Gainsborough (YN 1534), for the Ministry of War Transport (Redhead & Drys Tugs Ltd, Mgrs.) as *Empire Mustang.*
1944 : Managers France Fenwick Tyne & Wear Co. Ltd.
1946 : Owners Ministry of Transport.
1947 : Purchased by Tees Towing Co. Ltd. (Robinson & Crosthwaite, Mgrs.) for £16,250, renamed *Dundas Cross.*
1949 : Managers Wm. Crosthwaite & Son.
20. 1.1958 : Sold to Newport Screw Towing Co. Ltd., renamed *Duneagle.*
1965 : Sold to Tsavliris (Salvage & Towage) Ltd., renamed *Nisos Syros.*
c1975 : Owners Maritime Commercial Enterprises Ltd., Piraeus.
c1976 : Broken-up.

MARPLE.
(From "Humber Shipping" - A Dalesman Publication.)

59. MARPLE (1947)

O.N. 94094 123g, 53n; 91.0 x 20.1 x 8.5 feet

Two - C.2Cy. 15" & 28" x 18", 70 NHP. Twin Screw. NB 1921.
Earle's Co. Ltd., Hull.

P.O.R. 1888, Grimsby.

10.1888 : Completed by Earle's Co. Ltd., Hull (YN 313) for The Manchester, Sheffield & Lincolnshire Railway.
1. 8.1897 : Transfered to The Great Central Railway.
1. 1.1923 : Transfered to London & North Eastern Railway Co. Ltd.
21. 3.1947 : Purchased by Tees Towing Co. Ltd. (Robinson & Crosthwaite, Mgrs.) for £500.
1. 5.1947 : Sold to Clayton & Davie Ltd., Dunston for breaking-up for £160.

SILVER CROSS
passing Clarence Wharf. Captain T. Hood at the wheel, c. 1948.
(W. Haig Parry)

60. SILVER CROSS (1947 - 1958)

O.N. 127861 136g, 1n; 92.1 x 21.1 x 10.6 feet

C.2Cy. 17" & 43" x 27", 78 NHP, 750 IHP.
Baird Bros., North Shields.

P.O.R. 1910, Grimsby. 1947, Middlesbrough. 1958, Grimsby.

6.1910 : Completed by J.T. Eltringham & Co., South Shields (YN 275) for Great Central Railway as *Central No. 1.*
1. 1.1923 : Transfered to London & North Eastern Railway Co. Ltd.
21. 3.1947 : Purchased by Tees Towing Co. Ltd. (Robinson & Crosthwaite, Mgrs.) for £2,750, renamed *Silver Cross.*
1949 : Managers Wm. Crosthwaite & Son.
24. 3.1958 : Sold to J.H. Pigott & Son. Ltd., Grimsby, renamed *Lady Joan.*
6. 6.1964 : Arrived Inverkeithing in tow of tug 'Workman' for breaking-up by Thos. W. Ward Ltd.

TEMPLE CROSS
off Clarence Wharf in charge of Captain J. Purvis, c. 1948.
(W. Haig Parry)

61. TEMPLE CROSS (1947 - 1962)

O.N. 132122 137 g, Nil n; 92.2 x 21.1 x 10.6 feet

C.2Cy. 17" & 43" x 27", 66 NHP, 750 IHP.
Baird Bros., North Shields.

P.O.R. 1912, Grimsby. 1947, Middlesbrough.

3.1912 : Completed by J.T. Eltringham & Co., South Shields, (YN 287) for Great Central Railway as *Central No. 2*
1. 1.1923 : Transferred to London & North Eastern Railway Co. Ltd.
21. 3.1947 : Purchased by Tees Towing Co. Ltd., (Robinson & Crosthwaite, Mgrs.) for £2,750, renamed *Temple Cross.*
1949 : Managers Wm. Crosthwaite & Son.
25. 4.1962 : Sold for breaking-up at Hendrik-Ido-Ambacht, Rotterdam.

KINGS CROSS (2) in 1948. (W. Haig Parry)

62. **KINGS CROSS (2)** (1948-1957)

O.N. 146556 197 g, 14 n; 104.2 x 21.0 x 10.1 feet

T.3Cy. 12.6", 20.5" & 32.3" x 22.8", 99 NHP, 575 IHP.
Danziger Werft, Danzig.

P.O.R. 1922, London. 1948, Middlesbrough.

1921 : Completed by Danziger Werft, Danzig (YN 28) for G. Edgeley, Gravesend as *New Storm Cock.*
1928 : Sold to Gamecock Steam Towing Co. Ltd., (R.T. Lester, Mgr.)
1947 : Sold to Ocean Salvage & Towage Co. Ltd., London. (L.H.G. Walford, Mgr.)
10.11.1948 : Purchased by Tees Towing Co. Ltd. (Robinson & Crosthwaite, Mgrs.) for £12,850, renamed *Kings Cross* (2)
1949 : Managers Wm. Crosthwaite & Son.
1. 3.1957 : Sold to C.W. Dorkin & Co., Gateshead for breaking-up.

BANBURY CROSS (1) in 1950. (W. Haig Parry)

63. **BANBURY CROSS (1)** (1950 - 1955)

O.N. 169458 258 g Nil n; 105.9 x 30.1 x 12.4 feet

1945. T.3Cy. 16½", 27" & 46" x 30", 1000 BHP.
Plenty & Son Ltd., Newbury.

1975.Oil. 2SA. Vee16Cy. 146 x 146 mm.
General Motors Corpn., Detroit.

P.O.R. 1945, Glasgow. 1950, Middlesbrough. 1955, Fremantle. c.1975, Panama.

12.1945 : Completed by Scott & Sons, Bowling, (YN 375) for the Ministry of War Transport as *Empire Nan.*
1946 : Sold to Metal Industries Ltd., (T.M. McKenzie, Mgr), renamed *Metinda II.*
5. 6.1950 : Purchased by Tees Towing Co. Ltd. (Wm. Crosthwaite & Son., Mgrs.) for £47,000 renamed *Banbury Cross* (1).
12. 4.1955 : Sold to The Adelaide Steamship Co. Ltd. and Swan River Shipping Co. Ltd., Fremantle, renamed *Wilga*
8. 2.1973 : Sold to Consolidated Marine Developments (Australia) Pty. Ltd. for $A 11,500.
1973 : Sold to Prioper Shipping Pty Ltd., Frmantle for $A 19,500.
1975 : Sold to Straits Engineers (Singapore) Pte. Ltd., Singapore.
c1976 : Sold to World Dredging Ltd., Singapore.
1983 : Still in service.

CAEDMON CROSS on trials, 1953.

64. CAEDMON CROSS (1953 - 1966)

O.N. 169161 132 g. Nil n; 80.2 x 23.5 x 8.1 feet

1953. Oil. 2SA. 4Cy., 14½" x 19", 750 BHP.
Crossley Bros. Ltd., Manchester.

1970. Oil. 2SA. 8Cy. 220 x 380 mm
Appingedammer Brons, Appingedammer.

P.O.R. 1953, Middlesbrough. 1966, Swansea. 1970, Terneuzen.

11.1953 : Completed by Scott & Sons, Bowling, (YN 400) for Tees Towing Co. Ltd., (Wm. Crosthwaite & Son, Mgrs.)
27. 4.1966 : Sold to Alexandra Towing Co. Ltd., renamed *Margam.*
1970 : Sold to Sleepdienst Willem Muller N.V., Terneuzen, renamed *Rilland.*
1983 : Still in service.

GOLDEN CROSS on trials, 1955.
(A.T. Kelly & Co. Ltd.)

65. GOLDEN CROSS (1955 - 1968)

O.N. 169164 132 g, Nil n; 86'3" x 23'11" x 10'4"

Oil. 2SA, 4Cy., 14½" x 19", 750 BHP.
Crossley Bros. Ltd., Manchester.

P.O.R. 1955, Middlesbrough. 1968, Newport.

7.1955 : Completed by Scott & Sons, Bowling, (YN 407) for Tees Towing Co. Ltd. (Wm. Crosthwaite & Son., Mgrs.)
7. 8.1968 : Sold to Newport Screw Towing Co. Ltd., Newport, renamed *Dunheron.*
1971 : Sold to Cory Ship Towage Ltd.
1973 : Sold to A.C. Cranes Ltd., Dublin.
1978 : Sold to Carmet Tugs Co. Ltd., Birkenhead.
1983 : Still in service.

INGLEBY CROSS (2) on trials, 1955. (A.T. Kelly & Co. Ltd.)

66. INGLEBY CROSS (2) (1955 - 1968)

O.N. 187302 132 g, Nil n; 86'2" x 23'11" x 10'4"

Oil. 2SA, 4Cy., 14½" x 19", 750 BHP.
Crossley Bros. Ltd., Manchester.

P.O.R. 1955, Middlesbrough. 1968, Fowey.

10.1955 : Completed by Scott & Sons, Bowling, (YN 408), for Tees Towing Co. Ltd., (Wm. Crosthwaite & Son., Mgrs.)
6. 6.1968 : Sold to Fowey Harbour Commissioners, renamed *Gribbin Head*.
1983 : Still in service.

FIERY CROSS as built with original shape of funnel, passing Smith's Dock outward bound, 1958.

67. FIERY CROSS (1957 - 1981)

O.N. 187309 192 g, Nil n; 104'6" x 26'11" x 11'9"

Oil, 2SA, 6Cy., 14½" x 19", 1125 BHP. Kort rudder
Crossley Bros. Ltd., Manchester.

P.O.R. 1957, Middlesbrough. 1981, Terneuzen.

19. 5.1957 : Completed by Scott & Sons, Bowling, (YN 414) for Tees Towing Co. Ltd. (Wm. Crosthwaite & Son., Mgrs.)
20. 6.1981 : Sold to Sleepdienst Willem Muller, Terneuzen, renamed *Waterland*.
1983 : Still in service.

HUTTON CROSS (2) running stern first on arrival at Tees Wharf from Bowling, 1958.

68. HUTTON CROSS (2) (1958 - 1970)

O.N. 187313 105 g, Nil n; 82'8" x 23'11" x 12'1"

Oil. 2SA, 4Cy., 14½" x 19", 750 BHP. Single Voith-Schneider propeller.
Crossley Bros. Ltd., Manchester.

P.O.R. 1958, Middlesbrough. 1970, Terneuzen. 1973, Ghent.

24. 3.1958 : Completed by Scott & Sons., Bowling, (YN 417) for Tees Towing Co. Ltd. (Wm. Crosthwaite & Son., Mgrs.)
11. 8.1970 : Sold to Sleepdienst Willem Muller N.V., Terneuzen, renamed *Kamperland.*
1973 : Transferred to Sleepdienst Willem Muller (Belgie) S.A., Ghent.
1983 : Broken-up by Van Heyghen, Ghent.

BANBURY CROSS (2) on trials, 1958.

(N. Horne Ltd.)

69. BANBURY CROSS (2) (1958 - 1971)

O.N. 187314 106 g, Nil n; 82'4" x 23'11" x 10'9"

1958. Oil. 2SA. 4Cy., 14½" x 19", 750 BHP.
Crossley Bros. Ltd., Manchester.

1981. Oil, Type ESL6M. Single Voith-Schneider Propeller.
Mirlees Blackstone Ltd., Stamford.

P.O.R. 1958, Middlesbrough. 1971, Ravenna.

19. 5.1958 : Completed by Philip & Son. Ltd., Dartmouth (YN 1294) for Tees Towing Co. Ltd., (Wm. Crosthwaite & Sons., Mgrs.)
16. 9.1971 : Sold to Società Esercizio Rimorchi e Salvataggi S.p.A., Ravenna, (O. Turchi, Mgr.), renamed *Gatto.*
1982 : Still in service but subsequent history not known.

ERIMUS CROSS on trials, 1960. (W. Ralston Ltd.)

70. ERIMUS CROSS (1960 - 1976)

O.N. 187316 192 g, Nil n; 104'6" x 26'11" x 11'9"

Oil. 2SA, 6Cy., 14½" x 19", 1125 BHP. Kort rudder.
Crossley Bros. Ltd., Manchester.

P.O.R. 1960, Middlesbrough. 1976, Glasgow.

5. 2.1960 : Completed by Scott & Sons (Bowling) Ltd., Bowling (YN 423), for Tees Towing Co. Ltd., (Wm. Crosthwaite & Son, Mgrs.)
3. 5.1976 : Sold to Howard Doris Ltd., (R.F. Withey, Mgr.) renamed *Mairi of Kishorn.*

DANBY CROSS.

71. DANBY CROSS (1961 - 1975)

O.N. 187319 114 g, Nil n; 87'10" x 23'11" x 9'10"

Oil. 2SA, 4Cy., 14½" x 19", 750 BHP. Kort rudder.
Crossley Bros. Ltd., Manchester.

P.O.R. 1961, Middlesbrough. 1975, Terneuzen.

4. 8.1961 : Completed by J. Pollock, Sons & Co. Ltd., Faversham (YN 2123) for Tees Towing Co. Ltd., (Wm. Crosthwaite & Son Mgrs.)
6.1975 : Sold to Sleepdienst Willem Muller B.V., Terneuzen. renamed *Finland.*
1983 : Still in service.

MARTON CROSS.

72. MARTON CROSS (1963 - 1981)

O.N. 187325 133 g, Nil n; 93'10" x 24'11" x 9'11"

Oil. 2SA, 6Cy., 14½" x 19", 1125 BHP. Kort rudder.
Crossley Bros. Ltd., Manchester.

P.O.R. 1963, Middlesbrough. 1981, Terneuzen.

25. 4.1963 : Completed by R. Dunston (Hessle) Ltd., Hessle (YN S.794) for Tees Towing Co. Ltd., (Wm. Crosthwaite & Son, Mgrs.).
20. 6.1981 : Sold to Zeesleepdienst Willem Muller, Terneuzen, renamed *Waasland.*
1983 : Still in service.

AYTON CROSS
on trials 1967.
(Walter Fussey & Son)

73. AYTON CROSS (1967 -)

O.N. 187330 214 g, Nil n; 106'6" x 27'0" x 12'2"

Oil. 2SA, 9Cy., 10½" x 13½", 1800 BHP. Kort rudder.
Crossley Premier Engines Ltd., Manchester.

P.O.R. 1967, Middlesbrough.

9. 6.1967 : Completed by R. Dunston (Hessle) Ltd., Hessle, (YN S.844) for Tees Towing Co. Ltd., (Wm. Crosthwaite & Son, Mgrs.)
31.12.1983 : In the present fleet.

ORMESBY CROSS, 1983. (Richard Crosthwaite)

74. ORMESBY CROSS (1967 -)

O.N.187331 214 g, Nil n; 106'6" x 27'0" x 12'2"

Oil. 2SA, 9Cy., 10½" x 13½", 1800 BHP. Kort rudder.
Crossley Premier Engines Ltd., Manchester.

P.O.R. 1967, Middlesbrough.

27.10.1967 : Completed by R. Dunston (Hessle) Ltd., Hessle (YN S.845) for Tees Towing Co. Ltd., (Wm. Crosthwaite & Son, Mgrs.)
31.12.1983 : In the present fleet.

LEVEN CROSS, 1971.

75. LEVEN CROSS (1971 -)

O.N. 341853 141 g, Nil n; 94'0" x 25'5" x 13'0"

Oil. 2SA, 6Cy., 14½" x 19", 1235 BHP. Kort rudder.
Crossley Premier Engines Ltd., Manchester.

P.O.R. 1971, Middlesbrough.

24. 5.1971 : Completed by Fairmile Construction Co. Ltd., Berwick-upon-Tweed (YN 662) for Tees Towing Co. Ltd.
31.12.1983 : In the present fleet.

RALPH CROSS entering Tees Dock.
(J.K. Byass)

76. RALPH CROSS (1974 -)

O.N. 341861 244 g, Nil n; 105'11" x 27'7" x 12'4"

Oil. 4SA, Vee12Cy., 10" x 12", 2,640 BHP. Kort rudder.
Ruston Paxman Diesels Ltd., Newton-le-Willows.

P.O.R. 1974, Middlesbrough.

22. 2.1974 : Completed by Richards (Shipbuilders) Ltd., Yarmouth. (YN 515) for Tees Towing Co. Ltd.
31.12.1983 : In the present fleet.

GREATHAM CROSS on trials, 1976.
(W. Ralston Ltd.)

77. GREATHAM CROSS (1976 -)

O.N. 341868 193g, Nil n; 28.3 x 8.95 x 5.0 metres

Two - Oil. 4SA, each 6Cy., 10" x 12", 2,200 BHP total. Twin rudder propellers.
Ruston Paxman Diesels Ltd., Newton-le-Willows.

P.O.R. 1976, Middlesbrough.

16. 3.1976 : Completed by Scott & Sons (Bowling) Ltd., Bowling, (YN 452), for Tees Towing Co. Ltd.
31.12.1983 : In the present fleet.

SKELTON CROSS
leaving Middlesbrough Dock Cut
1976.
(Richard Crosthwaite)

78. SKELTON CROSS (1976 -)

O.N. 341869 | 193 g, Nil n; | 28.3 x 8.95 x 5.0 metres

Two - Oil. 4SA, each 6Cy., 10" x 12", 2,200 BHP total. Twin rudder propellers.
Ruston Paxman Diesels Ltd., Newton-le-Willows.

P.O.R. 1976, Middlesbrough.

22. 6.1976 : Completed by Scott & Sons (Bowling) Ltd., Bowling (YN 453) for Tees Towing Co. Ltd.
31.12.1983 : In the present fleet.

YARM CROSS
entering the water at Hessle,
1979.
(Walter Fussey & Son)

79. YARM CROSS (1979 -)

O.N. 341878 | 185 g, Nil n; | 28.3 x 9.0 x 5.0 metres.

Two - Oil. 4SA, each 6Cy., 10" x 12", 2,640 BHP total. Twin rudder propellers.
Ruston Paxman Diesels Ltd., Newton-le-Willows.

P.O.R. 1979, Middlesbrough.

8.1979 : Completed by R. Dunston (Hessle) Ltd., Hessle (YN 920), for Tees Towing Co. Ltd.
31.12.1983 : In the present fleet.

COATHAM CROSS
on trials, 1981.
(Walter Fussey & Son)

80. COATHAM CROSS (1981 -   )

O.N. 341886 | 186 g, Nil n; | 28.3 x 9.0 x 5.0 metres.

Two - Oil. 4SA, each 6Cy., 10" x 12", 2,640 BHP total. Twin rudder propellers.
Ruston Paxman Diesels Ltd., Newton-le-Willows.

P.O.R. 1981, Middlesbrough.

11.1981 : Completed by R. Dunston (Hessle) Ltd., Hessle, (YN H.931), for Tees Towing Co. Ltd.
31.12.1983 : In the present fleet.

NORTON CROSS
having her superstructure lowered into place whilst building at Hessle.
(Walter Fussey & Son)

81. NORTON CROSS

O.N. 341888 | 189 g, Nil n; | 28.3 x 9.0 x 5.0 metres

Two - Oil 4SA, each 6Cy., 10" x 12", 3,400 BHP total. Twin rudder propellers.
Ruston Paxman Diesels Ltd., Newton-le-Willows.

31.12.1983 : Building at R. Dunston (Hessle) Ltd., Hessle, (YN 941), for Tees Towing Co. Ltd. for delivery in 1984.

Apppendices

A. Source of Vessel Names.

B. Shipbuilders.

C. Engine Builders.

D. Funnel, flag and hull colours.

E. Legend of Seahorse Insignia.

F. Chart: Evolution of Tees Towing Co. Ltd.

G. Chart: Tug Ownership Chronology.

Appendix A

Source of Vessel Names

Whilst ship names do not necessarily have to follow any particular theme or pattern they nevertheless frequently do so. Tees Towing Co. Ltd. are no exception and currently have a clear and standard theme for the naming of their tugs.

The names are of two words, the first being of a Cleveland village or of an ancient cross, and the second is "Cross" which phonetically relates to the Crosthwaite ownership. However, this has not always been so since the ". . . . Cross" sequence did not appear until 1927 with *Ingleby Cross* (1) and there had been other transient themes such as the Duncan family names (five vessels), ". . . . dale" (four vessels) and ". . . . opolis" (three vessels).

It is not always possible to know why a vessel was given its particular name; some may have been chosen just because they sounded right. The list following gives the origins, where known, of the names used during the ownership of the companies covered by this history.

Ordnance Survey Map References of the villages named are given where applicable.

Future names are expected to continue with the ". . . . Cross" ending and to use village or small town names of the Cleveland area; and so much the better if the location has got a real cross. At any given time the initial letters must all be different and it is not intended that earlier names should be repeated.

1)	*Florence*	
2)	*Primrose*	
3)	*Charles Dickens*	– Named after the author of that name.
4)	*Challenger* (1)	
5)	*Clarissa*	
6)	*Empress of India*	– Probably named to commemorate the Diamond Jubilee of Queen Victoria.
7)	*Glen Rosa*	
8)	*Hero*	
9)	*Vixen* *Archdale*	– Built for Mr. T.W. Fox!
10)	*Champion*	
11)	*Challenger* (2)	
12)	*Liberia*	– One of a series of vessels with names ending "...*IA*" when owned by Wm. Watkins.
13)	*Triumph*	
14)	*Ida Duncan*	– Daughter of Chas. Wm. Duncan.
15)	*Lingdale*	– Cleveland Village. (NZ 674163.)
16)	*Frank*	
17)	*Dora Duncan*	
18)	*Adonis*	– The most beautiful of Greek Gods.

19) *Fifeshire* – Named after local county when working and owned at Kirkcaldy.

20) *Monsdale*

21) *Privateer*

22) *Lily*
Lily Duncan

23) *Betsy Duncan* – Sister of Chas. Wm. Duncan, operatic Prima Donna.

24) *Powerful*

25) *Athlete*

26) *Cleveland* – The geographical name given to the moorland area to the S.E. and S of Middlesbrough.

27) *George Peabody*

28) *George Robinson* – Name of owner prior to purchase by Tees Towing Co. Ltd.

29) *Nunthorpe* – Name of village to the south of Middlesbrough. (NZ 538151).

30) *Pendennis* – Named after Pendennis Castle when owned at Falmouth.

31) *Samphire Batts* – An area of tidal mud flats on the north side of the River Tees where Samphires used to grow.

32) *Borwick Rails* – Name of quay at Millom, Cumberland.
Ironopolis – Name given to Middlesbrough and surrounding areas because of their pre-eminence in iron making.

33) *Lord Warden* – Lord Warden of the Cinque Ports.

34) *Granite City* – Named after the City of Aberdeen.

35) *United*

36) *William Findley* – Possibly named after a relative of the shipbuilders who were named Findley.

37) *Laceby* – Named after a village to the SW of Grimsby.

38) *Electric Arc* – Named thus because of significance of being the first petrol-electric driven vessel.

39) *William Fallows* – Named after one of the founders of Middlesbrough. 6th Mayor of the town in 1859.

40) *Coalopolis* – The first vessel purchased new by Tees Towing Co. Ltd. Presumably refers to Middlesbrough and the Tees as a coal exporting centre.

41) *C.M. Palmer* – Charles (later Sir Charles), Mark Palmer was founder and first Mayor of Jarrow.

42) *Beattie Duncan* – Wife of Charles Chrystal Duncan.

43) *Vigilant*

44)	*Hurworth*	– Named after village near Darlington. (NZ 305102).
	Hutton Cross (1)	– Hutton Lowcross is a hamlet near Guisborough. (NZ 602138).
45)	*Bilsdale*	– A dale in the Cleveland Hills south of Middlesbrough, (SE 568920), which Sir William Crosthwaite always claimed to be the most beautiful dale in England.
46)	*Ingleby Cross* (1)	– Ingleby Greenhow is a village at the foot of the Cleveland Hills. (NZ 581063). First vessel to be given the "...*Cross*" series of names.
47)	*Kings Cross* (1)	– Named after the London terminus of the London and North Eastern Railway which in turn was named after the huge monument of King George IV which stood on the site from 1830 to 1845.
48)	*Glenthorpe*	
49)	*Graythorpe*	– May have been named after the village of Graythorp to the NW of the Tees Estuary.
50)	*Troon*	– Named after port of S.W. Scotland.
51)	*Steelopolis*	– Reflected the importance of the area as a steel-making centre.
52)	*Queens Cross*	– No doubt named to match *Kings Cross* (1) as a pair of sea-going tugs.
53)	*Acklam Cross*	– Acklam is a suburb of Middlesbrough.
54)	*Charing Cross*	– Named after the well known district and railway station of London.
55)	*Euston Cross*	– Possibly named to match with the London stations of Kings Cross and Charing Cross. If so then the local name themes had strayed somewhat.
56)	*Lady Howard Stepney*	– Named after local lady when owned by the Llanelly Pilots.
57)	*Flying Fish*	– Named in line with "*Flying* . . ." names of Clyde Shipping Co. Ltd.
58)	*Dundas Cross*	
59)	*Marple*	– Name of a town on the Manchester, Sheffield and Lincolnshire Railway when the vessel was owned by that company.
60)	*Silver Cross*	
61)	*Temple Cross*	
62)	*Kings Cross* (2)	– See 47) above.
63)	*Banbury Cross* (1)	– Banbury Cross of the nursery rhyme.

64) *Caedmon Cross* – An actual cross in St. Mary's churchyard Whitby. Caedmon was a Brother of St. Hilda's monastery in the 7th Century.

65) *Golden Cross* – Named to commemorate Sir William and Lady Crosthwaite's Golden Wedding.

66) *Ingleby Cross* (2) – See 46) above.

67) *Fiery Cross* – The mustering symbol of the Scottish Highlands.

68) *Hutton Cross* (2) – See 44) above.

69) *Banbury Cross* (2) – See 63) above.

70) *Erimus Cross* – "Erimus" is the Latin motto from the Middlesbrough coat of arms. It means "we shall be".

71) *Danby Cross* – Danby is a Cleveland village. (NZ 708087).

72) *Marton Cross* – Marton was a village just south of Middlesbrough and is now a suburb of that town. (NZ 515158). Village cross was given by Sir William Crosthwaite.

73) *Ayton Cross* – Great Ayton is a village to the south of Middlesbrough. (NZ 562107).

74) *Ormesby Cross* – Ormesby is a district of Middlesbrough (NZ 531169). Village cross was re-located at Sir William Crosthwaite's expense.

75) *Leven Cross* – Leven Bridge is a village to the south-west of Middlesbrough. (NZ 445121). The River Leven is a tributary of the River Tees joining it near Yarm.

76) *Ralph Cross* – An actual ancient cross standing at 1,400 feet on the moors south of Castleton. (NZ 677021).

77) *Greatham Cross* – Greatham is a village on the north side of the River Tees. (NZ 493275).

78) *Skelton Cross* – Skelton is a town in East Cleveland. (NZ 655188).

79) *Yarm Cross* – Yarm is a town on the River Tees upstream from Middlesbrough. (NZ 419128).

80) *Coatham Cross* – Coatham originally a village on the south bank of the River Tees. Now part of Redcar. (NZ 595251).

81) *Norton Cross* – Norton originally a village north of Stockton-on-Tees. Now part of the latter town. (NZ 446216).

Appendix B
Shipbuilders

Alphabetical list of the 44 shipbuilders of the 81 vessels covered by this history.

Shipbuilders	Tug history reference numbers
Allsup & Co. Ltd., Preston.	9. & 45.
Ash & Co., James; Cubitt Town.	30.
Bewley & Webb, Dublin.	22.
Butchard, George; Milton, Gravesend.	13. & 20.
Carmichael MacLean & Co., Greenock.	6.
Clark, Richard; Weston Point.	5.
Cochrane & Sons, Selby.	12.
Cook, William; Middlesbrough.	23.
Cox & Co., Falmouth.	56.
Craggs, R. & Sons; Middlesbrough.	16.
Cumming & Ellis, Inverkeithing.	31.
Danziger Werft, Danzig.	62.
Dunston, R., (Hessle) Ltd., Hessle.	72,73,74,79,80 & 81.
Duthie, J., Sons & Co., Aberdeen.	2.
Earles Co. Ltd., Hull.	59.
Earles Shipbuilding & Eng. Co. Ltd., Hull.	28.
Edwards, H.S., & Sons, Howden.	41.
Edwards & Symes, Millwall.	8.
Eltringham, J.T., South Shields.	10. & 29.
Eltringham, J.T., & Co., South Shields.	4,17,19,24,26, 42,44,46,57,60 & 61.
Fairmile Construction Co. Ltd., Berwick.	75.
Hall, A, & Co. Ltd., Aberdeen.	40.
Hall, Russell & Co. Ltd., Aberdeen.	53.
Hepple & Co., North Shields.	39.
Jonker, Gebroeders, Kinderdijk.	47.
Jonker & Stans, Hendrik-Ido-Ambacht.	43.
Liverpool Shipbuilding Co. Ltd., Liverpool.	32.
McLaren Bros. Ltd., Dumbarton.	38.
Nimmerzust, N.V. Schps, Lekkerkerk.	52.
Philip & Sons Ltd., Dartmouth.	69.
Pollock, J., Sons & Co. Ltd., Faversham.	71.
Readhead, Softley & Co., South Shields.	3,27 & 33.
Readhead, J., & Co., South Shields.	11.
Rennoldson, J.P., & Sons, South Shields	14,48,50 & 54.
Richards (Shipbuilders) Ltd., Lowestoft.	76.
Robertson, A.W., & Co., Canning Town, London.	51.
Scott & Sons, Bowling.	63,64,65,66,67 & 68.
Scott & Sons (Bowling) Ltd., Bowling.	70,77 & 78,
Shearer, J, & Son, Glasgow.	7.

Stewart, J, & Sons Ltd., Blackwall.	25.
Techlenbörg, J.C., Geestemünde.	37.
Thorneycroft, J.I., & Co. Ltd., Southampton.	55.
Tilkin, L., & Co., Liége.	49.
Toward, T. & W.; Newcastle.	21.
Watson, J.S., (Gainsborough) Ltd., Gainsborough.	58.
Westwood, Baillie & Co., Poplar.	15.
Williamson, T.; Harrington.	1.
Wouldhave & Johnson, North Shields.	18,34 & 36.

It is interesting to note that 21 of these vessels were built in South Shields.

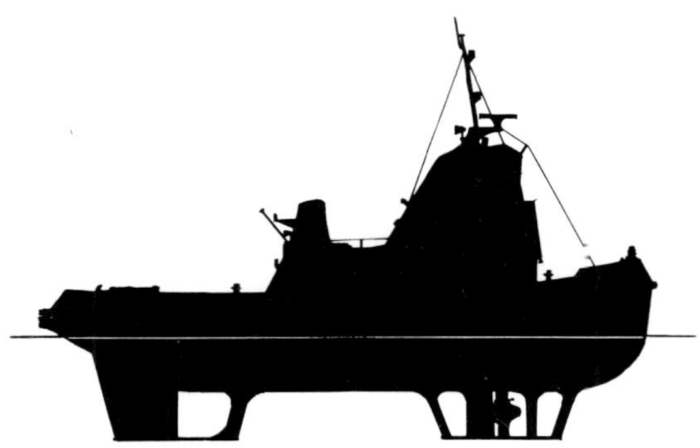

GREATHAM CROSS

Appendix C
Engine Builders

Alphabetical list of the 36 engine builders of the 81 vessels covered by this history.

Engine Builders	Tug History Reference Numbers
Allsup, W., and Sons, Preston.	9 & 45.
Almond, J.P., North Shields.	1.
Avontuur, Machinefabriek, Dordrecht.	52.
Baird and Barnsley, North Shields.	17 & 42.
Baird Bros., North Shields.	46,60 & 61.
Bolnes, N.V., Machinefabriek, Bolnes.	47.
Bow, McLachlan & Co., Paisley.	51.
Brotherhood, Peter, Ltd., Peterborough.	53.
Butchard, George, Milton, Gravesend.	13 & 20.
Cox & Co., Falmouth.	56.
Crossley Bros. Ltd., Manchester.	64,65,66,67, 68. 69,70,71 & 72.
Crossley Premier Engines Ltd., Manchester.	73,74 & 75.
Danziger Werft, Danzig.	62.
Earles Co. Ltd., Hull.	59.
Earles Shipbuilding & Eng. Co. Ltd., Hull	28.
Findley, R.B., & Son, North Shields.	34 & 36.
Foden, Edward, Sandbach.	5.
Forrester, G., & Co., Liverpool.	32.
Grey, G.T., South Shields.	12.
Hall, Russell & Co., Aberdeen.	2.
Hall, Russell & Co. Ltd., Aberdeen.	40.
Hepple, G.P., North Shields.	21.
Hepple & Co., North Shields.	39.
Hepple & Co., South Shields.	4 & 44.
Hepple & Co. Ltd., South Shields.	57.
Holmes, C.D., & Co. Ltd., Hull.	58.
Kincaid, J.G., & Co., Greenock.	6.
Mavor & Coulson, Ltd.	38.
Muir & Houston, Glasgow.	7 & 31
Plenty & Son, Newbury.	43.
Plenty & Son Ltd., Newbury.	63.
Readhead, Softley & Co., South Shields.	3,27 & 33.
Readhead, J., & Co., South Shields.	11.
Rennoldson, J.P., South Shields.	10 & 48.
Rennoldson, J.P., & Sons, South Shields.	14,19,24,26, 50,54 & 57.
Richardson & Westgarth & Co. Ltd., Middlesbrough.	49.
Ruston, Paxman Diesels Ltd., Newton-le-Willows.	76,77,78,79,80 & 81.

Appendix D

Funnel, Flag and Hull Colours of Tees Towing Co. Ltd. and its Constituent Companies.

1. The Florence Tugboat and Salvage Co. Ltd. (1902-1919)
   Funnel colours believed to be those shown. Hull colour – black.
2. George Petrie. (c.1880-1911)
   Paddle tugs owned by this company had a red star painted on the fore and aft faces of their paddle boxes. The firm was usually referred to as the Red Star Line Steamboats.
3. The Tees Tug Co. Ltd. (1909-1920)
   Hull colour – black with narrow light-coloured (white?) lines at rubbing strake and boot-topping.
4. George Robinson & Co. (c.1900-1909)
   The Robinson Tug Co. Ltd. (1909-1920)
5. Tees Towing Co. Ltd. (1920 to date)
   The colours used on the current series of twin-funnelled tugs are:–
   Hull – Black with red oxide boot topping flash towards the bow. Narrow lemon line around hull just above rubbing strake. Names and port of registry are in lemon sans-serif lettering.
   Superstructure – Deck housing, teak; "boat deck" and bridge bulwarks, white; lower sides of wheelhouse, red; upper sides and roof of wheelhouse, white.
   Deck and equipment – Deck, dull red; inside bulwark, teak; capstan and windlass, green; other fittings, black; handrails, white.
6. C.W. Duncan & Co. (c.1900-1914).
7. Charles Duncan & Sons Ltd. (1914-c.1928)
   After 1928 the Duncan vessels carried the Tees Towing Co. colours.
8. The Crosthwaite Steamship Co. Ltd. (1925-1935)
   Hull and superstructure colour – white.
9. George Alder Ltd. (? - 1929)

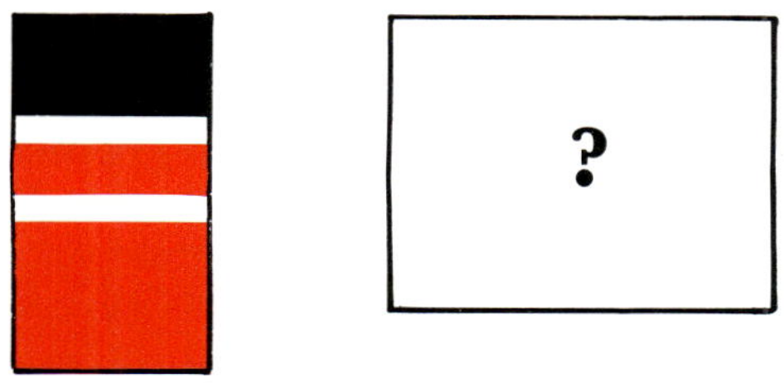

1

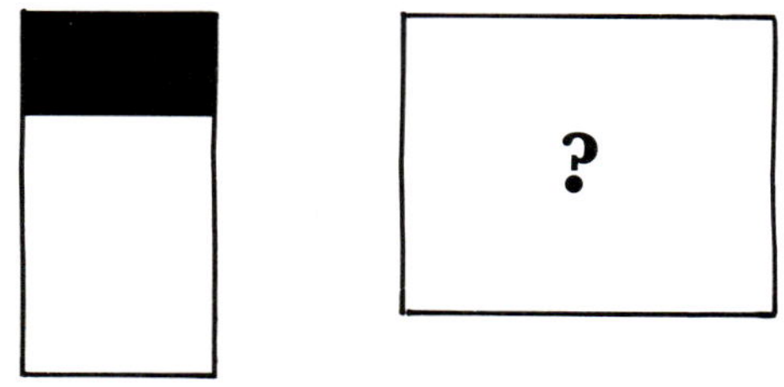

2

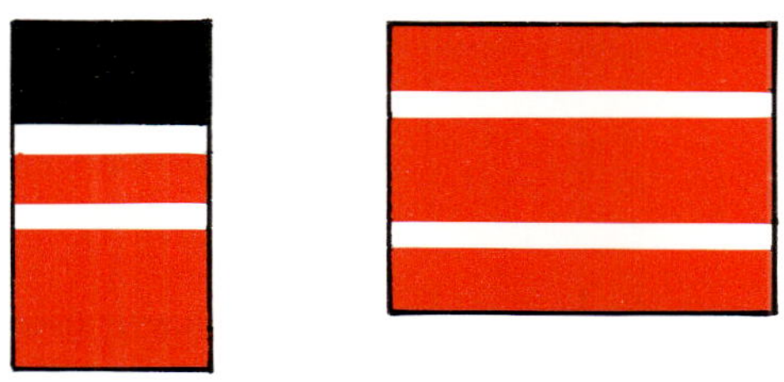

3

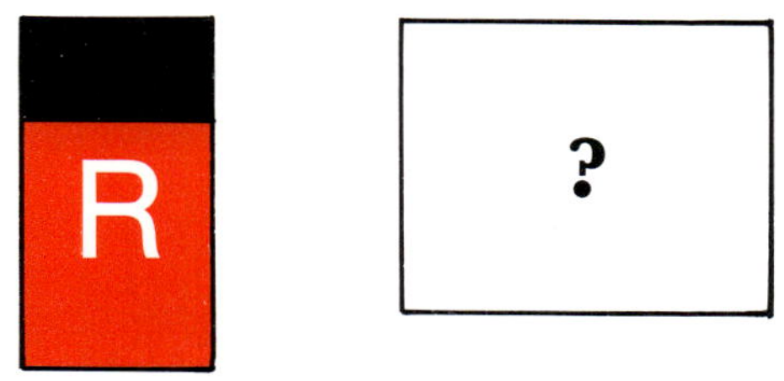

4

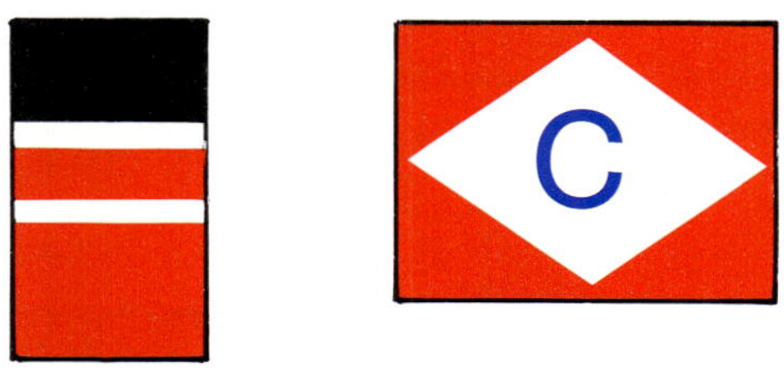

5

6

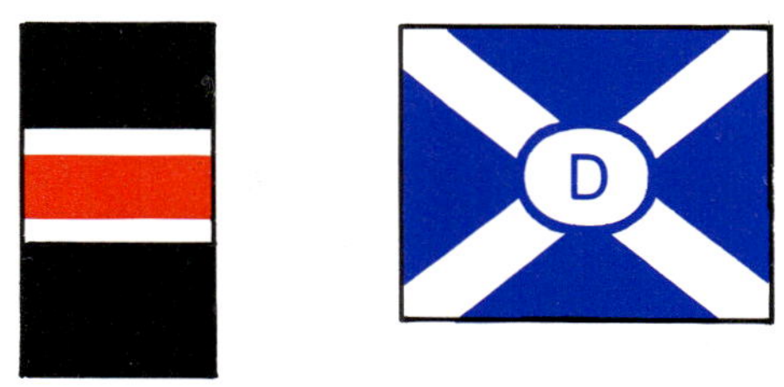

7

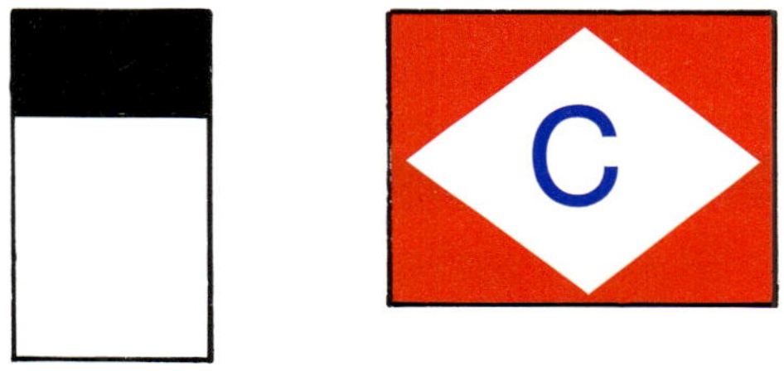

8

9

Appendix E
Tees Towing Company Limited

Legend of the Company's Badge, Insignia or Symbol

Symbol: *Hippocampus,* (Seahorse).
Motto: *Facta Non Verba,* (Deeds not Words).
Decoration,
Ends of scroll: *Rosa Alba Semi-Plena,* (White Rose of York).

1. It was quite a common practice in the days of the paddle tugs for owners to have a device and/or motto carved or painted on the piece of wood which secured the laths at the bottom on the outside of the paddle casings. Alternatively, a motif of some kind was worked in the scroll on the wooden board fixed on the outside of the bulwark close to the stem, or on the fore and/or after ends of both casings.

2. In 1840, a wooden clinker-built, square stern, single-engined paddle tug, 78 feet x 16 feet and of 26NHP, was built for the Middlesbrough-on-Tees Steam Tug Company by Andrew Woodhouse of South Shields. She was named *Seahorse* and had a painting of such on both casings fore and aft. She was sold to Joseph Gibson, a Middlesbrough auctioneer in 1848 who, in the same year sold her to the River Wear Commissioners who employed her until 1895 when she was sold to Mr. R.L. Cook, Sunderland, with whom she ended her days.

3. In 1903 the iron paddle tug *Florence* came to the River Tees. A seahorse and the motto "Facta non Verba" were carved on the place aforesaid and this must have been there since she was built in 1879.

4. In 1906 the *Florence* came under my management. I immediately adopted this motto, and when there was room, this symbol with a Yorkist Rose for decoration at each end of the scroll was painted or carved on the place aforesaid on all our paddle tugs – *Champion, Challenger, Conqueror* and all paddle tugs subsequently acquired, the last being the *Lingdale* which was bought from the Dover Harbour Board as the *Lady Vita* in 1914.

5. In 1916, the motto was chosen by a local gentleman for his Grant of Arms.

6. In 1929, the motto was chosen by the governors of the local Technical College.

7. On all our present tugs a fibre-glass casting of the complete badge is affixed to the front of the bridge bulwark. A sculpture of a seahorse in Springwell Sandstone, (Co. Durham), and executed by Gillian McLeod of Glasgow, is mounted on the architrave of the entrance to our town office.

8. A fibre-glass casting by McCarthy is affixed to the front and back of the tower on the top of our Riverside offices which is illuminated from sunset to sunrise.

William H. Crosthwaite, 1962.

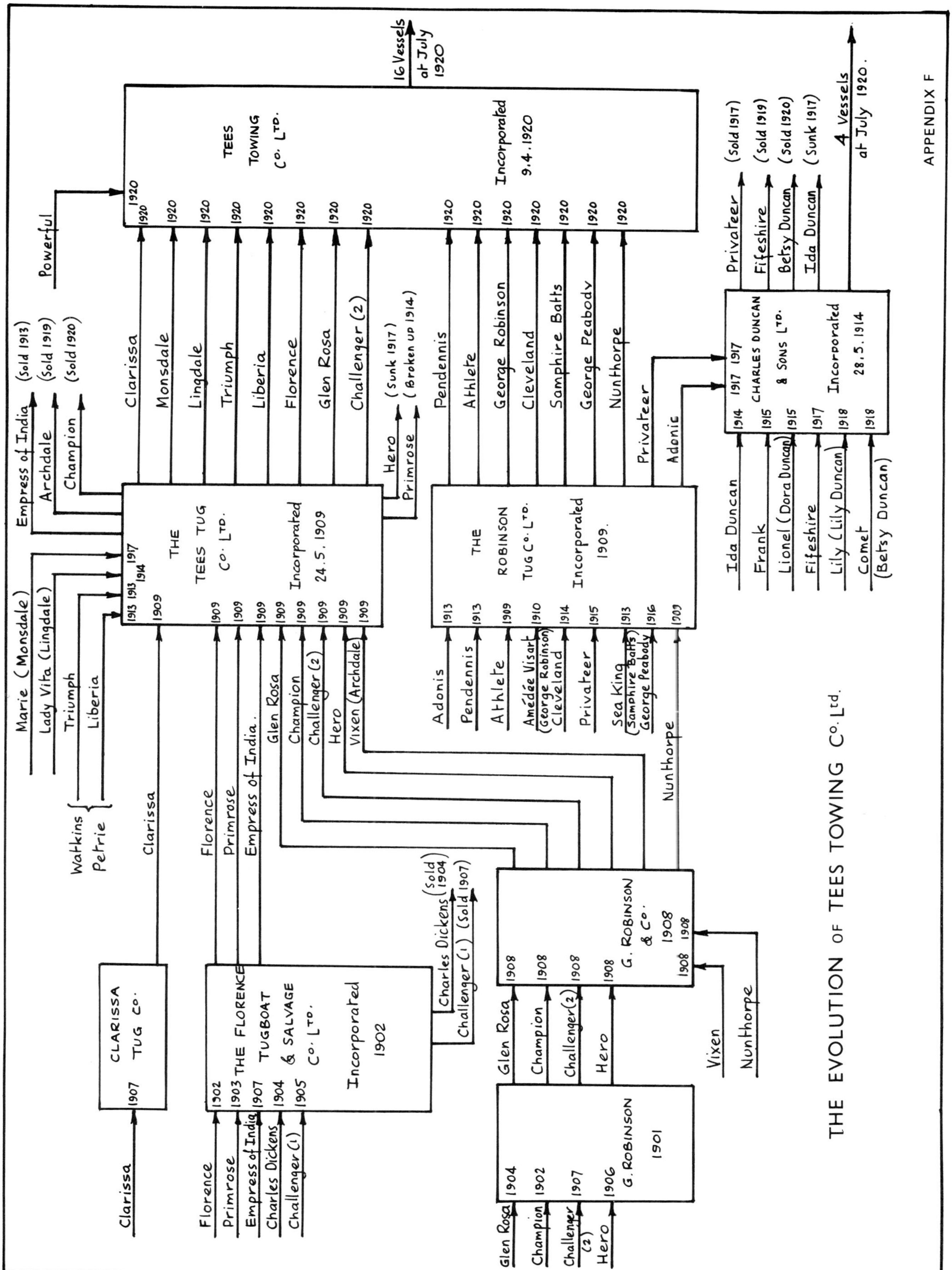
THE EVOLUTION OF TEES TOWING Co. Ltd.
APPENDIX F
G. ROBINSON 1901
G. ROBINSON & Co. 1908
CLARISSA TUG Co.
THE FLORENCE TUGBOAT & SALVAGE Co. Ltd. Incorporated 1902
THE TEES TUG Co. Ltd. Incorporated 24.5.1909
THE ROBINSON TUG Co. Ltd. Incorporated 1909.
CHARLES DUNCAN & SONS Ltd. Incorporated 28.5.1914
TEES TOWING Co. Ltd. Incorporated 9.4.1920
16 Vessels at July 1920
4 Vessels at July 1920.
Glen Rosa
Champion
Challenger (2)
Hero
Vixen
Nunthorpe
Clarissa
Florence
Primrose
Empress of India
Charles Dickens
Challenger (1)
Charles Dickens (Sold 1904)
Challenger (1) (Sold 1907)
Watkins
Petrie
Marie (Monsdale)
Lady Vita (Lingdale)
Triumph
Liberia
Vixen (Archdale)
Empress of India (Sold 1913)
Archdale (Sold 1919)
Champion (Sold 1920)
Powerful
Hero (Sunk 1917)
Primrose (Broken up 1914)
Monsdale
Lingdale
Adonis
Pendennis
Athlete
Amédée Visart (George Robinson)
Cleveland
Privateer
Sea King (Samphire Batts)
George Peabody
George Robinson
Samphire Batts
Adonic
Ida Duncan
Frank
Lionel (Dora Duncan)
Fifeshire
Lily (Lily Duncan)
Comet (Betsy Duncan)
Privateer (Sold 1917)
Fifeshire (Sold 1919)
Betsy Duncan (Sold 1920)
Ida Duncan (Sunk 1917)

Appendix F.

TUG OWNERSHIP CHRONOLOGY

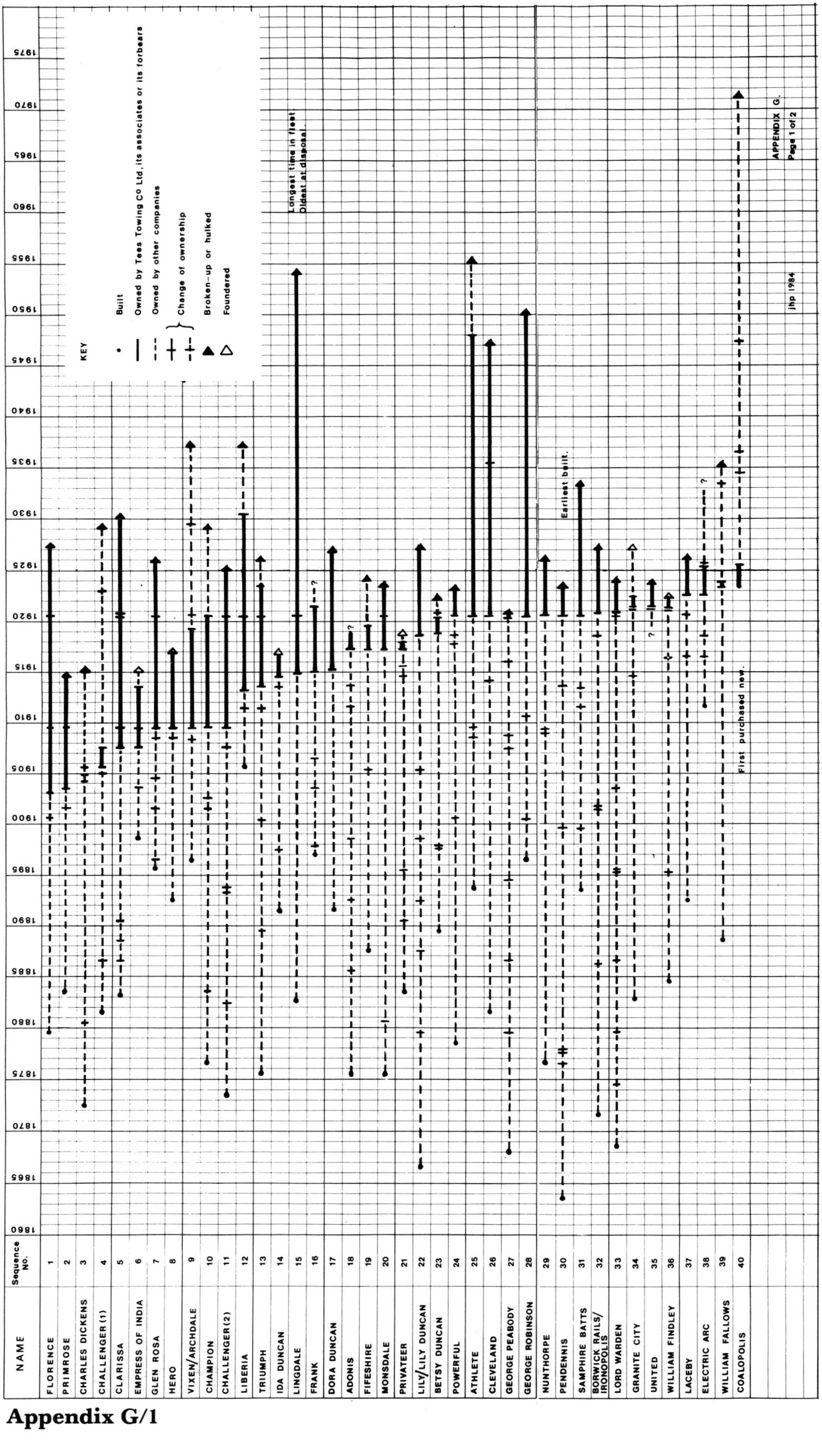

TUG OWNERSHIP CHRONOLOGY

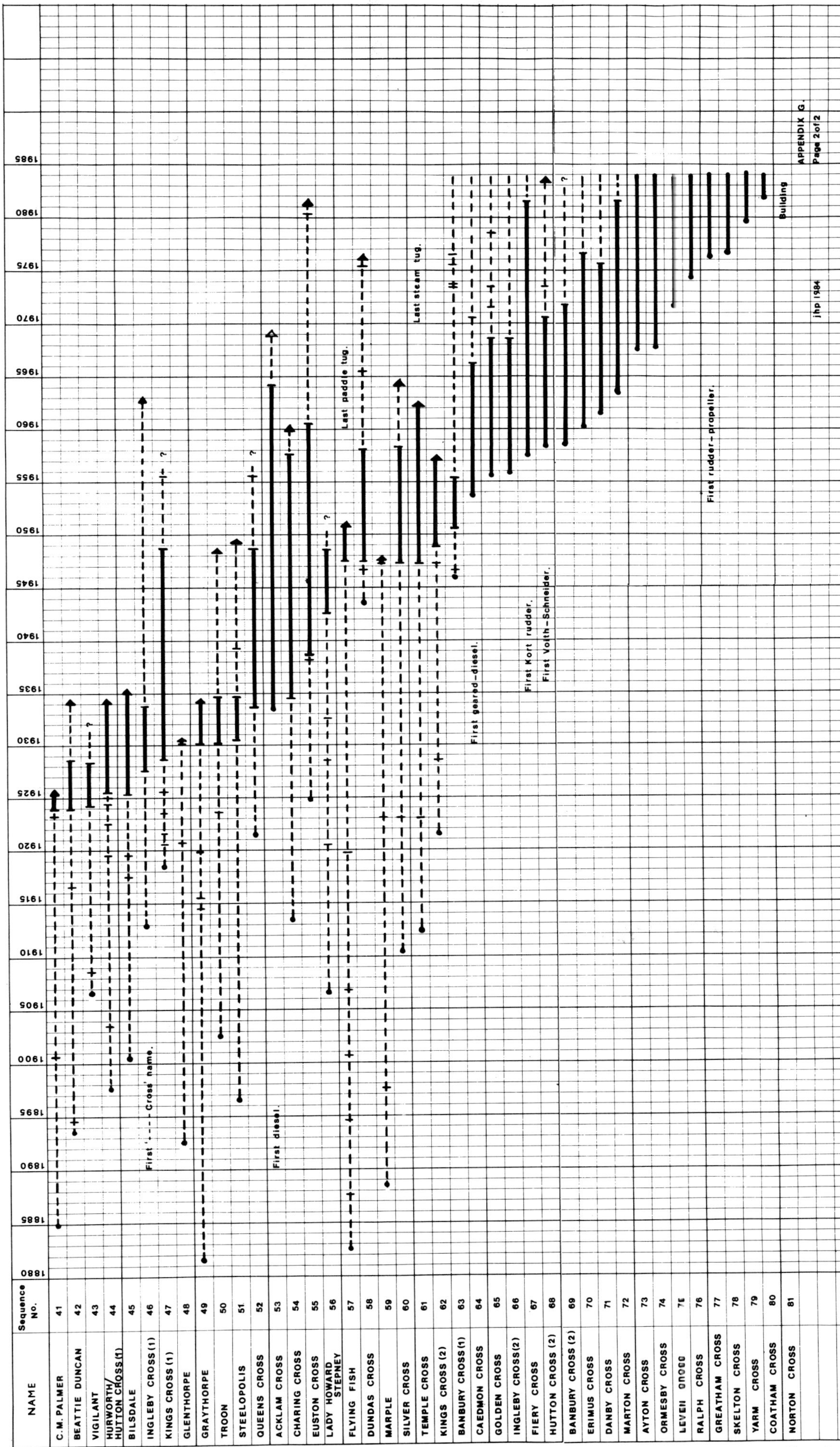

ANDALUSIAN

TEMPLE CROSS

Author

Stuart Dixon, IPMO-E, APMP, PRINCE2, P3O, is a PMO Consultant based in Crowborough, United Kingdom. He has more than 25 years' experience in PMO setup and management in a variety of sectors including retail, finance, and travel. He developed his first PMO Service catalogue over 12 years ago and has been enhancing it ever since. He was one of the reviewers for the P3O standard and has contributed to the development of the APM Body of Knowledge and their competency assessment. He has previously been the chair of the APM specific interest group for PMOs. Stuart has been one of the authors of the PMO competency framework. Stuart is a passionate supporter of PMOs and the difference they can make to the success of the organization

Contents

Introduction

Introduction to the second edition

This is the second edition of this book. The first edition was published back in March 2020 and this edition has seen a few tweaks and changes in the same way any service catalogue would. The first major change is to align the competencies with the PMO competency framework launched in early 2021.

The second change to this is the introduction of a new area for Process Improvement which has a single group of Process Improvement Operations. The purpose of introducing a new area was to make it a bit more obvious that continuous improvement is something that a PMO does focus on, not only to improve itself, but to refine the processes that are used by its customers. This introduced 2 new services of Map key value streams and processes and Automate Processes whereas the rest of the services in this grouping were previously in the Knowledge Management Operations section. This goes to prove that there is no perfect way to establish a PMO Service Catalogue and if when you are designing your list of services you feel like combining some of the services here into a new service that your customers understand then there is nothing wrong in doing that.

The other new service that got added was Provision of Management Dashboards as the PMO can be asked to produce management dashboards with data other than that included in a progress report.

My intention with this book is to try to codify and structure the tasks that a PMO is asked to do. As PMOs are still evolving one book cannot cover all of the items that a PMO can do, so if you find something you think I have missed then please reach out to me via Linked In (https://www.linkedin.com/in/stuartdixon1/) so that I can update this book (and credit you if you are happy with that)

I would like to thank John McIntyre, Ken Burrell, Nicole Reilly, Chris Walters, Eileen Roden and Lindsay Scott for their inspiration, support and encouragement in ensuring this book has been published

Book structure

Within the service section the services are divided up into 25 service areas. A service area is related to an area of knowledge.

Each area is then divided up into service groups. A service group is related to one of the 3 main activity types that the PMO is expected to do:

Design – a PMO can provide the standards, tools, templates, processes, procedures, help, guidance, framework that defines how work will operate within that particular service area.

Operate – a PMO can operate (or perform) some of the work on behalf of other people within the project (program or portfolio) team. If the PMO does not perform this service then, if this is performed at all, then this will be done by another member of the team.

Monitor – a PMO can review the work done by others (or even other parts of the PMO) and provide and independent quality assessment and check. They can provide reporting across the service area and highlight items that require escalation.

Not all the PMO activities fall neatly into the 3 groupings. For some of the services the operate activity is split up into different groups. Where this has been done it has been for ease of comprehension as it fits more naturally into how the service area operates.

Table 1.1 Service Group mapping to Design, Operate, Monitor

Area	**Design**	**Operate**	**Monitor**
Administration		Administration Operations	
Benefits Management	Benefits Management Design	Benefits Management Operations	Benefits Realization Monitoring
Capability Management	Capability Design	Capability Operations	Capability Monitoring
Capacity Management		Capacity Operations	Capacity Monitoring
Change control	Change Control Design	Change Control Operations	Change Control Monitoring
Change Management	Change Management Design		
Communications Management	Communications Design	Communications Operations	Communications Monitoring
Configuration Management	Configuration Management Design	Configuration Management Operations	Configuration Management Monitoring
Consultancy		Consultancy Operations	
Financial Management	Financial Management Design	Financial Management Operations	Financial Management Monitoring

Area	Design	Operate	Monitor
Governance	Governance Design	Governance Operations	
Issue Management	Issue Management Design	Issue Management Operations	Issue Management Monitoring
Knowledge and Innovation		Innovation Operations	
Knowledge Management	Knowledge Management Design	Knowledge Management Operations	Knowledge Management Monitoring
Methodologies	Method Design	Method Operations	
People Development	People Development Design	People Development Operations	
PMO Development	PMO Design	PMO Management Operations	PMO Monitoring
Portfolio Management	Portfolio Design	Portfolio Operations	Portfolio Monitoring
PPM Tool Support	PPM Tool Design	PPM Tool Operations	
Process Improvement		Process Improvement Operations	
Quality Management	Quality Management Design	Quality Management Operations	Quality Management Monitoring
Risk Management	Risk Management Design	Risk Management Operations	Risk Management Monitoring
Rollup reporting		Reporting Operations	
Schedule Management	Scheduling Design	Scheduling Operations	Scheduling Monitoring
Stakeholder Management	Stakeholder Management Design	Stakeholder Management Operations	
Supplier Management	Supplier Management Design	Supplier Management Operations	Supplier Management Monitoring

Within each service group there is one or more service. A service is the lowest level of offering that a PMO can provide. To avoid duplication services are linked to a single service group, however within each service we have indicated where services are related. Related services are typically performed together. A related service may in a different service grouping or even in a different service area.

Below it explains how you can use the information in the detailed services section of the book to construct your own service catalogue using the information from this book as a basis. The one thing that this book cannot provide you is context – how this will work within your organization. Just as each project is unique so is each PMO as it has to adapt to what the organization expects of it.

It is not expected that the reader will read this book from cover to cover, but they will use it as a reference book to be dipped into and referred back to when they need conformation of what a particular service should be, how to perform the service, and why it is important to the customer of that service.

How to read the services

Each of the areas, groups and services descriptions have been written with 2 distinct audiences in mind.

- For the PMO: they describe information about how the service should be performed and some hints and tips that the PMO should consider when performing the service.
- For the customer: they consider why would someone want to get this service, what would they expect to be delivered from this service and why would they benefit from having the PMO (as opposed to anyone else) deliver the service.

Understanding a service area

Each of the 25 service areas covers an area that the PMO is typically expected to cover. The brief explanation of the area can be used to review whether it is worth reading more about the service groups and the services that make up that service area.

As with the individual services the description for the area explains this from a PMO perspective and describes the value the service will provide the customer (and who the customers are likely to be). This can assist the reader in understanding whether this may be of value for the PMO to offer services within that particular area.

The rest of the information within the service area description provides some overall hints and tips around the delivery of the service area itself.

Understanding a service group

A service group sits within a service area and explains why the list of services have been grouped together. The groups are arranged into design (setting up the framework and training it out), operate (performing the tasks within the area) and monitor (reviewing how wel the area services are working).

The Responsibility Assignment Matrix is useful for working out who needs to be involved with each of the services. The PMO may be delivering the service, they do not work alone and need to deliver the service in conjunction with others.

Finally, there is a hints and tips section around the delivery of the service group itself.

Understanding a Service

The service is the lowest level of PMO offering. Each service has 2 audiences, although only one of those may read the book.

Each service is described for the PMO who will be delivering the service. It describes what the service is, how it can be delivered, who is involved in delivering it along with some detailed hints and tips. The related services section describes other services that the PMO may want to consider when putting together their service catalogue.

The service is described from the perspective of the recipient of the service. What can they expect to get from this service and why would they want the PMO to be able deliver this for them?

How to put together a service catalogue

Having read the book and dipped into the service listings, how do you convert this into something that will work for your PMO and your organization?

One of the quickest ways in approaching this is to do a review or audit of what your PMO is currently doing and see how that aligns to the services listed in this book. This will then give you a structure that you can work with.

It will be inevitable that the services that you are currently performing will not align 100% to the service as described within this book and that is fine as each of these services within this book can only be described in general terms as the authors do not understand the particular circumstances of your PMO. They will not understand the individual capabilities of the people within the PMO, the maturity of the organization, and the other factors that make each PMO unique.

For the initial service catalogue, it will be good enough to collate what you already have. This can then be subsequently refined. Having got a list of services together, unless you have a PMO of one individual, it is likely that some of these services are only delivered by particular people, or they are only delivered in particular circumstances (see Criteria for when the PMO will offer this service). Consideration should be given to ensuring that there is not just a single person who can perform a particular service from a business continuity and succession planning perspective (or even considering what happens when that person is on holiday, does that service stop?).

Once you have your initial service catalogue you should review this to see whether the number and blend of services seems right. Are you trying to do too much? It can be better to deliver a great service across a small number of services, rather than trying to stretch and deliver a poor service across a large number of services.

Tailoring the service information

For each of the services in this book we have used the same structure. When you convert this for your own usage you may want to revise this structure to include a few more pieces of information including:

- Who can deliver the service? – If this service is only delivered by a particular person or persons then add this to the list as it will ensure the right people are assigned
- Specific measures – this book lists how each service can be measured but does not put out specific metrics. It should be possible to expand that section to provide a specific measure
- Service Level – some of the services such as facilitation service or managing project management tools would benefit from having as service level given so people using the service are aware how long it will take to get something delivered, and what level of quality can this be delivered
- Process detail – this book provides a list of process names for each of the services but there is no detail to those processes. It would therefore be sensible to expand that and provide a process/procedure linked to each of the services you will be doing. That will ensure consistency in the provision of the service
- How to request – this may not be for all the services but some which are performed ad-hoc it may be useful to include something about how people can engage with the PMO for them to deliver the service. Consider whether people are going to contact the PMO via a central request mechanism (e.g. one email box) or do the requests go to any member of the PMO?

To make it easier to use you may consider changing the format of this catalogue and converting it to a spreadsheet format, or may be a SharePoint site, which can then give you the linkages to the process detail and allow for easier sorting and grouping of the services.

How to review the service catalogue

Having got a list of services together the next sensible question to ask is do the customers of the service actually want this? When doing this be careful as some services have more than one customer. It may be that the Project Manager may not want a service to be done as they see it as interfering. The Senior Management that require consistency may insist that the PMO do this service.

Do not confuse the want for a service with the need for the service. As an example, people may not want to go to the dentist, but if they want to keep their teeth nice, they will need to go. A person may want a nice car, but all they need is a bus ticket. It is useful for the PMO to probe this question to distinguish the wants (or not wants) from the need.

One of the ways to perform this is to do a Voice of the Customer (VOC) exercise where the PMO goes out to the people they are delivering the service for and ask them questions such as:

- Do you receive this service?
  This is a simple yes or no choice
- Do you want to continue to receive this service?
  This is applicable if they answer the first question as yes
- Do you want to start to receive this service?
  This is applicable if they answer the first question as no
- How important is this service to you?
  Rate this on a scale of Low, Medium, High. This question can be asked regardless of whether the person receives the service or not
- Why is this service important to you?
  What would happen to your business if this service were to stop being delivered by the PMO?
- If you already receive this service how do you rate it?
  Rate this on a scale of 1 = Very satisfied, 2 = Satisfied, 3 = Neutral, 4 = Dissatisfied, 5 = Very Dissatisfied
- In delivering this service, what does success look like?
  This allows you to understand what the person wants/values from the service

This information can then be used by the PMO Manager to look at the services they currently offer and see how useful this is to their customers.

Doing a VOC exercise can be quite daunting, this is why some PMOs get consultants in to run these exercises for them. At its essence it consists of going out to people you work with on a regular basis and asking the question 'Do you think I do a good job?'. Without this essential question being asked the PMO cannot hope to improve and you may be pleasantly surprised by the result.

There are other ways that the PMO can canvas their customers to find out what they want. Regardless of how it is done, the PMO need the detailed understand of what their customers want from them.

If the PMO is looking to move into new services, this exercise may be a suitable time to ask the questions about the new services. Rather than ask 'Do you receive this service?' ask 'Would you like to receive this service?'

Dealing with the feedback

Having got a service catalogue and asked the customers of those services 'Do you like it?' the PMO Manager will be faced with a set of responses ranging from 'Excellent keep doing this and more' through to 'Who are you and why are you asking me these questions?'. What does the PMO Manager do with this valuable information?

Unpopular services

There will be some services that the PMO delivers that are not valued. After all who really likes an audit. The PMO Manager will need to consider whether this is something they stop offering (this can be seen as a success as the PMO Manager can declare they have listened to feedback and will stop doing service A and focus instead their resources on service B which has got a better response). They could continue it because although the primary customer does not appreciate the service it is mandated/required by a secondary customer. E.g. a Project Manager may not appreciate going through a Gate Review process; however, the Portfolio Manager may want this to continue as it provides them assurance that the portfolio is progressing correctly.

Popular services

There are other services which are much appreciated by their customers. The PMO manager will need to consider whether they are able to focus their resources on delivering more of these services. It may not be possible to do this for all the popular services as some may be time bound e.g. the PMO could not offer a schedule update to 10 projects if they all needed them in the same 2 hours timeslot and they only had one person to do this service.

The PMO Manager may want to consider dropping services which are unpopular to deliver the popular ones.

Other services

Then there are services which are neither popular or unpopular and the customers are ambivalent about the service. For these services, the PMO Manager needs to consider how important they are. If they are of high importance, then the PMO Manager needs to consider still offering the service. If they are of low importance, then the PMO Manager should consider dropping them to focus on other services.

Implementing the service catalogue

The PMO now has a service catalogue, how do they implement this? There are several steps that the PMO Manager needs to consider in implementing the services within their service catalogue.

PMO capability

One of the first things to consider when implementing a new service is are the people delivering the service capable of delivering this service. If the answer is no, then they will need to gain the requisite skills before this service is offered. If the person offering the service cannot deliver, then it does not matter how much the customer wants the service they will not be happy. The PMO Manager needs to ensure they only offer the services that they can deliver, otherwise the reputation of the PMO will suffer.

Service demand

Having ensured the PMO can deliver this service the next thing the PMO Manager needs to consider is offering this service to a few of the customers who asked for it as part of the VOC exercise. Rather than provide this as a general offering the PMO may benefit from having a pilot in one or two areas and refining the service based on feedback from those people before offering it to a wider audience.

Service feedback

Having offered a service for a while the PMO needs to monitor and see how well this service is perceived, remembering that perceptions differ from reality. If the PMO has followed the service description contained within this book they will have gained insight into how they can monitor the success (or value) of this service. If the service is not performing as expected, then the PMO Manager will need to review the service and see how this can be tweaked to improve the service offering.

Reusing the service catalogue

The real value for the service catalogue comes when new people come to the PMO and ask what they can do for them. The PMO Manager is then able to use the service catalogue to enable them to have a discussion with the new customer about the services the PMO can offer and really answer the question 'What can the PMO do for me?'

Evolving the service catalogue

The service catalogue should not be a static document that never gets revised. The PMO Manager should take the opportunity of reviewing this on a regular basis. How often should the service catalogue be reviewed? The actual answer depends on lots of factors, but the minimum should be annually.

The other factors that the PMO could consider for reviewing their service catalogue include:

- PMO resource changes – have the capabilities changed?
- PMO sponsor changes - are the PMO required to do different things?
- PMO scope changes – have the PMO taken on a new area?
- PMO management changes – do the PMO report into a different management structure? I.e. moved from IT to business
- Demand changes – is there a request for extra PMO services?
- Technology changes – has the business recently implemented a new tool? Are there new opportunities to automate some of the repetitive work?
- Business context changes – has the business changed from an expansion policy to one of consolidation or reduction?
- Priority changes – has the business changed its focus to deliver a different type or style of project?

Factors to consider for service success

For each of the services listed in this book we have suggested how these services can be measured. The reason for this is that the PMO wants to be perceived as a success. How can you know whether you are successful as a PMO without measuring it?

Some of the services naturally lend themselves to being measured. If the PMO offers a service to setup a project within a project management tool, then this is an easy item to measure as there will be a request coming in and then sometime later the project will be setup and the person notified. This can then be measured, and a service level put together. This means that the person needing that particular service has an idea, before they even request this, how long it is likely to take to get this service delivered.

If this service is always delivering within the Service Level Agreement (SLA), then that may be judged by the PMO as a good thing. However, this can depend on whether the SLA matches what the customer expects. In the example above if the SLA were set at 1 month then that would be considered as unrealistic by the customer, although the PMO would deliver that every time. If the SLA was set at 1 hour, then although it would please the customer, it may be the PMO would not deliver that most of the time. Which then means that the service needs to escalate to the PMO manager, or even their manager.

When judging what the set the service level to be it needs to be realistic, both from the PMO's perspective and the perspective of the customer. In the example above a realistic SLA for setting up a project in a project management tool would be 1 working day. That gives enough time for the PMO to deliver given other work they may be doing. From the customer perspective it seems reasonable that if you ask for something today you would get it tomorrow.

Other services are a bit more subjective and can only be measured after the event. For example, delivery of a training session. This can be measured using feedback forms, but they only occur after the event. That would then have a target score using a customer satisfaction or Net Promoter Score, which the PMO could then review and judge whether they are doing a good job.

For some services it is a combination of things that make them successful. It is the time taken to respond to the original request, the manner in which this is done (polite, friendly, knowledgeable) and the outcome of the service – did this deliver what the customer expected? For those services e.g. the staffing of a help desk for PPM queries, the only true feedback on whether that service is a success is judged based on the feedback from the customers. Hence back to the voice of the customer survey.

Where a PMO is outsourced there is a temptation, driven by the contractual process, to put in an SLA for the PMO services. Whilst it is a good idea to have a service menu as part of the contract, so the organization which is buying in the outsourced PMO service knows what they are getting. It may not be a good thing to have a service level for each of those services. Perhaps there needs to be an overall SLA based on customer feedback of the PMO as well as a specific SLA on items that can easily and quickly be measured.

If every service required a measure, then there should be a service of measuring PMO services as this will take up time that could otherwise be spent on the delivery of other services.

As the PMO matures there will be less need for the SLA at the detailed level as the organization that is using the PMO will find themselves trusting that when the PMO says it will deliver it will actually happen. This does not mean that the PMO should stop measuring their services, just that it can be done on the service of the PMO as a whole, rather than listing every single thing and asking for a judgement on it.

Introducing the T model of PMOs

There are many types of PMOs out there, and each one of those is unique just like the projects they support. Previous models of PMO have tried to group them into categories based on whether they are directing, controlling, or supporting which as a simplistic way of grouping the services that the PMO provides, without going down, as this book has, and defining the individual PMO services and looking why this PMO exists.

Another way of grouping PMOs has been whether they are internal or external, which is a simple way of looking at whether the PMO belongs to the organization or whether the PMO has been brought in as a contracted service. This just tells you who is staffing the PMO and what their reporting lines are. It does not really help with what the PMO can do.

I am proposing that we need to look at the PMOs differently when we look at the services they could offer. What we need to look at is the depth and breadth that the PMO can cover. I see out there a lot of Project Offices [1]and they come in 2 types when looked at from a depth/breadth perspective.

First is the dedicated Project Office. This is where the Project Office has on or more individuals within it who just focus on a single project.

Second is the Delivery Office model where the Project Office supports one or more Project Managers [2]with a range of projects.

Hence the T model shown below. A Delivery Office will support a broad range of items but will not go into detail on them. A Project Office will support a small number of items, and will do so in detail

Picture 1.1 T Model

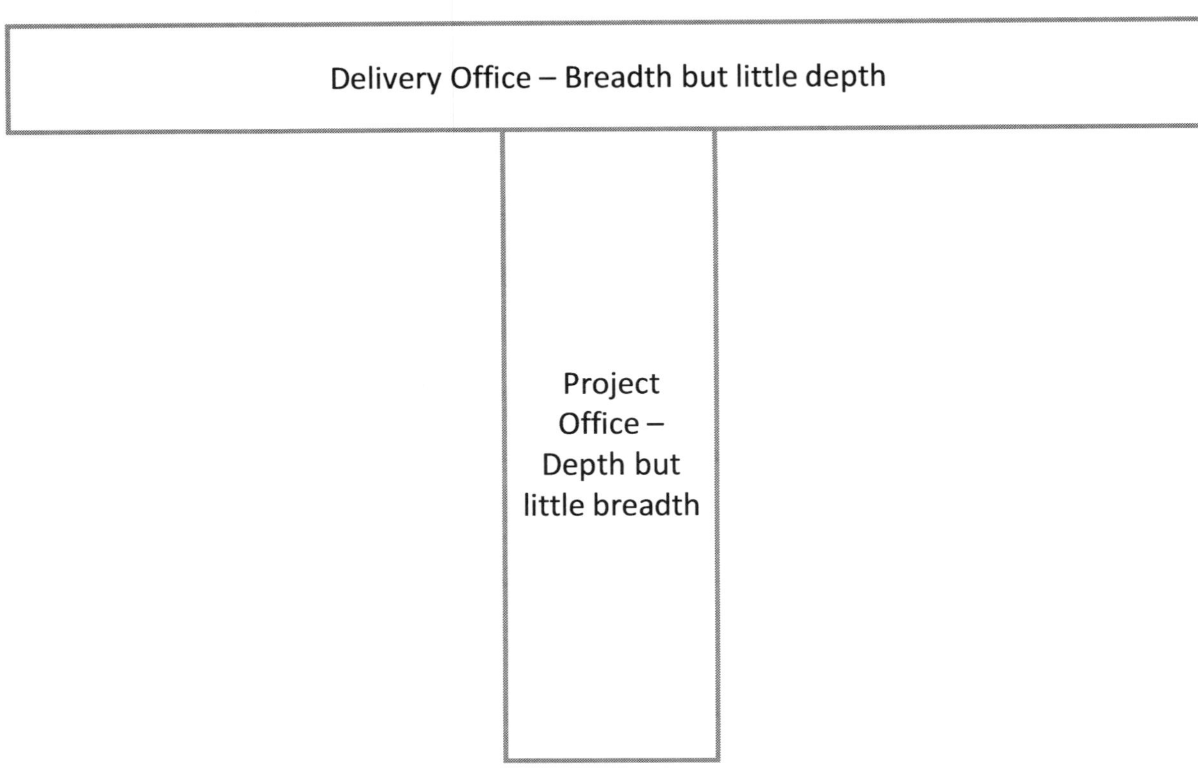

[1] For Project Office also read Program Office
[2] For Project Managers this can apply to Program Managers as well

What does this have to do with the development of a service catalogue? Well when putting together a service catalogue you are deciding what services you are going to offer and who to. This needs to be balanced off with the capability of the people delivering the service and the effort available to deliver this service.

If you have one person in the PMO and they are supporting a single project they will be more likely to take on more of the operate services, such as updating of registers, maintaining schedules, controlling assets, updating detailed financial plans.

If you have one person in the PMO and they are supporting multiple projects and Project Managers then they will be more likely to take on more of the monitor services, such as reviewing business cases, performing Gate Reviews, combining schedules, producing consolidated reporting.

If there is not a central PMO then both types of PMO will need to pick up the applicable design services to ensure that they can perform the operate and monitoring services.

This model does not assume that a particular style of Project Office will definitely perform a set of services, just that they will consider which services they will perform in light of the breadth or depth to which it makes sense to support them.

This model relates to Program or Project Offices.

Other types of PMO

As well as a Project or Program Office the other type of PMO that is quite common is a Portfolio Office, sometimes called an Enterprise PMO or a Strategic PMO. This Office is linked to a Portfolio Manager who has responsibility for ensuring the Portfolio is created, maintained and that the individual Projects and Programs within the Portfolio get delivered. A Portfolio Office can support this, and they tend to pick from the design and monitoring set of services, only looking at the operate services within the Portfolio Management service area.

AXELOS P3O ®came up with the concept of a PMO Centre of Excellence. In the context of this book a Centre of Excellence would look to pick up the design services. There will be many PMOs who do not have a dedicated Centre of Excellence. In those cases, the PMOs will need to look at the individual services they are wanting to perform and then they need to look at which are the related design services that they may need to add to their service catalogue.

Administration

Administration

Description

Provides portfolio, program, or project administrative support. This includes onboarding of resources, organizing, arranging, and documenting meetings.

What the services within the area provide for the customer

This covers a broad range of administrative services that is done on behalf of the portfolio, program, or project. These activities can be done by the portfolio, program or project manager or even other people within the organization. Where there is a large volume of requests it can be quicker to provide a dedicated service.

Helpful hints for when the PMO is delivering this service area

- These services are typically provided by a junior PMO individual. They are normally only provided for the larger projects and programs. If the PMO does not provide this service, then this work is picked up by the project or program manager
- It is generally only worth providing a dedicated service where there is a large volume of work, or the individual providing the service has other work they will be doing for the project or program

Administration Operations

Service group description

These services cover administrative tasks such putting on events, on boarding new individuals or organizing the facilities for the project or program team.

Why have these services been grouped together?

These services all relate to the provision of administration services on behalf of the portfolio, program, or project manager. These services can occur on a regular basis or ad-hoc basis. Where no PMO person is performing this service, they tend to be done by other members of the organization.

List of related services described in other areas

Provide training logistics support
Provide secretariat function to Change Control Board (CCB)

Responsibility Assignment Matrix

Service	Executive	Portfolio Manager	Program Manager	Project Manager	PMO	Sponsor	Other Stakeholder
Events management					R		
On boarding and induction		A	A	A	R		
Facilities management		I	I	I	R		
Provide a secretariat service for meetings		A	A	A	R		
Order office equipment and stationery			C	C	R		
Set up meetings on behalf of others		A	A	A	R	A	I (Meeting attendees)
Arrange travel for other people			A	A	R		C (travel suppliers)
Formatting documents					R		AC (document provider)
Chase up missing timesheets			A	A	R		I (PPM Team)

Helpful hints when delivering this service group

- These services relate to the co-ordination of other people's efforts. Ensure you identify who are the experts within the organization who can assist with these activities prior to starting. Even if you end up delivering these yourselves then their advice on approach will be valuable
- Having an acronym sheet to decode what different acronyms mean is useful in meetings to help understanding of what is being said
- If dealing with senior people, having a network of contacts with their secretaries or personal assistants can ensure that you get the attendance at the meetings that is required

Events management

Service description

Where a large number of people are required to get together a single point of contact is required to organize this and act as the contact on the day. This can fit in with the communication role a PMO can play within a program

What the service provides for the customer

This provides a focal point for the organization of the event on behalf of the Program or Project Manager. The PMO can deal with the details such as: organizing the venue, organizing the catering, sorting out attendees & no-shows, getting access, sorting audio-visuals, seating plans, confirming logistics and being the central point of contact on the day.

Why is this service being offered to the customer?

Organizing an event, such as a roadshow or even a workshop, is a time-consuming effort. Having a dedicated person to sort out the logistics will free the recipient of the service to focus on the content of the event

How PMO will apply this service

The PMO will require the following information prior to arranging the event:

- the purpose for the event – why is this being held
- the timings for the event – when will it start/finish. When will breaks be required, whether a working lunch is required, or a break is needed?
- the attendees – who is required to be there and who is optional, what happens if a required attendee cannot attend, is the event to be moved or can deputies attend. Are there any issues with access that need to be considered? Are all the attendees required for the full duration of the meeting?
- the proposed location – will this be on site or off site. This may depend on the volume of attendees as there may not be enough room on site to host a large meeting. Will separate areas be required for breakouts (this may not need to be done as separate rooms, which may incur extra expense, but could be done in communal areas such as coffee areas)
- the catering – are there any dietary requirements that need to be catered for
- the audio-visuals – will there be presentations, are flipcharts, pens etc. required. Will there need to be microphones to enable people to hear (and how many), will it be recorded, and how will people access that recording
- technical requirements - will access be required to the internet, the company network, will people be dialling in, will that be as a video conference or just audio?
- the materials – will copies of slides, writing materials be required, and how many copies (do not assume that it is just one per attendee). Will there be any giveaways/prizes required?
- the budget – make sure you know what monies are available for the event. Try to stick to this (or less)

Having got the basic information the PMO can then contact the venue and get that booked, it may require some flexibility to get a venue that can suit, depending on the notice given to organize the event.

The PMO will send out the invitation to the attendees with an outline of the purpose of the meeting, the likely agenda and the details of any preparation required from the attendees.

The PMO will liaise with the catering supplier to organize the food and drink requirements. For a basic event this may just be the PMO going to the shops and buying the food and drink themselves and charging the costs back to the project.

If there are any requirements for external people to provide audio-visual/technical access ensure this is arranged and agreed prior to the event – this may require a contract to be signed, so an understanding of how these are done (and paid) is useful

On the day of the event the PMO will need to arrive at the venue early and ensure that the room is setup according to the requirements. They need to check that any audio-visuals are in working order. Are all the presentations available and loaded for access? Do people know how to work the equipment. Do all the pens work for the flipcharts/whiteboards. Can you stick flipcharts to the walls (use white-tac rather blue-tac or sticky tape)?

If the event is being held externally are there signs directing people to the right place, do you need name badges (these need to have been printed and organized in advance).

Are you aware where the toilets are (if there is a security door between the venue and the toilets, how will people get there?). Is there a fire alarm expected, where is the nearest fire exit, and the rendezvous point?

During the event, the PMO can ensure that the timings are kept to, liaise with the speakers to let them know what signals will be provided to let them know their time is coming to an end. They can ensure that the catering is available at the appropriate times

At the end of the event, they can ensure that the venue is left clear.

After the event ensure that any external invoices are paid. If the audio/video was recorded that is has been processed, published, and communicated. Send any thank-you's if external speakers attended or you had volunteers help on the day/in the build-up.

Supplier	Input	Process	Output	Customer
Facilities Event suppliers Program manager Project manager	Event timing Event location Attendee list	Booking meetings	Event	Project team Program team

How the PMO will measure the value of this service

The success of the event can be measured using feedback forms with specific questions on how good the arrangements have been.

If an event has been well organized, then this tends not to be noticed as the attendees are focused on the content of the event. If an event has been badly organized, then the attendees will focus on the organization over the content of the event. If no-one mentions the event organization then the chances are it was very successful.

Criteria when the PMO will use this service

The PMO will be asked to perform this service when there is a large event that requires organizing. Typically, this will be done for events which are at least 1 day in length.

Helpful hints for the PMO when delivering the service

- Ask for as many details about the event up front, it will save time later
- Have a plan for the event – treat this just like a project
- Do not assume anything. If in doubt ask, the chances are the person you are asking has not thought of this (otherwise they would have told you), but by asking it will get a decision
- Ensure any printing is done with plenty of time. Allow at least 2 days more than the printers tell you to allow for unforeseen circumstances such as couriers not delivering
- Delegate – if possibly get people to help with the venue, printing, organizing on the day etc.

PMO Capabilities needed to fulfil this service

Competencies	Techniques and generic tools
P3M Administration Financial Management Planning and Scheduling Personal Integrity and reliability Personal Communication Relationships and engagement Teamwork Resourcefulness	Scheduling tool Work Breakdown Structure

Related services

Set up meetings on behalf of others Provide facilitation service	Support supplier liaison across portfolio, program, or project Provide training logistics support

Further Reading

Event Management for Dummies

On boarding and induction

Service description

The introduction of new staff in a project or program in a consistent manner. Ensuring they are aware of the purpose of the program, the governance structure, and rules.

What the service provides for the customer

This ensures that new staff are aware of what the project/program is there to deliver and how it will be delivered. It ensures that they become an efficient member of the team in the shortest time possible.

Why is this service being offered to the customer?

By the PMO providing this induction service it relieves the burden of the project/program manager having to do this themselves, or the service not being offered at all and therefore the new staff take a while to be productive.

How PMO will apply this service

The PMO should look to create a welcome or induction pack for the project/program. This can then be used by the PMO when they are performing this service and it will give the new people something to refer back to. The induction pack needs to contain information that is typically found in a Project Initiation Document such as purpose, approach, timelines, organizational structure, risk, issue, change procedures and regular meetings they will be expected to help with. If the person joining is external and has not worked in the organization before then having a view about where to find things in the office will be useful.

Having got the welcome pack then the PMO can either just hand this over, or better still they can sit with the new person for 30 minutes to give an overview of the contents of the pack and answer any questions the person may have. They can then leave the pack with the individual for them to refer to afterwards.

Supplier	Input	Process	Output	Customer
PMO	Project/program overview Governance structure Organization structure	Induction	Trained individual	Project Team Program Team

How the PMO will measure the value of this service

This can be a difficult one to measure as the most effective measure is the length of time taken for the new person to be productive. However, if this service is being offered consistently then there is a no baseline to measure against.

This can be measured by seeing how many questions come from new staff members as opposed to existing staff members. If the induction has been done well these two groups should have the same number of questions.

Criteria when the PMO will use this service

- When there are new staff working for the project/program

Helpful hints for the PMO when delivering the service

- If you are developing a welcome pack, this will need to be kept up to date as the project/program progresses
- Consider tailoring the induction depending whether the new starter is contract or permanent
- Tailor the induction for new people to the organization to include information about where to find things in the office, the tools used, how to get computer access etc.
- If there are people on the project in multiple locations cover the best ways of communicating, especially if different time zones are involved
- Use this as the time to get the contact details from the new people and introduce yourself and how you can help them

PMO Capabilities needed to fulfil this service

Competencies	Techniques and generic tools
P3M Administration Governance Frameworks Personal Communication	Prompt Lists

Related services

Order office equipment and stationery Assist in the recruitment of program and project managers	Assist in the recruitment and evaluation of PMO team members

Facilities management

Service description

During an office move the PMO can be asked to pick up the co-ordination of desk spaces, crate moves, telephone changes, directory changes, health & safety updates. These activities can be done by anyone, but due to the organizational ability of the PMO it can be given for them to co-ordinate.

What the service provides for the customer

This will provide a central point of contact within the project or program team for the co-ordination of the office move. The rest of the team can focus on the delivery of the project or program.

Why is this service being offered to the customer?

This service will be offered in the absence of a dedicated person to perform this role. This service requires attention to detail, planning and co-ordination skills. All these are found in PMO staff.

How PMO will apply this service

The PMO will meet with the people from facilities who will perform the actual move and will work out what is being moved where. Together with facilities, the PMO will draw up a moving checklist which will show all items to be moved, their original locations and their new ones. This will list any specific requirements for furniture and equipment. Some of this may not be obvious, for example the ability to dial particular numbers (e.g. international) from a phone or to have phones in pick-up groups.

Once the moving checklist has been agreed it can be passed to facilities for them to execute the move. After the move has occurred the PMO will check that everything is working as expected and acts as a central coordination point to deal with queries.

Supplier	Input	Process	Output	Customer
Facilities	Moving checklist	Desk relocation Move equipment	New office location	Project team Program team

How the PMO will measure the value of this service

This will be judged a success if the move goes well, all the equipment is where it is expected to be, and people arrive ready to work at the new location.

Criteria when the PMO will use this service

- If there is an office move that requires coordination
- If there is no one else more qualified to perform this role

Helpful hints for the PMO when delivering the service

Ensure you work closely with the team who are actually going to be performing the move on the day. Work out who will be around on the first working day after the move has happened to ensure there are people there to sort out any issues. Make sure you communicate with the people being moved about what to pack, and what not to pack. Ensure that everything that should be labelled is labelled with the new desk locations. Be aware of any people being on holiday during the move period and ensure someone is able to move their kit. Let people know when they can expect to receive the boxes for them to pack, and when they need to have unpacked by. Have a way of dealing with unwanted equipment. Ensure there are plenty of bins available for people to divest themselves of unwanted paperwork.

PMO Capabilities needed to fulfil this service

Competencies	Techniques and generic tools
P3M Administration Information Management Planning and Scheduling Personal Communication Teamwork Resourcefulness	None

Provide a secretariat service for meetings

Service description

To ensure that the meeting runs smoothly and is documented for audit purposes the PMO will ensure that meetings are setup with a location (real or virtual), provide an agenda and minutes (actions) and distribute to all attendees and invitees.

What the service provides for the customer

This ensures for each meeting that the attendees will be provided with agenda in advance and get the minutes distributed afterwards. These minutes can be circulated wider if required according to the communication plan.

Why is this service being offered to the customer?

This service allows the recipient to delegate the details of the meeting and enable them to focus on the content of the meeting and ensuring the correct decisions are made.

How PMO will apply this service

There are several parts to this service: The PMO will need to speak to the recipient of the service and find out which part(s) they are required to do in advance.

Booking the meeting

Prior to the meeting the PMO will need to find out who is expected to attend. Which of those people can send deputies, who is required and who is optional? They need to find out the expected length of the meeting and preferred timeslot.

The meeting can then be booked. Either as a virtual meeting (conference call) or at a physical location. If doing a video conference, then it may be necessary to book a room in each location where that can occur.

The PMO will need to ensure they keep track of attendees and whether they are attending.

Preparing the agenda

The PMO will work with the chair of the meeting to pull together an agenda. This should be sent out to all attendees at least 24 hours prior to the meeting maybe more depending on the amount of pre-reading that is required for the meeting.

Preparing the pack

The PMO will work with the chair of the meeting to pull together a pack. This can be pulled from existing material that the PMO has access to, as well as asking for contributions from others. With the individual contributions the PMO will pull this together ensuring that the pack is put together in advance to allow for a draft to be reviewed and a final presentation before the meeting starts. In some circumstances the pack will need to be sent out with the agenda.

Attending the meeting

To write the minutes this bit is compulsory. There may be other things the PMO is required to do during the meeting such as escort guests to and from the meeting room, dial people in for audio and video conferences, or make sure any microphones/videos/presentations are working.

Writing the minutes

After the meeting, the PMO will draft a copy of the minutes. This should be sent to the chair of the meeting for them to ratify. Where actions have been captured the PMO need to ensure that there is a clear owner and date for each of these actions.

Distributing the minutes

Once the chair has ratified the minutes they can be distributed to all invitees of the meeting as well as the attendees. The PMO should consult the communications plan to see where else these minutes may need to be sent.

Supplier	Input	Process	Output	Customer
Project Managers Program Managers Portfolio Managers	Meeting Agenda Calendar Invite	Taking minutes Booking meetings Preparing steering group packs	Meeting Minutes Decision Log	Steering Groups Project Approval Board

How the PMO will measure the value of this service

A simple measure could be the number of times an agenda is not sent out 24 hours prior or the number of times minutes have not been drafted within 2 working days.

If the meeting is a regular one, then the PMO can observe whether the meeting becomes more efficient over time as a result of this service.

Criteria when the PMO will use this service

This service is typically offered by an embedded PMO working directly for a single project or program. It can be offered by a portfolio PMO when supporting the project approval board.

Helpful hints for the PMO when delivering the service

- Ensure you have a standard template for the agenda and minutes
- Provide an easy way of transferring any decisions into a decisions log
- Review whether the actions can be put straight into an action log, rather than tracking through meeting minutes

PMO Capabilities needed to fulfil this service

Competencies	Techniques and generic tools
P3M Administration Personal Communication	None

Related services

Set up meetings on behalf of others Coordinate the internal communication Provide a secretariat service for meetings Facilitate independent change impact assessment workshops Carry out a strategy formulation session	Attendance at steering groups Provide facilitation service Run lessons-learned workshops Support the Project Approval Board Facilitate stakeholder identification and communication workshops Facilitate independent issue analysis and resolution workshops

Order office equipment and stationery

Service description

The ordering of items of office equipment (e.g. IT kit) or stationery items for use by people within the project or program.

What the service provides for the customer

As a result of this service the person will have the necessary equipment, they need to perform their role.

Why is this service being offered to the customer?

On a large program there may be lots of resources being on boarded. Having a single point of contact to get the necessary equipment setup can assist and would allow the program manager to focus on the delivery of the program rather than just administration.

How PMO will apply this service

If the PMO is aware that there will be a new starter then they can review the equipment required for that role and use the internal ordering process to ensure that the IT equipment is available for the person to use when they start.

The PMO can ensure that any stationery requirements (pens, pads etc.) is obtained and waiting on the person's desk for them to arrive.

Supplier	Input	Process	Output	Customer
IT department Stationery company	Order form	Order IT equipment Order stationery	Stationery Office Equipment	Project Team Program Team

How the PMO will measure the value of this service

If the PMO are aware of the individuals starting, then the measurement should be the equipment being available prior to the person starting.

Criteria when the PMO will use this service

- When there is a large project or program with lots of people being onboarded
- Where there is a dedicated PMO to a single project or program

Helpful hints for the PMO when delivering the service

- PMO should consider having a reserve of stationery items for the use of the project or program
- Consider having a workshop box which contains all the stationery items required to run a workshop
- If the office equipment is not provided by the PMO but the recruiting/line manager, then the PMO may decide to offer reminders to them to ensure all items have been correctly ordered

PMO Capabilities needed to fulfil this service

Competencies	Techniques and generic tools
P3M Administration Personal Integrity and reliability Resourcefulness	Prompt Lists

Related services

On boarding and induction Provide facilitation service	Place and track small orders for portfolio, program, or project Assist in the recruitment and evaluation of PMO team members

Set up meetings on behalf of others

Service description

The booking of meetings including sending out calendar invites, booking the rooms and/or audio-visual conference booking.

What the service provides for the customer

This provides a one stop shop to getting a meeting scheduled.

Why is this service being offered to the customer?

In a busy project or program it can be difficult to find the time to get meetings booked. Having a dedicated resource to provide this can ensure the smoother running of the management team, especially for organizations with limited meeting space.

How PMO will apply this service

Having got the details of the meeting such as purpose, time, location, attendees, and a brief description of the meeting the PMO will look to arrange this. They will try to schedule the meeting with all the attendees at the preferred time/location. If this is not possible then they will look to see when the meeting could be arranged and go back with some alternatives. Hopefully one of those alternatives will be suitable and the meeting can be booked. The PMO will then send out the calendar invites to the attendees and ensure the meeting rooms get booked and it necessary any audio or video conference details.

Supplier	Input	Process	Output	Customer
Project Managers Program Managers Portfolio Managers	Meeting details	Booking meetings	Calendar Invites	Project Managers Program Managers Portfolio Managers

How the PMO will measure the value of this service

This can be measured by recording the numbers of meetings that the PMO is asked to book. Occasionally the person who has asked for the meeting to be arranged may say thank you.

Criteria when the PMO will use this service

- When there are lots of meetings that need booking
- When there is a dedicated PMO for the project or program

Helpful hints for the PMO when delivering the service

- Consider booking regular meetings in the diaries of people once this has been agreed for the project/program
- Have some details of external room providers who can offer rooms at short notice (obviously that will come at a cost)

PMO Capabilities needed to fulfil this service

Competencies	Techniques and generic tools
P3M Administration Personal Communication Resourcefulness Negotiation Result Orientation	None

Related services

Provide a secretariat service for meetings Arrange travel for other people Events management Trigger post-program or project reviews	Run lessons-learned workshops Work with internal audit to ensure compliance with audit requirements Assist in the recruitment of program and project managers Provide training logistics support

Arrange travel for other people

Service description

The booking of travel arrangements including accommodation, rail or plane tickets or the hiring of cars.

What the service provides for the customer

This provides a single point of contact to get travel booked. Tickets can be provided in advance and discounts can be obtained for group travel etc.

Why is this service being offered to the customer?

By the provision of this service the PMO can ensure that the travel costs are in line with company rules. By booking travel for contract resources they can save the company money by not getting sales tax (VAT) applied to the invoice from the contractor. The PMO is able to accrue for these costs as part of the finances for the project/program.

How PMO will apply this service

Having received a request for travel the PMO should re-acquaint themselves with the company policy for booking travel. The PMO then need to confirm where the travel is from and to as this maybe from an individual's home rather than from an office location. For early meetings it may be better to book an overnight stay prior to the meeting rather than travel on the same day. The PMO should then use the preferred mechanism for booking the travel (some companies have negotiated organizations to do this for them, others can go direct). Once this has been booked the details will be sent to the individual(s) requesting travel.

If there is a need for a visa, then the PMO will inform the individual and it will be up to them to provide this.

Supplier	Input	Process	Output	Customer
Project Team Program Team	Travel Request	Book travel	Travel Booking	Project Team Program Team

How the PMO will measure the value of this service

By reducing the cost of travel this offers value to the project or program. This can be measured as savings on the travel budget.

The value to individual is of less hassle involved in booking the travel and then claiming the money back. This can be measured by asking the individual whether they value this service.

Criteria when the PMO will use this service

- Where there is lots of travel required by the project or program
- When there is a dedicated PMO for the project or program

Helpful hints for the PMO when delivering the service

- For people who travel abroad frequently consider having the details of their passport to make booking easier
- When booking travel tickets see if there are cheaper ways to go e.g. later train, slower train, split tickets
- Check to see whether a group discount can be achieved

PMO Capabilities needed to fulfil this service

Competencies	Techniques and generic tools
P3M Administration Personal Communication Relationships and engagement Resourcefulness Negotiation	Prompt Lists

Related services

Set up meetings on behalf of others Control adherence to accounting procedures	Advise on cost control and opportunities for savings Provide training logistics support

Formatting documents

Service description

The reformatting of documentation to meet the correct (and latest) template.

On behalf of the project, program or portfolio manager ensure that the documentation meets the correct (and latest) template. This means changing the formatting of the documents (e.g. layout & font) to meet the standards.

What the service provides for the customer

It ensures that documents are transferred into the correct template to meet internal standards.

Why is this service being offered to the customer?

If there are good reasons why the information needs to be added into the latest template, then having the PMO will save the project or program manager time and effort.

How PMO will apply this service

The PMO will identify the need to transfer the document into the correct format. This can be that it was a supplier written document but needs to be transferred to internal templates for formal approval. It could be that in the correct format the document can be fitted into automated routines or consolidations.

Having identified the need the PMO will perform the reformatting. If the new template is sufficiently different from the version supplied the PMO will need to go back to the originator for clarifications.

Once the document has been reformatted then the PMO need to ensure that this replaces the previous version of the document. The PMO will send the reformatted back to the originator with instructions to use the updated version of the document in future.

Supplier	Input	Process	Output	Customer
Project Managers Program Managers Portfolio Managers	Unformatted Documentation Documentation standards	Reformatting documents	Formatted documentation	Project Managers Program Managers Portfolio Managers

How the PMO will measure the value of this service

If a document needs to be reformatted, then someone will have to perform this. Having the PMO do this rather than the originator may be a cheaper option.

Criteria when the PMO will use this service

- When there are advantages to be obtained by having the documents in the correct template
- Where there are documents that need to be transferred into the latest template

Helpful hints for the PMO when delivering the service

- Try to reduce the number of requests to transfer documents into the latest template
- Encourage the project and program managers to pick the current document template from a central location each time they need to create the document
- Ensure once the document has been transferred to the new format that it is sent back to originator and they use the reformatted document in future, otherwise the exercise may need to be repeated in future

PMO Capabilities needed to fulfil this service

Competencies	Techniques and generic tools
P3M Administration Change Control Information Management Quality Management Professionalism and ethics Personal Integrity and reliability Relationships and engagement Result Orientation	None

Related services

Review Business cases for compliance	Capture and categorize new ideas

Chase up missing timesheets

Service description

On behalf of the project or program manager chase those individuals who have not submitted a timesheet on time.

What the service provides for the customer

This ensures that everyone who is responsible for entering a timesheet by the deadline either has done so, or has been reminded to fill one in. This means that the actuals will include all time recorded and there will be no surprises later for late booked actuals. Any individual who has yet to fill in a timesheet will be asked to complete one and will be assisted to do so.

Actuals recorded against a timesheet can be compared against the expected estimate of time and the remainder of the effort re-planned as part of the regular review cycle.

Why is this service being offered to the customer?

As the PMO looks after the PPM tool (if there is one) they can produce compliance reports showing who has yet to submit a timesheet. Where timesheets are required without a PPM tool (e.g. for contractor time recording) then the PMO will review and check who has not filled those timesheets in.

How PMO will apply this service

The PMO will confirm who needs to fill in a timesheet, and how those timesheets are submitted. They will produce a report on a regular basis which shows those people who have yet to submit a timesheet. The PMO will endeavour to contact the individual directly and ask them to fill a timesheet in. Where the individual is absent, the PMO will speak to their line manager and ask them to complete it on their behalf.

If there are persistent offenders who regularly miss the timesheet submission deadline the PMO can put in reminders ahead of time or escalate that non-compliance through to their direct line manager.

Supplier	Input	Process	Output	Customer
PMO Supplier	Timesheet compliance report	Chase timesheets	Chased individuals	Project Manager Program Manager

How the PMO will measure the value of this service

This can be measured by an increase in the timesheet compliance statistics.

Criteria when the PMO will use this service

- Where timesheets are required to be filled in
- Where it is important that actuals are collected on time

Helpful hints for the PMO when delivering the service

- Incentives can be given for those individuals or teams who have a good submission record
- Look to provide some rules around who needs to submit a timesheet, why and by when
- It is more likely that the worst offenders will be permanent members of staff as contractors need to submit a timesheet to be paid, whereas permanent staff members are paid regardless of timesheet submission
- If acting as a supplier to another organization the timesheet may be required to enable invoicing to occur. If timesheets are late then invoicing may not occur losing the company money
- Ensure it is clear when timesheets are required to be submitted and that is communicated when a person joins the organization
- If there are any changes to timesheet deadlines e.g. for public / national holidays or financial cut-offs, ensure this is clearly communicated in advance

PMO Capabilities needed to fulfil this service

Competencies	Techniques and generic tools
P3M Administration Information Management Reporting, Insights and Analysis P3M Tools Personal Communication Relationships and engagement Resourcefulness Negotiation Result Orientation	Categorized frequency analysis (Frequency plot, bar chart) Project Management Information System

Related services

Monitor and report on financial spend Manage invoicing processing for portfolio, programs, and projects	Prepare monthly financial reports

Benefits Management

Benefits Management

Description

Ensures that a consistent 'fit for purpose' approach to benefits and value management is applied across the portfolio or program and that benefits realization is optimized from the organization's investment in change.

What the services within the area provide for the customer

Having a consistent way of identifying and tracking benefits provides the program or portfolio manager reassurance that the projects and programs will deliver the value that the customer is expecting. Providing the structure ensures consistency in the approach to benefits management within the organization for the senior management. They ensure that the benefits being claimed are realistic and have a mechanism in place for tracking them.

Helpful hints for when the PMO is delivering this service area

- Ensure you link up with the finance department to ensure that benefits are properly recorded
- Look to develop a means of tracking different benefits by linking into the current recording mechanisms e.g. if tracking customer satisfaction link up with the sales department who may already be tracking this metric
- By providing the templates and standards it will be able to ensure consistency as you can control the benefit types and what can be claimed
- Consider how long you want to track the benefits of a project or program once it has finished
- Understand that there will be some enabling or mandatory projects for which tracking benefits is not possible

Benefits Management Design

Service group description

The setup of the benefits management standards, templates, processes and guidelines for the portfolio or program.

List of related services described in other areas

Develop Business Case process and templates
Automate Processes

Responsibility Assignment Matrix

Service	Executive	Portfolio Manager	Program Manager	Project Manager	PMO	Sponsor	Other Stakeholder
Develop benefits management framework	A	C	I	I	R	I	
Establish a benefit-variance escalation process		A	C		R	I	

Helpful hints for when the PMO is delivering this Service Group

- When developing the framework consider how this will fit in not only with the portfolio and program methodologies, but in with the business areas who have to deliver on the benefits. Consider how these will be tracked

Develop benefits management framework

Service description

Develop a benefits management framework consisting of process, procedures, standards, templates, help and tools.

What the service provides for the customer

This provides the program and portfolio managers with a set of templates and standards for benefits to be identified and tracked consistently, allowing projects and programs to be compared on an equal footing.

It provides a framework for the portfolio manager to enable benefits to be tracked after program closure.

Why is this service being offered to the customer?

It allows the program manager to codify what benefits will be delivered for their program. These can then be rolled up at portfolio level and the portfolio manager can see how each of the items within the portfolio will contribute to the overall benefits.

How PMO will apply this service

The PMO will review the external guidance on how to track benefits and will look to tailor this for their organization. The PMO should look to see the types of benefits that are applicable for their organization and this will then be codified, providing a benefit definition, a standard way that these benefits can be tracked. This will be built into the business case. Working with finance to ensure that they are able to provide a way to measure the financial side. Consideration should be given to how non-financial benefits will be considered, whether they will be given a nominal cost or treated separately.

The PMO will propose a process and procedures for identifying benefits, codifying the benefits, putting measures in place and KPIs to track the benefits through the program's life and finally tracking and reporting the benefits after the program has finished.

The PMO will provide templates for benefit profiles and ways to summarizing this information into consistent reporting.

Supplier	Input	Process	Output	Customer
PMO	Standards template	Develop Standard Develop Templates	Business Case Benefit drivers list Benefits realization plan template Benefits Management strategy template Benefits Management process	Project Managers Program Managers Portfolio Managers Project Approval Board

How the PMO will measure the value of this service

The value of this service is most easily measured by being able to report on the total expected benefit of the portfolio. Without the consistency that this service offered being able to report on the overall benefits will be difficult if not impossible to do.

Criteria when the PMO will use this service

- When the organization wish to be able to track benefits
- When the organization which to have business case consistency
- As part of developing a portfolio or program methodology

Helpful hints for the PMO when delivering the service

- Ask around the organization to find out how people are tracking benefits currently and see if those can be incorporated as standard tracking mechanisms
- Start with the basic way of recording and capturing the benefits, complexity can be added later
- Look to provide worked examples of the templates – not only do people have something to compare against, but it allows you to see whether the template will work in real world usage
- Look to trial any new templates or procedures out on a single program before distributing it to a wider audience
- Look to consolidate the questions (with the relevant answers) you get into a help document to accompany the process and templates

PMO Capabilities needed to fulfil this service

Competencies	Techniques and generic tools
Benefits and Value Management Business Case Information Management Delivery Methods Governance Frameworks	Cost/ Benefit Analysis Benefit realization analysis Flowcharts Proposal evaluation system Swim-lane flowcharts

Related services

Establish a benefit-variance escalation process Facilitate agreement of the program benefits documents Track and report on benefit realization Review post-program benefits against strategic investment decisions Review Business cases for compliance Define, maintain, and implement standard PPM framework Develop and maintain tailoring guidelines for standards, methods, and approaches	Identify duplicate and double counting of benefits Develop Business Case process and templates Develop and refine portfolio, program, or project business cases Manage the Process Improvement Plan Map key value streams and processes

Further Reading

Benefit Realisation Management: A Practical Guide to Achieving Benefits Through Change Gerald Bradley
Managing benefits: optimizing the return from investments Steve Jenner

Establish a benefit-variance escalation process

Service description

Establish a set of rules or guidance for when variances to benefits for a program or a portfolio will be escalated and who they will be escalated to.

What the service provides for the customer

Guidance (in advance) for when variances to benefits need to be escalated to the next level of management.

Why is this service being offered to the customer?

This enables the program or portfolio manager to understand what they will need to do if the benefits exceed the tolerances set. They can then put in place mechanisms for checking these variances as the program or portfolio progresses.

For the portfolio manager or executive, it allows for deviations from expected benefits to be reported up to a sufficient level to allow for corrections to be made to program delivery. Able to understand the impact of changes on the cost/benefit validity of the project or program. Allows for remedial actions to be taken whilst there is time to rectify the situation.

How PMO will apply this service

The PMO will work with the portfolio manager to establish some criteria by which changes to benefits can be judged. This will typically be a percentage based and is linked into the Red, Amber, Green reporting for a program report. An example of this would be a negative variance of under 5% would be Green, between 5% and 10% would be Amber and about 10% would be Red. The Amber items would need to be escalated to the portfolio manager and the Red items up to the portfolio board.

Supplier	Input	Process	Output	Customer
PMO Portfolio Manager	Standards template	Develop Standard	Benefits variance escalation standard	Business Department Project Approval Board

How the PMO will measure the value of this service

The PMO can monitor the numbers of projects or programs requiring escalating.

Criteria when the PMO will use this service

- When there is a portfolio board and /or a portfolio manager to escalate the variance to
- When the organization is looking to track benefits (as opposed just including them in a business case)

Helpful hints for the PMO when delivering the service

- It may be that an absolute number is used in conjunction with the percentage. A negative variance of more than x or 10% whichever is the greater get reported
- Think about how you want to report positive variances. Do these need to be escalated separately
- How will projects which have mostly non-financial benefits be reviewed and tracked

PMO Capabilities needed to fulfil this service

Competencies	Techniques and generic tools
Benefits and Value Management Reporting, Insights and Analysis Delivery Methods Governance Frameworks	Benefit realization analysis Performance variance report Stakeholder engagement assessment matrix Task responsibility matrix/RACI

Related services

Develop benefits management framework Track and report on benefit realization	Facilitate agreement of the program benefits documents

Benefits Management Operations

Service group description

Reviewing benefits identified within a program or project ensuring they can be measured and there are no duplicates or overlaps with other business cases within the portfolio.

List of related services described in other areas

Develop and refine portfolio, program, or project business cases

Responsibility Assignment Matrix

Service	Executive	Portfolio Manager	Program Manager	Project Manager	PMO	Sponsor	Other Stakeholder
Facilitate agreement of the program benefits documents	C	I	C	I	R	A	C (Business area managers)
Identify duplicate and double counting of benefits		A	I	I	R	I	
Review Business cases for compliance		I	A	A	R	C	

Helpful hints for when the PMO is delivering this Service Group

- It is possible to deliver both of these services together. They have been listed separately as they could be done in different PMO

Facilitate agreement of the program benefits documents

Service description

On behalf of the program manager get agreement between the program, the Sponsor, and the business areas responsible for achieving the benefits that the benefits listed in the business case (or benefit profile) can be delivered.

What the service provides for the customer

This service provides the program manager with the agreement that the benefits can be delivered by each of the relevant business areas.

Why is this service being offered to the customer?

Getting agreement from each of the business areas can be time consuming. The PMO can do this on behalf of the program manager allowing them to focus on the delivery of the program, which will enable the outputs to deliver the outcomes and measured as benefits.

How PMO will apply this service

For each of the benefits listed in the business case the PMO will, in conjunction with the program manager, identify the business area responsible for delivery of that benefit. Between the sponsor, the program manager and the PMO a named individual will be identified to represent that business area, and hence the benefit delivery. The PMO will approach that person, or their delegate and get them to agree to the delivery of the benefit. This may require some negotiation and if necessary, a benefits workshop may be called to resolve any conflicts.

Supplier	Input	Process	Output	Customer
Program Manager	Benefits management strategy Benefit profiles Benefits realization plan	Obtain agreement	Agreed Benefits management strategy Agreed Benefit profiles Agreed Benefits realization plan	Program Manager Sponsor

How the PMO will measure the value of this service

This service can only be measured by counting which areas have agreed benefit profiles and which ones do not. The aim being for 100% compliance.

Criteria when the PMO will use this service

- When the PMO is dedicated to a single program
- When the business case is initially written
- When the benefits have changed significantly

Helpful hints for the PMO when delivering the service

- If there is difficulty in gaining agreement, then call a facilitated benefits workshop and get agreement via the workshop
- Alternatively find someone more senior to get agreement with so the person responsible has to do it because they have been told to
- Get the Sponsor to help with arbitrations around benefit delivery

PMO Capabilities needed to fulfil this service

Competencies	Techniques and generic tools
Benefits and Value Management Information Management Stakeholder Engagement Personal Communication Relationships and engagement Resourcefulness Negotiation Result Orientation	Cost/ Benefit Analysis Benefit realization analysis

Related services

Establish a benefit-variance escalation process Develop benefits management framework	Review post-program benefits against strategic investment decisions

Identify duplicate and double counting of benefits

Service description

On behalf of relevant governance boards assess benefits planning and realization across several programs or projects within the portfolio to identify gaps, overlaps and conflicts and to eliminate double counting in the benefits plan of individual programs and projects.

What the service provides for the customer

This provides the portfolio manager with an assurance that benefits are not being duplicated across multiple projects.

It ensures that there are ways that each of the benefits in a business case can be tracked, which will enable the benefits tracking service to operate post benefit delivery.

Why is this service being offered to the customer?

If there are duplicated benefits, then the total benefits for the portfolio are being artificially inflated. The delivery of this service will ensure that all benefits are unique and can be accumulated to give an overall benefit position for the portfolio.

How PMO will apply this service

The PMO will accept the new business case to review. For each of the benefits being claimed they will look to see which business area is claiming the benefit. They will look at the business cases for all active projects within the portfolio to find out which of the other projects are claiming a similar benefit. For each of the similar benefits check whether they are actually the same – this can be done by speaking the business area concerned. If they are the same, then alert the portfolio manager or the project approval board of the duplication. It will be for them to deal with the issue.

Supplier	Input	Process	Output	Customer
Project Managers Program Managers	Business cases	Benefits Review	Benefits realization plan	Project Approval Board Portfolio Managers

How the PMO will measure the value of this service

The PMO can measure the numbers of business cases received with duplicated benefits. Over time this number should reduce.

Criteria when the PMO will use this service

- When there is a benefits framework in place
- When the portfolio manager wants to count the benefits for an entire portfolio
- When the organization wants to ensure clarity of benefits being claimed for the portfolio

Helpful hints for the PMO when delivering the service

- Be prepared for project and program managers to claim they have no duplication as they are interested in getting their business case approved
- Does the organization really want to know they are artificially inflating the benefits claimed? Or do they want to remain in ignorance?
- Have a repository of all the business cases for all approved projects to refer back to
- Ensure the repository has an easy way of classifying benefits by business area/budget centre, not just by area submitting the business case. It may be that a project run for one department has benefits for another department
- If you add up the cost savings for all the projects in the portfolio, are they greater than the cost of the area? For example, if you have 10 projects claiming half an FTE saving, but you only have 4 people in the area concerned then you will be able to run this with minus one person. This does not seem possible, so something is wrong somewhere
- The PMO can only highlight issues with benefits being duplicated, they are not able to actually resolve the problem. That will be the responsibility of the portfolio manager or project approval board

PMO Capabilities needed to fulfil this service

Competencies	Techniques and generic tools
Benefits and Value Management Business Case Assurance Professionalism and ethics Personal Integrity and reliability Conflict and Crisis	Cost/ Benefit Analysis Benefit realization analysis Document Analysis

Related services

Review Business cases for compliance Develop benefits management framework	Review post-program benefits against strategic investment decisions Develop Business Case process and templates

Review Business cases for compliance

Service description

Review Business Cases to ensure that the benefits are aligned to standard capture mechanisms and are aligned to benefits processes. Ensure that all benefit types are considered.

What the service provides for the customer

This is a sense check on the benefits part of the business case ensuring that all benefits listed are measurable using standard measures. Where these are not aligned the PMO can suggest different benefits that may be easier to quantify. The PMO will confirm that all the different benefit types have been considered and will suggest additional benefits that could be claimed.

Why is this service being offered to the customer?

This provides a second pair of eyes on the business case. Having this independent review ensures that all the benefits are valid and that no valid benefits have been missed.

How PMO will apply this service

The PMO will familiarize themselves with the benefits framework, in particular having a look at the benefit types and how they are tracked. They will then examine the business case and check for the following:

- Are all the benefits listed in line with the benefit types listed in the framework?
- Is there a standard measurement already available to track this benefit?
- If there is no measurement already available will the program create one?
- Have any benefits been missed?
- Are all the benefits achievable? Is the timescale for the benefits correct, will they start immediately, or will it require a ramp up period?
- Are the business areas responsible for delivering the benefits in agreement with the figures published in the business case?

The PMO will then feedback what they have found along with the potential corrections back to the project or program manager in order they are able to fix any issues prior to the business case being submitted.

Supplier	Input	Process	Output	Customer
Project Manager Program Manager	Business Cases Benefits standards	Business case review	Business Cases	Portfolio Manager Project Approval Board

How the PMO will measure the value of this service

The PMO can measure this service by counting the number of business cases which are subsequently rejected or queried because of issues with the benefits.

Criteria when the PMO will use this service

- When requested to review a business case by the project or program manager
- When there is a standard benefits framework that can be used to evaluate the business cases against

Helpful hints for the PMO when delivering the service

- If a business case gets revised, then this service can be offered again
- Dig to see if you can find what the assumptions are that the benefits have been built on. Check for flaws in the assumptions
- Check to see the baseline that the benefits are going to increase/decrease against. Does that make the benefits still valid? For example, if a 10% uplift in customer satisfaction is promised is that against a baseline of 30% or 80%. Against a baseline of 30% would seem easier to achieve

PMO Capabilities needed to fulfil this service

Competencies	Techniques and generic tools
Benefits and Value Management Business Case Information Management Personal Integrity and reliability Conflict and Crisis	Document Analysis Gap analysis Prompt Lists Check sheets

Related services

Identify duplicate and double counting of benefits Develop benefits management framework Review post-program benefits against strategic investment decisions	Formatting documents Develop Business Case process and templates Develop and refine portfolio program, or project business cases

Benefits Realization Monitoring

Service group description

Tracking and review of benefits on behalf of programs and the portfolio.

List of related services described in other areas

Feedback to senior management on the success of strategic initiatives
Reporting results linked to organizational strategy

Responsibility Assignment Matrix

Service	Executive	Portfolio Manager	Program Manager	Project Manager	PMO	Sponsor	Other Stakeholder
Review post-program benefits against strategic investment decisions	A	I			R	A	
Track and report on benefit realization	A	I			R		

Helpful hints for when the PMO is delivering this Service Group

- These services require a way of measuring each of the benefits. If a standard measure is not in place the measure needs to have been developed by the project or program during its life and handed over as one of the deliverables. For the standard measures consult the benefits framework

Review post-program benefits against strategic investment decisions

Service description

The checking of the actual benefit delivery against the planned delivery listed in the business case. Answering the question did the project/program deliver as expected?

What the service provides for the customer

This provides feedback to the portfolio manager and project approval board of the actual success of a project or program as measured by benefits delivered.

Why is this service being offered to the customer?

Reviewing the actual benefits against the business case and strategy allows the organization to understand whether the project and programs were as successful as they had predicted.

There may be further work to identify why the benefits delivered were different and to initiate any new projects/programs to deliver any deficit in benefits.

How PMO will apply this service

The PMO will get the business case for the project or program they are evaluating. They will then have a look at the benefit tracker for that project or program. They will compare the difference between the two.

Where there are discrepancies can these be attributed to a timing issue? i.e. were the benefits delivered a few months late just because the project delivered a few months late?

If the discrepancies cannot be explained as a timing issue, then the PMO should see whether anything can be done to accelerate the delivery, or will these gaps remain (or even get worse). This can be done by speaking to the benefit owner within the business area and getting their view on the matter.

With the information on the success or otherwise of the benefits delivery the PMO should prepare a report for the portfolio manager for them to take to the project approval board. This would include some statistics about how much the actual benefits differ from the projected benefits and any recommendations either for specific projects to rectify deficiencies or more generally for the project approval board to consider when approving future projects.

Supplier	Input	Process	Output	Customer
Project Managers Program Managers Finance Strategy	Business cases Benefits realization plan Individual benefit tracker Strategic plan	Benefits Realization	Benefits realization plan	Project Approval Board Portfolio Managers Strategy

How the PMO will measure the value of this service

The PMO can measure this by asking the portfolio manager or project approval board whether this is a service they value. It could be measured by seeing the numbers of projects that are initiated as a result of benefit actual vs planned gaps.

Criteria when the PMO will use this service

- When the organization has a strategic plan
- When there are business cases for each project
- When the portfolio manager or project approval board want to understand how well projects and programs have done
- When benefits are being tracked post project delivery

Helpful hints for the PMO when delivering the service

- Ensure that you have the latest approved version of the business case to evaluate against
- Ensure you have the copy of the strategic plan that was in place when the project was approved as well as the current strategic plan

PMO Capabilities needed to fulfil this service

Competencies	Techniques and generic tools
Benefits and Value Management Business Case Reporting, Insights and Analysis	Cost/ Benefit Analysis Benefit realization analysis Business value Analysis categorized frequency analysis (Frequency plot, bar chart) Performance variance report

Related services

Facilitate agreement of the program benefits documents Identify duplicate and double counting of benefits Review Business cases for compliance	Track and report on benefit realization Develop benefits management framework Feedback to senior management on the success of strategic initiatives

Track and report on benefit realization

Service description

The tracking of benefits on behalf of the program after the program or individual projects within the program have finished.

What the service provides for the customer

A central point for benefits tracking on behalf of the program or portfolio.

Why is this service being offered to the customer?

To ensure that benefits are tracked as part of a program this can be delegated to the PMO. Once a program has finished either the benefits can be tracked by the benefit owner or they can be tracked centrally by the PMO on behalf of the portfolio manager. It provides a way of then reporting on the benefits achieved for the portfolio.

How PMO will apply this service

For each of the projects that get delivered (and closed) within a program or for completed programs the PMO will be given the benefit profiles. This will list the benefits that are needing to be tracked and the mechanism by which they can be tracked. On a regular basis (normally monthly) the PMO will follow the instructions within the benefit profiles to measure the benefits. This information will then be consolidated so that an overall benefit measure can be produced for the portfolio as a whole.

Supplier	Input	Process	Output	Customer
Project Manager Program Manager	Benefit profiles Benefits realization plan	Benefits Realization	Benefits realization plan	Project Manager Program Manager

How the PMO will measure the value of this service

The PMO will be able to measure this service by reporting on the benefits delivered by the portfolio on a regular basis.

Criteria when the PMO will use this service

- When there is a portfolio manager that is interested in reviewing the delivery of the benefits
- Where there is a standard way of recording benefits
- Where benefits can be tracked within the organization

Helpful hints for the PMO when delivering the service

- Ensure that you have access to the benefit capture systems. If you do not have direct access, then build a set of contacts who can provide the information on a regular basis
- As projects close check to see that they have written some benefit profiles, or at least there is a way of knowing what benefits are due and how to track them
- Consider developing a template to enable benefits to be tracked in a consistent manner
- If possible, see if you can attribute the benefit back to the project or program that delivered it. This will assist when tracking the effectiveness of each project or program

PMO Capabilities needed to fulfil this service

Competencies	Techniques and generic tools
Benefits and Value Management Information Management Reporting, Insights and Analysis Teamwork Negotiation	Benefit realization analysis Trend Analysis categorized frequency analysis (Frequency plot, bar chart) Performance variance report Time series plots

Related services

Develop benefits management framework Review post-program benefits against strategic investment decisions Trigger post-program or project reviews Establish a benefit-variance escalation process	Set up and track portfolio, program, and project metrics (KPI's) Increase in accuracy of Profit & Loss & balance sheets Feedback to senior management on the success of strategic initiatives Provision of Management Dashboards

Capability Management

Capability Management

Description

Ensures current and future programs and projects are equipped with enough staff of the right skills.

What the services within the area provide for the customer

These provide the organisation an understanding of the capabilities required it to deliver the project and programs. This can allow the organization to develop staff into the roles thereby reducing costs from recruiting expensive short-term contract resource.

Helpful hints for when the PMO is delivering this service area

- Define a standard set of roles to track capability against

Capability Design

Service group description

Defining the roles and job descriptions for PPM staff. Providing a structure to enable skills to be assessed and improved.

List of related services described in other areas

Create and maintain PMO career paths
Develop and maintain PMO role profiles
Develop and maintain a PMO competence framework

Responsibility Assignment Matrix

Service	Executive	Portfolio Manager	Program Manager	Project Manager	PMO	Sponsor	Other Stakeholder
Provide standard role descriptions for PPM staff	A	C	C	C	R		
Define a process for selection of key PPM roles	A	R	R	R	C		
Define strategy for acquiring and developing skills	A	C	C	C	R		
Develop and maintain a PM Competence Framework	A		C	C	R		

Helpful hints for when the PMO is delivering this service group

- It can be more cost effective to promote and develop staff from within the organization rather than recruit from outside
- Look to liaise with the HR department to ensure that HR rules are adhered to when developing staff

Provide standard role descriptions for PPM staff

Service description

The writing of role descriptions for PPM staff including project, program, and portfolio managers.

What the service provides for the customer

This ensures there is consistency in what is expected from people performing the role. These role descriptions can then be used to recruit individuals to those roles.

Why is this service being offered to the customer?

As experts in PPM the PMO are able to create standard role descriptions for the main PPM roles. This will ensure that the people performing those roles have some guidelines as to what is expected of them.

How PMO will apply this service

The PMO will speak with HR to find the standard role description template. They will speak with the PPM staff who are performing this role to find out what behaviours, soft skills and training requirements are needed for the role. The PMO will examine the good practice manuals to see if they can find an example job description for the role.

The PMO will write up the role description using the template provided. They will confirm this with some senior individuals who are performing the role. Once they are happy that the role covers what people do then the PMO will send the role to HR for assessment. Once the assessment has been done and the role is signed off by HR, then the PMO can circulate this as required. They can make this available for when people are being recruited into the role.

Supplier	Input	Process	Output	Customer
HR	Role description template	Writing role descriptions	Role description	PPM Staff

How the PMO will measure the value of this service

This can be measured by evaluating the individuals performing those roles against the role profiles.

Criteria when the PMO will use this service

- If there are no standard role profiles written
- If the project management community are unable to write them themselves
- If a role profile is needed to recruit new individuals
- If the PMO needs to assess PPM individuals against a standard role description

Helpful hints for the PMO when delivering the service

- Speak to the people performing the role to confirm what the particulars of the role should be
- Use the external contacts the PMO has to see if you can find examples from other organizations
- Use job boards to see what other companies include in job role descriptions
- Do not get involved in job grading. Leave that to HR

PMO Capabilities needed to fulfil this service

Competencies	Techniques and generic tools
Capability Development Relationships and engagement	Organization charts & position descriptions

Related services

Define a process for selection of key PPM roles Define strategy for acquiring and developing skills Ensure HR practices and procedures are aligned to Agree a project management certification process Provide succession planning service for key roles	Assist in the recruitment of program and project managers Develop and maintain PMO role profiles Create and maintain PMO career paths Develop and maintain a PM Competence Framework Assess PMs against a Competence Framework

Further Reading

PRINCE2
Managing Successful Programmes (MSP)
PMI PMBoK (A Guide to the Project Management Body of Knowledge)
Praxis

Define a process for selection of key PPM roles

Service description

The creation of an interview pack to be used to recruit PPM individuals.

What the service provides for the customer

An interview pack including timing, interview questions, interview scenario and sample answers.

Why is this service being offered to the customer?

By defining a standard recruitment pack for the various levels of PPM role it allows for candidates to be interviewed fairly and gets improved standard of PPM individuals within the organization.

How PMO will apply this service

The PMO will speak to HR to find out their guidance around recruiting individuals, including any competency questions. They will look to see whether there are any existing questions that are being used. They will look to create a scenario based on a situation that is occurring within the organization currently. They will provide a suggested answer to the scenario.

The PMO will collate the questions, these will include competency-based questions as well as technical questions and career direction questions. They will provide a suggested timetable for interview to allow enough time for the questions, scenario, presentation (of the scenario answer) and any questions the interviewee may have.

The PMO will then make the pack available to the relevant resource managers.

Supplier	Input	Process	Output	Customer
HR PMO	Role profiles	Develop interview pack	PPM question set Interview pack Interview Scenarios	HR Resource managers

How the PMO will measure the value of this service

This can be measured in the quality of the individuals being recruited into the organization.

Criteria when the PMO will use this service

- When there are new people needing to be recruited
- Where there is no existing selection material

Helpful hints for the PMO when delivering the service

- Consider having a set of questions for telephone interviews as well as face to face interviews
- Consider having different questions for temporary individuals than permanent
- Find out what the agreed behaviours are for the organization and have some competency questions in the pack which draw out these behaviours
- The suggested answer to the scenario may not be a complete answer, but may just contain the list of points that the individual is expected to raise in their answer
- Suggest that the scenario is 'road tested' to find out whether someone currently doing the role could answer it in the time provided

PMO Capabilities needed to fulfil this service

Competencies	Techniques and generic tools
Capability Development Relationships and engagement Resourcefulness	None

Related services

Provide standard role descriptions for PPM staff Work with HR to provide a sourcing strategy Assist in the recruitment of program and project managers Assist in the recruitment and evaluation of PMO team members	Facilitate the management of consultants and interims contracts Provide succession planning service for key roles Ensure HR practices and procedures are aligned to Allocate resources directly to a program or project

Define strategy for acquiring and developing skills

Service description

The creation and maintenance of a strategy for skills development.

What the service provides for the customer

This provides an approach to the training and development of individuals within the department. Being aligned to the strategy ensures that the training is focused on skills that enable the strategy to be delivered, rather than just on skills that would just benefit the individual. It ensures the training budget is spent in the most effective way.

Why is this service being offered to the customer?

The PMO are central to the PPM delivery. They have connections with the strategy department to obtain the strategy. The PMO can develop the strategy, to cover external training and PMO provided internal training. The PMO can provide the coordination role required to ensure the training strategy gets delivered.

How PMO will apply this service

The PMO will obtain the strategic plan from the strategy department. They will speak with the training department to find out the list of available training, both internal and external. The PMO will speak to finance to find out the amount of monies set aside for training. The PMO will speak to the resource managers to find out the training requirements for their staff.

The PMO will then develop a plan for each of those individuals to attend the training. Where there is higher demand than available budget the PMO will check to see which skills, are required the most to deliver the strategy and prioritize accordingly.

Once the development plan has been produced the PMO will communicate that out to the resource managers and will start to get individuals booked on the relevant training courses.

Supplier	Input	Process	Output	Customer
HR PMO Training / Learning & Development department Strategy department Finance	Competency Framework Training catalogue Strategic plan Training Budget	Develop organizational training strategy	Organizational strategic training needs	Resource Managers Training / Learning & Development department HR

How the PMO will measure the value of this service

This can be measured by checking that all the training budget is assigned. It can be measured by assessing individuals against a competency framework to see if the training has had the desired effect.

Criteria when the PMO will use this service

- When there is a centralized budget for training
- Where there is higher demand for training than available budget
- Where the organization wishes to get the most out of their training budget
- When the PMO is permanent

Helpful hints for the PMO when delivering the service

- Look to see if savings can be made on training courses by getting a group discount
- See if courses can be run in-house rather than have an external course (would save on travel expenses)
- Look for alternatives to training courses such as webinars, attendance at conferences & meetups, subscription to professional organizations

PMO Capabilities needed to fulfil this service

Competencies	Techniques and generic tools
P3M Administration Financial Management Supplier Management Capability Development Professionalism and ethics Personal Integrity and reliability Personal Communication Relationships and engagement Leadership Teamwork Result Orientation	Alternatives analysis Alternatives generation Decision tree analysis Cost/ Benefit Analysis Business value Analysis Capability and Capacity analysis

Related services

Develop and maintain a PM Competence Framework Work with HR to provide a sourcing strategy Provide PPM training Provide training logistics support Identify skills shortages and recommend suitable development Assess PMs against a Competence Framework Perform organizational PPM maturity assessments Perform coaching of portfolio, program, or project managers	Promote good PPM within the organization External networking attendance at good practice events Develop external relationships to share lessons and experience Provide standard role descriptions for PPM staff Agree a project management certification process Provide succession planning service for key roles Organize buddy relationships and secondments Ensure HR practices and procedures are aligned to Create and maintain PMO career paths Develop individuals within the PMO team

Develop and maintain a PM Competence Framework

Service description

The creation and maintenance of a competence framework for project, program, and portfolio managers.

What the service provides for the customer

A framework to allow an objective assessment of the role of a project, program, or portfolio manager. This will cover knowledge as well as experience. It covers personal, process and technical skill areas.

Why is this service being offered to the customer?

Having a competence framework allows the organization and the individuals to assess how good they are at performing their role. Having the standard to evaluate against means it become and objective assessment rather than a subjective one. By seeing where an individual's strengths and weaknesses allows for training to be targeted. It allows for assignments to fit the individual's strengths and development needs.

How PMO will apply this service

The PMO will obtain a copy of the role profiles for the project, program, and portfolio manager roles. They will find and evaluate the different external competence frameworks to see which one is best aligned to the organization.

If there are multiple levels of each role e.g. junior project manager, project manager, senior project manager. The PMO will align each of these roles with the competence levels so it is clear what level of competence is required to perform at each of the levels.

If there are any competencies that are deemed as missing (e.g. behavioural ones) then the PMO should look to add those in and provide some definitions for each of the levels.

Once the framework has been produced then the PMO should look to start assessing individuals against the framework.

Supplier	Input	Process	Output	Customer
Professional organizations PMO/HR	External competence frameworks Role profiles	Develop competence framework	Competence framework	PPM Managers HR

How the PMO will measure the value of this service

This can be measured by being able to evaluate the members of the project management community to target training and assignments.

Criteria when the PMO will use this service

- When there is a desire for improvement in the way projects are run in the organization
- When there is a permanent PMO
- When the project management community are not providing this for themselves

Helpful hints for the PMO when delivering the service

- If possible, look to take an existing framework rather than create from scratch
- Align the framework chosen to the organization. This can include providing scoring for the organizational behaviours
- Link into the role profiles in order that it is clear what levels people need to be to perform each role. This links into career development
- Provide a link to training in order that people can see what they can do to improve either their knowledge or their experience

PMO Capabilities needed to fulfil this service

Competencies	Techniques and generic tools
Capability Development Leadership Result Orientation	Capability and Capacity analysis Check sheets

Related services

Provide standard role descriptions for PPM staff Agree a project management certification process Provide PPM training Identify skills shortages and recommend suitable development Assess PMs against a Competence Framework Develop and maintain a PM Competence Framework	Create and maintain PMO career paths Assess PMOs against a Competence Framework Perform organizational PPM maturity assessments Define strategy for acquiring and developing skills Ensure HR practices and procedures are aligned to

Further Reading

APM Competence framework
IPMA Competence baseline
PMI - Project Manager Competency Development (PMCD) Framework

Capability Operations

Service group description

The recruitment and training of individuals ensuring the individuals with the correct skills can be deployed on the projects and programs. This covers both permanent and contract resource deployment.

List of related services described in other areas

Perform mentoring and coaching of PMO staff
Ensure Continuing Professional Development of the PMO team
Assess PMOs against a Competence Framework
Develop individuals within the PMO team
Monitors the performance of individual team members and the team as a whole
Assist in the recruitment and evaluation of PMO team members

Responsibility Assignment Matrix

Service	Executive	Portfolio Manager	Program Manager	Project Manager	PMO	Sponsor	Other Stakeholder
Agree a project management certification process	A				R		C (HR)
Capture the resource requirements of portfolio, programs, and projects		A	A	A	R		
Work with HR to provide a sourcing strategy	A				R		C (HR)
Facilitate the management of consultants and interims contracts	A				R		C (HR)
Provide 'help squads' for projects and programs			C	C	A, R		
Provide succession planning service for key roles	A		C	C	R		
Assist in the recruitment of program and project managers	A	R	R		C		
Provide PPM training					A, R		
Provide training logistics support					A, R		
Organize buddy relationships and secondments	A		C	C	R		C (PPM team)
Identify skills shortages and recommend suitable development	A	C	C	C	R		
Assess PMs against a Competence Framework	A		C	C	R		
Maintain resource database					A, R		

Agree a project management certification process

Service description

Prior to the assignment of individuals as project and program managers, ensure they have the correct level of knowledge and experience to perform the role.

What the service provides for the customer

This provides the sponsor with a level of reassurance that the person asked to run the project or program is capable of performing the role.

Why is this service being offered to the customer?

As the PMO is independent they can ensure that the certification is objective. The assessment may be done against a competence framework, it may be done via external PPM qualifications, or it can be done via an internal accreditation scheme.

How PMO will apply this service

The PMO will decide on how they are going to perform the assessment, what criteria will be used. If there is a PM competence framework the PMO will use that to do the assessment. If there is no framework in place then the PMO will use the external qualifications e.g. PMP, APMP, PRINCE2 etc. to decide what level of complexity that each person can manage. It may be possible for an individual who has had lesser experience/knowledge to manage a more complex project, but then guidance/mentoring should be available from a more experienced member of the PPM community.

Once the PMO have decided on the assessment criteria they should publish this. As each new project or program gets approved the PMO should suggest the level required to manage that piece of work.

Supplier	Input	Process	Output	Customer
PMO	Project Management Framework	Certify project managers	Certification Accreditation	Project Manager Program Manager Sponsor

How the PMO will measure the value of this service

This can be measured via the project and program success rates. If you have the right people assigned, then the projects and programs should be more successful.

Criteria when the PMO will use this service

- When the organization wants to improve its project management expertise
- When dealing with complex projects to get the right individuals assigned
- When starting projects

Helpful hints for the PMO when delivering the service

- Some organizations have bronze, silver and gold level project and program managers. This says what size and complexity of project each of those levels is able to run. In addition, a silver level person must mentor a bronze level person. A gold level person must mentor a silver level or a couple of bronze level people. The assessment is then done as part of the regular HR review of the individual
- Get input from the project management community as to what they think are the appropriate levels to manage the common project types
- If going for external certification, ensure there is a training budget to get individuals through the certification

PMO Capabilities needed to fulfil this service

Competencies	Techniques and generic tools
Resource Management Capability Development Governance Frameworks	Capability and Capacity analysis

Related services

Define strategy for acquiring and developing skills Develop and maintain a PM Competence Framework Assess PMs against a Competence Framework	Identify skills shortages and recommend suitable development Assist in the recruitment of program and project managers Provide standard role descriptions for PPM staff Actively monitor the deployment cf staff

Capture the resource requirements of portfolio, programs, and projects

Service description

Obtain the numbers, types and skills of people required to work on the projects and programs within the portfolio.

What the service provides for the customer

This allows for the demand by resource type (e.g. contract, permanent) alongside the skills (e.g. project manager, business analyst) by period (week/month/quarter) to be gathered in a consistent manner.

Why is this service being offered to the customer?

By capturing the resource demand this allows for forecasting of required capacity against known demand. As this is split down by resource skills and type then this ensures the right people are recruited to deliver the projects and programs within the portfolio.

How PMO will apply this service

The PMO will speak with the portfolio manager to confirm what they are trying to forecast. This will give the PMO an idea of the data they need to capture to produce the overall report. Once the PMO understands the level of detail required they can design a template to be sent out to the project and program managers.

The PMO will ask for the information back in a given timescale. They will chase up any project or program manager who has not returned their information. Once they have the information returned the PMO will collate this information.

They will look to do some preliminary analysis on this information such as:

- Skills in demand – a view of the most common skills required
- Resource types required – a view of the split between permanent and contract. Are contract resources just being used to flex the resource pool or are they being relied on over and above the permanent resources
- Data quality – does the information returned look correct e.g. 2 resources in period 1, 20 resources in period 2 and 3 resources in period 3 would suggest that period 2 data is incorrect. For each potential error, the PMO will check back with the person who provided the data to confirm

They will then pass the information and the details of any analysis they have done to the portfolio manager.

Supplier	Input	Process	Output	Customer
Project Managers Program Managers	Resource demand	Capture resource requirements	Consolidated resource demand	Resource Managers Portfolio Manager

How the PMO will measure the value of this service

This can be measured by seeing recruitment being planned, rather than reactive.

Criteria when the PMO will use this service

- When the PMO is aligned to the portfolio manager
- Where the portfolio manager is trying to work out the demand vs capacity of the portfolio

Helpful hints for the PMO when delivering the service

- Be wary of going into too much detail, it may be difficult to obtain the information, especially if you are trying to plan out the next 18 months by week. The information you receive back (if at all) will be at a spurious level of accuracy
- Find out what level of detail is required, and who will use this before asking for the information
- Work out how to profile out projects and programs which have just started and not much information is known. Do you use a standard profile where no other detail is available, or do you leave it blank? Either decision will have an impact on the resultant summary report
- If using a PPM or scheduling tool see if the information can be obtained directly from this tool

PMO Capabilities needed to fulfil this service

Competencies	Techniques and generic tools
Planning and Scheduling Reporting, Insights and Analysis Resource Management Capability Development P3M Tools Relationships and engagement Teamwork Resourcefulness Negotiation Result Orientation	Capability and Capacity analysis Project Management Information System Resource breakdown structure Scheduling tool Time series plots

Related services

Identify skills shortages and recommend suitable development Maintain resource database Provide a view of resource commitments that will impact delivery Provide resource tracking and capacity reports Forecast future resource needs	Capture the resource requirements of portfolio, programs, and projects Actively monitor the deployment of staff Allocate resources directly to a program or project Provide 'what if' resource capacity analysis

Work with HR to provide a sourcing strategy

Service description

The creation and maintenance of an approach to the upskilling and recruitment of individuals to work on projects and programs within the portfolio.

What the service provides for the customer

This ensures that the cost for resources is reduced by planning for the types and source of individuals required rather than having to go for expensive short-term contracts.

Why is this service being offered to the customer?

A better mix of resources between permanent, contract, fixed price reduces the overall cost of delivery. It ensures that peaks and troughs in demand are handled in the most flexible manner.

How PMO will apply this service

The PMO will obtain the demand by role for the projects and programs. They will work with HR and senior management to discuss which roles require a permanent person and which can be done by temporary resources. They will discuss the lowest level of resource demand/available budget over the next few years and ensure the permanent recruitment does not exceed that demand level. They will then explore the different options for flexing the resource model including: Contract, temporary, fixed price, fixed term, voluntary.

For the permanent roles they will discuss whether these will be done by recruitment, converting contract to permanent or upskilling permanent individuals to perform a new role.

For the contract resources they will discuss where those will be sourced from, will they need to be from the current location, or will they come from a low-cost location. They will discuss whether they have preferred suppliers for their resources or whether they will go onto the open market each time.

Once all these questions have been decided the PMO will ensure that this is written up as a sourcing strategy and communicated out to all the individuals responsible for recruiting individuals to work on projects and programs.

Supplier	Input	Process	Output	Customer
Project Managers Program Managers HR/Senior Management	Forecast demand & capacity split by role and resource type Sourcing policy	Design sourcing strategy	PPM sourcing strategy	HR Senior Managers Resource Managers

How the PMO will measure the value of this service

This can be measured by a reduced cost profile for the portfolio.

Criteria when the PMO will use this service

- When the PMO is aligned to the portfolio manager
- Where there is pressure to reduce the cost for resources
- Where there is a perceived reliance on external resources
- Where there is a demand from HR for consistency in recruitment
- Where there is a need to understand the skills training requirements

Helpful hints for the PMO when delivering the service

- Having developed a strategy, work with the resource managers to see how they can transition to the new strategy
- Look to link to the training of resources to ensure the skills required are being trained
- If the strategy includes skilling of individuals, look to sell this as a plus point to the permanent staff
- Look to revisit this at least annually in line with the budgeting for the following financial year

PMO Capabilities needed to fulfil this service

Competencies	Techniques and generic tools
Reporting, Insights and Analysis Resource Management Capability Development Relationships and engagement Leadership	Alternatives analysis Alternatives generation Cost/ Benefit Analysis Comparative advantage analysis Gap analysis Scenario analysis Capability and Capacity analysis

Related services

Ensure HR practices and procedures are aligned to Capture the resource requirements of portfolio, programs, and projects Provide succession planning service for key roles Assist in the recruitment of program and project managers Define strategy for acquiring and developing skills	Define a process for selection of key PPM roles Facilitate the management of consultants and interims contracts Allocate resources directly to a program or project Assist in the recruitment and evaluation of PMO team members

Facilitate the management of consultants and interims contracts

Service description

Ensure that when temporary staff are recruited that their details are captured to enable payment. Confirm notice periods and renewal/termination dates.

What the service provides for the customer

This ensures that the rates for contractors/consultants are added into any financials for the project or program. That timesheets are approved confirming the hours/days worked by the individual and the details of the program/projects/tasks the individual has worked on. It ensures that invoices for consultants and contractors are paid according to the terms of the contract. It ensures that contractor start/end dates are maintained and communicated to the resource manager in time for any renewal process to commence.

Why is this service being offered to the customer?

The PMO are able to ensure that the resource managers are aware of the contractors and consultants renewal/termination dates to enable renewal to happen (if required) in a timely manner, to prevent the individual leaving before the work is finished.

How PMO will apply this service

When the PMO have been notified of a new contractor or consultant joining they will find out the key details including: Start and end dates; rate (including any agency commission and sales tax); role; location; resource manager.

The PMO will ensure that information about the financials gets included in any costing of actuals/forecast.

The PMO will ensure that the contract resource fills in timesheets (if applicable) in the correct system(s) to allow for prompt payment of the individual. If the resource submits an invoice, then the PMO will ensure this gets directed to the correct person to approve (and that it does get approved).

Prior to the contractor end date, the PMO will send a reminder to the resource manager informing them that the individual is due leave on a particular date. They will include links to the renewal process (if required) and information on what to do should the person no longer be required.

If the contractor is renewed, then the PMO will update their records. If the contractor is not renewed, then as well as updating the records the PMO will ensure the leaving process is followed.

Supplier	Input	Process	Output	Customer
External Supplier HR	Contractor details	Maintain resource information	Contractor financials Contractor end dates Renewal reminders	Resource Manager

How the PMO will measure the value of this service

This can be measured by a reduction in the number of contractors or consultants who have not been renewed as expected. It can be measured by asking for feedback from the resource managers.

Criteria when the PMO will use this service

- Where a PMO is maintaining a PPM tool
- Where a PMO is aligned to a single project or program
- Where the PMO is tracking contractor information
- Where the PMO are expected to maintain resource information

Helpful hints for the PMO when delivering the service

- Ensure the contractor details are stored securely and the information (especially the rates) is only available to those people who should have access to it
- When individuals leave it can be useful to get a quick summary of what the hiring manager and project manager they worked with thought of the individual. This can then be used if that person applies for a different role this can be used as reference material
- When keeping details of resources be aware of any data protection compliance required

PMO Capabilities needed to fulfil this service

Competencies	Techniques and generic tools
P3M Administration Information Management Resource Management Supplier Management Professionalism and ethics Personal Integrity and reliability Relationships and engagement Teamwork	Cash flow analysis Prompt Lists Check sheets Resource breakdown structure

Related services

Work with HR to provide a sourcing strategy Ensure HR practices and procedures are aligned to Define a process for selection of key PPM roles	Assist in the recruitment of program and project managers Maintain resource database

Provide 'help squads' for projects and programs

Service description

Provide resources from the PMO to provide consultancy skills for the project or program.

What the service provides for the customer

This provides the project or program manager with expertise to help with the delivery of the project or program.

Why is this service being offered to the customer?

The PMO can provide PPM expertise at short notice (they are already working for the organization). As they have a good understanding of all the process, able to get down into the detail and provide senior consultancy they make a flexible resource which can be used on a variety of tasks for the project or program. They may facilitate the recruitment of other resources to join the program due to their understanding of the competencies and availability of all the resources within the portfolio.

How PMO will apply this service

The PMO manager will be approached by a project or program manager to provide resources to assist with their project or program. The PMO will ascertain what the resource is required to perform, how much of the resource is required and how long the deployment is going to be.

The PMO manager will look to see whether they have the people who could perform this role. If they do, then the manager will look to see how the individual(s) can be freed up to deliver this service. Once this is agreed, the PMO manager will agree a start date with the project or program manager.

When the assignment is due to end the PMO manager will review this with the individual(s) and the project or program manager. If this is still required and the individual(s) are happy to stay a new end date can be agreed. If the need has gone then the PMO will need to be reassigned back to other PMO services when they return into the team.

Supplier	Input	Process	Output	Customer
Project Manager Program Manager	Resource request	Provide Consultancy	Deployed resources	Project Manager Program Manager

How the PMO will measure the value of this service

This can be measured by obtaining feedback from the project or program manager on the success of the deployment. If there is a request to extend the assignment, that can indicate a successful deployment.

Criteria when the PMO will use this service

- When the project or program requires immediate access to resource to deliver
- Where the PMO has capacity and skills to be available to help

Helpful hints for the PMO when delivering the service

- If allocating part of a resource's effort look to assign on a set number of days/half-days per week. Allocating a resource on Monday is better than saying they can have 8 hours for the week. This means both parties know when the resource is available, and the 8 hours does not expand into 10 or 15 (without prior agreement)
- If the PMO is losing individuals to help with projects and programs they will need to consider backfill requirements, or a reduction in the services offered
- If working on a recharge model, then ensure that the PMO person is billed for correctly

PMO Capabilities needed to fulfil this service

Competencies	Techniques and generic tools
Depending on the resource requirement depends on the competencies required	Capability and Capacity analysis Resource breakdown structure

Related services

Allocate resources directly to a program or project	Provide project or program rescues

Provide succession planning service for key roles

Service description

Identify which roles are crucial for the delivery of the portfolio and ensure that there are other people able to perform the role should the person doing this leave.

What the service provides for the customer

This provides a list of crucial roles/skills/knowledge for the delivery of portfolio. It provides a list of people (deputies) who would want to step up into those roles. It provides a list of training/experience requirements for those deputies.

Why is this service being offered to the customer?

By having a plan for succession, it reduces the impact on the portfolio delivery should an individual choose to move on. As the PMO can see from other the capacity and capability services who are the individuals who are in most demand, they can start to plan for their succession, should they leave.

How PMO will apply this service

The PMO will look to find out which resources are considered critical to the continued running of the portfolio. They will find out what knowledge and experience the resource has that makes them critical. They will look to see whether new people can be recruited (internally or externally) to support the critical individuals. They will look to define how individuals can gain the knowledge and experience. This could be by the provision of training, giving the individual project experience or providing a mentor.

The PMO will try to work out the timescale for the succession. This can be easier to establish if the succession plan covers a retiree or a current contractor as they will have leaving dates. For permanent staff this will be an educated guess from the PMO in consultation with the resource manager.

Once the succession plan has been produced it should be circulated to the resource managers to ensure they give the people the necessary opportunities to receive the training or be assigned to the correct projects to gain the experience.

Supplier	Input	Process	Output	Customer
Resource managers HR/PMO	Role profiles Career development plans PPM sourcing strategy Resource demand	Succession Planning	Career development plans Training plans	Resource Managers Training Department

How the PMO will measure the value of this service

A reduction in the time taken to find individuals to replace key roles. A reduction in red risks due to resource unavailability.

Criteria when the PMO will use this service

- When the organization has high turnover
- Where there is a desire to promote people from within, rather than use external contractors
- When this is not being done by the senior management

Helpful hints for the PMO when delivering the service

- When deciding who are the crucial individuals, look for those people who are assigned to the most projects at one time
- Check the resource database (if present) to see which skills are in short supply. Cross check this with the strategy to see if those are still required
- Although this service is related to succession planning for PPM staff, a similar succession plan will be required by the user community
- Find out from HR what the typical time period is for a resource to remain in the same role (this may differ based on seniority)
- Ensure that the people being earmarked as potential replacements actually want to perform the role
- Do ensure that the succession plan is reviewed on a regular basis to check that it is still current
- When one of the people leaves then that is the time to use the succession plan

PMO Capabilities needed to fulfil this service

Competencies	Techniques and generic tools
Resource Management Capability Development Relationships and engagement Leadership Resourcefulness	Capability and Capacity analysis

Related services

Define a process for selection of key PPM roles Define strategy for acquiring and developing skills Actively monitor the deployment of staff Work with HR to provide a sourcing strategy	Assist in the recruitment of program and project managers Provide PPM training Identify skills shortages and recommend suitable development Organize buddy relationships and secondments Provide standard role descriptions for PPM staff

Assist in the recruitment of program and project managers

Service description

Helping with the recruitment of project and program managers. This can include providing administrivia assistance with booking of rooms, meetings, scheduling interviews, provision of scenario packs, conducting telephone interviews, being part of the recruitment panel.

What the service provides for the customer

It provides administrative assistance with the recruitment of project and program managers. By delegating the entire recruitment process to the PMO the portfolio manager gets the project and program managers they require.

Why is this service being offered to the customer?

It provides a standard way of assessing a program or project manager. Ensures a consistency in the quality of program and project managers.

How PMO will apply this service

The PMO will confirm how much of this service they are being asked to perform to ensure expectations are met.

If the PMO is being asked to provide administrative assistance, then the PMO will work with the recruiting manager to find a series of available slots to perform the interview. They will pencil in those slots with the people on the interview panel (to ensure that they do not double book) and book a room. The PMO will then coordinate with HR to assign the people to be interviewed into those slots. The PMO will then confirm which one of the interviewees is attending which slot. They will print out any of the relevant interview information including CV, interview questions, scenario pack, scenario answers. They will arrange with reception for the person to be greeted when they arrive. The PMO will arrange to pick the person up from reception and take them to the interview room. They will provide drinks and indicate where the rest rooms are. They will ensure that introductions are performed.

If the PMO is being asked to provide the scenario pack they will use the define a process for selection of key PPM roles service to produce the pack, along with the standard answers.

If the PMO is being asked to perform the telephone interviews they will confirm what the questions are. They will arrange, via HR, the date, time, and duration of the interview. At the agreed time they will contact the person being interviewed, explain about the role, the organization and obtain answers to the interview questions. After the interview they will prepare their feedback and share that with the recruiting manager. They will ensure that the decision made whether to pursue the recruitment of the individual is shared back with HR.

If the PMO is being asked to assist with an assessment centre, then the PMO will have a role as an observer. They will pay attention to what is being done, and how individuals are interacting. They will make notes as they go. At the end of the assessment centre then the PMO will compare notes with the other observers and a decision can be made on who to recruit.

If the PMO is asked to run the face-to-face interview then they will perform their own administration, they may even shortlist the CVs. They will perform any telephone interviews. They will conduct the interview including any scenarios and at the end make a fact-based decision. After all the interviews are finished the PMO manager will decide who to recruit, and who not to and why. The PMO will ensure the candidates gain the appropriate feedback. The PMO will then follow through to ensure the individual(s) recruited are onboarded successfully.

Supplier	Input	Process	Output	Customer
HR Recruiting manager	CVs Skills questionnaires Assessment centre packs Recruitment scenarios	Interviewing Running assessment centres Arranging meetings	Selected project and program managers	Program managers Portfolio manager Resource managers

How the PMO will measure the value of this service

This can be measured by looking at the slickness of the interview process. If the PMO are in charge of all the recruitment this can be measured based on the effectiveness of the individuals being recruited.

Criteria when the PMO will use this service

- Where there are people to be recruited
- Where consistency is required in the recruitment process
- If the PMO has experience in interviewing

Helpful hints for the PMO when delivering the service

- When confirming the interview person add the name of the person being interviewed to the invite. Add the CV and the recruitment pack to the invite so the person has a copy of all the information in one place

PMO Capabilities needed to fulfil this service

Competencies	Techniques and generic tools
P3M Administration Capability Development Professionalism and ethics Personal Integrity and reliability Personal Communication Relationships and engagement Resourcefulness Result Orientation	Check sheets

Related services

Define a process for selection of key PPM roles On boarding and induction Set up meetings on behalf of others Assist in the recruitment and evaluation of PMO team members Provide standard role descriptions for PPM staff	Ensure HR practices and procedures are aligned to Work with HR to provide a sourcing strategy Facilitate the management of consultants and interims contracts Agree a project management certification process Provide succession planning service for key roles Organize buddy relationships and secondments

Provide PPM training

Service description

The provision of training for PPM staff, primarily project, program, and portfolio managers on the PPM framework. Basic project management related training on how to be a better project manager.

What the service provides for the customer

This provides training to improve the individuals who are responsible for running projects, programs, and portfolios within the organization. This training is aligned to the way the organization runs its projects.

Why is this service being offered to the customer?

This training will allow the individuals to be more effective in their role. As the PMO is responsible for the creation of the frameworks, they are best place to provide the training on this.

How PMO will apply this service

The PMO can provide training on the PPM framework, or on one element of it. They may decide to offer some bespoke PPM training courses for new starters or on specific elements of running the project e.g. risk management, stakeholder management.

The PMO will write a brief course outline explaining what the training will cover and what the recipient will get from the training. The PMO will create the training slides and any additional courseware e.g. exercises, handouts. They will then book the training and advertise this to the relevant PPM community.

The PMO will book the rooms and assign people onto the courses. They will deliver the training according to the course outline. Once the training has been completed, they will review its effectiveness by asking for feedback.

Supplier	Input	Process	Output	Customer
PPM team Resource Manager	Request for training	Provide Training	Trained individuals	PPM team

How the PMO will measure the value of this service

This can be measured by satisfaction scores after the training has been delivered. It can be measured in the improvement in the PPM maturity of individuals and the organization as a whole.

Criteria when the PMO will use this service

- When the PPM framework (or one of its parts has been updated)
- When there are new starters
- When the PMO has experience in offering training

Helpful hints for the PMO when delivering the service

- Some of the training e.g. configuration management may be compulsory for all individuals
- If the organization does a large recruitment exercise look to offer training after they have all joined
- Have a series of courses that can be offered. These should be advertised via the PMO intranet site, or posters
- As the PPM framework changes then ensure the training gets updated

PMO Capabilities needed to fulfil this service

Competencies	Techniques and generic tools
P3M Administration Capability Development P3M Tools Personal Communication Relationships and engagement Result Orientation	Capability and Capacity analysis

Related services

Provide training logistics support Communicate the change control framework Communicate change management framework Train people in configuration management Train the issue management framework Train the Quality Control Framework Train the risk management framework Introduce tools for managing risks Communicate PPM purchasing Framework Perform organizational PPM maturity assessments	Perform coaching of portfolio, program, or project managers Define strategy for acquiring and developing skills Develop and maintain a PM Competence Framework Provide succession planning service for key roles Identify skills shortages and recommend suitable development Ensure Continuing Professional Development of the PMO team Develop individuals within the PMO team

Provide training logistics support

Service description

Provide support to organize training courses including booking of rooms, organizing travel/hotels, providing refreshments, booking training courses.

What the service provides for the customer

This provides a one-stop shop to organize the training. The individual can come to the PMO with the training request and they will arrange the training, sort out the travel/accommodation and then inform the individual.

For internally run courses the PMO will book the trainer (internal or external), book the meeting rooms, print all course material (if required), arrange refreshments, organize the room layout, process the feedback forms.

Why is this service being offered to the customer?

Having one place to go to organize the training makes it easier, and more cost effective for the individual and the organization.

How PMO will apply this service

The PMO will receive a request to organize some training. They will confirm whether this is an internally run course or an external course. They will confirm the number of attendees, the suggested dates and proposed location.

If this is an external course, then the PMO will liaise with the external training organization to book the individual on the training. If required, they will arrange for the travel and any accommodation to be booked. They will communicate to the individual the date and location of the course and confirm what travel/accommodation has been booked.

If this is an internal course, then the PMO will confirm whether this is an internal or external trainer. If it is an external trainer the PMO will need to arrange for security passes for that individual. The PMO will book the meeting room(s) for the duration of the training. The PMO will confirm whether any courseware is required to be printed, and if necessary, arrange that to be done. If people are coming from different locations, then the PMO will (if required) book the travel and accommodation. The PMO will arrange for refreshments to be available. On the day of the training the PMO will be on hand to arrange the room appropriately. They will meet the trainer (if external then ensure they are met at reception and get through security through into the room). At the end of the training the PMO will ensure feedback forms get filled in and return the room to its previous state.

Supplier	Input	Process	Output	Customer
Individual Resource manager PMO	Request for training	Organize training	Training course booking Room booking Travel / accommodation details Printed course material Feedback forms	Individual

How the PMO will measure the value of this service

This can be measured by looking at the answers to the feedback forms on how easy it was to sort the logistics out.

Criteria when the PMO will use this service

- If lots of training courses are to be booked
- When the PMO is organizing any training courses
- If the PMO is in charge of the organizational PPM training

Helpful hints for the PMO when delivering the service

- Consider sending an invite to the individual with the details of the training – this will then provide a reminder of the information in their calendar
- If an internal course requires IT equipment, the PMO should ensure that this can be provided within the room. This could be providing PC equipment in the room, or ensuring each attendee has a laptop they can bring and use in the room with access to the relevant IT software
- If lots of internal IT training courses are required, then suggest to the senior management that a dedicated training room is setup and equipped
- When booking refreshments, it could be just the use of existing facilities, or catering provided to the room

PMO Capabilities needed to fulfil this service

Competencies	Techniques and generic tools
P3M Administration Personal Integrity and reliability Personal Communication Relationships and engagement Resourcefulness Negotiation	Prompt Lists Check sheets

Related services

Provide PPM training Communicate the change control framework Train people in configuration management Train the issue management framework Train the Quality Control Framework Train the risk management framework Introduce tools for managing risks	Communicate change management framework Communicate PPM purchasing Framework Set up meetings on behalf of others Events management Arrange travel for other people Define strategy for acquiring and developing skills Ensure Continuing Professional Development of the PMO team

Organize buddy relationships and secondments

Service description

Provide a way that individuals can gain a buddy or mentor to assist them with their personal development. Arrange for individuals to be seconded into new roles.

What the service provides for the customer

Having a buddy or a mentor provides the individual with someone they can go to who will assist and advise them with difficulties they may be experiencing within their current role.

Having secondment opportunities allows individuals to try a new area/skill out and can help with succession planning.

Why is this service being offered to the customer?

As the PMO is central to PPM within the organization they are able to see what roles are available. They can act as a centralized clearing house for secondment opportunities and buddy relationships.

How PMO will apply this service

The PMO will receive a request for a person to be seconded onto a project. They will publish the list of all secondments in a central place. This will include: a description of the secondment, the recruiting manager, the closing date for applications, the type of role required. On a regular basis the PMO will update the list removing secondments that have been filled. Where a secondment closing date has passed the PMO will confirm with the recruiting manager whether the Position has been filled if the position has not been filled then the PMO will confirm with the manager whether the secondment needs to be updated with a new closing date or whether it can be removed from the list.

The PMO will put out a request for mentors. As a new person comes into the organization the PMO will direct them through to the list of mentors and the individual can then be assigned to have one of these people as their mentor. The PMO will publish a list of available mentors in a central location. Once an individual has been assigned one or two people, they can be removed from the list temporarily to avoid a single mentor getting all the people assigned to them.

Supplier	Input	Process	Output	Customer
Project Manager Program Manager Individual	Secondment opportunity Mentoring requirement Mentor list	Manage secondments Organize mentors	Arranged secondment Assigned mentor	Project Manager Program Manager Individual

How the PMO will measure the value of this service

This can be measured by the number of successful secondments that have been arranged. This can be measured by the number of mentor or buddy relationships that have been organized.

Criteria when the PMO will use this service

- Where there is a need for more development of individuals
- Where there is a succession plan in place
- Where the PMO operate in a centralized role
- Where there is a culture of development of individuals

Helpful hints for the PMO when delivering the service

- As well as publishing the information in a central place, consider offering a subscription service so individuals can sign up to see the new roles
- The success secondment process can depend on the willingness of the resource managers to let people go to try new things. There can be a temptation to hold onto good people and let the poorer people move on. The key to success for this can depend on the resource managers understanding the people development requirements

PMO Capabilities needed to fulfil this service

Competencies	Techniques and generic tools
P3M Administration Resource Management Capability Development Professionalism and ethics Personal Communication Relationships and engagement Negotiation	Capability and Capacity analysis

Related services

Define strategy for acquiring and developing skills Actively monitor the deployment of staff Ensure HR practices and procedures are aligned to Provide succession planning service for key roles	Assist in the recruitment of program and project managers Assist in the recruitment and evaluation of PMO team members Identify skills shortages and recommend suitable development

Identify skills shortages and recommend suitable development

Service description

Review the skill requirements to deliver the projects and programs within the portfolio against the available skillsets and look to see where there is the greatest need for development.

What the service provides for the customer

This enables the training department to plan for training events to support the increase in skills. It assists the organization by providing more people with the relevant skills. It enables the portfolio to deliver with the existing people and saving on recruitment/contractor costs.

Why is this service being offered to the customer?

By having a coordinated approach to the delivery of training, relating it to the skills that organization requires ensures that the training budget is spent wisely.

How PMO will apply this service

The PMO will obtain the output from the PM capability assessments. They will look at the strategic plan to see what skills will be required to deliver the portfolio. The PMO will examine the gap between the skills required and the skills available. They will prioritize those skills which are most needed to deliver the portfolio.

The PMO will look at the ways in which those skills can be obtained including training course, reading blogs, forums, white papers, and books, having a mentor/buddy relationship, being seconded to gain experience, attending conferences and workshops, webinars. The PMO will put their recommendations into a training and development plan which will list the names of the individuals requiring training and the suggested timescale for the training to occur. The PMO will pass this plan over to the team responsible for agreeing and organizing the training.

Supplier	Input	Process	Output	Customer
PMO Strategy department	PM capability assessment Strategic plan Resource database	Identify skills shortages	Training and development plan	HR Training department

How the PMO will measure the value of this service

This can be measured by an increase in the skills of people within the PPM community. It can be measured by a reduction in the external spend as the right people are already available in house.

Criteria when the PMO will use this service

- When there are PM competency assessments being done
- Where the training is coordinated via the PMO
- Where there is a desire to increase the capability of internal staff
- Where the PMO performs a centralized role

Helpful hints for the PMO when delivering the service

- When prioritizing the skills look to see not only which skills are missing, but when they are required
- Not all 'training' needs to be an external course, there are there ways that individuals can learn
- When suggesting ways to learn link that through to an individual's learning style

PMO Capabilities needed to fulfil this service

Competencies	Techniques and generic tools
Reporting, Insights and Analysis Resource Management Capability Development Relationships and engagement	Root Cause Analysis Gap analysis Capability and Capacity analysis Scheduling tool

Related services

Define strategy for acquiring and developing skills Agree a project management certification process Provide succession planning service for key roles Provide PPM training Organize buddy relationships and secondments Assess PMs against a Competence Framework	Maintain resource database Perform coaching of portfolio, program, or project managers Develop and maintain a PM Competence Framework Capture the resource requirements of portfolio, programs, and projects Actively monitor the deployment of staff Allocate resources directly to a program or project Develop individuals within the PMO team

Further Reading

Honey, Peter; Mumford, Alan. Learning styles questionnaire

Kolb, David A. Experiential learning: experience as the source of learning and development

Assess PMs against a Competence Framework

Service description

The assessment of project managers against a competence framework.

What the service provides for the customer

This provides an objective assessment of the skills experience and knowledge of project managers. This can be assessed against the standard role profile for the role. Improvements can therefore be suggested to what the project manager may do to improve the knowledge and experience move through to the next role or perform the current role better.

Why is this service being offered to the customer?

As the PMO have created the PM competence framework they are in a good position to be able to assess the individuals against that. They have also had a role in producing the role descriptions for the PPM manager roles, so are able to align the role descriptions with the PM competence framework.

How PMO will apply this service

The PMO will find the latest copy of the PM competence framework. They will book time with the person being assessed and go through the questions within the framework. They will find examples of where the project manager has delivered the particular competence or skill. They will assign a score for each of the elements of the framework and this will lead to an overall score.

Based on the assessment the PMO to look at the role profile for the individual and the role profile for the role they want to achieve. They will suggest improvements in the knowledge or experience they have for each of the skills in the framework to allow them to deliver their desired role.

Supplier	Input	Process	Output	Customer
PMO	PM Competence framework	Perform competence assessment	Assessment scoring Suggestions for further development	Project Manager Program Manager Portfolio Manager Training department

How the PMO will measure the value of this service

This can be measured by the number of project managers being assessed.

Criteria when the PMO will use this service

- When there is PM competence framework
- Where the PMO has experience in PPM
- Where there is a desire to improve the skills of the PPM managers

Helpful hints for the PMO when delivering the service

- Look for examples of where the skills have been used or learnt
- Be realistic with the assessment, do not over or under rate individuals based on what they want to do. Be objective and list what the individual can (and cannot) do
- Note that getting to the top assessment level in a competency assessment can be related to the complexity of the project. If the person has not run complex projects, they will not be able to be assessed against the highest levels of the framework

PMO Capabilities needed to fulfil this service

Competencies	Techniques and generic tools
Reporting, Insights and Analysis Capability Development Relationships and engagement Negotiation	Check sheets

Related services

Develop and maintain a PM Competence Framework Identify skills shortages and recommend suitable development Provide standard role descriptions for PPM staff Perform organizational PPM maturity assessments	Perform coaching of portfolio, program, or project managers Promote good PPM within the organization Define strategy for acquiring and developing skills Agree a project management certification process

Maintain resource database

Service description

Maintain a list of resources with associated details to enable reporting.

What the service provides for the customer

This provides a list of all the individuals who have worked in the organization, along with their current status and other details. This helps with capacity management as it can be used to confirm who is currently working, when do they leave, what is their employment type, status, and role. Additional information can be captured including rate, skills, location, secondary role, current assignments, resource/line manager, cost centre, organizational structure, hours worked, working patterns.

Why is this service being offered to the customer?

This enables capacity management It can be linked into skills capture and development options. As the PMO operate in a central role they are able to keep the authoritative version of the resource information for PPM staff. This can combine information from HR and contract databases into a single source.

How PMO will apply this service

The PMO will assess whether they need a separate resource database or whether the resource information should be stored within the PPM tool. The PMO will work out which resource elements they wish to capture. They will work out where the source for the information will be provided from. If it is to come from other database such as HR or a contractor database, the PMO will need to speak to the individuals responsible for maintaining that database. The PMO will need to arrange for regular extracts of the data to be provided. The PMO will need to be aware of how to update the information in the source databases.

The PMO will populate the information in the resource database. Where there are changes the PMO will be informed, either directly or via new extracts coming from the source databases. The PMO will then apply the relevant changes.

On a regular basis the PMO will audit the resource database to ensure there is no missing information. That resources have leaving dates in the future if they are still marked as active (or the resource becomes inactive). They will chase up any incorrect information with the resource and their line manager. These changes will then need to be applied to the database.

The PMO will look to provide some regular extracts of the resource information in order that it can be used in other reporting such as any capacity vs demand reporting.

Supplier	Input	Process	Output	Customer
Resource Managers HR	Resource details	Maintain Resource Information	Resource Database	PMO Senior management

How the PMO will measure the value of this service

This can be measured in the ease of reporting on resource information.

Criteria when the PMO will use this service

- When the PMO needs to work out who is in the organization
- Where there is a PPM tool being used
- Where the PMO needs a definitive version of the resource information
- Where the PMO operates in a centralized role

Helpful hints for the PMO when delivering the service

- Resource database may be included as part of a PPM tool
- Ensure that names are recorded consistently. Is someone called Michael, Mick or Mike? Or do they use their middle or nickname instead?
- Where there are duplicate individuals e.g. David Smith ensure that they have a unique identifier (or middle initials) to ensure the right information gets updated
- Exactly what information to store will depend on what the information will be used for
- Do not look to store information that is not required
- When new people start then, ensure the new starter request captures all the relevant detail for the database
- Consider whether you need to have history of when changes were made, by whom and under what authority. In case the information is questioned, can you revert to a prior version of the record
- If combining data from HR and contract databases, then ensure you know which one the source is, and which one is a copy of the data. This ensures that the data need only get updated in one place, rather than 2 which will lead to discrepancies

PMO Capabilities needed to fulfil this service

Competencies	Techniques and generic tools
P3M Administration Information Management Quality Management Reporting, Insights and Analysis Resource Management Supplier Management Relationships and engagement	Capability and Capacity analysis Swim-lane flowcharts

Related services

Facilitate the management of consultants and interims contracts Manages project management tools (systems admin) Capture the resource requirements of portfolio, programs, and projects Identify skills shortages and recommend suitable development Actively monitor the deployment of staff Ensure HR practices and procedures are aligned to	Forecast future resource needs Allocate resources directly to a program or project Develop resource plans to underpin the portfolio plan Set up and track portfolio, program, and project metrics (KPI's) Provide 'what if' resource capacity analysis Provide resource tracking and capacity reports

Capability Monitoring

Service group description

The monitoring and review of individuals on projects ensuring that HR processes are followed, and the right people assigned.

Why have these services been grouped together?

These services relate to the monitoring of the assignment of people to projects

Responsibility Assignment Matrix

Service	Executive	Portfolio Manager	Program Manager	Project Manager	PMO	Sponsor	Other Stakeholder
Actively monitor the deployment of staff		A			R		
Ensure HR practices and procedures are aligned to					R		A (HR)

Actively monitor the deployment of staff

Service description

Review which projects and programs individuals are assigned to ensuring that they have the requisite skills to perform the role.

What the service provides for the customer

This ensures that the right people are assigned to the project or program. This is based on skillset and availability.

Why is this service being offered to the customer?

By reviewing where individuals are assigned the PMO can confirm that they have the skills to deliver. The PMO can review the training needs of the individual as well as the skills needs of the project or program.

How PMO will apply this service

When an individual is assigned to a project or program the PMO will review the role to which the individual has been assigned. They will check the skills required to perform the role, the skills of the individual, the training needs of the individual and review any alternatives who may be available to fill the role.

If there are individuals who would be better suited to the role who are available, the PMO would speak to the project or program manager to let them know of the alternatives.

If there are no suitable alternatives, but the individual is not the best fit, the PMO will speak to the project or program manager to suggest where additional assistance may be required. The PMO may suggest offering some training or a mentor to aid the individual and to help the project or program succeed.

Supplier	Input	Process	Output	Customer
Resource Managers PMO	Resource assignments Training and development plan Resource database	Monitor assignments	Assignment suggestions	Project Manager Program Manager Individual

How the PMO will measure the value of this service

This can be measured by checking to see a reduction in lessons identified due to the incorrect resource assignment. It can be measured by feedback from the project or program manager and the individual concerned.

Criteria when the PMO will use this service

- Where the PMO are involved with resource management
- Where the PMO are involved with skills development
- Where the PMO are independent from the project or program

Helpful hints for the PMO when delivering the service

- Any assessment must be made objectively based on the fit for the role and not as a judgement on the individual concerned
- Where the individual is the correct person for the role then no recommendations are required
- Consider including in the assessment to number of other projects the resource is assigned to. Although they may have the right skills for the role, they may not have the time to be able to perform the role

PMO Capabilities needed to fulfil this service

Competencies	Techniques and generic tools
Resource Management Assurance Capability Development Professionalism and ethics Personal Integrity and reliability Personal Communication Relationships and engagement Negotiation Result Orientation	Decision tree analysis Gap analysis Capability and Capacity analysis Prioritization matrices

Related services

Allocate resources directly to a program or project Identify skills shortages and recommend suitable development Maintain resource database Agree a project management certification process	Capture the resource requirements of portfolio, programs, and projects Provide succession planning service for key roles Organize buddy relationships and secondments

Ensure HR practices and procedures are aligned to

Service description

When recruiting, developing, and releasing staff ensure this is done in line with the HR rules and regulations.

What the service provides for the customer

This provides reassurance that when developing and assessing role profiles, recruiting individuals, offering training and development, organizing secondments that this is done in a fair way. Any potential risks will be flagged up to the relevant people to stop them happening.

Why is this service being offered to the customer?

Ensures that the organization will not be prosecuted for failing to adhere to due process. Ensures that people are dealt with fairly when it comes to recruitment and development.

How PMO will apply this service

The PMO will obtain the latest copy of the HR policy. For each of the items which involve an HR element e.g. recruitment, role profiles, skills development, managing secondments, overtime, working hours. The PMO will review the current process against the HR guidelines. Where it is not clear whether the current process follows the rules the PMO will speak to a member of HR to clarify the rules.

If there are any circumstances where the current process violates the HR policy, then the PMO will need to ensure the process gets updated. Once the process has been updated the PMO will confirm that this meets the HR rules by consulting with a member of HR. The PMO will need to make sure that any changes to process have been communicated to the relevant people.

Supplier	Input	Process	Output	Customer
HR	HR practices and procedures	Review HR compliance	HR compliance	Resource Manager Line manager HT

How the PMO will measure the value of this service

This can be measured by the absence of issues regarding HR compliance with no grievances raised.

Criteria when the PMO will use this service

- When the PMO has a role in producing role profiles, recruiting individuals, or offering training to individuals
- Where there is a clearly defined HR policy

Helpful hints for the PMO when delivering the service

- If in doubt about whether something is HR related contact a member of HR to get them to confirm (or deny)
- Ask the HR contacts to inform you if there are any major changes planned to the HR policy in order that the PMO processes can be updated at the same time

PMO Capabilities needed to fulfil this service

Competencies	Techniques and generic tools
Resource Management Capability Development Personal Communication Relationships and engagement Teamwork	Document Analysis Process Analysis

Related services

Provide standard role descriptions for PPM staff Define a process for selection of key PPM roles Define strategy for acquiring and developing skills Develop and maintain a PM Competence Framework Work with HR to provide a sourcing strategy	Facilitate the management of consultants and interims contracts Assist in the recruitment of program and project managers Maintain resource database Organize buddy relationships and secondments Create and maintain PMO career paths Develop and maintain PMO role profiles Develop and maintain a PMO competence framework

Capacity Management

Capacity Management

Description

Ensures current and future programs and projects are equipped with enough staff, at the time they are needed, and that those resources are used as efficiently as possible.

What the services within the area provide for the customer

These provide the portfolio manager with an understanding of when programs and projects can start and when they are likely to finish depending on the availability of resources. It allows the organization to 'right-size' the numbers and skills of people to deliver the projects.

Tips and tricks for when the PMO is delivering this service area

- Define a standard set of roles to track capacity against
- Try to ensure that there are no more than 10 roles to track against
- Develop guidelines for productivity to ensure that you are not overloading people
- Do not wait until you have 'accurate' information before starting capacity management, some information is better than none and will allow for indicative information to be provided
- Understand how capability and demand are linked. Develop some rules for how competent the average person performing a role may be
- Decide whether you want to do capacity management bottom up (from individual project estimates) or top down (review of strategic demand)
- Remember when looking at resource bottlenecks that a 'resource' may be equipment or a person

Capacity Operations

Service group description

These services over the provision of demand information on projects, programs, and portfolios to enable capacity monitoring to happen.

List of related services described in other areas

Develops scenario modelling to reduce commitments or increase capacity
Provide tools and analysis for Business Capacity Management

Responsibility Assignment Matrix

Service	Executive	Portfolio Manager	Program Manager	Project Manager	PMO	Sponsor	Other Stakeholder
Forecast future resource needs		A	C	C	R		
Allocate resources directly to a program or project					A, R		
Provide 'what if' resource capacity analysis		A	C	C	R		
Identify over commitment of changes to the business	A	I	C	C	R		

Forecast future resource needs

Service description

For each project and program within the portfolio ensure they have a profile of the resource requirements by role by period.

What the service provides for the customer

Having a forecast profile by role and period allows the data to be summarized to enable demand vs capacity reporting to be produced. This will then allow the scheduling of the portfolio according to resource availability as well as by priority.

Why is this service being offered to the customer?

Ensures resources are in place to do the work required and the necessary recruitment can take place. If resources are under-utilized, they can be re-allocated or removed. It can be used to drive recruitment plans for the organization.

How PMO will apply this service

The PMO will speak with the project and program managers and ask them to forecast out their projects and programs. Where the budget has not been approved for the entirety of the project or program then the PMO should profile out the expected full cost of the project or program in a separate pipeline plan.

For each project which has been approved in principle, but not started a pipeline plan should be created. Ideally the portfolio manager should maintain this plan, but it may be delegated to the PMO.

Once all the forecasts have been entered then the PMO can check this for consistency and see if there are any glaring data errors. If there are any errors the PMO should speak to the project or program manager responsible and get them to update the information.

Having got the details, the PMO can then consolidate this to portfolio level to compare against the available demand. This information can then be passed on to the portfolio manager for them to review and potentially reschedule the projects and programs to enable delivery within resource constraints.

Supplier	Input	Process	Output	Customer
Project Managers Program Managers Strategy department	Pipeline plans Demand from projects, BAU, Small change Strategic plan	Forecast resources Produce demand vs capacity report	Demand vs capacity reporting	Portfolio Manager Resource Managers Senior Managers

How the PMO will measure the value of this service

This can be measured by evaluating how effective the forward planning is for the organization. It can be measured by who easy it is to collect the data.

Criteria when the PMO will use this service

- When the PMO are aligned to the portfolio manager
- When the organization is interested in resource/demand management

Helpful hints for the PMO when delivering the service

- Where there is no PPM tool in use the PMO need to devise a spreadsheet (or equivalent) to enable the data to be collected in a consistent manner to allow for rollup to occur
- Decide whether BAU data needs to be forecast out. If BAU staff are separate from staff working on changes then the forecasts can be separated. If individual could work on BAU or changes then the BAU forecast will be required
- Assume that the BAU profile is static across the year. Either use the profile from last year's actuals or profile as the same percentage for each period
- The PMO will need to communicate the level of detail that is required for the forecast and how far in advance the forecast is required
- The PMO may need to chase project or program managers to provide the information by the requisite timescale

PMO Capabilities needed to fulfil this service

Competencies	Techniques and generic tools
Information Management Reporting, Insights and Analysis Resource Management Capacity Management Personal Communication Relationships and engagement	Capability and Capacity analysis

Related services

Provide 'what if' resource capacity analysis Develop resource plans to underpin the portfolio plan Capture the resource requirements of portfolio, programs, and projects Maintain resource database	Provide resource tracking and capacity reports Allocate resources directly to a program or project Provide a view of resource comm tments that will impact delivery Develops scenario modelling to reduce commitments or increase capacity

Allocate resources directly to a program or project

Service Description

The assignment of resources to a project or program based on the skills required.

What the service provides for the customer

The PMO can act in a resource manager role. Based on a role requirement from the project or program manager they can review who is suitable for the role and have availability. They can then allocate the person to the project or program.

Why is this service being offered to the customer?

This ensures that people get allocated to the projects and programs based on skills and needs of the project or program. As the PMO have a view of the portfolio and the skills of the individuals they can ensure the correct people get assigned. It saves the project or program manager the effort of finding the right resource for the change.

How PMO will apply this service

The PMO will receive a resource request from a project or program manager. This will list the role/skills required, the amount of effort required and the time period that the resource is required for. It may include other information such as location and business knowledge.

The PMO will examine the resource database to see who matches the requisite skill/knowledge levels. They will look to see of those individuals who has available capacity to be assigned. The PMO will look to see whether there are any development opportunities required for individuals (e.g. for succession planning reasons).

Having selected the individual, the PMO will inform the person concerned and the project or program manager.

If there are no suitable people available, then the PMO will review whether individuals can be reassigned, or whether there is a need to recruit individuals to deliver this project or program. If the PMO decide to reallocate an individual the project or program manager that will be impacted will be contacted and the PMO will assign a different person to the impacted project or program. The individual will be informed and be reassigned. If there is a need to recruit an individual, then the PMO will inform the project or program manager and they can look to recruit a person directly.

Supplier	Input	Process	Output	Customer
Project Manager Program Manager	Resource request	Allocate resources	Allocated resource	Project Manager Program Manager

How the PMO will measure the value of this service

This can be measured by the speed with which individuals are assigned to project or program. This can be measured by checking with the project or program manager that the right people have been assigned.

Criteria when the PMO will use this service

- When there is a resource management process in use
- Where the PMO have been asked to take a central role in ensuring the right people get assigned to projects and programs

Helpful hints for the PMO when delivering the service

- If there is a PPM tool in use the PMO will allocate the individuals to the project or program within the PPM tool
- If recruiting a new individual, ensure the line manager of the team the person will work in is included in the recruitment
- Keep a skills/knowledge database in order that you know the right people to assign

PMO Capabilities needed to fulfil this service

Competencies	Techniques and generic tools
Reporting, Insights and Analysis Resource Management Capability Development Capacity Management P3M Tools Professionalism and ethics Personal Integrity and reliability Relationships and engagement Teamwork Resourcefulness Negotiation Result Orientation	Capability and Capacity analysis Project Management Information System

Related services

Work with HR to provide a sourcing strategy Define a process for selection of key PPM roles Maintain resource database Identify skills shortages and recommend suitable development	Capture the resource requirements of portfolio, programs, and projects Forecast future resource needs Provide 'help squads' for projects and programs Actively monitor the deployment of staff Provide a view of resource commitments that will impact delivery

Provide 'what if' resource capacity analysis

Service Description

Provision of a series of scenarios to examine the impact on the resource demand/capacity.

What the service provides for the customer

Working with the portfolio manager to run through the different scenarios and see the impact on the portfolio using the data available. Such scenarios include level of funding changing, level of resources changing, scope changes, delivery dates changing.

Why is this service being offered to the customer?

Having the various different options on what can happen with the portfolio demand/capacity provides the portfolio manager with an understanding of the impact of these changes on the portfolio.

How PMO will apply this service

The PMO will find the current resource capacity/demand information. They will speak to the portfolio manager to review what scenarios they are wanting to see. These scenarios could include reduction of x% on budget, increase of y% on budget, change in the mix between projects & BAU, change in the mix of resource types (contractor & permanent).

For each of the scenarios the PMO will take the current demand and try to fit this into the capacity for the scenario. This may include changing the start/finish/duration of projects. As well as providing the new capacity/demand information the PMO will provide some analysis and commentary as to the impact of the scenario on the current capacity/demand.

Based on the different 'what if' scenarios the portfolio manager can then make some decisions on what needs to be done. It may mean that the PMO is asked to run some new scenarios with slightly different parameters.

Supplier	Input	Process	Output	Customer
Project Managers Program Managers	Resource Demand Schedules Financial plans	Provide 'what if' analysis	'What if' analysis	Portfolio Managers Project Approval Board

How the PMO will measure the value of this service

This can be measured by asking for feedback from the portfolio manager. If can be measured by seeing whether any of the options are adopted.

Criteria when the PMO will use this service

- When the PMO is aligned to a portfolio manager
- Where there are challenges to the budget for the portfolio
- Where there is the option to expand the budget for the portfolio

Helpful hints for the PMO when delivering the service

- Look to see whether there are any tools which can help re-profile the schedule if extending the duration of a project
- If reprofiling a project with a different duration look to see whether there are any standard profiles that can be used, rather than just flat phase the demand
- If looking to reduce the budget by a percentage, consider whether entire projects could be removed rather than reduce the demand of all projects by a given percentage
- If extending projects into the next financial year, see whether there will be budget in that year to complete the project
- If extending project durations, see whether there is any impact e.g. projects which are required to deliver legislative changes probably cannot be moved without having a negative impact

PMO Capabilities needed to fulfil this service

Competencies	Techniques and generic tools
Reporting, Insights and Analysis Resource Management Capacity Management P3M Tools Resourcefulness Result Orientation	Alternatives analysis Alternatives generation Change Impact Analysis Scenario analysis Capability and Capacity analysis Prioritization matrices Project Management Information System

Related services

Forecast future resource needs Capture the resource requirements of portfolio, programs, and projects Maintain resource database	Provide resource tracking and capacity reports Develops scenario modelling to reduce commitments or increase capacity Provide tools and analysis for Business Capacity Management

Identify over commitment of changes to the business

Service Description

The review of the changes impacting the different areas of the business to ensure there is not too much change going on at once.

What the service provides for the customer

An independent review of the changes that are going to be delivered to each of the business areas. This provides a check to see whether the balance of change is correct. Either too much or too little change can have a negative impact on the business area concerned.

Why is this service being offered to the customer?

Too much change leads to change fatigue which means the business are unable to absorb the changes that are due. By understanding the impact of the change, the portfolio manager can adjust the schedule to balance out the change impact.

How PMO will apply this service

The PMO will obtain all the schedules for the projects and programs within the portfolio. They will use those schedules to find out when they are due to deliver. They will look at the documentation to find out which of the business areas that will be impacted.

The PMO will then look to show this information in a visual way (see figure 04.01) in order that the volume of change can be shown. If there are key times of the year where changes cannot be released, then the PMO may decide to provide a visual to reflect this (see figure 04.02)

It is not only about the number of changes, but it is about the size of the change. A few minor changes may be able to be absorbed rather one larger change.

Having provided the report, the PMO should provide some analysis and commentary about how the deliveries can be adjusted to smooth the impact that change is happening on the business area.

Department	Month 1	Month 2	Month 3	Month 4	Month 5	Month 6
Department 1	Project A	Project D		Project H		Project J
	Project B	Project E		Project I		
	Project C	Project F				
		Project G				
Department 2	Project K	Project L	Project M		Project P	
			Project N		Project Q	
			Project O			
Department 3		Project R	Project T	Project U	Project V	Project W
		Project S				Project X

Figure 04.01 Report showing project delivery by month, by department

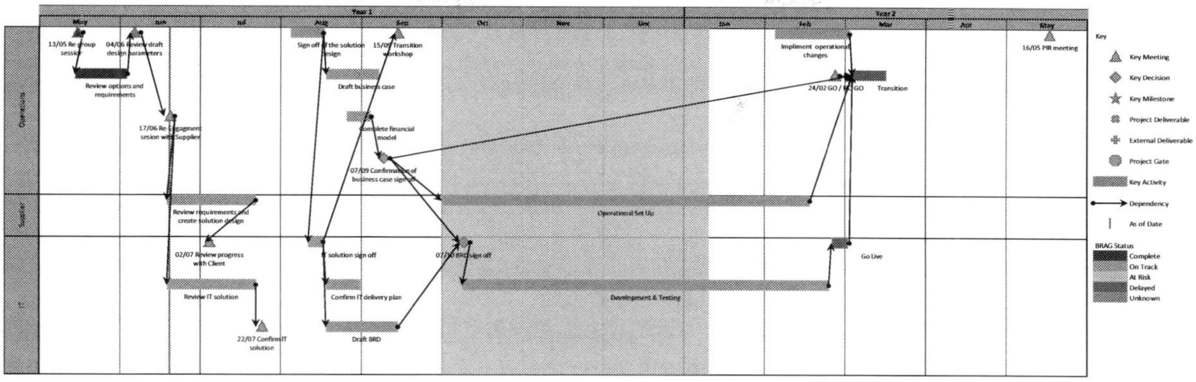

Figure 04.02 – release plan example with change freeze

Supplier	Input	Process	Output	Customer
Project Managers Program managers	Portfolio delivery schedule	Analyse business change impact	Release plan Recommendations	Portfolio Managers

How the PMO will measure the value of this service

This can be measured by looking at the revised impact of the change on the business. It can be measured by an increase in the ability of the business areas to absorb the change. It can be measured by getting feedback from the portfolio manager.

Criteria when the PMO will use this service

- Where the PMO is aligned to a portfolio manager
- Where there is a large volume of change within the organization
- Where the benefits are failing to be delivered

Helpful hints for the PMO when delivering the service

- Consider how to display the impact of the change to the various business areas
- Where a single project is delivering to multiple business areas ensure that this change is shown for each of the areas
- Where a single project is delivering multiple releases (e.g. for office software upgrade) then show each of the releases as a separate item per business area
- If there are business areas which are not having changes delivered to them, consider evaluating the decision matrix when initially prioritizing projects

PMO Capabilities needed to fulfil this service

Competencies	Techniques and generic tools
Change Management Planning and Scheduling Reporting, Insights and Analysis Capacity Management Relationships and engagement Negotiation Result Orientation	Change Impact Analysis Diagramming techniques Swim-lane flowcharts

Related services

Business strategy and roadmap maintenance Support the Project Approval Board	Perform data analysis of project selection and delivery performance Maintain a register for current and potential programs and projects

Capacity Monitoring

Service group description

The tracking of capacity against demand and reporting on this at both program and portfolio levels

Responsibility Assignment Matrix

Service	Executive	Portfolio Manager	Program Manager	Project Manager	PMO	Sponsor	Other Stakeholder
Provide a view of resource commitments that will impact delivery		I	I	I	A, R		
Provide resource tracking and capacity reports		I	I	I	A, R		

Provide a view of resource commitments that will impact delivery

Service Description

The review of the commitments of resources on other projects, programs, BAU which is reducing the availability for assignment to a particular project or program.

What the service provides for the customer

This is a report showing what a resource is assigned to outside of this particular project or program. It shows the amount and percentage of effort that this individual is spending on other activities.

Why is this service being offered to the customer?

Each project or program manager may want their resource fulltime on their work. However, most resources have other things they are asked to do. By understanding this the project or program manager can understand the impact on their project or program and if required escalate this to get the resource released from their other commitments or get another resource assigned who is able to commit the amount of time required.

How PMO will apply this service

The PMO will obtain the resource commitment of all resources on projects and programs, as well as other commitments such as Business as Usual (BAU), non-productive tasks like performance reviews, holidays.

The PMO will then look to display the information to the project manager so they can clearly see how much effort the individual is spending on their project and how much effort they are spending on other things (see figure 04.03)

Resource Name	Line Manager	Role	Grouping	Project Name	Project Manager	Month 1	Month 2	Month 3	Month 4	Month 5	Month 6	Month 7	Month 8	Month 9	Month 10	Month 11	Month 12
Resource 1	Line Mgr 1	Role 1	Projects	Project 1	PM 1	14.1 d	8.2 d	14.0 d	10.6 d	16.1 d	18.4 d	18.4 d	18.4 d	18.4 d	17.1 d	17.1 d	16.2 d
Resource 1	Line Mgr 1	Role 1	Projects	Project 2	PM 1				1.8 d								
Resource 1	Line Mgr 1	Role 1	BAU	BAU	PM 2					2.3 d	6.0 d	6.0 d	6.5 d	5.4 d	6.5 d	5.7 d	5.1 d
Resource 1	Line Mgr 1	Role 1	Non-Discretionary	Overhead	N/A	14.9 d	16.2 d	16.8 d	12.3 d	11.4 d							
Resource 1	Line Mgr 1	Role 1	Total committed			29.1 d	24.4 d	30.8 d	24.7 d	29.8 d	24.4 d	24.4 d	25.0 d	23.9 d	23.7 d	22.8 d	21.4 d
Resource 1	Line Mgr 1	Role 1	Projects	Project 1	PM 1						11.9 d	13.0 d	13.6 d	11.9 d	13.6 d		
Resource 1	Line Mgr 1	Role 1	Total Pipeline								11.9 d	13.0 d	13.6 d	11.9 d	13.6 d		
Resource 1	Line Mgr 1	Role 1	Overall Total			29.1 d	24.4 d	30.8 d	24.7 d	29.8 d	36.3 d	37.5 d	38.6 d	35.7 d	37.3 d	22.8 d	21.4 d
Resource 1	Line Mgr 1	Role 1	Capacity			22.5 d	20.4 d	23.6 d	22.5 d	23.6 d	22.5 d	22.5 d	24.6 d	20.4 d	24.6 d	21.4 d	19.3 d
Resource 1	Line Mgr 1	Role 1	Available			-6.6 d	-4.1 d	-7.2 d	-2.2 d	-6.2 d	-13.8 d	-15.0 d	-14.0 d	-15.3 d	-12.7 d	-1.4 d	-2.1 d

Figure 04.03 – Resource commitment report

The PMO can then present this to the project manager and provide some suggestions as to what can be done about getting the person to be available for the amount of time they are required.

Supplier	Input	Process	Output	Customer
Project Managers Program Managers	Resource Demand	Review resource commitments	Resource utilization report	Project Manager Program Manager Portfolio manager

How the PMO will measure the value of this service

This can be evaluated by seeing the changes to individual's allocations to projects based on the knowledge of what there are doing vs what they should be doing.

Criteria when the PMO will use this service

- When the PMO has a role in resource management
- Where there is an issue with resources not being as productive as they should be
- Where is necessary to ensure that work is focused on delivery of a single project or program

Helpful hints for the PMO when delivering the service

- Consider using a PPM tool to store and provide this information to make the consolidation easier and more consistent
- If historical actuals are shown in conjunction with current forecast, it can be easier to spot whether the individual is really spending as much time as envisaged on the project concerned
- The PMO will need to ensure the accuracy of the forecast information, just because there is no forecast does not mean there is no demand, it could mean that the information has not been provided/updated
- Consider different ways of showing the information (apart from the one shown above) to emphasize the effort that is being spent elsewhere

PMO Capabilities needed to fulfil this service

Competencies	Techniques and generic tools
Reporting, Insights and Analysis Resource Management Capacity Management P3M Tools Resourcefulness Negotiation Result Orientation	Capability and Capacity analysis

Related services

Forecast future resource needs Allocate resources directly to a program or project Develop resource plans to underpin the portfolio plan	Capture the resource requirements of portfolio, programs, and projects Provide resource tracking and capacity reports

Provide resource tracking and capacity reports

Service Description

Provision of reports and analysis showing what individuals are assigned to, what they are working on. Provision of summary data showing demand vs capacity at a consolidated level.

What the service provides for the customer

This provides a suite of reports showing capacity vs demand at various levels of detail including individual resource, role, team, resource type. This should show actual effort as well as forecast effort over time.

Why is this service being offered to the customer?

The PMO can assist the portfolio or program manager by showing them what the resources are working on and helping them smooth the resource utilization.

How PMO will apply this service

The PMO will speak to the portfolio or program manager to find out what level of analysis they require. The PMO will gather the details of the actuals and forecast by resource. They will gather the resource availability (capacity).

The PMO will produce reports showing the demand vs capacity at various levels from an overall level (figure 1) to a summary level (figure 2) to an individual resource level (figure 3).

To look at the planned resource utilization and provide some smoothing for this then the portfolio manager may need to use the 'provide a view of resource commitments that will impact delivery' service to drill down into the detail of exactly what an individual is working on.

Once the reporting has been passed to the program or portfolio manager the PMO may be called upon to provide some insights and analysis of the information. If required, the PMO should provide some suggestions about the moving and rescheduling of projects and programs to smooth out the overall resource utilization across the program or portfolio.

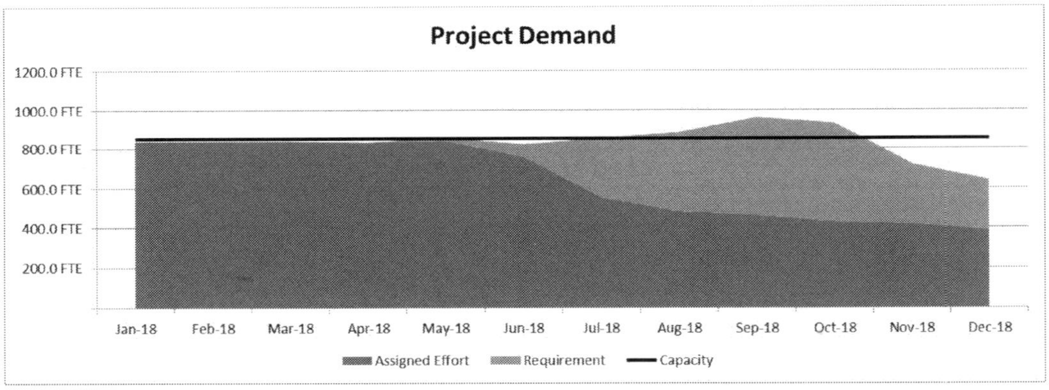

Figure 04.04 – Overall demand vs capacity report

Role	Month 1	Month 2	Month 3	Month 4	Month 5	Month 6	Month 7	Month 8	Month 9	Month 10	Month 11	Month 12
Role 1	111%	100%	106%	105%	95%	109%	95%	95%	95%	95%	95%	95%
Role 2	105%	100%	100%	90%	91%	100%	100%	100%	100%	100%	100%	Unavailable
Role 3	105%	91%	105%	100%	154%	228%	228%	228%	217%	21%	21%	21%

Figure 04.05 – summary of resource utilization by role

Line Manager	Resource Name	Role	Resource Type	Month 1	Month 2	Month 3	Month 4	Month 5	Month 6	Month 7	Month 8	Month 9	Month 10	Month 11	Month 12
Manager 1	Resource 1	Role 1	Permanent	110%	100%	105%	95%	120%	139%	110%	110%	110%	110%	110%	110%
Manager 1	Resource 2	Role 2	Contractor	105%	100%	100%	90%	91%	100%	100%	100%	100%	100%	100%	Unavailable
Manager 1	Resource 3	Role 1	Permanent	113%	100%	107%	114%	70%	80%	80%	80%	80%	80%	80%	80%
Manager 2	Resource 4	Role 3	Permanent	105%	91%	105%	100%	154%	228%	228%	228%	217%	21%	21%	21%

Figure 04.06 – detailed resource utilization by person

Supplier	Input	Process	Output	Customer
Project Managers Program Managers Resource Managers	Resource Demand Resource Capacity	Produce resource utilization report	Resource utilization report	Portfolio manager Program manager

How the PMO will measure the value of this service

This can be measured by reviewing the overall resource utilization and seeing whether the remedial actions suggested by the PMO have made any difference to the figures.

Criteria when the PMO will use this service

- When the PMO is aligned to the portfolio or program manager
- When there is a focus on resource utilization
- Where there is a desire to understand what people are working on and how busy they are

Helpful hints for the PMO when delivering the service

- The exact splits of the resource level information depend on what is important to manage. If it is important to see how busy a team is then the split should be team. If this how busy a role is then the split should by role etc.
- Although the summary reports are useful, the next question is who is busy, so it needs to be possible to drill down into the detail (and come up to a summary level)
- Use the resource database to provide information on the available capacity
- Look to assign the information as Full Time Equivalent (FTE). An individual who works 4 days a week would by 0.8 FTE. This will ensure the report can be viewed in a consistent manner
- There should be an assumption for forecast effort that there will be a certain amount of unavailability due to holidays, sickness, training etc. Decide whether you want to subtract that from the capacity, or add it in as a demand item, but not both
- If possible, use a PPM tool to source the information in order that the information used is timely. If it takes weeks to collate and produce the reports, then by the time decisions have been made the information is out of date

PMO Capabilities needed to fulfil this service

Competencies	Techniques and generic tools
Reporting, Insights and Analysis Resource Management P3M Tools Relationships and engagement	Capability and Capacity analysis Time series plots

Related services

Maintain resource database Provide a view of resource commitments that will impact delivery Forecast future resource needs Provide 'what if' resource capacity analysis	Develop resource plans to underpin the portfolio plan Capture the resource requirements of portfolio, programs, and projects Develops scenario modelling to reduce commitments or increase capacity

Change Control

Change control

Description

Ensuring that the portfolio, program, or project has effective processes in place to identify, monitor and deliver changes.

What the services within the area provide for the customer

Change is inevitable, however if properly controlled they can work to the advantage for the project or program. The PMO can provide the structure and the discipline to ensure that change is tamed, and projects and programs do not go out of control.

Helpful hints for when the PMO is delivering this service area

- Ensure the change control process is similar across projects, programs and the portfolio allowing changes to be escalated up the different level

Change Control Design

Service group description

The setup and communication of a change control framework consisting of process, procedures, standards, templates, help and tools.

Why have these services been grouped together?

These services relate to the establishment of a change control framework. The organization will then require training in the use of this framework, together with any tailoring for specific projects or programs.

List of related services described in other areas

Automate Processes

Responsibility Assignment Matrix

Service	Executive	Portfolio Manager	Program Manager	Project Manager	PMO	Sponsor	Other Stakeholder
Develop the overall change control framework	A	C	C	C	R		I (PPM team)
Introduce tools for controlling changes	A	C	C	C	R		I (PPM team)
Communicate the change control framework	I	I	I	I	A, R		I (PPM team)

Helpful hints for when the PMO is delivering this service group

The framework will need to be developed before it can be communicated, or any tools introduced. Ensure the tools are aligned to the change control process.

Develop the overall change control framework

Service description

Develop a change control framework consisting of process, procedures, standards, templates, and help.

What the service provides for the customer

This provides the program and project managers with the process for managing change requests on their programs and projects. It provides a set of templates to allow changes to be recorded and tracked through their lifecycle.

Why is this service being offered to the customer?

Having a consistent way of managing and controlling change across the portfolio allows the information on changes to be rolled up and reported on consistently. It means that when moving from project to project the project manager, and their teams do not need to learn or develop this afresh for each project.

How PMO will apply this service

The PMO will review the external guidance on how to manage changes for projects and programs and will look to tailor this for their organization. They will develop a standard approach to managing change requests and suggest some tailoring options that can be taken depending on the size of project or program.

They will produce a standard change request form and a linked change register together with some help guides for their usage. This may be incorporated within the documents themselves.

The PMO will consider any common reporting requirements and will try to ensure these can be delivered using the information in the change register.

Supplier	Input	Process	Output	Customer
PMO	Standards template	Develop Standard Develop Templates	Change control framework Change Register Change Request Form Change control process	Project Manager Program Manager Portfolio Manager PMO

How the PMO will measure the value of this service

The PMO can measure the value of this service by looking how widely the documents produced by this service have been used. i.e. how many people are using the change request form, or are they developing their own?

Criteria when the PMO will use this service

- When there is no consistent change control process
- Where there is a desired to have some standardization in approach across the portfolio
- If the existing change control process needs a review

Helpful hints for the PMO when delivering the service

- Link this service with the Introduce tools for controlling changes service to introduce a tool at the same time as the process is being introduced
- When developing the change request form, divide this into sections to link to the steps in the process
- Trial the change request form and register on a real change, or two, to see how workable this is. Has this been made too complex or too simplistic?
- Provide guidance on how the change control approvals process can be tailored depending on the type and scale of the project or program being run
- Assume that every project will have a change on it at some point

PMO capabilities needed to fulfil this service

Competencies	Techniques and generic tools
Change Control Information Management Reporting, Insights and Analysis Delivery Methods Governance Frameworks	Change Impact Analysis Process Analysis Change control tools Stakeholder checklist Swim-lane flowcharts Task responsibility matrix/RACI

Related services

Introduce tools for controlling changes Communicate the change control framework Maintain the change control register Control escalation of changes to higher authority Provide a secretariat service for meetings Facilitate cross-program impact analysis Ensure quality of change requests	Develop configuration management standards and processes Define, maintain, and implement PPM governance framework Manage the Process Improvement Flan Map key value streams and processes

Further Reading

PMI PMBoK (A Guide to the Project Management Body of Knowledge)
PRINCE2
Managing Successful Programmes (MSP)
APM BoK
Praxis

Introduce tools for controlling changes

Service description

The sourcing/developing/tailoring of tools to manage change control aligned to the change control process. Ensuring that the users get trained in the use of these tools.

What the service provides for the customer

This will provide the project or program manager with a tool which will support the change control process. Ensuring all the steps in the process have been followed, help track where the change is in the process and possibly provide automated approval functionality.

Why is this service being offered to the customer?

Rather than just relying on Word and Excel to record changes, having a tool can provide a more integrated view of change allowing the information to be recorded once, increasing accuracy, and reducing data errors. Depending on the tool chosen it may be possible to have a workflow built in which will guide the user through the change lifecycle.

How PMO will apply this service

The PMO will check to see whether there is an existing tool that can be configured to support the change control process (the organization may already have a PPM tool in place). If there is not, then they will review whether they want to develop something in-house (if they have the skills) or whether they want to get a vendor supplied tool.

If this is being developed in house then the PMO will supply the developer with the requirements (generally this will consist of the change control process, the existing change request form and change register). Once the development has finished the PMO will perform the testing, ensuring it meets the requirements before accepting the tool into use.

If this is being sourced from a vendor, then the package will need to be customized to ensure it fits in with the processes that are in use for change control. Once this has been done the PMO can start rolling out the usage of the tool.

Regardless of how the tool was obtained it will need to have some training developed and some guidelines for use. The PMO should look to develop the training and be prepared to deliver the training alongside the rollout of the tool. The PMO should consider how frequently they want to deliver the training once the initial training has finished. Do they want to run regular sessions or individual session as and when new users are identified?

The process for cutover of existing changes needs to be considered. Will there be an initial load, or conversion of existing change registers, will it just be applied to new projects and programs. If there is a data load will it be the PMO who will be doing this, or will each project be expected to load their own changes?

The existing change process will need to be updated to have appropriate references to the new tool and the links to the change request form and the change register will need to be discontinued.

Supplier	Input	Process	Output	Customer
Vendor In house developers	Vendor software In house software	Software implementation	Change control tool	Project Manager Program Manager PMO

How the PMO will measure the value of this service

This can be measured by increase the data quality of change control information. The reduction in time taken to access change control information. Reduction in changes not following change control process.

Criteria when the PMO will use this service

- When there is desire for consistency across the portfolio
- Where a change control framework has been developed
- Where there is funding to purchase a vendor tool

Helpful hints for the PMO when delivering the service

- Factor the cost of supporting the tool as well as the initial purchase
- Work out how much tailoring a tool will require to be aligned to the change control process
- Fit the tool to the process not the other way around
- Work out how people will be trained in the use of the tool, both on initial rollout and when new people join and are required to use it

PMO Capabilities needed to fulfil this service

Competencies	Techniques and generic tools
Change Control Information Management Reporting, Insights and Analysis Delivery Methods P3M Tools Relationships and engagement	Make or buy analysis Communication requirements analysis Change control tools Stakeholder checklist Stakeholder engagement assessment matrix

Related services

Develop the overall change control framework Develops in-house project management tools Tailors and configures project management tools Implements vendor provided project management tools	Manages project management tools (systems admin)Facilitate cross-program impact analysis Maintain the change control register Advise on PPM tools and software Automate Processes

Communicate the change control framework

Service description

Clearly communicate the change control framework, and the benefits of following it, to all, personnel involved with the portfolio, program, and projects, including Business Operations.

What the service provides for the customer

This ensures that everyone who is involved with the change control process knows how it works, who is responsible for each part of the process. This will cover what reporting and monitoring is done. If this is tailored for an individual project or program, due to size, complexity, or lifecycle type then this needs to be explained as well.

Why is this service being offered to the customer?

As this is a central process common across the portfolio, having a central team (the PMO) to explain it ensures there is consistency of training.

How PMO will apply this service

The PMO will identify the key people in each project or program that need training. Typically, this will include the project and program managers along with any team leaders, the members of the steering group and change controls.

Once the PMO have a list of who requires training/communication about the process they will decide the best means of doing this. Will it be a full training course or is it just sending a link out to the process?

If it has been decided that training session(s) are required, they need to be booked in the diary and people invited. The PMO can then prepare the training material that will be used. At the training course take note of who has attended and who has not and be prepared to organize further training sessions.

If it has been decided to send out a communication then the PMO will draft this communication, ensuring it covers why this is important as well as when and how to use the process. Some frequently asked questions could be included in the communication to help cover some of the basic questions that are likely to arise.

Supplier	Input	Process	Output	Customer
Project Manager Program Manager	Change Control Framework	Deliver training Communication	Informed people	Project teams Program teams

How the PMO will measure the value of this service

This can be measured by numbers of people trained and the satisfaction with the training.

Criteria when the PMO will use this service

- When there is a change to the change control framework, or the change control framework is new
- When new people are added to the project teams

Helpful hints for the PMO when delivering the service

- Deciding whether to hold a training course or just to send a communication out will depend on how the organization typically manages changes to process. More adoption will be gained by providing dedicated training, but it takes more time from the PMO and the attendees. There is always the chance that not everyone will be able to make a training session
- If there is a tool that needs to be used, then show that at the same time
- Ensure that there are worked examples of change requests which have been filled in at different stages of the process, so people can understand what is expected
- If providing a training course, make it a repeatable one so that it can be given to any new starters
- Use the questions from the training courses to help devise a frequently asked questions or help document
- Gain feedback from the training course on how effective the training was and use that as a measure for the service

PMO Capabilities needed to fulfil this service

Competencies	Techniques and generic tools
Change Control Professionalism and ethics Personal Communication Leadership Result Orientation	Communication requirements analysis Change control tools Stakeholder checklist Stakeholder engagement assessment matrix

Related services

Develop the overall change control framework Train the issue management framework Train the risk management framework Control escalation of changes to higher authority	Provide secretariat function to Change Control Board (CCB) Provide PPM training Provide training logistics support

Change Control Operations

Service group description

The operation of the change control process including updating the change control register, performing impact analysis, ensuring changes get evaluated, recording the decisions made and if necessary, escalating decisions up to the next level.

Why have these services been grouped together?

These services relate to the day to day running of the change control process on behalf of the project or program manager and the Change Control Board.

List of related services described in other areas

Maintain details of changes to budget baseline

Responsibility Assignment Matrix

Service	Executive	Portfolio Manager	Program Manager	Project Manager	PMO	Sponsor	Other Stakeholder
Control escalation of changes to higher authority	A	R	R	R	C	C	C (CCB)
Provide secretariat function to Change Control Board (CCB)	C		C	C	R	A	A (CCB)
Facilitate independent change impact assessment workshops	I		A	A	R	I	I (CCB)
Facilitate cross-program impact analysis		A	C		R	C	I (CCB)
Maintain the change control register	I		A	A	R	I	I (CCB)

Helpful hints for when the PMO is delivering this service group

Consider the use of a tool to store the change requests and provide easy access for reporting on the status of change requests.

Control escalation of changes to higher authority

Service description

The control of the approval of change request by the appropriate body. The level at which changes need approving is normally defined by cost levels. PMO to ensure that changes are approved according to the approval levels of the boards.

What the service provides for the customer

This ensures that changes can be approved by the appropriate body. If they need approving by a previous person or group, the PMO can ensure this happens in the correct sequence.

Why is this service being offered to the customer?

To enable changes to get approved according to the governance setup for the project or program.

How PMO will apply this service

The PMO will receive a change request to be approved and this will have been assessed so that the cost, timescale, scope, benefits, and quality impacts are known.

The PMO will review this against the change control framework to see which approvals are required. The PMO will ensure that the change request is approved by the lower levels (if applicable) prior to the being approved by the required level. The PMO will produce a timeline for these approvals to occur, considering any 'fast-track' approval process that may be built in. This timeline will be communicated back to the change request owner. They (or the PMO) can then follow the timeline and ensure that the change request gets the necessary approvals. The PMO will monitor the outcome of each approval level and record this. Only when the change has been approved by a lower level should it be sent to the higher level for approval.

If there are any alterations required to the change request prior to it being approved, then the PMO will need to confirm whether the approvals cycle starts again from scratch or whether the alterations are cosmetic or minor and do not require a lower-level re-approval.

Supplier	Input	Process	Output	Customer
Project Manager Program Manager Finance	Change Register Change control framework Communication Management Strategy Approval levels		Change control framework Communication Management Strategy	Project Manager Program Manager Portfolio Manager

How the PMO will measure the value of this service

The PMO will measure this by reviewing which changes are not authorized by the correct bodies as a proportion of the number of changes submitted.

Criteria when the PMO will use this service

- When there is a dedicated PMO for a single project or program
- Where there is a series of change approval levels e.g. Project Manager, CCB, Steering Group
- Where the PMO provide a secretariat service for the CCB

Helpful hints for the PMO when delivering the service

- Ensure that changes are not sub-divided, yet need to be delivered together, just get under any approval thresholds
- Maintain an overall view of change spend by project and program to confirm whether the totality of the change spend exceeds the change budget
- Ensure there are clear rules as to how and why a change needs to be escalated to the next level of approval. It could be about timescale, scope, benefits as well as just cost

PMO Capabilities needed to fulfil this service

Competencies	Techniques and generic tools
P3M Administration Change Control Information Management Personal Communication	Change control tools

Related services

Provide secretariat function to Change Control Board (CCB) Maintain the change control register Ensure quality of change requests	Develop the overall change control framework Communicate the change control framework Define, maintain, and implement standard PPM framework Define, maintain, and implement PPM governance framework

Provide secretariat function to Change Control Board (CCB)

Service description

The administration around the CCB including the setup of the meeting, managing the attendee list, providing the agenda, minuting the meeting, and recording any decisions taken.

What the service provides for the customer

Ensures that changes to projects and programs follow the prescribed process. Documents decisions made and communicates this to the change owner, project/program manager and other appropriate stakeholders.

Why is this service being offered to the customer?

This provides an independent person to document the meeting and ensures that the chair can focus on the role of getting decisions made and the rest of the CCB can focus on critically assessing the changes.

How PMO will apply this service

Once the frequency of the CCB has been agreed the PMO can arrange these meetings with the attendees. Prior to the meeting the PMO will confirm with the CCB chair the list of changes that will be submitted for the CCB to review. These changes will come from the change register and will be dependent on their status.

The PMO will agree the agenda with the chair of the CCB and then issue that along with the details of the changes needing considering and the minutes of the prior meeting (if there was one).

The PMO will attend the meeting and record the decisions made. After the meeting, the PMO will ensure the change register gets updated with the details of the change decisions. They will document the decisions made and any actions in the CCB minutes. These will then get distributed to all CCB attendees. The PMO should ensure that they communicate the decision made on each of the changes back to the change author and anyone else listed in the relevant section of the communications plan.

Supplier	Input	Process	Output	Customer
Change Request authors	Change Request Forms Previous CCB minutes CCB Agenda	Taking minutes Booking meetings	CCB minutes	Change Control Board Program Manager Project Manager Portfolio Manager Audit

How the PMO will measure the value of this service

The PMO can measure this in a similar way to other meetings such as the number of times an agenda is not sent out 24 hours prior or the number of times minutes have not been drafted within 2 working days.

Criteria when the PMO will use this service

- When there is a dedicated PMO looking after a single project or program
- When there is a CCB in place
- When there is a CCB meeting

Helpful hints for the PMO when delivering the service

- Consider doing this service and the Maintain the change control register service together
- Confirm who the chair of the CCB is, it may not be the project or program manager
- Ensure that you set deadlines for changes to be submitted to the CCB to ensure that the attendees get time to read the changes prior to them attending the meeting
- Set a Service Level Agreement (SLA) for decisions and minutes to be communicated after the CCB
- Have a central place to store the CCB minutes that is accessible to the project or program team

PMO Capabilities needed to fulfil this service

Competencies	Techniques and generic tools
P3M Administration Change Control Information Management Personal Communication	Change control tools

Related services

Maintain the change control register Develop the overall change control framework Communicate the change control framework	Provide a secretariat service for meetings Control escalation of changes to higher authority

Facilitate independent change impact assessment workshops

Service description

Provide a facilitation service to enable a change request to be discussed and the response be devised.

What the service provides for the customer

This provides a facilitation service to enable tricky change impacts to be discussed and solutions devised.

Why is this service being offered to the customer?

This provides an independent person to conduct the facilitation and allows the other participants to focus on finding a solution to deal with the change request.

How PMO will apply this service

Having identified the need for a facilitated workshop the PMO will liaise with the project or program manager to work out who needs to attend the workshop. The PMO will then book the meeting and invite all the attendees. The purpose of the workshop will be clearly stated prior to the workshop commencing. Any background documentation should be sent to the participants in advance to give them time to read the materials prior to the meeting.

In the meeting the PMO will set the ground rules and re-state the objective of the meeting to ensure everyone has a clear understanding of what they are being expected to do. During the meeting, the PMO, as facilitator, will ensure that everyone gets a chance to speak and put forward their views. The PMO should ensure that decisions are recorded and capture all the workshop outputs.

After the meeting, the PMO will communicate the result of the meeting out to all participants and document the solution in the change request and update the change register (if applicable).

Supplier	Input	Process	Output	Customer
Project Manager Program Manager	Change Request	Facilitating a meeting	Change Register Updated Change Request	Project Manager Program Manager

How the PMO will measure the value of this service

The value of this service comes in finding a solution to the change request.

Criteria when the PMO will use this service

- Where there is a dedicated PMO assigned to a single project or program
- If there is a change request where multiple solutions have been proposed and it cannot be agreed which one is the best solution

Helpful hints for the PMO when delivering the service

- Consider having a facilitation/workshop kit (pens, post-its, blue-tac, flipchart paper etc.)
- Assign one of the flipcharts as a parking lot to avoid wasting time discussing an intractable issue
- Consider training individuals within the PMO to deliver this service

PMO Capabilities needed to fulfil this service

Competencies	Techniques and generic tools
P3M Administration Change Control Personal Communication Relationships and engagement Teamwork Negotiation Result Orientation	Change Impact Analysis

Related services

Ensure quality of change requests Facilitate cross-program impact analysis Provide a secretariat service for meetings	Provide facilitation service Facilitate independent issue analysis and resolution workshops

Facilitate cross-program impact analysis

Service description

The review of changes across programs to check whether there are similar change requests which would benefit from having a project raised to fix. Checking to see if there are conflicting change requests which would cancel each other out.

What the service provides for the customer

This provides an independent check on behalf of the portfolio manager to see whether there are conflicting or common change requests.

Why is this service being offered to the customer?

By getting into the detail the PMO are able to spot duplication and highlight to the portfolio potential conflicts or items of re-work and ensure there is a smoother more unified portfolio delivery.

How PMO will apply this service

The PMO will gain access to all the open change requests for the programs they are looking to review. They will read the summary information from the change register to see which changes to investigate and which ones are looking to change the scope of the program. For each of the changes which have an impact on the scope of the program they will review the detail in the change request form. Where there is potential overlap the PMO can make a list of these, together with the conflict area and highlight that to the portfolio manager.

Supplier	Input	Process	Output	Customer
Program Manager	Change Request forms Change Register	Reviewing a change request	List of Changes with conflict or duplication	Portfolio Manager

How the PMO will measure the value of this service

This can be measured by a reduction of duplicate or conflicting change requests.

Criteria when the PMO will use this service

- When requested by the portfolio manager
- Where the PMO have access to all change requests for the programs they are looking to review
- Where programs have dependencies on each other or are dealing with the same business area(s)

Helpful hints for the PMO when delivering the service

- Consider using a tool to store all change requests in a single place
- The PMO will need to understand the original scope of the program to understand the impact the change will have on that scope
- To make this service ongoing as opposed to one-off, have a way of being informed when a new change request gets raised in order that this service can be done before too much effort is put in to consider the change
- If delivering is as an ongoing service, consider reporting changes with conflicts back to the program directly as well as to the portfolio manager
- The PMO may find after doing this review that there are no change requests with conflicts or duplications. If this is the case, then report that to the portfolio manager

PMO Capabilities needed to fulfil this service

Competencies	Techniques and generic tools
Change Control Reporting, Insights and Analysis Assurance Governance Frameworks Relationships and engagement Teamwork	Change Impact Analysis

Related services

Maintain the change control register Develop the overall change control framework	Introduce tools for controlling changes Facilitate independent change impact assessment workshops

Maintain the change control register

Service description

Keep the change control register up to date with the details of each change including approval statuses. Add the details of each new change as it gets raised.

What the service provides for the customer

This provides the project or program manager with an up-to-date change register. This acts a summary of the change request forms.

Why is this service being offered to the customer?

Having the PMO perform this, rather than the project or program manager, allows them to focus on the overall delivery of the project or program. They get the knowledge that the information is accurate and can be reviewed at any point. It gives confidence that this reflects the true approval status of each of the changes.

How PMO will apply this service

For a new change, the PMO will receive a copy of the change request form from the change author. They will take the relevant information from the change request and transfer this into change register. They will ensure the change has been assigned a unique reference number and if necessary, update the change request form with that unique reference number. They will ensure that the change request form has been stored according the configuration management policy explained as part of the change control framework. If the change request has been updated, then they will ensure a copy of this gets back to the change request author.

Prior to the agenda for the CCB meeting being sent out the PMO will review the change register and update the status of any changes going to the meeting.

After the CCB meeting the PMO will review the minutes for the decisions made and update change register with the details of the approval status and the dates when that decision was made. If the approvals information is also stored in the change request form itself, they will ensure that gets updated to be in line with the change register.

When a change has been implemented then the PMO will update the status of the change within the change register.

Supplier	Input	Process	Output	Customer
Change Request authors CCB	Change Request Forms CCB minutes	Maintaining a register	Change Register	Project Manager Program Manager

How the PMO will measure the value of this service

The measure will be that the change register reflects the status and contents of the individual change request forms.

Criteria when the PMO will use this service

- When there is a dedicated PMO supporting a single project or program
- When the project or program manager is happy to delegate this responsibility
- Where there a change request process in place
- When changes have been raised or require updating

Helpful hints for the PMO when delivering the service

- Consider using a tool to store the change requests
- Review the reporting requirements for change requests and ensure that can be driven from the change register rather than having to review each form
- Look to offer this service in conjunction with the Provide secretariat function to Change Control Board (CCB) service so the PMO is aware of the CCB decisions

PMO Capabilities needed to fulfil this service

Competencies	Techniques and generic tools
P3M Administration Change Control Information Management Reporting, Insights and Analysis Personal Integrity and reliability	Change control tools

Related services

Ensure quality of change requests Provide secretariat function to Change Control Board (CCB) Develop the overall change control framework Introduce tools for controlling changes	Control escalation of changes to higher authority Facilitate cross-program impact analysis Hold master copies of all portfolio, program, or project information Support contracts monitoring and management

Change Control Monitoring

Service group description

The review of change requests for quality purposes.

Why have these services been grouped together?

This service relates to the review of change requests that have been submitted for the project or program.

Responsibility Assignment Matrix

Service	Executive	Portfolio Manager	Program Manager	Project Manager	PMO	Sponsor	Other Stakeholder
Ensure quality of change requests			A	A	R	C	

Ensure quality of change requests

Service description

The review of change requests to ensure there is enough information contained within them for the Change Control Board (CCB) to make an informed decision.

What the service provides for the customer

This enables the attendees for the CCB to read the change request and make an informed decision based on the information contained in the change request.

Why is this service being offered to the customer?

Without this time may be wasted at the CCB by reviewing a change request only for the decision be taken to go back and find more information. If this review was done in advance this will reduce the time taken for the CCB to come to a decision, it can be done in a single meeting rather than several.

As changes are raised, ensure that there is enough information to make an informed decision. Where this is not the case go back to the change request author and advise them of what is required. This means that when the change goes to the CAB, they are in the best place to make an informed decision.

How PMO will apply this service

The PMO will receive a change request for validation. They will check that this uses the correct, current template. If not, they will look to copy the change request over into the new template and advise the change request author of the need to submit in the correct format for future changes.

The PMO will then check to see whether there is enough information in to come to a decision. If this is the first time the change has come to the CCB the PMO should check:

- Is there a business driver for the change?
- Are the change request classifications such as priority, severity, category all filled in correctly?
- Does it adequately explain what the alternatives are?
- Are there acceptance criteria for the change?

If this is the second time that the change has come to the CCB then the PMO should check:

- Are there details about the solution and approach for the change?
- Does it have details of how the timescale, costs, benefits, quality etc. will be impacted by this change? i.e. is there a cost and a timescale for the implementation of this change

If the change is lacking in quality, then the PMO will need to feed this back to the change request author with details of the changes required.

Supplier	Input	Process	Output	Customer
Change Request authors	Change Request Forms	Change Request review	Validated Change Request Forms	Project Manager Program Manager Change Control Board

How the PMO will measure the value of this service

The PMO can measure this service by reviewing the numbers of changes that get rejected by the CCB due to poor data quality. This should go down over time as the service gets introduced.

Criteria when the PMO will use this service

- When the PMO is dedicated to a single project or program
- Where there is a CCB in place
- When any change request gets submitted

Helpful hints for the PMO when delivering the service

- The PMO will need to change this depending on the format of the change request template in place. They will need to change this to align to the change request process
- The PMO could develop a checklist so they have consistency in the way they check for change request quality

PMO Capabilities needed to fulfil this service

Competencies	Techniques and generic tools
Change Control Quality Management Reporting, Insights and Analysis Assurance	Cost/ Benefit Analysis Change Impact Analysis Assumption and constraint analysis Prompt Lists Check sheets

Related services

Develop the overall change control framework Control escalation of changes to higher authority Automate Processes	Facilitate independent change impact assessment workshops Maintain the change control register

Change Management

Change Management

Description

This service area covers the setup of change management within the organization. Change management has a wider remit than project management which is about the delivery of something. Change management covers the adoption of that thing by individuals and takes people through the change journey.

What the services within the area provide for the customer

These services ensure that change management is defined and trained out across the organization. As experts in doing change management for their service catalogue the PMO are ideally experienced to provide this setup for the rest of the organization.

Helpful hints for when the PMO is delivering this service area

- Understand and communicate the difference between project management and change management
- Ensure that you understand the difference between change control and change management

Change Management Design

Service group description

The design and setup of change management within the organization.

Why have these services been grouped together?

These services relate to the design and communication of the change management framework.

Responsibility Assignment Matrix

Service	Executive	Portfolio Manager	Program Manager	Project Manager	PMO	Sponsor	Other Stakeholder
Create Change Management Framework	I	I	C	C	R	I	
Communicate change management framework	I	I	I	I	R, A	I	

Helpful hints for when the PMO is delivering this service group

The PMO will need to develop the framework before communicating it. These 2 services should go together. As there will be new people joining the organization then the PMO may communicate the change framework to new people without having the change it every time.

Create Change Management Framework

Service description

The creation of the process, procedures, standards, templates and help that enable change management to be performed in a consistent way in the organization.

What the service provides for the customer

This provides a way for the change managers to run their change projects and programs in a consistent manner. It provides the process, templates, hints, and tips that are needed when introducing change into the organization.

Why is this service being offered to the customer?

Without change management the organization will not be able to successfully embed the changes they require to deliver the benefits. Having advice and guidance available will enable this to be done consistently and will help the change delivery improve.

How PMO will apply this service

The PMO will review the external guidance on how the different change management models and will choose one that is suited to their organization. They may decide to provide some tailoring optioned depending on the type of project being run. Having decided which change management model to follow the PMO can provide more detailed processes, help and templates aligned to that model.

The PMO will review the existing guidance on how projects and programs are run to include references to the change management model within that guidance and vice versa. The PMO may consider writing role descriptions for change manager and project manager roles to differentiate them in the minds for of the people performing the 2 roles.

Supplier	Input	Process	Output	Customer
PMO	Standards template	Develop Standard Develop Templates	Change story Change Management Strategy Change impact Sustainment plan	Change Manager

How the PMO will measure the value of this service

The PMO can measure this by looking at the numbers of projects incorporating the change management framework.

Criteria when the PMO will use this service

- When the organization wants to introduce change management
- When the organization wants to update its change management framework
- When there is a drive to manage change in a consistent manner

Helpful hints for the PMO when delivering the service

- Change management is not the same as project management, but will contain some of the same elements
- Aligning the change management process to an existing model can help when it comes to detailed training and certification of change management individuals within the organization
- Consider writing specific roles for change manager and project manager to emphasize the differences in the 2 roles

PMO Capabilities needed to fulfil this service

Competencies	Techniques and generic tools
Change Management Delivery Methods Governance Frameworks	Process Analysis Change control tools Swim-lane flowcharts Task responsibility matrix/RACI

Related services

Communicate change management framework Define, maintain, and implement standard PPM framework Define, maintain, and implement PPM governance framework	Define, maintain, and implement reporting framework Manage the Process Improvement Plan Map key value streams and processes

Further Reading

Prosci (https://www.prosci.com)
Lewin's Change Management Model
The McKinsey 7S Model
Kotter's 8 Step Change Model
The Kubler Ross Change Curve
The ADKAR Model

Communicate change management framework

Service description

Clearly communicate the change management framework, and the benefits of following it, to all, personnel involved with the program and projects, including Business Operations.

What the service provides for the customer

This ensures that the people who need to use the change management framework understand what it is and how it can be applied.

Why is this service being offered to the customer?

Change managers will be expected to prepare the organization for change and help the change get embedded, by having a consistent framework including help and templates provides the change managers with the structure they need to deliver the change into the organization.

How PMO will apply this service

The PMO will identify the change managers who require detailed training along with other people such as project and program managers who may require awareness training. For the detailed training, the PMO will put together a training package explaining the change management process and the steps within it, the use of any templates, with worked examples. Consideration should be given to providing the opportunity for change managers to practice using what they have learnt on a case study example that would be applicable to their organization.

The PMO will look to book the training sessions and invite people to attend. At the end of the training course take note of who has attended and who has not and be prepared to organize further training sessions.

Supplier	Input	Process	Output	Customer
PMO	Change Management Framework	Deliver training Communication	Informed people	Change Managers Project Managers

How the PMO will measure the value of this service

The PMO can measure this by recording the numbers of individuals who have attended training.

Criteria when the PMO will use this service

- When there is a new change management framework
- When there have been changes to the change management framework
- When new people need to know about the change management framework

Helpful hints for the PMO when delivering the service

- Consider having a video on demand introduction to the framework. This could be done by recording a session that was given and making it more widely available. This would work well for the awareness training where only an overview would be required
- Deciding whether to hold a training course or just to send a communication out will depend on how the organization typically manages changes to process. More adoption will be gained by providing dedicated training, but it takes more time from the PMO and the attendees. There is always the chance that not everyone will be able to make a training session
- If providing a training course, make it a repeatable one so that it can be given to any new starters
- For the detailed training, the PMO may consider sending people on an external accredited course
- Use the questions from the training courses to help devise a frequently asked questions or help document
- Gain feedback from the training course on how effective the training was and use that as a measure for the service
- Provide examples of success stories where people have followed the framework and it has made a difference to the organization (and the change manager)
- Consider using the change management framework to help manage the change, this way the PMO can say they are following the process they are training out and people can see this in action
- Split out the detailed training and the awareness sessions due to the differences in the level of detail and time required to explain. This way the PMO can focus their efforts on the people who need the most training

PMO Capabilities needed to fulfil this service

Competencies	Techniques and generic tools
Change Management Delivery Methods Governance Frameworks Professionalism and ethics Personal Communication Leadership Result Orientation	Communication requirements analysis Change control tools Stakeholder checklist Stakeholder engagement assessment matrix

Related services

Create Change Management Framework Define, maintain, and implement PPM governance framework	Manage the Process Improvement Plan Provide PPM training Provide training logistics support

Communications Management

Communications Management

Description

Communications Management is the collection of tasks which relate to the communication of information about the project, program, or portfolio out to the relevant stakeholders.

What the services within the area provide for the customer

These services provide a convenient way of ensuring that the communications go out on the regular basis to the required individuals. This will enable them to focus on their primary role knowing that the stakeholders are being communicated to correctly.

Helpful hints for when the PMO is delivering this service area

- If you are embarking on a communications campaign ensure you know where the sources of information are being provided from, and what happens when that source is not available (e.g. the person has gone on holiday)

Communications Design

Service group description

The development of the standards and templates associated with communicat ons on project, programs, and the portfolio.

Why have these services been grouped together?

These services are related to the setup of the templates to enable communications to occur in a consistent manner across the portfolio.

Responsibility Assignment Matrix

Service	Executive	Portfolio Manager	Program Manager	Project Manager	PMO	Sponsor	Other Stakeholder
Enable the formulation of communication plans		A	A	A	R		
Develop and maintain the communication framework		C	C	C	A, R		

Helpful hints for when the PMO is delivering this service group

Ensure that the communication and stakeholder engagement frameworks are linked.

Enable the formulation of communication plans

Service description

Ensures that communication plans are written for the project, program, or portfolio.

What the service provides for the customer

This will provide a communication plan which will detail how the project, program or portfolio will communicate with its stakeholders. It will cover the format and frequency of the communication alongside who will be responsible for handling that communication.

Why is this service being offered to the customer?

Communication is vital for the project, program, or portfolio to be successful. It is not good enough to have a stakeholder list without working out how to communicate with them. By creating a communication plan, it will document how that communication will occur. This plan can then be used throughout the life of the project, program, or portfolio to manage those communications.

How PMO will apply this service

The PMO will find the stakeholder matrix for the project, program, or portfolio. They will discuss with the relevant manager what communications will be required for each stakeholder and stakeholder group. They will look to create a communication plan with all this information in it.

The communication plan will include:

- Stakeholder details – who will be communicated to. This will be taken from the stakeholder list
- Frequency of communication – how often will this stakeholder be communicated with
- Means of communication – how will the stakeholder be communicated with
- Who is responsible – who is going to do the communication?

Once the communication plan has been written it will then be the responsibility of the manager concerned to ensure that it is followed and updated as required.

Supplier	Input	Process	Output	Customer
PMO Project Manager Program Manager Portfolio Manager	Communication plan template Stakeholder management plan	Write communication plan	Communication plan	Project Manager Program Manager Portfolio Manager

How the PMO will measure the value of this service

Th is can be measured by ensuring that the communication plan is followed.

Criteria when the PMO will use this service

- When the PMO is aligned with a project, program, or portfolio manager
- Where there is no communication plan already written
- Where the PPM manager does not do this themselves

Helpful hints for the PMO when delivering the service

- Ensure that once the communication plan is written that it is actually followed. There is no point in producing a communication plan that no one uses
- Look to produce the communication plan alongside the stakeholder matrix

PMO Capabilities needed to fulfil this service

Competencies	Techniques and generic tools
Stakeholder Engagement Personal Communication Relationships and engagement	Communication requirements analysis Salience model Stakeholder checklist Stakeholder engagement assessment matrix

Related services

Develop and maintain the communication framework Monitor the effectiveness of communications Coordinate the internal communication Facilitate stakeholder identification and communication workshops Facilitate the formulation of stakeholder engagement strategies Develop stakeholder plans, profiles, and matrices	Manage Customer Interfaces Provide answers and briefings to queries and information requests Support press enquiries Manages social media activities Advise on key stakeholders and influencing strategies

Develop and maintain the communication framework

Service description

The development and maintenance of the communication plan template and communication strategy.

What the service provides for the customer

This provides the project and program managers with a template to assist them in communicating with their stakeholders.

Why is this service being offered to the customer?

By having a standard communications plan, the information can be consolidated to program or portfolio level to have a common understanding of who is being communicated to. This then then prevent conflicting or duplicate messages going to the same individuals. Having a template ensures that there will be nothing forgotten about how and when the communication will occur.

How PMO will apply this service

The PMO will review the external guidance about communications management and see which templates are suitable for the organization to use. Based on the selected template they will revise this for the organization.

As well as providing the template they will provide guidance on the approach to communications management and the use of the template.

Supplier	Input	Process	Output	Customer
PMO	Standards template	Develop standard Develop templates	Communications plan Guidance	Project Manager Program Manager Portfolio Manager

How the PMO will measure the value of this service

This can be measured by the numbers of people using the templates provided.

Criteria when the PMO will use this service

- Where consistency is needed in the communication to stakeholders
- Where there is a need to roll up information across a program or portfolio

Helpful hints for the PMO when delivering the service

- Ensure that the communication plan template aligns with the stakeholder identification template to ensure that information can be copied from one to the other
- Ensure that it is possible to develop the reporting from the template to show how effective the communication has been

PMO Capabilities needed to fulfil this service

Competencies	Techniques and generic tools
Stakeholder Engagement Delivery Methods Personal Communication	Communication requirements analysis

Related services

Enable the formulation of communication plans Monitor the effectiveness of communications Develop and maintain the stakeholder engagement framework	Develop stakeholder plans, profiles, and matrices Facilitate stakeholder identification and communication workshops Manage Customer Interfaces Map key value streams and processes

Communications Operations

Service group description

The delivery of communications on behalf of the project, program, or portfolio

Why have these services been grouped together?

These services relate to the day-to-day management of the communications on behalf of the project, program, or portfolio.

Responsibility Assignment Matrix

Service	Executive	Portfolio Manager	Program Manager	Project Manager	PMO	Sponsor	Other Stakeholder
Coordinate the internal communication		A	A	A	R		
Provide answers and briefings to queries and information requests		A	A	A	R		
Support press enquiries			A	A	R		C (Legal)
Establish and maintain the intranet site or information portal		I	I	I	A, R		
Manages social media activities			A	A	R		

Coordinate the internal communication

Service description

Ensures the communications listed in the communication plan get produced and issued according to the communication plan.

What the service provides for the customer

This provides the project, program, or portfolio manager with a reassurance that the communications will occur as per the communications plan.

Why is this service being offered to the customer?

There is no use in having a communications plan that does not get followed. By having the PMO distribute the communications as per the plan ensures that the project, program, or portfolio will be perceived as more successful.

How PMO will apply this service

The PMO will obtain the communication plan from the project, program, or portfolio manager. They will look to see what communications are required, and who is responsible for providing the information. If the communication is face-to-face then the PMO will speak to the person responsible for the communication and gain assurance that this is happening. If it is not happening the PMO will find out the reason behind this and if possible, resolve the issue. If necessary, the PMO can escalate the matter to the project, program, or portfolio manager.

If the communications are electronic then the PMO can speak to the person responsible for the communication and offer to issue the communication on their behalf. If they accept this offer, then the PMO will ensure they have the details of all the people to whom they need to communicate with. They will work with the content provider to ensure that the PMO has the necessary information in time. The PMO will then ensure the communication is sent to the necessary individuals and a copy of the communication is stored within the documentation repository.

If the communications are due to happen on regular basis e.g. for a monthly newsletter, then the PMO will setup a reminder in the diary to ensure these happen on schedule. They will provide a reminder for the content providers before the content is due to enable them to produce the content in time for the overall communication to be distributed.

Supplier	Input	Process	Output	Customer
Project Manager Program Manager Portfolio Manager	Communications plan	Issue communications	Individual communications	Various stakeholders Portfolio Managers Program Managers Project Managers

How the PMO will measure the value of this service

This can be measured by verifying that the communications occur according to the plan. It can be measured by gaining feedback from the project, program, or portfolio manager.

Criteria when the PMO will use this service

- When the PMO is aligned with the project, program, or portfolio manager
- Where this role is not being performed by the project, program, or portfolio manager
- Where there is a communications plan in place

Helpful hints for the PMO when delivering the service

- The PMO is not necessarily responsible for putting the communications together, but they need to speak to the people responsible to ensure that it does happen
- Once they have sent out the communication the PMO may update the communications plan with the information of when the last communication occurred
- If required the PMO will update the project, program, or portfolio manager on the status of the communication

PMO Capabilities needed to fulfil this service

Competencies	Techniques and generic tools
P3M Administration Stakeholder Engagement Professionalism and ethics Personal Integrity and reliability Personal Communication Relationships and engagement Teamwork	Communication requirements analysis

Related services

Enable the formulation of communication plans Establish and maintain the intranet site or information portal Hold master copies of all portfolio, program, or project information Support press enquiries	Manages social media activities Provide a secretariat service for meetings Support supplier liaison across portfolio, program, or project Provide answers and briefings to queries and information requests

Provide answers and briefings to queries and information requests

Service description

On behalf of the project or program manager provide information about the project or program that can be released under confidentiality rules.

What the service provides for the customer

This provides the stakeholders with information they require on the status of the project or program.

Why is this service being offered to the customer?

By delegating the provision of information to the PMO it will save the time and effort of the project or program manager.

How PMO will apply this service

The PMO will receive a request for some information on the project or program. They will check to see whether this is some information that they are allowed to communicate (there may be a Non-Disclosure Agreement (NDA) in place prohibiting the sharing of information, except with those individuals who have also signed the NDA). If they can share the information, then the PMO will find the necessary information and provide this to the stakeholder. The PMO will confirm with the stakeholder that the information provided is what they actually required and that they are happy.

Supplier	Input	Process	Output	Customer
Stakeholders	Information request	Answer questions	Information answer	Stakeholders

How the PMO will measure the value of this service

This can be measured by the numbers of requests for information which have been processed by the PMO without impacting on the project or program manager. It can be measured by gaining feedback from the project or program manager.

Criteria when the PMO will use this service

- When the PMO is aligned to a single project or program manager
- Where there are lots of requests for information about the project or program

Helpful hints for the PMO when delivering the service

- If the PMO is getting regular requests for information from a particular stakeholder consider adding them into the communication plan so they can get the information sent to them, rather than having to request it all the time
- If the request is for a status update, then the PMO should provide them with the latest progress report. There should be no need to create a new report specifically for each stakeholder request
- If there are requests coming in for the same or similar information then consider creating an intranet page or information leaflet that can be sent out, saving time for the PMO in finding the information each time

PMO Capabilities needed to fulfil this service

Competencies	Techniques and generic tools
P3M Administration Information Management Professionalism and ethics Personal Integrity and reliability Personal Communication Relationships and engagement Teamwork Resourcefulness	Communication requirements analysis

Related services

Coordinate the internal communication Support press enquiries	Establish and maintain the intranet site or information portal Enable the formulation of communication plans

Support press enquiries

Service description

The point of contact between the press office and the program.

What the service provides for the customer

This provides the press office with a single contact to route any queries about the program to. It provides the program manager with a reassurance that simple messages are being dealt with and they only need to be involved with the larger ad-hoc questions.

Why is this service being offered to the customer?

Where a program has a wider impact outside of the organization, the press office for the organization will be involved in distributing the information outside of the organization. Having a single point of contact means that they can be assured that the information they are distributing is correct. It allows the program manager to know that only information that is not confidential is being released to the press office.

How PMO will apply this service

The PMO will receive a request for information from the press office. The PMO will confirm the scope of the information required. Is it to answer a specific question, provide Frequently Asked Questions answers or marketing/sales information about the program? The PMO will source the information from the documentation they already have access to and will clarify the validity of the information with the experts within the team.

The PMO will prepare the draft briefing and will pass this to the press office for them to make the final adjustments, before confirming with the program manager that the item is fit for release.

Supplier	Input	Process	Output	Customer
Press Office	Request for information	Prepare press briefing	Draft press briefing	Press Office

How the PMO will measure the value of this service

This can be measured by the numbers of briefings that have been produced. If can be measured by getting feedback from the press office and the program manager.

Criteria when the PMO will use this service

- When the program the PMO is associated with has a high-profile presence outside of the organization
- Where there are multiple/regular requests for information from the press office
- Where the information being requested is routine

Helpful hints for the PMO when delivering the service

- Depending on the information being shared, the PMO may want to review the content of any briefing note with the program manager before issuing to the press office
- On a larger program, where regular communication is required there may be a dedicated person or team providing communications for the program
- If regular communication is required by the press office, they should be listed as a stakeholder and added into the communication plan

PMO Capabilities needed to fulfil this service

Competencies	Techniques and generic tools
Personal Communication Relationships and engagement Teamwork Resourcefulness Negotiation	Communication requirements analysis Stakeholder checklist

Related services

Provide answers and briefings to queries and information requests Coordinate the internal communication	Enable the formulation of communication plans Manages social media activities

Establish and maintain the intranet site or information portal

Service description

The creation and maintenance of an online repository for information about and for the project, program, or portfolio.

What the service provides for the customer

This provides a single place that the members of the PPM team can find out information about the project, program, or portfolio. It can provide access to the processes, procedures, standards, templates, and help related to the standard methodologies in place within the organization to deliver change. A portfolio level site may contain information about the portfolio itself e.g. project list, dashboards. A project or program site may contain background information about the project or program being delivered and advice for new starters.

Why is this service being offered to the customer?

Having a centralized repository provides a single place for people to look for information regarding the project, program, or portfolio. It saves time for the PMO in having to find the information to provide to team members each time. By having access to the methodology, it ensures that change is delivered in a consistent manner.

How PMO will apply this service

The PMO will find out how to create an intranet site or information portal. They will review who the stakeholders are for the site and therefore what the content for the site should contain. The PMO will review who should have access to the information within the site. Will this be available to everyone, or is it limited to the people within the project or program?

Once the content has been decided and the audience been defined the PMO should look to see how the information can be structured. With the structure defined the PMO can then start to create the site. They should design each of the pages and make sure the navigation around the site is clear. Having designed the pages the PMO can then apply any security before adding the content, that way it will ensure that no one can inadvertently access something they are not allowed to.

With the security in place the PMO can start to add the content to the site and add the information into the site's pages.

On a regular basis the PMO should review the information that is shown on the site to see whether this is still current e.g. has the list of projects changed? When items have changed the PMO should update the content to the latest version. If something is no longer required, then this information needs to be removed.

If the site goes through a redesign, or lots of new information is made available then the PMO should consider notifying the regular users of the information in order that they are aware of the changes made.

Supplier	Input	Process	Output	Customer
Project Managers Program Managers Portfolio Managers	Project List Status reports Processes Procedures Templates Standards Help	Maintaining intranet site	Intranet site pages	PPM team PMO Senior Management

How the PMO will measure the value of this service

This can be measured by tracking how many people visit the site. It can be measured by seeing how many people have this as a bookmarked site.

Criteria when the PMO will use this service

- When there is information which needs sharing to a wide audience
- Where access is required to the methodology

Helpful hints for the PMO when delivering the service

- It may be possible to have a site split out with different levels of security access. There could be parts which are open to all and other part which have a particular set of individuals who have access
- When providing a structure for the site the PMO may want to produce a strawman of the design and review it internally as well as with a few stakeholders to see whether the design allows people to access the information and the path around the site is clear
- It is not necessary to have all the information available when the site is first created. The information can be added to over time
- Consider having a way that people can submit requests to the PMO directly from the site e.g. email links, contact forms
- The site content will depend on the level of the PMO. The PMO may want to consider having a separate site for the methodology and one for information about the project, program, or portfolio

PMO Capabilities needed to fulfil this service

Competencies	Techniques and generic tools
P3M Administration Information Management P3M Tools Personal Communication	Communication requirements analysis Project Management Information System

Related services

Capture good practice examples for inclusion in good practice repository Define, maintain, and implement standard PPM framework	Provide answers and briefings to queries and information requests Coordinate the internal communication

Manages social media activities

Service description

Keeping people informed about the project or program via the use of social media.

What the service provides for the customer

Social media is a way for keeping people up to date on the status of the project or program. Having a specific media account for the project or program can allow people to subscribe to receive the updates.

Why is this service being offered to the customer?

Having the PMO manage the social media activities provides a single point to control the message and reputation of the project. This ensures that the focus of the project and program managers can be on delivery.

How PMO will apply this service

The PMO will review the communications plan to see what messages should be sent over social media. The PMO will ensure that there is a specific account that is setup that is associated with the project or program. They will ensure that they have the ability to access the social media platform concerned as part of their IT setup.

The PMO will use social media to communicate according to the communications plan. They will monitor the account and deal with any replies they get to their postings. Where they get posts in from other people, they will deal with these in an appropriate manner.

The PMO will be responsible for curating the contacts that the account has, ensuring that this is only used for work and not leisure purposes.

Supplier	Input	Process	Output	Customer
Project Managers Program Managers	Press Releases Communications plan	Update social media	Social Media postings	External stakeholders

How the PMO will measure the value of this service

This can be measured by seeing the number of times the information is shared or viewed on the social media platform.

Criteria when the PMO will use this service

- Where the organization uses social media to update on the status of the projects and programs
- Where social media tools are used as a communication mechanism internally within the project or program
- Where there is a social media account for the project or program

Helpful hints for the PMO when delivering the service

- Communications should come from an official address; this will ensure that this can be transferred to other people should the person in charge of doing this leave the organization
- The PMO should ensure that all postings fit the culture of the organization they are representing
- The PMO should ideally find a person to perform this role who is used to using the service already and is therefore aware of the best way of getting the information seen

PMO Capabilities needed to fulfil this service

Competencies	Techniques and generic tools
P3M Administration Professionalism and ethics Personal Integrity and reliability Personal Communication	Communication requirements analysis

Related services

Coordinate the internal communication Monitor the effectiveness of communications	Enable the formulation of communication plans Support press enquiries

Communications Monitoring

Service group description

Tracking the effectiveness of the communications of the project, program, or portfolio.

Why have these services been grouped together?

This service is related to monitoring how well the communications are being received.

Responsibility Assignment Matrix

Service	Executive	Portfolio Manager	Program Manager	Project Manager	PMO	Sponsor	Other Stakeholder
Monitor the effectiveness of communications		A	A	A	R		

Monitor the effectiveness of communications

Service description

The review of how effective the communications are for the project, program, or portfolio.

What the service provides for the customer

This provides an objective review of the communications for the project, program, or portfolio. Based on this review and an assessment of the communications plan the PMO can suggest some recommendations on the style, format, and frequency of the communications.

Why is this service being offered to the customer?

Understanding whether the communications are reaching the individuals they are supposed to enables the communications plan to be tweaked to increase the impact of that communication. If the communication is working as expected, then no change will be required.

How PMO will apply this service

The PMO will obtain a copy of the communications plan. They will check to see whether any of the communications listed have actually been produced and sent out. Where a communication has gone out to a stakeholder, or group of stakeholders the PMO will find out from them (or a sample of them) whether they received it, and what they thought of it. Do the recipients have any suggestions as to how it can be improved? Would they want to receive this information in future? Did they like the format that was used, or would they have found a different way more useful? Was the frequency about right or would they want the information more or less often?

The PMO will summarize the feedback from the stakeholders and compare what the stakeholders have said against the communications plan. Based on the comparison they will look to make some recommendations to improve the level of communication. These recommendations should then be included within the communications plan.

Supplier	Input	Process	Output	Customer
Project Manager Program Manager Portfolio Manager	Communications plan	Monitor communications	Recommendation	Project Manager Program Manager Portfolio Manager

How the PMO will measure the value of this service

This can be measured by looking at the recommendation for change to the communications plan that have actually been picked up and included in the plan.

Criteria when the PMO will use this service

- Where there is a communications plan
- Where the PMO is aligned to a project, program, or portfolio manager
- As a project or program is going into a new phase is a good time to review the communications offered
- For a portfolio look to review this at least every 6 months

Helpful hints for the PMO when delivering the service

- If none of the communications have been distributed as per the communications plan, then the advice would be to update the plan to include the current communication list and then follow the plan in future
- When gaining the feedback, it is possible for this to be contradictory as individuals have different preferences for how they like to receive and absorb information
- This should be done on a regular basis as different levels of communication are needed at different points in a project or program lifecycle

PMO Capabilities needed to fulfil this service

Competencies	Techniques and generic tools
Reporting, Insights and Analysis Stakeholder Engagement Personal Communication Relationships and engagement Teamwork	Communication requirements analysis

Related services

Develop and maintain the communication framework Enable the formulation of communication plans Support supplier liaison across portfolio, program, or project	Manage Customer Interfaces Clearly communicates the PMO vision and objectives Manages social media activities Develop stakeholder plans, profiles, and matrices

Configuration Management

Configuration Management

Description

The custodian and guardian of all master copies of the portfolio, program, or project's information. This setup how documents will be accessed, named, indexed, and stored including the archival and retrieval of these files.

What the services within the area provide for the customer

These services provide a way of ensuring the correct documentation is available at all times. They provide a standard way of managing version control for documents and cover where they should be stored and under what circumstances new approvals are required for change controlled documents. Where support is provided to a specific project or program the PMO can manage this on behalf of the team for approved documents.

Helpful hints for when the PMO is delivering this service area

- Ensure where any tool is used that this is trained out alongside the configuration management process
- Understand that configuration management affects all people within the PPM domain, so training must be given to all people who will be expected to work with an item under configuration control

Configuration Management Design

Service group description

The setup of configuration management including policy, process, standards, templates, and tools.

Why have these services been grouped together?

These services relate to the design and setup of the way configuration management will work in the organization.

List of related services described in other areas

Automate Processes

Responsibility Assignment Matrix

Service	Executive	Portfolio Manager	Program Manager	Project Manager	PMO	Sponsor	Other Stakeholder
Develop information management policy	A	I	I	I	R		I (PPM team)
Develop configuration management standards and processes		I	I	I	R, A		I (PPM team)
Create standard information library structures and templates		C	C	C	R, A		C (PPM team)
Develop or source tools for PPM document configuration management		I	C	C	R, A		I (PPM team)
Train people in configuration management		I	I	I	R, A		I (PPM team)

Helpful hints for when the PMO is delivering this Service Group

- The information management policy needs to be in place before the other services to ensure that the configuration management standards adhere to the that policy
- Look to have the tool to support the configuration management process. If it cannot then you will have to change the process so that it fits. The two must work in harmony. If possible, have the tool as easy to use as possible. If using check-out/check-in facilities within the tool, ensure this has an override to cope for when people are unavailable for an extended period of time
- When training people in configuration management ensure that the process, tool, and standards are trained at the same time, so people can see how the process and tool fit together

Develop information management policy

Service description

The creation of the policy about information storage and retrieval. This covers data retention and archiving timescales as well as confidentially and access rights for documentation.

What the service provides for the customer

This sets the overall guidance for how documents will be classified, stored, and retained. Without this the configuration management standards would not be possible.

Why is this service being offered to the customer?

This takes the company level guidance and explains how this applies to project related documentation.

How PMO will apply this service

The PMO will look and see if they can find a copy of the company level information management policy. If there is no policy, then they will need to start to develop one for themselves.

Using a standard policy template (if one is available) they will create the information management policy which will cover the following items:

- Scope – what does this cover, is it just PPM documentation, does it differ between physical copies or electronic? Does this cover just official PPM documentation, or would this cover working copies of documents as well?
- Roles and responsibilities – the type of people involved and what they are expected to do, including third parties. This needs to cover Confidentiality, Integrity, Availability and Accountability
- Sensitivity levels – what levels of access is required to documents and under what circumstances
- Overview of document lifecycle – showing the life from creation, use, closure, archival and destruction
- Archival policy – when will PPM documents be archived. Is that based on the age of the individual document or will the time not kick in until the project has closed
- Retention policy – after they are archived how long will the documents be stored
- Retrieval policy – how can the documents be retrieved once they have been archived
- Sharing – who can see the documents – this is linked to sensitivity levels and roles section
- Destruction of records – when they are no longer required how will documents be deposed of
- Monitoring and conformance – how will this policy be policed and what happens if the policy is not followed

Once the policy has been written it will need to be reviewed and signed by the Executive (the senior management of the department) as they are ultimately responsible for this policy.

Supplier	Input	Process	Output	Customer
Legal department	Company policy	Develop policy	Information management policy	Project team Program team Portfolio team PMO

How the PMO will measure the value of this service

The PMO will be able to measure the value of this when they come to create the configuration management standards. Having a specific PPM information management policy will make this process easier.

Criteria when the PMO will use this service

- When the PMO is looking to create a configuration management process and standards
- When there are questions asked about how the company level policy applies to PPM
- When the PMO is looking to source a configuration management tool

Helpful hints for the PMO when delivering the service

- If the PMO do not provide a specific information management policy, then by default they will be using the one for the entire organization
- Having a specific information management policy for PPM allows this to be more focused and omit some of the things from the overall policy that are not applicable. It will clarify exactly what circumstances the various sensitivity levels will need to be used
- Whenever the overall policy is changed this one will need to be reviewed to see if there are any items which need changing

PMO Capabilities needed to fulfil this service

Competencies	Techniques and generic tools
Information Management Assurance Governance Frameworks	None

Related services

Develop configuration management standards and processes Develop or source tools for PPM document configuration management Train people in configuration management Control the issue of portfolio, program, or project deliverables	Hold master copies of all portfolio, program, or project information Undertake configuration audits Manage archives of portfolio, program, or project documentation Provision of Management Dashboards

Develop configuration management standards and processes

Service description

The creation of the Configuration Management processes and standards to ensure that the correct documents are available for use at all times.

What the service provides for the customer

This provides the guidance on how documents are stored, access is obtained, how version control works, which documents require version control, and which are just managed documents.

Why is this service being offered to the customer?

Having standards ensures that configuration management can happen in a consistent manner across all projects and programs within the portfolio.

How PMO will apply this service

The PMO will find the information management policy, either the specific one for the PPM environment or the company one. This can then be referenced to ensure the configuration management process does not conflict.

The PMO will then create the configuration management process which will classify documents into 2 main types. Those under change control (such as a business case) which need formal approval to be changed) and managed documents (such as risk registers or progress reports) which are dynamic documents and do not require formal approval to be changed.

The standard will need to consider:

- The naming convention for change controlled documents
- The naming convention for managed documents
- The folder structure for change controlled and managed documents
- The linkage between approvals and change control
- How version control works – when to increment the number and the format of the version number
- What a Configuration Item Index is and how it should be created
- How and when to take baselines
- Performing a configuration management audit

If necessary (because a tool is not being used), the PMO may consider creating a Configuration Item Index template along with instructions for usage.

Supplier	Input	Process	Output	Customer
PMO	Standards Template Information management policy	Develop Standard	Configuration management procedures Configuration Management Standard CI Index template	PPM Managers PMO

How the PMO will measure the value of this service

The PMO will measure this by conducting configuration management audits to see compliance with the standards.

Criteria when the PMO will use this service

- When consistency is required on how documents are managed
- Where there is no existing process and standards, or they require updating

Helpful hints for the PMO when delivering the service

- It allows for a standard that can then be verified when performing a configuration audit
- If in an IT environment the configuration management process will need to cover software configuration items
- Version control numbers may be dictated by the tool if you are using a tool to manage the change-controlled documentation

PMO Capabilities needed to fulfil this service

Competencies	Techniques and generic tools
Information Management Quality Management Assurance Governance Frameworks	Process Analysis Project Management Information System Swim-lane flowcharts Task responsibility matrix/RACI

Related services

Develop information management policy Create standard information library structures and templates Develop or source tools for PPM document configuration management Train people in configuration management Control the issue of portfolio, program, or project deliverables Undertake configuration audits	Develop the overall change control framework Establish and administer portfolio, program, or project baselines Establish and maintain the CI index Manage the Process Improvement Plan Manage archives of portfolio, program, or project documentation Establish and maintain the CI index Map key value streams and processes

Create standard information library structures and templates

Service description

The setup of a standard document library for a project or program.

What the service provides for the customer

This ensures that when a project or program starts that the document library is setup according to the configuration management standard.

Why is this service being offered to the customer?

To ensure projects are setup correctly and to save the project manager having to create this structure as part of their kick-off work.

How PMO will apply this service

The PMO will find the configuration management standards which will have the standard folder structure for documents. If using a tool, then PMO will ensure that this structure is setup using the tool. Otherwise the PMO will set up the structure within the project folder on the network drive. If it is not provided automatically as part of any tool used the PMO will setup the configuration item index as well.

Once everything has been setup correctly the PMO will then inform the project or program manager and remind them about the configuration management process and standard.

Supplier	Input	Process	Output	Customer
PMO	Configuration management standard	Setup project Setup program	Standard folder structure	Project Manager Program Manager

How the PMO will measure the value of this service

This can be measured by the number of projects passing the folder structure part of the configuration management audit.

Criteria when the PMO will use this service

- When a new project or program is being setup

Helpful hints for the PMO when delivering the service

- This is typically done at the start of the project or of a phase
- This may involve the creation of a template within a tool to make this process easier and more consistent

PMO Capabilities needed to fulfil this service

Competencies	Techniques and generic tools
P3M Administration Information Management Quality Management Governance Frameworks	Project Management Information System

Related services

Develop configuration management standards and processes Train people in configuration management Undertake configuration audits	Establish and maintain the CI index Manage archives of portfolio, program, or project documentation Control the issue of portfolio, program, or project deliverables

Develop or source tools for PPM document configuration management

Service description

Creating or making available a tool to support the configuration management procedure and standards.

What the service provides for the customer

A tool to support configuration management of documents on the project or program. This should automatically create a Configuration Item (CI) Index for the project or program manager.

Why is this service being offered to the customer?

This will make it easier to the version and status of each document. It will ensure the standards are adhered to and create the CI Index for the project manager.

How PMO will apply this service

The PMO will look at the configuration management standards to find out what the requirements of the tool should be. They will do a review of existing tools that may be available to them. They can review the external marketplace to see what is available. Working with the senior management to find out what the budget for a tool could be they will draw up a shortlist of possible options with their positives and negatives and take that back to the senior management for a decision.

Having decided on a tool to select the PMO will look to install this, integrate it with the other tools they have for the project and update the configuration management process and standard to reflect the usage of the tool in performing configuration management.

Supplier	Input	Process	Output	Customer
PMO Senior management	Configuration management standard Budget	Decision making Develop Standard	Configuration Management Tool Updated configuration management standard	Project team Program team Portfolio team PMO

How the PMO will measure the value of this service

All projects and programs are using the tool. There is a high level of satisfaction in tool usage. The tool requires little or no training.

Criteria when the PMO will use this service

- When there is a desire to have a tool to support configuration management
- When the configuration audits are returning a high degree of errors with the compliance with the configuration management standards

Helpful hints for the PMO when delivering the service

- If there is a PPM tool in place, consider whether this could also work for configuration management
- Depending on the way version control works it may be necessary to update the configuration management standard to fit the way the tool works
- Ensure archive and retrieval is included as part of the requirements for the tool

PMO Capabilities needed to fulfil this service

Competencies	Techniques and generic tools
Information Management Supplier Management P3M Tools	Make or buy analysis Project Management Information System

Related services

Develop information management policy Develop configuration management standards and processes Train people in configuration management Advise on PPM tools and software Tailors and configures project management tools	Implements vendor provided project management tools Undertake configuration audits Manage archives of portfolio, program, or project documentation Administer document tools

Train people in configuration management

Service description

Training people in the PPM teams in how to do configuration management of documents according to the standard using any tools that may be available.

What the service provides for the customer

This ensures that everyone involved in PPM is aware how to do version control of documents. Which documents are under version control and which are merely managed documents? If there is a tool to be used for document control, then the people are aware of how to access it and how it works.

Why is this service being offered to the customer?

This ensures there is consistency in the way documents are handled in the life of the project. This enables the project and program manager to understand the status and location of all the project documentation.

How PMO will apply this service

The PMO will take the configuration management process, standards, and tool (if there is one) to develop a training course. They will arrange for the training to be given to all the people working in PPM in the organization. They will develop some help documentation (in the form of crib sheets) which can be handed out at the training course. They may decide to put together a test at the end to ensure that people have learnt how to perform the task correctly.

Supplier	Input	Process	Output	Customer
PMO	Configuration management standard Configuration management tool Configuration management process	Develop training Deliver training	Training course Help documentation Trained people	PPM team

How the PMO will measure the value of this service

The PMO can measure this based on the numbers of people trained. They can measure this via configuration audits to check adherence to process.

Criteria when the PMO will use this service

- When the configuration management standard has been written or has changed
- When a tool is introduced to help do configuration management

Helpful hints for the PMO when delivering the service

- If using a tool make sure the process, standard and tool is trained out in a single session. This works better taking a document through its lifecycle, creating a new version, updating it, approving it, and then having a subsequent change
- Unlike the other training services this one will need to be delivered to everyone working in PPM as they will all be dealing with documents at some point

PMO Capabilities needed to fulfil this service

Competencies	Techniques and generic tools
Information Management Capability Development P3M Tools Personal Communication Relationships and engagement Result Orientation	Communication requirements analysis Project Management Information System Stakeholder checklist Stakeholder engagement assessment matrix

Related services

Develop configuration management standards and processes Develop or source tools for PPM document configuration management Develop information management policy	Create standard information library structures and templates Undertake configuration audits Provide PPM training Provide training logistics support

Configuration Management Operations

Service group description

Performing configuration management on documents within the project, program, or portfolio.

Why have these services been grouped together?

These services relate to the day-to-day operation of configuration management, including baselining, archiving, and indexing of documents under control.

Responsibility Assignment Matrix

Service	Executive	Portfolio Manager	Program Manager	Project Manager	PMO	Sponsor	Other Stakeholder
Hold master copies of all portfolio, program, or project information		A	A	A	R	I	
Establish and administer portfolio, program, or project baselines		A	A	A	R	I	
Control the issue of portfolio, program, or project deliverables		A	A	A	R	I	I (PPM team)
Establish and maintain the CI index		A	A	A	R		I (PPM team)
Manage archives of portfolio, program, or project documentation					A, R		
Administer document tools	A	C	C	C	R		

Helpful hints for when the PMO is delivering this Service Group

- Ensure the roles and responsibilities for performing configuration management have been made clear before starting
- Ensure that the configuration management process (including the use of any tool) has been trained out

Hold master copies of all portfolio, program, or project information

Service description

Ensure that master copies of the key documentation are not updated without the appropriate governance, according the configuration management standards.

What the service provides for the customer

Ensure that all master copies of documentation are held securely and cannot be updated without appropriate authority.

Why is this service being offered to the customer?

This provides reassurance to the project, program, or portfolio manager that key documentation is being correctly secured, and access to update this is being controlled according to the guidance provided.

How PMO will apply this service

The PMO will review the configuration management standards and the configuration management plan (if there is one) to ensure they know how to perform this service. They will be aware of the rules governing when a document can be updated.

When a change-controlled document has been initially approved they will store this in the document repository along with the documented approvals. If a request comes to change the document, they will ensure that there is an approved change request prior to releasing the document for update. They will ensure that the configuration item index gets updated with the current status of the document.

Supplier	Input	Process	Output	Customer
Project Managers Program Managers Portfolio Managers	Documentation Configuration Management Plan Configuration Management Standards Approved Change Request	Maintaining a Configuration Management library	Configuration Item Index	Project Managers Program Managers Portfolio Managers

How the PMO will measure the value of this service

The PMO can measure this by validating the process is being followed by passing a configuration audit. They can ask the project or program manager this is being done on behalf of whether they find the service of value.

Criteria when the PMO will use this service

- When there is a PMO who is dedicated to a single project or program
- Where the PMO performs the role of portfolio office
- Where there is a large amount of documentation requiring to be managed

Helpful hints for the PMO when delivering the service

- If the PMO did not do this then this would be the responsibility of the project, program, or portfolio manager
- The PMO may use a tool to assist them in control of the documentation if there is one available

PMO Capabilities needed to fulfil this service

Competencies	Techniques and generic tools
P3M Administration Change Control Information Management P3M Tools	Project Management Information System

Related services

Establish and maintain the CI index Control the issue of portfolio, program, or project deliverables Maintain the change control register	Develop information management policy Work with internal audit to ensure compliance with audit requirements Coordinate the internal communication

Establish and administer portfolio, program, or project baselines

Service description

On a regular basis, according to the configuration management strategy, the PMO should take a baseline copy of the documentation so that the information can be restored if required.

What the service provides for the customer

This will provide a snapshot of the documentation at a particular time in the project. This can then be referred back to and may be used in any project audits that occur.

Why is this service being offered to the customer?

This ensures there is a prior copy of the documentation that can be reverted to should it be required. For example, if a change request were approved and work started to revise the documentation, if that change request got revoked then it would be necessary to revert to the latest approved documentation i.e. the baseline copy.

How PMO will apply this service

The PMO will review the configuration management strategy to work out under what circumstances a baseline will be taken. They will review the configuration management standards to ensure they are aware how to store the baselined information.

When they are ready to take a baselined copy of the documentation, they will take a snapshot of the documentation along with the CI index at that particular time and store this somewhere which will allow the information to be restored. If working on a network drive this may just involve taking an archived copy of the files. If using a tool, they would follow the instructions provided within the tool.

The PMO will ensure they name and store the baseline according to the convention described in the configuration management standards. They will then make the project, program, or portfolio manager aware that this has been performed.

Supplier	Input	Process	Output	Customer
Project Managers Program Managers Portfolio Managers	Documentation Schedules Configuration Management Strategy Configuration Management standard	Performing a baseline	Baselined documentation Baselined CI index	Project Managers Program Managers Portfolio Managers

How the PMO will measure the value of this service

This can be measured by reviewing whether this comes up as an issue in a configuration audit. They can ask the person the baseline is being performed for whether they find it of value. If an item can be restored from the baseline, then this is a certain way of ensuring the value of the service.

Criteria when the PMO will use this service

- Where there is a dedicated PMO for a single project or program
- Where it is specified in the configuration management strategy as the role of the PMO
- When the project or program is being baselined

Helpful hints for the PMO when delivering the service

- This service should be performed at the end of each stage as a minimum
- If this service is not performed by the PMO it will be the responsibility of the project or program manager
- As well as storing a copy of the documentation the Configuration Item Index should be stored to ensure that it is clear which versions of the documentation are available
- It may be possible to use a tool to facilitate the provision of this service
- If taking an archived copy of the documentation, then consideration should be given to making this information read-only or putting a password on this to prevent unauthorized update of the baseline copy
- A periodic check should be made to see that information from a baseline can be restored
- A check should be made whether just one item or the whole baseline information can be restored

PMO Capabilities needed to fulfil this service

Competencies	Techniques and generic tools
P3M Administration Change Control Information Management Assurance Delivery Methods Governance Frameworks P3M Tools	Change control tools Project Management Information System

Related services

Establish and maintain the CI index Administer document tools	Undertake configuration audits Develop configuration management standards and processes

Control the issue of portfolio, program, or project deliverables

Service description

The controlled distribution of deliverables (documents) to individuals within the project, program or portfolio provided they have the authority to access them.

What the service provides for the customer

This ensures that people have access to the information when they need it.

Why is this service being offered to the customer?

Unauthorized access to information can cause problems for projects. Some projects may have non-disclosure agreements (NDAs) in place so that only certain people have access to the information. If information gets out that should not, it can have negative consequences not only to the project, but to the organization itself. Having the PMO check this prior to issuing information will prevent this occurring.

How PMO will apply this service

Before granting access to any of the deliverables the PMO will check whether there is an NDA in place. If there is then the PMO will check to see whether the person concerned has signed the NDA, if not then they will not be given access to the information until it has been signed.

If the NDA has been signed, or there is no NDA in place then the PMO will check whether the person ought to have access to the deliverable. If the answer is no, then access will not be provided. If the person is authorized to have access to the deliverable, then the PMO will provide access.

The PMO may decide to record who has had access to the deliverable if that is required by the configuration management standard.

Supplier	Input	Process	Output	Customer
Project Managers Program Managers Portfolio Managers	Deliverables Configuration Management Index NDAs Configuration Management Standard	Maintaining a Configuration Management library	Updated Configuration Management Index	Project Managers Program Managers Portfolio Managers

How the PMO will measure the value of this service

This can be measured by conformance at a configuration management audit. It is easier to measure where this has not occurred as projects can be leaking information without being aware of it.

Criteria when the PMO will use this service

- Where there is a dedicated PMO working for a single project or program
- Where the PMO is working as a portfolio office
- Where there is a high degree of confidentiality required
- Where NDAs have been signed
- Where access to the information is specified as part of a contract

Helpful hints for the PMO when delivering the service

- If using a tool to provide a configuration management service, then ensure access requirements can and are setup within the tool. This can normally be controlled down to the individual deliverable level.
- Consider having a list of all the people who have signed the NDA (if one is required) to make it easy to check whether individuals are authorized

PMO Capabilities needed to fulfil this service

Competencies	Techniques and generic tools
P3M Administration Information Management Resource Management Stakeholder Engagement Supplier Management Governance Frameworks Professionalism and ethics Relationships and engagement	Organization charts & position descriptions Project Management Information System Stakeholder checklist

Related services

Develop configuration management standards and processes Create standard information library structures and templates Hold master copies of all portfolio, program, or project information	Establish and maintain the CI index Develop information management policy Work with internal audit to ensure compliance with audit requirements

Establish and maintain the CI index

Service Description

The provision of an electronic index of the status of all the deliverables on a project or program. This may list deliverables which have not yet been produced. If the deliverable is in progress, then the name(s) of the individuals assigned to this work can be listed in the index. The CI Index may provide access to get to the detail of the latest copy of each deliverable.

What the service provides for the customer

Access to an up-to-date CI Index ensures that the project or program manager can have a single place to get the overview of the deliverable status in order that progress can be quickly ascertained.

The CI Index is a useful document when doing a configuration audit.

Why is this service being offered to the customer?

Where there is no tool providing this facility, creating the CI Index is time consuming work. Although the CI Index is of value to the project or program manager, they could be spending their time more usefully elsewhere. Having the PMO do this for them is a saving of time for the project or program manager.

How PMO will apply this service

The PMO may be notified of change to deliverables, if they are not, they will need to do a regular review of the deliverable storage area. If they find an updated deliverable, they will add the reference to the deliverable into the CI Index. They will add in details such as:

- Deliverable name – what the deliverable is called
- Deliverable reference number – a unique reference number for the item
- Status – normally chosen from a defined list as referenced in the configuration management standard e.g. Not produced, in progress, approved
- Version – as per the configuration management standard
- Date of last update – when was this changed
- Approval links – references/links to any approvals (if required)
- Deliverable link – a link to so that access can be gained to the deliverable directly from the CI index

Supplier	Input	Process	Output	Customer
Project Managers Program Managers	Configuration Management Index Deliverables	Maintaining a Configuration Management library	Updated Configuration Management Index	Project Managers Program Managers

How the PMO will measure the value of this service

The PMO can measure this service as a cost saving. The time taken to do this will be the same regardless of who does it. Assigning this to a cheaper resource will provide a cost saving.

Criteria when the PMO will use this service

- Where there is a dedicated PMO working for a single project or program
- Where there is no tool to automatically provide a CI Index

Helpful hints for the PMO when delivering the service

- Consider using a tool for configuration management and the CI Index will be automatically produced
- Ensure when people update a document, they notify you, which will make the job easier
- Rather than constantly updating the CI index, look to do this at the start or end of the day. Having something that is only 1 working day out of date is normally OK for most projects

PMO Capabilities needed to fulfil this service

Competencies	Techniques and generic tools
P3M Administration Information Management	Project Management Information System

Related services

Develop configuration management standards and processes Undertake configuration audits Hold master copies of all portfolio, program, or project information Establish and administer portfolio, program, or project baselines	Control the issue of portfolio, program, or project deliverables Create standard information library structures and templates Work with internal audit to ensure compliance with audit requirements Automate Processes

Further Reading

PRINCE2 Configuration Item Record

Manage archives of portfolio, program, or project documentation

Service Description

The archival and retrieval of electronic documentation according to the information management policy.

What the service provides for the customer

Archiving the information ensures that only current information is available for immediate access. This increases the space available on file shares etc. for current documentation. Information from archived projects can be retrieved if required and is controlled via the PMO.

Why is this service being offered to the customer?

Archiving tends to take place a while after the project or program has finished. As the project or program has closed there needs to be a central role to do this. The PMO is ideally positioned to know what items need archiving, what the rules for archiving are and be able to perform this archival.

How PMO will apply this service

The PMO will consult the information management policy to find out the circumstances under which project related data should be archived and how it needs to be stored for. They will provide a list of projects and programs that they are planning to archive and circulate this to ensure there are no valid reasons why this information cannot be archived.

Once they have a list of information to archive, they will follow the archival process to ensure the project data is archived. Once all the information is archived, they will confirm that this has been done.

If a request comes in for some information on an archived project, they will find the particular project in the archive and retrieve the information requested and provide it to the person who asked.

Supplier	Input	Process	Output	Customer
Project Managers Program Managers	Documentation Information management policy	Archiving documentation	Archived documentation	Auditors PMO
Auditors PPM Staff	Request for archived project information	Archiving documentation	Project documentation	Auditors PPM Staff

How the PMO will measure the value of this service

The PMO can measure this by looking at the space they have managed to save within network drives. They could measure this by seeing how much easier it is to access information on existing projects.

Criteria when the PMO will use this service

- When there is a centralized PMO
- As part of the year end processes to review what projects will require archiving
- When information is required for archived projects

Helpful hints for the PMO when delivering the service

- Have an SLA in place for how long it will take to retrieve the information from an archived project
- Consider doing the archival process as part of the year end process
- Understand whether the archived documentation is made read-only or just moved to a separate place
- Understand who needs access to the archived documentation
- If the information is password protected ensure that information is not lost when people leave the organization
- If a configuration management tool is in place, then ensure archive and retrieval is included as part of the requirements for the tool

PMO Capabilities needed to fulfil this service

Competencies	Techniques and generic tools
P3M Administration Information Management P3M Tools	Prompt Lists Check sheets Project Management Information System

Related services

Develop information management policy Develop configuration management standards and processes	Develop or source tools for PPM document configuration management Trigger post-program or project reviews

Administer document tools

Service Description

The administration of tools used to manage configuration management. This includes setup/removal of users, control of access to particular documents, updates to dropdowns and lists, setup/closure of projects, standard folder structures.

What the service provides for the customer

This ensures that the configuration management tool is available for the project team to use.

Why is this service being offered to the customer?

PPM tools, including configuration management tools, are centrally managed. The PMO can do this on behalf of all PPM users. As changing the tool would require administrative access letting anyone do this would contradict the principles of information only being available to those people who need it.

How PMO will apply this service

The PMO will receive a request to change the configuration management tool, this may be from a member of the PPM team, or it could be from the PMO as part of their setup process for new projects. The request types include:

- New user
- Change to user access
- Remove a user
- Add a new project
- Close a project
- Change access for a project/user combination
- Add/change/remove dropdown information
- Baseline project documentation
- Archive documentation

The PMO will perform the necessary changes and inform the user of the change that has been made. It could be that a request comes in that cannot be done (e.g. the person is asking for confidential information they are not privileged to see), in these circumstances the PMO need to refuse the request and explain why this has been declined.

Supplier	Input	Process	Output	Customer
Project managers Program managers Portfolio managers PMO PPM team	Vendor Software Tool change request	Adding / removing a user Adding / closing a project Drop down updates	Updated configuration management tool	Project managers Program managers Portfolio managers PMO PPM team

How the PMO will measure the value of this service

The PMO can measure this service by checking that the tool is able to be accessed by those people who require it.

Criteria when the PMO will use this service

- When there is a central tool for configuration management
- When there is a centralized PMO
- When there is a need for changes to the tool e.g. user changes, project changes, dropdown changes

Helpful hints for the PMO when delivering the service

- Consider having an SLA for how long it takes for each type of request to be delivered
- If you have an SLA, ensure compliance to that SLA is monitored so the PMO can evidence how well they are doing
- Have a standard form for requests to changes to the tool
- Add in changes to the configuration management tool as part of the checklist when projects start-up or close
- If there is a request to give a person access to a project in a configuration management tool, then the PMO need to check whether there are any NDAs in place. If an NDA is required, but has not been signed, the PMO will have to refuse the request

PMO Capabilities needed to fulfil this service

Competencies	Techniques and generic tools
P3M Administration Information Management P3M Tools Professionalism and ethics Personal Integrity and reliability	Prompt Lists Project Management Information System

Related services

Program or project fast-track mobilization service Develop or source tools for PPM document configuration management	Manages project management tools (systems admin) Establish and administer portfolio, program, or project baselines Automate Processes

Configuration Management Monitoring

Service group description

The monitoring and review to check that the project or program is following the configuration management process.

Why have these services been grouped together?

There is currently only one service within this service group, which relates to auditing of the configuration management process.

Responsibility Assignment Matrix

Service	Executive	Portfolio Manager	Program Manager	Project Manager	PMO	Sponsor	Other Stakeholder
Undertake configuration audits	I	A	A	A	R		C (PPM team)

Helpful hints for when the PMO is delivering this Service Group

- This cannot be performed without a defined standard for configuration management having been agreed up front

Undertake configuration audits

Service description

The review of the documents produced for a project or program to ensure they are adhering to the configuration management standard. The review may cover whether baselines have been correctly taken and stored; whether the configuration item index is accurate; whether items have been correctly classified according to the information management policy.

What the service provides for the customer

This checks that documents are being correctly classified and stored. If not, it will suggest remedies to prevent any reoccurrence.

Why is this service being offered to the customer?

Knowing that the correct documents are available and in use will prevent any errors caused by individuals working on different versions of the same document.

How PMO will apply this service

The PMO will find copies of the configuration management standard and the information management policy. If there is a standard audit checklist, they will use that as a basis to conduct the audit. They will confirm with the project or program manager the scope of the audit:

- Will this just cover change-controlled items, or will it cover managed items?
- Will this cover the compliance with the information management policy?
- Will this review the baselines as well as the current versions of the documents
- Will this use random sampling of the documents or will each on be checked?

Once the scope has been clearly defined the PMO will use the Configuration Item (CI) Index as the basis of all the available documents and will check these to ensure that the contents of the document are actually the same version within the document as the CI index claims. If a document states it has been approved are the approvals recorded, and are they stored correctly? If a document has been re-approved under change control, was the change approved prior to the work starting?

The PMO will build up a set of compliance issues and suggest some recommendations to resolve these and prevent any future issues.

Supplier	Input	Process	Output	Customer
Project Managers Program Managers	Deliverables Configuration Management Index Audit Checklist Configuration management standard Information management policy	Auditing a project or program	Updated Audit Checklist Recommendations	Project Managers Program Managers

How the PMO will measure the value of this service

The PMO can measure this by looking at whether compliance or adherence to the configuration management standard is improving over time.

Criteria when the PMO will use this service

- When there is a configuration management standard in place
- At the end of a stage
- As part of a wider audit on the health of the project
- When asked to by senior management or the project/program manager

Helpful hints for the PMO when delivering the service

- Consider having a checklist to ensure consistency in the audit
- Look to have recommendations for any issues that have been identified in the audit
- Remember it is about preventing future issues occurring, you cannot change what has already happened, but you can improve for the future

PMO Capabilities needed to fulfil this service

Competencies	Techniques and generic tools
P3M Administration Information Management Assurance P3M Tools Relationships and engagement	Document Analysis Prompt Lists Check sheets Project Management Information System

Related services

Develop information management policy Develop configuration management standards and processes Develop or source tools for PPM document configuration management Train people in configuration management	Establish and maintain the CI index Create standard information library structures and templates Establish and administer portfolic, program, or project baselines

Consultancy

Consultancy

Description

Provides consultancy and expertise in PPM and organizational processes focused at maintaining minimum standards and achieving target performance.

What the services within the area provide for the customer

These services provide the customer with targeted applied knowledge enabling them to speed up delivery, resolve difficult issues or return a project/program back to a green status. This advice is based on knowledge of the subject matter, and first-hand practical experience in getting the job done.

Helpful hints for when the PMO is delivering this service area

To perform these services a PMO must have first-hand experience of the service being provided. They do not necessarily need to have run the service themselves, but they must have participated to understand what will work and how to adjust the service to the circumstances. The PMO individual will need to keep abreast of the PMO trends and be aware of how things are done in other organizations and general good practice around the subject. If they do not have direct experience outside their current job, then they should use their network to provide them with the experience necessary to give a rounded view.

Consultancy Operations

Service group description

The provision of consultancy services to assist in the delivery and rescue of ind vidual projects and programs.

Why have these services been grouped together?

These services relate to the PMO delivering a consultancy service to others by executing a particular technique.

List of related services described in other areas

Provide 'help squads' for projects and programs

Responsibility Assignment Matrix

Service	Executive	Portfolio Manager	Program Manager	Project Manager	PMO	Sponsor	Other Stakeholder
Facilitate outcome relationship modelling			A, R		C		
Set up and track portfolio, program, and project metrics (KPI's)		A	A	A	R		
Provide facilitation service			A	A	R		C (PPM team)
Provide project or program rescues		A	C	C	R	I	C (PPM team)
Perform organizational PPM maturity assessments	A		C	C	R	I	C (PPM team
Recommend ways to reduce or shorten project lifecycle times			A	A	R		
Perform coaching of portfolio, program, or project managers	A	C	C	C	R		
Provide a help desk manned by experts in PPM	I	I	I	I	A, R	I	I (PPM Team)
Promote good PPM within the organization	I	I	I	I	A, R	I	I (PPM team)
Advise Sponsors and Management Boards of appropriate frameworks and governance models	I		C	C	A, R	I	
Provide advice and guidance to prevent project or program failure	A		I	I	R	A	

Helpful hints for when the PMO is delivering this service group

These services require a good knowledge of PPM and its practical application.

Facilitate outcome relationship modelling

Service description

The creation of a model to map the activities and milestones in a program to the outcomes which deliver the strategy.

What the service provides for the customer

A way of visualizing the outcomes of a program in order that the value of those outcomes can be seen. It provides a poster for the program that can be displayed and increases awareness of the program goals.

Why is this service being offered to the customer?

This allows the program manager and senior stakeholders to better understand the purpose of the program. In creating this model, it provides a way of driving out the benefits for the program and allows discussion on how those benefits can be measured.

How PMO will apply this service

The PMO will read the program vision to find out the list of benefits for the program. They will read the program blueprint to find out the outcomes for the program. They may organize a workshop which will get the key stakeholders in the room along with the program manager and they will try to link the outcomes to the benefits. This in turn may drive more outcomes and benefits identified. To deliver the outcomes, they will need to have a list of outputs that will deliver those outcomes.

For each of the benefits the PMO will seek to understand and document how these can be measured and whether there are any Key Performance Indicators (KPIs) that can be created to track those benefits.

The PMO will document the linkage of the outcomes to the benefits. This model can then be shared with the key stakeholders and the program manager.

Supplier	Input	Process	Output	Customer
Program Manager	Program Vision Program Blueprint	Outcome relationship modelling	Outcome Relationship Model	Senior Stakeholders Program Manager

How the PMO will measure the value of this service

This can be measured by an increased awareness of the program outcome and goals and how they align to the strategic direction of the organization.

Criteria when the PMO will use this service

- When the PMO is aligned to a single program
- When the program is starting up

Helpful hints for the PMO when delivering the service

- The PMO could deliver a benefits map instead of an outcome relationship model
- Look to link up the schedule, the activities, and milestones to the outcomes
- Check to see how each of the outcomes will deliver benefits and how they will be measured
- To deliver the workshop the PMO may run this as a facilitated session
- The outcome relationship model can be used as a poster to aid understanding of the benefits

PMO Capabilities needed to fulfil this service

Competencies	Techniques and generic tools
Benefits and Value Management Reporting, Insights and Analysis Governance Frameworks Relationships and engagement Negotiation	Alternatives analysis Alternatives generation Benefit realization analysis Business value Analysis Scenario analysis Flowcharts Diagramming techniques

Related services

Provide facilitation service	Set up and track portfolio, program, and project metrics (KPI's)

Set up and track portfolio, program, and project metrics (KPI's)

Service description

The creation and maintenance of Key Performance Indicators (KPIs) to monitor the success of a portfolio, program, or project.

What the service provides for the customer

A way of understanding the effectiveness of a portfolio, program or project being delivered. It allows the project, program, or portfolio manager to be in control.

Why is this service being offered to the customer?

The PMO has access to the information used to create the KPIs. They are experienced in the creation of reports and understand how to present the information in a way that effective decisions can be made.

How PMO will apply this service

The PMO will speak with the customer of this service to understand what decisions are needing to be made based on the KPI dashboard being created. Based on that discussion the PMO will draft a KPI dashboard. Depending on what is required the KPIs could include:

- Milestone data – to show how effective the project or program is on delivering
- Cost – to show actuals/forecast vs baseline to show whether this will deliver on budget
- Benefits – to show whether the portfolio will deliver the expected benefits
- Change – to show the volume and cost of change within the project or program
- Story points – to show whether the project is going to deliver the expected velocity within the sprint
- Risk – to show the risk exposure for the project, program, or portfolio
- Issues – to show the volume of outstanding issues and how fast those issues are getting resolved
- Prioritization – to show how effective the portfolio is in delivering its objectives
- Strategic alignment – to show how effective the portfolio is on delivering the strategic objectives
- Quality – to show the progress of the quality testing for the project or program. Is this being done at the expected rate, how much is failing and therefore generating re-work
- RAG Status – to show the trend information across prior time periods, allows an understanding of whether information is improving
- Resources – to show whether enough and the right resources are available when required
- Governance – to show whether the projects and programs are aligned to the governance framework

Having drafted a dashboard the PMO will present that to the customer and ensure that this can be clearly understood. The PMO should check that the dashboard is suitable for the decisions to be made.

The PMO will make changes to the dashboard based on the feedback from the customer. They will agree the frequency of the dashboard update and how the dashboard will be accessed.

The PMO will review the content of the dashboard on a regular basis and confirm it still meeting customer needs.

Supplier	Input	Process	Output	Customer
Project Managers Program Managers	Milestone Dates Project/program costs/benefit targets & actuals Risk, Issue, Change, Quality Registers Prioritization Strategy	Creating a dashboard	KPI dashboard	Project Managers Program Managers Portfolio Managers Steering Group Project Approval Board

How the PMO will measure the value of this service

This can be measured by looking at the demand for the dashboard. If people are asking for the dashboard then that means they are finding the information useful.

Criteria when the PMO will use this service

- When there is a need to monitor the state of the portfolio, program, or project
- Where there is a KPI dashboard already in place that needs revising

Helpful hints for the PMO when delivering the service

- Look to have a series of KPIs that can be included into a dashboard depending on what is relevant to show at that part of the project or program
- The KPI dashboard should ideally be one page
- Consider using an interactive software tool to allow for drill down to individual KPI elements
- Consider where the data will come from and who will provide the data as part of the KPI design
- Inform the individuals providing the data what is required and when – consider developing a reporting schedule
- If possible, align the collection of data with the regular reporting cycle(s)
- Ensure it is clear which data source is being used
- Clean up the data at source rather than for the dashboard as that will prevent the clean up having to be done each time
- Find out whether the dashboard is to be pushed out to the customer or will it be accessed on demand
- Consider putting a date on the dashboard indicating when the data was last refreshed
- Consider using trend/historical information as well as snapshot progress information in the dashboard
- Consider adding analysis/commentary from the PMO on the dashboard

PMO Capabilities needed to fulfil this service

Competencies	Techniques and generic tools
Change Control Financial Management Information Management Issue Management Planning and Scheduling Quality Management Reporting, Insights and Analysis Resource Management Risk Management Capacity Management Governance Frameworks P3M Tools Relationships and engagement Resourcefulness Negotiation Result Orientation	Benefit realization analysis Categorized frequency analysis (Frequency plot, bar chart) Stratified data plots or scatter plots

Related services

Track and report on benefit realization Maintain resource database Monitor and report on financial spend Define, maintain, and implement reporting framework	Reporting results linked to organizational strategy Facilitate outcome relationship modelling Sets PMO team targets

Provide facilitation service

Service description

The provision of a facilitator for a meeting or workshop.

What the service provides for the customer

A facilitator is a neutral individual with an understanding of the subject matter being discussed. This allows the participants to focus on the outcome of the workshop or meeting. The facilitator can ensure that the group arrives at the answer or decision that will achieve the best result.

Why is this service being offered to the customer?

As an independent individual with a knowledge of PPM and the individual project, program or portfolio being discussed the PMO make an ideal candidate for facilitating a meeting or workshop. Having seen a variety of projects or programs delivery they can offer the wisdom based on other related scenarios.

How PMO will apply this service

The PMO will receive a request to facilitate a meeting. They will speak to the person beforehand to understand what the required outcome of the meeting should be. They will review any documentation needed during the meeting beforehand. The PMO will understand who has been invited and why.

At the start of the meeting the facilitator will introduce themselves and set the ground rules for the meeting. They will outline the outcomes required from the meeting. They will ensure that all people know each other and why they have been invited.

During the meeting they will ensure that all opinions are listened to and respected. They will enable everyone to have a voice and ensure that no one can dominate the session. Any unresolvable issues will be parked to enable the session to move onwards.

At the end of the session the facilitator will recap on the decisions made during the meeting. If there are any actions, they will ensure these are assigned to individuals present and dates agreed.

Supplier	Input	Process	Output	Customer
Project Managers Program Managers Portfolio Managers PMO	Facilitation request	Facilitating a meeting	Facilitated meeting	Project Managers Program Managers Portfolio Managers

How the PMO will measure the value of this service

This can be measured by the number of requests to provide a facilitator for a meeting.

Criteria when the PMO will use this service

- When the PMO is aligned to a single project or program
- When the PMO is aligned to a portfolio manager
- When there is potential for a conflict within a meeting or workshop
- Where the meeting or workshop requires an independent voice to allow for clarity in decision making

Helpful hints for the PMO when delivering the service

- The PMO may provide this service themselves or they may link into other people within the organization who can have these skills
- Consider having a facilitation box with items like post-its, flipchart pens, sticky tape, blu-tak to enable a meeting to be facilitated at short notice
- The PMO may get involved in organizing the meeting and inviting the attendees

PMO Capabilities needed to fulfil this service

Competencies	Techniques and generic tools
P3M Administration Stakeholder Engagement Personal Integrity and reliability Personal Communication Relationships and engagement Leadership Conflict and Crisis Resourcefulness Negotiation Result Orientation	Mind Mapping Swim-lane flowcharts

Related services

Provide a secretariat service for meetings Facilitate independent change impact assessment workshops Facilitate outcome relationship modelling Facilitate independent issue analysis and resolution workshops Facilitate independent risk workshops	Facilitate the formulation of stakeholder engagement strategies Facilitate stakeholder identification and communication workshops Trigger post-program or project reviews Run lessons-learned workshops

Provide project or program rescues

Service description

Perform the role of project or program manager and turn around a failing project or program.

What the service provides for the customer

This ensures that a failing (or potential failing) project or program gets turned around and put back on track.

Why is this service being offered to the customer?

As experts in PPM the PMO are able to perform the role of project or program manager. They are able to go in and stabilize a project or program. Being independent, but internal, they are in an ideal place to quickly provide an objective view about what is wrong with a project or program and the steps that are needed to turn this around.

How PMO will apply this service

The PMO will receive a request for assistance with a project or program. They will come in and review the documentation. They will interview the team and ask their thoughts on the causes of the failure and the potential solutions. They will speak to the sponsor and the steering group to get their thoughts on the issues. They will put any work on hold until such time as a plan has been developed and agreed upon.

They will look to document what the issues are and get those agreed with the majority of stakeholder (it may not be possible to agree the issues with everyone). For each of the issues identified they will prioritize the order in which a resolution needs to be agreed (as you cannot tackle all the issues at once).

They identify potential solutions to each of the issues. They will confirm with the steering group and the sponsor whether the solution will assist with getting the project or program back on track. They will then combine each of these solutions together to come up with a plan. This plan will need to be agreed by the team as well as the steering group and sponsor.

Having got a plan to put this back on track the PMO will start to execute this plan. They will look for a project or program manager to assist with the delivery of this plan. The PMO can then exit knowing that there will be someone who can follow through with the delivery of this plan.

Supplier	Input	Process	Output	Customer
Senior Management Portfolio managers Program Managers	Request for assistance Assessment checklist	Project rescue	Action plan	Project Managers Program Managers Portfolio Managers

How the PMO will measure the value of this service

This can be measured by the numbers of projects and programs using this service which have been helped to achieve their goals.

Criteria when the PMO will use this service

- When a project or program is failing, or perceived to be failing
- Where a PMO has the expertise to act as project or program manager

Helpful hints for the PMO when delivering the service

- Once the project or program has been stabilized and put back on track the PMO need to handover delivery back to project or program manager. They should not stay until the project or program has delivered
- The PMO can use their assurance service to identify projects or programs which may need this support
- Consider providing some training around the root cause of the failure to prevent a similar failure happening to other projects or programs
- The PMO must be prepared to consider closing the project or program down if a suitable approach to rescue the project or program cannot be found
- The PMO should document what steps have been taken and add this to the knowledge repository to assist other projects and prevent a similar reoccurrence

PMO Capabilities needed to fulfil this service

Competencies	Techniques and generic tools
Change Control Financial Management Information Management Issue Management Knowledge Management Planning and Scheduling Quality Management Reporting, Insights and Analysis Resource Management Risk Management Stakeholder Engagement Supplier Management Assurance Capability Development Governance Frameworks Professionalism and ethics Personal Communication Relationships and engagement Leadership Teamwork Conflict and Crisis Resourcefulness Negotiation Result Orientation	Root Cause Analysis Capability and Capacity analysis Assumption and constraint analysis Communication requirements analysis Risk Register Project Management Information System Salience model Scheduling tool Stakeholder checklist Stakeholder engagement assessment matrix Work Breakdown Structure

Related services

Provide advice and guidance to prevent project or program failure Advise on program or project assurance services Provide project and program health checks	Provide project and program audits Provide project and program assurance checks Develop and maintain the overall Quality Assurance Framework Provide 'help squads' for projects and programs

Perform organizational PPM maturity assessments

Service description

The assessment of the organization, or part of the organization using a recognized PPM maturity assessment with the view to baseline the maturity and suggest actions for improvement.

What the service provides for the customer

This provides a greater understanding of the strengths and weakness of the PPM delivery ability within the organization.

Why is this service being offered to the customer?

The PMO as an independent body, knowledgeable in PPM will be able to provide an objective assessment of the organizational maturity. They will be able to identify the best one of the available maturity models to use to conduct the assessment.

How PMO will apply this service

The PMO will investigate the different available maturity models and look at their strengths and weaknesses. They will look to choose the assessment which most aligns to the way that the organization runs the business.

Having selected the assessment, the PMO will look to identify the scope of the assessment. Will this cover all the PPM within the organization, or only just part of it? They will identify the relevant people talk to as part of the assessment. They will book up sessions to go through and ask the questions as part of the assessment.

The PMO will then interview the relevant people, they may look for examples of documents and look at the PPM framework. They will assess to see whether the PPM framework is actually being used as expected. They will look for any feedback loops to improve the PPM framework.

As well as asking the questions in the assessment the PMO will aim to get to the bottom of the reasons behind the views from the people being assessed.

Once all the people have been questioned, the PMO will collate the overall assessment. As well as providing an overall scoring using the maturity assessment scoring matrix the PMO will look to justify their assessment. The PMO will look to suggest a series of suggestions how the organization can improve, or at least maintain their current assessment.

Supplier	Input	Process	Output	Customer
External supplier	Maturity model questionnaire	Assessing maturity	Maturity assessment scoring Recommendations	Executive Portfolio Manager PMO

How the PMO will measure the value of this service

This service can be measured by looking at the number of suggestions for improvement that have been taken up by the organization.

Criteria when the PMO will use this service

- When the organization wants to improve the way, it runs projects and programs
- When the organization is looking to gain a contract, which requires a particular maturity

Helpful hints for the PMO when delivering the service

- The PMO may decide to get a consultancy in to perform the actual assessment to provide the necessary independence of the assessment
- If going for an accreditation (e.g. CMMI), then an external assessor will be required
- The ad-hoc comments can be more revealing about the state of PPM in the organization than the mere answers to the questions
- Maturity levels normally range from 1 to 5 where 1 is the lowest and 5 is the highest
- It is important to have someone with experience perform this assessment as some of the models are open to interpretation
- It is useful to have the same person/people to perform the assessments to ensure consistency
- If applying for a contract which needs a particular maturity level, the PMO may be forced to use a particular maturity assessment

PMO Capabilities needed to fulfil this service

Competencies	Techniques and generic tools
Knowledge Management Reporting, Insights and Analysis Assurance Capability Development Delivery Methods Governance Frameworks Relationships and engagement	Multi-Criteria Scoring Model Capability and Capacity analysis Check sheets

Related services

Define strategy for acquiring and developing skills Develop and maintain a PM Competence Framework	Provide PPM training Assess PMs against a Competence Framework Assess the Knowledge Management maturity

Further Reading

CMMI- Capability Maturity Model Integration
OPM3 – Organizational Project Management Maturity Model
P3M3 - Portfolio, Programme and Project Management Maturity Mode
Gartner Organizational Maturity
Kerzner's Project Management Maturity Model

Recommend ways to reduce or shorten project lifecycle times

Service description

The provision of advice and guidance to tailor the PPM framework for a particular project.

What the service provides for the customer

A tailored PPM framework to deliver the particular project quicker, whilst ensuring effective governance and control, taking due account of the risk involved.

Why is this service being offered to the customer?

As creators of the PPM framework the PMO will be best placed to suggest a tailoring pattern to suit the project (and the project manager). Having an agreed tailoring pattern ensures the project can deliver what is expected in a quicker timescale, without increasing the risk of delivery.

How PMO will apply this service

The PMO will speak to the project manager to find out about the project. They will read the PPM framework, the governance framework, and the tailoring patterns. Based on an assessment of the risk of the project the PMO will look to see which one of the tailoring patterns will be most appropriate. They will suggest ways that the governance can be tailored to reduce the times taken to decide about the project direction.

The PMO will discuss all the possible options to reduce the time taken with the project manager and ensure that the project manager documents this in the PID (or equivalent) for the project.

The PMO will look at the schedule for the project and look to see whether tasks could be performed in parallel or with an overlap. They will look at the sequencing of tasks to see whether these could be re-ordered to deliver faster. They will look at the resourcing to see whether adding more resources could deliver the tasks faster.

Supplier	Input	Process	Output	Customer
PMO	PPM framework Governance framework PID	Tailoring	PID Tailoring plan	Project Manager

How the PMO will measure the value of this service

This can be measured by the reduction in scheduled time to deliver the project after delivering this service.

Criteria when the PMO will use this service

- When a project is starting up
- Where there is a standard PPM framework in place

Helpful hints for the PMO when delivering the service

- Take into consideration the knowledge and experience of the project manager when tailoring the PPM framework for the project
- Use the experience gained from previous projects as to what works and what does not when tailoring a project
- Look at the impact of re-ordering the schedule will this help or just create confusion?
- Adding more resource may not help as the people may not be able to do the work in parallel

PMO Capabilities needed to fulfil this service

Competencies	Techniques and generic tools
Governance Frameworks Delivery Methods Relationships and engagement Resourcefulness	Alternatives analysis Capability and Capacity analysis Component milestones Scheduling tool Work Breakdown Structure

Related services

Tailor standard processes and template to the program or project Program or project fast-track mobilization service	Develop and maintain tailoring guidelines for standards, methods, and approaches

Perform coaching of portfolio, program, or project managers

Service Description

Provide coaching for portfolio, program or project managers in PPM processes, tools, and techniques.

What the service provides for the customer

This increases the capability level of project, program and portfolio managers in PPM processes, tools, and techniques.

Why is this service being offered to the customer?

As experts in PPM the PMO are ideally placed to provide mentoring and coaching on aspects of PPM to project, program, and portfolio managers to improve the overall capability within the organization.

How PMO will apply this service

Having identified a need for coaching the PMO will arrange for a time to speak to the individual directly. They will discuss the best approach to deliver the coaching, this may be a couple of sessions in quick succession or more sessions over a longer time period. The PMO will focus on one or two specific points that require coaching.

In the coaching session the PM may ask open questions such as 'How can I get better at identifying and mitigating risks'. The PMO can then dig into the responses to assist the individual with understanding how they can best approach the subject. They can provide the individual being coached with some examples and ideas to follow up on.

There will need to be more than one coaching session in order that the effectiveness of the coaching can be recognized and tailored to the individual.

Supplier	Input	Process	Output	Customer
Portfolio Managers Program Managers Project Managers	Capability Assessment gaps	Coaching	Coaching sessions	Portfolio Managers Program Managers Project Managers

How the PMO will measure the value of this service

This can be measured by an increase in the capability of project, program, and portfolio managers.

Criteria when the PMO will use this service

- When there are new PPM processes or tools being made available
- When there are new PPM managers in the organization
- Where there are capability assessment gaps identified
- Where a PPM manager is wanting to increase their skills to move to a more senior position

Helpful hints for the PMO when delivering the service

- Recognize that coaching is different from training (direct teaching) and mentoring (long term and generalized help)
- Consider the location of the coaching session, perhaps the sessions can be conducted in a local coffee shop, or park outside of the work environment. This avoids disturbance and can provide a calming atmosphere

PMO Capabilities needed to fulfil this service

Competencies	Techniques and generic tools
Capability Development Personal Integrity and reliability Personal Communication Relationships and engagement Leadership	Capability and Capacity analysis

Related services

Define strategy for acquiring and developing skills Provide PPM training Identify skills shortages and recommend suitable development Assess PMs against a Competence Framework	Program or project fast-track mobilization service Provide planning assistance to portfolio, programs, or projects Perform mentoring and coaching of PMO staff

Further Reading

The Project Management Coaching Workbook – Susanne Madsen

Provide a help desk manned by experts in PPM

Service description

Provision of advice and guidance on PPM related questions. This can cover how it works within the organization and how it is done across other organizations.

What the service provides for the customer

A single place to go to get a definitive answer on PPM related questions.

Why is this service being offered to the customer?

PMO are experts in how to run project, programs, and portfolios. The PMO have been involved in the creation of the PPM framework and are looking after the knowledge repository. They have links through into other organizations via their knowledge network which enables them to provide comprehensive answers to the questions that get asked.

How PMO will apply this service

The PMO will get asked a question. This is normally related to how PPM works within the organization or the application of the PPM framework. It could be a question about a service that the PMO offers. The PMO may need to clarify the question or put the question into context before providing an answer. Once the PMO understands the question they can then consult the PPM framework, governance framework, answers to previous questions or the knowledge base. They can then provide an answer to the question they have received.

There may be follow up question(s) which would seek further clarification of the initial response. If there are multiple people who could answer the question, then it is best that the same individual replies to keep the consistency of the response.

Supplier	Input	Process	Output	Customer
PPM team	PPM question PPM framework	PMO help desk	PPM answer	PPM team

How the PMO will measure the value of this service

This can be measured by the number of questions that get asked. It can be measured by the number of people who would go to the PMO first to ask the question because they know they will get a correct answer.

Criteria when the PMO will use this service

- Whenever there is a PMO
- If there was more than one person in the PMO

Helpful hints for the PMO when delivering the service

- Consider having a generic/shared mailbox for people to submit questions if there is more than one person in the PMO. These can then be answered by the most appropriate person within the team
- Consider aggregating the questions into a Frequently Asked Questions file which can then be shared via the PMO intranet site or wiki
- Consider whether it is worth organizing some specific training if there are common questions which keep occurring

PMO Capabilities needed to fulfil this service

Competencies	Techniques and generic tools
P3M Administration Benefits and Value Management Business Case Change Control Change Management Financial Management Information Management Issue Management Knowledge Management Planning and Scheduling Quality Management Reporting, Insights and Analysis Resource Management Risk Management Stakeholder Engagement Supplier Management Assurance Capability Development Delivery Methods Governance Frameworks P3M Tools Personal Communication Relationships and engagement Resourcefulness Result Orientation	Project Management Information System

Related services

This can be related to any one of the other services that the PMO delivers.

Promote good PPM within the organization

Service description

The promotion of good PPM practice within the organization to increase the skills, capability, and organizational maturity in PPM.

What the service provides for the customer

This provides a way of increasing the skills and knowledge of people working in a PPM environment. By promoting good practice, especially linked with external guidance can ensure the smoother running of PPM within the organization. An increase in the PPM maturity will lead to fewer PPM failures.

Why is this service being offered to the customer?

As experts in PPM and having the connection with groups outside the organization the PMO are ideally placed to offer advice and support on good PPM practice.

How PMO will apply this service

As new project, program or portfolio managers get appointed the PMO will offer to sit down and discuss with them the different ways that they can perform the role. The PMO can use opportunities to provide updates on what is considered as good practice in PPM outside the organization, with reference to new guidance that may be available. If the PMO attend an external event e.g. webinar, training course, conference they can feedback a summary of the updates.

There are many different ways the PMO can promote PPM good practice across the organization including:

- Newsletters – the PMO may already produce a newsletter and that can contain hints and tips about PPM
- Training sessions – these can be formal training when rolling out a new or updated framework or tool. They can be informal lunch and learn activities
- Webinars – the PMO could look to put on a webinar for people to dial into to learn more about a particular subject. They can provide details of external webinars
- Events – the PMO can contact one of the PPM professional organizations and host an event. The professional organization can help by providing a speaker
- Conferences – the PMO can distribute details of the conferences and meetups that are available for people to attend
- Team updates – the PMO can come along to a team/group meeting and provide information about PPM and how the PMO can help

Supplier	Input	Process	Output	Customer
External PPM professional organizations	PPM Good practice	Provide guidance	PMO Advice and suggestions	Project Managers Program Managers Portfolio Managers

How the PMO will measure the value of this service

This can be measured in the long term by an increase in PPM maturity in the organization. In the short term it can be measured by attendance at any of the sessions the PMO has put on.

Criteria when the PMO will use this service

- Where the organization wishes to increase its maturity
- Where the PMO has linkages with an external PPM professional body
- Where the PMO has the knowledge and experience in PPM that it can share the information to others
- Where there are people in the organization being asked to run a project, who would not consider themselves to be project managers

Helpful hints for the PMO when delivering the service

- Look to subscribe to mailing lists which keep the PMO informed about the state of PPM across different organizations

PMO Capabilities needed to fulfil this service

Competencies	Techniques and generic tools
Knowledge Management Capability Development Delivery Methods Personal Communication Relationships and engagement	Stakeholder checklist Stakeholder engagement assessment matrix

Related services

Capture good practice examples for inclusion in good practice repository External networking attendance at good practice events Develop external relationships to share lessons and experience Define strategy for acquiring and developing skills Assess PMs against a Competence Framework	Provide advice and guidance to prevent project or program failure Tailor standard processes and template to the program or project Program or project fast-track mobilization service Support closure process Document project and program success stories

Further Reading/Contacts

Association of Project Management (APM)
Project Management Institute (PMI)
International Project Management Association (IPMA)
PMO Flashmob
AIPMO
Global PMO Alliance
AXELOS

Advise Sponsors and Management Boards of appropriate frameworks and governance models

Service Description

Suggest to sponsors and management boards how programs and projects can be governed and what their role is in that governance.

What the service provides for the customer

This ensures that programs and projects are correctly governed to ensure that control is maintained, aligned to the risk of the endeavour and the competence of the individuals involved. This ensures a balance is maintained between rigid conformity and laissez-faire. It ensures that the sponsors and management boards understand their role and responsibilities in the project or program.

Why is this service being offered to the customer?

As the creators of the governance framework and the PPM framework the PMO are best placed to offer advice on how this can be applied to a particular project or program. They can offer support, advice and training for the sponsors and management boards to ensure they are setup for success.

How PMO will apply this service

The PMO will identify the sponsors and the management board for a particular project or program. The PMO will arrange for a time to meet and discuss with them, either individually (preferable) or as a group to review the way the project or program will be governed. The PMO will walk the individuals through the governance roles and responsibilities. They will show the governance structure and the individual's place in that structure. They will educate the individuals about the role good governance plays in the success of projects and programs. They will emphasize the importance of sticking to what has been setup and the issues that may be encountered if the processes are not followed.

They will explain any tailoring that has been done of the framework and why this has been decided. They will run through what feedback and information the sponsor and management board are likely to expect from the project and program. They will cover the sort of questions that will help them drive out a greater understanding of the status of the project or program in order that the sponsor and management boards can make the best decisions.

Supplier	Input	Process	Output	Customer
PMO	PPM Framework Governance Framework	Tailoring	Trained people Tailored governance framework	Sponsors Steering Groups Management Boards

How the PMO will measure the value of this service

This can be measured via the lessons learned to see whether the governance was setup correctly. It can be measured via feedback from the sponsors and management boards.

Criteria when the PMO will use this service

- Where a PMO is aligned to a single project or program
- Where there has been feedback about poor program and project governance
- Where there is a desire to improve the PPM knowledge of sponsors

Helpful hints for the PMO when delivering the service

- Consider developing some training for sponsors on their role in projects and programs
- Consider providing some written guidance on what to look for to see that a project or program is going well (or badly) and what to do about it
- Consider developing a sponsor charter for the sponsor to sign to provide evidence that they have received the information and have understood it. This can then be used later if there are governance issues
- If the membership of the management board or sponsor changes this will need to be repeated

PMO Capabilities needed to fulfil this service

Competencies	Techniques and generic tools
Assurance Capability Development Delivery Methods Governance Frameworks Personal Communication Relationships and engagement	Process Analysis

Related services

Provide advice and guidance to prevent project or program failure Provide guidance on how the governance framework can be tailored Define, maintain, and implement PPM governance framework	Define, maintain, and implement standard PPM framework Develop and maintain tailoring guidelines for standards, methods, and approaches

Provide advice and guidance to prevent project or program failure

Service Description

Provision of advice and guidance to project and program managers to keep the project or program on track and to prevent the need for the project or program to be rescued.

What the service provides for the customer

Timely advice on how to deal with troublesome aspects of the project. By heeding the advice, it will keep the project and program on track and prevent the need to rescue the project or program at a later date.

Why is this service being offered to the customer?

PMOs see lots of projects and can identify where a project or program may be heading into trouble. By offering advice when it is needed it becomes more relevant to the person receiving the advice. This means they are more likely to use the information to stabilize the project or program.

How PMO will apply this service

The PMO will review the health of the project or program by examining the information contained (or not contained) within the progress report. If they spot a project or program which looks like it needs some assistance they will arrange to speak to the project or program manager.

Based on the knowledge of the project or program, their knowledge of how to rescue projects or programs that are in trouble the PMO can provide targeted advice to the project or program manager. They can give them hints and tips in how to deal with particular situations. They can suggest different approaches which may help remove some of the roadblocks that were impacting the project or program.

Having provided the advice then the PMO should continue to monitor the situation until the project or program is stabilized. They may need to offer further advice should the initial advice not complete resolve the issue.

Supplier	Input	Process	Output	Customer
PMO	Knowledge database Potential risks Progress reporting	Provide guidance Analyse reports Knowledge management	Advice	Project Manager Program Manager

How the PMO will measure the value of this service

If this service is successful, then there should be no need to use the 'provide project or program rescue' service.

Criteria when the PMO will use this service

- When the PMO perceive that a project or program is getting into difficulties

Helpful hints for the PMO when delivering the service

- When projects and programs start to go wrong it can be difficult to get correct information, or information is not provided in a timely manner. The PMO should identify these projects or programs as potentials for this service
- If a project looks too perfect with everything being correct and on track, then it may be worth looking at those to see why
- When looking at the progress report there can be times when it does not contain information it may be expected to e.g. confirmation of milestone dates, hinting about risks that are not raised. These should raise concern to the PMO
- Do not confuse a red project with an out-of-control project. It is possible for a project to be flagging as red, and getting the help required and once the necessary decisions have been made it will be back on track

PMO Capabilities needed to fulfil this service

Competencies	Techniques and generic tools
Change Control Financial Management Information Management Issue Management Knowledge Management Planning and Scheduling Quality Management Reporting, Insights and Analysis Resource Management Risk Management Stakeholder Engagement Supplier Management Assurance Capability Development Governance Frameworks Professionalism and ethics Personal Communication Relationships and engagement Leadership Teamwork Conflict and Crisis Resourcefulness Negotiation Result Orientation	Root Cause Analysis Failure Modes and Effects Analysis (FMEA)

Related services

Provide project or program rescues Make constructive challenge and recommendations on collated progress reports Make constructive challenge and recommendations on combined progress reports Promote good PPM within the organization Advise Sponsors and Management Boards of appropriate frameworks and governance models	Provide project and program health checks Provide project and program audits Develop and maintain the overal Quality Assurance Framework Establish and maintain an efficient flow of information regarding risk handling and escalation

Financial Management

Financial Management

Description

Ensure that the financials for the portfolio, program or project are accurate and operate according to the organizational financial controls.

What the services within the area provide for the customer

These services enable the project, program, or portfolio manager to know that the financials being reported are accurate and will enable them to deal with any discrepancies in a timely manner.

Helpful hints when the PMO is delivering this service area

- The PMO may need to work closely with the finance function within the organization to ensure that the data provided is accurate and is processed according to the accounting rules
- For a large project or program, it may be necessary to recruit dedicated financial people to perform these services

Financial Management Design

Service group description

The design and setup of the financial governance for projects, programs, and the portfolio.

Why have these services been grouped together?

These services are concerned with the control and approval of finances within a project, program, and the portfolio.

List of related services described in other areas

Automate Processes

Responsibility Assignment Matrix

Service	Executive	Portfolio Manager	Program Manager	Project Manager	PMO	Sponsor	Other Stakeholder
Develop Business Case process and templates	A	I	I	I	R	I	C (Finance)
Develop and maintain the PPM financial framework	A	I	I	I	R	I	C (Finance)

Helpful hints when delivering this service group

The PMO will need to consult with the finance department to deliver these services.

Develop Business Case process and templates

Service description

Creation of a standard business case for approving projects and programs. Creation of guidance on business case approval process.

What the service provides for the customer

A standard business case template with some guidance on how this is to be filled in. The associated process will describe what the approval steps are, which may differ depending on the costs requested.

Why is this service being offered to the customer?

As projects and program require a business case to be approved to start having a clearly defined process to achieve that will help the project or program manager understand what is required in advance.

How PMO will apply this service

The PMO will review the governance framework and check with the finance department to find out the delegated approval levels. They will provide an approvals process aligned to the governance framework and the size of the project.

They will look to develop the business case template which will have sections for:

- Description – containing the background, reasons for doing the project or program, any executive summary
- Costs – the cost of doing the work and supporting it, shown for the duration of the work and the next few years
- Benefits – both financial and non-financial, shown over the next few years after the work finishes
- Risks – any known risks along with actions to deal with them
- Options – different options that were thought of and discarded (along with a reason why)
- Investment appraisal – a calculation of costs vs benefits using techniques such as payback period, return on investment, net present value

Within each section the PMO will look to provide help notes in order that it is easier to fill in.

Once they have the business case designed, they will check this with finance to see that it meets their requirements. They should check that any formulas included work correctly.

Supplier	Input	Process	Output	Customer
Finance PMO	Approval levels PPM Framework Governance Framework	Develop Standard Develop Templates	Business Case template Approval levels	Project Manager Program Manager

How the PMO can measure the value of this service

The effectiveness can be measured by a reduced number of questions in the use of the template or the approvals process.

Criteria when the PMO will use this service

- When projects and programs need approving
- Where consistency is required to evaluate different projects and programs against the same criteria

Helpful hints for the PMO when delivering the service

- The greater the spend request the more rigor is required in the Business Case. A Business Case template should be able to cope for the request of more information without making the lower approval level Business Cases to complicated and time consuming to use
- Most organizations have levels of delegated approval. The Business Case approval process needs to align to those
- As a business case contains financial information it is typically created using a spreadsheet program or a PPM tool
- To have consistency the business case should run for several years, this will vary per organization, but 3 or 5 years is typical
- Consider locking the template down to prevent changes and deletions of formulae or drop-down choices
- Consider having a worked example so people using the template know how it should be filled in

PMO Capabilities needed to fulfil this service

Competencies	Techniques and generic tools
Benefits and Value Management Business Case Financial Management Governance Frameworks Relationships and engagement Negotiation	Cost/ Benefit Analysis Business value Analysis Flowcharts Check sheets Swim-lane flowcharts Task responsibility matrix/RACI

Related services

Develop and maintain the PPM financial framework Review Business cases for compliance Identify duplicate and double counting of benefits	Develop benefits management framework Develop and refine portfolio, program, or project business cases Calculate the Total Cost of Ownership Automate Processes

Further Reading

PRINCE2
Managing Successful Programmes (MSP)
PMI PMBoK (A Guide to the Project Management Body of Knowledge)
Praxis

Develop and maintain the PPM financial framework

Service Description

The development of the PPM level financial controls. This includes guidance on approval levels, financial coding, finance tracking, purchasing rules, accruals, month & year-end requirements.

What the service provides for the customer

A simplified version of the financial controls for a project or program.

Why is this service being offered to the customer?

Unless you have dedicated financial staff within a project or program most financial controls are too complex for what is required to manage a project or program. The PMO working with Finance can provide a simplified version of the controls, which can be understood by a Project or Program Manager as well as a Finance person.

How PMO will apply this service

The PMO will speak to the project and program managers to find out what financial advice they require. The PMO will then speak to finance to get them to explain how this works in financial terms. The PMO will then interpret that information and produce a simplified guide for PPM staff to follow.

The framework can include:

- Approval levels – who needs to approve signoff of spend, dependent on size and type of spend
- Accruals – how and when to raise. What evidence is needed
- Capitalization – what can be capitalized and what cannot. How this works and the impact it has on the financial tracking
- Finance coding – how to link project references to finance reference numbers. How these can be requested (if applicable)
- Actual extracts – how they can be obtained, how they can be interpreted, what frequency they will be available
- Budget trackers – how finance will review the costing for your project within their systems, and what information they require and when they need it. Whether they will require any reforecasts from the projects
- Month/Quarter/Year-end – What needs to be done at month, quarter, and year end, including what happens with budget surpluses or overruns. The timetable of events. Information on budget updates required for finance
- Purchasing rules – some organizations have rules around who can purchase items (i.e. they must be a permanent staff member, or there must be a requester and an approver). These need to be clearly laid out
- Roles and responsibilities – who can do what. Where is the division between the PPM manager, the PMO and finance?

As well as the process (how to do something) the PMO will provide a timetable of events (when to do something) and the templates that are required to be used.

Supplier	Input	Process	Output	Customer
Finance	Approval levels Audit requirements Financial controls	Develop Standard Develop Templates	PPM Financial Framework	Project Manager Program Manager Project Approval Board

How the PMO can measure the value of this service

This can be measured by a reduction in the questions going directly to finance. It can be measured by the compliance of projects to the finance guidance during project audits/health checks.

Criteria when the PMO will use this service

- When there is not a dedicated financial resource within the PMO
- Where consistency is required in financial control
- Where finance is not able to support the questions coming from PPM managers and staff

Helpful hints for the PMO when delivering the service

- Look to keep the framework up to date with any changes announced by finance
- Check whether there is anything missing by looking at comments raised as part of the lessons learned process

PMO Capabilities needed to fulfil this service

Competencies	Techniques and generic tools
Business Case Financial Management Reporting, Insights and Analysis Supplier Management Relationships and engagement Teamwork Negotiation	Cash flow analysis Categorized frequency analysis (Frequency plot, bar chart) Time series plots

Related services

Develop Business Case process and templates Control adherence to accounting procedures Monitor and report on financial spend Manage invoicing processing for portfolio, programs, and projects Oversee capitalization of capital assets Facilitate timely calculation of accruals, forecasts, and anticipated cash flow Maintain details of project credit transfers between business units	Gather, review, and edit submissions for budget cycles Track expenses on behalf of business units Define, maintain, and implement PPM governance framework Challenge spend profile and forecast spend profile Forecast portfolio, program or project spend Advise on cost control and opportunities for savings Manage the Process Improvement Plan Map key value streams and processes

Financial Management Operations

Service group description

The updating the financial information on behalf of the project, program, portfolio, or business units.

Why have these services been grouped together?

Due to their links with finance the PMO can update the financial information on behalf of the project, program, or portfolio manager.

List of related services described in other areas

Review Business cases for compliance
Ensure invoices are paid according to the contract terms

Responsibility Assignment Matrix

Service	Executive	Portfolio Manager	Program Manager	Project Manager	PMO	Sponsor	Other Stakeholder
Forecast portfolio, program or project spend		A	A	A	R		
Manage invoicing processing for portfolio, programs, and projects		A	A	A	R		
Prepare monthly financial reports	A	A	A	A	R		
Administer and track budget allocations		A	A	A	R		
Develop and refine portfolio, program, or project business cases		A	A	A	R		
Advise on cost control and opportunities for savings	S	C	C	C	R		
Oversee capitalization of capital assets		A	A	A	R		I (Finance)
Facilitate timely calculation of accruals, forecasts, and anticipated cash flow		A	A	A	R		C (Finance)
Maintain details of project credit transfers between business units	A				R		C (Finance)
Gather, review, and edit submissions for budget cycles	A				R		C (Finance)
Maintain details of changes to budget baseline		C	C	C	A, R		
Increase in accuracy of Profit & Loss & balance sheets		C	C	C	R		A (Finance)
Calculate the Total Cost of Ownership	A				R		I (Finance)
Track expenses on behalf of business units	A				R		C (Finance)

Helpful hints when the PMO is delivering this service group

The PMO delivering these services would benefit from having some finance experience.

Forecast portfolio, program or project spend

Service description

Creation or updating of a financial forecasted spend profile for a portfolio, program, or project.

What the service provides for the customer

This ensures that the financial forecast represents the expected spend, by type, by period for the project, program, or portfolio. They can apply the actuals and re-profile the remaining forecast. The forecast will be aligned to when expected expenditure will occur.

Why is this service being offered to the customer?

The PMO can ensure that the financial profile is created and updated in accordance with the PPM financial framework. The PMO have access to the actuals recorded and can apply this to the forecast on behalf of the project, program, or portfolio manager.

Using the actual spend to date and the standard profile of a project/program provide an estimate of the expected cost of a project/program. This can then be compared to the forecast from the Project/Program Manager and the approved budget. Any significant variations would then warrant further investigation.

How PMO will apply this service

When creating the initial forecast, the PMO individual will sit with the PPM manager and discuss all the items that could be included within the financial profile. Having a look at the scope of the project and the business case will provide suggestions as to what should be included.

Having got all the categories and the total amounts the PMO should work with the PPM manager to ascertain when these costs are likely to be spent. Some items like resourcing costs will be profiled across, whereas hardware costs may be incurred as a one-off expense. If there is any contingency in the profile, ensure this is back loaded.

Once the PMO has drafted the initial profile they will confirm this with the PPM manager. Once this has been approved this can be then baselined.

On a regular basis, aligned to when financial actuals are available, the PMO will apply the actuals to the forecast. The forecast for the previous period will be replaced by the actuals and any differences will be applied to the rest of the forecast (see hints section). The PMO will then look to see whether the rest of the forecast has changed. Are there any new items that need adding? Does the profile still reflect when spend is likely to occur? Are there any items which are no longer required? The PMO will check for these and apply the changes to the profile. Once all the changes have been made the PMO will confirm these with the PPM manager.

Supplier	Input	Process	Output	Customer
Project Managers Program Managers PMO	Actual Spend Project/Program duration Standard project/program cost profile PID	Forecast Financials	Financial variance report	Project Approval Board Portfolio Managers Program Managers

How the PMO can measure the value of this service

This can be measured by asking for feedback from the PPM manager.

Criteria when the PMO will use this service

- When the PMO is aligned to a single project or program
- When the PMO supports a portfolio manager
- Where a detailed financial profile is required

Helpful hints for the PMO when delivering the service

- When the original profile is setup work out how actuals are going to be added in and the forecast re-profiled. It is not just a matter of replacing the forecast with the actuals as any deviations will mean that the forecast will need to be amended
- If the actuals are greater than the forecast for a month, can this be put back on track by using some of the contingency, or will this need to be shown and an overspend
- If the actuals are less than the forecast for the month, does that mean:
    - The costs will never occur, in which case this could be claimed as a saving
    - The costs will never occur in which case it could get absorbed back into contingency
    - The timing was wrong, the costs were expected in the month, but have been deferred to later in the project
- Consider having a standard list of items that would go into a financial profile. This would be based on the finance categories, but would be cut down to only include the standard items expected
- Look at the scoping document to work out the sort of items that may need to be included
- Relate the initial profile back to the business case to ensure that the profile aligns with the budget that has been approved

PMO Capabilities needed to fulfil this service

Competencies	Techniques and generic tools
Business Case Financial Management Planning and Scheduling Reporting, Insights and Analysis Personal Communication Relationships and engagement Teamwork Negotiation	Cash flow analysis Performance variance report Scheduling tool

Related services

Gather, review, and edit submissions for budget cycles Maintain details of changes to budget baseline Develop and maintain the PPM financial framework Monitor and report on financial spend Develop and refine portfolio, program, or project business cases Prepare monthly financial reports	Advise on cost control and opportunities for savings Oversee capitalization of capital assets Develop and maintain an estimating framework Challenge spend profile and forecast spend profile Manage invoicing processing for portfolio, programs, and projects Facilitate timely calculation of accruals, forecasts, and anticipated cash flow

Manage invoicing processing for portfolio, programs, and projects

Service description

Tracking, accruing, and paying invoices according to the accounting procedures and approved contracts on behalf of a project, program, or portfolio. Includes rejection of incorrect invoices.

What the service provides for the customer

This allows the PPM manager to know that invoices are being dealt with according to the invoicing rules.

Why is this service being offered to the customer?

Having the PMO chase down the status of invoices allows the PPM manager to focus on other issues. The PMO will have access to the procurement and ledger systems to check on the status of an invoice.

How PMO will apply this service

The PMO will gain access to the procurement systems in order they can track the order of the goods. They look to check that the goods have been receipted. Once the goods have been receipted, they will look to raise an accrual if an invoice is not expected immediately. They will assign themselves (if possible) as a contact to be notified once an invoice has been raised and sent to the organization.

Once the PMO is notified about the invoice they will check to see whether this matches the expected amount and is aligned to any contract that may be in place. If there are any discrepancies then that needs to be fed back to the supplier and the invoice rejected, or at least, put on hold. Once the invoice correctly reflects the amount that has been spent then the PMO can approve this, either directly or get the correct approver to process this.

If an invoice has been set to be paid, then the PMO should ensure that any accrual that was raised to cover the invoiced amount is reversed from the ledger. They need to ensure that this information gets updated in the financial tracker.

Supplier	Input	Process	Output	Customer
Suppliers	Invoices Contracts PPM Finance Framework	Paying an invoice	Invoice payment	Project Manager Program Manager Portfolio Manager Supplier

How the PMO can measure the value of this service

This can be measured by looking to see how many unpaid invoices there are for a particular project, program, or portfolio where this service is offered.

Criteria when the PMO will use this service

- Where the PMO is aligned to a single project or program
- Where the PMO is supporting a portfolio manager
- Where there are external costs expected

Helpful hints for the PMO when delivering the service

- If this were not done by the PMO then the PPM manager would need to complete this task
- If expecting an invoice, think about adding a calendar reminder to check before the financial month end close

PMO Capabilities needed to fulfil this service

Competencies	Techniques and generic tools
P3M Administration Financial Management Supplier Management Assurance Relationships and engagement Negotiation	Cash flow analysis

Related services

Develop and maintain the PPM financial framework Monitor and report on financial spend Forecast portfolio, program or project spend Facilitate timely calculation of accruals, forecasts, and anticipated cash flow Ensure invoices are paid according to the contract terms	Control adherence to accounting procedures Increase in accuracy of Profit & Loss & balance sheets Oversee the quality review process for contractual supplier deliverables Chase up missing timesheets

Prepare monthly financial reports

Service description

The provision of standard reports showing the actual spend on a project or program. This information can then be used to reprofile forecasts or be compared against the approved spend.

What the service provides for the customer

This provides a standard way of viewing the actuals for a project or program. It is formatted in a way that allows ease of use into other reports.

Why is this service being offered to the customer?

By providing the actuals information in a consistent format this allows the data to be used to reforecast projects. It saves time as each project or program manager does not need to reformat this themselves.

How PMO will apply this service

The PMO will gain access to an extract of the ledger actuals. They will look to reformat this, so it is in a more useful format for the project and program managers. This can include:

- Adding project information in – translating the codes used by finance to denote the project into ones that the project or program manager would understand. This includes adding in the project manager name, the unique ID, the PMO name
- Decoding the financial categories – changing the codes used by the ledger to categories the project manager would understand like resource costs, travel etc.
- Removing unnecessary data – smoothing out the ins and out and providing a single figure (useful for accruals). Excluding the transfers to other cost centres (if using a recharge model)
- Aligning to the time periods – ensuring that the time periods on the report match the time periods that the project manager is expected to report on

The final report can then be published or distributed as applicable.

Supplier	Input	Process	Output	Customer
Finance	Ledger Actuals	Producing financial actuals report	Financial actuals report	Project Manager Program Manager PMO

How the PMO can measure the value of this service

This can be measured by the ease with which this information can be reused to produce other financial reports.

Criteria when the PMO will use this service

- When the PMO are responsible for reporting financial information
- When consistency is needed in the actuals used for financial reporting

Helpful hints for the PMO when delivering the service

- Consider adding the production of this report into the reporting schedule so people who want the data know when and where they can find it
- Discuss with the recipients what they are going to do with the data and see if it can be re-arranged into the correct format to save them time later

PMO Capabilities needed to fulfil this service

Competencies	Techniques and generic tools
Financial Management Reporting, Insights and Analysis Relationships and engagement	Categorized frequency analysis (Frequency plot, bar chart) Time series plots

Related services

Monitor and report on financial spend Forecast portfolio, program or project spend Collate individual progress reports	Combine individual progress reports Chase up missing timesheets Automate Processes

Administer and track budget allocations

Service description

Maintain a register of agreed budget allocations for projects and programs as part of the overall portfolio budget.

What the service provides for the customer

An approved in principle agreement of the potential costs for an entire project or program. This can then be used to compare against current forecast figures. It can be useful to compare this figure against the baselined cost or total cost for the project or program.

Why is this service being offered to the customer?

Knowing the budget allocations allows the program manager to know how much has been set aside for the entire program, even if all the individual projects have yet to be approved.

Knowing the budget allocation allows a project manager to know how much has been set aside for the entire project even if the approvals happen gate by gate.

How PMO will apply this service

Following a project approval board meeting then the PMO will make a note of the approval of each of the projects and programs. They will track to see whether this is a full allocation for the entirely of the project or whether this has been only given for part of the work. If a program allocation has been approved, they will note how much of that has already been assigned to the individual projects within that program.

The PMO should look to store at least the following information:

- Unique ID – to the project or program
- Name – of the project or program
- Amount – this would need to be listed as a total, and if available the split by financial year
- Type of approval – is this just an allocation, is it the full amount or has this been drawn down if it is a project within an overall program
- Date of approval – when was this approved – this can then help with links to the minutes of the meeting in case of queries

This information should be shared with the portfolio, program, and project manager.

Supplier	Input	Process	Output	Customer
Project approval board	Potential costs	Track budget allocations	Budget Allocation tracker	Portfolio Manager Program Manager Project Manager

How the PMO can measure the value of this service

This will be measured by the consistency of the information about the allocated budget for a particular item. This can be measured by the reduction in time it will take for the PMO to verify an allocated budget figure.

Criteria when the PMO will use this service

- Where the PMO supports a portfolio manager
- Where the PMO supports a project approval board

Helpful hints for the PMO when delivering the service

- There can be 5 different figures used when reviewing a project or program
    - Allocated cost – this is the amount set aside or ring-fenced for the program
    - Baselined cost – this is the amount that have been formally approved for the program based on business cases and agreed changes
    - Actual cost – this is the amount that has been spent
    - Forecast cost – this is the amount that is still left to spend, according to the program manager
    - Total cost – this is the actual cost plus the forecast cost for the program,
- This service is primarily about recording the allocated cost, but may as part of this track the baselined figure as well
- If the portfolio has an overall budget, consider drawing down from that overall figure in order that you can track the total amount allocated and know whether you will exceed the overall portfolio budget

PMO Capabilities needed to fulfil this service

Competencies	Techniques and generic tools
P3M Administration Financial Management Governance Frameworks Relationships and engagement	None

Related services

Develop and refine portfolio, program, or project business cases Maintain details of changes to budget baseline Monitor and report on financial spend	Maintain a register for current and potential programs and projects Support the Project Approval Board Gather, review, and edit submissions for budget cycles

Develop and refine portfolio, program, or project business cases

Service description

The creation or updating of the business case for the project, program, or portfolio.

What the service provides for the customer

A business case that can be used for approval of the project, program, or portfolio.

Why is this service being offered to the customer?

The PMO can work with the senior users and finance department to ensure that the business case contains all the costs and benefits. By getting the PMO to out the detail into the business case the PPM manager can focus on the bigger picture. As the PMO got involved in the creating the business case template they will be able to know how it works and therefore be quicker in filling the information in.

Work with senior user and finance departments to ensure that the costs and benefits are all accounted for. That any sensitivity analysis has been done. Ensure that the Business Case aligns to the finance procedures.

How PMO will apply this service

The PMO will be asked to create or update the business case. If this is a new business case, then the PMO will find the template. If the business case requires updating, then the PMO will find the latest version of the business case.

For a new business case the PMO will fill in the background information. This can normally be obtained from the scoping document They will look at the risk register and extract the major risks. They will work with the PPM manager to update the costs section of the business case. This will need to contain any ongoing support costs as well as the cost of delivery. The PMO will work with the senior users to work out what the potential benefits will be. They will then apply any calculations to work out the cost vs benefits, as detailed in the business case. Once they have produced the draft business case, they will send it to the PPM manager for them to review and send off for approval.

For an existing business case the PMO will look to see whether any of the background information needs changing and amend appropriately. They will review the risks section against the risk register and add in any new risks and delete old ones. They will speak to the senior users to confirm the benefits are still correct and amend to align to the expected benefit values and phasing. For the costs section they will update this with actuals and the revised forecasted costs. Once the PMO has produced the draft business case they will send it to the PPM manager for them to review and send off for approval.

Supplier	Input	Process	Output	Customer
Project Manager Program Manager Portfolio Manager	Business case template Current business case Benefit drivers list	Complete business case	Updated Business Case	Project Manager Program Manager Portfolio Manager Project Approval Board

How the PMO can measure the value of this service

This service can be measured by feedback from the PPM manager. This can be measured by reduced or no feedback when the business case is reviewed for compliance.

Criteria when the PMO will use this service

- Where the PMO is aligned to a single project or program
- Where the PMO supports a portfolio manager
- Where there is a business case to be written or updated

Helpful hints for the PMO when delivering the service

- Consider doing a sensitivity analysis on the figures to see how well the business case stacks to, and therefore how likely it may be to be approved
- If the business case is difficult to update, consider making changes to the template as that will benefit everyone

PMO Capabilities needed to fulfil this service

Competencies	Techniques and generic tools
P3M Administration Business Case Change Control Financial Management Information Management Governance Frameworks Relationships and engagement Negotiation	Cost/ Benefit Analysis Benefit realization analysis Cash flow analysis Sensitivity analysis Risk Register

Related services

Review Business cases for compliance Develop Business Case process and templates Maintain details of changes to budget baseline Support the Project Approval Board	Develop benefits management framework Forecast portfolio, program or project spend Administer and track budget allocations Calculate the Total Cost of Ownership

Advise on cost control and opportunities for savings

Service description

The review of the costs for the portfolio, program, or project to identify cost savings, which will not impact delivery.

What the service provides for the customer

It provides a way of reducing the cost, allowing the monies to be spent on other items within the portfolio, or to be seen as an overall cost saving.

Why is this service being offered to the customer?

As the PMO understands the accounting procedures it can advise on items such as capitalization to reduce the operating costs. The PMO has an overview across the entire portfolio they are ideally positioned to see where saving can be made by combining purchases across multiple projects.

How PMO will apply this service

The PMO will have a look at the financial plans to see whether there are items which can be combined. They will then look to see whether these items are shared with other projects within the program or portfolio. To do that they will need to find the financial plans for the other projects.

If the PMO think there is a possibility of combining items then they will speak to the project manager of the other project to see whether this will be feasible i.e. do they require this in the same timescale, will there be cost savings if items are brought in bulk. If they can be combined, then the PMO will suggest that to both project managers and offer to coordinate the purchase of those items as one order.

The PMO will examine the financial plan to see if there are items which can be capitalized or depreciated, which have not already been marked as such. They will confirm this with finance and advise the project manager of the impact on their project financials. The PMO will then offer to update the financial plan to reflect the saving and work with finance to ensure the necessary accounting procedures have been followed.

The PMO will look at the travel and expenses section to see whether there are any opportunities to cut costs by reducing the numbers of trips, perhaps face to face meetings could be replaced by video or audio conferencing. By booking people into hotels at a group rate, rather than individual bookings would save money.

Supplier	Input	Process	Output	Customer
Finance PMO	Accounting procedures Financial Framework Financial Plans	Review financials	Cost saving suggestions	Project Manager Program Manager Portfolio Manager

How the PMO can measure the value of this service

This can be measured by the amount of saving possible.

Criteria when the PMO will use this service

- Where the PMO is aligned to a single project or program
- Where the PMO is aligned to a portfolio manager
- Where there is a cost savings challenge

Helpful hints for the PMO when delivering the service

- It is more likely that non-resource spend e.g. hardware or software can be combined
- Ensure that when potential savings are identified that they do not have an impact on delivery timescales for the projects. Sometimes it may be better to have a higher cost to achieve delivery sooner, and start getting the benefits earlier

PMO Capabilities needed to fulfil this service

Competencies	Techniques and generic tools
Financial Management Reporting, Insights and Analysis Supplier Management Resourcefulness	Alternatives analysis Cash flow analysis

Related services

Develop and maintain the PPM financial framework Control adherence to accounting procedures Forecast portfolio, program or project spend	Oversee capitalization of capital assets Arrange travel for other people Challenge spend profile and forecast spend profile

Oversee capitalization of capital assets

Service description

Ensuring that capital assets can get written down over the life of the asset rather than being expensed when purchased.

What the service provides for the customer

This provides a way of spreading the costs of assets between the project and business as usual. This will reduce the cost impact to the project, but it will increase the impact to business as usual.

Why is this service being offered to the customer?

As the PMO have created the Financial PPM framework they will be able to offer advice on whether an asset can be capitalized. They have the connections with finance to ensure this gets done. They can notify the business-as-usual area to ensure these costs get included in any budget for that area.

How PMO will apply this service

The PMO will look at the financial plan to see what items could be capitalized. They will look at the accounting rules to see whether the item meets the criteria for capitalization. They will look at the procedure for capitalizing and speak to the finance department to get them to process the accounting. They will then update the financial plan with the new profile for the costs. They will inform the business-as-usual area of the costs that will be depreciated over the life of the asset.

Supplier	Input	Process	Output	Customer
Suppliers	Invoices Accounting procedures	Capitalization of assets	Capitalization schedule Depreciation schedule	Project Manager Program Manager

How the PMO can measure the value of this service

This can be measured by the reduction in accounting errors. It can be measured by getting feedback from the project or program manager.

Criteria when the PMO will use this service

- Where the PMO is aligned to a single project or program
- Where there is the possibility of capitalizing spend

Helpful hints for the PMO when delivering the service

- Ensure you have a good working relationship with the finance department
- Be prepared that not all items can be capitalized and instead will need to be treated as expense costs

PMO Capabilities needed to fulfil this service

Competencies	Techniques and generic tools
Financial Management Stakeholder Engagement Supplier Management Professionalism and ethics Personal Integrity and reliability Relationships and engagement Negotiation	Cash flow analysis

Related services

Control adherence to accounting procedures Facilitate timely calculation of accruals, forecasts, and anticipated cash flow Increase in accuracy of Profit & Loss & balance sheets Develop and maintain the PPM financial framework	Challenge spend profile and forecast spend profile Forecast portfolio, program or project spend Advise on cost control and opportunities for savings

Facilitate timely calculation of accruals, forecasts, and anticipated cash flow

Service Description

Ensuring that the financial plan represents the expected spend within the project or program. Ensuring accruals get raised within the ledger after goods are receipted.

What the service provides for the customer

An accurate financial record for the project or program.

Why is this service being offered to the customer?

The PMO has access to the ledger and the procurement systems and can identify where items need accruing. They may be responsible for reforecasting costs on behalf of the project or program manager.

How PMO will apply this service

The PMO will identify that goods have been receipted. They will then either raise the accrual on the project or program managers behalf or chase up to ensure this is raised. The PMO will ensure that the financial plan has been updated to reflect actuals that have been booked. They will ensure that the financial plan will reflect the expected delivery of the cost for the project or program.

Supplier	Input	Process	Output	Customer
Project Manager Program Manager	Financial plan	Update financial plan	Updated financial plan Accruals	Project Manager Program Manager

How the PMO can measure the value of this service

This can be measured by checking there is no variance between the figures in the financial plan and those in the ledger.

Criteria when the PMO will use this service

- Where a PMO is aligned to a single project or program
- Where the PMO has been asked to assist with the finances
- Where there is external spend that needs accruing

Helpful hints for the PMO when delivering the service

- Consider being the person to receipt the goods, thereby ensuring you know when to raise the accrual and for how much
- Ensure the accrual correctly deals with any tax or currency exchange rates
- As accruals automatically reverse each month the PMO should check whether the invoice has been paid. If it has not, then they should resubmit the accrual. If the invoice has been paid, then the accrual must not be resubmitted

PMO Capabilities needed to fulfil this service

Competencies	Techniques and generic tools
Financial Management Relationships and engagement Teamwork Resourcefulness Result Orientation	Cash flow analysis

Related services

Forecast portfolio, program or project spend Monitor and report on financial spend Ensure invoices are paid according to the contract terms Develop and maintain the PPM financial framework	Challenge spend profile and forecast spend profile Manage invoicing processing for portfolio, programs, and projects Oversee capitalization of capital assets Increase in accuracy of Profit & Loss & balance sheets

Maintain details of project credit transfers between business units

Service description

Keep a track of who is paying for a project across the different business units.

What the service provides for the customer

Where a project is due to be paid for out of multiple business units. This ensures those costs are correctly apportioned. Where change requests get raised and they are apportioned out individually the PMO can ensure the overall cost gets aggregated.

Why is this service being offered to the customer?

The PMO have access to the original approved split between business unit and the change register. They can ensure that the costs are correctly split. Where a change is paid for by one department the PMO will ensure those costs do not get charged to the other departments erroneously.

How PMO will apply this service

Where a project is going to be paid for by multiple business units/cost centres the PMO will maintain a spreadsheet showing the proportional split. They will ensure that this has been agreed (and documented) at the project approval board. When change requests get raised, they will ensure that the split for each of those changes gets shown. Once the change request has been approved, they will add this to the spreadsheet. If no split is mentioned, then the PMO can assume that this will be the same as the original project. However, it may be that a change has been raised that will be paid for by a single business unit. The PMO should record that in their spreadsheet.

Before the recharge occurs each month the PMO should send the finance department an updated spreadsheet with the information of how the splits should be applied.

Supplier	Input	Process	Output	Customer
Project Approval Board Change Board Steering Group	Business Case Approval splits Change Requests	Apportion costs	Project charges	Business Units

How the PMO can measure the value of this service

This can be measured by the accuracy of the recharge.

Criteria when the PMO will use this service

- Where the organization uses cross charging
- Where multiple departments are paying for a single project

Helpful hints for the PMO when delivering the service

- It may be sensible to maintain this spreadsheet for all projects, even the ones that will be paid 100 by a single business unit as that will ensure none of the project splits are missed. If a project needs to be recharged that is not on the list the PMO can go and find the details of the split before the recharge occurs
- When change requests have a different split than the entire project consider identifying those separately. If the change request cannot be identified separately then the PMO should alter (from that the change request has been approved) the percentage split between business units, based on the approved cost of the change request. For example, if a project costing 100 was split 50/50 between 2 business units then the original percentage for each would be 50%. If a change request were approved for 10 that a single business unit was paying for this would make the split 55/45 to the business unit who was paying for the change request

PMO Capabilities needed to fulfil this service

Competencies	Techniques and generic tools
P3M Administration Financial Management Governance Frameworks Relationships and engagement Result Orientation	Cash flow analysis

Related services

Increase in accuracy of Profit & Loss & balance sheets	Develop and maintain the PPM financial framework

Gather, review, and edit submissions for budget cycles

Service description

Ensure that each project and program has submitted their budgets for the next year or quarter.

What the service provides for the customer

This provides finance with the expected budget for each project or program for the remainder of the year, or the following year. It ensures that the project or program manager gets the budget figures they expect.

Why is this service being offered to the customer?

This provides finance a single point of contact. The PMO will ensure the data goes to finance on schedule. The PMO will ensure the project and program managers get confirmation of the budget figures recorded by finance.

How PMO will apply this service

The PMO will speak with the finance department to find out what the budget cycle will be. The PMO will overlay on the budget timetable the actions required by the project and program managers.

The PMO will find the proposed budget template expected by finance. They will see how this aligns to the standard financial plan template in use by the project and programs. They will look to see if they can adjust this so that if the financial plan gets included that the budget template will be updated automatically.

The PMO will provide some guidance for the project and program manager in how the template is to be used, and the timescale for completing the information.

According to the timetable the PMO will expect the responses in from the projects and programs. Where no response has been provided the PMO will chase these up. Before submitting them to finance the PMO will perform a sense check to ensure that they are aware of any deviances between the prior budget and this one. This ensures that the PMO can answer some of the questions finance may have. They can go back to the project or program to confirm any changes.

Once the budgets have been submitted to finance they will decide and agree the figures. Once the decision has been made the PMO will find the agreed figures and compare that with the submissions. The PMO will inform the projects and programs of the new financial budget along with any variance, and reason for the variance from the submission. The PMO will work with the project and program to suggest how those changes get incorporated into the current financial plan

Supplier	Input	Process	Output	Customer
Finance	Budgeting timetable Budget template	Manage budget cycle	Budget instructions Budgeting timetable Budget template	Project Manager Program Manager
Project Manager Program Manager	Financial forecast profile Budget template	Manage budget cycle	Expected budget profile	Finance
Finance	Agreed budget	Manage budget cycle	Financial plan updates	Project Manager Program Manager

How the PMO can measure the value of this service

This can be measured by the numbers of budget templates submitted on time with the correct data quality (i.e. not returned with queries). This can be measured based on feedback from the finance department.

Criteria when the PMO will use this service

- When a budget cycle is due
- When the PMO is looking after a range of projects
- Where the PMO is aligned to a portfolio manager

Helpful hints for the PMO when delivering the service

- The budget cycle will be annual, but additional cycles may be required quarterly
- Where the budget returned does not agree with the financial plan of the project or program then the PMO will need to provide advice to the project or program manager how this can become aligned

PMO Capabilities needed to fulfil this service

Competencies	Techniques and generic tools
P3M Administration Change Control Financial Management Information Management Reporting, Insights and Analysis Personal Communication Relationships and engagement Teamwork Conflict and Crisis Resourcefulness Negotiation Result Orientation	Cash flow analysis Swim-lane flowcharts Task responsibility matrix/RACI

Related services

Maintain details of changes to budget baseline	Administer and track budget allocations
Forecast portfolio, program or project spend	Develop and maintain the PPM financial framework

Maintain details of changes to budget baseline

Service description

Keeping an up-to-date record of the agreed baseline for each project and program within the portfolio.

What the service provides for the customer

This ensures that there is one figure that can be relied upon as the agreed one for each project and program. This will show the original agreed amount, the amount of approved change requests and the current agreed amount.

Why is this service being offered to the customer?

The PMO will know the original cost for the project or program. They will be informed of the approved changes. They will be responsible for the baselining within any PPM tool. The PMO provide an independent place where the baseline figure can be confirmed.

How PMO will apply this service

Following a project approval board, the PMO will note the agreed budget baseline figure for the project or program. They will store this information in the baseline budget tracker. When the project or program has an approved change request, the PMO will make a note of the change to the budget figure.

The budget baseline tracker should include the following information:

- Unique ID – to the project or program
- Name – of the project or program
- Original Amount – this would need to be listed as a total, and if available the split by financial year
- Cumulative change request amount – this is the total of all the approved change requests
- Current baseline figure – this is the Original Amount + Cumulative change request amount

Once the budget baseline tracker has been updated the project or program manager needs to be informed of the new budget baseline amount. The project or program manager will need to reflect the new budget baseline amount within their reporting.

Supplier	Input	Process	Output	Customer
Project Approval Board Change board Steering group	Approved Business case Approved change request	Baseline projects	Budget baseline tracker	Project Manager Program Manager Portfolio Manager Finance

How the PMO can measure the value of this service

This will be measured by the consistency of the information about the budget baseline for a project or program. This can be measured by the reduction in time it will take for the PMO to verify the budget baseline figure.

Criteria when the PMO will use this service

- Where the PMO supports a portfolio manager
- Where the PMO is responsible for baselining projects
- Where the PMO supports a project approval board

Helpful hints for the PMO when delivering the service

- Change requests can move the budget up or down
- It may be required to store the budget split by year. If so, then this will need to be done for change requests as well
- When creating the budget baseline tracker, the PMO will need to consider what reporting they will require from this information
- The budget baseline tracker needs to be held under configuration management in order that the correct version is always in use

PMO Capabilities needed to fulfil this service

Competencies	Techniques and generic tools
P3M Administration Business Case Change Control Financial Management Information Management Governance Frameworks P3M Tools Professionalism and ethics Personal Integrity and reliability Personal Communication Relationships and engagement Teamwork	Cash flow analysis Project Management Information System

Related services

Monitor and report on financial spend Prepare monthly financial reports Administer and track budget allocations	Develop and refine portfolio, program, or project business cases Forecast portfolio, program or project spend Gather, review, and edit submissions for budget cycles

Increase in accuracy of Profit & Loss & balance sheets

Service description

Ensure the costs and benefits from PPM get included into the profit and loss accounting for the organization.

What the service provides for the customer

This enables finance to correctly report on the profit and loss for an organization or part of an organization.

Why is this service being offered to the customer?

The PMO are aware of the PPM costs and can track the benefits from PPM deliveries. The PMO can ensure that the PPM data is correctly reflected within the ledger.

How PMO will apply this service

The PMO will look at the actuals that have been recorded in the ledger for the projects and programs. They will ensure that the costs that are in the ledger are directly attributable to the projects or programs. Any items which are not correctly associated with the individual project or program they will work with the finance department to ensure they are correctly recorded within the ledger.

The PMO will look at the financial benefits that should have been achieved, using the benefits realization plan. For each of these benefits they will confirm what has been delivered. They will examine the ledger to see that this has been correctly captured (or not). If the benefits have not been correctly recorded the PMO will work with the finance department to ensure they get recorded correctly.

Where benefits are due to the forgoing of expenditure if this has not happened the PMO will chase up to find out why this has not been done. They may escalate this to senior management and alert them that the benefits have not been achieved, and the necessary steps to get this delivered.

Supplier	Input	Process	Output	Customer
Project Manager Program Manager	Benefits realization plan Financial plan	Track finances Benefits Realization	Ledger submissions	Finance

How the PMO can measure the value of this service

This can be measured by looking at the accuracy of the cost/benefit trackers compared with the ledger information.

Criteria when the PMO will use this service

- Where the PMO is involved with benefits realization
- Where the PMO gets involved with financial reconciliation

Helpful hints for the PMO when delivering the service

- If an item has been incorrectly accrued the PMO can get the accrual removed
- If an item has been booked against the wrong project, then the PMO can raise a request to get this reversed and assigned to the correct project
- If the incorrect amount has been recorded, then the PMO can raise a journal to reverse this. The PMO should ensure they have evidence to back this up
- Some of the benefits will represent a saving. Savings will not be shown on the ledger. For example, if a benefit is listed as not paying for a service, the PMO need to check the ledger to see whether the contract got cancelled and the service was not paid for

PMO Capabilities needed to fulfil this service

Competencies	Techniques and generic tools
Benefits and Value Management Financial Management Result Orientation	Cost/ Benefit Analysis Benefit realization analysis Cash flow analysis

Related services

Track and report on benefit realization Monitor and report on financial spend Manage invoicing processing for portfolio, programs, and projects	Oversee capitalization of capital assets Facilitate timely calculation of accruals, forecasts, and anticipated cash flow Maintain details of project credit transfers between business units

Calculate the Total Cost of Ownership

Service Description

Calculate what the lifetime costs are of a new investment. Rather than just consider the costs of delivery, this will include the costs of support and upgrades at the end of the lifecycle.

What the service provides for the customer.

This provides an understanding of the true cost of the investment, giving the profitability of the investment over time.

Why is this service being offered to the customer?

By calculating this for each investment it allows the project approval board to understand where they should be investing their funds to create the most benefit.

How PMO will apply this service

The PMO will examine the business case for a project or program. They will find the cost for each of these along with the associated support costs. They will find out from the sponsor the expected life of the product. Based on the cost of delivery, the support costs, and the length of the product they will look to calculate the Total Cost of Ownership (TCO).

Supplier	Input	Process	Output	Customer
Project Manager Program Manager	Business case	Calculate Total Cost of Investment	Total Cost of Ownership	Project Approval Board

How the PMO can measure the value of this service

This can be measured by the feedback from the project approval board on the usefulness of the service.

Criteria when the PMO will use this service

- Where the PMO supports a project approval board
- Where the PMO is aligned to a portfolio manager
- Where the organization is interested in the support costs of the investment as well as the delivery costs

Helpful hints for the PMO when delivering the service

- In itself the TCO is not very useful, its use becomes relevant when compared against other possible investments. Ensure that the TCO for a single investment is shown against the other current approved investments to allow the project approval board to show a comparison
- To ensure like for like comparisons it may be useful to calculate a TCO over the same timescale (e.g. 5 or 10 years). If the investment will be replaced before the timescale ends, then the cost of replacement needs to be included in the TCO figure
- The cost of replacement should include the cutover costs, delivery cost and support costs over the same time period
- Do not just rely on the TCO figure. Other decisions about the worth of the investment need to be considered including Payback period and regulatory compliance (sometimes you just need to deliver a project)
- It may be useful to put in different scenarios for the TCO, including the cost of support over the timescale and the cost of support and then replacement over the timescale

PMO Capabilities needed to fulfil this service

Competencies	Techniques and generic tools
Benefits and Value Management Business Case Financial Management Reporting, Insights and Analysis	Cost/ Benefit Analysis Benefit realization analysis Cash flow analysis Sensitivity analysis

Related services

Develop Business Case process and templates Develop and refine portfolio, program, or project business cases	Support the Project Approval Board Establish a portfolio management framework

Track expenses on behalf of business units

Service description

The tracking and reporting of expenses for business units. Ensuring that the actual and projected spend does not exceed the budgeted figures.

What the service provides for the customer

Early warning for the business units of any over/under spend on expenses within their department.

Why is this service being offered to the customer?

As the PMO understand Management Information and finances they can provide early warning for the business units of any projected overspend. The PMO can suggest some actions that the business unit head can take to prevent any overruns.

How PMO will apply this service

The PMO will work with finance to get an extract of the appropriate ledger information. The PMO will speak with finance and the business unit head to get a copy of the budget. The PMO will look to provide some reports and analysis to show how well the business unit achieving its expense figures. This will be shown year to date as well as a projection for the full year. This will allow the business unit head to see whether they are likely to exceed their target for the year.

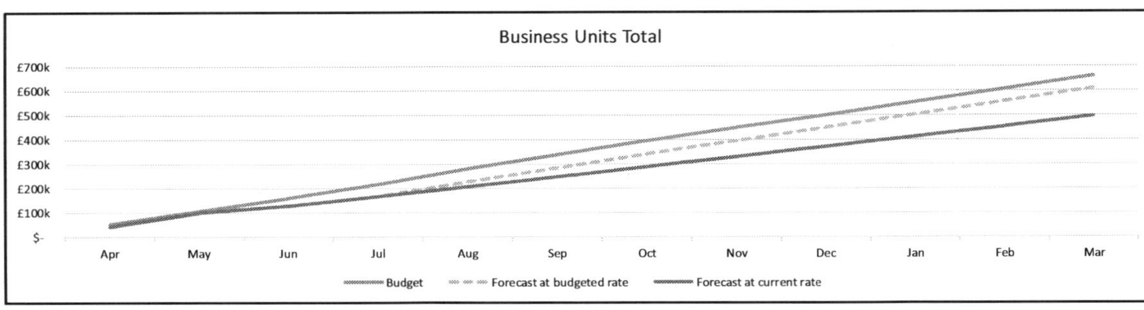

Figure 10.1 – graph showing budget versus actual projections over the year for all expense.

The PMO will provide more detailed analysis allowing the business unit head to work out which of the expense types require more oversight.

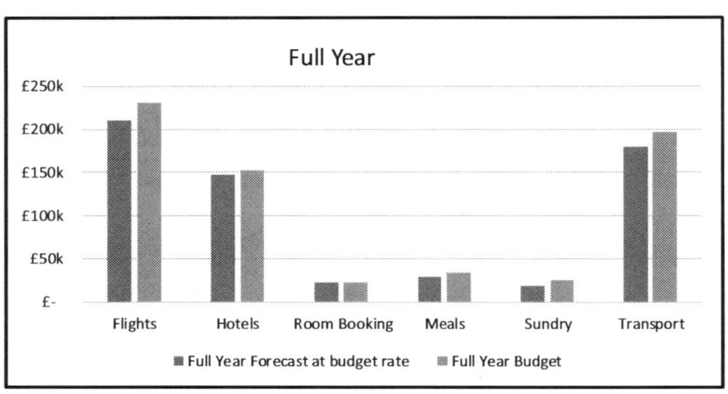

Figure 10.2 – graph showing budget versus actual by expense type.

Supplier	Input	Process	Output	Customer
Finance	Ledger extracts	Track expenses	Expense Reports	Business Unit Managers

How the PMO can measure the value of this service

This can be measured by the reduction on any overruns on expense budget for each business unit.

Criteria when the PMO will use this service

- When the PMO supports the business units
- When the PMO is asked to look after cost control for the business units

Helpful hints for the PMO when delivering the service

- Look to provide details of exceptional spend by person for the business unit head to have a conversation (if required) to the individual concerned
- Consider providing reports to the department head so they can compare the spend across the different business units in their control
- The PMO may consider providing reports on the individuals who are spending the most, to enable the business unit head to have the conversation with them about alternative ways of working to avoid expenses being incurred

PMO Capabilities needed to fulfil this service

Competencies	Techniques and generic tools
Financial Management Reporting, Insights and Analysis	Cash flow analysis Categorized frequency analysis (Frequency plot, bar chart) Time series plots

Related services

Develop and maintain the PPM financial framework

Financial Management Monitoring

Service group description

The review of the status of the finances and reporting on that information.

Why have these services been grouped together?

These services relate to the PMO monitoring the financial information and providing commentary to senior management.

Responsibility Assignment Matrix

Service	Executive	Portfolio Manager	Program Manager	Project Manager	PMO	Sponsor	Other Stakeholder
Monitor and report on financial spend		A	A	A	R	I	
Control adherence to accounting procedures	A				R		C (Finance)
Challenge spend profile and forecast spend profile	A	A	A	A	R		

Helpful hints when the PMO is delivering this Service Group

The PMO will need an understanding of financial accounting procedures. They will need to agree on which is the source of information used in the financial reports and whose responsibility it is to ensure data accuracy.

Monitor and report on financial spend

Service description

Provision of reports to show how much has been spent against the approved budget.

What the service provides for the customer

This provides a series of reports to check whether the finances for a project, program or portfolio are in control. Any added commentary will provide reasons for this happening and suggestions to keep the financials under control.

Why is this service being offered to the customer?

The PMO understand how to obtain and interpret the financial data. They can delve into the detail to analyse reasons for the actual/projected spend not being on budget. They can provide suggestions as to how the projected spend can be brought back on budget.

These should be split down both by financial year and over the life of the project/program. This allows for further analysis of the data and recommendations to keep within the tolerances set.

How PMO will apply this service

The PMO will find the latest approved spend for the project/program or portfolio being reported on. They will find the actual spend and the projected spend. They will then show this, often with an associated RAG status and commentary. The PMO may need to examine the data to find out the root cause for any over or underspend

Name	Phase	($000) Latest Agreed Spend	($000) Actuals to Date	($000) Projected Cost	($000) Variance	RAG	Commentary
Project 3	Execute	798	798	798		G	
Project 4	Execute	649		812	(163)	R	
Project 5	Execute	731			731	G	
Project 6	Execute	989			989	G	
Program 1 Sub Total		3,167	798	1,611	1,556	G	
Project 7	Closed	117	117	117		G	
Project 8	Closed	58	95	95	(37)	R	
Project 9	Embed	1,402	855	1,402		G	
Project 10	Execute	36	01	03	33	G	
Project 11	Execute	446	129	497	(41)	A	
Project 12	Define	64	42	62	02	G	
Project 13	Execute	982	493	1,080	(98)	G	
Program 2 Sub Total		3,105	1,731	3,256	(141)	G	
Portfolio Total		6,272	2,529	4,867	1,415	G	

Figure 10.3 – example of financial budget vs actual report with RAG status. Commentary to be added by PMO before sending.

They may decide to show this information over time

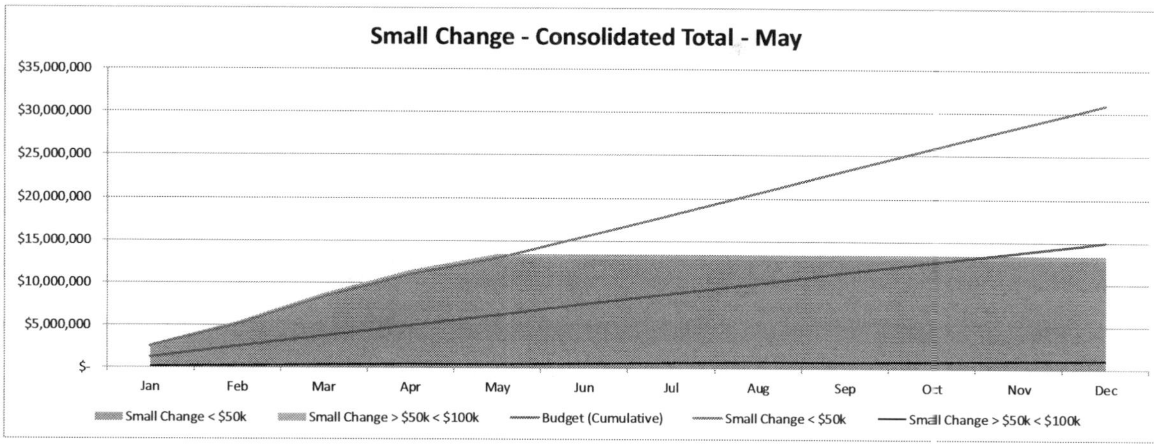

Figure 10.4 – example of a small change report showing actual spend against budget, with a projection of where the final figure is likely to be. This can then be added into an overall presentation deck with additional commentary explaining the actions taken.

They may decide to show this as a waterfall style report showing how much of the available budget has been allocated, spent, and still remaining.

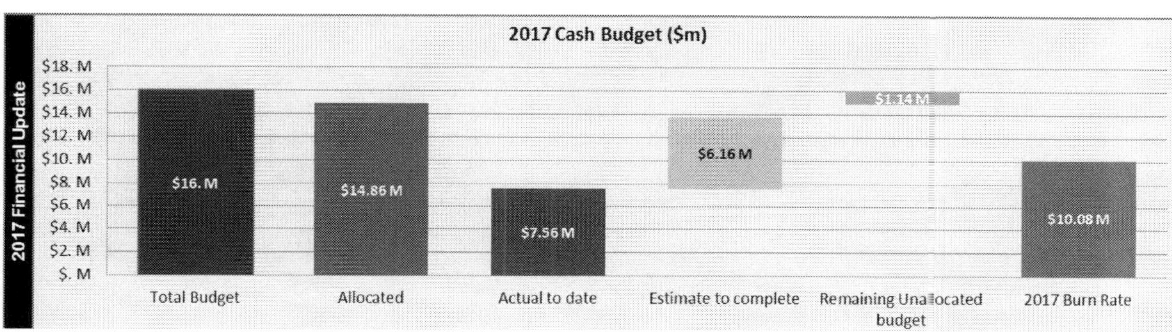

Figure 10.5 – example of a portfolio level budget vs actual report shown as a waterfall style report. Showing how much has been allocated out of the budget as well as actual and remaining figures.

Supplier	Input	Process	Output	Customer
Project Managers Program Managers Portfolio Managers	Financial Plans Approved Budgets Actual Spend Forecast Spend	Track finances	Management Dashboard Budget vs Actual report	Project Approval Board Portfolio Managers Program Managers

How the PMO can measure the value of this service

The PMO can measure this by asking the users of the reports whether they find it useful and easy to understand and interpret.

Criteria when the PMO will use this service

- When the PMO is asked to report on financials
- As part of any in-depth review of the project, program, or portfolio

Helpful hints for the PMO when delivering the service

- Use the latest agreed spend rather than the original budget as the latest agreed spend includes the cost of all the agreed change requests
- Decide whether the actual spend will come from a PPM system, the information collated by the project/program manager or the ledger
- Where there are discrepancies between the data reported by the PMO and that reported by finance or the project/program manager this can be down to using different data sources. Ensure that the reporting uses a constant source and that any changes are made directly at source and not in the production of the report

PMO Capabilities needed to fulfil this service

Competencies	Techniques and generic tools
Financial Management Reporting, Insights and Analysis	Root Cause Analysis Cash flow analysis Categorized frequency analysis (Frequency plot, bar chart) Performance variance report Time series plot

Related services

Forecast portfolio, program or project spend Administer and track budget allocations Facilitate timely calculation of accruals, forecasts, and anticipated cash flow Develop and maintain the PPM financial framework Collate individual progress reports Combine individual progress reports	Set up and track portfolio, program, and project metrics (KPI's) Challenge spend profile and forecast spend profile Manage invoicing processing for portfolio, programs, and projects Maintain details of changes to budget baseline Increase in accuracy of Profit & Loss & balance sheets Chase up missing timesheets Provision of Management Dashboards

Control adherence to accounting procedures

Service description

A review of the financials of a project or program to ensure that it has followed accounting good practice.

What the service provides for the customer

Assurance that the financials for the project or program are accurate and will not need amending. It confirms that the finances will pass any audits.

Why is this service being offered to the customer?

As the PMO have developed the PPM financial framework they will be familiar with good accounting practice. They can ensure that any financials meet the accounting criteria and cannot be challenged.

How PMO will apply this service

Having been asked to review the finances for a project or program the PMO will examine the accounting procedures and the PPM financial framework to remind themselves of the current rules. They will then look at the actual spend, and forecast spend on the project or program.

The typical items the PMO will look to review compliance for include:

- Accruals – have the accruals that have been raised been done with sufficient paperwork? Can the project or program evidence the purchase and receipt of the goods? Have accruals been raised for all items that have been receipted, but not paid? Have accruals been released once payment has occurred?
- Capitalization – Have the rules been followed for what can be capitalized? Are the rules followed consistently? Is the project or program capitalizing all it can?
- Depreciation – If equipment is purchased, can the cost of this be depreciated? If so, is this being done according to the financial rules laid down
- Coding structure – When items have been purchased have, they been coded up correctly so that the costs go to the ledger correctly? E.g. if an IT server has been purchased, have the costs been separated out between hardware (for the server), software (for the operating system) and consultancy (for the person installing the server)?
- Expenses – When booking travel and accommodation have the rules been followed e.g. correct class of train travel, hotel through preferred supplier

If the PMO finds any exceptions where the process has not been followed, then the PMO will work with the finance department to try and rectify the error. The PMO will speak with the project or program manager to ensure they understand what the problem is, how it will be rectified and the steps they need to take to prevent this from happening again.

Supplier	Input	Process	Output	Customer
Finance	Accounting procedures PPM Financial Framework	Validate financials	Exceptions	Project Manager Program Manager Finance

How the PMO can measure the value of this service

This can be measured by the project or program passing any financial audit.

Criteria when the PMO will use this service

- When the PMO is aligned to a single project or program
- Where there is external spend on the project or program
- Where the project or program manager is not experienced in PPM finance rules
- When looking to close a project down
- When ordering items on behalf of the project or program
- When receipting or paying invoices

Helpful hints for the PMO when delivering the service

- Consider providing someone to one training with the project or program manager before they look to purchase any external items for the first time to review the process

PMO Capabilities needed to fulfil this service

Competencies	Techniques and generic tools
Financial Management Reporting, Insights and Analysis Supplier Management Capability Development Relationships and engagement	Expected monetary value analysis Check sheets Task responsibility matrix/RACI

Related services

Develop and maintain the PPM financial framework Manage invoicing processing for portfolio, programs, and projects Oversee capitalization of capital assets Arrange travel for other people Support closure process	Place and track small orders for portfolio, program, or project Ensure invoices are paid according to the contract terms Challenge spend profile and forecast spend profile Advise on cost control and opportunities for savings

Challenge spend profile and forecast spend profile

Service description

A critical review of the planned expenditure for a project, program, or portfolio.

What the service provides for the customer

This provides confirmation that the expected spend could happen as projected. Any potential under or over-spend is highlighted early to allow for action to be taken.

Why is this service being offered to the customer?

This provides an independent check on the financial profile of a project, program, or portfolio. As you come the end of a financial year there can be more pressure to profile when spend is likely to occur. With pressure to spend approved budgets the PMO can assist the Project or Program Manager in deciding which year spend can occur, or whether the cost is required (is it being held onto as contingency?).

How PMO will apply this service

The PMO will find the financial profile for the project, program, or portfolio. They will want to see this information broken down into months and have a line-by-line listing of the potential spend. This should be listed at the lowest possible level to allow for detailed analysis to take place.

The checks that the PMO will do include:

- Contingency - is there any contingency within the forecasted profile. Is it likely that this will be used up? If so then, can this be assigned to a specific spend, rather than being left as contingency? If not, can this be removed?
- Timing – is it likely that the spend will happen when it is predicted? The PMO will need to look at the resource profile to see whether the ramp up of people is possible. Are you suddenly going to go from 2 to 20 people? If so, have they been recruited? With external spend, the PMO will look at the schedule to see whether the delivery of the goods is linked into the expected delivery in the schedule
- Missing items – this can be more difficult to ascertain, but by asking questions of the project or program manager the PMO can look to work out whether all the costs have been included. For example, if equipment has been purchased, does it need a person to install it, will there be servicing or licensing costs?
- Double counting – have items been included more than once? This can be a way of hiding contingency within the profile as it would avoid the casual observer finding the contingency and removing it

Having reviewed the forecast spend profile the PMO will feedback any comments they have and can work with the project or program manager to get the forecast profile updated.

Supplier	Input	Process	Output	Customer
Project Managers Program Managers	Forecast spend profile Schedule Resource profile Contracts	Review financials	Updated forecast spend profile	Program Managers Portfolio Managers Project approval board

How the PMO can measure the value of this service

This will be measured by the accuracy of the forecasted profile against what occurred.

Criteria when the PMO will use this service

- As part of any year-end process
- When accruals are needing to be raised
- Where there is pressure on budgets to spend monies in the correct year
- Where funds are being challenged and costs are wanting to be removed

Helpful hints for the PMO when delivering the service

- Timing of spend becomes more critical as you reach year end to ensure they monies are spent as budgeted. If not, that can leave a gap in the following year's budget where the unplanned spend will have to be accounted for

PMO Capabilities needed to fulfil this service

Competencies	Techniques and generic tools
Financial Management Planning and Scheduling Reporting, Insights and Analysis Resource Management Supplier Management Assurance Relationships and engagement Resourcefulness	Cash flow analysis Reserve analysis

Related services

Develop and maintain the PPM financial framework Monitor and report on financial spend Control adherence to accounting procedures	Forecast portfolio, program or project spend Advise on cost control and opportunities for savings Facilitate timely calculation of accruals, forecasts, and anticipated cash flow Oversee capitalization of capital assets

Governance

Governance

Description

Governance is required to ensure that appropriate stakeholders take the decisions relating to change initiatives, including decisions whether to initiate, continue with, and/or alter the scope of the initiatives.

What the services within the area provide for the customer

These services provide a structure to the setup and running of projects, programs, and portfolios. It enables decisions to be made in a consistent manner and provides control. For the senior management in the organization it enables them to have confidence that money and effort is spent where it is needed and that any overruns will be highlighted so they can deal with them appropriately. It provides them a framework in which decisions can be made.

Helpful hints for when the PMO is delivering this service area

- PPM Governance must work within the decision-making structures of the organization. Within most organizations there are existing governance rules, it will be the PMO's job to codify these and document the exceptions
- Governance is about keeping the decision makers honest. Those decision makers can think that governance is something that applies to people below them rather than to themselves. The PMO must walk a fine line to ensure that governance can apply to everyone, without irritating anybody

Governance Design

Service group description

The setup and design of the project and program governance framework.

Why have these services been grouped together?

These services relate to the way projects and programs are governed. They provide the standards for how they should be governed along with suggestions about how those standards can be tailored depending on the size and style of the project.

List of related services described in other areas

Automate Processes

Responsibility Assignment Matrix

Service	Executive	Portfolio Manager	Program Manager	Project Manager	PMO	Sponsor	Other Stakeholder
Define, maintain, and implement PPM governance framework	A	C	C	C	R		I (PPM team)
Provide guidance on how the governance framework can be tailored		C	C	C	A, R	I	I (PPM team)

Helpful hints for when the PMO is delivering this service group

- Work with the senior management to get agreement on why these standards are important
- Consult with external group like finance and risk for their advice on how projects can be governed
- Are there any rules that need to be followed, either internally or externally that have a bearing on how the governance framework can be implemented?

Define, maintain, and implement PPM governance framework

Service description

The creation of governance framework for projects and programs. A governance framework provides the guidance for who needs to sanction what level of expenditure (risk). How progress needs to be reported and how frequent, according to the scale of the piece of working being delivered. It provides a set of rules for how deviations from approved spend or delivery need to be escalated up to senior levels within the organization.

What the service provides for the customer

This provides a set of rules and guidelines related to the control and approval of projects and programs within a portfolio.

Why is this service being offered to the customer?

The PMO are ideally positioned to provide the translation between the financial and risk areas and the project management area as they understand all areas. This then allows the project, program, or portfolio manager to focus on operating within those controls.

How PMO will apply this service

The PMO will speak with the risk and finance departments to find out their rules for control of risk and the authorization of spend/approval limits. They will look at the PPM and change methodologies to see where approvals are required. These include:

- Initial approval
- Changes
- Risk budgets
- External spend/purchases/contracts
- Escalations
- Closure
- Gate reviews

The PMO should put together a set of guidelines/standards which deals with each of these and lay down who is authorized to approve these, depending on the type of project being run, who is running it and the amounts involved. The amounts involved should be looked at per item and as an overall amount.

Once the guidelines have been written the PMO will need to ensure this is communicated to the relevant people. This can be done by publishing the information in a central location, normally the PMO intranet site, and sending out a communication to the key people (PPM managers) who requiring a decision to be made.

Supplier	Input	Process	Output	Customer
PMO Finance Risk	Financial standards Risk standards	Develop Standard Develop Templates	Governance processes, standards, templates, and help	PPM teams PMO Executive

How the PMO will measure the value of this service

The PMO can measure the value of this service by looking at the numbers of questions they get and the number of exceptions that they need to deal with.

Criteria when the PMO will use this service

- When there is no clear governance framework in place
- Where there have been changes to finance or risk procedures
- When going through a year end to verify the framework is valid for the next year
- When a senior manager decides to change the approval limits

Helpful hints for the PMO when delivering the service

- Befriend the finance and risk departments to ensure you get detailed advice from them about their rules and guidance
- Confirm where rules may be different for different types of spend e.g. Capital Expenditure versus Operational Expenditure. Internal spend versus external spend
- Verify the rules apply to project and/or business as usual approvals
- Check who can deputize for named authorities
- Think about the loopholes and try to find ways to plug the gaps e.g. projects being put through under the approval level, but having to be run as one item
- Be aware when a senior manager decides to change the approval limits for their staff and insists all items after a certain amount need to be signed by that manager. This should trigger a review of this governance and a temporary framework being put in place

PMO Capabilities needed to fulfil this service

Competencies	Techniques and generic tools
Reporting, Insights and Analysis Governance Frameworks Professionalism and ethics Personal Communication Relationships and engagement Teamwork	Communication requirements analysis Complexity Matrix Controls Assessment Matrix Matrix diagrams Organization charts & position descriptions Stakeholder checklist Stakeholder engagement assessment matrix Swim-lane flowcharts Task responsibility matrix/RACI

Related services

Develop and maintain tailoring guidelines for standards, methods, and approaches Tailor standard processes and template to the program or project Control escalation of changes to higher authority Develop the overall change control framework Create Change Management Framework Develop and maintain the PPM financial framework Automate Processes Map key value streams and processes	Define, maintain, and implement standard PPM framework Define, maintain, and implement reporting framework Provide guidance on how the governance framework can be tailored Advise on program or project assurance services Advise Sponsors and Management Boards of appropriate frameworks and governance models Manage the Process Improvement Plan Provide guidance on quality criteria, reviewers, and sign-off authority to ensure consistency

Provide guidance on how the governance framework can be tailored

Service description

Provision of guidance to the project or program manager on how their project or program can be governed. Ensuring that the governance is within the framework set down and has the right level of control.

What the service provides for the customer

The provision of the right level of control for the project or program. Ensures that the governance is not too restrictive and therefore preventing the project or program manager from being able to suitable manage. Ensures the governance is not too lose which would allow the project or program to get out of control without prior notice being given.

Why is this service being offered to the customer?

As the PMO are responsible for the PPM governance framework they are best placed to know how this can be flexed. They can work with the project or program manager to provide a good overall framework suited to the project or program being delivered.

How PMO will apply this service

The PMO will review the current PPM Governance Framework. They will speak to the project or program manager to get an understanding of the project and program. They will suggest how the governance framework can be best applied to their project of program. The PMO will ensure that there is a balance between the level of control required by the senior management and the ability to retain decisions within the project or program.

The PMO will ensure the suggested governance framework is written down and agreed by the sponsor on behalf of the steering group.

Supplier	Input	Process	Output	Customer
PMO	PPM Governance Framework	Tailoring	Tailored PPM Governance Framework	Project Manager Program Manager Sponsor Steering group

How the PMO will measure the value of this service

The PMO can measure this service by asking for feedback from the project or program manager. It can be measured by looking at the feedback from the lessons learned reviews to see how effective the governance was for the project or program.

Criteria when the PMO will use this service

- When a project or program is starting
- When an audit or gate review highlights issues with the project or program governance
- When there is a PPM governance framework in place
- Where the PMO is asked for advice by the project or program manager

Helpful hints for the PMO when delivering the service

- Ensure that you are aware of any external governance requirements for this project or program. Some large projects may have additional requirements imposed on them
- Consider using diagrams to explain how the governance flow will work. This can enable the PMO to spot issues or potential overlaps in governance

PMO Capabilities needed to fulfil this service

Competencies	Techniques and generic tools
Assurance Governance Frameworks Personal Communication Relationships and engagement Negotiation	Process Analysis

Related services

Define, maintain, and implement PPM governance framework Program or project fast-track mobilization service	Advise Sponsors and Management Boards of appropriate frameworks and governance models Provide guidance on quality criteria, reviewers, and sign-off authority to ensure consistency

Governance Operations

Service group description

The application of the governance framework to a particular project or program.

Why have these services been grouped together?

These services relate to how governance is applied throughout to the life of a project or program.

List of related services described in other areas

Advise Sponsors and Management Boards of appropriate frameworks and governance models

Responsibility Assignment Matrix

Service	Executive	Portfolio Manager	Program Manager	Project Manager	PMO	Sponsor	Other Stakeholder
Program or project fast-track mobilization service		I	C	C	A, R	I	
Advise on program or project assurance services			C	C	A, R		
Ensure scope is clear and delineated			R	R	C	A	
Attendance at steering groups			R	R	R	A	
Trigger post-program or project reviews		A	A		R	A	
Support closure process			R	R	C	A	

Helpful hints for when the PMO is delivering this service group

Ensure that the governance requirements are set up at the start of the project or program. That way it means people know what to expect when it comes to the control required.

Program or project fast-track mobilization service

Service Description

The provision by the PMO of some consultancy to get a project or program kick started.

What the service provides for the customer

This enables the project or program to start right. It gets the basic governance and structure of the project or program decided ensuring the basics are in place such as funding, governance structures, approach, scope, milestones, reporting. This will speed up the start of the project or program and ensures it is under control from the start.

Why is this service being offered to the customer?

With their work in setting up the frameworks and their view across the other projects and programs the PMO are best place to offer this advice. They can use the information from the lessons learned to create a start-up checklist which can go through the necessary questions and generate the outline documentation in a short space of time. A project manager may only start one or two projects a year, but the PMO see them start all the time and can see what works and share that experience across the project management community.

How PMO will apply this service

The PMO will look to develop a standard checklist which will cover the basic information including:

- Project Governance - have you agreed the governance structure and roles and responsibilities?
- Project cadence – Have you worked out what the reporting cycle should be and scheduled the meetings in the diary?
- Project Definition – Have you got agreement on the scope, business drivers, benefits, and any key dependencies
- Project Schedule – is there an outline schedule with key milestones. Do you have necessary estimates and actual resources?
- Project controls – have the risk, issue, change registers and controls been setup
- Communications – have the stakeholders been identified and the communications plan created. Have the initial briefings occurred with the sponsor, core team?
- Finances – has the budget been finalized and the spend profile been agreed. Have the structures been setup to monitor this

Having got a checklist, the PMO will sit down with the Project or Program Manager and review all the items. Where there is not the item in place, the PMO will work with the individual to go through and create the draft version of the item. Just by asking the pertinent questions the PMO can assist the project or program manager in clarifying the necessary details.

The PMO may be able to help in the form of templates for risk, issue, change registers. They can provide suggestions for governance and team structures. They can help by booking some of the regular meetings on behalf of the project or program manager.

Supplier	Input	Process	Output	Customer
PMO	Start-up checklist	Project Start-up Program Start-up	Tailored PPM Framework Tailored Governance Framework	Project Manager Program Manager

How the PMO will measure the value of this service

The PMO can measure this by reviewing the reduction in time taken to start a project.

Criteria when the PMO will use this service

- When new projects and programs are due to start
- Where there is pressure to deliver a project or program quickly

Helpful hints for the PMO when delivering the service

- Keep the checklist of items to review when mobilizing a project or program up to date
- The full level of detail that the PMO can provide the project or program manager is determined by the level of experience of the PMO in starting projects and the position of the PMO. If the PMO is working as part of the project or program they will be able to pick up more of the detail of the start-up tasks e.g. booking meetings
- Use the feedback from lessons learned to work out which are the crucial parts where it is important that the setup is done correctly
- Link into the tailoring guidelines in order there are some standard ways of tailoring suggested

PMO Capabilities needed to fulfil this service

Competencies	Techniques and generic tools
Business Case Financial Management Issue Management Knowledge Management Planning and Scheduling Quality Management Reporting, Insights and Analysis Risk Management Stakeholder Engagement Delivery Methods Governance Frameworks Personal Communication Relationships and engagement Teamwork Resourcefulness Negotiation Result Orientation	Prompt Lists Complexity Matrix Project Management Information System Resource breakdown structure Scheduling tool Stakeholder checklist Task responsibility matrix/RACI

Related services

Ensure scope is clear and delineated Tailor standard processes and template to the program or project Perform coaching of portfolio, program, or project managers Promote good PPM within the organization Provide guidance on how the governance framework can be tailored	Develop and maintain tailoring guidelines for standards, methods, and approaches Administer document tools Advise on program or project assurance services Recommend ways to reduce or shorten project lifecycle times

Advise on program or project assurance services

Service description

The definition of the level of assurance required for a particular project or program to ensure that the project or program will be well managed and will deliver what is required.

What the service provides for the customer

An agreement of the level of assurance that will be applied to the project or program by the PMO on behalf of the portfolio manager or senior management.

Why is this service being offered to the customer?

All projects and programs within the portfolio will need assurance. By agreeing with the PMO the assurance at the outset then the project or program manager can plan adequately to ensure they are in control.

How PMO will apply this service

The PMO will review the PPM Governance Framework to check how projects and programs are normally assured. For example, will there be a Gate Review, will the project be audited?

The PMO will book a session with the project or program manager to discuss the expected assurance level. If necessary, the PMO can go through a standard review checklist so the project or program manager is aware the sort of things that are checked. The PMO will explain what happens to these assurance reviews and the expected time for the corrections to occur.

Once the PMO and the project/program manager have agreed the level of assurance required this will then be described as part of the quality management strategy.

Supplier	Input	Process	Output	Customer
PMO	PPM Governance Framework	Assurance	Quality Management Strategy Project Initiation Document	Project Manager Program Manager

How the PMO will measure the value of this service

The PMO can measure this by checking to see whether the level of assurance has been appropriate by checking the lessons learned.

Criteria when the PMO will use this service

- When a project or program is being initiated
- Where the PMO have a role in the assurance of projects and programs

Helpful hints for the PMO when delivering the service

- If the project or program is likely to be audited, then the assurance that the PMO agree must include the requirements of the auditors
- Ensure that the level of assurance is documented somewhere. Either within the PID or by the PMO in their assurance list
- If the PMO cannot get the project/program manager to agree with the level of assurance, then they will need to agree this with the sponsor

PMO Capabilities needed to fulfil this service

Competencies	Techniques and generic tools
Quality Management Assurance Governance Frameworks Personal Communication Negotiation	Complexity Matrix Task responsibility matrix/RACI

Related services

Program or project fast-track mobilization service Define, maintain, and implement framework for monitoring and review Define, maintain, and implement PPM governance framework	Provide a Stage Gate Review or Gateway support service Provide project or program rescues Develop and maintain the overall Quality Assurance Framework Provide project and program audits

Ensure scope is clear and delineated

Service description

The definition of what is in scope, and what is out of scope for the project or program along with the documentation of the assumptions that come with that.

What the service provides for the customer

A clear understanding of what is within (and out of) scope of the project or program. A way of tracing what all the requirements are.

Why is this service being offered to the customer?

Documenting the scope ensures that the project or program can ensures that the project can deliver what is expected. Alterations to scope can then be managed under change control, thereby preventing 'scope creep'. The PMO can deliver this in the absence of a business analyst to perform this role.

How PMO will apply this service

The PMO will obtain a copy of the mandate. They will speak with the area that the project is being delivered for. They will confirm the detail of the requirements. Using the requirements template that has been defined they will document the requirements. They will note down any assumptions that have been made, recording them in the assumptions register. They will note down the level of the requirement, is this a detailed or high-level requirement?

The PMO will attempt to put a boundary around the scope of the project by confirming what is out of scope. They will then ensure this gets included in the relevant document and that that document gets approved by the steering group/sponsor. This ensures that the scope can then be put under change control.

Supplier	Input	Process	Output	Customer
Project Manager Business Analysts	Mandate	Document requirements	Requirements tracker Project Initiation Document	Project Managers Program Manager Steering Group

How the PMO will measure the value of this service

The PMO can speak to the project or program manager to confirm their satisfaction with the service level. If the scope has been clearly defined, then the project or program will not be subject to 'scope creep' as any changes can be handled under change control.

Criteria when the PMO will use this service

- Where there is no business analyst able to deliver this
- When the scope is not entirely clear
- Where the PMO is aligned to a single project or program

Helpful hints for the PMO when delivering the service

- This can be done by a business analyst. If this is not done, then the PMO can do this instead
- Ensure that the out of scope is clearly documented
- Document any assumptions in the assumptions register so they can be confirmed as the project progresses
- Provide a requirements traceability matrix so the requirements can be tracked throughout the lifecycle

PMO Capabilities needed to fulfil this service

Competencies	Techniques and generic tools
Information Management Governance Frameworks Relationships and engagement Negotiation	5 Whys

Related services

Program or project fast-track mobilization service

Attendance at steering groups

Service description

Having the PMO attend the steering group to support the program or project manager.

What the service provides for the customer

The PMO can attend the steering group to provide services such as minute taking. They can assist the project or program manager by having access to the details of the item being discussed to ensure that the relevant information is available within the meeting. This helps the steering groups run more efficiently.

Why is this service being offered to the customer?

The PMO can act as the right-hand person for the project or program manager, able to have to hand the necessary information to support them whilst in the steering group. By the PMO providing secretariat support it allows the project or program manager to focus on the task of driving the project forward and getting answers to the issues that are presented to the steering group to resolve.

How PMO will apply this service

The PMO will speak to the project or program manager and confirm they can attend the steering group meeting. The PMO will offer to provide a secretariat service for meetings. During the meeting, in addition to the secretariat service the PMO may assist the project or program manager by having access to background information on the topics under discussion. The PMO should be able to pull up details of risks, issues, changes, financials, schedule, scope etc. to provide the project or program manager details within the meeting. This will enable the discussions to conclude within the meeting rather than have to have an action and come back at a later date.

Supplier	Input	Process	Output	Customer
Project Manager Program Manager	Steering group agenda	Write Minutes	Steering Group Minutes	Steering Group Attendees

How the PMO will measure the value of this service

The PMO can gain feedback from the project or program manager on the value of the service. If a PMO is doing a good job, then it is unlikely that people will notice as it will 'just happen'. The PMO can measure this being effective by the numbers of requests for a similar service on other projects and programs.

Criteria when the PMO will use this service

- When the PMO is dedicated to a single project or program
- Where there is a steering group meeting to support

Helpful hints for the PMO when delivering the service

- Consider offering a full secretariat role and book the meeting, prepare the agenda/pack, write the minutes
- Be able to deputize for the project or program manager if required
- Know who all the people are in the steering group and their roles

PMO Capabilities needed to fulfil this service

Competencies	Techniques and generic tools
P3M Administration Reporting, Insights and Analysis Personal Integrity and reliability Personal Communication Relationships and engagement Teamwork Resourcefulness	Risk Register

Related services

Provide a secretariat service for meetings

Trigger post-program or project reviews

Service description

Trigger post-program or project reviews to assess return on investment/benefits for the portfolio.

What the service provides for the customer

This provides the portfolio manager with a way of getting the information they require to deliver the benefits realization process. Assisting with Post Implementation Reviews allows a consistent way of checking the success (or otherwise) of programs and projects. Doing this in a consistent manner provides an easy way of rolling this up for the portfolio itself.

Why is this service being offered to the customer?

As the project or program will have finished by the time these reviews are triggered the PMO is a constant that will be around to assist with getting these reviews done. As they will have been involved with the closure of the project or program, they will have access to the benefit maps or business case needed to work out how to track the benefits, and who will need to be involved.

How PMO will apply this service

When a project or program finishes the PMO will make a note of when the post program or project reviews will need to occur. The PMO should ensure they are aware of how to track any benefits and who is responsible for doing this before the project program closes.

The PMO will then diarize the event and ensure it gets added onto the calendar. When the event occurs the PMO will get in touch with the relevant people who will be supplying the benefits information. The PMO will explain what is required, and why.

If the information is not forthcoming the PMO will need to escalate that to the portfolio manager for them to deal with.

Once the PMO have all the necessary information they can provide the consolidated report up to the portfolio manager.

Supplier	Input	Process	Output	Customer
Project Managers Program Managers Finance	Business Case Benefit Maps Post implementation review template	Benefits Realization	Benefit realization sheet Completed post implementation review form	Portfolio Managers Finance

How the PMO will measure the value of this service

The PMO can ask the portfolio manager on what they think the value of this service is.

Criteria when the PMO will use this service

- Where the PMO supports the portfolio
- Where projects or programs have finished
- Where benefits are being tracked

Helpful hints for the PMO when delivering the service

- Ensure that when projects and programs are closed that a note is diarized to trigger the reviews after a defined period
- Ensure the benefit maps and business cases of closed projects are available (i.e. not archived) to deliver this service
- Typically, projects or programs are reviewed after 3 or 6 months after they have been implemented
- To support the benefits realization process, it may be decided to the review the benefits of closed projects each month
- The PMO will need to work with the portfolio manager to review when the best time to trigger these reviews are as part of the closure service
- As part of the closure service the PMO should contact the people who will be providing information for this. They should inform them that they will be asked for benefits information and when they will be asked for that information
- The PMO should consider adding the required benefits information into a central tracker to make the job of collating all the information easier. If there are multiple projects that one person needs to supply the information for it is best that this is done as one request rather than individual ones
- If the person who is due to supply the information moves roles/leaves then the PMO will need to find out who will be supplying this in future

PMO Capabilities needed to fulfil this service

Competencies	Techniques and generic tools
Benefits and Value Management Business Case Knowledge Management Reporting, Insights and Analysis Personal Communication Relationships and engagement Teamwork Resourcefulness Result Orientation	Failure Modes and Effects Analysis (FMEA) Prompt Lists Performance variance report

Related services

Track and report on benefit realization Support closure process Manage archives of portfolio, program, or project documentation Set up meetings on behalf of others Provide facilitation service Create and maintain knowledge management framework Maintain lesson register	Facilitate lessons learning Run lessons-learned workshops Capture good practice examples for inclusion in good practice repository Analyse lessons to identify items to be added to the Process Improvements Plan Document project and program success stories

Support closure process

Service Description

Support closure process through independent lessons workshops, archiving of libraries, handover of documentation into the support arena.

What the service provides for the customer

An assurance that the information on the project or program has been dealt with according to the information management framework. It ensures the lessons identified are incorporated into the knowledge of the organization and can be applied to other projects as applicable.

Why is this service being offered to the customer?

Either the person doing this role has left or has moved onto another project or program, so they have little time to do this work. The PMO can not only pick this work up, but ensure it is done according to the guidelines set down. This ensures that projects and programs are closed in a consistent manner.

How PMO will apply this service

The PMO will consult the information management framework to find out when and how to archive the documentation. They will follow the framework to ensure the information is archived properly. Some of the documentation may be required by the support teams and these items will need to be identified and a copy handed over to them.

If there are any exemplar documents, then the PMO should consider making that available as examples for the methodology so other people can see what a successful document looks like.

The PMO will ensure that a lesson learned workshop has been run and that the outputs have been documented. The PMO will ensure that these lessons have been incorporated in any central lessons log or knowledge base. If there are any action plans that are required to be followed through the PMO can add that to a central register and ensure that those lessons are identified.

The PMO will ensure that all risks, assumptions, actions, dependencies, issues, and changes are closed. If required the PMO will hand over any open items to another project, or to the support areas for them to pick up prior to closing the information for this project or program.

The PMO will chase through and ensure all the financials are dealt with. They will check whether all the invoices have been paid, and whether the necessary accruals have been made if not. They will make a note to close down any cost codes that have been setup against the project once all the finances have been booked.

The PMO will ensure that the benefit maps or equivalent have been provided to those people expected to track the benefits after the project or program has completed.

If there is a PPM tool in place the PMO will ensure that the project/program is closed within the tool and no further updates will be allowed.

Supplier	Input	Process	Output	Customer
Project Managers Program Managers	Project Documentation Information management framework Lessons identified	Project Closure Program Closure	Archived documentation Updated knowledge database Benefit maps	Program Managers Portfolio Managers

How the PMO will measure the value of this service

The PMO can measure the value of this service in the number of projects or programs that are closed down successfully and cleanly.

Criteria when the PMO will use this service

- When a project or program is closing
- When the PMO will continue after the life of the project or program
- Where the project or program manager is unable to perform this role

Helpful hints for the PMO when delivering the service

- Consider having a closedown checklist to ensure that all the necessary activities have been performed

PMO Capabilities needed to fulfil this service

Competencies	Techniques and generic tools
Benefits and Value Management Change Control Financial Management Information Management Issue Management Knowledge Management Risk Management Governance Frameworks P3M Tools Personal Integrity and reliability Relationships and engagement Teamwork	Prompt Lists Check sheets Project Management Information System

Related services

Trigger post-program or project reviews Run lessons-learned workshops Maintain lesson register Capture good practice examples for inclusion in good practice repository Promote good PPM within the organization	Analyse lessons to identify items to be added to the Process Improvements Plan Facilitate lessons learning Control adherence to accounting procedures Ensure program and project supplier relationships are embedded in Business as Usual Maintain a register for current and potential programs and projects

Issue Management

Issue Management

Description

Ensuring that the portfolio, program, or project has effective processes in place to identify, monitor and resolve issues.

What the services within the area provide for the customer

These services enable the project or program manager to delegate resolution of issues to the PMO enabling them to focus on other matters. By providing the tools, templates, and approach to issue management the project and program managers can resolve or escalate issues consistently, saving time and providing the necessary focus on resolution.

Helpful hints for when the PMO is delivering this service area

If performing this service in conjunction with the risk management service think about how risks are escalated into issues and how these can be tied back to provide traceability.

Issue Management Design

Service group description

The setup and communication of an issue management framework consisting of process, procedures, standards, templates, help and tools.

Why have these services been grouped together?

These services relate to the establishment of an issue management framework. The organization will then require training in the use of this framework, together with any tailoring for specific projects or programs.

List of related services described in other areas

Automate Processes

Responsibility Assignment Matrix

Service	Executive	Portfolio Manager	Program Manager	Project Manager	PMO	Sponsor	Other Stakeholder
Develop the overall issue management framework	A	C	C	C	R	I	I (PPM team)
Introduce tools for managing issues	A	C	C	C	R		I (PPM team)
Train the issue management framework	I	I	I	I	A, R	I	I (PPM team)

Helpful hints for when the PMO is delivering this service group

- The framework will need to be developed before it can be communicated, or any tools introduced. Ensure the tools are aligned to the issue management process
- When looking at a tool, consider whether this can be done as part of the existing PPM tool

Develop the overall issue management framework

Service description

Develop an issue management framework consisting of process, procedures, standards, templates, and help. This will include suggested escalation routes for issues, which will need to be tailored for each project.

What the service provides for the customer

This provides the project and program managers a standard way of recording issues and tracking issues through to resolution. It provides a process and procedures for them to follow. It shows how to convert a risk into an issue and have the links between issues and changes.

Why is this service being offered to the customer?

Having a consistent way of raising, managing, tracking, and resolving issues across the portfolio allows the information on issues to be rolled up and reported on consistently. It means that when moving from project to project the project manager, and their teams do not need to learn or develop this afresh for each project.

How PMO will apply this service

The PMO will review the external guidance about issue management for projects and programs and will look to tailor this for their organization. They will suggest a typical escalation route for getting issues resolved, with tailoring options that can be considered.

They will produce a standard issue register with a help guide for its usage. The PMO will consider any common reporting requirements (e.g. inclusion in steering group packs and progress reports) and will try to ensure these can be delivered using the information in the issue register.

Supplier	Input	Process	Output	Customer
PMO	Standards template	Develop Standard Develop Templates	Issue management strategy Issue Register Issue Management process	Project Manager Program Manager Portfolio Manager PMO

How the PMO will measure the value of this service

The PMO can measure the value of this service by looking how widely the documents produced by this service have been used. They can judge this by how easy it is to provide a rolled-up view of the issues across the portfolio.

Criteria when the PMO will use this service

- When there is a need for a consistent issue management process
- Where the existing issue management framework requires review
- Where there is a centralized PMO
- If there is no centralized PMO then this may need to be developed for each program and project separately

Helpful hints for the PMO when delivering the service

- Link this service with the Introduce tools for managing issues service to introduce a tool at the same time as the process is being introduced
- Link this with the develop the risk management framework to ensure that risks can be easily turned into issues and there is traceability of which ones have occurred
- When looking at the reporting required such as feed into to progress report templates and steering group packs, look to see whether the information can be transferred with the minimum of reformatting on the project managers behalf. Look out for locked cells, merged columns etc.

PMO Capabilities needed to fulfil this service

Competencies	Techniques and generic tools
Information Management Issue Management Reporting, Insights and Analysis Delivery Methods Governance Frameworks	Swim-lane flowcharts Task responsibility matrix/RACI

Related services

Introduce tools for managing issues Train the issue management framework Perform logging and tracking to resolution of issues Review effectiveness of issue identification and resolution processes	Examine Issue Registers for common issues Manage the Process Improvement Plan Develop the overall risk management framework Automate Processes Map key value streams and processes

Further Reading

PMI PMBoK (A Guide to the Project Management Body of Knowledge)
PRINCE2
Managing Successful Programmes (MSP)
APM BoK
Praxis

Introduce tools for managing issues

Service description

The sourcing/developing/tailoring of tools to manage, report and escalate issues aligned to the issue management framework. Ensuring that the users get trained in the use of these tools.

What the service provides for the customer

This will provide the project or program manager with a tool which will allow them to register, track, escalate and resolve issues. This will allow them to use this information to add to progress reports or steering group packs.

Why is this service being offered to the customer?

Rather than just relying on Word or Excel to record issues, having a tool can provide a way of ensuring consistency between an issue report and the issue register. This can provide automation to automatically identify issues which need attention or escalation. Having validation built in will reduce data errors and make reporting easier.

How PMO will apply this service

The PMO will check to see whether there is an existing tool that can be configured to support the issue management process (the organization may already have a PPM tool, or a risk management tool in place). If there is not, then they will review whether they want to develop something in-house (if they have the skills) or whether they want to get a vendor supplied tool.

If this being developed in house the PMO will supply the developer, the requirements (typically the current issue templates and the escalation process along with standard report extracts required). Once the development has finished the PMO will perform the testing, ensuring it meets the requirements before accepting the tool into use.

If this is being sourced from a vendor, then the package will need to be customized to include the necessary fields and dropdowns. The PMO need to review how the data can be extracted for inclusion in standard reporting. Once this has been done the PMO can start rolling out the usage of the tool.

Regardless of how the tool was obtained it will need to have some training developed and some guidelines for use. The PMO should look to develop the training and be prepared to deliver the training alongside the rollout of the tool. The PMO should consider how frequently they want to deliver the training once the initial training has finished. Do they want to run regular sessions or individual session as and when new users are identified?

The process for loading up existing issues needs to be dealt with as part of the initial rollout. Will this be the PMO, will there be an automated load? Do all issues need to be loaded or just the open ones? What about existing issue numbering, can that be kept?

The existing issue management process will need to be updated to have appropriate references to the new tool and the links to the issue report and the issue register will need to be discontinued. The risk management process would need to be looked as well to see whether that references turning risks into issues and therefore may need to include references to the new tool.

Supplier	Input	Process	Output	Customer
Vendor In house developers	Vendor software In house software	Software implementation	Issue management tool	Project Manager Program Manager PMO

How the PMO will measure the value of this service

This can be measured by increase the data quality of issue information. It can be measured by the use of the tool over the existing templates. The PMO can ask the users of the service whether they prefer the tool (and why).

Criteria when the PMO will use this service

- When there is desire for consistency across the portfolio
- Where an issue management framework has been developed
- Where there is funding to purchase a vendor tool
- Where there is capability within the PMO to build an issue management tool in-house

Helpful hints for the PMO when delivering the service

- Factor the cost of supporting the tool as well as the initial purchase
- Work out how people will be trained in the use of the tool, both on initial rollout and when new people join and are required to use it
- Check to see whether the same tool can be used to manage risks and issues. That will make it easier to convert a risk into an issue and keep track of which issues have resulted as risks that were not dealt with and which were new issues
- Consider having extracts that enable issues to be easily imported into steering group packs or progress reports

PMO Capabilities needed to fulfil this service

Competencies	Techniques and generic tools
Information Management Issue Management Reporting, Insights and Analysis Delivery Methods P3M Tools Relationships and engagement	Project Management Information System Stakeholder checklist Stakeholder engagement assessment matrix

Related services

Develop the overall issue management framework Train the issue management framework Perform logging and tracking to resolution of issues Examine Issue Registers for common issues Control escalation of issues to higher authority Develops in-house project management tools	Tailors and configures project management tools Implements vendor provided project management tools Manages project management tools (systems admin) Advise on PPM tools and software Develop the overall risk management framework Introduce tools for managing risks Automate Processes

Train the issue management framework

Service description

Train the people responsible for raising and resolving issues about the issue management framework. This includes the issue management process, procedures, templates, tools, standards, and help.

What the service provides for the customer

This ensures that everyone who is involved with raising and resolving issues knows how it works, who is responsible for each part of the process. This will cover under what circumstances issues are escalated and reported. Escalation and reporting may be tailored for a particular project or program.

Why is this service being offered to the customer?

As the PMO have been responsible for producing the framework and the associate tool (if there is one) then they will know how the framework should be implemented and be able to answer any questions individuals may have around this.

How PMO will apply this service

The PMO will identify the key people who need training in each project or program. Typically, this will be the project and program managers along with any team leaders.

Once the list of people is available the PMO will book the training sessions and invite the people. The PMO can then prepare the training material to be used. At the training course take note of who has attended and who has not and be prepared to organize further training sessions.

Supplier	Input	Process	Output	Customer
PMO	Issue Management framework	Deliver training Communication	Informed people	PPM Teams

How the PMO will measure the value of this service

This can be measured by numbers of people trained and the satisfaction with the training.

Criteria when the PMO will use this service

- When there is a new issue management framework
- When there is a change to the issue management framework
- When new people are added to the project teams

Helpful hints for the PMO when delivering the service

- If there is a tool that needs to be used, then show that at the same time
- Use the questions from the training courses to help devise a frequently asked questions or help document
- Gain feedback from the training course on how effective the training was and use that as a measure for the service
- Demonstrate how risks can get raised into issues and what then happens to the risk
- Show how issues can be reported in the progress report and steering group packs
- Consider training the sponsor and steering group members about their role in resolving issues
- If there are minor changes to the issue management framework then the PMO may consider just providing a communication explaining the changes
- Consider having a sweep up session(s) to get to those people who were unable to get the original sessions when booked
- For 'hard to get' people consider doing one to one training to ensure the framework gets trained out to everyone

PMO Capabilities needed to fulfil this service

Competencies	Techniques and generic tools
Issue Management Capability Development P3M Tools Personal Communication Relationships and engagement Result Orientation	Communication requirements analysis Project Management Information System Stakeholder checklist Stakeholder engagement assessment matrix

Related services

Develop the overall issue management framework Introduce tools for managing issues Perform logging and tracking to resolution of issues Review effectiveness of issue identification and resolution processes	Communicate the change control framework Train the risk management framework Manage the Process Improvement Plan Provide PPM training Provide training logistics support

Issue Management Operations

Service group description

The operation of the issue management process, including updating of the issue register, escalation of issues and the resolution of issues.

Why have these services been grouped together?

These services are all related to the day to day running of the issue management process.

Responsibility Assignment Matrix

Service	Executive	Portfolio Manager	Program Manager	Project Manager	PMO	Sponsor	Other Stakeholder
Perform logging and tracking to resolution of issues		A	A	A	R	I	
Facilitate independent issue analysis and resolution workshops			A	A	R	I	
Control escalation of issues to higher authority	I	A	A	A	R	I	C (Issue owner)

Perform logging and tracking to resolution of issues

Service description

The raising and updating of issues in the issue register on behalf of a project or program.

What the service provides for the customer

This ensures that the issue register has an up-to-date reflection of the state of the issues within the project or program.

Why is this service being offered to the customer?

The issues will need to be tracked using the issue register. Having the PMO perform this, rather than the project or program manager, allows them to focus on the overall delivery of the project or program. They get the knowledge that the information is accurate and can be reviewed at any point.

How PMO will apply this service

The PMO will be notified of an issue. They will raise that issue in the issue register ensuring it is properly classified according to the issue management strategy. They will assign it a unique reference number to ensure that it can be tracked.

For each of the issues in the register they will ensure they get assigned an owner and have one or more actions associated with them to bring the issue through to resolution.

The PMO will on a regular basis chase up the status of each of the issues focusing on the important ones first. They will find out what the status of each of the actions is and clarify with the issue owner that if all the actions have been done whether the issue can be closed.

If there is an issue which is not getting resolved, then the PMO will look to escalate this as per the issue management strategy. In the first instance they will confirm with the project or program manager that the escalation is required.

At each stage of the process the PMO will update the issue register with the current details and status.

Supplier	Input	Process	Output	Customer
Project Manager Program Manager PPM team	Issue Issue management strategy	Identify and record an issue	Issue Register	Project Manager Program Manager

How the PMO will measure the value of this service

The PMO can measure this by checking that the issue information is current and passes any audit.

Criteria when the PMO will use this service

- When there is a dedicated PMO supporting a single project or program
- When the project or program manager is happy to delegate this responsibility

Helpful hints for the PMO when delivering the service

- Consider using a tool to store the issues in, which will aid with validation and can alert for issues which need attention
- Review the reporting requirements to ensure this information can be taken from the issue register to go into the individual progress report or steering group packs
- An issue can be deemed important because a due date is imminent (or has passed), it has a high severity, or it has a red or amber status attached

PMO Capabilities needed to fulfil this service

Competencies	Techniques and generic tools
P3M Administration Issue Management Reporting, Insights and Analysis P3M Tools Personal Integrity and reliability Relationships and engagement Teamwork	Project Management Information System

Related services

Examine Issue Registers for common issues Develop the overall issue management framework Control escalation of issues to higher authority Introduce tools for managing issues	Train the issue management framework Facilitate independent issue analysis and resolution workshops Support contracts monitoring and management Maintain the Risk Register

Facilitate independent issue analysis and resolution workshops

Service description

The facilitation of a workshop to enable issues to be analysed and actions identified to resolve the issue.

What the service provides for the customer

This provides an independent individual able to facilitate a workshop.

Why is this service being offered to the customer?

A facilitator needs to be independent to ensure they get the best out of the meeting. They need to understand what is required in terms of resolution. As the PMO has expertise in PPM they are ideally placed to provide this service.

How PMO will apply this service

The PMO will be requested to facilitate an issue resolution workshop. They will speak to the issue owner to find out who the most appropriate people are to attend the workshop. They will use the provide a secretariat service for meetings service to ensure that the meeting is booked, and people invited.

During the meeting they will use the provide facilitation service to ensure the meeting is properly facilitated and the outcome that is desired is obtained.

After the meeting they will ensure that the actions that were decided on during the meeting are communicated. They may use the perform logging and tracking to resolution of issues to track the status of the issue in the issue register. If this is not the PMO's role then they will pass the information back to the issue owner in order that they can get the information updated.

Supplier	Input	Process	Output	Customer
Issue Owner	Issue	Facilitating a meeting	Issue register Actions log	Project Manager Program Manager

How the PMO will measure the value of this service

The PMO can measure the value of this by reviewing the number of times they are asked to perform this service as opposed to other people in the PPM team.

Criteria when the PMO will use this service

- When the PMO has the skills to facilitate a meeting
- When there are issues where the best approach cannot be easily identified
- Where there is a dedicated PMO aligned to a single project or program

Helpful hints for the PMO when delivering the service

- Have a facilitation kit (pens, post-its, blu-tak etc.) to hand to be able to deliver a workshop quickly and effectively
- Set the ground rules at the start of the workshop
- Communicate clearly what is required as an output of the workshop

PMO Capabilities needed to fulfil this service

Competencies	Techniques and generic tools
Issue Management Reporting, Insights and Analysis Personal Communication Relationships and engagement Teamwork Resourcefulness Negotiation Result Orientation	Root Cause Analysis Proposal evaluation system

Related services

Provide a secretariat service for meetings Provide facilitation service Perform logging and tracking to resolution of issues	Review effectiveness of issue identification and resolution processes Facilitate independent change impact assessment workshops

Control escalation of issues to higher authority

Service description

The escalation of issues to a higher authority to get the actions confirmed and endorsed. By escalating an issue to the correct level any barriers preventing the successful resolution should be removed and the issue resolved and closed.

What the service provides for the customer

A way of getting the actions associated with issues agreed and resolved.

Why is this service being offered to the customer?

The PMO have the connections within the organization to ensure that issues can be escalated to the correct level. They are able (if required) to bypass levels of management in order that the actions can be agreed. This will enable the issue owner to get speedier resolution to their issue.

How PMO will apply this service

The PMO will identify an issue that requires escalation, or they may be informed about one. They will speak to the project or program manager to confirm that escalation is required. Once there is agreement that this issue requires escalation the PMO will follow the escalation process set out in the issue management strategy.

The PMO will list out the issue and the proposed actions to resolve the issue. The person/group the issue is being escalated to will decide on the actual actions to be carried out and who will be responsible for performing those actions and by when. This information will be documented in the issue register. The people responsible for carrying out the actions will be informed and be told by when they needed to have done these by.

The project or program manager will need to confirm that the actions agreed on will resolve the issue, otherwise further, or different actions will be required and should be decided at the point of escalation.

Supplier	Input	Process	Output	Customer
Project Manager Program Manager Issue Owner	Issue Register Issue management strategy Communication Management Strategy	Escalate issues	Issue Register Agreed actions	Project Manager Program Manager Portfolio Manager Issue Owner

How the PMO will measure the value of this service

The PMO can measure this by reviewing the numbers of issues escalated that are then resolved versus the number that are not resolved. They can gain feedback from the issue owner on their view of the success of the service.

Criteria when the PMO will use this service

- When there is an issue requiring escalating
- When the PMO is dedicated to a single project or program

Helpful hints for the PMO when delivering the service

- Not all issues require escalation, only the important ones. By defining what important is in the context of the program or portfolio (e.g. severity, RAG) permits management by exception
- Any issue where there are blockers preventing the actions from being affected will require escalation to the level above the blockage, this ensure that the people causing the blockage are then given direction from their management on the course of action
- If the project or program manager refuses to escalate an issue the PMO may decide to overrule them and speak, privately, to the level above and see whether something can be done to engineer the escalation. This is not to embarrass the person blocking the escalation, just to ensure that the issue does get dealt with and does not fester unresolved

PMO Capabilities needed to fulfil this service

Competencies	Techniques and generic tools
Issue Management Reporting, Insights and Analysis Stakeholder Engagement Personal Communication Relationships and engagement Teamwork Conflict and Crisis Resourcefulness Negotiation Result Orientation	Organization charts & position descriptions Project Management Information System

Related services

Perform logging and tracking to resolution of issues Review effectiveness of issue identification and resolution processes	Introduce tools for managing issues Support contracts monitoring and management

Issue Management Monitoring

Service group description

The review of issues and the success of the issue management framework across a program or portfolio.

Why have these services been grouped together?

These services relate to the external review of the way issues are identified, tracked, and managed across a program or portfolio.

Responsibility Assignment Matrix

Service	Executive	Portfolio Manager	Program Manager	Project Manager	PMO	Sponsor	Other Stakeholder
Examine Issue Registers for common issues		A	A, I	I	R		
Review effectiveness of issue identification and resolution processes	A	C	C	C	R		

Helpful hints for when the PMO is delivering this Service Group

To perform these services, it is required to have an issue management framework in place first.

Examine Issue Registers for common issues

Service description

The review of issue registers across a program or portfolio to find common issues.

What the service provides for the customer

This provides the program or portfolio manager with issues that have a common root cause. The program or portfolio manager can then propose actions to deal with the root cause, thereby preventing future similar issues arising.

Why is this service being offered to the customer?

The PMO will have access to the issue registers for each project in the program, or even over the entire portfolio. They have the time available to review the entire issue registers to find issues with a similar root cause. These can then be reported, along with some suggested actions to the program or portfolio manager for resolution.

How PMO will apply this service

The PMO will gain access to each of the issue registers within a program or group of related projects. They will examine, in detail, each of the issues to see if there are any underlying root causes of these issues. These may relate to a particular team not performing, a set of processes that are not aligned or to poor risk management. The PMO will analyse the information and produce a set of recommendations to try and resolve the root cause of these issues.

The PMO will take the recommendations through to the program manager or portfolio manager in order that they can deal with the root cause, and therefore prevent any similar issues occurring in future.

If the root cause is down to poor management or a defective PPM process, then the PMO should look to rectify this themselves by implementing changes to the PPM framework and following that up with training. The training needs to cover not only the team impacted but to the rest of the department as well. This will ensure that having done something to resolve the immediate root cause that this does not move into another area instead.

Supplier	Input	Process	Output	Customer
Project Manager Program Manager	Issue Register	Identify and record an issue	Recommendations	Program Manager Portfolio Manager

How the PMO will measure the value of this service

The PMO can measure this service by reviewing the numbers of similar issues found on future projects and programs.

Criteria when the PMO will use this service

- When the PMO supports a portfolio of projects or a single program
- Where there is a belief that there are common causes of issues
- Where similar lessons are being identified on projects

Helpful hints for the PMO when delivering the service

- Having access to all issues in a single tool will make this process easier, at least in terms of access to the information
- Speaking to the program or portfolio manager prior to starting work will help identify which areas should be looked at first
- Not only review the issues but look at the related actions. Perhaps it is not the issues that are the problem, but the fact that actions are not getting progressed
- Review to see which issues are getting regularly escalated, can a pattern be spotted here

PMO Capabilities needed to fulfil this service

Competencies	Techniques and generic tools
Information Management Issue Management Reporting, Insights and Analysis Assurance P3M Tools Resourcefulness	Root Cause Analysis Trend Analysis Project Management Information System

Related services

Introduce tools for managing issues Develop the overall issue management framework	Analyse lessons to identify items to be added to the Process Improvements Plan

Review effectiveness of issue identification and resolution processes

Service description

The review of the issue management framework against real world usage. This check provides the feedback from users into improving the framework.

What the service provides for the customer

This ensures the issue management framework is kept up to date. It enables help to be written based on real world cases, showing the impact of following the process on the success of projects.

Why is this service being offered to the customer?

As the PMO created the Issue Management framework they are the best people to ensure the feedback from projects and programs using this is fed back into the process.

How PMO will apply this service

On a regular basis the PMO will examine the issue registers to see how many of the issues came from risks and which ones were raised directly. Of the ones which were raised directly the PMO will look and see whether these could have been dealt with as risks and therefore prevented the issue occurring. If there are then they would feed those into the risk management framework as suggestions for risk categories for projects.

The PMO will have a look at the actions related to the issues to see how well they were being delivered. They will look to see whether there are actions that should have been escalated earlier, and if they had been then would that have resulted in the quicker resolution of the related issue. They can then add some guidance into the framework to suggest under what circumstances escalations should occur.

They will ask the people involved in the projects, how well they thought the processes worked. Where there any suggestions that they would have which would improve the process?

Having reviewed all the available information the PMO will see whether there are any changes to the framework required, or whether it is just a refresher training that is required. They will then use the services develop the overall issue management framework and train the issue management framework to deliver those improvements.

Supplier	Input	Process	Output	Customer
Project Manager Program Manager	Issue register	Revising a process	Revised Issue Management Framework	Project Manager Program Manager

How the PMO will measure the value of this service

The PMO can measure the value of this service by looking at how many improvements have been made to the issue management framework.

Criteria when the PMO will use this service

- Where there is an existing issue management framework in place
- When the framework has not been reviewed for a while
- As a result of problems with the framework being identified as part of a lessons learned review

Helpful hints for the PMO when delivering the service

- This is linked into Knowledge Management and continuous improvement. It enables the PMO to provide regular updates to the framework and tailor to the organization
- This service could be performed as part of the year end process
- Feedback from PPM staff on the issue identification and resolution process can be obtained as part of the lessons learned review sessions

PMO Capabilities needed to fulfil this service

Competencies	Techniques and generic tools
Issue Management Knowledge Management Reporting, Insights and Analysis Assurance	Process Analysis Trend Analysis

Related services

Develop the overall issue management framework Train the issue management framework	Facilitate independent issue analysis and resolution workshops Control escalation of issues to higher authority

Knowledge and Innovation

Knowledge and Innovation

Description

Innovation is the process by which new ideas (projects) are formulated before being submitted into the portfolio. From a PMO perspective this differs from portfolio management which is about the categorization of someone else's ideas. This is about getting the ideas in the first place.

What the services within the area provide for the customer

By providing a way of generating new ideas for the organization this provides the senior management with a means of identifying which of these ideas will drive the organization forward the most.

Helpful hints for when the PMO is delivering this service area

This service area is a precursor to the portfolio management area.

Innovation Operations

Service group description

The formulation of new ideas (projects) to drive the organization forward.

Why have these services been grouped together?

These services are related to the running of the innovation sessions and grouping the ideas that originate and forming them into projects to be submitted into the portfolio.

List of related services described in other areas

Maintain a register for current and potential programs and projects

Responsibility Assignment Matrix

Service	Executive	Portfolio Manager	Program Manager	Project Manager	PMO	Sponsor	Other Stakeholder
Capture and categorize new ideas	A	C			R	C	C (Staff)
To run an innovation competition	A				R	C	C (Staff)
Carry out a strategy formulation session	A				R	C	R (Strategy team)

Helpful hints for when the PMO is delivering this service group

- If you are doing either of 2 last services, you will need to ensure you categorize the ideas that get generated
- There must be a link from these services into the portfolio to ensure ideas can get delivered as projects

Capture and categorize new ideas

Service description

The way of ensuring new ideas get raised and codified in a consistent manner to be added into the portfolio.

What the service provides for the customer

This ensures that the ideas are recorded in a consistent manner allowing the portfolio manager to evaluate them as part of the portfolio review process.

Why is this service being offered to the customer?

This helps the portfolio manager as it ensures the ideas are in a fit state to be reviewed. The PMO can ensure these ideas are recorded and tracked allowing for the portfolio manager to give feedback to the idea generator on progress for their ideas.

How PMO will apply this service

The PMO will receive an idea. They will ensure that this is entered into the correct idea form format. If there is information missing from the form, then the PMO will go back to the originator of the idea for clarification. The PMO will update the form with any additional information they receive.

Once the idea form is filled in the PMO will attempt to classify the idea according to the classification used for project types within the portfolio. The PMO will confirm the classification of the idea with the Portfolio Manager and the originator.

The PMO will ensure they have a unique reference for the idea and the details of the originator are captured. This will help when additional information or clarifications are required later in the process the portfolio manager can go back to the originator directly.

Supplier	Input	Process	Output	Customer
Staff	Idea	Capture idea Formatting documents	New idea form	Portfolio Manager

How the PMO will measure the value of this service

The PMO can measure this by recording the numbers of ideas submitted through this service.

Criteria when the PMO will use this service

- When ideas need to be tracked
- When the portfolio manager is not doing this role for themselves
- When there is a portfolio level PMO in place

Helpful hints for the PMO when delivering the service

- Develop a standard idea form to record the important parts of the idea. It allows for a consistent evaluation of the idea
- Ensure each idea has a unique reference number and originator details to allow for feedback to be given and trackability for that idea. This will be needed if the originator of a successful idea is due a reward

PMO Capabilities needed to fulfil this service

Competencies	Techniques and generic tools
P3M Administration Benefits and Value Management Information Management	Alternatives generation Cash flow analysis Sensitivity analysis Comparative advantage analysis Proposal evaluation system

Related services

To run an innovation competition Maintain a register for current and potential programs and projects	Formatting documents Horizon scan for impending policy or strategy changes

To run an innovation competition

Service description

To run a competition to get new ideas, to be turned into projects, which can move the organization forward. The ideas ideally will be step changes rather small incremental changes.

What the service provides for the customer

This provides the organization, as represented by the Executive, ideas which will drive the organization. Ideas can come from anywhere; an innovation competition can harness these ideas in order they can be turned into reality.

Why is this service being offered to the customer?

The portfolio PMO can provide a central point to co-ordinate the competition. They can ensure that all ideas are captured, tracked, and passed onto the portfolio manager for approval.

How PMO will apply this service

The PMO will speak to the Portfolio Manager or the person responsible for suggesting the competition and find out the basic information such as:

- Who is the competition aimed at – internal staff, customers, general public
- What prizes are, and under what circumstances will they be given out? – is this just for entering (chosen at random) or just for successful ideas?
- When is the deadline for entries?
- Is there a scope for what the ideas will be about? – you may want to focus this to get the best out of the suggestions
- Who will be judging the entries – this will be required should there be a prize on offer?
- What format should entries be submitted in
- How can people find out what happened to their idea?

Once the PMO have the basic information they can go about putting together the competition details, any entry forms that will be required along with setting up the submission details and the promotional materials (leaflets, websites, posters).

The PMO will confirm all this before sending it out. The PMO will then monitor any suggestions that come in. They will respond to requests for information or clarification of details. This may involve them creating or updating a Frequently Asked Questions document and making it available on the website.

Once the competition is over the PMO will remove and dispose of the promotional material. They will send the collated suggestions to the portfolio manager, using the Capture and categorize new ideas service.

If there is a prize to be won, then the PMO will ensure that the entries which meet the criteria are submitted through to the people who will be judging the prizes. They will ensure the prizes are drawn and then distributed to the winners. They will make available the list of winners, as per the competition rules.

Supplier	Input	Process	Output	Customer
Portfolio Manager Executive	Competition rules Prizes Deadline	Run competition	Entry form Submission details Promotional material	Staff Customers

How the PMO will measure the value of this service

The PMO will measure this based on the number of submissions they receive.

Criteria when the PMO will use this service

- When there is a portfolio level PMO in place
- When it is decided to run an innovation competition

Helpful hints for the PMO when delivering the service

- If dealing with external competitions, then it is best to get the legal department and marketing departments involved

PMO Capabilities needed to fulfil this service

Competencies	Techniques and generic tools
P3M Administration Financial Management Stakeholder Engagement Personal Communication Relationships and engagement	Alternatives generation Scheduling tool

Related services

Capture and categorize new ideas

Carry out a strategy formulation session

Service description

The provision of a meeting to enable the key players to come up with a new or revised strategic direction for the organization, or part of the organization.

What the service provides for the customer

This ensures there is focus on the development and agreement of the strategy. The PMO can organize and facilitate the session. They can convert the output into a strategy for the organization.

Why is this service being offered to the customer?

The PMO can facilitate the meeting, as independent but knowledgeable people. The PMO have experience with the current strategy and the portfolio and can contribute their understanding of the impact of the proposed strategy on the existing portfolio.

How PMO will apply this service

The PMO will be asked to assist with a strategy formulation session. They will work with the Executive to work out who will attend and get the scope of the session sorted. They will work with the strategy manager and the portfolio manager to agree the format for the ideas that will be required in advance of the meeting. The PMO will assist by developing any templates that will be required to ensure consistent information capture in advance of the meeting. They will send out any templates used to gather the information in advance of the meeting. They will then ensure that this is all collated and organized so it can be used as input to the meeting itself.

The PMO will use the provide a secretariat service for meetings service to ensure the meeting is organized and run efficiently. During the meeting they will use the provide facilitation service to ensure the meeting is properly facilitated and the outcome that is desired is obtained.

After the meeting, the PMO will draft the outputs into a strategic plan working with the strategy manager and the portfolio manager to help develop this document.

Supplier	Input	Process	Output	Customer
Business areas Strategy Manager Portfolio Manager	Ideas Current strategy	Facilitating a meeting	Revised Strategy	Executive

How the PMO will measure the value of this service

The PMO can measure this by getting feedback from the attendees on the value of the session.

Criteria when the PMO will use this service

- When there is a portfolio PMO in place
- When a new strategy is required
- When the meeting requires facilitation
- When the portfolio manager requires support to deliver this session

Helpful hints for the PMO when delivering the service

- When getting senior management, it can be easier to get them for a full day rather than part of a day
- Ensure the agenda/scope for the meeting is defined in advance
- Send out details of preparations required out with sufficient time for people to provide the information in advance of the meeting
- Understand what format the strategy needs to be documented, and in what detail prior to the meeting to enable the outputs to be easily turned into the strategic plan after the meeting

PMO Capabilities needed to fulfil this service

Competencies	Techniques and generic tools
P3M Administration Reporting, Insights and Analysis Personal Communication Relationships and engagement Conflict and Crisis Resourcefulness Negotiation Result Orientation	Alternatives generation Multi-Criteria Scoring Model Comparative advantage analysis Scenario analysis Prioritization matrices

Related services

Provide a secretariat service for meetings Provide facilitation service Horizon scan for impending policy or strategy changes	Business strategy and roadmap maintenance To run an innovation competition

Knowledge Management

Knowledge Management

Description

Knowledge management is about taking what is learnt both inside and outside the organization any applying this to how change is run within the organization.

What the services within the area provide for the customer

By sharing the experience across the PPM domain ensures that projects and programs can be run in a more efficient and productive way. They can take advantage of the wisdom of others to prevent issues occurring and find speedier, more effective ways to deliver.

Helpful hints for when the PMO is delivering this service area

Knowledge management is more than just recording lessons learned, it is about taking the essence of those lessons and applying it to the way projects, programs and the portfolio is managed within the organization. Following on from knowledge gathering there needs to be knowledge dissemination.

Remember that lessons can be positive, in which case we need to understand how to repeat the successes, as well as negative, in which case we need to understand how to avoid them.

Knowledge Management Design

Service group description

The approach to the way knowledge will be handled within the organization.

Why have these services been grouped together?

This service relates to the setup of knowledge management within the organization.

Responsibility Assignment Matrix

Service	Executive	Portfolio Manager	Program Manager	Project Manager	PMO	Sponsor	Other Stakeholder
Create and maintain knowledge management framework	A	I	I	I	R	I	I (PPM Team)

Create and maintain knowledge management framework

Service description

The creation of the approach to knowledge management within the organization.

What the service provides for the customer

This explains who is involved in knowledge management and how it is performed. It provides some tools to enable knowledge management within the organization.

Why is this service being offered to the customer?

As the PMO are normally the custodians of the PPM knowledge as they can complete the circle from project end to project start, they are ideally placing to develop the processes and tools to support PPM related knowledge management within the organization.

How PMO will apply this service

The PMO will look to see how (if at all) knowledge management is done in the organization currently. They will consult their wider network to find out how knowledge management is done in other organizations and see what can be transferred into this organization.

They will look to create a lesson learned register, both to be applied at an individual project level and for a central register. They will look to incorporate the lessons learned review into the PPM framework, not only at the end, but as part of start-up in order that the central lessons register is consulted as projects begin. They will develop a process to ensure that examples of good practice (e.g. templates that have been filled in and worked well) are captured and shared. They will develop a process to ensure that actions get taken from the lessons learned and fed back into the existing processes.

The PMO will look to see what tools are available to support the knowledge management processes. If there is nothing available, then they will look to see what can be created in house.

Supplier	Input	Process	Output	Customer
PMO	Standards template	Develop Standard Develop Templates	Knowledge Management Tools Knowledge Management Process Lessons Learned Register	PPM Teams PMO

How the PMO will measure the value of this service

This can be measured by the numbers of good practice examples that are captured and improvements that are raised to existing processes as a result of actions taken from lessons learned.

Criteria when the PMO will use this service

- When the organization is looking to improve the project management maturity
- Where the organization is looking to move beyond just capturing lessons learned

Helpful hints for the PMO when delivering the service

- Consider having groups (communities of practice) where colleagues can share hints and tips
- When looking at the knowledge management tools, consider how people will get information out as well as getting information in

PMO Capabilities needed to fulfil this service

Competencies	Techniques and generic tools
Knowledge Management Reporting, Insights and Analysis Delivery Methods Governance Frameworks P3M Tools Relationships and engagement Teamwork	Root Cause Analysis 5 Whys Process Analysis Swim-lane flowcharts Task responsibility matrix/RACI

Related services

Analyse lessons to identify items to be added to the Process Improvements Plan Facilitate lessons learning Trigger post-program or project reviews Maintain lesson register Capture good practice examples for inclusion in good practice repository Map key value streams and processes	Manage the Process Improvement Plan Enable sharing of good practice Assess the Knowledge Management maturity Assess the usage of the central lessons register

Knowledge Management Operations

Service group description

The codification, storage and distribution of the knowledge that has been gathered.

Why have these services been grouped together?

These services relate to the sharing knowledge and information with others, both in and outside the organization.

Responsibility Assignment Matrix

Service	Executive	Portfolio Manager	Program Manager	Project Manager	PMC	Sponsor	Other Stakeholder
Analyse lessons to identify items to be added to the Process Improvements Plan					A, R		
Facilitate lessons learning			A	A	R		
Run lessons-learned workshops			A	A	R		C (PPM Team)
Maintain lesson register			A	A	R	I	C (PPM Team)
Capture good practice examples for inclusion in good practice repository			C	C	A, R		
Enable sharing of good practice	A	I	I	I	R	I	I
External networking attendance at good practice events					A, R		
Develop external relationships to share lessons and experience					A, R		
Develop case study material			C	C	A, R		
Document project and program success stories			C	C	A, R		

Helpful hints for when the PMO is delivering this service group

- There is no point gathering in the information without being able to share it
- Consider setting up communities of practice, both internally and externally to share what has been learnt

Analyse lessons to identify items to be added to the Process Improvements Plan

Service description

A review of the central lessons registers to identify items where action needs to be taken to improve the PPM framework.

What the service provides for the customer

This ensures that the PPM framework is updated based on comments from the lessons identified on projects and programs.

Why is this service being offered to the customer?

This ensures the PPM framework is maintained. It means that actions identified from lessons register are taken forward and resolved. As the PMO will remain in place after the project or program has closed, they are ideally positioned to own these changes and ensure they get applied.

How PMO will apply this service

The PMO will review all the items in the central lessons register. They will see whether an action needs to be taken forward. If they do, then then they will add this to the Process Improvement Plan. This plan will contain a list of all the planned changes for the various frameworks. For each of the actions raised they will be assigned to an individual to resolve and given a date by which the action is expected to have been done by.

Supplier	Input	Process	Output	Customer
PMO	Central Lessons Register	Analyse lessons register	Process Improvement Plan	PMO

How the PMO will measure the value of this service

This can be measured in the numbers of lessons in the central register that have been actioned. It can be measured in the number of improvements to the PPM framework.

Criteria when the PMO will use this service

- Where there is a central lesson register
- Where there is a culture of continuous improvement
- Where the PMO is permanent

Helpful hints for the PMO when delivering the service

- Consider reviewing the central lessons register on a regular basis e.g. every 3 or 6 months
- If uncertain as to whether a lesson should be perused, ask for advice from the project management community as to whether they think a change is required
- Make the Process Improvement Plan public so that people who have submitted requests for change can see when they are likely to get the change implemented

PMO Capabilities needed to fulfil this service

Competencies	Techniques and generic tools
Change Control Knowledge Management Reporting, Insights and Analysis Delivery Methods	Root Cause Analysis Process Analysis Change control tools

Related services

Manage the Process Improvement Plan Run lessons-learned workshops Maintain lesson register Trigger post-program or project reviews Examine Issue Registers for common issues	Support closure process Create and maintain knowledge management framework Monitor use of corporate guidance and standards to identify improvements Assess the usage of the central lessons register

Facilitate lessons learning

Service description

Ensure that lessons are learnt throughout the lifecycle.

What the service provides for the customer

A reminder when reaching the end of a sprint the value in conducting a retrospective.

A reminder when planning the next stage to learn from any lessons identified in the previous stage.

Why is this service being offered to the customer?

If lessons are just recorded, then the value of learning the lesson is lost to the project or program and the organization. If the PMO maintain the lesson register they are in a position to provide the detail of the lessons that have already been captured.

How PMO will apply this service

When the PMO is working on an agile project they should speak to the scrum master and ensure they have booked time aside to perform a retrospective at the end of the sprint. The PMO should remind the scrum master of the importance of carrying the learnings from the current sprint into the next sprint planning sessions. This should incorporate not only the reasons for any blockers, but the successes as well.

When working in a waterfall manner, when it is coming to the end of the stage the PMO should remind the project manager to update the lessons register. The project manager needs to see which one of those lessons could be incorporated into the planning of the next stage.

When planning the next stage or sprint the PMO should see whether there are any lessons identified in the central register that could be applicable. If there are then the PMO should share these with the project manager so they can incorporate them into their planning process.

Supplier	Input	Process	Output	Customer
PMO	Lessons Register Central lessons register	Learn lessons	Lessons learned	PPM Team

How the PMO will measure the value of this service

This can be measured by seeing the numbers of lessons that have been incorporated into the planning of the next stage/sprint.

Criteria when the PMO will use this service

- When the PMO is aligned to a single project or program
- Where the project is coming to the end of a stage or sprint

Helpful hints for the PMO when delivering the service

- Although the end of a stage or sprint gives a suitable time to learn lessons, these can be incorporated at any stage

PMO Capabilities needed to fulfil this service

Competencies	Techniques and generic tools
Knowledge Management Personal Integrity and reliability Personal Communication Relationships and engagement Teamwork Result Orientation	None

Related services

Maintain lesson register Run lessons-learned workshops Trigger post-program or project reviews Enable sharing of good practice	Assess the usage of the central lessons register Support closure process Create and maintain knowledge management framework

Run lessons-learned workshops

Service description

The delivery of a lessons learned workshop on behalf of a project or program.

What the service provides for the customer

This provides an independently run workshop which will help drive out any lessons (good or bad) and good practice examples that will prove useful to other projects or programs.

Why is this service being offered to the customer?

Having an independent person run the workshop can ensure that all sides are heard, and the root causes of any issues can be brought out.

How PMO will apply this service

The PMO will get a request to run a lessons-learned workshop. They will speak to the project or program manager to agree a location, time, and date. They will work out who is relevant to be invited. The PMO can use the 'Provide a secretariat service for meetings' to get the meeting arranged and minuted. During the meeting, the PMO can use the 'Provide facilitation service' to ensure that everyone is engaged, and the root cause of the issues can be identified.

During the meeting, the PMO will see if they can identify any good practice documents that would be useful to share with others. The actual documents can be obtained after the meeting. They would then ensure those documents were made available via the good practice repository.

As a result of the meeting the PMO should ensure that the lessons register was updated with any lessons that came out of the meeting. They would then pass a copy of the lessons register through to the central PMO function to ensure they get added to the central lessons register.

Supplier	Input	Process	Output	Customer
Project Manager Program Manager	Workshop request	Facilitating a meeting	Central Lessons Register Good practice examples	PPM Team PMO

How the PMO will measure the value of this service

This can be measured by asking for feedback from those attending the workshop.

Criteria when the PMO will use this service

- When a project or program is ending
- When a project is going through a stage gate

Helpful hints for the PMO when delivering the service

- The key attendees for the workshop could be obtained from the stakeholder list

PMO Capabilities needed to fulfil this service

Competencies	Techniques and generic tools
P3M Administration Knowledge Management Reporting, Insights and Analysis Personal Integrity and reliability Personal Communication Relationships and engagement Negotiation	Root Cause Analysis 5 Whys Alternatives analysis Alternatives generation Failure Modes and Effects Analysis (FMEA) Process Analysis Scheduling tool Stakeholder checklist Stakeholder engagement assessment matrix Task responsibility matrix/RACI

Related services

Provide a secretariat service for meetings Set up meetings on behalf of others Provide facilitation service Support closure process	Facilitate lessons learning Trigger post-program or project reviews Capture good practice examples for inclusion in good practice repository Analyse lessons to identify items to be added to the Process Improvements Plan

Maintain lesson register

Service description

Capture of any lessons during a project or program within a lesson register.

What the service provides for the customer

The capture of lessons in a consistent format for use later in the project or program.

Why is this service being offered to the customer?

Lessons do not only come up at the end of a project or program, but during it as well. Rather than let lessons slip by the PMO can capture these and record them to assist the project or program. Lessons identified can be used to improve the project or program delivery.

How PMO will apply this service

When the project or program manager identifies a lesson the PMO will capture this and record it into the lessons register. The lessons register should include:

- ID – a unique reference for the lesson
- Issue – what was the issue that is being captured
- Impact – What impact did the issue have on the project or program. Was it a positive or negative impact?
- Resolution – how was the issue resolved?
- Cause – what was the root cause of the issue
- Recommendation – what would you look to different next time
- Date logged – when was this lesson identified. This can tie the issue back to a particular place in the lifecycle
- Logged by – who raised the issue. This can be useful if you need to find out more about the issue

Supplier	Input	Process	Output	Customer
PMO Project	Lessons Register	Record lessons	Updated Lessons Register	Project Manager Program Manager PMO

How the PMO will measure the value of this service

This can be measured by the number of lessons that have been recorded during the lifecycle of the project or program as opposed to just captured at the end.

Criteria when the PMO will use this service

- When a PMO is aligned to a single project or program
- Where there are lessons identified
- At a retrospective
- As part of an end of stage/gate review

Helpful hints for the PMO when delivering the service

- Ensure that positive lessons (things that went well) are captured as well as the negative lessons
- It may be useful to capture the lessons in stages i.e. record the Issue, impact, and cause. Once the item has resolved itself then capture the resolution and recommendation

PMO Capabilities needed to fulfil this service

Competencies	Techniques and generic tools
P3M Administration Knowledge Management Reporting, Insights and Analysis	Root Cause Analysis 5 Whys Decision tree analysis Process Analysis

Related services

Create and maintain knowledge management framework Facilitate lessons learning Analyse lessons to identify items to be added to the Process Improvements Plan	Support closure process Trigger post-program or project reviews

Capture good practice examples for inclusion in good practice repository

Service description

Finding good examples of documents, based on standard templates, that can be added into the good practice repository to act as examples for others.

What the service provides for the customer

This provides worked examples to go into the good practice repository.

Why is this service being offered to the customer?

Having worked examples provides a reference for the project or program manager when they are looking to fill in the relevant document. If the project or program manager is uncertain as to what is required in a particular heading, they can look at the worked example.

How PMO will apply this service

The PMO will review the documents that the project or program has produced. Where they have used one of the standard templates the PMO will see whether they think this is a good example. If they think it is then the PMO will ask the project or program manager whether they think it was a helpful document. If both the PMO and the manager think it was helpful/successful, then this will be considered as part of the good practice repository.

Having got the document, the PMO should create a link from the PPM framework to the good practice repository. If possible where each type of document template is shown there should be some examples of each of those templates filled in.

Supplier	Input	Process	Output	Customer
Project Manager Program Manager	Filled in templates	Update good practice repository	Good practice examples	Project Manager Program Manager

How the PMO will measure the value of this service

This can be measured by the numbers of worked examples available in the good practice repository.

Criteria when the PMO will use this service

- When a project or program is closing
- As part of a lessons-learned workshop
- When the project goes through a gate
- Where there is a good practice repository

Helpful hints for the PMO when delivering the service

- Not every document will be a good practice example
- There may be some documents that are good examples but did not use the template. Consider changing the template to align to the good example
- It may be that the good example uses an older version of the template. That should not stop the example being included in the good practice repository. However, you may need to mention that the template has been updated since this document was produced

PMO Capabilities needed to fulfil this service

Competencies	Techniques and generic tools
Information Management Knowledge Management P3M Tools Resourcefulness	None

Related services

Run lessons-learned workshops Support closure process Trigger post-program or project reviews Promote good PPM within the organization Create and maintain knowledge management framework Enable sharing of good practice External networking attendance at good practice events	Develop case study material Document project and program success stories Assure the development of portfolio, program, and project quality plans Provide project and program assurance checks Feedback to senior management on the success of strategic initiatives Establish and maintain the intranet site or information portal

Enable sharing of good practice

Service description

Ensure that good practice on how PPM runs is shared across the PMM community. This can include examples from inside or outside the organization.

What the service provides for the customer

This helps the PPM teams with their delivery by providing hints and tips on the different approaches. The advice can save PPM teams effort by sharing quicker ways to perform the task in hand. It can prevent re-work by helping the PPM manager to know where to focus their efforts to get it right first time.

Why is this service being offered to the customer?

We want to learn from the wisdom of others. As the PMO see the different projects and programs across the portfolio and participate in the lessons capture sessions they are ideally positioned to find the information and share it across the portfolio.

How PMO will apply this service

The PMO will attend the lessons review sessions and glean some hints and tips. They can attend external sessions (e.g. workshops, conferences, webinars, training courses) to pick up hints and tips.

When a new project or program starts then the PMO can advise the project or program manager on the different approaches and share those hints and tips. When going through a gate review or retrospective the PMO can use this as an opportunity to pick-up and share tips.

When the PMO is speaking to the PPM manager they will find out how the work is going and look to see if there are any ways that what the PPM manager is doing can be used elsewhere. If there is then the PMO will find out the details and use that information to share with the other teams.

Supplier	Input	Process	Output	Customer
External organizations PPM teams PMO	Worked examples Advice Checklists Lessons Registers	Knowledge Management	Good practice examples	PPM teams

How the PMO will measure the value of this service

This can be measured by the number of times the PMO is asked whether they have any good practice to share.

Criteria when the PMO will use this service

- When projects or programs start
- When going through a gate review
- When speaking to the PPM manager

Helpful hints for the PMO when delivering the service

- If there is a project management community within the organization, consider having the PMO attend to hear what the pain points are. A slot for the PMO to speak and share information can be useful
- Consider sharing across the different roles that make up a PPM team e.g. business analyst, tester. Do not just restrict yourself to the project management community
- Attendance at external events can help with bringing in new ideas to the organization
- Speak to new starters in the PMO and new project managers to ask them what information they would have wanted to know when they started. Then incorporate that into the new starter pack

PMO Capabilities needed to fulfil this service

Competencies	Techniques and generic tools
Knowledge Management Stakeholder Engagement Capability Development Governance Frameworks Professionalism and ethics Personal Communication Relationships and engagement Teamwork Resourcefulness	Capability and Capacity analysis

Related services

Develop external relationships to share lessons and experience External networking attendance at good practice events Capture good practice examples for inclusion in good practice repository Create and maintain knowledge management framework Document project and program success stories	Provide a Stage Gate Review or Gateway support service Facilitate lessons learning Develop case study material Provide project and program assurance checks Feedback to senior management on the success of strategic initiatives Review the effectiveness of risk mitigation actions

External networking attendance at good practice events

Service description

Attendance at conferences, training, meetups, webinars with a view to learning information to take back into the organization. Making of new connections who can assist with learning experiences.

What the service provides for the customer

This provides a way of getting new experience into the organization. It allows the PMO to validate and expand their knowledge. It provides a way that the PMO can gain new connections outside of the organization.

Why is this service being offered to the customer?

The PMO need to be able to improve their knowledge and build new contacts they can call on for advice and expertise.

How PMO will apply this service

The PMO will find and attend PPM related conferences, training, meetups, or webinars. They will look to share the details of these events with other people in the PMO and where applicable in the PPM community.

At the event, the PMO will make notes and check to see how this can be applied to the way PPM is run within the organization. During the breaks, the PMO will chat to other attendees and share their experiences. If relevant the PMO will swap details with the other attendees and see how information can be shared after the event.

After the event, the PMO will look to contact the individuals who they met at the event and link to them across the social networks/email.

If there were any presentations that were shown at the event the PMO should try to obtain a copy and circulate this to others in the PMO and PPM community.

Supplier	Input	Process	Output	Customer
Conferences Training Meetups	Speakers Slides Attendees	Networking Knowledge management	New connections Good practice examples	PMO PPM team

How the PMO will measure the value of this service

This can be measured by the number of new contacts the PMO has built up. It can be measured by the numbers of good practice examples the PMO has brought back into the organization.

Criteria when the PMO will use this service

- When the PMO is looking to improve what they do

Helpful hints for the PMO when delivering the service

- Sign up for events with the major project management organizations
- Look for webinars advertised on social networks (twitter, linked in etc)

PMO Capabilities needed to fulfil this service

Competencies	Techniques and generic tools
Knowledge Management Capability Development Professionalism and ethics Personal Integrity and reliability Personal Communication Relationships and engagement Resourcefulness	None

Related services

Enable sharing of good practice Develop external relationships to share lessons and experience Capture good practice examples for inclusion in good practice repository Ensure Continuing Professional Development of the PMO team	Define strategy for acquir ng and developing skills Promote good PPM within the organization Develop case study material Communicates regularly with the PMO team and wider networks

Develop external relationships to share lessons and experience

Service description

Building a network of individuals external to the organization to share lessons and experience.

What the service provides for the customer

By developing their network, the PMO are able to leverage the real-world practical experience of others to be combined with their theoretical knowledge to improve the services they offer.

Why is this service being offered to the customer?

By getting experience from outside the organization the PMO can have a sounding board to review the PMO and identify areas for improvement. By sharing what the PMO knows with others can consolidate the understanding of the PMO.

How PMO will apply this service

The PMO will speak to people at external events (conferences, meetups, training) and connect with them. On a regular basis the PMO should look to maintain contact with those individuals, if possible, meeting up in person.

Whenever they do contact the individuals the PMO should be willing to share their own experiences with others before asking for help. Where a request comes in for assistance the PMO should offer their experience in the matter. They should listen to what others have to say and add positive contributions.

Supplier	Input	Process	Output	Customer
External PMO groups PMO	Experience Request for assistance	Knowledge Management Networking	Knowledge Lessons learned	PMO External PMO groups

How the PMO will measure the value of this service

This can be measured by the size of the network and the effectiveness of that network in being able to provide answers that the PMO require.

Criteria when the PMO will use this service

- When the PMO wants to have external knowledge as a sounding board
- Where the PMO is looking to improve their skills and knowledge
- Where the PMO has information to share

Helpful hints for the PMO when delivering the service

- The knowledge sharing must be bilateral otherwise the network will not be maintained
- Social networks like Linked In are useful for maintain contact with other professionals
- If the PMO is constantly taking from individuals within the network, the PMO will quickly lose touch with those individuals. No one likes to be exploited
- Try not to undermine others with your contribution. Even if you think they are wrong, this can be challenged in a positive way by getting to understand the other's point of view
- As there are lots of different PMOs there are likely to be many different ways of doing things depending on the context of the organization
- Even where organizations appear to be different, talking to individuals can bring out similarities. These can be then shared across different organizations
- Due to commercial conflicts it may not be possible to share specific templates, however the contents of a template can be discussed, and the headings shared
- Within the public sector it may be more possible to share information due to lack of conflict of interest

PMO Capabilities needed to fulfil this service

Competencies	Techniques and generic tools
Knowledge Management Stakeholder Engagement Capability Development Professionalism and ethics Self-reflection and self-management Personal Integrity and reliability Personal Communication Relationships and engagement	None

Related services

Enable sharing of good practice External networking attendance at good practice events Promote good PPM within the organization Ensure Continuing Professional Development of the PMO team	Define strategy for acquiring and developing skills Carries out PMO benchmarking activities Communicates regularly with the PMO team and wider networks

Develop case study material

Service description

The development of case studies based on the use of the PPM framework within the organization.

What the service provides for the customer

This provides a blog, training example or white paper which can take one (or several) elements of the PPM framework and explain how useful this has been. By getting examples and sound bites from practitioners allows the process to come alive for the recipients.

Why is this service being offered to the customer?

As the PMO reviews the good PPM practice and is responsible for the training of PPM users, this is another way the PMO can get this message across. This information can then be used at external events to demonstrate the knowledge and experience of the PMO to other companies.

How PMO will apply this service

Having identified the area to deliver a case study for the PMO will look to see what information they have available. They will look back through the recently delivered projects to pick out documentation which has worked well, and that which has not to provide a comparison between the two. They will speak to project and program managers as well as users and the sponsor to find some good quotes to use. They will look back through the lessons registers to find evidence of the success or failure of the area of the case study.

The case study should look to have the following elements:

- Background – what were the circumstances that led to the issue that you are writing the case study about
- Approaches taken – what approaches were taken to resolve the problem
- Outcome – Having taken the approach what happened
- Conclusion – what were the learning points from last time
- More information – if others want to follow the route to success how do they go about it?

Depending on the case study there may be several approaches and outcome sections. If so, then look to add in an intervention section which explains why a different approach was taken.

Supplier	Input	Process	Output	Customer
PPM Teams PMO	Project Reviews Project documentation	Create case study material	White Paper Blog pieces Training examples	PPM Teams

How the PMO will measure the value of this service

This can be measured by the numbers of people who read the articles that get created. Of those people who read the articles they could be asked how relevant and useful it has been having this information.

Criteria when the PMO will use this service

- Where the PMO want to share information about PPM to a wider audience
- Where there is a desire to do something different to train people in PPM
- Where the PMO has been asked to deliver a session on PPM to an external audience

Helpful hints for the PMO when delivering the service

- Try to tell this as a story, rather than a collection of facts as it will engage the audience better
- When picking an area for a case study, either focus it on a success or focus it on an area that not many people know about. Hence showcasing this to a wider audience

PMO Capabilities needed to fulfil this service

Competencies	Techniques and generic tools
Knowledge Management Capability Development Delivery Methods Self-reflection and self-management Personal Communication	Root Cause Analysis Failure Modes and Effects Analysis (FMEA) Communication requirements analysis

Related services

External networking attendance at good practice events Document project and program success stories	Enable sharing of good practice Capture good practice examples for inclusion in good practice repository

Document project and program success stories

Service description

Where projects or programs have been particularly successful then provide a write-up to share this with a wider audience.

What the service provides for the customer

This provides a blog piece which celebrates success and shares the reasons behind this in order that this can be repeated across other projects and programs.

Why is this service being offered to the customer?

It is good to celebrate success. As the PMO can look after the training and communication of good PPM practice they are in a position to be able to share this widely across the organization.

How PMO will apply this service

Having found a successful project or program the PMO will speak to the project or program manager to find out why they thought it was successful and to highlight a few key points about they delivery they thought could be transferred to other projects. They will speak to the sponsor and the users of the products to find out what they thought of the finished product and their involvement in the success of the project or program.

The PMO will create a blog piece which will set the context of the project or program, explain what was successful and why. They will highlight the key individuals involved and the role they played to make it a success. They will bring out the key transferable points. They will provide references so that people can look to repeat this for other projects and programs.

Once the blog piece has been written they will validate this with the sponsor and the project or program manager to ensure that the information is correct. The PMO will then publish this out to a wider audience.

Supplier	Input	Process	Output	Customer
Project Manager Program Manager	Project Reviews Project documentation	Document success	Blog piece	PPM Teams

How the PMO will measure the value of this service

This can be measured in the numbers of people who read the blog piece. In the longer term this can measured by the success story being repeated in other projects.

Criteria when the PMO will use this service

- When a project or program has been successful
- Where there is a mechanism to share success stories across the organization

Helpful hints for the PMO when delivering the service

- Decide whether a project or program has been successful as part of the post implementation review process
- Consider using the intranet or in-house magazine to publicize the success of the project or program

PMO Capabilities needed to fulfil this service

Competencies	Techniques and generic tools
Knowledge Management Personal Communication Relationships and engagement	Root Cause Analysis

Related services

Enable sharing of good practice Develop case study material Promote good PPM within the organization	Trigger post-program or project reviews Capture good practice examples for inclusion in good practice repository Feedback to senior management on the success of strategic initiatives

Knowledge Management Monitoring

Service group description

Monitoring the effectiveness of knowledge management within the organization.

Why have these services been grouped together?

These services relate to ensuring the knowledge management framework is effective.

Responsibility Assignment Matrix

Service	Executive	Portfolio Manager	Program Manager	Project Manager	PMO	Sponsor	Other Stakeholder
Assess the Knowledge Management maturity	A	C	C	C	R	I	C (PPM Team)
Assess the usage of the central lessons register			C	C	A, R		C (PPM Team)

Helpful hints for when the PMO is delivering this service group

Feedback the knowledge gained from these services back into the knowledge management framework.

Assess the Knowledge Management maturity

Service description

Assess how good the organization is at doing knowledge management and suggest items for improvement.

What the service provides for the customer

This allows an independent assessment of how well the organization is on sharing knowledge. With the suggestions for improvement it allows the organization to improve.

Why is this service being offered to the customer?

As an independent body the PMO are ideally positioned to assess the capability of the organization.

How PMO will apply this service

The PMO will investigate the different available maturity models and look at their strengths and weaknesses. Having selected the assessment, the PMO will look to identify the scope of the assessment. Will this cover the entire portfolio or just a specific program?

They will identify the relevant people talk to as part of the assessment. They will book up sessions to go through and ask the questions as part of the assessment. The PMO will then interview the relevant people, they may look for examples of where knowledge management has been successful.

Once all the people have been questioned, the PMO will collate the overall assessment. As well as providing an overall scoring using the maturity assessment scoring matrix the PMO will look to justify their assessment. The PMO will look to suggest a series of suggestions how the organization can improve, or at least maintain their current assessment.

Supplier	Input	Process	Output	Customer
External supplier	Knowledge Management Maturity questionnaire	Assessing maturity	Maturity Assessment scoring Recommendations	Executive PMO

How the PMO will measure the value of this service

This can be measured by looking at the improvements in the knowledge management maturity of the organization.

Criteria when the PMO will use this service

- When the organization wants to improve the way, knowledge is shared
- Where there is a desire for improvement
- Where the PMO has a role as an independent assessor

Helpful hints for the PMO when delivering the service

- Review whether it is just the knowledge management maturity that needs assessing or is it the whole PPM maturity
- When looking for recommendations link them into improvements in the current knowledge management framework

PMO Capabilities needed to fulfil this service

Competencies	Techniques and generic tools
Knowledge Management Reporting, Insights and Analysis Assurance Personal Communication Relationships and engagement	Multi-Criteria Scoring Model Capability and Capacity analysis Check sheets

Related services

Perform organizational PPM maturity assessments	Create and maintain knowledge management framework

Further Reading

wisdomsource.com: K3M the Knowledge Management Maturity Model
APQC's Levels of Knowledge Management Maturity
Siemens Knowledge Management Maturity Model (KMMM)
Infosys Knowledge Management Maturity Model (KMMM)
Paulzen and Perc's Knowledge Process Quality Model (KPQM)
Kulkarni and Freeze's Knowledge Management Capability Assessment Model (KMCA)
Forrester Group KM maturity
Fujitsu organizational Maturity

Assess the usage of the central lessons register

Service description

Review the effectiveness of the central lessons register in enabling lessons to be shared across the organization.

What the service provides for the customer

It provides a review of the usefulness of the lessons register to work out what can be done to ensure that this is used more by the project and program managers. The PMO can work out who has been looking at it and suggest what will ensure the lessons can be learnt.

Why is this service being offered to the customer?

If no one is using the central lessons register, then it means that the lessons are not being learnt.

How PMO will apply this service

The PMO will look to see who has reviewed the central lessons register. They will look to see how many individual lessons registers have been added to the central one. Where there any projects or programs which did not get the lessons added? If not, why not? The PMO will look to see whether all the lessons have follow-on actions, if they do not, should they?

The PMO will ask a couple of project and program managers who have used the central lessons register how effective they found using it. They will ask the project and program managers who have not used the central lessons register why not. They will ask the project and program managers to suggest ways the access to the register could be improved.

Based on the feedback from the project and program managers and the access records the PMO will suggest some improvements in the usage of the register. They will ensure that these suggestions get acted upon and amend the knowledge management framework, as necessary.

Supplier	Input	Process	Output	Customer
PMO	Central Lessons Register	Analyse lessons register	Recommendations	PMO PPM team

How the PMO will measure the value of this service

This can be measured in the increased usage of the central lessons register.

Criteria when the PMO will use this service

- Where there is a central lesson register
- Where the organization wants to improve the way, it manages it lessons learned
- Where the PMO has an interest in knowledge management

Helpful hints for the PMO when delivering the service

- Consider adding a section to the project documentation for lessons learned, so that it can be evidenced which lessons have been reviewed and incorporated into each project
- Rather than have a spreadsheet to record the lessons consider using an online repository linked into the PPM framework

PMO Capabilities needed to fulfil this service

Competencies	Techniques and generic tools
Information Management Knowledge Management Reporting, Insights and Analysis Relationships and engagement Teamwork	Root Cause Analysis 5 Whys Failure Modes and Effects Analysis (FMEA) Process Analysis

Related services

Analyse lessons to identify items to be added to the Process Improvements Plan	Create and maintain knowledge management framework Facilitate lessons learning

Methodologies

Methodologies

Description

Provides a set of processes, procedures, standards, templates, worked examples and help which allow the organization to run projects, programs and portfolios in a consistent manner.

What the services within the area provide for the customer

By providing a standard way of working it ensures time is not wasted in having to create the templates for every project or program being run in the organization. Having consistency in the way projects and programs are run means staff are more productive as they do not need to learn a new way of working for every project or program they are assigned to. This is more applicable where staff are working on more than one change initiative at a time.

Helpful hints for when the PMO is delivering this service area

- Look to align the internal methodology with external standards as this will make training and recruitment easier
- When providing templates, having worked examples and help text to enables the user to understand how to fill the templates in
- Although the PMO may be very familiar with the methodology, expect that the project or program manager may not be as they do not deal with the individual process and templates on as regular basis as the PMO, and since they last used this the information may have been updated. Be prepared to offer coaching and training to the project and program managers if they require it

Method Design

Service group description

The setup, maintenance and training of processes, procedures, templates, standards, and help relating to a consistent way of running projects and programs within the organization.

Why have these services been grouped together?

These services provide the structure and backbone of the way PPM operates within the organization.

List of related services described in other areas

Develop the overall change control framework
Create Change Management Framework
Develop configuration management standards and processes
Develop and maintain the PPM financial framework
Define, maintain, and implement PPM governance framework
Develop the overall issue management framework
Create and maintain knowledge management framework
Establish a portfolio management framework
Develop and maintain the overall Quality Control Framework
Develop the overall risk management framework
Define planning standards and templates
Develop and maintain an estimating framework
Develop and maintain the communication framework
Develop and maintain the stakeholder engagement framework
Work with Procurement teams to agree PPM purchasing Framework
Automate Processes

Responsibility Assignment Matrix

Service	Executive	Portfolio Manager	Program Manager	Project Manager	PMC	Sponsor	Other Stakeholder
Define, maintain, and implement standard PPM framework	A	C	C	C	R		I (PPM team)
Define, maintain, and implement reporting framework	A	C	C	C	R		I (PPM team)
Define, maintain, and implement framework for monitoring and review		I	I	I	A, R		
Develop and maintain tailoring guidelines for standards, methods, and approaches	A	C	C	C	R		I (PPM team)

Helpful hints for when the PMO is delivering this service group

These services are linked into a lot of the other service groups within the other domains that form the detailed approach to performing PPM tasks in a consistent manner in the organization.

Define, maintain, and implement standard PPM framework

Service description

The definition and documentation related to running projects in a consistent manner.

What the service provides for the customer

This provides the project, program and portfolio manager and their teams ways of running projects or programs in a consistent manner. Where multiple methodologies are available the PMO will provide a way of helping the selection.

Why is this service being offered to the customer?

Having standards to run projects and programs against provides consistency and professionalism in the way the organization approaches their delivery. It gives greater control and allows the organization to understand the effectiveness of the deliver allowing them to intervene early should the delivery being going out of tolerance.

How PMO will apply this service

The PMO will review the sorts of projects and programs the organization is running and wants to run. They will look and see what the current good practice standards are available to run projects, programs, and portfolios. They may get external expertise in to see how this is organized in other companies. If there is an existing framework, they will have a look at this. They will have a look at the feedback coming out of the lessons learned reviews.

Based on all the research they have done and talking to the people who are running the projects and programs they will start to put together a framework. This framework will have:

- Processes - A set of high-level activities that together performs a recognizable function within an organization. Defines what needs to be done to perform that function
- Procedures - A detailed step-by-step description of how to perform a particular activity within a process
- Checklists - Used to help practitioners and project managers ensure that all appropriate activities have been carried out (and if not, why not)
- Templates - Document skeletons that must be used when building the process or project deliverables
- Help - Help files/documents, Frequently Asked Questions (FAQs) or reference materials for guidance
- Standards - Mandatory requirements employed and enforced to prescribe a disciplined uniform approach to process usage

Once the framework is defined the PMO will need to train the people in its use. They will identify and organize training for the people needing it. When the framework is updated the PMO will send out a communication to all the people using the framework explaining the changes made. The PMO should be prepared to update any training material they have and give detailed training for new users.

Supplier	Input	Process	Output	Customer
PMO	PPM good practice Standards Template Current PPM framework	Develop Standard Develop Templates	PPM process, procedure, standards, checklists, templates, and help	Project team Program team Portfolio team PMO

How the PMO will measure the value of this service

The PMO can measure this by seeing how many comments come back as part of the lessons learned process about the effectiveness of the framework. These can be reviewed as the effectiveness of the framework as opposed the understanding of the framework.

Criteria when the PMO will use this service

- When the organization wants to adopt a new method
- On a regular basis as part of the continuous improvement cycle to incorporate feedback from practitioners
- When there is no consistently used method and the organization is looking to drive consistency

Helpful hints for the PMO when delivering the service

- Consider how the framework will be trained out. If the methodology is tailored too much from the standard guidance it will mean developing bespoke training
- Do you need a 'light' version of the methodology for smaller pieces of work?
- Consider having a way that anyone can suggest improvements/changes to the framework
- Put the framework in a centralized location and encourage all users to check for the latest copy of the templates prior to use
- Ensure the framework is under configuration management in order that the latest versions of artefacts can be identified

PMO Capabilities needed to fulfil this service

Competencies	Techniques and generic tools
Reporting, Insights and Analysis Governance Frameworks Professionalism and ethics Personal Communication Relationships and engagement Teamwork	Communication requirements analysis Risk Register Probability and impact matrix Stakeholder checklist Stakeholder engagement assessment matrix Swim-lane flowcharts Task responsibility matrix/RACI

Related services

Develop and maintain tailoring guidelines for standards, methods, and approaches Define, maintain, and implement PPM governance framework Develop benefits management framework Create Change Management Framework Communicate change management framework Define, maintain, and implement reporting framework Tailor standard processes and template to the program or project	Define planning standards and templates Advise Sponsors and Management Boards of appropriate frameworks and governance models Manage the Process Improvement Plan Develop and maintain the overall Quality Control Framework Provide guidance on quality criteria, reviewers, and sign-off authority to ensure consistency Establish and maintain the intranet site or information portal Automate Processes Map key value streams and processes

Further Reading

PMI PMBoK (A Guide to the Project Management Body of Knowledge)
PRINCE2
PRINCE2 Agile
AgilePM, AgilePGM, AgilePFM
Managing Successful Programmes (MSP)
Scrum
Management of Portfolios (MoP)
APM BoK
Praxis
ITIL

Define, maintain, and implement reporting framework

Service description

The development of a standard way of reporting progress on projects and programs to allow the portfolio rollup reporting to happen consistently. It should include a definition of what the source of the data is to be used for the rollup reports and whose responsibility it is to provide it. This will include the standard definitions for any indicators used e.g. RAG Status.

What the service provides for the customer

It provides a template for the progress report and definitions for RAG statuses.

Why is this service being offered to the customer?

As the custodians of the PPM and governance frameworks the PMO are ideally placed to define the reporting framework. The PMO are asked to produce standard collated reports and therefore need to be able to define the data they will need to include in those reports.

How PMO will apply this service

The PMO will look at the governance, PPM, and change frameworks. They will look at the consolidated reporting they are asked to produce before looking at designing a reporting framework.

As part of the framework the PMO should consider putting together a reporting flowchart to show where the information comes from and who it goes to. Often the individuals filling in the report may not be aware of this and making them aware may help improve the quality of the information that is contained in the report.

The PMO will produce a report template, if using a tool, they may provide screens for data capture and have a report which is produced from the data within the tool. The PMO need to provide a worked example of the template explaining what information is required and what detail is needed. If the information in the report is coming from other sources e.g. risk registers, then the PMO need to ensure that this works consistently, and the data can be easily copied or imported without requiring reformatting.

The PMO need to provide standard definitions of data used within the report e.g. RAG status. These need to be clearly defined and easy to calculate and interpret.

Once the PMO has the source report template produced they need to look at all the reports that are expected to come from the source report. Is all the information available, will the report template need to be revised to incorporate these details, or should the destination report be changed to use different information?

The PMO need to provide a timetable which shows when the reports are required and when summary reports are available.

When the reporting framework has been designed then the PMO will need to communicate this to the report providers and to the report recipients.

Supplier	Input	Process	Output	Customer
PMO	PPM Governance Framework PPM Delivery Framework Change management framework	Develop Standard Develop Templates	Reporting templates Traffic light definitions Reporting timetable	PPM Managers Senior Management Governance Boards PMO

How the PMO will measure the value of this service

The PMO can measure this by how easy it is to perform the collated reporting for a program or portfolio.

Criteria when the PMO will use this service

- When there is no reporting framework existing
- As part of year end
- When there have been changes to the Governance Framework
- When there is feedback about the effectiveness of the reporting framework

Helpful hints for the PMO when delivering the service

- Link the use of any PPM tool into the reporting framework
- Consider when developing the traffic light definitions what additional colours are required e.g. Orange/Yellow rather than Amber. Blue for completed, Grey for unavailable, Black for worse than Red
- Are the traffic light colours calculated?
- Will the overall RAG status be derived from the individual statuses or independently assessed?
- Will there need to be different templates dependent on different project types/sizes
- It is easier to remember if the reports are required on the same day each week/month

PMO Capabilities needed to fulfil this service

Competencies	Techniques and generic tools
Reporting, Insights and Analysis Governance Frameworks P3M Tools Professionalism and ethics Personal Communication Relationships and engagement Teamwork	Communication requirements analysis Categorized frequency analysis (Frequency plot, bar chart) Scheduling tool Stakeholder checklist Stakeholder engagement assessment matrix Time series plots

Related services

Define, maintain, and implement PPM governance framework Define, maintain, and implement standard PPM framework Create Change Management Framework Develops in-house project management tools Tailors and configures project management tools Automate Processes	Implements vendor provided project management tools Collate individual progress reports Combine individual progress reports Set up and track portfolio, program, and project metrics (KPI's) Manage the Process Improvement Plan Provision of Management Dashboards Map key value streams and processes

Define, maintain, and implement framework for monitoring and review

Service description

The development of a framework for the monitoring and review of projects and programs within a portfolio. This will provide circumstances under which projects or programs will be monitored, advice on how this can be done and checklists to confirm this is done consistently.

What the service provides for the customer

This means that the project or program manager knows what to expect when they go through a gate review or a project audit. They will know under what circumstances they are likely to receive a review. They will know the purpose of the review in advance.

Why is this service being offered to the customer?

To ensure the monitoring and review is done in a consistent manner and defined frequencies with a defined outcome a process for doing a review needs to be developed along with a timetable of when the reviews will happen, how to select items for review and a checklist to evidence that the check has happened along with a standard template for recording the recommendations and actions.

How PMO will apply this service

The PMO will speak to the portfolio manager and to the senior management (executive) and work out what their requirements are for projects to be reviewed. They will agree the circumstances by which projects can be selected for review and the level of detail the review can take.

The PMO will come up with some detailed review criteria (how are projects selected for review). They will publish a list of projects that are going to be reviewed.

The PMO will consult the PPM framework and the governance framework to enable them to create the checklist of items to review. These checks may include talking to the people on the project and finding out from them any issues that are concerning them.

Each review may result in items being found and actions needing to be taken. As part of the process the PMO will cover how these actions can be followed up and any remaining non-conformance dealt with.

Supplier	Input	Process	Output	Customer
PMO Executive Portfolio Manager	Standards template Monitoring requirements	Develop Standard Develop Templates	Monitoring and review process Monitoring and review template Monitoring and review checklist Monitoring and review timetable	PMO Project Manager Program Manager Portfolio Manager

How the PMO will measure the value of this service

The PMO can measure this by seeing how many reviews are done and the outcome of those reviews. Has it led to an improvement in the way projects are run?

Criteria when the PMO will use this service

- When there is a need for a regular review of projects
- Where consistency is needed in the review process

Helpful hints for the PMO when delivering the service

- Train the PMO staff in the use of the process
- Advertise the review timetable to allow the project or program manager to prepare. The aim is to get the project or program delivered not blame individuals. Do not make it personal
- The PMO may decide to perform a light review of all projects or a detailed review of a select number of projects. They may decide to do both

PMO Capabilities needed to fulfil this service

Competencies	Techniques and generic tools
Reporting, Insights and Analysis Assurance Governance Frameworks Professionalism and ethics Personal Communication Relationships and engagement Teamwork	Cost/ Benefit Analysis Benefit realization analysis Cash flow analysis Communication requirements analysis Stakeholder checklist Stakeholder engagement assessment matrix

Related services

Provide project and program health checks Provide project and program audits Provide project and program assurance checks Provide a Stage Gate Review or Gateway support service	Advise on program or project assurance services Manage the Process Improvement Plan Develop and maintain the overall Quality Assurance Framework Map key value streams and processes

Develop and maintain tailoring guidelines for standards, methods, and approaches

Service description

The provision of some standard/typical ways of tailoring the PPM framework.

What the service provides for the customer

This provides some suggestions of how the PPM framework might work as applied to this project or program.

Why is this service being offered to the customer?

As every project is unique the standards need to be tailored to the specific project being run. The PMO to provide some guidelines, tailoring patterns based on the sorts of projects being run to enable the project or program manager to adapt the standards to ensure they are effective for their project.

How PMO will apply this service

The PMO will look at the PPM framework and at the types of projects and programs run in the organization. They will review the lessons learned to see how other projects and programs have used the framework and have adapted it. From this the PMO will look to provide a set of typical project styles and show how the PPM framework can work for each of these styles. The PMO will then publish this as part of the PPM framework.

Supplier	Input	Process	Output	Customer
PMO	PPM Framework	Tailoring	Tailored PPM Framework Tailoring pattern	Project Managers Program Managers PMO

How the PMO will measure the value of this service

When projects are reviewed it can be ascertained as to whether the tailoring pattern fits the way the project is trying to deliver.

Criteria when the PMO will use this service

- When there is a PPM framework in place

Helpful hints for the PMO when delivering the service

- Use the feedback from the lessons learned to work out suitable tailoring patterns
- This will not cover all the possible permutations, but will cover common project types e.g. small projects, process only projects

PMO Capabilities needed to fulfil this service

Competencies	Techniques and generic tools
Assurance Delivery Methods Governance Frameworks	Process Analysis Prompt Lists Check sheets

Related services

Define, maintain, and implement standard PPM framework Tailor standard processes and template to the program or project Define, maintain, and implement PPM governance framework Program or project fast-track mobilization service	Develop benefits management framework Recommend ways to reduce or shorten project lifecycle times Advise Sponsors and Management Boards of appropriate frameworks and governance models Provide guidance on quality criteria, reviewers, and sign-off authority to ensure consistency Map key value streams and processes

Method Operations

Service group description

The application and adoption of the standard methodology to a single project or program.

Why have these services been grouped together?

These services relate to the application of the methodology to an active project or program.

List of related services described in other area

Provide guidance on how the governance framework can be tailored

Responsibility Assignment Matrix

Service	Executive	Portfolio Manager	Program Manager	Project Manager	PMO	Sponsor	Other Stakeholder
Tailor standard processes and template to the program or project		A	A	A	R	I	I (PPM Team)

Helpful hints for when the PMO is delivering this service group

Where possible use the tailoring guidelines to assist with how the standard methodology can be aligned to a particular project or program. Although all projects are different they can be delivered within a framework.

Tailor standard processes and template to the program or project

Service description

The provision of consultancy to enable the project or program manager to tailor the PPM framework for this project or program.

What the service provides for the customer

A tailored PPM framework with guidance that allows the project or program to achieve, retaining control, without tying the change up with unnecessary governance.

Why is this service being offered to the customer?

As the PMO have created the PPM Framework and the standard tailoring guidelines they will be best positioned to offer advice as to how to tailor the framework for this project.

How PMO will apply this service

The PMO will look at the PPM framework and the standard tailoring guidelines. They will speak to the project or program manager to find out about their project or program. They will then discuss what the is proposed to be delivered for this project or program.

If the PMO feel that there are additional items required, they will suggest those to the project or program manager along with the reasonings for that choice. If the PMO feels that there are extra items that may not be required or could be combined, then the PMO will suggest those along with the reasoning for this.

The PMO and the project/program manager will agree a list of deliverables and the governance structure and that can then be baselined and put under change control.

Supplier	Input	Process	Output	Customer
PMO	PPM process, procedure, standards, checklists, templates, and help Tailored PPM Framework	Tailoring	Tailored PPM Framework	Project Managers Program Managers PPM Team

How the PMO will measure the value of this service

The PMO can measure this by seeking feedback from the project or program manager. They can measure this by looking at the lessons learned and seeing whether the framework was appropriately tailored.

Criteria when the PMO will use this service

- When there is a PPM framework in place
- As part of setting up a project or program
- When they are asked for advice by the project or program manager

Helpful hints for the PMO when delivering the service

- Look to review the standard tailoring guidelines. If there is a new tailoring option, then look to revise the standard tailoring guidelines to add in this option
- Discuss the proposed framework with the project or program manager so they understand why something needs to be included/excluded. Some items in the framework are mandatory e.g. a Business Case
- Be open and flexible about how the items in the framework can be achievec. E.g. a scoping statement does not have to be in the prescribed format, but one will be required
- Have a deliverable tailoring list so you can quickly review which deliverables will be produced and see if there are any gaps
- Use the baselined deliverables list as input to any gate review to confirm what should have been delivered has been delivered

PMO Capabilities needed to fulfil this service

Competencies	Techniques and generic tools
Assurance Delivery Methods Governance Frameworks Personal Communication Relationships and engagement Resourcefulness Negotiation Result Orientation	Process Analysis Risk Register Probability and impact matrix

Related services

Define, maintain, and implement standard PPM framework Develop and maintain tailoring guidelines for standards, methods, and approaches Promote good PPM within the organization Automate Processes	Program or project fast-track mobilization service Define, maintain, and implement PPM governance framework Recommend ways to reduce or shorten project lifecycle times

People Development

People Development

Description

People Development is about the development of individuals with the PMO and providing them a structured career path to follow.

What the services within the domain provide for the customer

These services provide the individuals working within the PMO, and prospective PMO people a structured career path to follow.

Helpful hints for when the PMO is delivering this service domain

- Look to link up with training providers to provide a standard suite of course to improve the individuals within the team
- Do not forget that training will cover the softer skills as well as the technical skills
- Link up with industry bodies to utilise their capability frameworks

People Development Design

Service group description

The setup of PMO competency frameworks and career paths for those people within a PMO or wanting to be in a PMO.

Why have these services been grouped together?

These relate to the setup of the PMO career and people structure.

Responsibility Assignment Matrix

Service	Executive	Portfolio Manager	Program Manager	Project Manager	PMO	Sponsor	Other Stakeholder
Create and maintain PMO career paths					A, R		
Develop and maintain PMO role profiles					A, R		C (HR)
Develop and maintain a PMO competence framework					A, R		C (HR)

Helpful hints for when the PMO is delivering this service group

When developing this information look to tie in with the role profiles, framework, and career paths of the project management community.

Look to align these to the maturity of the organization, allowing room for growth.

Create and maintain PMO career paths

Service description

The creation of a career path for PMO people. This shows the route an individual can take from junior to senior PMO roles. It will show the cross over to and from related roles e.g. Project Manager, Business Analyst.

What the service provides for the customer

This provides the members of the PMO team with an understanding of where they can go to in their careers and the means by which this can be done.

Why is this service being offered to the customer?

By having a career path, it allows the individuals within the PMO to develop. It promotes the PMO as a profession. It provides a path to move individuals up into senior roles.

How PMO will apply this service

The PMO will find the role profiles for all the PMO roles. They will show this as a hierarchy, moving from junior to senior roles. They will show what the related roles are for each of the other professions e.g. project management, business analysts. They will show what needs to be done to move from one role to the next.

As well as the list of roles and the capability requirements there needs to be advice on how to get the necessary training and experience to move into one of the new roles.

Once the career paths have been built then they need to be publicized, not only within the PMO, but within the related roles.

Supplier	Input	Process	Output	Customer
PMO HR	PMO Role Profiles	Develop career path	PMO Career Path	PMO

How the PMO will measure the value of this service

This can be measured by the numbers of people using the career path to move on in the organization.

Criteria when the PMO will use this service

- When there is more than one person performing a PMO role
- Where there are teams of PMO people
- Where the PMO has a desire to improve the individuals within it

Helpful hints for the PMO when delivering the service

- Ensure you consider the overlaps with other related roles e.g. project management, business analysis, testing, administrators
- Ensure the linkages with other roles come in and go out. Allow for sideways moves as well as upwards moves
- If there is a competency framework then that can be used to show what the differences are between the roles as differences in the ability level for each of the relevant competencies
- If there are specialist roles, then they should be shown on the relevant level with a view how those roles can be moved to/from
- Whenever there are new roles created then the PMO career path will need to be revised

PMO Capabilities needed to fulfil this service

Competencies	Techniques and generic tools
Skills development PMO Management People/ Line Management Professionalism and ethics Relationships and engagement Leadership	Capability and Capacity analysis Flowcharts Hierarchical charts Organization charts & position descriptions Swim-lane flowcharts

Related services

Develop and maintain PMO role profiles Develop and maintain a PMO competence framework Ensure Continuing Professional Development of the PMO team Assess PMOs against a Competence Framework Develop individuals within the PMO team Assist in the recruitment and evaluation of PMO team members	Ensure HR practices and procedures are aligned to Define strategy for acquiring and developing skills Provide standard role descriptions for PPM staff Develop and maintain a PM Competence Framework Perform mentoring and coaching of PMO staff

Develop and maintain PMO role profiles

Service description

The writing of role profiles for all PMO individuals.

What the service provides for the customer

This ensures there is consistency in what is expected from people performing the role. These role descriptions can then be used to recruit individuals to those roles. These roles can be used as part of the PMO career path.

Why is this service being offered to the customer?

Each PMO individual needs to understand what is expected of them within the role. Having standard role profiles allows for guidelines as to the possible breadth and depth of the role.

How PMO will apply this service

The PMO will speak with HR to find the standard role description template. They will work out what the required roles are to be developed from junior to senior including any specialist roles within those levels e.g. planning risk. The PMO will examine the good practice manuals to see if they can find an example job description for each of the roles.

The PMO will work out what technical skills, behaviours, soft skills, and training requirements are needed for the role. The PMO will write up the role description using the template provided.

Once they are happy that the role covers what people do then the PMO will send the role to HR for assessment. Once the assessment has been done and the role is signed off by HR, then the PMO can circulate this as required. They can make this available for when people are being recruited into the role.

Supplier	Input	Process	Output	Customer
HR	Role description template	Writing role descriptions	Role description	PMO Staff

How the PMO will measure the value of this service

This can be measured by evaluating the individuals performing those roles against the role profiles. It can be measured by the ability to recruit individuals into the PMO using the role profiles.

Criteria when the PMO will use this service

- If there are no standard role profiles written
- If a role profile is needed to recruit new individuals
- Where a role profile is needed to create a PMO career path
- Where there is more than one person performing a PMO role in the organization

Helpful hints for the PMO when delivering the service

- Use the external contacts the PMO has, to see if you can find examples from other organizations
- Use job boards to see what other companies include in job role descriptions
- Do not get involved in job grading. Leave that to HR

PMO Capabilities needed to fulfil this service

Competencies	Techniques and generic tools
Capability Development PMO Management Relationships and engagement Leadership	Organization charts & position descriptions

Related services

Create and maintain PMO career paths Develop and maintain a PMO competence framework Provide standard role descriptions for PPM staff Ensure HR practices and procedures are aligned to	Develops PMO team objectives and ways of working with the team Assist in the recruitment and evaluation of PMO team members Assess PMOs against a Competence Framework

Further Reading

P3O Manual

Develop and maintain a PMO competence framework

Service description

The creation and maintenance of a competence framework for PMO individuals.

What the service provides for the customer

A framework to allow an objective assessment of PMO individuals. This will cover knowledge as well as experience. It covers personal, process and technical skill areas.

Why is this service being offered to the customer?

Having a competence framework allows the organization and the individuals to assess how good they are at performing their role. Having the standard to evaluate against means it become and objective assessment rather than a subjective one. By seeing where an individual's strengths and weaknesses allows for training to be targeted. It allows for assignments to fit the individual's strengths and development needs.

How PMO will apply this service

The PMO will obtain a copy of the PMO role profiles for all the PMO roles. They will find and evaluate the different external competence frameworks to see which one is best aligned to the organization.

For each of the roles the PMO will align them with the competence levels so it is clear what level of competence is required to perform at each of the levels. If there are any competencies that are deemed as missing (e.g. behavioural ones) then the PMO should look to add those in and provide some definitions for each of the levels.

Once the framework has been produced then the PMO can assess the PMO individuals against the framework.

Supplier	Input	Process	Output	Customer
Professional organizations PMO/HR	External competence frameworks Role profiles PMO career path	Develop competence framework	PMO Competence framework	PMO HR

How the PMO will measure the value of this service

This can be measured by being able to evaluate the PMO to target training and assignments. It can be measured by the number of times the framework is used as part of a PMO career path to improve individuals within the PMO.

Criteria when the PMO will use this service

- Where there is a desire to assess the PMO individuals against a skills benchmark
- Where the PMO has a desire to improve the knowledge and experience of the individuals within the PMO

Helpful hints for the PMO when delivering the service

- If possible, look to take an existing framework rather than create from scratch
- Align the framework chosen to the organization. This can include providing scoring for the organizational behaviours
- Link into the role profiles in order that it is clear what levels people need to be to perform each role
- This links into career development
- Provide a link to training in order that people can see what they can do to improve either their knowledge or their experience

PMO Capabilities needed to fulfil this service

Competencies	Techniques and generic tools
Capability Development PMO Management Leadership Result Orientation	Capability and Capacity analysis Check sheets

Related services

Create and maintain PMO career paths Develop and maintain PMO role profiles Assess PMOs against a Competence Framework Develop individuals within the PMO team	Ensure Continuing Professional Development of the PMO team Develop and maintain a PM Competence Framework Ensure HR practices and procedures are aligned to

People Development Operations

Service group description

These services relate to the development of the individuals within the PMO.

Why have these services been grouped together?

These relate to the recruitment, evaluation, and development of individuals within the PMO.

List of related services described in other areas

Provide succession planning service for key roles
Organize buddy relationships and secondments
Identify skills shortages and recommend suitable development

Responsibility Assignment Matrix

Service	Executive	Portfolio Manager	Program Manager	Project Manager	PMO	Sponsor	Other Stakeholder
Perform mentoring and coaching of PMO staff					A, R		
Ensure Continuing Professional Development of the PMO team					A, R		
Assess PMOs against a Competence Framework					A, R		
Develop individuals within the PMO team					A, R		
Monitors the performance of individual team members and the team as a whole		C	C	C	A, R		
Assist in the recruitment and evaluation of PMO team members		C	C	C	A, R		

Helpful hints for when the PMO is delivering this service group

- If individuals within the PMO team are not developing, then there is the potential that the PMO will stagnate. PMOs should look to evolve and develop in line (or just ahead) of the organization's PPM maturity level

Perform mentoring and coaching of PMO staff

Service description

Provide coaching for PMO individuals in order they can improve their knowledge. Provide a mentor for PMO individuals to enable professional growth.

What the service provides for the customer

This provides mechanisms for the individuals within the PMO to improve their capabilities.

Why is this service being offered to the customer?

To develop more junior individuals within the PMO they may need to be mentored and/or coached by more senior individuals within the PMO.

How PMO will apply this service

The PMO Manager will work with the individuals within the team to work out the need for coaching or mentoring.

If the individual requires a mentor, then the PMO manager will either perform this role themselves or will find one of their peers to be a mentor. The individual will then set up time with the mentor. They will discuss how long they want the mentor/mentee relationship to be. The individual will then look to drive those session to ensure they get the best out of them.

If the individual requires coaching, then the PMO manager will focus on one or two issues which require coaching. They will book the initial session with the individual and agree how many and how frequent the subsequent sessions will be.

In the coaching session the individual may ask open questions such as 'How can I get better at identifying and mitigating risks'. The PMO can then dig into the responses to assist the individual with understanding how they can best approach the subject. They can provide the individual being coached with some examples and ideas to follow up on.

Supplier	Input	Process	Output	Customer
PMO	Capability Assessment gaps	Mentoring Coaching	Mentoring Sessions Coaching Sessions	PMO

How the PMO will measure the value of this service

This can be measured by an improvement in the individual's capability assessment.

Criteria when the PMO will use this service

- When the PMO individuals are looking to improve their knowledge
- When there is more than one individual within the PMO

Helpful hints for the PMO when delivering the service

- A mentor does not necessarily need to be from within the PMO but could be another individual within the organization. It could even be someone outside the organization who could perform a mentoring role
- For the mentoring to work both individuals need to be committed to the sessions

PMO Capabilities needed to fulfil this service

Competencies	Techniques and generic tools
Capability Development PMO Management Professionalism and ethics Personal Integrity and reliability Personal Communication Relationships and engagement Leadership	Capability and Capacity analysis

Related services

Perform coaching of portfolio, program, or project managers Ensure Continuing Professional Development of the PMO team Create and maintain PMO career paths	Assess PMOs against a Competence Framework Develop individuals within the PMO team

Ensure Continuing Professional Development of the PMO team

Service description

Ensure that each PMO team member has a professional development plan and follows it.

What the service provides for the customer

Learning is not just about attending training courses, but can cover reading, presenting, sharing knowledge, volunteering, informal learning. As a professional the individuals within the PMO should strive to continually improve themselves over the course of their career.

Why is this service being offered to the customer?

To be considered a professional a PMO should commit to performing the equivalent of a week's work of Continuing Professional Development (CPD) per year. By developing themselves individuals within the PMO then will have more to offer the people they are supporting.

How PMO will apply this service

The individuals within the PMO will assess themselves against the PMO competency framework to understand their areas for improvement. For permanent members of staff, they may have a career development plan as part of their annual review.

Having worked out where the gaps are, and where their strengths are each individual should see how they can improve their weaknesses and share their areas of strength with others.

Each person should look to create a CPD plan. This should not focus solely on one area, but can include:

- Formal training – e.g. courses, workshops, conferences
- Work based learning – e.g. job shadowing, secondments, acting up
- Self-directed learning – e.g. reading articles/journals/blogs, contributing to online groups, reviewing books
- Professional activity – e.g. being a mentor, giving training, giving presentations at conferences
- Voluntary work – e.g. involvement in a professional body, performing the role for a volunteer organization

Having decided which items are suitable the individual should record these in a CPD log to provide evidence of the development obtained.

As part of any regular career discussion between the PMO manager and their team members they can review the CPD log and the PMO manager may offer advice or suggestions on how to further develop the individual.

Supplier	Input	Process	Output	Customer
PMO	Capability Assessment Career Development plan	Develop staff	Continual Professional Development Log	PMO

How the PMO will measure the value of this service

This can be measured by the numbers of individuals who complete the requisite number of CPD hours in the year. It can be measured in the increase in the capability of the individuals within the PMO.

Criteria when the PMO will use this service

- Where the PMO individual is serious about being professional
- Where the PMO is a member of a professional organization that requires CPD
- Where the PMO individual is looking to improve their capabilities

Helpful hints for the PMO when delivering the service

- Generally speaking, each hour spent on self-development is worth one hour of CPD
- Some training organizations and websites offer the ability to obtain Professional Development Units (PDUs) to make it easier to record in the CPD log
- Do not force the individuals to maintain a log if they do not see the need. The drive for training has to come from the individual themselves

PMO Capabilities needed to fulfil this service

Competencies	Techniques and generic tools
Knowledge Management Capability Development PMO Management Professionalism and ethics Self-reflection and self-management Personal Integrity and reliability Leadership	Gap analysis Capability and Capacity analysis

Related services

Create and maintain PMO career paths Assess PMOs against a Competence Framework Develop individuals within the PMO team Monitors the performance of individual team members and the team as a whole Provides leadership for the PMO team Sustains an environment that encourages high performance and empowers team members	Define strategy for acquiring and developing skills Provide PPM training Provide training logistics support External networking attendance at good practice events Develop external relationships to share lessons and experience Develop and maintain a PMO competence framework Perform mentoring and coaching of PMO staff

Assess PMOs against a Competence Framework

Service description

The assessment of PMO individuals against the PMO competence framework.

What the service provides for the customer

This provides an objective assessment of the skills experience and knowledge of individuals performing a PMO role. By assessing this against their role profile, improvements can therefore be suggested to what the individual may do to improve the knowledge and experience move through to the next role or perform the current role better.

Why is this service being offered to the customer?

By performing the assessment, it allows the individual to work out what their strengths and weaknesses will be. That information can then be used to provide a training plan for that individual.

How PMO will apply this service

The PMO will find the latest copy of the PMO competence framework. They will book time with the person being assessed and go through the questions within the framework. They will find examples of where the individual has delivered the competence or skill. They will assign a score for each of the elements of the framework and this will lead to an overall score.

Based on the assessment the PMO to look at the role profile for the individual and the role profile for the role they want to achieve. They will suggest improvements in the knowledge or experience they have for each of the skills in the framework to allow them to deliver their desired role.

Supplier	Input	Process	Output	Customer
PMO	PMO competence framework	Perform competence assessment	Assessment scoring Suggestions for further development	PMO Training department

How the PMO will measure the value of this service

This can be measured by the number of project managers being assessed.

Criteria when the PMO will use this service

- Where there is a PMO competence framework
- Where the PMO desire to improve the capabilities of the individuals within the team
- Where an individual has a Continuing Professional Development plan

Helpful hints for the PMO when delivering the service

- Look for examples of where the skills have been used or learnt
- Be realistic with the assessment, do not over or under rate individuals based on what they want to do. Be objective and list what the individual can (and cannot) do

PMO Capabilities needed to fulfil this service

Competencies	Techniques and generic tools
Reporting, Insights and Analysis Capability Development PMO Management Professionalism and ethics Relationships and engagement Leadership Negotiation	Check sheets

Related services

Develop and maintain a PMO competence framework Ensure Continuing Professional Development of the PMO team Monitors the performance of individual team members and the team as a whole Provides leadership for the PMO team Develop and maintain PMO role profiles	Define strategy for acquiring and developing skills Develop and maintain a PM Competence Framework Create and maintain PMO career paths Perform mentoring and coaching of PMO staff Develop individuals within the PMO team

Develop individuals within the PMO team

Service description

Provide a development plan for individuals within the PMO team.

What the service provides for the customer

This provides a series of development opportunities to enable the PMO team member to grow as an individual and add more value into the PMO services they offer. It provides the PMO manager with more engaged staff.

Why is this service being offered to the customer?

The PMO manager has a responsibility to develop individuals within the team in order that they can improve the service their deliver their customers. This should address the requirements, circumstances and interests of team members whilst balancing individual needs with those of the team as a whole.

How PMO will apply this service

The PMO will find a copy of the role profile for the individual, the PMO career path, the individual's current objectives and their competency assessment. The PMO will book some time with the individual to discuss where they want to go in the short to medium term (next 3 years). They will listen to what the individual wants and balance that off against the requirements for the team as a whole and the other individuals.

Based on the discussion the PMO Manager will suggest items that the individual may consider adding to their Continuing Professional Development (CPD) plan. Between them they will work out the best time for these suggestions to be enacted. This may include secondments and job shadowing as well as formal training options.

At the next review session, the PMO Manager and the individual will look back and reflect on how well the CPD has helped the individual to progress towards their goals. They will revise the CPD plan to enable the individual to meet their short to medium term goals.

Supplier	Input	Process	Output	Customer
PMO	Competency assessment Role profile Career path Objectives	Develop team member	Continuing Professional Development plan	PMO

How the PMO will measure the value of this service

This can be measured by looking at how successful the individual has been in meeting their goals. It can be measured by looking at the competency assessment improvements. It can be measured by asking for feedback from the individual being developed.

Criteria when the PMO will use this service

- When there is more than one person in the PMO
- Where the PMO Manager has line management responsibilities for PMO staff
- Where there are permanent members of staff in the PMO team

Helpful hints for the PMO when delivering the service

- It could be that the individual is happy in their role and requires no further development
- This is normally done as part of a permanent member of staff's performance review
- The CPD plan should be revisited at least every 6 months

PMO Capabilities needed to fulfil this service

Competencies	Techniques and generic tools
Capability Development PMO Management Professionalism and ethics Relationships and engagement Leadership	Capability and Capacity analysis

Related services

Assess PMOs against a Competence Framework Ensure Continuing Professional Development of the PMO team Perform mentoring and coaching of PMO staff Monitors the performance of individual team members and the team as a whole Provides leadership for the PMO team Develops PMO team objectives and ways of working with the team Sustains an environment that encourages high performance and empowers team members	Provide PPM training Identify skills shortages and recommend suitable development Define strategy for acquiring and developing skills Create and maintain PMO career paths Develop and maintain a PMO competence framework Encourages an open discussion to address challenges Consistently models desirable behaviours

Monitors the performance of individual team members and the team as a whole

Service description

The monitoring and review of the performance of individuals within the PMO team.

What the service provides for the customer

This provides feedback on how the individuals within the PMO are performing their role. This feedback will come from the PMO Manager, other PMO team members and the individuals they are working with on a regular basis.

Why is this service being offered to the customer?

The PMO can have a difficult message to give, especially when things are not going well. However, the way that that message is given is important. By getting feedback on how the individuals within the team are performing allows the individuals to improve the way they are providing the services.

How PMO will apply this service

The PMO individual will ask for feedback from a range of stakeholders. This will include customers, team members and their direct boss. This feedback will be shared with the PMO Manager.

Based on the feedback the PMO Manager may put the individual forward for an award (if the feedback has been particularly great).

If the feedback has been poor, then the PMO Manager will need to provide some detailed suggestions for improvement. These suggestions will be discussed with the individual concerned and an action plan devised on how performance can be improved. The PMO Manager (and the individual) will then review progress against the plan to track improvements.

Supplier	Input	Process	Output	Customer
PMO team PPM Managers PPM team HR Finance Procurement	Feedback	Monitor performance	Rewards Performance improvement suggestions	PMO individuals

How the PMO will measure the value of this service

This can be measured by seeing an improvement in performance. It can be measured by the accolades that are received by individuals within the PMO.

Criteria when the PMO will use this service

- As part of the annual performance review of permanent members of staff
- When a project or program ends and the PMO is reassigned to a new role
- When the PMO member has done something praiseworthy
- If there are disciplinary issues

Helpful hints for the PMO when delivering the service

- It is important to get views from the people that the PMO works with regularly as they see how the PMO is delivering the service on a regular basis
- By getting views from multiple people, reduces the effect of bias in the reviews
- As for feedback from those people who have been critical as well as helpful to get a rounded view of performance
- Feedback may be sought by the PMO Manager on behalf of the PMO individual
- Never offer feedback indirectly, always share the feedback with the individual concerned
- Consider monitoring performance on a regular (monthly) basis, rather than just as part of an annual performance review cycle
- Feedback should cover how the person is delivering the service as well as what services the person is delivering

PMO Capabilities needed to fulfil this service

Competencies	Techniques and generic tools
PMO Management Professionalism and ethics Self-reflection and self-management Personal Integrity and reliability Personal Communication Relationships and engagement Leadership Conflict and Crisis	Capability and Capacity analysis

Related services

Develop individuals within the PMO team Sets PMO team targets Provides leadership for the PMO team Develops PMO team objectives and ways of working with the team Sustains an environment that encourages high performance and empowers team members	Encourages an open discussion to address challenges Consistently models desirable behaviours Measure PMO performance Ensure Continuing Professional Development of the PMO team Assess PMOs against a Competence Framework

Assist in the recruitment and evaluation of PMO team members

Service description

The recruitment of individuals, both permanent and temporary to be members of the PMO team.

What the service provides for the customer

This provides individuals who will work within the PMO. By being involved in the recruitment the PMO Manager can ensure the individuals recruited not only are capable of performing the role but have a good fit to the culture of the organization they will be working within.

Why is this service being offered to the customer?

This ensures the correct people are recruited into the PMO team. The people recruited need to have the correct fit for now and where the PMO is going.

How PMO will apply this service

The PMO Manager will write up a job specification based on the role profile of the role being recruited. They will work with HR to get the role advertised. When the CVs arrive the PMO Manager will review these against the job specification and reduce them down to a short list of candidates. The PMO Manager may decide to conduct a telephone interview to reduce this list down further.

When the PMO Manager has a list of candidates they wish to interview they will contact the individuals concerned and invite them for a face-to-face interview. The PMO Manager may decide to include a scenario, an assessment centre, competency-based questions within the interview process.

Following the interview, the PMO Manager will select a candidate. If none of the candidates was deemed to be good enough for the role then they will need to repeat this service until they do get a suitable person. The PMO Manager will contact the successful candidate and arrange a suitable time for them to start in the role.

Supplier	Input	Process	Output	Customer
External Candidates HR	Job specification CVs Skills questionnaires Assessment centre packs	Interviewing	Selected PMO Staff	PMO Manager

How the PMO will measure the value of this service

This can be measured by getting good feedback on the new recruits from existing team members and the customers of the PMO.

Criteria when the PMO will use this service

- When new PMO people are required

Helpful hints for the PMO when delivering the service

- As well as evaluating their technical skills and knowledge the PMO Manager should evaluate their people skills
- When rejecting an individual, the PMO Manager should give constructive feedback on why the individual was unsuccessful
- After selecting the person to join the PMO Manager should ensure they put together a new starter induction pack so they have a plan for what the individual will do over the first 2 weeks after joining
- The PMO manager will need to ensure that equipment and logons have been requested for the new starter

PMO Capabilities needed to fulfil this service

Competencies	Techniques and generic tools
P3M Administration PMO Management Professionalism and ethics Personal Integrity and reliability Personal Communication Relationships and engagement Leadership Result Orientation	Prompt Lists Check sheets Organization charts & position descriptions

Related services

On boarding and induction Order office equipment and stationery Work with HR to provide a sourcing strategy Assist in the recruitment of program and project managers Organize buddy relationships and secondments	Develop and maintain PMO role profiles Define a process for selection of key PPM roles Create and maintain PMO career paths Set up PMO

PMO Development

PMO Development

Description

PMO Development is about setting up, maintaining, and improving the PMO.

What the services within the domain provide for the customer

These services provide the PMO manager and team with a way to improve what and how they deliver. These provide a structured way in which the PMO can develop and increase not only the breadth, but also the depth of the services they offer.

Helpful hints for when the PMO is delivering this service domain

- Unlike the other service domains this one is unusual in having the PMO as its own customer. It is focused on self-improvement
- Usage of this book will help the PMO work out what it is offering and why

PMO Design

Service group description

The design, setup, and subsequent improvement of the PMO.

Why have these services been grouped together?

These relate to the way the PMO is initially designed and subsequently improved.

Responsibility Assignment Matrix

Service	Executive	Portfolio Manager	Program Manager	Project Manager	PMO	Sponsor	Other Stakeholder
Carries out PMO benchmarking activities					A, R		
Sets PMO team targets					A, R		I (PMO Team)
Set up PMO	A				R		
PMO imitation and evolvement					A, R		
Develop PMO Operating Procedures & Workflows					A, R		

Helpful hints for when the PMO is delivering this service group

Ensure that the PMO designs itself to support the current and desired maturity of the organization in its PPM delivery.

Carries out PMO benchmarking activities

Service description

The comparison of the services offered and the perceived value of the PMO with other PMOs either internally or externally. This benchmarking can be done formally via a consultancy or informally via the PMO network.

What the service provides for the customer

A benchmark provides a view of how PMOs operate in other organizations, or in other parts of the same organization.

Why is this service being offered to the customer?

Having a benchmark allows the PMO manager to compare and contrast how their PMO is performing. With this information the PMO manager can set new PMO targets and set the direction for improvement for this PMO.

How PMO will apply this service

The PMO will decide whether they want to benchmark formally, using some external consultants or benchmark informally by contacting individuals within their external network. The PMO will decide what is the basis for the benchmark. If this is done by an external consultancy, they may be able to offer guidance as to the sensible/available options for benchmarking.

The areas for benchmarking include:

- Cost of the PMO – how much does the PMO cost as a proportion of the overall portfolio cost. This will help the PMO understand whether they are getting value for money
- PMO Maturity – how does the PMO do in the scope of the services they offer. Be aware that the PMO maturity needs to align to organizational maturity
- Individual competencies – how well do individuals in the PMO score against the competency framework
- Satisfaction levels – how well are the PMO thought of in the organization

Having worked out what they are going to benchmark and how, the PMO will ensure the benchmark occurs. The PMO manager should ensure that the same benchmark is used for their PMO in order they can compare like with like.

Once the figures have been obtained the PMO manager needs to put a plan of action in place. If this PMO is behind its peers, then the PMO manager needs to consider a plan of action to gain places in the benchmark. If this PMO is significantly ahead of its peers, then the PMO manager should think out sharing this within the organization (celebrate success) and outside the organization to share the information with their peers.

Supplier	Input	Process	Output	Customer
External consultants PMO network	Questionnaire	Benchmarking	PMO assessment	PMO Manager

How the PMO will measure the value of this service

This can be measured by looking at the improvement in the PMO services and maturity. It can be measured by looking at the increase in the PMO scores against the benchmark figures.

Criteria when the PMO will use this service

- When the PMO is looking to improve
- When the value of the PMO is being called into question
- When the PMO requires reassurance that it is doing the right things

Helpful hints for the PMO when delivering the service

- When choosing a type of benchmark have a think about what use this will be in helping your PMO improve. It is possible to assess the PMO against criteria that have no inherent value e.g. how long the PMO has existed. These will not help the PMO drive improvements
- To make the benchmarking more relevant the other PMOs should work in the same sector as this PMO
- An informal benchmark will carry less weight than a formal one. However, it may be all that is required to allow the PMO Manager to assess the progress of their PMO
- Having a benchmark is no use, unless there is an action plan resulting from this

PMO Capabilities needed to fulfil this service

Competencies	Techniques and generic tools
PMO Management Professionalism and ethics Relationships and engagement Leadership Resourcefulness	Failure Modes and Effects Analysis (FMEA) Comparative advantage analysis Market / Competitor Analysis

Related services

Develop external relationships to share lessons and experience PMO imitation and evolvement	Provides leadership for the PMO team Measure PMO performance

Further Reading

PMO Maturity cube

Sets PMO team targets

Service description

Provides targets for the PMO to deliver. The targets can be for an individual service, for the numbers of people the PMO help, the customer satisfaction score or for reaching a particular maturity level, either as an organization or just the PMO.

What the service provides for the customer

This provides a target that the PMO can then measure themselves against to see how effective they have been in delivering their plan.

Why is this service being offered to the customer?

Without having a target, it can be difficult to understand whether the PMO is achieving what is required.

How PMO will apply this service

The PMO Manager will review what behaviours they wish to drive. They will review the services that are performed. They will look at any existing targets that may be in place. They will see whether there is a need to contribute to any organizational or departmental metrics. They will review at what level they wish to set the targets. They will discuss whether they want to apply a target value and a stretch target value so the PMO have something to aim for if they achieve the normal target.

The targets could include the following areas:

- Time to deliver a service – this would be a Service Level Agreement, which can then be tracked e.g. time to setup a new project within the PPM tool
- Staff turnover – how well the PMO is doing at retaining staff
- Customer satisfaction – how happy are people with the services provided by the PMO
- Cost – this could be expenses e.g. travel or cost of the people delivering the service. These targets are normally driven by the organization
- Maturity – to drive an increase in the maturity of individuals within the PMO or of the PMO itself
- Number of services delivered – if the PMO wants to move into a new area they could look to put a target for those e.g. number of gate reviews delivered
- Recognition – if the PMO wants to make a name for themselves they could submit themselves for external (or internal) awards, either for the PMO as a whole or for individuals within the PMO

Having set and agreed the targets the PMO manager should ensure that these are communicated to the PMO team. They will need to ensure that there are measures in place to review how well the PMO is delivering against those targets and take corrective measures as necessary to keep on track.

Supplier	Input	Process	Output	Customer
Senior Management PMO	Departmental metrics PMO Service catalogue	Set PMO target	PMO targets	PMO Manager

How the PMO will measure the value of this service

This can be measured by gaining feedback about the PMO performance.

Criteria when the PMO will use this service

- When the PMO is starting out
- Where there are organizational and departmental targets to be delivered
- Where the PMO wants to improve and drive behaviours

Helpful hints for the PMO when delivering the service

- Not everything will require a target. It could be OK to provide an overall target for the PMO, rather than provide targets for each individual service
- Ensure you are measuring the right things. By putting in a measure you are driving behaviour. If you just measure the numbers of requests received, then there is no incentive to deal with those requests. If the measure is for those people satisfied with the service, then this can ensure that the people will care about giving good customer service
- Ensure you understand how to measure the item to reach the target
- Ensure measure collection is done as part of the normal PMO activity rather than a service in its own right
- Look to provide a realistic target i.e. something that is not too easy or too tough

PMO Capabilities needed to fulfil this service

Competencies	Techniques and generic tools
PMO Management Professionalism and ethics Leadership Result Orientation	Performance variance report

Related services

Set up PMO PMO imitation and evolvement Develop PMO Operating Procedures & Workflows Set up and track portfolio, program, and project metrics (KPI's)	Monitors the performance of individual team members and the team as a whole Provides leadership for the PMO team Develops PMO team objectives and ways of working with the team Sustains an environment that encourages high performance and empowers team members

Set up PMO

Service description

The design and creation of a new PMO. This could be at portfolio, program, or project level.

What the service provides for the customer

This provides a new PMO to assist the project, program, or portfolio, depending on the level the PMO is being created for.

Why is this service being offered to the customer?

All PMOs need to start from somewhere. Where a new project or program is being created the existing permanent PMO can assist in designing and staffing a PMO to support.

It is better that a PMO is designed and staffed correctly from the outset as this will increase the chances of PMO success.

How PMO will apply this service

There will be a request to setup a PMO. The PMO designer will work with the requestor to work out what level the PMO will be required to be operating. The PMO designer will use this manual to design the service catalogue for the PMO.

The PMO designer will review the numbers of individuals required to deliver the required service. They will agree what the structure of the new PMO will look like and who they will report into. Once that has been agreed then they will look to recruit individuals to work within the PMO.

They will work out who the stakeholders are of the PMO and what will be the communication plan.

They will agree the start date for the PMO and put together a plan for the initial few months of the PMO with the likely deliverables.

Supplier	Input	Process	Output	Customer
Senior management Program Manager Project Manager	Request for new PMO	Setup PMO	PMO	Portfolio Manager Program Manager Project Manager

How the PMO will measure the value of this service

This can be measured by asking for feedback on the success of the PMO.

Criteria when the PMO will use this service

- Where there is a request for a new PMO

Helpful hints for the PMO when delivering the service

- Use this book to assist with designing the service catalogue for the new PMO
- Use the advice from the IPMO-E course to help design the PMO to fit the organization

PMO Capabilities needed to fulfil this service

Competencies	Techniques and generic tools
Change Management Financial Management Planning and Scheduling Resource Management Stakeholder Engagement Capability Development Governance Frameworks PMO Management Professionalism and ethics Personal Communication Relationships and engagement Leadership Teamwork Negotiation Result Orientation	Capability and Capacity analysis Communication requirements analysis Organization charts & position descriptions Resource breakdown structure Salience model Scheduling tool Stakeholder checklist Stakeholder engagement assessment matrix Work Breakdown Structure

Related services

Sets PMO team targets PMO imitation and evolvement Clearly communicates the PMO vision and objectives Provides leadership for the PMO team	Assist in the recruitment and evaluation of PMO team members Communicates regularly with the PMO team and wider networks Develop PMO Operating Procedures & Workflows Sustains an environment that encourages high performance and empowers team members

PMO imitation and evolvement

Service description

The review and assessment of other PMOs to improve this PMO.

What the service provides for the customer

By reviewing what other PMOs do and how they deliver those services it will provide suggestions for this PMO to improve.

Why is this service being offered to the customer?

This allows the PMO to understand how other organizations approach their PMO and the services that they offer. These can be used as insights to see what is applicable for this PMO.

How PMO will apply this service

The PMO will read books and blogs. They will attend conferences and read white papers. They will talk to other PMOs via their external networks. Based on all this information the PMO may identify something that they want to pursue.

The PMO should understand what were the circumstances that the other PMO had that required this service. They should look and see whether there are similar circumstances for this PMO. If there are then the PMO Manager needs to look and see how this service can be applied. They will look to see whether the current PMO has the capabilities to deliver the new service, if not they will need to consider how those can be obtained.

Having decided that there is the need and ability for the new service the PMO manager should develop an action plan to introduce that new service. The manager should communicate the driver behind it and the value it will offer.

Supplier	Input	Process	Output	Customer
External PMOs	PMO success stories	Review PMO services	Updated service catalogue	PMO

How the PMO will measure the value of this service

This can be measured by the changes to the PMO that are viewed as successful.

Criteria when the PMO will use this service

- When the PMO is looking to improve its service offering

Helpful hints for the PMO when delivering the service

- This is not about replicating exactly what is done in another PMO as the PMO Manager needs to be aware of the context of this PMO. Just because something was a success in another organization or even another PMO within this organization does not mean it would be successful in this PMO
- There needs to be a need or driver within the current organization to pick up these new services

PMO Capabilities needed to fulfil this service

Competencies	Techniques and generic tools
Knowledge Management PMO Management Relationships and engagement Leadership	Comparative advantage analysis Capability and Capacity analysis Market / Competitor Analysis Stakeholder engagement assessment matrix

Related services

Set up PMO Provides leadership for the PMO team Sets PMO team targets	Carries out PMO benchmarking activities Clearly communicates the PMO vision and objectives Measure PMO performance

Develop PMO Operating Procedures & Workflows

Service description

The creation of the operating procedures for how the PMO will perform each of its agreed services.

What the service provides for the customer

This provides a standard way of performing each of the services. It enables the person performing the service to do so consistently.

Why is this service being offered to the customer?

By documenting how a service is performed it allows new individuals to understand how to deliver the service. It provides a consistent experience for the customer as they will get the same service each time.

How PMO will apply this service

The PMO will assess which services are being performed by multiple individuals within the PMO to prioritize which services to document first.

The PMO will consult with the individuals who are performing the service to document the steps they take to deliver the service. The PMO will draft the procedure and ask the people who perform the service to review it. Based on their feedback the PMO will revise the procedure.

The PMO will provide a flow diagram which will help explain the steps taken, by whom and include this within the procedure.

Having documented the procedure, the PMO will share this with the PMO team as part of the service catalogue. Any new person who is asked to perform the service will then have the details of how to deliver this.

Supplier	Input	Process	Output	Customer
PMO	Procedure template	Create procedure	Operating procedure	PMO

How the PMO will measure the value of this service

This can be measured by having a consistency of performance for the PMO services. It can be measured by getting feedback from the customers of the PMO services

Criteria when the PMO will use this service

- Where there is more than one person in the PMO
- Where there is a need for consistency
- Where the PMO is likely to handover to another individual

Helpful hints for the PMO when delivering the service

- As well as documenting the procedure the PMO will look to see whether a Service Level could be associated with the service
- If the service requires information from other people, or feedback to others then the PMO should look to see whether it is worth creating a template for this to get the information in a consistent manner, to make the service easier

PMO Capabilities needed to fulfil this service

Competencies	Techniques and generic tools
P3M Administration Information Management PMO Management Professionalism and ethics Leadership	SIPOC Diagramming techniques Mind Mapping Swim-lane flowcharts Task responsibility matrix/RACI

Related services

Set up PMO Provides leadership for the PMO team Develops PMO team objectives and ways of working with the team	Sets PMO team targets Measure PMO performance

PMO Management Operations

Service group description

The day to day running of the PMO team by the PMO Manager.

Why have these services been grouped together?

These services relate to how the PMO Manager provides the environment for the PMO team to develop and flourish. They relate to how the PMO Manager will communicate the vision and direction of the PMO to the team and the wider group of stakeholders.

List of related services described in other areas

Monitors the performance of individual team members and the team as a whole

Responsibility Assignment Matrix

Service	Executive	Portfolio Manager	Program Manager	Project Manager	PMO	Sponsor	Other Stakeholder
Clearly communicates the PMO vision and objectives	I	I	I	I	A, F	I	I (PPM teams)
Provides leadership for the PMO team					A, F		
Develops PMO team objectives and ways of working with the team					A, F		C (PMO Team)
Communicates regularly with the PMO team and wider networks	I	I	I	I	A, F	I	I
Sustains an environment that encourages high performance and empowers team members					A, F		C (PMO Team)
Encourages an open discussion to address challenges					A, F		C (PMO Team)
Consistently models desirable behaviours					A, F		C (PMO Team)

Helpful hints for when the PMO is delivering this service group

The PMO manager needs to provide the right day to day management to get the best of out the PMO team.

Clearly communicates the PMO vision and objectives

Service description

The communication of the PMO vision and objectives to the PMO team and key stakeholders.

What the service provides for the customer

This provides a means of communication the purpose and value of the PMO to a wider audience.

Why is this service being offered to the customer?

By communicating the vision of the PMO the purpose of the PMO and the value it offers will be clearly understood. The vision statement is aspirational, so should inspire the team to deliver a good service.

How PMO will apply this service

The PMO will develop a set of objectives and link that to a vision statement. The PMO will use the stakeholder and communication templates to work out who to communicate the vision to. The PMO will prepare some communications to go out to the key stakeholders and to the PMO team.

Whenever the PMO is asked what they do, then they should be prepared to have a conversation about the PMO vision and then go into detail about the objectives.

Supplier	Input	Process	Output	Customer
PMO Manager	PMO vision PMO objectives	Communication	Communicated vision statement	PMO team Key stakeholders

How the PMO will measure the value of this service

This can be measured by asking members of the PMO team or any of the key stakeholders what the PMO vision is and they are able to respond with the correct answer.

Criteria when the PMO will use this service

- When the PMO is starting up
- When the PMO as a vision statement
- When the PMO is trying to create an impact in the organization

Helpful hints for the PMO when delivering the service

- Make the vision statement short and sweet to enable it to be remembered and easily recited
- Link the vision statement of the PMO with the vision statement of the organization (if there is one)

PMO Capabilities needed to fulfil this service

Competencies	Techniques and generic tools
Stakeholder Engagement PMO Management Personal Communication Relationships and engagement Leadership	Communication requirements analysis Salience model Stakeholder checklist Stakeholder engagement assessment matrix

Related services

Set up PMO PMO imitation and evolvement Provides leadership for the PMO team Communicates regularly with the PMO team and wider networks Advise on key stakeholders and influencing strategies Develop stakeholder plans, profiles, and matrices	Facilitate the formulation of stakeholder engagement strategies Monitor the effectiveness of communications Develops PMO team objectives and ways of working with the team Measure PMO performance

Provides leadership for the PMO team

Service description

The leadership of the PMO team by the PMO Manager to gain and maintain the trust, confidence, commitment, and collaboration of others.

What the service provides for the customer

This provides the direction for the PMO team.

Why is this service being offered to the customer?

Without leadership the PMO team will lack direction and the PMO will not be a success. Having a strong leader gives a sense of purpose to the PMO. It provides development opportunities for those within the team.

How PMO will apply this service

The PMO manager will review the vision of the PMO and look to communicate this to the team. When delivering the message, tailor this to the circumstances so the delivery of the message is tailored to the listener. The PMO manager will confirm that the message has been understood and the people owning the actions understand how they are needing to achieve them.

The PMO manager will deal with any conflicts within the team and give praise where it is due. They will listen to any feedback and act on it.

When assigning tasks, the PMO manager will balance the need for the task to be done with the strengths of the individuals within the team. The PMO manager will keep the team informed of any changes, or potential changes in advance to give time for people to adopt and manage the change.

Supplier	Input	Process	Output	Customer
PMO Manager	PMO Vision PMO Objectives	Lead PMO team	Team trust PMO direction	PMO team

How the PMO will measure the value of this service

This can be measured in the morale and direction of the PMO team. It can be measured by asking for feedback from the PMO team.

Criteria when the PMO will use this service

- Where there is more than one person in the PMO
- When there is a PMO manager

Helpful hints for the PMO when delivering the service

- Do not be afraid to ask for advice on leadership from others
- Consider getting some leadership skills training

PMO Capabilities needed to fulfil this service

Competencies	Techniques and generic tools
PMO Management Professionalism and ethics Personal Communication Relationships and engagement Leadership Conflict and Crisis	Communication requirements analysis Stakeholder checklist Stakeholder engagement assessment matrix

Related services

Develops PMO team objectives and ways of working with the team Communicates regularly with the PMO team and wider networks Encourages an open discussion to address challenges Consistently models desirable behaviours Sets PMO team targets Set up PMO Monitors the performance of individual team members and the team as a whole	Ensure Continuing Professional Development of the PMO team Assess PMOs against a Competence Framework Develop individuals within the PMO team Develop PMO Operating Procedures & Workflows Carries out PMO benchmarking activities PMO imitation and evolvement Clearly communicates the PMO vision and objectives Sustains an environment that encourages high performance and empowers team members Measure PMO performance

Develops PMO team objectives and ways of working with the team

Service description

The creation, review, and maintenance of objectives for individuals within the PMO team.

What the service provides for the customer

This provides some specific goals for the individuals within the PMO to achieve. These include some measures of performance. In setting the objectives the PMO manager will provide guidance as to the ways to approach and deliver those objectives.

Why is this service being offered to the customer?

Having specific objectives it ensures that the individuals within the PMO understand exactly what their goals are for the year. They provide structure and a means of measuring performance.

How PMO will apply this service

The PMO Manager will find the role profile for the individual. They will find the current PMO objectives and the service catalogue. The PMO Manager will draft out some objectives based on which services the individual is responsible for and how they help deliver the overall PMO objectives. For each of the objectives the PMO manager will ensure they are SMART (Specific, Measurable, Achievable, Realistic and Timebound).

The PMO manager will draft out the objectives and share them with the individual concerned. They will then arrange a meeting to review these in detail, make any changes and agree the objectives.

On a regular basis the PMO manager and the individual will review the progress against the objectives and offer advice as to how these can be achieved.

Supplier	Input	Process	Output	Customer
PMO Manager	Role profile PMO vision PMO objectives Service catalogue	Set objectives	Objectives	PMO team

How the PMO will measure the value of this service

This can be measured by checking how well the team are performing against those objectives.

Criteria when the PMO will use this service

- Where there is a PMO Manager who has staff working for them
- As part of the annual review cycle for the permanent individuals within the team

Helpful hints for the PMO when delivering the service

- Objectives for permanent members of staff will contribute towards a performance review and may be linked into a pay review cycle
- As well as getting feedback on the objectives it is useful to gain feedback on the way the individual has been working from their peers and customers

PMO Capabilities needed to fulfil this service

Competencies	Techniques and generic tools
Capability Development PMO Management Professionalism and ethics Personal Communication Relationships and engagement Leadership Result Orientation	None

Related services

Sets PMO team targets Clearly communicates the PMO vision and objectives Consistently models desirable behaviours Develop and maintain PMO role profiles Develop individuals within the PMO team	Monitors the performance of individual team members and the team as a whole Develop PMO Operating Procedures & Workflows Provides leadership for the PMO team Sustains an environment that encourages high performance and empowers team members

Communicates regularly with the PMO team and wider networks

Service description

The regular communication by the PMO Manager with the PMO team and key stakeholders. Communication out to the external PMO network.

What the service provides for the customer

This provides information to the customer on what is going on with the PMO, how the PMO can assist them, what services they have to offer.

Why is this service being offered to the customer?

Without communication no one will know what the PMO can offer. The PMO is the central hub to PPM within an organization and is there to share information widely and help break people out of a silo mentality.

How PMO will apply this service

The PMO will find their communications plan. This will have a list of all the stakeholders, the frequency, method, and content of the communications. The PMO will tailor the communication mechanism according to the recipients. The PMO team may handle communications in a team meeting. For key stakeholders, such as the project management community the PMO may produce a regular newsletter with hints and tips. For senior management this may end up being face to face one to one sessions. For the external PMO network, that may involve communicating at conferences or via online messaging forums and blogs.

The PMO will review the success, or otherwise, of their communication. Are the people getting the message they want, are they getting it at the required frequency and level of detail? Based on the feedback the PMO will make changes to their communication plan.

Supplier	Input	Process	Output	Customer
PMO Manager	Communications plan	Communication	Communications	PMO team Key stakeholders PMO network

How the PMO will measure the value of this service

This can be measured by the number of times PMO is asked to assist.

Criteria when the PMO will use this service

- When the PMO has some new services to offer
- On a regular basis as per the communications plan

Helpful hints for the PMO when delivering the service

- Ensure you tailor the message to the group or individual who is being communicated to
- Consider having mailing lists to which people can get added, and then send out communications using the mailing list

PMO Capabilities needed to fulfil this service

Competencies	Techniques and generic tools
Stakeholder Engagement PMO Management Professionalism and ethics Personal Communication Relationships and engagement Leadership	Salience model Stakeholder checklist Stakeholder engagement assessment matrix

Related services

Clearly communicates the PMO vision and objectives Set up PMO Develop external relationships to share lessons and experience	External networking attendance at good practice events Provides leadership for the PMO team

Sustains an environment that encourages high performance and empowers team members

Service description

The provision of a positive working environment that allows the individuals within the PMO team to achieve their full potential.

What the service provides for the customer

This provides a good working environment. It allows the individuals to prosper and to achieve success, not only for them as individuals, but for the team as a whole. An individual who is empowered to deliver will deliver greater value than one who is micromanaged.

Why is this service being offered to the customer?

It ensures the PMO team are able to deliver for the organization. Having a good working environment contributes to reduced staff turnover.

How PMO will apply this service

The PMO manager will provide guidance to their staff on the services that need to be delivered. They will provide clear communication to the team of who is involved in delivering a particular service and how they can contribute. They will promote healthy discussion within the team, allowing individuals to suggest new ideas and ways of working. They will arrange time for social events, both within the team and involving the individuals they work closely with.

The PMO manager will promote respect for all members of the team and will value their contributions. They will promote a culture of trust and consistency within the team.

Supplier	Input	Process	Output	Customer
PMO Manager	PMO vision Positive feedback Individual objectives	Performance review Conducting meetings	Empowered individuals	PMO Team

How the PMO will measure the value of this service

This can be measured by increased satisfaction of the PMO team members. It can be measured in the increase in positive feedback from others about the PMO.

Criteria when the PMO will use this service

- When there is more than one person in the PMO

Helpful hints for the PMO when delivering the service

- The PMO manager should look to lead by example and promote the behaviours they wish the team to emulate
- Although the PMO manager can lead on this it does take the contribution of all team members to make this a success

PMO Capabilities needed to fulfil this service

Competencies	Techniques and generic tools
Stakeholder Engagement PMO Management Professionalism and ethics Personal Communication Relationships and engagement Leadership Teamwork	None

Related services

Provides leadership for the PMO team Sets PMO team targets Develop individuals within the PMO team Monitors the performance of individual team members and the team as a whole Set up PMO	Develops PMO team objectives and ways of working with the team Encourages an open discussion to address challenges Consistently models desirable behaviours Ensure Continuing Professional Development of the PMO team

Encourages an open discussion to address challenges

Service description

Encourages and facilitates open discussion in order that any difficulties or challenges are identified and addressed in a timely manner.

What the service provides for the customer

This provides a way of identifying and airing any issues that are currently being experienced by individuals within the team. By discussing this openly and getting to understand the root cause of the problems an action plan can be devised to overcome or come to terms with the issues.

Why is this service being offered to the customer?

If issues are left unresolved then they can lead to resentment from the individuals concerned towards the rest of the team and the manager. This in turn can lead to disharmony and a poor working environment. By having an open and honest discussion the problems can be aired and a resolution sought.

How PMO will apply this service

Whenever there are issues within the team, the PMO manager should talk to the individual concerned. If the issues affect multiple individuals within the team then this can be done as a part of the team meeting.

The PMO manager will clarify what the issue is. They will dig down into the issue to find out whether there are any underlying issues and look to discuss those as well. Once the issue has been described in objective terms then all parties to the discussion can suggest ideas that could be done to tackle the issue. For each of the ideas that are suggested they will be evaluated as to whether this will resolve the issue, partially resolve it, not make a difference, or make it worse. For those ideas which contribute to the resolution these will be included on the action plan, along with an owner and due date.

Having concluded what the actions should be, the discussion should be closed, and the action plan followed. This may be revisited at a later date, after all the actions have been done if the issue is still present.

Supplier	Input	Process	Output	Customer
PMO team	Challenges	Discussion	Action plan	PMO team

How the PMO will measure the value of this service

This can be measured in the morale of the team. It can be measured by the number of challenges faced that have had a successful resolution.

Criteria when the PMO will use this service

- When there is more than one person in the PMO

Helpful hints for the PMO when delivering the service

- Not all problems can be resolved. For issues which cannot be directly resolved, alternatives need to be discussed about how the individual (or team) can deal with the situation in a professional manner
- The PMO manager needs to understand which items can be discussed in an open forum, and which ones will require more delicate handling
- The PMO manager should ensure the discussion happens in a positive manner and remains focused on finding a successful outcome

PMO Capabilities needed to fulfil this service

Competencies	Techniques and generic tools
Stakeholder Engagement PMO Management Professionalism and ethics Personal Integrity and reliability Personal Communication Relationships and engagement Leadership Conflict and Crisis Resourcefulness Negotiation	Root Cause Analysis 5 Whys Alternatives analysis Alternatives generation Communication requirements analysis Stakeholder engagement assessment matrix

Related services

Develop individuals within the PMO team Monitors the performance of individual team members and the team as a whole Provides leadership for the PMO team	Consistently models desirable behaviours Sustains an environment that encourages high performance and empowers team members

Consistently models desirable behaviours

Service description

Consistently model desirable behaviours to encourage similar behaviour from others.

What the service provides for the customer

This provides the PMO team member something to emulate. By acting as a role model, the PMO Manager demonstrates how they would like their team to behave.

Why is this service being offered to the customer?

Having consistent positive behaviour traits will lead to improved team morale. This positivity ensures that the team will work better together.

How PMO will apply this service

The PMO Manager will decide which are the positive behaviour traits they wish to present. These could include:

- Meeting deadlines – agreeing when items need to be delivered and ensuring the work is done by those dates
- Being consistent – dealing with each of the team members in a similar way, not having favourites
- Courteous and friendly – being welcoming to people coming over and asking questions
- Taking responsibility – not everything goes well, so an individual will need to own up to making mistakes
- Punctuality – turning up on time, especially to meetings

Having chosen the behaviours that, they want to see within their team the PMO Manager should start to display those traits.

Supplier	Input	Process	Output	Customer
PMO Manager	Behaviours	Modelling behaviours	Behaviours	PMO team

How the PMO will measure the value of this service

This can be measured by increase team morale. This can be measured by an increase in positive behaviour from all team members.

Criteria when the PMO will use this service

- When there is more than one person in the PMO

Helpful hints for the PMO when delivering the service

- If an organization has their own list of behaviours, they wish their staff to follow the PMO Manager should try to model those ones
- The PMO Manager should ask for feedback to ensure that they are actually modelling the behaviours that they think they are

PMO Capabilities needed to fulfil this service

Competencies	Techniques and generic tools
PMO Management Professionalism and ethics Personal Communication Relationships and engagement Leadership	None

Related services

Provides leadership for the PMO team Sustains an environment that encourages high performance and empowers team members Encourages an open discussion to address challenges	Develop individuals within the PMO team Monitors the performance of individual team members and the team as a whole Develops PMO team objectives and ways of working with the team

PMO Monitoring

Service group description

The review of PMO performance with a view to improving it.

Why have these services been grouped together?

This service is related to the what the PMO does and whether it is achieving its objectives.

Responsibility Assignment Matrix

Service	Executive	Portfolio Manager	Program Manager	Project Manager	PMO	Sponsor	Other Stakeholder
Measure PMO performance	C	C	C	C	A, R		C (PPM teams)

Measure PMO performance

Service description

Provide an assessment of whether the PMO is performing as expected. Are the services meeting the requirements of the PMO customers?

What the service provides for the customer

This provides an assessment of the value of the PMO in the eyes of those people who receive services from the PMO.

Why is this service being offered to the customer?

This enables the PMO manager to understand what is working with the PMO and what needs to change. It gives them a view of any additional services that may be required by the customers of the PMO. With this understanding the PMO manager can make change to the service catalogue and/or the way those services are offered. This will lead to improvements in the perception and value of the PMO.

How PMO will apply this service

The PMO will identify who they are going to ask for feedback from. They will look to develop a questionnaire which they will send out to the stakeholders. They will then send the questionnaire out to the people identified. If necessary, following up with a face-to-face session to understand the meanings behind some of the scoring.

Having got the scores and the underlying reasons behind those scores the PMO manager can then review to see whether this meets their expectations. If it falls short, or the PMO manager strives to deliver improved service then the PMO Manager will come up with an action plan (in conjunction with the team) to address the issues the survey highlighted. They will then look to make the changes they have come up with and they can look to redo the survey to see whether those changes have had the desired effect.

Supplier	Input	Process	Output	Customer
PMO Manager PPM managers Senior Management	Feedback forms Voice of the Customer survey	Evaluate PMO performance	PMO assessment PMO action plan	PMO Manager

How the PMO will measure the value of this service

This can be measured in the changes to the PMO service catalogue. It can be measured in increases in the customer satisfaction with the PMO services.

Criteria when the PMO will use this service

- As part of the PMO's annual review process
- When the PMO wants to understand how effective they are

Helpful hints for the PMO when delivering the service

- As painful as it may be, look to conduct a voice of the customer survey in person to understand why people are scoring what they are. It is not just about the score; it is understanding the underlying reasons behind that score
- Look to conduct the survey on a regular (annual) basis in order that improvements can be shown
- Feedback can be subjective, but it is important to understand how the PMO is perceived. If you believe that perception to be wrong, then you can do something about changing that perception
- Consider tailoring the questionnaire depending on the stakeholder and the interactions the PMO are having with them
- Do not forget to ask the team how well they think the PMO is doing, they are a key stakeholder as well
- If there are lots of issues look to prioritize and focus on the important issues first

PMO Capabilities needed to fulfil this service

Competencies	Techniques and generic tools
Reporting, Insights and Analysis Stakeholder Engagement PMO Management Professionalism and ethics Personal Communication Relationships and engagement Leadership Conflict and Crisis Result Orientation	Root Cause Analysis 5 Whys Failure Modes and Effects Analysis (FMEA)

Related services

PMO imitation and evolvement Develop PMO Operating Procedures & Workflows Clearly communicates the PMO vision and objectives	Provides leadership for the PMO team Monitors the performance of individual team members and the team as a whole Carries out PMO benchmarking activ ties

Portfolio Management

Portfolio Management

Description

The framework by which projects and programs are selected to deliver the strategic direction of the organization. As the projects and programs progress it ensures they remain aligned to that strategy and provide regular feedback on the progress. Ensuring that the changes are properly transitioned into Business as Usual

What the services within the area provide for the customer

These services provide support for the portfolio manager by ensuring that there is a structure by which projects can be assessed. They provide assurance to the senior management that the right projects are selected, and that money and effort is not wasted.

Helpful hints for when the PMO is delivering this service area

- It is very difficult to support portfolio management without having a clear strategy to evaluate the effectiveness of the portfolio against
- Ensure the PMO has a linkage to the strategy development process and is aware of potential changes to ensure they can communicate the impact on the current portfolio

Portfolio Design

Service group description

The setup and maintenance of the processes, tools, standards, templates and help to enable portfolio management.

Why have these services been grouped together?

These services relate to the setup of the rules by which the portfolio will be governed and managed.

Responsibility Assignment Matrix

Service	Executive	Portfolio Manager	Program Manager	Project Manager	PMO	Sponsor	Other Stakeholder
Establish a portfolio management framework	I	A			R		
Develops scenario modelling to reduce commitments or increase capacity	C	A	I	I	R		
Provide tools and analysis for Business Capacity Management		A			R		

Helpful hints for when the PMO is delivering this service group

Ensure that the rules laid down are clear and that everyone is following them, otherwise that can lead to issues when trying to perform portfolio management.

Establish a portfolio management framework

Service description

The creation and maintenance of the process, procedures, standards, templates and help to enable a portfolio to be created, maintained, and run.

What the service provides for the customer

This provides a project and program prioritization matrix, allowing them to be evaluated according to the value to the organization. It sets up the project approval board which will approve, or reject, each project or program. It allows for delegated approval based on value and risk. It provides the form which will need to be completed to submit a project or program for approval.

Why is this service being offered to the customer?

Ensures that projects get approved against a consistent set of criteria. Weeds out 'pet' projects or programs which deviate from the strategy.

How PMO will apply this service

The PMO will talk to finance to find out the financial approval levels (i.e. who has authority to approve a certain amount of money). They will speak to the risk team to find out what the risk assessment levels are. They will speak with the strategy department to find out what the strategic drivers are.

The PMO will come up with a prioritization matrix, which can include the cost, benefit, risk, strategic driver, whether the item is mandatory or not. This matrix can then be used to evaluate each of the items for approval against a common set of criteria.

The PMO will develop a project approval form which will be used to submit items for approval. This can contain: a project title, description of the project, why the project is required, what problems it will solve, any alternatives, information to help with prioritization.

The PMO will create a simple process to get an idea to be considered by the project approval board. This may include initial reviews before the project goes for approval. This process will cover what happens if an idea is not selected.

The PMO will design a set of criteria for a project to be approved to start. They will create criteria which would cause a project to be halted.

The PMO will design the reports which will enable the portfolio manager and the project approval board to manage and understand the status of the portfolio.

Once the framework has been created then the PMO will ensure this is published in order that it can start to be used.

Supplier	Input	Process	Output	Customer
Strategy Risk Finance	Strategic plan Financial approval signoff levels Risk assessment levels	Develop Standard Develop Templates	Prioritization matrix Project approval guidelines Project approval form	Project approval board Senior Management PPM Managers PMO

How the PMO will measure the value of this service

This can be measured by ensuring that all projects and programs are approved in a consistent manner using the framework developed.

Criteria when the PMO will use this service

- When the PMO is aligned to the portfolio manager
- Where there is no approval process defined or the approval process requires updating

Helpful hints for the PMO when delivering the service

- Each time the finance approval level, risk assessment levels or strategic drivers change the framework will require updating
- The information in the project approval form should give enough information for those being asked to approve it, to understand what the project is about and why is should (or should not be approved)
- A project may meet the prioritization criteria and be approved. It does not necessarily mean that the project will start immediately after approval. There may be a delay between approval and start-up due to resource availability or conflicts with other projects. When a project is approved it should be scheduled to start. Having project start-up criteria will make this clearer to all concerned
- If a project is no longer required, it does not meet the strategic direction, no longer has enough benefits, is costing too much, or is unlikely to complete then it should be stopped. Having these criteria clearly listed will make it easier to understand why a project has been halted, and make it easier to do

PMO Capabilities needed to fulfil this service.

Competencies	Techniques and generic tools
Benefits and Value Management Business Case Financial Management Governance Frameworks Professionalism and ethics Teamwork	Multi-Criteria Scoring Model Cost/ Benefit Analysis Probability and impact matrix Prioritization matrices Proposal evaluation system

Related services

Maintain a register for current and potential programs and projects Support the Project Approval Board Calculate the Total Cost of Ownership Review of delivery schedules against Business as Usual	Manage the Process Improvement Plan Develops scenario modelling to reduce commitments or increase capacity Perform data analysis of project selection and delivery performance Reporting results linked to organizational strategy

Develops scenario modelling to reduce commitments or increase capacity

Service description

The creation of scenarios to enable the project approval board and the portfolio manager to understand the impact of different decisions that can be made about the portfolio.

What the service provides for the customer

A set of scenarios which allow the senior management to understand the impact on changing the numbers (and types) of resource available on project delivery. i.e. if we increase the resource pool by x% how many more projects could we deliver. If we have less money to spend next year what will that do to the portfolio.

Models the impact of changes to the strategic direction e.g. if we invest in growth rather than cost reduction what will be the impact to the portfolio.

Why is this service being offered to the customer?

By having the different scenarios, it allows the portfolio manager and project approval board to understand the impact of decisions they want to make on the portfolio before they have been made. Allows for medium to long term planning on the portfolio.

How PMO will apply this service

The PMO will speak with the portfolio manager to find out what scenarios they are requiring modelling. These could include changes in resource types, changes in budget (increases and decreases), changes in strategic direction.

For each of the scenarios the PMO will model the impact on the projects included (and excluded), the duration and the timings (start and finish dates) of those projects. As well as just providing the new model the PMO will provide commentary on the differences and the impact on the resources being asked to deliver the work.

Based on the different 'what if' scenarios the portfolio manager and project approval board can then make some decisions on what needs to be done. It may mean that the PMO is asked to run some new scenarios with slightly different parameters.

Supplier	Input	Process	Output	Customer
Project Managers Program Managers Portfolio Manager	Resource Demand Schedules Financial plans Strategic decisions Scenarios to model	Provide 'what if' analysis	'What if' analysis	Portfolio Manager Project Approval Board

How the PMO will measure the value of this service

This can be measured by asking for feedback from the portfolio manager. If can be measured by seeing whether any of the options are adopted.

Criteria when the PMO will use this service

- When the PMO is aligned to a portfolio manager
- Where there are challenges to the budget for the portfolio
- Where there is the option to expand the budget for the portfolio
- Where there are changes planned to the strategic direction

Helpful hints for the PMO when delivering the service

- Look to see whether there are any tools which can help re-profile the schedule if extending the duration of a project
- If reprofiling a project with a different duration look to see whether there are any standard profiles that can be used, rather than just flat phase the demand
- If looking to reduce the budget by a percentage, consider whether entire projects could be removed rather than reduce the demand of all projects by a given percentage
- If extending projects into the next financial year, see whether there will be budget in that year to complete the project
- If extending project durations, see whether there is any impact e.g. projects which are required to deliver legislative changes probably cannot be moved without having a negative impact
- If changing the strategic direction ensure that existing projects, and those in the pipeline are linked to a particular strategic driver

PMO Capabilities needed to fulfil this service

Competencies	Techniques and generic tools
Reporting, Insights and Analysis Resource Management Capacity Management Governance Frameworks P3M Tools Resourcefulness Result Orientation	Alternatives analysis Alternatives generation Change Impact Analysis Scenario analysis Capability and Capacity analysis Prioritization matrices Project Management Information System

Related services

Provide 'what if' resource capacity analysis Establish a portfolio management framework Maintain a register for current and potential programs and projects	Provide resource tracking and capacity reports Forecast future resource needs Provide tools and analysis for Business Capacity Management

Provide tools and analysis for Business Capacity Management

Service description

Provision of tools which allow for the demand and capacity to be managed. Using these tools to provide 'what if' scenarios and detailed analysis of the demand and supply variances.

What the service provides for the customer

Provides a set of tools which allows a view of the demand vs supply across the portfolio to understand whether the correct resources are available to enable the projects to deliver what they need to.

Why is this service being offered to the customer?

Having tools will make the process of providing the 'what if' scenarios and analysis much easier and quicker. This means that decisions can be made in a quicker timescale.

How PMO will apply this service

The PMO will evaluate what tools are available to provide demand versus capacity modelling. They will look to see what reporting is available and how flexible the 'what if' modelling is. The PMO will recommend to the organization that they invest in the chosen tool. If accepted, then the PMO will help implement and configure the software for use.

If the PMO cannot find or implement a tool, then the PMO could consider developing and using spreadsheets to provide the modelling capability. The PMO should design this so that it can easily take inputs from the demand and capacity sources. They should allow for projects to be added in or removed. They need to allow for durations to changed, and therefore reprofile the detail. They need to allow for the project start date to be moved to start earlier/later. They need the option to save scenarios and compare 2 scenarios against each other. They need to option to revert to the current setup, should they want to start a new scenario model.

The PMO will provide training for any individuals who are required to use the software.

Supplier	Input	Process	Output	Customer
External suppliers PMO	Modelling software PPM tools Spreadsheets	Software implementation Software development	Modelling tool	PMO Portfolio Manager

How the PMO will measure the value of this service

This can be measured by seeing the decrease in time taken to produce a 'what if' scenario.

Criteria when the PMO will use this service

- When the PMO is being asked to provide 'what if' modelling
- When the PMO is aligned to the portfolio manager

Helpful hints for the PMO when delivering the service

- If possible, see whether the modelling can be done within any existing PPM toolset
- Ensure the data within the tool can be refreshed easily, from existing sources
- Consider whether standard scenarios (e.g. resource constraints, x% increase in project costs/duration) should be created so that the models can be used as part of the approvals process

PMO Capabilities needed to fulfil this service

Competencies	Techniques and generic tools
Information Management Planning and Scheduling Reporting, Insights and Analysis Resource Management Capacity Management P3M Tools Resourcefulness Result Orientation	Make or buy analysis Capability and Capacity analysis Project Management Information System

Related services

Advise on PPM tools and software Develops in-house project management tools Tailors and configures project management tools	Implements vendor provided project management tools Develops scenario modelling to reduce commitments or increase capacity Provide 'what if' resource capacity analysis

Portfolio Operations

Service group description

The operation of the portfolio management framework. Related to the maintenance of the portfolio registers, recording approval statuses, and performing portfolio prioritization.

Why have these services been grouped together?

These services relate to the day-to-day operation of portfolio management within the organization, with the PMO supporting the portfolio manager and senior management in making and communicating the decisions about the portfolio.

List of related services described in other areas

Develop resource plans to underpin the portfolio plan
Capture the resource requirements of portfolio, programs, and projects
Monitor the portfolio's total exposure to risk
Develop and maintain schedules for the portfolio, program, or project

Responsibility Assignment Matrix

Service	Executive	Portfolio Manager	Program Manager	Project Manager	PMO	Sponsor	Other Stakeholder
Maintain a register for current and potential programs and projects	I	A	I	I	R		
Support the Project Approval Board		A			R		
Ensure quality of project requests		A			R		
Business strategy and roadmap maintenance		C			R		A (Strategy Department)
Manage Customer Interfaces		A			R	C	
Perform data analysis of project selection and delivery performance	A	C			R		

Helpful hints for when the PMO is delivering this service group

The PMO will be acting in a supporting role in the delivery of these services. The final decision will be made by the executive or delegated down to the Project Approval Board and the portfolio manager.

Maintain a register for current and potential programs and projects

Service description

The creation and maintenance of a list of projects and programs with their relevant details and status.

What the service provides for the customer

Provides a list (in one place) of all change activity going on the organization, its status, cost and expected delivery date.

Why is this service being offered to the customer?

This is a pre-requisite for developing a prioritization framework. Having a list of all the change activities ensures that duplicate projects do not get raised. It provides a record of the approval decisions made by the Project Approval Board.

How PMO will apply this service.

The PMO will create the initial register and populate this will the active projects and programs. They will then expand this to include the ideas and projects that have not yet been approved or started.

The register could include:

- Unique reference – to ensure that there are no duplicates and provide a quick way of referencing a project as names may change
- Name – what is the idea, project or program called
- Status – this would reflect the statuses defined in the portfolio framework e.g. idea, awaiting approval, approved, in flight, closed, cancelled, withdrawn
- Originator – who raised this. This could be a name of an individual or group. This person will know about the idea to help with approval
- Business area – which area of the business will this deliver into
- Strategic driver – which area of the strategy does this relate to
- Project manager – who is running this, who can we go to find out more information
- Delivery date – this will be the expected date that this will deliver
- Cost – Approved cost, could include current forecast as well
- Benefits – Approved/expected benefits

The PMO will update the register whenever the following happens:

- As new ideas get thought of – the initial information will get added
- As ideas are due to be approved – the status will be updated
- The project approval board decisions – the status will be update
- The project starts - the current status and details of the project manager will be updated
- The costs/benefits/dates change – this will be reflected in the register
- The project finishes – the status will be updated

Supplier	Input	Process	Output	Customer
Portfolio Manager Program Managers Project Managers Project Approval Board	Project approval form Approval decisions Project and program updates	Maintain Project Register	Project register	PMO Senior Managers Portfolio Manager

How the PMO will measure the value of this service

This can be measured by the ease with which the current status of a project or program can be obtained

Criteria when the PMO will use this service

- Where the PMO is aligned to a portfolio manager
- Where the PMO has a role in portfolio management
- Where the PMO supports the Project Approval Board

Helpful hints for the PMO when delivering the service

- Consider storing this information in a PPM tool
- The exact details of the information needing to be stored will depend on the organization and different ways that are required to segment the data
- Consider publishing a simplified extract of this register to allow a better understanding of the changes expected within the organization

PMO Capabilities needed to fulfil this service

Competencies	Techniques and generic tools
P3M Administration Information Management P3M Tools	Project Management Information System

Related services

Establish a portfolio management framework Support the Project Approval Board Capture and categorize new ideas Support closure process	Develops scenario modelling to reduce commitments or increase capacity Identify over commitment of changes to the business Business strategy and roadmap maintenance Ensure quality of project requests Reporting results linked to organizational strategy

Support the Project Approval Board

Service description

Provide administrative support for the Project Approval Board, who are responsible for approving projects and programs within the portfolio. Ensure the projects and programs are approved according to the portfolio management framework.

What the service provides for the customer

A meeting where new projects and programs can be approved. The project approval forms will have been quality checked and the prioritization algorithm will have been processed prior to their submission. The PMO will provide updates on the status of the active projects and programs within the portfolio. Any project or program escalations will be raised, and action decided upon.

Why is this service being offered to the customer?

Having a project approval board ensure that known risks are surfaced, and realistic costs, benefits and timescales are considered. It verifies that projects and programs will deliver the strategic intent of the organization. Having a record of the decisions agreed can be useful to disseminate the information and could be used for auditing purposes.

How PMO will apply this service

The PMO will discuss with the portfolio manager who should attend the Project Approval Board. They will setup the meetings and invite the attendees. The PMO will publish the dates for the meetings in advance in order that those people who need to submit an item for approval know when to target their documentation for.

Prior to the meeting the PMO will agree the agenda with the portfolio manager. They will review all the submissions and ensure they meet the required quality prior to them being approved for submission. The PMO will send out the agenda and the documents for approval in advance of the meeting to allow attendees to review the information in advance.

During the meeting, the PMO will ensure the meeting runs smoothly, with all items being discussed and reviewed. Each decision will be noted and be included in the minutes.

After the meeting, the PMO will update the project register with the decisions. They will write and distribute the minutes. They will ensure that each project which asked for a decision to made gets informed of the result.

Supplier	Input	Process	Output	Customer
Project Managers Program Managers	Project Approval form Prioritization criteria Strategic plan Financial plan Consolidated portfolio level report Escalation reports Approval process Business cases	Support Project Approval Board Writing Minutes	Updated Project Register Update Project Approval Form Meeting minutes	Project Approval Board Portfolio Manager

How the PMO will measure the value of this service

This can be measured by the smoothness with which the meeting runs. If all projects get discussed and decisions made and minuted then this can be considered a success.

Criteria when the PMO will use this service

- When the PMO supports a portfolio manager
- Where the portfolio manager is not providing this service themselves

Helpful hints for the PMO when delivering the service

- The Project Approval Board has different names in each company. It does not matter what the meeting is called. The role it performs is the important
- The Project Approval Board will have a core of decision makers attend and then individuals may be called upon to attend part of the meetings to present their projects to the board
- The PMO may decide to publish a condensed set of the minutes with just the decisions if some of the actions are considered confidential

PMO Capabilities needed to fulfil this service

Competencies	Techniques and generic tools
P3M Administration Benefits and Value Management Business Case Change Control Quality Management Governance Frameworks Professionalism and ethics Personal Integrity and reliability Personal Communication Relationships and engagement Teamwork Resourcefulness Negotiation	Multi-Criteria Scoring Model Cost/ Benefit Analysis Prioritization matrices

Related services

Maintain a register for current and potential programs and projects Provide a secretariat service for meetings Coordinate quality reviews of deliverables Administer and track budget allocations Develop and refine portfolio, program, or project business cases	Calculate the Total Cost of Ownership Identify over commitment of changes to the business Establish a portfolio management framework Ensure quality of project requests Be aware of stakeholders with an interest in the organization's delivery portfolio

Ensure quality of project requests

Service description

Provide a review of the project approval form to ensure the information contained within it is accurate and represents value to the organization.

What the service provides for the customer

This provides an independent assessment of the value of the proposed project to the organization. It will look at whether this fits with the strategy, has business value and assesses the risk of delivery and risk to delivery.

Why is this service being offered to the customer?

Prior to a project being approved, the project approval form needs to be independently assessed to ensure that the information contained in it accurate. It helps the project approval board when they come to decide on whether to approve this piece of work.

How PMO will apply this service

The PMO will receive a Project Approval Form. They will ensure that the idea has been properly risk assessed. The risk needs to be viewed from the perspective of risk of the project being able to deliver successfully. The risk also needs to be viewed from the impact if the project does or does not deliver i.e. the risk to the business of delivery (what opportunities will this bring?).

The PMO should ensure that the idea aligns with the strategy, if not they will go back to the originator and advise them that they need to update the form.

The PMO will ensure that the prioritization of the idea has been done and that the form is updated with the relative ranking, prior to going for approval.

The PMO will review to see whether there are any overlaps between this idea and other ideas that have been submitted. They will check to see if this represents an idea which has previously been reviewed and rejected in the past. This will save time in the Project Approval Board considering a project which has not been successful before.

Supplier	Input	Process	Output	Customer
Originator	Project Approval Form	Evaluate Project Approval Form	Updated Project Approval Form	Project Approval Board

How the PMO will measure the value of this service

This can be measured in a reduction in the numbers of project approval forms which are sent back for clarification.

Criteria when the PMO will use this service

- When the PMO is aligned to a portfolio manager
- Where the PMO support the Project Approval Board

Helpful hints for the PMO when delivering the service

- Consider developing a checklist of items to review to ensure consistency in the review process
- Ensure that if there are any changes required to the Project Approval Form that the reasons behind the change, as well as the actual change are communicated back to the originator

PMO Capabilities needed to fulfil this service

Competencies	Techniques and generic tools
Business Case Quality Management Reporting, Insights and Analysis Professionalism and ethics Personal Communication Relationships and engagement Negotiation Result Orientation	Document Analysis Prompt Lists Prioritization matrices

Related services

Maintain a register for current and potential programs and projects	Support the Project Approval Board

Business strategy and roadmap maintenance

Service description

Turning the business strategy into a release or product roadmap in order that the organization knows how and when the strategy is to be delivered.

What the service provides for the customer

This ensures that the strategy is turned into a visual representation via a roadmap to aid communication out to a wider audience.

Why is this service being offered to the customer?

Having a visual representation of the strategy will bring this to life and ensure greater buy-in to the company vision and strategy.

How PMO will apply this service

The PMO will obtain the latest copy of the strategy from the strategy department. They will obtain the latest copy of the portfolio delivery schedule (the schedule which shows when each of the projects and programs within the portfolio will be delivered).

Using the project register the PMO can associate each of the active projects and programs with an element from the strategy. They can use that information to provide a visual representation of when each element of the strategy will be delivered. For the parts of the strategy which are not represented by active projects the PMO will check the project register to see if there is any information that can be used to verify which projects to be created to deliver those part of the strategy and add those to the roadmap.

There will be items within the strategy that will not have been formulated enough to be raised as a project. The PMO can work with the strategy department and the portfolio manager to get those items scoped in order that they can be included within the roadmap and added to the project register.

Supplier	Input	Process	Output	Customer
Strategy department PMO	Business strategy Delivery schedule Project Register	Update roadmap	Strategic roadmap	Portfolio Manager

How the PMO will measure the value of this service

This can be measured in an increase awareness of the strategy.

Criteria when the PMO will use this service

- When the PMO is aligned to the portfolio manager
- Where there is a desire to increase strategic awareness

Helpful hints for the PMO when delivering the service

- Look to update the roadmap on a regular (quarterly or monthly) basis
- Consider printing a copy of the roadmap and putting it on display
- Ensure the roadmap gets communicated throughout the organization to increase awareness of its existence and to ensure a wider awareness of the strategy turning into reality

PMO Capabilities needed to fulfil this service

Competencies	Techniques and generic tools
Planning and Scheduling Reporting, Insights and Analysis Personal Communication Relationships and engagement	Time series plots

Related services

Maintain a release schedule Maintain a register for current and potential programs and projects	Identify over commitment of changes to the business Horizon scan for impending policy or strategy changes

Manage Customer Interfaces

Service description

The evaluation of customer satisfaction scores on behalf of the portfolio manager. The managing of the customer relationships for the portfolio.

What the service provides for the customer

At the simplest level this provides a way that the portfolio manager can keep track of how well the objectives of the portfolio are meeting customer needs by looking at the customer satisfaction scores. The PMO could go the step further and actually manage the relationship with the customers of the portfolio on behalf of the portfolio manager.

Why is this service being offered to the customer?

To make a success of the portfolio the customers of the portfolio (those people to whom the projects are delivering) need to be happy. By managing the communications and reviewing their satisfaction with the delivery the PMO are able to see whether they are happy. The PMO can then make the necessary communication adjustments to increase customer satisfaction.

How PMO will apply this service

The PMO will decide what sort of customer satisfaction survey they are wanting to do. These choices include:

- A simple customer satisfaction question (rate how satisfied you are between 1 & 5 where 1 is Very dissatisfied and 5 is very satisfied)
- A Net Promoter Score (rated on a score of 0-10, Detractors have scores in the 0-6 scores range; Passives are in the 7-8 range; Promoters have scores in the 9-10 range)
- A Customer Effort Score (CES) (How much effort did you personally have to put forth to handle your request on a scale of 1-5? Where 1 indicates very low effort and 5 indicates very high effort)

Having chosen the questions then the PMO will send out the questionnaire to the customers of the portfolio. They will collate the results and look to publish this on a regular basis.

If the PMO has been asked to manage the customer relationships, they will find the latest stakeholder framework. They will discuss with the portfolio manager who the stakeholders are and the relationship/communications that are required. The PMO will fill in the stakeholder matrix and the communications plan. The PMO will then ensure that the communications plan gets followed and the relevant communications get sent to the stakeholders according to the plan.

Supplier	Input	Process	Output	Customer
PMO	Customer Satisfaction questionnaire	Evaluate customer satisfaction	Customer Satisfaction scores	Portfolio Manager
PMO	Communications framework Stakeholder framework	Manage stakeholders	Communication plan Stakeholder matrix	Portfolio Manager PMO

How the PMO will measure the value of this service

This can be measured by seeing an increase in the customer satisfaction scores. It can be measured by gaining feedback from the portfolio manager.

Criteria when the PMO will use this service

- When the PMO is aligned with a portfolio manager
- Where the organization is focused on customer service
- When the portfolio manager wants to work closely with their customers

Helpful hints for the PMO when delivering the service

- Look to send out the questionnaire just after a project or program has delivered to get feedback from those customers
- Look to compare how the customer satisfaction rating has changed over time

PMO Capabilities needed to fulfil this service

Competencies	Techniques and generic tools
P3M Administration Reporting, Insights and Analysis Stakeholder Engagement Personal Communication Relationships and engagement	Communication requirements analysis Categorized frequency analysis (Frequency plot, bar chart) Salience model Stakeholder checklist Stakeholder engagement assessment matrix Stratified data plots or scatter plots

Related services

Develop and maintain the communication framework Monitor the effectiveness of communications Facilitate the formulation of stakeholder engagement strategies Develop stakeholder plans, profiles, and matrices	Facilitate stakeholder identification and communication workshops Advise on key stakeholders and influencing strategies Enable the formulation of communication plans Be aware of stakeholders with an interest in the organization's delivery portfolio

Perform data analysis of project selection and delivery performance

Service description

A systemic review of the delivery of the portfolio to examine any root causes of poor project selection or poor performance with a view to providing recommendations to prevent further examples.

What the service provides for the customer

This provides examples of poor project selection or poor project performance. It provides an action plan to resolve the root causes of the performance issues.

Why is this service being offered to the customer?

Rather than looking at the performance of each item in the portfolio independently, examining performance holistically ensures that fundamental issues with selection and delivery can be identified. Once these have been identified then an action plan can be created to resolve and prevent those issues occurring.

How PMO will apply this service

The PMO will look at all the projects which closed in the last year (or 18 months). They will examine to see which proportion of those were not considered a success. Of those projects the PMO will examine why they were not considered successful. The PMO will identify the root causes of these failures.

Having got the root causes of all the unsuccessful projects the PMO will examine to see whether there is any commonality between the root causes. For those ones where there are common issues the PMO will create an action plan to try and resolve these underlying issues.

The PMO will take this plan to the portfolio manager and the Project Approval Board for their support in taking the action plan forward. They will assign the owners to the actions and the PMO can then track the progress of the action plan, in conjunction with the portfolio manager.

Supplier	Input	Process	Output	Customer
Project Managers Program Managers	Status Reports Schedules Financial plans	Review portfolio performance	PMO Recommendations Action Plan Process Improvement Plan	Portfolio Managers Project Approval Board

How the PMO will measure the value of this service

This can be measured by seeing the performance of the portfolio improve. It can be measured by a reduction in the number of project failures.

Criteria when the PMO will use this service

- When the PMO is aligned to a portfolio manager
- When the organization is interested in increasing its maturity
- When the organization has had a series of project failures

Helpful hints for the PMO when delivering the service

- Need to define what success will be, by project. A project may deliver on time, on budget, on scope, but still be considered a failure as the benefits where not achieved. A project which did deliver the benefits, but was over budget and time may be considered a success
- Without senior management backing it will be difficult to take forward any of the actions within the action plan
- If any of the root causes are linked to poor project selection, especially if this appears to criticize any of the members of the Project Approval Board then these actions need to be handled diplomatically for them to have any chance of successful implementation
- If any of the actions relate to process improvement, consider adding them to the Process Improvement Plan and tracking them via that route

PMO Capabilities needed to fulfil this service

Competencies	Techniques and generic tools
Knowledge Management Reporting, Insights and Analysis Delivery Methods Professionalism and ethics Personal Integrity and reliability Personal Communication Relationships and engagement Leadership Conflict and Crisis Resourcefulness Negotiation Result Orientation	Root Cause Analysis 5 Whys Failure Modes and Effects Analysis (FMEA) Process Analysis

Related services

Manage the Process Improvement Plan Establish a portfolio management framework Identify over commitment of changes to the business	Feedback to senior management on the success of strategic initiatives Reporting results linked to organizational strategy

Portfolio Monitoring

Service group description

The review and feedback on the performance of the portfolio.

Why have these services been grouped together?

Introduction to the Service Group, why is it grouped in the way it creates value.

List of related services described in other areas

Perform data analysis of project selection and delivery performance

Responsibility Assignment Matrix

Service	Executive	Portfolio Manager	Program Manager	Project Manager	PMO	Sponsor	Other Stakeholder
Feedback to senior management on the success of strategic initiatives	I	A			RI		
Reporting results linked to organizational strategy	I	A			R		I (Strategy department)
Horizon scan for impending policy or strategy changes		I			A, R		C (Strategy department)

Helpful hints for when the PMO is delivering this service group

Ensure that any feedback on the success or failure of the chosen initiatives is fed back into the portfolio management framework in order that there is more chance of selecting successful initiatives in future.

Feedback to senior management on the success of strategic initiatives

Service description

The assessment of the success of each completed project and program within the portfolio in their delivery of the strategic goals.

What the service provides for the customer

This provides an independent assessment of the project and program delivery. This review covers the how well the project or program was delivered as well as the contribution it made to the delivery of the strategic benefits.

Why is this service being offered to the customer?

This allows the organization to understand (retrospectively) the success of the projects (collectively) in delivery of the strategic objectives. Further analysis made be required to understand the underlying reasons for any deviation from the expected success levels.

How PMO will apply this service

The PMO will review the benefits realization plan for the projects which have just delivered to see whether they are delivering the expected benefits. They will find the details from the project which has delivered including: the schedule, the financial plan, the business case, the lessons register. They will review the post implementation review to assess the general success of the project – did it deliver as expected?

Based on all the information the PMO will provide feedback to the portfolio manager and the Project Approval Board on whether the project was delivered in a successful manner. They will provide feedback on whether the project is likely to deliver the expected benefits. They will assess whether there are any gaps in the delivery of the strategy that this project will not be able to achieve. The PMO will provide recommendations about how any gaps can be filled.

Supplier	Input	Process	Output	Customer
Strategy Project Manager	Latest approved Business case Financial plan Schedule Benefits realization plan Strategic plan Lessons register	Benefits Realization Review portfolio performance	Portfolio level benefits realization plan	Senior Management Project Approval Board Strategy Portfolio Manager

How the PMO will measure the value of this service

This can be measured by feedback from the portfolio manager. This can be measured by an increase in the benefits realization across the portfolio.

Criteria when the PMO will use this service

- When the PMO is aligned to a portfolio manager
- Where the organization has a strategic plan
- Where the organization wishes to track the delivery of the strategy

Helpful hints for the PMO when delivering the service

- Separate out the success in the delivery of the project from the successful delivery of the benefits
- If projects have been particularly successful, see if any lessons can be learnt and transferred to other ongoing projects
- For project failures, see if root causes can be identified and actions raised to prevent this happening in other projects

PMO Capabilities needed to fulfil this service

Competencies	Techniques and generic tools
Knowledge Management Reporting, Insights and Analysis Assurance Personal Communication Relationships and engagement	Root Cause Analysis Failure Modes and Effects Analysis (FMEA)

Related services

Review post-program benefits against strategic investment decisions Track and report on benefit realization Enable sharing of good practice Capture good practice examples for inclusion in good practice repository	Manage the Process Improvement Plan Document project and program success stories Perform data analysis of project selection and delivery performance Reporting results linked to organizational strategy

Reporting results linked to organizational strategy

Service description

Provision of reporting showing how the portfolio is delivering against strategy.

What the service provides for the customer

This provides reports to show how well the portfolio is delivering the strategic aims for the organization.

Why is this service being offered to the customer?

By understanding how well the strategy is being delivered the portfolio manager along with the Project Approval Board can decide which new projects and programs to approve which will ensure the rest of the strategy can be delivered. It will allow them to make decisions on which items to stop as they are no longer delivering strategic value.

How PMO will apply this service

The PMO will obtain a copy of the strategic plan. They will find the latest copy of the portfolio delivery plan showing which projects are being delivered and how they align with the strategy. The PMO reporting can include:

- Strategic alignment – how well the portfolio aligns with the strategy
- Benefits realized – how much of the strategy has already been delivered vs how much is left to be done
- RAG status – how well the portfolio is delivering, using the RAG status of the projects and programs as guidance
- Delivery dates – when the existing portfolio is expected to deliver the strategic objectives

The reports, along with any analysis and commentary will be shared with the portfolio manager and the Project Approval Board.

Supplier	Input	Process	Output	Customer
Strategy department Portfolio Manager	Strategic plan Portfolio delivery plan	Analyse Strategic delivery	Strategic delivery report	Portfolio Manager Project Approval Board

How the PMO will measure the value of this service

This can be measured by the increase of the portfolio in the strategic deliverables. It can be measure by feedback from the Project Approval Board and the portfolio manager.

Criteria when the PMO will use this service

- When the PMO is aligned to a portfolio manager
- Where the organization has a published strategic plan
- Where the PMO supports the Project Approval Board

Helpful hints for the PMO when delivering the service

- The actual reports produced will be tailored to what decisions the portfolio manager and Project Approval Board are trying to make based on review of strategy

PMO Capabilities needed to fulfil this service

Competencies	Techniques and generic tools
Benefits and Value Management Reporting, Insights and Analysis Relationships and engagement Teamwork	Gap analysis Tornado diagram Categorized frequency analysis (Frequency plot, bar chart) Prioritization matrices

Related services

Feedback to senior management on the success of strategic initiatives Maintain a register for current and potential programs and projects Perform data analysis of project selection and delivery performance	Establish a portfolio management framework Set up and track portfolio, program, and project metrics (KPI's)

Horizon scan for impending policy or strategy changes

Service description

A review of the upcoming legislation, industry trends, internal announcements for changes that may impact the portfolio or affect the strategic direction of the organization.

What the service provides for the customer

This provides a list of changes that may impact the delivery of the portfolio, both positive and negative.

Why is this service being offered to the customer?

By having a wider awareness of what is going on the PMO can provide early warning to the portfolio manager on changes that will have an impact (positive or negative) on the portfolio. This will allow the portfolio manager to deal with the situation before it occurs.

How PMO will apply this service

The PMO will be aware of what is coming up on the horizon including:

- Legislation changes – are there any laws that are being discussed which will impact the organization, and therefore for portfolio
- Organizational changes – have there been changes to the way the organization is lead, which will have an impact on portfolio delivery, or at least stakeholder management
- Policy changes – are there any changes to the internal policies e.g. financial approvals, purchasing, external recruitment which will have an impact on the portfolio
- Industry trends – is the industry going in a particular direct which will force the organization to react e.g. different sales outlets, new technology
- Competitor changes – are the direct competitors trying something new that this organization may want to follow suit, or offer an alternative, which will mean new projects will need to be added in

For each of these, the PMO will assess what impact (if any) the changes are likely to have, and when they are likely to materialize. Depending on the level of change the PMO may want to raise this as a risk to the portfolio with the portfolio manager. They may want to suggest a new project to be added to the portfolio.

Supplier	Input	Process	Output	Customer
Strategy Industry specific groups Government	Strategic Plan Legislation changes Industry trends	Review strategic horizon	Risks Project Approval Form	Portfolio Manager Strategy

How the PMO will measure the value of this service

This can be measured by seeing how many portfolio level changes are identified in advance of them being announced. This can be measured by asking for feedback from the portfolio manager.

Criteria when the PMO will use this service

- Where the PMO is aligned to a portfolio manager
- Where the PMO works closely with the strategy department
- Where there is a published strategic plan

Helpful hints for the PMO when delivering the service

- Consider subscribing to newsfeeds and webinars that are related to the industry that organization operates within
- Ensure you are up to date on any of the organizational changes
- Be aware of upcoming legislation within all the countries/sectors that the organization operates
- Be aware of any of the policy changes within the organization

PMO Capabilities needed to fulfil this service

Competencies	Techniques and generic tools
Knowledge Management Reporting, Insights and Analysis Governance Frameworks Professionalism and ethics Relationships and engagement Teamwork Resourcefulness	Comparative advantage analysis Gap analysis Market / Competitor Analysis Organization charts & position descriptions

Related services

Capture and categorize new ideas Strategic Risk Assessment	Contribute to the identification of risks Business strategy and roadmap maintenance

PPM Tool Support

PPM Tool Support

Description

This service domain covers the PMO's ability to implement, maintain and use Portfolio, Program and Project Management tools. These tools can be commercial off-the-shelf tools or can be ones that have been developed in house. This may cover a single tool or a group of tools, which may or may not be integrated.

What the services within the domain provide for the customer

By using a PPM tool, the PMO is able to offer consistency in the information provided. These tools provide a way of validating the information being entered and having the information in a single place enables visibility and transparency. A PPM tool is linked into the processes being used and therefore not only is the information consistent, but it helps ensure the processes are being followed.

Helpful hints for when the PMO is delivering this service domain

When using commercial tools, the PMO will need to ensure the license and support costs are factored into the cost of running the PMO or are costed elsewhere within the organization.

The PMO will need to be aware of any restrictions on usage of the tool.

These tools may be implemented by related departments such as finance or procurement or may just cover the PPM domain. The PMO can benefit from having all their information in a central location therefore saving time in locating information.

Any tool will need to have technical support from the supplier (even if this is internal), IT support for the technical platform this resides (if this is done as Software as a Service (SaaS) then this may be the same people, and support to ensure individuals have the correct access to information within the tool. It can fall to the PMO to be responsible for the user support and training of the tool usage.

PPM Tool Design

Service group description

This group of services is concerned with the creation, implementation, and rollout of PPM tools. These tools can be developed in-house or could be commercial off-the-shelf tools.

Why have these services been grouped together?

These services enable the PMO to ensure they have the appropriate tool(s) to perform their role. If the tool is not directly implemented for PPM e.g. a finance or procurement tool the PMO needs to be aware how the tool can be utilized for the benefit of PPM within the organization.

List of related services described in other areas

Automate Processes

Responsibility Assignment Matrix

Service	Executive	Portfolio Manager	Program Manager	Project Manager	PMO	Sponsor	Other Stakeholder
Advise on PPM tools and software	A	C	C	C	R	I	I (PPM Staff)
Develops in-house project management tools		C	C	C	R		R (Developer)
Tailors and configures project management tools		I	I	I	R		

The head of PMO (PMO Manager/PMO lead) is typically involved with the selection and the implementation of the tool(s). if in-house tools are used these may or may not be created by the PMO themselves or another member of the PPM community.

Helpful hints for when the PMO is delivering this service group

- When selecting the right tool for the organization to use the PMO must be aware of the maturity of the organization and select one that fits in with their current maturity level whilst leaving space for the organization to grow. If an overly complex tool is chosen compared with the ability of the key users to operate it will result in frustration. If a too simplistic tool is chosen it may not be flexible enough to support the different process permutations that the organization uses
- The tool chosen should be able to support the processes rather than the processes changed so the tool can work in the organization
- Care must be taken to work out how the tool can be supported, both technically and from a user access perspective. What if any training will be required, both with the initial rollout and when new people need to use this?
- Sometimes it can be better not to implement any tool rather than implement one that does not fit the organization
- If moving from one tool to another what is the cost to the users & the data of moving. Will it give the chance for the organization to move forward or will it lead to organizations maintaining the data in multiple places?

Advise on PPM tools and software

Service description

The PMO can advise on how tools can support the PPM process set. Based on their experience, the PPM software market, and services like Gartner the PMO can help the organization choose a PPM tool which will align to the maturity of the organization.

What the service provides for the customer

The recipients of this service include project & program managers, portfolio managers, PPM staff (if the tool includes a time sheeting element) and the senior management who would need to pay for the tool and gain the reports from the data.

They would be getting advice on what is the appropriate PPM tool for their organization. This may include in-house offerings (e.g. SharePoint sites) as well as vendor software. As well as tool choice this would include information on how the tool would support or enhance the processes, how the tool will be supported and what training is available for the users.

Why is this service being offered to the customer?

The PMO understands the organizational maturity and understands how a tool will support the project/program managers. They may have previously used a variety of PPM tools.

The PMO will typically be the place where a PPM tool is supported in terms of user administration (maintaining drop downs etc.). They will be expected to train the people in the use of the tool and will alter the procedures to incorporate references to the tool. The PMO will be expected to use the information from the tool to create consolidated reports which are used by senior individuals and groups within the organization.

To gain the most advantage a PPM tool needs to be implemented centrally as it will need to be administered, amended and training provided. It is important that any tool implemented meets to maturity of the organization, whilst allowing room to expand.

How PMO will apply this service

The PMO will need to go and speak to the customers of the tool to find out the requirements, what the tool is expected to support. The PMO will then review the market to see what tools are available, if none are suitable then consideration should be given as to whether something developed in house should be selected, or even no tool used.

If an external tool supplier is selected, then consideration should be given as to whether this needs to be run as a project using the existing project management framework.

Supplier	Input	Process	Output	Customer
PPM staff Tool/Software vendors In house developers	Tool requirements Tool abilities	Decision making	PMO Advice	Project Managers Program Managers Portfolio Managers PPM Staff Senior Management

The PMO need to consider:

- How the training in the use of the tool & the related processes will be done for the customers of the tool?
- How the information will be extracted in the form of reports?
- How extensible is the tool (to allow room for expansion)?
- Who will technically support this (backup/restores/tool availability)?

How the PMO will measure the value of this service

For larger tool selection this should follow the normal business case / benefits management processes. For smaller decisions, the PMO may consider taking some customer feedback prior to the tool decision and afterwards to see whether the advice has helped the customers in their tool usage.

Criteria when the PMO will use this service

This service is typically used when the organization has reached a level of maturity or complexity that it is becoming difficult to manage the control of projects just through the use of office tools such as Excel.

It can be used when the organization is trying to consolidate the usage of tools across multiple projects to provide some consistency of data captured.

Helpful hints for the PMO when delivering the service

- Ensure that you have processes already in place that the tool can support
- Understand the motivation for the organization in wanting to move to use a tool
- Understand the maturity of the organization to select something that is not too advanced, yet not too basic
- Be prepared to recommend that no tool is used until the process has been fully defined
- Take recommendations from the people who will use the tool as they may already be using a basic product they have been using for free and now require this to be moved to the paid service
- Understand the people who may benefit from the tool being introduced may not be the people using the tool e.g. senior managers may like the information to come out, but they may not be putting the data in
- Ensure it is confirmed who will enter the data, who will keep it current and who will use the data
- Remember when putting in an interim tool that it may be in place for serval years before it is replaced

PMO Capabilities needed to fulfil this service

Competencies	Techniques and generic tools
Supplier Management P3M Tools	Make or buy analysis Comparative advantage analysis Gap analysis Capability and Capacity analysis Market / Competitor Analysis Process Analysis Flowcharts Project Management Information System Scheduling tool

Related services

Develops in-house project management tools Tailors and configures project management tools Develop or source tools for PPM document configuration management Implements vendor provided project management tools Automate Processes	Develop or source tools for Quality Control Introduce tools for controlling changes Provide tools and analysis for Business Capacity Management Introduce tools for managing risks Provision of Management Dashboards

Further Reading

Gartner magic quadrant for PPM vendors

Develops in-house project management tools

Service description

For organizations without a single source of the truth or where the vendor tool needs extending the PMO develops tools to fill the gaps. These will need supporting, documenting, and training by the PMO.

What the service provides for the customer

This will provide the project and program managers with a tool or series of tools to support their PPM processes. These can range from the simple risk/issue registers up to a PPM reporting suite. As these are developed in-house, they can be very closely aligned to the PPM processes they are needing to support.

Why is this service being offered to the customer?

These tools are developed to support the gaps where either no central tool exists or where the central tool does not provide the functionality required.

How PMO will apply this service

Having identified a gap in the provision of tools the PMO will consult with the potential users of the tool and gain a set of requirements. This can be brief such as we want a risk register to support the risk process. This helps understand what the need is for the tool.

Once the PMO has a set of requirements they will then identify the software used to create the tool. Once the tool has been developed the PMO will try this out (test it) internally before engaging with the customer for the tool. The PMO can then incorporate any feedback received to enhance the tool.

The PMO will ensure there is a user guide and training available to support the tool.

Supplier	Input	Process	Output	Customer
Project Managers PMO Resource Managers	Requirements	Software development	Excel macro sheets SharePoint sites Access Databases	Project managers Program managers Portfolio managers Resource managers PMO

How the PMO will measure the value of this service

The main measure will be in the uptake of the tool by the customer.

Value can be measured by the numbers of customers suggesting the tool usage and coming to the PMO to see how they can get the best out of the tool. If the customers are suggesting enhancements to the tool that shows, they are using it and want to make it better.

Criteria when the PMO will use this service

This would only be used where there is no central tool, or the central tool does not support the functionality of the tool being developed.
The PMO will need to be sufficiently technical proficient to think about using this service. Although it can be easy to develop a risk register in Excel or SharePoint it will need to be maintained. An understanding of how the tool can support the methodology being used will be required to ensure the tool adequately supports the process.

Helpful hints for the PMO when delivering the service

- If this tool is being developed by an external contractor think about how this will be supported when they leave
- Think about how this will be maintained. Do you have a central tool which can be updated for all (like SharePoint) or is distributed so there may be multiple copies (like a spreadsheet)?
- What are the reporting requirements from the data within the tool? Are these built into the tool itself or will the data be exported and used elsewhere e.g. risks being copied into a progress report/presentation
- Do we need some people to be editors and others to just read the information?
- Does the content within the tool need to be made secure (as it contains confidential information)?
- What training is required for people to use the tool? Is the training going to cover the tool or will it cover the process and the tool usage?
- Consider piloting the tool with a subset of users prior to making it available to all as this will allow you to see the flaws (if there are any) early and will give a set of users who can help the PMO promote the use of the tool

PMO Capabilities needed to fulfil this service

Competencies	Techniques and generic tools
Information Management Reporting, Insights and Analysis Delivery Methods P3M Tools Relationships and engagement	Gap analysis Process Analysis Risk Register Performance variance report Project Management Information System Scheduling tool Stakeholder checklist Stakeholder engagement assessment matrix Work Breakdown Structure

Related services

Tailors and configures project management tools Manages project management tools (systems admin) Introduce tools for controlling changes Advise on PPM tools and software Introduce tools for managing issues	Define, maintain, and implement reporting framework Develop or source tools for Quality Control Provide tools and analysis for Business Capacity Management Introduce tools for managing risks

Tailors and configures project management tools

Service description

Most large third-party vendors provide a way for the tool to be customized which still allows for the tool to be upgraded. Additional fields, screens and reports allow the PMO to make the most of the tool and bend the tool to support the process rather the other way around.

What the service provides for the customer

The customer will get an improved tool. This may be a slicker way of doing something they already have, new or enhanced functionality or reporting.

Why is this service being offered to the customer?

The PMO typically support the PPM tools within the organization hence they are best placed to update the tool and configure this in a way that will improve the tool usage. Enhancements to the tool ensure that the tool usage grows in line with the maturity and expectations of the organization.

How PMO will apply this service

The PMO will identify a need to make a change to the PPM tool. Using the administration screens provided by the vendor software the PMO will look to make the required changes. Once the changes have been made the PMO will review this internally to ensure that it is fit for purpose. The changes can then be tested by a subset of the PPM tool users before being rolled out to everyone.

Supplier	Input	Process	Output	Customer
PMO PPM tool users	Vendor software Requirements	Creating new screens Creating new reports	New screens New reports Updated screens Updated reports	Project managers Program managers Portfolio managers Resource managers PPM tool users PMO

How the PMO will measure the value of this service

KPI examples, satisfaction measurement, or any other way of proving the effect of this service.

Criteria when the PMO will use this service

- A PPM tool is in use
- A change to the PPM tool has been identified

Helpful hints for the PMO when delivering the service

- Although this is mainly focused on vendor software, this may be applicable to in-house developed tools as well
- Consideration should be made to making changes to the PPM tool within a test environment, so they can be developed and tested without impacting the regular use of the tool
- If lots of changes are requested to the tool, consider creating a change process to evaluate the need for each of the changes
- Ensure the PMO is trained up in the use of the administration screens
- Ensure that any changes to the tool are accompanied by changes to the documentation and training

PMO Capabilities needed to fulfil this service

Competencies	Techniques and generic tools
Change Management Information Management Reporting, Insights and Analysis P3M Tools	Gap analysis Process Analysis Change control tools Project Management Information System Swim-lane flowcharts

Related services

Implements vendor provided project management tools Manages project management tools (systems admin) Introduce tools for controlling changes Develop or source tools for PPM document configuration management Advise on PPM tools and software Develops in-house project management tools	Introduce tools for managing issues Define, maintain, and implement reporting framework Develop or source tools for Quality Control Introduce tools for controlling changes Provide tools and analysis for Business Capacity Management Introduce tools for managing risks

PPM Tool Operations

Service group description

These services are concerned with the implementation and management of PPM tools, whether in-house or vendor supplied. The management consists of ensuring the right people have access and controlling the lists of data within the tool. Depending on the size and scope of the tool this may include setting up new projects, resources, users within the tool.

Why have these services been grouped together?

If the organization is using a PPM tool the user admin tends to reside within the PMO area. There are 2 main services here. One to ensure the tool is implemented and the other to maintain the access and the lists of data within this. The implementation is done infrequently; however, the maintenance is an ongoing responsibility. Without the tool being present the maintenance will not be needed.

List of related services described in other areas

Chase up missing timesheets
Develop or source tools for PPM document configuration management
Administer document tools
Introduce tools for managing issues
Provide tools and analysis for Business Capacity Management
Develop or source tools for Quality Control
Introduce tools for managing risks

Responsibility Assignment Matrix

Service	Executive	Portfolio Manager	Program Manager	Project Manager	PMO	Sponsor	Other Stakeholder
Implements vendor provided project management tools	A	C	C	C	R	I	R (Technical Support)
Manages project management tools (systems admin)	A	I	I	I	R		

The senior management in the organization are typically responsible for the decision to implement a tool. The responsibility for maintaining the tool fits under the PMO manager.

Access is controlled on behalf of the PPM staff within the organization.

Helpful hints for when the PMO is delivering this service group

When maintaining the data within a PPM tool ensure there is a clear understanding about how access is provided and under what circumstances lists of data change. This may be linked to changes to processes and procedures and related training. If the tool is distributed rather than centrally available (e.g. a risk register) think about how the users will receive updated versions of the tool and the impact of them using an outdated version of the tool, especially if the processes have changed to align to the new version of the tool.

Implements vendor provided project management tools

Service description

This covers the implementation of a chosen tool within the organization. The decision on which tool to implement can be taken outside the PMO, typically involving representatives of the project and portfolio management community. The PMO will typically be involved with the training of the PPM staff who use the tool and the linkages between the tool and the procedures the tool is expected to support.

What the service provides for the customer

The result of this service will be a PPM tool which will provide a standard way of controlling projects. There are a variety of customers for this service. This includes the PMO who will have a single source of the truth. The Project, Program and Portfolio Managers who will use the tools to aid them in running their projects (the extent to which this helps depends on the capabilities of the tool being implemented). It will aid Sergio Rossi management who can use the data entered into the tool to provide reports to make decisions about the status of the projects, programs, and the portfolio.

Why is this service being offered to the customer?

The PMO understand the PPM processes and work with the Project, Program and Portfolio Managers. The PMO can assist the tool vendor with understanding how the tool needs to be tweaked to align to the processes and update the procedures to incorporate references to the tool. Once the tool has been implemented the PMO will pick up future training of new people as they turn up. The PMO is typically expected to support the tool in terms of system administration (providing access, updating data lists). If the PMO is involved in the initial implementation they will then be in a position to provide this support once the tool is in use.

How PMO will apply this service

Once a decision has been made to implement a PPM tool the PMO will need to be involved as customers of the PPM tool, in-house trainers in the use of the tool, future system administrators and as representatives of the other users of the tool.

The PMO will need to work with the tool supplier to develop the specific training for the users. The training should focus on how the tool supports the procedures of the organization and if necessary, the PMO should look to provide some user guides and quick reference material. The training may vary depending how much of the tool the users are expected to use e.g. a project manager will typically use more of a PPM tool than a timesheet user.

As part of the implementation the PMO will need to ensure that the data lists are populated, and they understand how these can be updated in future. This includes understanding how access is controlled to the tool and to items within the tool.

Depending on the scope of the tool it may be necessary to create new projects (and close them) as well as new resources. The PMO need to develop procedures explaining how these items get created, who does this and how the PMO will be notified that these need creating/updating/closing.

Supplier	Input	Process	Output	Customer
Vendors	Vendor Software	Software implementation	Project management tool	Project managers Program managers Portfolio managers Timesheet users Resource managers PMO

How the PMO will measure the value of this service

If the tool is implemented and the users understand how the tool works, then this service is a success. An alternative way of measuring this could be to measure the number of people trained in the use of the system as a proportion of users. This would be split by resource type e.g. Project Managers, Timesheets users.

The people using the tool may not be happy they have to use the tool as they may want to do things their own way or use a different tool so customer satisfaction may be the wrong measurement to use to understand the success of this service.

Criteria when the PMO will use this service

- This service should be used once a decision has been made to implement a new PPM tool

Helpful hints for the PMO when delivering the service

The PMO will need to understand how the tool is being technically supported, what is the route for escalations in case of a defect in the tool and the service level agreement (SLA) to get fixes applied. The tool support may be directly through the vendor or there may be an internal technical team who provides initial support prior to escalating through to the vendor.

The PMO needs to be aware of the contractual arrangements for support costs, licensing fees, upgrades in order that this is budgeted for.

If these items are not done by the PMO directly then the PMO will need to know who in the organization has that responsibility in order, they can contact them should circumstances change.

PMO Capabilities needed to fulfil this service

Competencies	Techniques and generic tools
Stakeholder Engagement Supplier Management P3M Tools Personal Communication	Risk Register Component milestones Project Management Information System Scheduling tool Stakeholder checklist Stakeholder engagement assessment matrix Work Breakdown Structure

Related services

Advise on PPM tools and software Tailors and configures project management tools Manages project management tools (systems admin) Introduce tools for controlling changes Develop or source tools for PPM document configuration management Automate Processes	Introduce tools for managing issues Define, maintain, and implement reporting framework Develop or source tools for Quality Control Provide tools and analysis for Business Capacity Management Introduce tools for managing risks

Manages project management tools (systems admin)

Service description

If a PPM tool is in use then the core data within this tool, such as projects, resources, data lists will require regular updating to add in new information and to close or archive old information. The PMO will do this via standard screens only accessible by individuals with an administration logon. The actual data needing to updated will depend on the tool in use.

What the service provides for the customer

The individuals using the PPM tool (typically project, program, and portfolio managers) will have access to the correct information. Any drop downs that are available within the tool are linked to the processes and procedures for PPM management. Without this being done the PPM tool will not be as usable and may even be unused.

Why is this service being offered to the customer?

A PPM tool, whether in-house or vendor supplied will require some administration of core data such as resources, users, projects, rates, and drop-down lists. The PMO will typically have access to these screens that allow this to be done and will be able control who has access to what within the tool. This means the PPM staff, including Project Managers, Program Managers and Portfolio Managers will have the correct access to use the tool. By having the information set up correctly allows the PMO to slice their reporting in different ways. For example, if projects need to be aligned to the strategic aims when they change the alignment of the projects will need to be changed in the tool. The PMO can ensure this is done centrally without burdening each project manager with the responsibility.

If access is security controlled, then the PMO can be responsible for adding/removing/changing users' access.

How PMO will apply this service

The request to change an item within the tool may come from inside or outside the PMO. The PMO will then decide whether this is a change that should/can be performed within the tool. They will then follow the documented procedures in making the change. Once the change has been made, they will inform the requestor that this change has been performed.

If the change cannot be made the PMO will need to explain to the requestor the reason behind this decision and any alternative ways, the request may be performed.

Supplier	Input	Process	Output	Customer
PPM Tool users PMO	Vendor Software	Adding / removing a user Adding / removing a resource Adding / closing a project Resource rate updates Drop down updates	Updated project management tool	Project managers Program managers Portfolio managers Timesheet recorders Resource managers PMO

How the PMO will measure the value of this service

This service is typically measured by the length of time taken to make the change. This is calculated as the time between the request going in and the notification back to the requestor of the change being made.

Criteria when the PMO will use this service

- This will be done when there is a PPM tool to support

Helpful hints for the PMO when delivering the service

- If a drop down is changing it may be necessary for the PMO to go through and update not only the drop down but other information within the system e.g. if the list of applicable strategies is changed the PMO will need to go through and re-align all open projects to the new strategy list. Or if a project manager leaves and a new one joins then the PMO will need to reassign the projects from the old project manager to the new one
- The actual items to be updated will depend on the tool being supported. There are lots of different vendor supplied tools, as well as in-house developed tools. The procedures shown above are a typical example. The actual procedures will need to be changed to cover the different parts of the tool that need to be changed
- The PMO should ensure they write a procedural guide to ensure that administrative changes are made in a consistent manner
- The PMO may need to provide an externally focused guide which explains to PPM tool users how they would request an administrative change gets made and any necessary approvals required before this update is performed. The PMO may consider providing a template for individuals to fill in when requesting an update
- Sometimes changes will be asked for that cannot be done within the tool, either because the tool does not support this or because it goes against the governance agreement or against the agreed procedures. The procedures need to cover this eventuality
- Failure to provide this service (or have someone in the organization who does this) means that the tool may not be used
- The PMO should set a Service Level Agreement (SLA) so that requestors will know how long it takes to make a change. If they have set an SLA this will need to be monitored and where items take longer than the SLA that the root cause for this is understood and a solution found to ensure it does not occur in future

PMO Capabilities needed to fulfil this service

Competencies	Techniques and generic tools
P3M Administration Information Management Governance Frameworks P3M Tools	Capability and Capacity analysis Process Analysis Prompt Lists Check sheets Project Management Information System

Related services

Implements vendor provided project management tools Introduce tools for controlling changes Develops in-house project management tools Tailors and configures project management tools Administer document tools	Introduce tools for managing issues Develop or source tools for Quality Control Maintain resource database Introduce tools for managing risks

Process Improvement

Process Improvement

Description

The review and improvement of processes used in the delivery of projects, programs, and portfolios.

What the services within the area provide for the customer

These provide the organisation a means of improving the processes, tools, templates, help, and guides. This allows the organisation to take stock of what is working and enhance and refine this, so it works better than before

Tips and tricks for when the PMO is delivering this service area

- When changing a process ensure that people using the process are involved with the change as they will be more aware of what works and what does not
- Ensure that after changing the process all the relevant people are trained
- If a process is changed check whether any automation needs to be updated
- Remember the drivers for process improvement can come from changes to corporate governance as well as suggestions from people using the existing processes

Process Improvement Operations

Service group description

The improvement and automation of existing processes

Why have these services been grouped together?

These services relate to the identification of process improvements. Process improvements are not done in isolation, an improvement to the risk process may have a knock-on impact to the change or issue processes.

List of related services described in other domain groups

Develop benefits management framework
Develop the overall change control framework
Communicate the change control framework
Create Change Management Framework
Communicate change management framework
Develop and maintain the communication framework
Develop configuration management standards and processes
Train people in configuration management
Develop and maintain the PPM financial framework
Define, maintain, and implement PPM governance framework
Develop the overall issue management framework
Train the issue management framework
Create and maintain knowledge management framework
Define, maintain, and implement standard PPM framework
Define, maintain, and implement framework for monitoring and review
Develop and maintain the overall Quality Control Framework
Train the Quality Control Framework
Develop and maintain the overall Quality Assurance Framework
Develop the overall risk management framework
Train the risk management framework
Develop and maintain the stakeholder engagement framework
Define, maintain, and implement reporting framework
Define planning standards and templates
Develop and maintain tailoring guidelines for standards, methods, and approaches
Work with Procurement teams to agree PPM purchasing Framework
Communicate PPM purchasing Framework

Responsibility Assignment Matrix

Service	Executive	Portfolio Manager	Program Manager	Project Manager	PMO	Sponsor	Other Stakeholder
Map key value streams and processes	C	C	C	C	R	A	
Automate Processes		C	C	C	A, F		
Monitor use of corporate guidance and standards to identify improvements					A, F		
Manage the Process Improvement Plan					A, F		

Tips and tricks for when the PMO is delivering this service group

Be willing to accept assistance from people who are using the current processes as they can help identify improvements

Sometimes it can be better to completely replace or remove a poorly performing process rather than try to fix what cannot be mended

Map key value streams and processes

Service description

The review and mapping of processes in order to identify and reduce waste

What the service provides for the customer

This ensures that the processes are leaner and any 'waste' activities are removed. This will improve the productivity of people using those processes

Why is this service being offered to the customer?

Improved processes will make the people using them and the organisation more productive. By cutting out the waste it can increase the morale of individuals as they will feel that their time is not being wasted by performing unnecessary tasks.

How PMO will apply this service

For each process the PMO are mapping, they will lay out the steps in the process, who they are being performed by and identify how long it takes for each step to be performed, both elapsed and actual. It is worth collecting information about repeated steps due to mistakes made in previous steps.

Having laid out the map of the current process then the future map of the process should be produced. What will it look like if all of the waste activities could be removed?

Having identified the waste items that could be removed e.g. waiting times, defects/mistakes the PMO will then prioritise the order in which those items can be removed. The PMO will look to incorporate the changes required into the processes and ensure the people using the processes are retrained on the changes that have been made.

Supplier	Input	Process	Output	Customer
PMO Project Manager Program Manager Portfolio Manager	Existing processes	Value stream mapping	Updated process New process	PMO Project Manager Program Manager Portfolio Manager

How the PMO will measure the value of this service

- Reduction in time to perform the process after the mapping activity has been done and the waste removed

Criteria when the PMO will use this service

- When designing a new process
- When reviewing or updating an existing process

Tips and tricks for the PMO when delivering the service

- Consider getting an experienced Lean Six Sigma practitioner in to assist with the mapping
- Some of the waste activities could be down to the training of the individuals performing the process rather than any defects in the process itself

PMO Capabilities needed to fulfil this service

Competencies	Techniques and generic tools
Change Control Knowledge Management Delivery Methods Governance Frameworks	Root Cause Analysis Failure Modes and Effects Analysis (FMEA) Process Analysis Value-add/non-value-add analysis SIPOC Task responsibility matrix/RACI Value stream map

Related services

Develop benefits management framework Develop the overall change control framework Create Change Management Framework Develop and maintain the communication framework Develop configuration management standards and processes Develop and maintain the PPM financial framework Define, maintain, and implement PPM governance framework Develop the overall issue management framework Create and maintain knowledge management framework	Define, maintain, and implement standard PPM framework Define, maintain, and implement framework for monitoring and review Develop and maintain the overall Quality Control Framework Develop and maintain the overall Quality Assurance Framework Develop the overall risk management framework Develop and maintain the stakeholder engagement framework Define, maintain, and implement reporting framework Develop and maintain tailoring guidelines for standards, methods, and approaches Work with Procurement teams to agree PPM purchasing Framework

Automate Processes

Service description

The development and enhancement of automation for existing PMO processes

What the service provides for the customer

Automating a process can ensure the process is performed in a consistent manner. It can reduce the time taken to perform that process. It can increase the accuracy of the data required for the process

Why is this service being offered to the customer?

Automation of a process will provide a simplified and consistent way of performing the actions required in the process. Time that was previously spent in executing that process can be spent elsewhere

How PMO will apply this service

The PMO will identify which processes are worth automating. To decide this, they will look at: the time taken to perform the process; the value of the process; the frequency the process is likely to change; the frequency that the process is used; the ability to codify the instructions in the process.

Once the processes have been identified they will look to decide on how much automation to apply. This could be a simple matter of providing some dropdown selections all the way through a Robotic Process Automation solution with embedded Artificial Intelligence.

They will select the tool they are going to use to perform the automation and ensure they have the necessary skills to use the tool.

They will develop, test, and deploy the automation including the training of any individuals who are required to use the process with the new tool.

Whenever the process changes, consideration must be given as to whether the automation requires updating.

Supplier	Input	Process	Output	Customer
PMO Project Manager Program Manager Portfolio Manager	Issue Management framework PPM framework Risk Management Framework Progress Reports Automation Software	Automate Process	Automation	PMO Project Manager Program Manager Portfolio Manager

How the PMO will measure the value of this service

- Accuracy of data provided
- Reduction in time to perform the process

Criteria when the PMO will use this service

- When the PMO has the skills to produce and update the automation
- When the value of automating the process is greater than performing this manually
- When the process can be codified and is not subject to a 'it depends' decision

Tips and tricks for the PMO when delivering the service

- Ensure the process being automated is well understood and unlikely to change significantly (at least while the process is being automated)
- Look to see if the steps in the process can be simplified as part of the automation
- Work out who will be responsible for verifying that the automation has been successful
- Consider what will happen should the automation fail. Will you know? Who can fix this? Is there a manual workaround in the event of a total automation failure?
- Ensure that automation is reviewed and updated when the process changes
- If the automation has been updated does the process still align with the automation?
- The more frequent and repetitive the process the greater the case for automation

PMO Capabilities needed to fulfil this service

Competencies	Techniques and generic tools
Business Case Change Control Financial Management Information Management Issue Management Planning and Scheduling Quality Management Reporting, Insights and Analysis Resource Management Risk Management Stakeholder Engagement Delivery Methods Governance Frameworks P3M Tools Personal Communication Relationships and engagement Teamwork Result Orientation	Business value Analysis Process Analysis Value-add/non-value-add analysis Change control tools Project Management Information System Swim-lane flowcharts

Related services

Develop the overall change control framework Introduce tools for controlling changes Ensure quality of change requests Develop or source tools for PPM document configuration management Establish and maintain the CI index Administer document tools Develop Business Case process and templates Prepare monthly financial reports Define, maintain, and implement PPM governance framework Develop the overall issue management framework Introduce tools for managing issues	Define, maintain, and implement reporting framework Define, maintain, and implement standard PPM framework Tailor standard processes and template to the program or project Advise on PPM tools and software Implements vendor provided project management tools Develop and maintain the overall Quality Control Framework Develop the overall risk management framework Introduce tools for managing risks Collate individual progress reports Provision of Management Dashboards Monitor use of corporate guidance and standards to identify improvements

Monitor use of corporate guidance and standards to identify improvements

Service description

The provision of feedback to the other departments (e.g. procurement, finance, HR) on improvements to their standards based on feedback from the PPM community.

The monitoring of changes in corporate standards which will require the frameworks to be updated.

What the service provides for the customer

For the PMO this ensures that the frameworks are kept up to date in alignment with the corporate standards.

For the other departments it ensures that the standards do not contain any ambiguity and they benefit from the feedback from real world usage.

Why is this service being offered to the customer?

This ensures that the guidance on offer is still relevant, useful, and workable. As the PMO are responsible for reviewing the lessons they can identify those that relate back to the corporate standards.

The PMO are responsible for the maintenance of the frameworks and need to ensure that they are aligned to the corporate standards.

How PMO will apply this service

The PMO will look at the lessons register to see how many actions relate to the changing of the corporate guidance. For each of the actions that suggest changes to the corporate guidance the PMO will contact the relevant department and inform them of the suggested change. The PMO will monitor to see whether this change gets adopted. If it does, then the PMO may need to change their framework to incorporate the change.

The PMO will monitor any changes to the corporate guidance. If they see any changes then they will have a look and see whether this means that any of the frameworks need to change. If they do, then they will add details of what needs to change to the Process Improvement Plan. They will assign this an owner and a delivery date.

Supplier	Input	Process	Output	Customer
PMO	Lessons Register	Analyse Lessons Register	Improvement suggestions	Other departments
Other departments	Corporate Standards	Monitor standards	Process Improvement Plan	PMO

How the PMO will measure the value of this service

This can be measured by looking at the alignment of the corporate standards with the various PPM frameworks.

Criteria when the PMO will use this service

- As part of the review process when looking at the lessons register to add items to the Process Improvement Plan
- Where the PMO is permanent
- Where there are changes to corporate guidance

Helpful hints for the PMO when delivering the service

- As well as informing the related department of the change suggested they will communicate the background to the change. They will explain why making the change would add value to the organization
- Look to perform this service with the 'Analyse lessons to identify items to be added to the Process Improvements Plan' service

PMO Capabilities needed to fulfil this service

Competencies	Techniques and generic tools
Knowledge Management Delivery Methods Governance Frameworks Relationships and engagement Teamwork	Document Analysis Process Analysis

Related services

Analyse lessons to identify items to be added to the Process Improvements Plan Manage the Process Improvement Plan	Develop and maintain tailoring guidelines for standards, methods, and approaches Automate Processes

Manage the Process Improvement Plan

Service description

Ensuring that the items in the Process Improvement Plan get actioned and the individual frameworks will get updated.

What the service provides for the customer

This provides a way of getting the frameworks updated with feedback from the lessons learned reviews.

Why is this service being offered to the customer?

Without updating the frameworks, they will become stale and out of date. The Process Improvement Plan provides a structured way of getting these frameworks updated.

How PMO will apply this service

The Process Improvement Plan will contain items that have come from the lesson's registers. In addition, there will be a way people using the frameworks can submit their own suggestions. The PMO will triage the items and if they are not duplicating or conflicting other items in the plan they will be added and assigned an owner.

The PMO will look at the Process Improvement Plan and check the status of each of the actions. They will contact each of the owners of the actions. They will update the comments section in the Process Improvement Plan with the current status. They will assign a date when they expect this action to be delivered.

The PMO will look to have regular releases of the frameworks. The PMO will ensure that each of the updates to the frameworks can be traced back to the reference in the Process Improvement Plan. When the PMO release a new version of the framework they can use the information from the Process Improvement Plan to provide the communications. Once an action has been delivered then the PMO can marked this as closed.

On a regular basis the PMO will review the old actions from the Process Improvement Plan to see whether they are still relevant. They will check with the action owner to see what the current status is. If the action is no longer relevant, they will look to remove this from the Process Improvement Plan.

Supplier	Input	Process	Output	Customer
PMO	Process Improvement Plan	Update frameworks	Governance Framework Financial PPM Framework Change Management Framework PPM Framework Information management framework PPM Purchasing Framework PPM Procurement Framework Benefits Management Framework Estimating Framework Portfolio Management Framework Change control framework Issue Management Framework Change Management Framework	PPM Teams PMO

How the PMO will measure the value of this service

This can be measured by looking at the numbers of actions in the Process Improvement Plan that have been delivered. This can be measured by the number of updates to the frameworks that can be traced back to a Process Improvement.

Criteria when the PMO will use this service

- Where there is a Process Improvement Plan
- Where there is a culture of continuous improvement
- Where the PMO is permanent

Helpful hints for the PMO when delivering the service

- Consider reviewing old items within the Process Improvement Plan at least every 6 months
- Have a standard point in the month where frameworks are updated, in order that people know when to expect the updates
- Make the Process Improvement Plan visible so individuals who have submitted an improvement can see the status of it
- Ensure that each time the framework is updated that the relevant people receive the necessary communication informing them what has changed

PMO Capabilities needed to fulfil this service

Competencies	Techniques and generic tools
P3M Administration	Communication requirements analysis
Change Control	Process Analysis
Change Management	Change control tools
Information Management	Check sheets
Knowledge Management	Salience model
Stakeholder Engagement	Stakeholder checklist
Delivery Methods	Stakeholder engagement assessment matrix
Governance Frameworks	
Self-reflection and self-management	
Personal Integrity and reliability	
Personal Communication	
Relationships and engagement	
Leadership	
Result Orientation	

Related services

Analyse lessons to identify items to be added to the Process Improvements Plan	Define, maintain, and implement framework for monitoring and review
Create and maintain knowledge management framework	Establish a portfolio management framework
Develop benefits management framework	Develop and maintain an estimating framework
Develop the overall change control framework	Work with Procurement teams to agree PPM purchasing Framework
Create Change Management Framework	Communicate PPM purchasing Framework
Communicate change management framework	Monitor use of corporate guidance and standards to identify improvements
Develop and maintain the PPM financial framework	Ensure compliance with quality standards and good practice
Develop the overall issue management framework	Analyse feedback from quality reviews
Train the issue management framework	Perform data analysis of project selection and delivery performance
Define, maintain, and implement reporting framework	Feedback to senior management on the success of strategic initiatives
Define, maintain, and implement PPM governance framework	Review the effectiveness of risk mitigation actions
Define, maintain, and implement standard PPM framework	
Automate Processes	

Quality Management

Quality Management

Description

Ensures that the new products or services delivered by the portfolio, program or project are fit for purpose and can deliver the benefits required by the relevant board/management level.

What the services within the area provide for the customer

By providing a standard approach to quality the project or program manager can be reassured that deliverables will be produced to the required quality level.

By tracking the evidence of these quality reviews and highlighting deviances the project or program manager can focus on dealing with the exceptions to the quality standard rather have to review each item.

By assessing the quality of the project delivery, the program manager can be assured that the project is delivering as expected and can trust the information they are receiving on the status of the project.

Helpful hints for when the PMO is delivering this service area

Before assessing the quality of anything it is necessary to have a definition of what quality looks like. This can vary from project to project and needs to be defined in conjunction with the recipient of the projects' outputs. Do not make the mistake of assuming that everything needs to be the same quality level.

Quality Management Design

Service group description

The setup and communication of a quality management framework consisting of process, procedures, standards, templates, help and tools.

Why have these services been grouped together?

These services relate to the establishment of a quality management framework. The organization will then require training in the use of this framework and any associated tools.

List of related services described in other areas

Automate Processes

Responsibility Assignment Matrix

Service	Executive	Portfolio Manager	Program Manager	Project Manager	PMO	Sponsor	Other Stakeholder
Develop and maintain the overall Quality Control Framework	A	C	C	C	R		I (PPM Team)
Develop or source tools for Quality Control	A	C	C	C	R		I (PPM Team)
Train the Quality Control Framework	I	I	I	I	A, R	I	I (PPM Team)
Develop and maintain the overall Quality Assurance Framework	A		I	I	A, R	I	

Helpful hints for when the PMO is delivering this service group

- The framework will need to be developed before it can be communicated, or any tools introduced. Ensure the tools are aligned to the quality management process.
- When looking at a tool, consider whether this can be done as part of the existing PPM tool

Develop and maintain the overall Quality Control Framework

Service description

Develop and maintain a quality control framework consisting of process, procedures, standards, templates, and help.

What the service provides for the customer

This provides the project and program managers a standard way of controlling the quality reviews. It provides them a process and procedure to follow using a standard template.

Why is this service being offered to the customer?

The quality control framework allows the projects and programs to assess the quality and ensure they deliver what is expected for the customer.

How PMO will apply this service

The PMO will review the external guidance about quality control and quality management for projects and programs and will look to tailor this for their organization.

They will produce a standard quality register with a help guide for its usage. The PMO will consider any common reporting requirements (e.g. steering group packs, progress reports, rework statistics) and try to ensure that these can be delivered using the information in the quality register. They will develop a quality control process and look to embed this into the overall PPM framework.

Supplier	Input	Process	Output	Customer
PMO	Standards template	Develop Standard Develop Templates	Quality control process Quality control help Quality Register	Project Manager Program Manager Portfolio Manager PMO

How the PMO will measure the value of this service

This can be measured by assessing the numbers of projects and programs using the quality control framework.

Criteria when the PMO will use this service

- When there is a need for consistent quality control framework
- Where there is a centralized PMO

Helpful hints for the PMO when delivering the service

- Ensure the quality control framework covers rework. Make sure those statistics can be captured for further analysis

PMO Capabilities needed to fulfil this service

Competencies	Techniques and generic tools
Quality Management Delivery Methods	Process Analysis Check sheets

Related services

Define, maintain, and implement standard PPM framework Assure the development of portfolio, program, and project quality plans Analyse feedback from quality reviews Develop or source tools for Quality Control Oversee the quality review process for contractual supplier deliverables	Coordinate quality reviews of deliverables Train the Quality Control Framework Work with procurement to ensure effective interface with supplier's quality systems Ensure compliance with quality standards and good practice Monitor quality performance Automate Processes Map key value streams and processes

Further Reading

PMI PMBoK (A Guide to the Project Management Body of Knowledge)
PRINCE2
Managing Successful Programmes (MSP)
APM BoK
Praxis

Develop or source tools for Quality Control

Service description

The provision of tools to record and monitor quality on a project or program.

What the service provides for the customer

This will provide them a tool which will allow the project or program manager to manage the quality of the deliverables. It will provide them with the necessary reporting for steering group, progress report and rework statistics.

Why is this service being offered to the customer?

Having a tool will allow better control of the quality and will allow for traceability back to the original requirements. It can provide automation to allow focus on the items that need the project or program managers attention or escalation.

How PMO will apply this service

The PMO will check to see whether there are any existing tools that can be used to manage quality. If there are not, then they will review the external marketplace for tools (if there is not budget or the appetite to have an external tool then they may look to create something in house).

If developing something in house the PMO will supply the developer with the requirements (from the quality control process, quality register and reporting requirements). Once the development has finished the PMO will perform the testing, ensuring it meets the requirements before accepting the tool into use.

If this is being sourced from a vendor, then the package will need to be customized to include the necessary fields and dropdowns. The PMO need to review how the data can be extracted for inclusion in standard reporting. Once this has been done the PMO can start rolling out the usage of the tool.

Regardless of how the tool was obtained it will need to have some training developed and some guidelines for use. The PMO should look to develop the training and be prepared to deliver the training alongside the rollout of the tool. The PMO should consider how frequently they want to deliver the training once the initial training has finished. Do they want to run regular sessions or individual session as and when new users are identified?

The existing quality control process will need to be updated to have appropriate references to the new tool and the links to the quality register will need to be discontinued.

Supplier	Input	Process	Output	Customer
Vendor In house developers	Vendor software In house software	Software implementation	Quality Control tool	Project Manager Program Manager PMO PPM Team

How the PMO will measure the value of this service

This can be measured in the use of the tool and any improvements in the management of quality within the projects and programs.

Criteria when the PMO will use this service

- Where there is a quality control framework in place
- Where there is a desire to purchase a vendor tool
- Where there is a desire for improved quality control

Helpful hints for the PMO when delivering the service

- Some of the tools which manage requirements can be configured to look at quality as well
- Ensure that as new people start, they are trained in the use of the tool
- Ensure there is the ability to extract information from the tool to include in reporting packs
- See if there can be a linkage between the quality control tool and the tool to manage requirements

PMO Capabilities needed to fulfil this service

Competencies	Techniques and generic tools
Quality Management Reporting, Insights and Analysis Supplier Management P3M Tools Relationships and engagement Leadership Teamwork	Make or buy analysis Architecture / cost trade-off analysis Gap analysis

Related services

Develop and maintain the overall Quality Control Framework Train the Quality Control Framework Monitor quality performance Analyse feedback from quality reviews Advise on PPM tools and software Develops in-house project management tools Tailors and configures project management tools	Implements vendor provided project management tools Manages project management tools (systems admin) Coordinate quality reviews of deliverables Work with procurement to ensure effective interface with supplier's quality systems Oversee the quality review process for contractual supplier deliverables

Train the Quality Control Framework

Service description

Train the people responsible for managing quality on the project or program. This covers the quality control process, templates, tools, standards, and help.

What the service provides for the customer

This ensures that everyone who is involved with the management of quality on a project or program understands how the process, tools, and reporting works.

Why is this service being offered to the customer?

As the PMO have been responsible for producing the framework and the associate tool (if there is one) then they will know how the framework should be implemented and be able to answer any questions individuals may have around this.

How PMO will apply this service

The PMO will identify the key people who need training in each project or program. Typically, this will be the project and program managers along with any team leaders.

Once the list of people is available the PMO will book the training sessions and invite the people. The PMO can then prepare the training material to be used. At the training course take note of who has attended and who has not and be prepared to organize further training sessions.

Supplier	Input	Process	Output	Customer
PMO	Quality control process Quality control help Quality Register Quality Control tool	Deliver training Communication	Informed people	PPM Teams

How the PMO will measure the value of this service

This can be measured by numbers of people trained and the satisfaction with the training.

Criteria when the PMO will use this service

- When there is a new quality control framework
- When there are changes to the quality control framework
- When new people are added to the project teams

Helpful hints for the PMO when delivering the service

- If there is a tool that needs to be used, then show that at the same time
- Use the questions from the training courses to help devise a frequently asked questions or help document
- Gain feedback from the training course on how effective the training was and use that as a measure for the service
- Show how statistics on quality control can be reported in the progress report and steering group packs
- If there are minor changes to the quality control framework then the PMO may consider just providing a communication explaining the changes
- Consider having a sweep up session(s) to get to those people who were unable to get the original sessions when booked
- For 'hard to get' people consider doing one to one training to ensure the framework gets trained out to everyone

PMO Capabilities needed to fulfil this service

Competencies	Techniques and generic tools
P3M Administration Quality Management Capability Development P3M Tools Personal Communication Relationships and engagement Result Orientation	Communication requirements analysis Project Management Information System Salience model Stakeholder checklist Stakeholder engagement assessment matrix

Related services

Develop and maintain the overall Quality Control Framework Develop or source tools for Quality Control Ensure compliance with quality standards and good practice	Monitor quality performance Analyse feedback from quality reviews Provide PPM training Provide training logistics support

Develop and maintain the overall Quality Assurance Framework

Service description

Develop and maintain a quality assurance framework consisting of process, procedures, standards, templates, and help.

What the service provides for the customer

It provides the PMO with a method of assuring the quality of the projects and programs within the portfolio. It provides some checklists and assessment criteria for delivering gate reviews, health checks, audits, and general assurance.

Why is this service being offered to the customer?

The quality assurance framework gives the senior management confidence that the projects and programs will deliver in a timely manner to budget and scope.

How PMO will apply this service

The PMO will review what quality assurance of the projects and programs is required. Is the PMO only doing gate reviews and general assurance, or will it get involved with health checks and audits as well? For each of the assurance items the PMO will look to put together a checklist and some guidance for how this can be used. The PMO will provide a process for delivering the assurance and following up on any remedial actions

Supplier	Input	Process	Output	Customer
PMO	Standards template	Develop Standard Develop Templates	Health Check checklist Gate Review checklist Assurance checklist Audit checklist Assurance trigger criteria	PMO

How the PMO will measure the value of this service

The assurance framework can be measured by the times that the PMO use the various checklists instead of creating their own.

Criteria when the PMO will use this service

- Where the PMO have been asked to provide a quality assurance role
- Where there is a centralized PMO

Helpful hints for the PMO when delivering the service

- Decide how much assurance is required for the organization. It is about getting the balance right between letting the projects deliver in their own way, and having consistency of delivery
- Ensure that the triggers for the assurance are clear
- Ensure it is clear the value that the assurance will bring. Make sure it is clear what the follow ups and escalation routes are based on the assurance review

PMO Capabilities needed to fulfil this service

Competencies	Techniques and generic tools
Assurance Delivery Methods	Process Analysis Check sheets

Related services

Provide project and program health checks Provide project and program audits Provide project and program assurance checks Advise on program or project assurance services	Define, maintain, and implement framework for monitoring and review Provide project or program rescues Provide advice and guidance to prevent project or program failure Provide a Stage Gate Review or Gateway support service Map key value streams and processes

Further Reading

PMI PMBoK (A Guide to the Project Management Body of Knowledge)
PRINCE2
Managing Successful Programmes (MSP)
APM BoK
Infrastructure and Projects Authority: assurance review toolkit
Praxis

Quality Management Operations

Service group description

The operation of the quality control and assurance process. Providing quality assurance checks on projects and projects. Assisting with the tracking of quality within projects and programs.

Why have these services been grouped together?

These services are related to the day to day running of the quality control processes.

List of related services described in other areas

Ensure quality of change requests
Ensure quality of project requests
Review Business cases for compliance
Monitor dependency register
Monitor assumptions register
Monitor the Risk Register
Advise on program or project assurance services
Trigger post-program or project reviews

Responsibility Assignment Matrix

Service	Executive	Portfolio Manager	Program Manager	Project Manager	PMO	Sponsor	Other Stakeholder
Coordinate quality reviews of deliverables			A	A	R		C (PPM team)
Work with internal audit to ensure compliance with audit requirements			A	A	C	I	R (Internal Audit)
Provide a Stage Gate Review or Gateway support service	A		C	C	R		
Provide project and program health checks	A		C	C	R	I	C (PPM team)
Assure the development of portfolio, program, and project quality plans	A	C	C	C	R		
Provide guidance on quality criteria, reviewers, and sign-off authority to ensure consistency			I	I	A, R		
Work with procurement to ensure effective interface with supplier's quality systems			A	A	R		C (Supplier) C (Procurement)
Provide project and program audits	A		C	C	R	I	C (PPM team) C (Internal Audit)
Provide project and program assurance checks	A		C	C	R		

Coordinate quality reviews of deliverables

Service description

The coordination of the quality reviews of deliverables on behalf of the project or program manager.

What the service provides for the customer

This ensures that each of the deliverables is reviewed for quality by the appropriate individuals, if necessary, using a checklist. The outcome of the quality review is then recorded, and any remedial actions are chased up through to resolution.

Why is this service being offered to the customer?

The PMO are able to provide a tracking service on behalf of the project or program manager. This will allow them to focus on the overall delivery of the project or program.

How PMO will apply this service

The PMO will be notified of deliverables requiring a quality review. They will find out from the deliverable author who needs to review the deliverable. The PMO will check whether there is a related checklist which needs to be used as part of the review process.

The PMO will distribute the deliverable, the checklist and the review form out to the reviewers, giving them a target date to reply. As each of the reviews has been completed then the PMO will collate those into a combined review form.

When the deadline for the review is approaching the PMO will chase any reviewers who have yet to reply. Once the deadline has passed (or all the reviews have been returned) the PMO will send the combined review form along with any annotated deliverables through to the deliverable author. If any reviews are missing, then the PMO will send details through to the author explaining what actions had been taken to chase up the review.

Supplier	Input	Process	Output	Customer
Deliverable author	Deliverables Compliance checklist Review form template	Coordinate quality review	Combined Review form Remedial actions	Deliverable author Program Manager Project Manager

How the PMO will measure the value of this service

This can be measured by feedback from the deliverable authors.

Criteria when the PMO will use this service

- Where the PMO is aligned to a single project or program
- Where there are lots of deliverables to review
- Where traceability is required of the deliverables review process

Helpful hints for the PMO when delivering the service

- Consider sending the requests for review out from a central email to ensure cover in times of absence
- Consider putting a tracking spreadsheet together to ensure that all the reviewers get chased on time
- This is not about asking the PMO to review the deliverable (although they may do that), it is about ensuring that everyone who should review the deliverable has done so

PMO Capabilities needed to fulfil this service

Competencies	Techniques and generic tools
P3M Administration Information Management Quality Management Professionalism and ethics Personal Communication Relationships and engagement Resourcefulness Negotiation Result Orientation	Check sheets

Related services

Analyse feedback from quality reviews Develop or source tools for Quality Control Develop and maintain the overall Quality Control Framework	Oversee the quality review process for contractual supplier deliverables Provide guidance on quality criteria, reviewers, and sign-off authority to ensure consistency Support the Project Approval Board

Work with internal audit to ensure compliance with audit requirements

Service description

Assist internal audit by providing the necessary documentation, setting up meeting with team members and providing them with the necessary support to enable them to complete their audit in a timely manner.

What the service provides for the customer

This aids the project or program manager as the PMO are able to provide what internal audit need without distracting them from the delivery of the project or program. Internal audit is able to get what they need to get the audit done. Once the audit has finished the PMO can co-ordinate the responses to any audit actions and feed those back to the audit team.

Why is this service being offered to the customer?

As the PMO have access to all the information on a project or program they are able to find the information and provide it for internal audit. They know the availability of team members and can arrange a suitable time for meetings to be booked in. This eases the impact of the audit on the project or program.

How PMO will apply this service

The PMO will be aware of the audit by the internal audit team. They will get a request from internal audit for some documentation. The PMO will confirm exactly what is required and send this across.

If internal audit requires any meetings to be setup to interview members of the team, the PMO will look at the diaries of the individuals and arrange to set up the meetings at the least inconvenient time.

Supplier	Input	Process	Output	Customer
Internal Audit	Audit request	Auditing a project or program	Audit report Audit Actions	Program Manager Project Manager Internal Audit

How the PMO will measure the value of this service

This can be measured by looking at the impact of the audit on the project or program. It can be measured by asking for feedback from the project or program manager.

Criteria when the PMO will use this service

- When the project or program is being audited by internal audit
- Where the PMO is aligned to a single project or program

Helpful hints for the PMO when delivering the service

- Ask internal audit for a copy of their scope, this way the PMO can provide the necessary documentation up front
- Consider attending any interviews, that way any requests for additional documentation can be noted and the PMO can send those through after the meeting

PMO Capabilities needed to fulfil this service

Competencies	Techniques and generic tools
P3M Administration Information Management Assurance Professionalism and ethics Personal Integrity and reliability Personal Communication Relationships and engagement Teamwork Resourcefulness Negotiation Result Orientation	None

Related services

Set up meetings on behalf of others Hold master copies of all portfolio, program, or project information Control the issue of portfolio, program, or project deliverables	Establish and maintain the CI index Provide project and program audits

Provide a Stage Gate Review or Gateway support service

Service description

The provision of an assurance review at the end of a stage to confirm suitability of the project or program to continue.

What the service provides for the customer

This provides a point of validation that the project or program is OK to continue.

Why is this service being offered to the customer?

Gate reviews may be required to gain funding to proceed to the next stage of the project or program. The PMO are able to assess the project on behalf of the project approval board. Being independent the PMO are able to perform this review in an objective manner.

How PMO will apply this service

The PMO will know when a project or program is due to pass into the next stage. Prior to that time, they will review the state of the project or program against the gate review checklist. They will check the state of the documentation to confirm that it has been produced as required and approved. They will check to see that a schedule and estimate for the next phase have been produced.

If there are any items which have not been produced as expected the PMO will list those out and provide a set of remedial actions that the project or program manager will need to complete prior to gate review having been marked as successful. Once those actions have been completed then the PMO will complete the gate review checklist again just to confirm that everything has been completed as expected.

Once the gate review checklist has been completed and the PMO are satisfied that everything is complete the project or program should be moved into the next stage. If the completion of the gate review means that funding is authorized, then the budgets for the project or program need to be updated accordingly.

Supplier	Input	Process	Output	Customer
PMO UK Government	Stage gate review checklist Gateway assessment	Performing a Gate review	Stage gate recommendations Stage gate Actions	Program Manager Portfolio Manager Project Approval Board

How the PMO will measure the value of this service

This can be measured by the number of projects or programs that have been evaluated. It can be measured in a reduction in the failure rate for projects and programs caused by starting a stage too early.

Criteria when the PMO will use this service

- When there is a gate review process
- When a project or program is due to complete a stage
- Where the PMO is independent of the project or program being reviewed

Helpful hints for the PMO when delivering the service

- For UK public sector this applies to Gateway reviews as well
- For the final gate there will not be a next phase, therefore there will not be a schedule and estimate to be produced
- Consider allowing the project or program to proceed 'at risk' if the gate review is not perfect. In this circumstance ensure the risk is clearly described and added to the risk register

PMO Capabilities needed to fulfil this service

Competencies	Techniques and generic tools
Quality Management Reporting, Insights and Analysis Assurance Delivery Methods Governance Frameworks Professionalism and ethics Personal Integrity and reliability Relationships and engagement Result Orientation	Root Cause Analysis Failure Modes and Effects Analysis (FMEA) Prompt Lists Check sheets

Related services

Develop and maintain the overall Quality Assurance Framework Provide project and program audits Provide project and program assurance checks Advise on program or project assurance services	Define, maintain, and implement framework for monitoring and review Enable sharing of good practice Assure the development of portfolio, program, and project quality plans Provide project and program health checks

Further Reading

OGC Gateway review

Provide project and program health checks

Service description

The review of the potential success of the project or program.

What the service provides for the customer

This provides a critical and independent review on the likelihood of success for the project or program. It provides a series of recommendations that can be implemented to allow the project or program to get back on track. This service is not focused on blame or searching for scapegoats. It is focused on getting the project or program to deliver.

Why is this service being offered to the customer?

To prevent a project or program rescue, a health check can intervene and provide corrections to get the project or program back on course. As experts in PPM the PMO are ideally positioned to be the helpful expert to work alongside the project or program manager to ensure a successful delivery.

How PMO will apply this service

The PMO will receive a request for a health check. They will go in and look at the documentation and the approach being taken. They will speak to members of the team to get their thoughts on what is wrong, and the potential ways this can be improved.

The PMO will need to consider all aspects of the project or program including:

- People – have we got the right people for the roles, are they experienced, do they need extra help, what is morale like. Do people understand their roles?
- Business Objective – Is this (and the overall business case) still valid
- Project Management lifecycle – has the right one been chosen, is it being followed
- Governance and control – Are the scope, cost, quality, schedule, benefits under strict control, and what actions are required to ensure they are
- Documentation – do we have some, is it being used consistently, its it managed under change control
- Risks & Issues – are these being managed or just recorded and ignored? Are there even any recorded?

Having understood where the weaknesses are the PMO should suggest some ways in which these can be strengthened. When looking at recommendations the PMO need to consider the timescale and cost of these to ensure they can be applied in a timely manner with the people available.

The PMO need to present their findings not only to the person/group who has requested the health check, but to the project or program manager to ensure they are aware of the actions suggested and to get their buy-in to delivering them.

Supplier	Input	Process	Output	Customer
PMO Portfolio manager Program manager	Request for health check	Provide health check	Health check recommendations Action plan	Portfolio manager Program manager Project manager

How the PMO will measure the value of this service

This can be measured by a reduction in the numbers of project and program rescues required. It can be measured by the number of suggestions that get adopted.

Criteria when the PMO will use this service

- When the project or program is perceived not to be going well
- When the PMO has the ability to provide a critical review
- When the PMO is independent of the project or program being reviewed

Helpful hints for the PMO when delivering the service

- Do not search for blame. Look to find the required actions to get back on track
- Listen to the people in the team, they often know what is wrong and how to fix it. The problem is that they are not being given the time to do this
- Consider recommending a firebreak in delivery. Time for the project or program to process the items in the action plan before continuing on. Having the time for reflection maybe all that is needed to allow the project or program to catch up with itself
- Do not be scared to recommend that the project or program be re-scoped or even closed. It can be better to close something than pour more money in and still not fix the problems
- Consider having a checklist, or guidance on items to check when performing a health check
- Look to perform the health check quickly to ensure that the actions and recommendations can be acted as quickly as possible
- Look for overlaps and gaps in the roles and responsibilities. Draw diagrams to allow people to see where these may be
- If something more formal is required, then look to audit the project or program

PMO Capabilities needed to fulfil this service

Competencies	Techniques and generic tools
Business Case	Root Cause Analysis
Change Control	5 Whys
Financial Management	Alternatives generation
Information Management	Failure Modes and Effects Analysis (FMEA)
Issue Management	Communication requirements analysis
Planning and Scheduling	Risk Register
Quality Management	Prompt Lists
Reporting, Insights and Analysis	Diagramming techniques
Resource Management	Organization charts & position descriptions
Risk Management	Salience model
Stakeholder Engagement	Scheduling tool
Supplier Management	Stakeholder checklist
Assurance	Stakeholder engagement assessment matrix
Delivery Methods	Swim-lane flowcharts
Governance Frameworks	Task responsibility matrix/RACI
Professionalism and ethics	Work Breakdown Structure
Personal Communication	
Relationships and engagement	
Result Orientation	

Related services

Provide project and program audits Provide project and program assurance checks Provide a Stage Gate Review or Gateway support service Develop and maintain the overall Quality Assurance Framework	Provide project or program rescues Provide advice and guidance to prevent project or program failure Define, maintain, and implement framework for monitoring and review

Assure the development of portfolio, program, and project quality plans

Service description

A critical and constructive review of the quality plan for the portfolio, program, or project with a view to suggesting improvements.

What the service provides for the customer

An independent review of the quality plan for the portfolio, program, or project.

Why is this service being offered to the customer?

Having an independent review assures that all aspects of quality have been considered. As the PMO have experience of the pitfalls that other projects and program have experienced, via their review of the central lessons register they can transfer that experience through to the quality plan they are currently reviewing.

How PMO will apply this service

The PMO will read the quality plan alongside the project or program scoping documentation. They will ensure that the quality plan covers all aspects of quality, not only in the depth, but also the breadth of the coverage. They will ensure that the quality reviews are fit for purpose and check that the people doing the reviews have the necessary experience. The PMO will check to see that the quality plan includes information on the recording of defects, and that quality criteria are built into the go/no-go decisions for the project or program. This will ensure that the project or program will not proceed unless the relevant quality criteria have been met or exceeded.

The PMO will review the central lessons register to see whether there have been any suggestions on what works/does not work regarding quality. They will look to see whether any of those suggestion would be applicable for this circumstance.

Having done the review, the PMO will suggest items for improvement back to the author of the quality plan and to the PPM manager.

Supplier	Input	Process	Output	Customer
Project Managers Program Managers Portfolio managers	Quality Plan Quality Standards Central lessons register Project/program documentation	Review documentation	Updated Quality plan	Project Managers Program Managers Portfolio managers

How the PMO will measure the value of this service

This can be measured by the numbers of improvements incorporated into the quality plan. It can be measured by a reduction in the numbers of negative lessons identified due to poor quality planning.

Criteria when the PMO will use this service

- Where quality plans have been written
- As part of the gate review services
- As part of an assurance review

Helpful hints for the PMO when delivering the service

- Consider having a good practice example quality plan that can be referred to, to ensure that no items are missed

PMO Capabilities needed to fulfil this service

Competencies	Techniques and generic tools
Quality Management Reporting, Insights and Analysis Assurance	Document Analysis Gap analysis Assumption and constraint analysis Value-add/non-value-add analysis

Related services

Capture good practice examples for inclusion in good practice repository Provide project and program assurance checks	Provide a Stage Gate Review or Gateway support service Develop and maintain the overall Quality Control Framework

Provide guidance on quality criteria, reviewers, and sign-off authority to ensure consistency

Service description

The provision of advice and guidance to project and program managers about the expected quality criteria, reviewers, and approvers for deliverables.

What the service provides for the customer

This provides a suggested RACI (Responsible, Approvers, Consulted, Informed) for all deliverables. It provides a quality checklist for each of the standard deliverables.

Why is this service being offered to the customer?

Having a quality checklist provides consistency with the deliverables. Being provided in advance of the deliverable creation it allows the author to understand what is important and what will be reviewed. It ensures each reviewer checks the deliverable in a consistent manner.

How PMO will apply this service

As part of the PPM framework the PMO will provide a generic RACI for each of the deliverables. This will be listed by role. As part of the guidance the PMO will obtain the organizational structure and ensure that each person is assigned to a role. They will assist the project or program manager in turning the generic RACI into a specific one for that project or program.

As part of the PPM framework the PMO will look to create some quality review criteria for each deliverable. When it comes to the specific deliverable the PMO can review that criteria to see whether there are any changes required and agree those changes up front with the project or program manager before the deliverable gets sent for review.

Each of the deliverables will have an approver listed. The PMO can confirm with the project or program manager whether the right person/group is chosen for the deliverable. It may be possible in some circumstances to delegate authority to a lower level. In other circumstances (e.g. business case approval) it may be necessary to escalate to a higher level.

Supplier	Input	Process	Output	Customer
Project Managers Program Managers	Quality Checklists Quality criteria RACI Organizational structure	Provide guidance	Advice Updated Quality Checklist	Project Managers Program Managers

How the PMO will measure the value of this service

This can be measured via an assurance review. This can be measured by asking for feedback from the project and program managers.

Criteria when the PMO will use this service

- Where there is a standard RACI used for all the deliverables
- Where there is a review checklist for a deliverable
- Where clarity is required in approval levels

Helpful hints for the PMO when delivering the service

- Look to agree the reviewers and approvers as part of the project or program start-up
- Confirm the reviewers and approvers as part of the gate review process
- As well as confirming the reviewers check that the schedule has allowed time for the review and any rework (and second review) prior to approval

PMO Capabilities needed to fulfil this service

Competencies	Techniques and generic tools
Quality Management Assurance Delivery Methods Governance Frameworks Professionalism and ethics Personal Communication Relationships and engagement Negotiation	Value-add/non-value-add analysis Check sheets Organization charts & position descriptions Task responsibility matrix/RACI

Related services

Define, maintain, and implement PPM governance framework Define, maintain, and implement standard PPM framework Develop and maintain tailoring guidelines for standards, methods, and approaches	Provide guidance on how the governance framework can be tailored Coordinate quality reviews of deliverables Oversee the quality review process for contractual supplier deliverables Monitor quality performance

Work with procurement to ensure effective interface with supplier's quality systems

Service Description

The alignment of the quality control systems between the supplier and the project or program.

What the service provides for the customer

It ensures that the project or program manager can look in one place to keep track of how quality control is going for the project or program.

Why is this service being offered to the customer?

The PMO has working relationships with procurement and with the supplier. They understand the importance of quality control. They can ensure that the quality control reporting for the project or program encompasses all quality information.

How PMO will apply this service

The PMO will speak to procurement prior to the contract being signed to ensure there is a clause in the contract which enables the client to get access to the quality control data from the supplier.

The PMO will speak to the supplier and ask for an extract of the quality control data on a regular basis. The PMO will look to specify what information is required (aligned to the quality register or quality control tool).

When the PMO receives the data, they will add any new records and update the information that has changed within the internal quality control tool.

Supplier	Input	Process	Output	Customer
Procurement Suppliers	Contract Quality plan Supplier quality control system	Update Quality Register	Quality Register Quality Control System	Project Managers Program Managers Suppliers

How the PMO will measure the value of this service

This can be measured by only having one place to find out the quality control progress for the project or program.

Criteria when the PMO will use this service

- If there is an external supplier on the project or program
- If the external supplier uses their own quality control system
- If the PMO is aligned to a single project or program

Helpful hints for the PMO when delivering the service

- If the supplier has access to the client's systems, it may be easier for them to use the client's quality control system directly
- The PMO should specify exactly what the format should be, including details like date, currency, and name formats
- The PMO should specify the frequency of the data collection. This should be aligned to the reporting cycle. Hence if the report is weekly the data should be provided weekly the day prior to the report day to allow for the internal quality system to be updated
- Specify unique references for each item to allow merging of data to be easier
- If possible, look to automate the merging of data from the supplier
- Ensure that the supplier's data is not updated directly within the internal tool, but only from the data coming from the supplier. Only have one source of the information, even if it has to be stored in 2 places

PMO Capabilities needed to fulfil this service

Competencies	Techniques and generic tools
P3M Administration Information Management Quality Management Reporting, Insights and Analysis Supplier Management P3M Tools Relationships and engagement Teamwork Negotiation	None

Related services

Develop and maintain the overall Quality Control Framework Develop or source tools for Quality Control	Oversee the quality review process for contractual supplier deliverables Analyse feedback from quality reviews

Provide project and program audits

Service description

The audit of a project or program against set criteria.

What the service provides for the customer

This will provide assurance that the deliverables are at the requisite quality. There are no issues with the management of the project or program. That the risk of unsuccessful delivery is minimized. It provides a point of reflection and renewed impetus for delivery.

Why is this service being offered to the customer?

The PMO are able to provide an independent review of the project or program status and provide recommendations for improvement. As experts in PPM the PMO are ideally positioned to provide that constructive challenge.

How PMO will apply this service

The PMO will receive a request to audit a project or program. They will speak to the requestor and to the project or program manager and confirm the scope of the audit. The scope will include what is being audited, what are the criteria to be used, how long the audit will take and who needs to be involved.

Having agreed the scope of the audit the PMO will conduct the review using their audit checklist. The audit will look to include the following areas:

- Documentation – do we have evidence for what is being said
- Interviews – are people delivering the project as expected. Is there any deviation between the way the project or program is planned versus the way it is being executed?
- Governance and control – are the projects and programs proceeding under control. Is the scope agreed, are changes being controlled with the relevant approvals? Are risks and issues being dealt with
- Reporting – are there any gaps between what is being reported and what is being done on the ground

Once the documentation (evidence) has been collated and the interviews with the relevant people have been conducted the PMO will write this up as a report. The report will typically include:

- Background – a review of the scope of the project or program being audited, the reasons for the audit and the scope of the audit
- Audit process – an overview of the documentation collected; a summary of the interviews taken
- Findings – what the audit has found, this will include positives, negatives, and neutral findings
- Recommendations – from the negative findings the audit will recommend some actions that need to be taken

The draft audit report will be discussed with the project or program manager just to confirm whether this is a true representation of the state of play. It gives the manager time to confirm and actions already taken and ensures that the audit is open.

The final audit report will then be presented back to the requestor and to the project or program manager. The actions from the audit will need to be chased up and cleared by the dates agreed. If they cannot be then potentially another audit may be required with a different remit.

Supplier	Input	Process	Output	Customer
PMO Portfolio manager Program manager Internal Audit	Request for audit Audit checklist	Auditing a project or program	Audit report Recommendations	Portfolio manager Program manager Project manager

How the PMO will measure the value of this service

This can be measured by a reduction in the numbers of project and program rescues required. The reduction in number of projects and programs being audited by internal audit, as the PMO audit is deemed sufficient.

Criteria when the PMO will use this service

- When the PMO is independent of the project or program being audited
- When the project or program is not being audited by internal audit
- When a request comes in for a project or program audit
- When the PMO has the ability to provide a critical review

Helpful hints for the PMO when delivering the service

- When auditing a project or program be aware that the people being interviewed are still trying to deliver. Try not to take too much more of their time than is required
- Ensure you agree the scope of the audit up front so that the project or program manager is aware of why they are being audited
- Consider writing an audit checklist to provide consistency in the audit
- Consider having more than one person involved in the audit from the PMO (if available) to avoid accusations of bias and provide the opportunity for junior PMO people to learn the service

PMO Capabilities needed to fulfil this service

Competencies	Techniques and generic tools
Business Case Change Control Financial Management Information Management Issue Management Planning and Scheduling Quality Management Reporting, Insights and Analysis Resource Management Risk Management Stakeholder Engagement Supplier Management Assurance Delivery Methods Governance Frameworks Professionalism and ethics Personal Communication Relationships and engagement Result Orientation	Root Cause Analysis 5 Whys Risk Register Prompt Lists Performance variance report Scheduling tool Task responsibility matrix/RACI

Related services

Provide project and program assurance checks Provide a Stage Gate Review or Gateway support service Develop and maintain the overall Quality Assurance Framework Provide project and program health checks Advise on program or project assurance services	Provide project or program rescues Provide advice and guidance to prevent project or program failure Define, maintain, and implement framework for monitoring and review Work with internal audit to ensure compliance with audit requirements

Provide project and program assurance checks

Service description

The independent review of projects and programs to ensure compliance with the agreed ways of working.

What the service provides for the customer

This provides the project and program managers a way of assessing how well their projects and programs are being run. For the PMO it provides feedback on the uptake and applicability of the delivery frameworks.

Why is this service being offered to the customer?

As the PMO wrote the frameworks they are able to review how well they are being used. By objectively reviewing the adherence and usage of the frameworks the PMO can provide recommendations to the project and program managers on ways to improve the delivery of their changes.

How PMO will apply this service

The PMO will decide which projects and programs to review. They will speak to the project or program manager and inform them they are doing a review of their project or program, and the reason behind this review. They will review the assurance checklist to see which elements are applicable for review. They will follow the guidance in the checklist and assess the individual project or program.

Once the PMO have completed the assessment they will speak to the project or program manager and inform them of the outcome. They will go through any of the recommendations that the assurance review has uncovered and work with the project or program manager on the action plan to embed the recommendation into the project or program delivery.

The PMO will follow up on each of the agreed actions and ensure that these have been acted on and incorporated into the project or program delivery.

Supplier	Input	Process	Output	Customer
PMO	Assurance checklist	Assure project Assure program	Assessment Recommendations	PMO Project Manager Program Manager

How the PMO will measure the value of this service

This can be measured by adherence to process. It can be measured by the increase in the success of the projects and programs.

Criteria when the PMO will use this service

- Where there is a desire to improve project and program delivery within the organization
- Where the PMO are independent of the project or program being assessed
- When the PMO has the ability to provide a critical review

Helpful hints for the PMO when delivering the service

- Consider doing spot checks on the projects and programs if they have a long time between gate reviews
- Do not look to assure all projects and programs, review them based on a risk basis. The higher the impact of failure, the more important the assurance review should be
- Consider doing a partial assurance review on a particular area e.g. finance, risk, change control, if this has come up as a concern area in the lessons learned reviews
- Consider using the gate review checklist as a basis for the assurance checklist
- If the PMO finds any examples where there is good adherence to the process, then this can be used as examples in the good practice repository

PMO Capabilities needed to fulfil this service

Competencies	Techniques and generic tools
Reporting, Insights and Analysis Assurance Personal Communication Relationships and engagement Negotiation Result Orientation	Check sheets

Related services

Capture good practice examples for inclusion in good practice repository Enable sharing of good practice Develop and maintain the overall Quality Assurance Framework Provide project and program health checks Provide project and program audits	Provide a Stage Gate Review or Gateway support service Define, maintain, and implement framework for monitoring and review Provide project or program rescues Provide advice and guidance to prevent project or program failure Assure the development of portfolio, program, and project quality plans

Quality Management Monitoring

Service group description

The review of quality control to ensure compliance with the quality management process and standard.

Why have these services been grouped together?

These services relate to the PMO monitoring the success of quality control across the portfolio.

List of related services described in other areas

Monitor supplier performance

Responsibility Assignment Matrix

Service	Executive	Portfolio Manager	Program Manager	Project Manager	PMO	Sponsor	Other Stakeholder
Ensure compliance with quality standards and good practice	A				A, R		
Oversee the quality review process for contractual supplier deliverables			A	A	R	I	C (Supplier)
Monitor quality performance	A		C	C	R		
Analyse feedback from quality reviews			C	C	A, R		

Ensure compliance with quality standards and good practice

Service description

The review of projects and programs adherence to the quality control process and templates.

What the service provides for the customer

This provides feedback to the PMO on any improvements that may be required to the quality control framework. It provides guidance and recommendations for the project and program managers on how to improve the way quality is controlled within the project or program.

Why is this service being offered to the customer?

By reviewing compliance, the PMO can ensure that the projects and programs are delivering to the correct quality level. As the PMO created the framework they are best placed to review its usage and suggest improvements.

How PMO will apply this service

The PMO will look at the quality management strategy for the project or program. They will look at the quality register and review how this is being managed. They will look at the reporting that is being produced to see if this can be improved.

If the PMO find any deviations between what is being used in the project or program and what is shown in the standard they will speak with the project or program manager. If the deviance is down to lack of understanding, then the PMO will provide some advice. If the deviance is due to tailoring, then the PMO may look to include this as guidance in the quality control framework.

Supplier	Input	Process	Output	Customer
PMO	Quality control process Quality control help Quality Register Quality management documentation	Review compliance with standard	Process improvements Recommendations	PMO Project Managers Program Managers

How the PMO will measure the value of this service

This can be measured by looking at the lessons to see a reduction in negative lessons due to issues with quality control. It can be measured by asking for feedback from the project or program manager.

Criteria when the PMO will use this service

- Where there is a quality control framework in place
- Where there have been lessons identified about improvements required in quality control

Helpful hints for the PMO when delivering the service

- There may be a good reason why the project or program is deviating from the standard. By talking with the manager concerned, the PMO can understand the reason for the deviation and may incorporate this into the standard
- If there are updates required to the process, then ensure these are controlled via the Process Improvement Plan

PMO Capabilities needed to fulfil this service

Competencies	Techniques and generic tools
Quality Management Assurance Personal Communication Relationships and engagement Negotiation Result Orientation	Document Analysis Process Analysis

Related services

Manage the Process Improvement Plan Develop and maintain the overall Quality Control Framework	Train the Quality Control Framework Analyse feedback from quality reviews

Oversee the quality review process for contractual supplier deliverables

Service description

Ensure that the supplier deliverables are reviewed for quality and meet (or exceed) the quality criteria set down in the contract in order that payment is triggered.

What the service provides for the customer

The project or program manager knows that the supplier deliverables will be quality reviewed according to the quality control framework. They will be assured that the supplier will not get paid until the quality of those deliverables reach the contractually agreed level.

Why is this service being offered to the customer?

The PMO are able to track the quality of the deliverables. They have access to the supplier contracts and know how to use the quality control tool/quality register to review the status of quality checks. By delegating this to the PMO the project or program manager can focus on the overall delivery.

How PMO will apply this service

The PMO will list each of the deliverables requiring a quality review in the quality register (or quality control tool). This will list what they required quality should be, who is responsible for the review and when the review is scheduled. Once the review has occurred the quality register will get updated with the outcome (pass/fail) and may list any remedial actions.

The PMO will produce regular reports on the status of the quality control process. This will include information on the numbers of deliverables for review, the numbers passed/failed. The report may contain information on any underlying reasons for failure to allow the project or program manager to consider some follow-up actions.

Once the deliverables have reached the required/agreed quality, then any invoice which is dependent on the required quality being reached can be paid.

Supplier	Input	Process	Output	Customer
Project Managers Program Managers	Documentation Compliance checklist Review form template Supplier Contract Quality Management strategy Quality Register	Coordinate quality review	Review form Remedial actions Updated Quality Register	Project Managers Program Managers

How the PMO will measure the value of this service

This can be measured by reviewing how many supplier invoices are paid correctly. If can be measured by gaining feedback from the project or program manager. It can be measured by tracking the accuracy if the quality control reporting.

Criteria when the PMO will use this service

- Where there is an external supplier responsible for some deliverables
- Where the PMO is aligned to a single project or program
- Where the PMO has been asked to oversee the quality control process

Helpful hints for the PMO when delivering the service

- If this is not done by the PMO it will need to be done by the project or program manager
- The PMO may assist the supplier with getting the deliverable reviewed
- The PMO may update the quality register/quality control tool on behalf of the supplier
- As well as the quality aspect, there may be other triggers in the contract which specify when payment should be made to the supplier

PMO Capabilities needed to fulfil this service

Competencies	Techniques and generic tools
P3M Administration Financial Management Quality Management Supplier Management Assurance Professionalism and ethics Personal Integrity and reliability Relationships and engagement Teamwork Result Orientation	Cash flow analysis

Related services

Develop and maintain the overall Quality Control Framework Develop or source tools for Quality Control Work with procurement to ensure effective interface with supplier's quality systems Support contracts monitoring and management	Monitor supplier performance Ensure invoices are paid according to the contract terms Coordinate quality reviews of deliverables Manage invoicing processing for portfolio, programs, and projects Provide guidance on quality criteria, reviewers, and sign-off authority to ensure consistency

Monitor quality performance

Service description

The review of the quality register to see how good the project or program is on getting it 'right first time' when doing quality reviews.

What the service provides for the customer

This provides the project or program manager with some insight into the success of the delivery by understanding how much time is wasted in re-work and re-checking deliverable quality. By providing some insight into the root cause of the quality review failures the PMO can suggest some remedial actions that the project or program manager can take to get quality 'right first time'.

Why is this service being offered to the customer?

The PMO are able to dig into the detail of the quality reviews and find out the underlying causes of any review failures. By getting quality 'right first time' saves on the cost and time associated with rework.

How PMO will apply this service

The PMO will look at the quality register to review how many reviews complete first time as a proportion of all the reviews completed. They will look to see how much extra time and effort the rework has cost the project or program.

If there have been a significant number of deliverables requiring rework, or the cost or time has been significant then the PMO should look to understand the root cause of the poor performance. The root causes could include:

- Misunderstanding of expected quality – to correct the project manager should ensure that quality criteria are agreed up front. This expected quality needs to be shared to the deliverable creator and to the reviewer to ensure they are both working to the same criteria
- Lack of time for internal quality checks – the deliverable has been rushed out for review before it was ready. To correct the project manager should ensure that deliverables have an interim quality review before being released for full review
- Inexperienced people – the people assigned to produce the deliverable did not have the necessary expertise. The project manager should ensure the correct people are assigned, or that junior people are mentored so they can improve
- Too high demands for quality – it could be that the required quality cannot be achieved and that the customer for the deliverable will need to accept a lower quality

Once the PMO has worked out the root causes of the delay due to rework because of quality defects they will pass this information back to the project or program manager along with some suggestions for actions to resolve the underlying issues.

Supplier	Input	Process	Output	Customer
Project Managers Program Managers	Quality Plan Quality Reviews Quality Register	Monitor Quality Performance	Quality compliance report	Project Managers Program Managers PMO

How the PMO will measure the value of this service

This can be measured by looking at the improvement in the numbers of quality reviews which do not require rework.

Criteria when the PMO will use this service

- When the PMO is aligned to a single project or program
- Where there is a perceived issue with quality control

Helpful hints for the PMO when delivering the service

- As well as cost and time, reworking deliverables if they are not of the requisite quality can have a negative impact on the morale of the team and the perception of the project or program
- If there is little rework or the cost/time of the rework is minor, then the PMO should try to find out why. Is there anything that can be taken as good practice from this project or program that can then be used on other projects or programs?
- Some of the root causes have been listed above, there will be others and it is likely there will be a mixture. The PMO should ascertain which one of the root causes is most prevalent and look to get that fixed first and then work on the other root causes
- If the same root causes come up across different project and programs the PMO should consider providing some more training out to project and program managers on things to look out for. They should update the quality control framework to incorporate these suggestions

PMO Capabilities needed to fulfil this service

Competencies	Techniques and generic tools
Quality Management Reporting, Insights and Analysis Result Orientation	Root Cause Analysis 5 Whys Failure Modes and Effects Analysis (FMEA) Categorized frequency analysis (Frequency plot, bar chart)

Related services

Develop and maintain the overall Quality Control Framework Train the Quality Control Framework Provide guidance on quality criteria, reviewers, and sign-off authority to ensure consistency	Develop or source tools for Quality Control Analyse feedback from quality reviews

Analyse feedback from quality reviews

Service description

Review of the usage of the quality control framework to provide suggestions for improvement.

What the service provides for the customer

This provides an objective review of the quality control process with a view to improving its value within the organization.

Why is this service being offered to the customer?

By reviewing the usage of the quality control framework, the PMO can spot good practice that can be used elsewhere. The suggestions for improvement ensure that the quality control framework will continue to be maintained.

How PMO will apply this service

The PMO will examine the lessons registers, stage gate reviews and progress reports to look for examples of where the quality control framework is not being used.

The PMO will look at the quality performance and see if there are any underlying root causes for poor quality that could be rectified by updating the quality control framework.

The PMO will look at the detail of the feedback from the quality reviews to see whether the same or similar comments are coming up.

The PMO will add all the suggestions for improvement into the Process Improvement Plan in order that the quality control framework get updated.

Supplier	Input	Process	Output	Customer
Project Managers Program Managers PMO	Stage gate reviews Gateway assessment Post Implementation Reviews Lessons Identified Progress Reports	Review quality process	Process Improvement Plan	PMO

How the PMO will measure the value of this service

This can be measured by counting the number of improvements to the quality control framework.

Criteria when the PMO will use this service

- When there is a culture of continuous improvement
- Where there are perceived issues with quality control

Helpful hints for the PMO when delivering the service

- Consider whether the quality control framework needs amending, or whether it is not understood and therefore further training is required
- Look to perform this service on a regular basis when the lessons registers are reviewed for process improvements

PMO Capabilities needed to fulfil this service

Competencies	Techniques and generic tools
Knowledge Management Quality Management Reporting, Insights and Analysis	Root Cause Analysis Failure Modes and Effects Analysis (FMEA) Process Analysis

Related services

Develop and maintain the overall Quality Control Framework Train the Quality Control Framework Manage the Process Improvement Plan Monitor quality performance	Ensure compliance with quality standards and good practice Develop or source tools for Quality Control Coordinate quality reviews of deliverables Work with procurement to ensure effective interface with supplier's quality systems

Risk Management

Risk Management

Description

The Risk Management service area contains the services associated with the identification, analysis, planning/risk responses and monitoring of risks within and across one or more projects, programs, and portfolios.

What the services within the area provide for the customer

Organizations require a holistic and structured view of risks that cover all types of risks within and outside the organization. Specialist competencies are required to design and populate a risk framework with the risk types that can impact an organization. The PMO is ideally positioned to offer risk management capabilities because of the direct involvement with projects and programs. In organizations with several PMOs, to ensure consistency of applying the risk framework, one or two PMOs may take the lead in offer this Service Domain across the organization.

Helpful hints for when the PMO is delivering this service area

- Define and test the risk framework with manual processes and a risk tool that can easily be changed and improved before creating or deciding on buying an enterprise-wide solution
- Understand the applicability of the proposed risk framework within the area that it is being applied
- Test the framework in a portfolio, program, and project context to see how the risks flow within the portfolio and outside the portfolio and if the defined governance is effective in dealing with the changes of risk assessments and situations of risks being triggered
- Know the risk understanding (maturity) of the organization and define or agree on risk levels in terms of risk thresholds, risk tolerance and risk appetite, per project type
- The risk management framework should be approved by internal risk, compliance, and any other organizational governance entity. This will go down to the risk appetite, risk threshold and risk tolerance of the project sponsor/project steering committee

Risk Management Design

Service group description

The development of standards, processes, procedures, templates, and help associated with the management of risks for projects and programs.

Why have these services been grouped together?

These services relate to the setup of risk management within the organization.

List of related services described in other areas

Automate Processes

Responsibility Assignment Matrix

Service	Executive	Portfolio Manager	Program Manager	Project Manager	PMO	Sponsor	Other Stakeholder
Develop the overall risk management framework	A	C	C	C	R	I	I (PPM team)
Introduce tools for managing risks		C	C	C	A, R		I (PPM team)
Train the risk management framework		I	I	I	A, R		I (PPM team)

Helpful hints for when the PMO is delivering this service group

When introducing a tool to manage risks ensure that this aligns to the risk management framework.

Develop the overall risk management framework

Service description

Develop a risk management framework consisting of process, procedures, standards, templates, and help. This will include suggested escalation routes for risks, which will need to be tailored for each project. It will cover the conversion of risks into issues.

What the service provides for the customer

This provides the project and program managers a standard way of recording risks and providing adequate risk responses to ensure that risks do not turn into issues. It provides a process and procedures for them to follow.

Why is this service being offered to the customer?

Having a consistent way of raising, responding, and monitoring risk across the portfolio allows the information on risks to be rolled up and reported on consistently. It means that when moving from project to project the project manager, and their teams do not need to learn or develop this afresh for each project.

How PMO will apply this service

The PMO will review the external guidance about risk management for projects and programs and will look to tailor this for their organization. They will suggest a typical escalation route for getting risks actions resolved, with tailoring options that can be considered.

They will produce a standard risk register with a help guide for its usage. The PMO will consider any common reporting requirements (e.g. inclusion in steering group packs and progress reports) and will try to ensure these can be delivered using the information in the risk register. They will provide a standard set of risk assessment definitions including those for impact, probability, and proximity.

Supplier	Input	Process	Output	Customer
PMO	Standards template	Develop Standard Develop Templates	Risk management strategy Risk register Risk management standard Risk management process	Project Manager Program Manager Portfolio Manager PMO

How the PMO will measure the value of this service

The PMO can measure the value of this service by looking how widely the documents produced by this service have been used. They can judge this by how easy it is to provide a rolled-up view of the risks across the portfolio.

Criteria when the PMO will use this service

- When there is a need for a consistent risk management process
- Where the existing risk management framework requires review
- Where there is a centralized PMO

Helpful hints for the PMO when delivering the service

- Link this service with the Introduce tools for managing risks service to introduce a tool at the same time as the process is being introduced
- Link this with the develop the issue management framework to ensure that risks can be easily turned into issues and there is traceability of which risks have turned into issues
- When looking at the reporting required such as feed into to progress report templates and steering group packs, look to see whether the information can be transferred with the minimum of reformatting on the project managers behalf. Look out for locked cells, merged columns etc.

PMO Capabilities needed to fulfil this service

Competencies	Techniques and generic tools
Information Management Reporting, Insights and Analysis Risk Management Delivery Methods Governance Frameworks	Risk Register Probability and impact matrix Swim-lane flowcharts Task responsibility matrix/RACI

Related services

Develop the overall issue management framework Introduce tools for managing issues Introduce tools for managing risks Train the risk management framework Monitor the Risk Register Maintain the Risk Register Facilitate independent risk workshops	Contribute to the identification of risks Contribute to the assessment of risks Strategic Risk Assessment Provide dependency analysis Advise on risk mitigation and contingency planning Establish and maintain an efficient flow of information regarding risk handling and escalation Automate Processes Map key value streams and processes

Introduce tools for managing risks

Service description

The sourcing/developing/tailoring of tools to manage, report and track risks aligned to the risk management framework. Ensuring that the users get trained in the use of these tools.

What the service provides for the customer

This will provide the project or program manager with a tool which will allow them to register, track, report and resolve risks. This will allow them to use this information to add to progress reports or steering group packs.

Why is this service being offered to the customer?

Rather than just relying on Word or Excel to record risks, having a tool can provide a way of ensuring consistency by having validation built in to reduce data errors and make reporting easier. This can provide automation to automatically identify risks which need attention or escalation. It can trigger a risk to be converted into an issue should the risk materialize.

How PMO will apply this service

The PMO will check to see whether there is an existing tool that can be configured to support the risk management process (the organization may already have a PPM tool, in place). If there is not, then they will review whether they want to develop something in-house (if they have the skills) or whether they want to get a vendor supplied tool.

If this being developed in house the PMO will supply the developer, the requirements (typically the current risk templates, the probability and impact matrix, the escalation process along with standard report extracts required). Once the development has finished the PMO will perform the testing, ensuring it meets the requirements before accepting the tool into use.

If this is being sourced from a vendor, then the package will need to be customized to include the necessary fields and dropdowns. The PMO need to review how the data can be extracted for inclusion in standard reporting. Once this has been done the PMO can start rolling out the usage of the tool.

Regardless of how the tool was obtained it will need to have some training developed and some guidelines for use. The PMO should look to develop the training and be prepared to deliver the training alongside the rollout of the tool. The PMO should consider how frequently they want to deliver the training once the initial training has finished. Do they want to run regular sessions or individual session as and when new users are identified?

The process for loading up existing risks needs to be dealt with as part of the initial rollout. Will this be the PMO, will there be an automated load? Do all risks need to be loaded or just the open ones? What about existing risk numbering, can that be kept?

The existing risk management process will need to be updated to have appropriate references to the new tool and the links to the risk register will need to be discontinued. The issue management process would need to be looked as well to see whether that references turning risks into issues and therefore may need to include references to the new tool.

Supplier	Input	Process	Output	Customer
Vendor In house developers	Vendor software In house software	Software implementation	Risk management tool	Project Manager Program Manager PMO

How the PMO will measure the value of this service

This can be measured by increase the data quality of issue information. It can be measured by the use of the tool over the existing templates. The PMO can ask the users of the service whether they prefer the tool (and why).

Criteria when the PMO will use this service

- When there is desire for consistency across the portfolio
- Where a risk management framework has been developed
- Where there is funding to purchase a vendor tool
- Where there is capability within the PMO to build an issue management tool in-house

Helpful hints for the PMO when delivering the service

- Factor the cost of supporting the tool as well as the initial purchase
- Work out how people will be trained in the use of the tool, both on initial rollout and when new people join and are required to use it
- Check to see whether the same tool can be used to manage risks and issues. That will make it easier to convert a risk into an issue and keep track of which issues have resulted as risks that were not dealt with and which were new issues
- Consider having extracts that enable risks to be easily imported into steering group packs or progress reports

PMO Capabilities needed to fulfil this service

Competencies	Techniques and generic tools
Information Management Reporting, Insights and Analysis Risk Management Delivery Methods P3M Tools Relationships and engagement	Make or buy analysis Risk Register Probability and impact matrix Project Management Information System Stakeholder engagement assessment matrix

Related services

Develop the overall risk management framework Train the risk management framework Introduce tools for managing issues Maintain the Risk Register Develops in-house project management tools Tailors and configures project management tools Implements vendor provided project management tools Manages project management tools (systems admin)	Advise on PPM tools and software Provide PPM training Provide training logistics support Contribute to the identification of risks Contribute to the assessment of risks Strategic Risk Assessment Provide dependency analysis Advise on risk mitigation and contingency planning Monitor the Risk Register Communicate with stakeholders affected either by the risk or the risk mitigations Automate Processes

Train the risk management framework

Service description

Train the people responsible for identifying, assessing, and responding to risk about the risk management framework. This includes the risk management process, procedures, templates, tools, standards, and help.

What the service provides for the customer

This ensures that everyone who is involved with identifying, assessing, and responding to risks knows how the risk management framework can be applied. This will cover under what circumstances risks are escalated, reported, and transferred into issues. Escalation and reporting may be tailored for a particular project or program.

Why is this service being offered to the customer?

As the PMO have been responsible for producing the framework and the associate tool (if there is one) then they will know how the framework should be implemented and be able to answer any questions individuals may have around this.

How PMO will apply this service

The PMO will identify the key people who need training in each project or program. Typically, this will be the project and program managers along with any team leaders.

Once the list of people is available the PMO will book the training sessions and invite the people. The PMO can then prepare the training material to be used. At the training course take note of who has attended and who has not and be prepared to organize further training sessions.

Supplier	Input	Process	Output	Customer
PMO	Risk Management framework	Deliver training Communication	Informed people	PPM Teams

How the PMO will measure the value of this service

This can be measured by numbers of people trained and the satisfaction with the training.

Criteria when the PMO will use this service

- When there is a new risk management framework
- When there is a change to the risk management framework
- When new people are added to the project teams
- When there is a new tool to be used alongside the risk management framework

Helpful hints for the PMO when delivering the service

- If there is a tool that needs to be used, then show that at the same time
- Use the questions from the training courses to help devise a frequently asked questions or help document
- Gain feedback from the training course on how effective the training was and use that as a measure for the service
- Demonstrate how risks can get raised into issues and what then happens to the risk
- Show how risks can be reported in the progress report and steering group packs
- Consider training the sponsor and steering group members about their role in responding to risk actions to prevent them becoming issues
- If there are minor changes to the risk management framework then the PMO may consider just providing a communication explaining the changes
- Consider having a sweep up session(s) to get to those people who were unable to get the original sessions when booked
- For 'hard to get' people consider doing one to one training to ensure the framework gets trained out to everyone

PMO Capabilities needed to fulfil this service

Competencies	Techniques and generic tools
P3M Administration Risk Management Capability Development P3M Tools Personal Communication Relationships and engagement Result Orientation	Communication requirements analysis Risk Register Probability and impact matrix Project Management Information System Stakeholder checklist Stakeholder engagement assessment matrix

Related services

Develop the overall risk management framework Introduce tools for managing risks Train the issue management framework Provide PPM training	Provide training logistics support Maintain the Risk Register Communicate the change control framework Communicate with stakeholders affected either by the risk or the risk mitigations

Risk Management Operations

Service group description

The series of steps required to identify, record, assess, provide responses to, and analyse the risks that can directly and indirectly impact a project, program or portfolio, or any other entity utilizing this service group.

Why have these services been grouped together?

These services relate to the identification, assessment and management of r sks and dependencies on a regular basis for the project or program to prevent, if possible, risks turning into issues.

Responsibility Assignment Matrix

Service	Executive	Portfolio Manager	Program Manager	Project Manager	PMO	Sponsor	Other Stakeholder
Provide dependency analysis		A	A	A	R		
Strategic Risk Assessment		A			R		
Contribute to the assessment of risks		A, R	A, R	A, R	C		
Facilitate independent risk workshops		A	A	A	R		C (PPM team)
Contribute to the identification of risks		A	A	A	R		C (PPM team)
Maintain the Risk Register	A	C	C	C	R		I (PPM team)
Advise on risk mitigation and contingency planning		C	C	C	A, R		

Helpful hints for when the PMO is delivering this service group

- Prepare for the engagement of the stakeholders as first impressions to your preparation will influence the way they perceive the importance of this service group as well as your ability to influence and steer the PPP or entity through all the service groups
- Ensure the tools i.e. registers can be use interactively during the facilitation sessions

Provide dependency analysis

Service description

The review of dependencies between projects within a program or programs and projects within a portfolio.

What the service provides for the customer

This provides an independent assessment of the dependencies across a program or portfolio. Dependencies which are identified are recorded in the relevant dependency registers.

Why is this service being offered to the customer?

As the PMO have an overview of all the projects within a program or all the items within a portfolio they are able to have an independent assessment of the linkages between these items. By identifying the dependencies and making the relevant managers aware it can ensure that they are managed correctly.

How PMO will apply this service

The PMO will find the list of projects and programs they are looking to see the dependencies between. They will look to find out all the existing dependencies that are in the registers. Where the dependency references another project or program the PMO will check the dependency register for that project or program to see whether this dependency exists. If the dependency does not exist, then the PMO will inform the project or program manager in order that they can add the dependency into their register.

The PMO will examine the scoping statements and other relevant documentation explaining the scope of the projects and programs. They will examine to see if they can spot any potential dependencies with other projects and programs. If they manage to identify some then they will speak with the project or program manager to confirm whether this is correct. If it is correct, then the PMO will ensure that the dependency gets added to both dependency registers.

Supplier	Input	Process	Output	Customer
Project Managers Program Managers	Dependency register Scoping statements	Assess dependencies	Dependency register	Program Managers Portfolio Managers

How the PMO will measure the value of this service

This can be measured by a greater alignment of the projects and programs across the portfolio. It can be measured by the numbers of dependencies that are identified.

Criteria when the PMO will use this service

- When the PMO is aligned to a project or program manager
- Where there is the potential for a large number of dependencies to exist within a program or portfolio

Helpful hints for the PMO when delivering the service

- Sometimes organizations record dependencies as risks rather than in their own register. If this is the case, then substitute the dependency register for the risk register
- Ensure the direction of the dependency is recorded correctly. For each inbound dependency there must be an equivalent outbound dependency from another project or program
- It is possible that one outbound dependency has more than one inbound dependency on different projects

PMO Capabilities needed to fulfil this service

Competencies	Techniques and generic tools
Reporting, Insights and Analysis Risk Management Relationships and engagement Resourcefulness	Document Analysis Risk Register

Related services

Monitor dependency register	Introduce tools for managing risks
Develop the overall risk management framework	Review cross project and p-ogram dependencies

Strategic Risk Assessment

Service description

The assessment of risks that are likely to impact the delivery of the strategy and therefore the portfolio.

What the service provides for the customer

This provides an assessment of the risks associated with the delivery of the portfolio.

Why is this service being offered to the customer?

The portfolio exists to deliver the strategy. If there are risks to the strategy that implies that there are risks to the portfolio. By understanding and managing those risks the portfolio will have a more likely chance of success.

How PMO will apply this service

The PMO will obtain a copy of the strategic plan. They will assess the external environment that the organization operates in and the short to medium term horizon. They will see what is likely to impact the delivery of the strategy. They will assess which of these risks have already been identified, either at the portfolio level, or within the project and program risk registers. Where risks have not been previously identified then they will need to be raised and added to the portfolio risk register.

Supplier	Input	Process	Output	Customer
Strategy department	Strategic plan Risk Register	Identify risks Assess risks	Risk Register	Portfolio Manager

How the PMO will measure the value of this service

This can be measured by the numbers of portfolio risks identified. It can be measured by feedback from the portfolio manager.

Criteria when the PMO will use this service

- Where the PMO is aligned to a portfolio manager
- Where there is a strategic plan
- Where the portfolio manager requires assistance with risk identification and assessment

Helpful hints for the PMO when delivering the service

- If there are portfolio level risks held within the individual project and program registers, then they need to be escalated to the portfolio level and managed there

PMO Capabilities needed to fulfil this service

Competencies	Techniques and generic tools
Reporting, Insights and Analysis Risk Management	Risk Register Probability and impact matrix

Related services

Contribute to the identification of risks Contribute to the assessment of risks Horizon scan for impending policy or strategy changes	Develop the overall risk management framework Introduce tools for managing risks

Contribute to the identification of risks

Service description

The identification and raising of risks for the project, program, or portfolio.

What the service provides for the customer

This provides a fuller record of the risks for the project, program, or portfolio. These risks can then be recorded, assessed, and tracked.

Why is this service being offered to the customer?

As the PMO works in a project or program they can help by identifying risks and ensure they are recorded in the Risk. Register. Having a more complete list of risks will allow for improved management and hopefully a reduction in the issues raised.

How PMO will apply this service

The PMO will review the progress report and the risk register to see if there are any items which have been added as commentary to the progress report that have not be raised as risks.

The PMO will review the schedule, finances, scope, change register and quality register to see if they can identify any new risks that should be considered.

For any of the items which are potential risks the PMO will discuss this with the project, program, or portfolio manager to get them to add the risk to the risk register and perform the necessary assessment and risk response.

Supplier	Input	Process	Output	Customer
PMO	Potential risk Risk register	Identify and record a risk	Risk Register	Project Manager Program Manager Portfolio Manager

How the PMO will measure the value of this service

This can be measured by seeing an increase in the numbers of risks in the risk register. It can be measured by seeing a reduction in the issues as risks are being identified and managed before they can become issues.

Criteria when the PMO will use this service

- When the PMO reviews the progress reports
- When the PMO performs a gate review for the project or program

Helpful hints for the PMO when delivering the service

- Consider reviewing the risks as part of the gate review for the project or program
- If a project, program, or portfolio is unwilling to add the risk to their register review whether the risk is too low level/detailed for inclusion, or whether risks are being managed correctly

PMO Capabilities needed to fulfil this service

Competencies	Techniques and generic tools
Reporting, Insights and Analysis Risk Management Professionalism and ethics Personal Integrity and reliability Relationships and engagement Negotiation	Risk Register Probability and impact matrix

Related services

Maintain the Risk Register Communicate with stakeholders affected either by the risk or the risk mitigations Develop the overall risk management framework Introduce tools for managing risks	Horizon scan for impending policy or strategy changes Facilitate independent risk workshops Strategic Risk Assessment

Facilitate independent risk workshops

Service description

The Service 'Facilitate Risk Workshop' includes all the steps in the preparation, facilitation, and follow-up to achieve the agreed goals.

What the service provides for the customer

This provides a facilitation service to enable risks to be identified, assessed and action plans devised.

Why is this service being offered to the customer?

Understanding the concepts of risks, the frameworks, principles, embedded techniques, and supporting tools required a high level of organizational capability. PPP stakeholders will never get to the same level of competencies as a risk professional within the PMO offering this service, because experience, frequency of use and understanding of risks across the PPP can only be achieved by an entity that have the governance and capabilities to achieve this.

How PMO will apply this service

Having identified the need for a facilitated workshop the PMO will liaise with the project or program manager to work out who needs to attend the workshop. The PMO will then book the meeting and invite all the attendees. The purpose of the workshop will be clearly stated prior to the workshop commencing. Any background documentation should be sent to the participants in advance to give them time to read the materials prior to the meeting.

In the meeting the PMO will set the ground rules and re-state the objective of the meeting to ensure everyone has a clear understanding of what they are being expected to do. During the meeting, the PMO, as facilitator, will ensure that everyone gets a chance to speak and put forward their views. The PMO should ensure that decisions are recorded and capture all the workshop outputs.

The PMO will look to provide a structured risk identification, assessment, and resolution approach to ensure that all risks are considered. The PMO will look to fill in the risk register as they go through the workshop, ensuring all parts are considered.

After the meeting, the PMO will distribute the risk register and remind the risk owners and the actionees of their responsibility to resolve the risks by the agreed dates.

Supplier	Input	Process	Output	Customer
PMO	Risk Register template	Facilitating a meeting	Risk Register	Project Manager Program Manager

How the PMO will measure the value of this service

Customer satisfaction in the preparation and execution of the workshop.

Ratio of risks identified from the risk workshops to existing risks that were identified later on in the PPP lifecycle, that existed since in first risk workshop.

Criteria when the PMO will use this service

- When a project or program is being initiated and the risks are being gathered
- When a project or program is moving to the next phase
- When there are difficulties in understanding the actions to take to respond to a risk

Helpful hints for the PMO when delivering the service

- Consider having a facilitation/workshop kit (pens, post-its, blue-tac, flipchart paper etc.)
- Consider having a structured set of questions to drive out risk identification based around PESTEL

PMO Capabilities needed to fulfil this service

Competencies	Techniques and generic tools
Risk Management Governance Frameworks Personal Communication Negotiation	5 Whys Risk Register Probability and impact matrix

Related services

Develop the overall risk management framework Contribute to the identification of risks Maintain the Risk Register Communicate with stakeholders affected either by the risk or the risk mitigations	Advise on risk mitigation and contingency planning Provide facilitation service Contribute to the assessment of risks

Contribute to the assessment of risks

Service description

Assisting the risk owner by using a variety of risk techniques to analyse the identified risks and their characteristics, related and through interactive sessions provides charts and reports.

What the service provides for the customer

The facilitated review of identified risks using a structured risk management approach to map the risks onto a risk severity/probability matrix.

Determining and/or using the risk governance thresholds and risk strategies to determine a risk profile that is acceptable to the steering committee.

Why is this service being offered to the customer?

The PMO can offer an independent review of the risk and the assessment of that risk considering everything else that is happening in the organisation. The PMO understands the related projects and programs and how related risks have been dealt with. As they can see what has happened in other areas, they can suggest assessments which will potentially prevent this risk occurring in the current project or program

How PMO will apply this service

When a new risk is raised the PMO can review it and assign a probability and impact. They will review the risk standards to ensure that the risk is correctly classified. They will examine the risk tolerance to ensure that the risk fits within the tolerance, if not this should be escalated to the next level of management. They will review effective suggestions which have resulted in mitigation of the risk against other projects or programs to suggest how this risk may be resolved.

They will ensure that the information is agreed with the risk owner and updated within the risk register.

Supplier	Input	Process	Output	Customer
Project Manager Program Manager Portfolio Manager PMO	Risk Register Risk tolerance Risk standards	Risk Analysis	Simulations and reports	Project Manager Program Manager Portfolio Manager

How the PMO will measure the value of this service

Customer satisfaction in the approach and understanding. The ability to provide options to achieve meet the risk governance levels.

Criteria when the PMO will use this service

- When new risks are raised

Helpful hints for the PMO when delivering the service

- Consider using a tool to provide the Monte Carlo analysis
- Only use the tools and techniques that you are comfortable using

PMO Capabilities needed to fulfil this service

Competencies	Techniques and generic tools
Risk Management P3M Tools Result Orientation	Risk Register Probability and impact matrix

Related services

Maintain the Risk Register Strategic Risk Assessment Facilitate independent risk workshops	Develop the overall risk management framework Introduce tools for managing risks

Further Reading

Avon, T. Foundations of risk analysis.
Robert, C. P. Monte Carlo methods.

Maintain the Risk Register

Service description

The update of the risk register on behalf of the project, program, or portfolio manager.

What the service provides for the customer

This provides the project, program, or portfolio manager with an updated risk register. The PMO can ensure that the data quality is accurate, that there is no missing data, risk action dates are not in the past, action updates are chased up and updated within the register.

Why is this service being offered to the customer?

By delegating the updating of the risk register to the PMO the PPM manager can focus on ensuring the right risks are identified and the actions and owners are in place to resolve those risks.

How PMO will apply this service

The PMO will receive a request from the project, program, or portfolio manager to update the risk register on their behalf. They will review the data quality and look to fill in any of the missing data (in conjunction with the PPM manager). They will chase down for updates to risk actions by contacting the named actionee and will update the dates and the status for the risks.

They will participate in risk identification and review sessions and ensure the register is updated after each session. They will alert the PPM manager to any risks which need their attention and ensure the updated information gets put into the register.

They may provide extracts of the risk register for regular reporting and risk review sessions.

If a risk has materialized and become an issue, they will update the register to close the risk and raise this within the issue register.

Supplier	Input	Process	Output	Customer
PPM team	Identified risks Risk Register	Identify and record a risk	Risk Register	Project Manager Program Manager

How the PMO will measure the value of this service

This can be measured by checking the data quality of a risk register which has this service versus on that has not. It can be measured in a reduction in the numbers of risks which turn into issues.

Criteria when the PMO will use this service

- When a PMO is aligned to a project, program, or portfolio manager
- Where the PPM manager is not performing this role themselves
- Where there is a large volume of risks that need managing

Helpful hints for the PMO when delivering the service

- Look to book in regular review sessions with the PPM manager where an update is done of all the open risks, or at least the ones which are the highest priority
- Once the update has been done, consider sending the latest copy of the risk register to the PPM manager for their information
- Consider using reporting or automation to identify risks which need immediate attention

PMO Capabilities needed to fulfil this service

Competencies	Techniques and generic tools
P3M Administration Information Management Quality Management Reporting, Insights and Analysis Risk Management P3M Tools Professionalism and ethics Personal Communication Relationships and engagement Resourcefulness	Risk Register Probability and impact matrix

Related services

Facilitate independent risk workshops Contribute to the identification of risks Communicate with stakeholders affected either by the risk or the risk mitigations Develop the overall risk management framework Introduce tools for managing risks Perform logging and tracking to resolution of issues	Train the risk management framework Contribute to the assessment of risks Advise on risk mitigation and contingency planning Monitor the Risk Register Proactively look across Risk Registers identify common themes and mitigations

Advise on risk mitigation and contingency planning

Service description

The provision of advice on the ways an individual risk could be mitigated and how to manage the risk budget for the mitigating actions.

What the service provides for the customer

This provides the PPM manager with some options to respond to particular risks as part of their risk register. The PMO can provide alternative options to deal with the risks.

Why is this service being offered to the customer?

Having the experience and knowledge across multiple projects and programs allows the PMO to provide a set of alternatives which have been used in other projects to deal with similar risks, along with an understanding of how effective these actions have been.

How PMO will apply this service

The PMO will find the risk register and see if there are any risks without risk responses, they will review the risk and suggest the different responses that could be taken to deal with the risk. As well as looking at the response the PMO will suggest the actions (and the actionees) to be followed to implement the suggested response. The PMO may suggest different responses and related actions to the risk.

The PMO will look at the central lessons register to see if they can find any examples of where a similar risk has appeared and review how that was dealt with, and how successful that approach was. They can then use that information to suggest alternatives to the risk responses that have already been suggested.

The PMO will share their analysis with the PPM manager and persuade them to accept the response and the actions. The PMO will then ensure that the information gets updated within the risk register.

Supplier	Input	Process	Output	Customer
Project Managers Program Managers Portfolio Managers PMO	Risk Register Lessons Register	Assess risks	Risk Register	Project Managers Program Managers Portfolio Managers

How the PMO will measure the value of this service

This can be measured by checking to see how effective the actions that have been suggested were in the mitigation of the risks.

Criteria when the PMO will use this service

- When the PMO is performing a review of the risks for a project, program, or portfolio
- As part of a risk workshop
- When identifying and assessing new risks

Helpful hints for the PMO when delivering the service

- The PMO may review other risk registers to see if similar risks have been identified and the actions taken. They will review whether those risks turned into issues, meaning the risk responses were not as successful as they were meant to be

PMO Capabilities needed to fulfil this service

Competencies	Techniques and generic tools
Issue Management Knowledge Management Reporting, Insights and Analysis Risk Management Relationships and engagement Teamwork	Risk Register

Related services

Review the effectiveness of risk mitigation actions Monitor the Risk Register Maintain the Risk Register Facilitate independent risk workshops Proactively look across Risk Registers identify common themes and mitigations	Develop the overall risk management framework Introduce tools for managing risks Communicate with stakeholders affected either by the risk or the risk mitigations Establish and maintain an efficient flow of information regarding risk handling and escalation

Risk Management Monitoring

Service group description

The review of the success of risk management across the portfolio.

Why have these services been grouped together?

These services relate to the review of the risks and dependencies across a portfolio of projects and programs.

Responsibility Assignment Matrix

Service	Executive	Portfolio Manager	Program Manager	Project Manager	PMO	Sponsor	Other Stakeholder
Monitor dependency register		C	C	C	A, R		
Monitor assumptions register		C	C	C	A, R		
Monitor the Risk Register		C	C	C	A, R		
Communicate with stakeholders affected either by the risk or the risk mitigations		A	A	A	R		I (affected stakeholders)
Review the effectiveness of risk mitigation actions		C	C	C	A, R		
Establish and maintain an efficient flow of information regarding risk handling and escalation		A	A	A	R		
Proactively look across Risk Registers identify common themes and mitigations		C	C	C	A, R		
Monitor the portfolio's total exposure to risk		A	C	C	R		

Monitor dependency register

Service Description

A review of the dependencies within the dependency register to validate for data accuracy and integrity.

What the service provides for the customer

Ensures that the information contained in a dependency register is accurate with the owner, dates and status being accurately recorded.

Why is this service being offered to the customer?

By having the correct information against the dependency, it helps the project or program to correctly manage it. The PMO are able to provide an independent assessment of the quality and integrity of the data, highlighting areas of concern and focus for the project or program manager.

How PMO will apply this service

The PMO will get access to the dependency register. They will check for any data quality issues including:

- Missing data – items which have not been filled in when they should have been
- Incorrect data – are items still assigned to individuals who have left
- Dates in the past – items that have not been updated, can they be closed, or does the date need to be in the future
- Inconsistent data – the dependency is marked as closed, however the related actions are outstanding and future dated

They will highlight all the items they find and report those back to the project or program manager for them to provide the correct information to resolve the issue.

Supplier	Input	Process	Output	Customer
Project Managers Program Managers	Dependency register	Validate Dependencies	Dependency register	Project Managers Program Managers

How the PMO will measure the value of this service

This can be measured by reviewing how many data issues have been identified with the dependency register. It can be measured by the feedback from the project or program manager.

Criteria when the PMO will use this service

- As part of a regular review of the project status
- As part of a gate review

Helpful hints for the PMO when delivering the service

- The PMO may offer to update the information in the register on behalf of the project or program manager
- The PMO may check the related project or program dependency register to see if the dependency is listed on there. They may check to see if that register has more information or different information on the dependency

PMO Capabilities needed to fulfil this service

Competencies	Techniques and generic tools
Information Management Quality Management Reporting, Insights and Analysis Risk Management Assurance Relationships and engagement Teamwork	Document Analysis Risk Register

Related services

Provide dependency analysis	Review cross project and program dependencies

Monitor assumptions register

Service description

Review the individual assumption registers to see whether there are assumptions that are no longer valid, or common assumptions that are shown on multiple registers.

What the service provides for the customer

Ensures the accuracy of the information within the assumptions register. Checks to see whether assumptions should be resolved, turned into risks, or confirmed as fact.

Why is this service being offered to the customer?

Assumptions often get raised at the beginning of the project or program and do not get reviewed as it proceeds. By monitoring them the PMO can ensure that the assumptions get dealt with and closed as the project or program progresses.

How PMO will apply this service

The PMO will get access to the assumptions register. They will check for any data quality issues including:

- Missing data – items which have not been filled in when they should have been
- Old assumptions – items that have either been confirmed as fact or have materialized as risks still appearing on the register as open items
- Dates in the past – items that have not been updated, can they be closed, or does the date need to be in the future

They will highlight all the items they find and report those back to the project or program manager for them to provide the correct information to update the register.

Supplier	Input	Process	Output	Customer
Project Managers Program Managers	Assumptions register	Validate assumptions	Assumptions register	Project Managers Program Managers

How the PMO will measure the value of this service

This can be measured by checking how many assumptions can be closed. It can be measured by feedback from the project or program manager.

Criteria when the PMO will use this service

- As part of a regular review of the project status
- As part of a gate review
- When the project or program moves into the next stage

Helpful hints for the PMO when delivering the service

- Consider reviewing the risk register to check whether an assumption has been raised as a risk
- Consider reviewing the issue register to check whether an assumption has been raised as an issue
- Review the meeting minutes to confirm that an assumption has been verified as fact

PMO Capabilities needed to fulfil this service

Competencies	Techniques and generic tools
Information Management Quality Management Reporting, Insights and Analysis Risk Management Assurance Relationships and engagement	Document Analysis Risk Register

Related services

Monitor the Risk Register

Monitor the Risk Register

Service description

A review of the risks within the risk register to validate for data accuracy and integrity. It confirms that actions are being followed to prevent risks becoming issues.

What the service provides for the customer

Ensures that the information contained in the risk register is accurate with the actions, dates and status being accurately recorded. It confirms that the actions are being followed to prevent the risk materializing.

Why is this service being offered to the customer?

Once a risk has been identified and recorded a plan for how to deal with this risk is required. The PMO can ensure that not only has this been identified, but the actions are assigned to individuals who are performing those actions. The PMO are able to provide an independent assessment of the quality and integrity of the data, highlighting areas of concern and focus for the project or program manager.

How PMO will apply this service

The PMO will get access to the risk register. They will check for any data quality issues including:

- Missing data – items which have not been filled in when they should have been
- Incorrect data – are items still assigned to individuals who have left
- Dates in the past – actions that have not been updated, can they be closed, or does the date need to be in the future
- Inconsistent data – the risk is marked as closed; however, the related actions are outstanding and future dated
- Materialized risks – risks which have been raised as issues, but still appear on the risk register

They will highlight all the items they find and report those back to the project or program manager for them to provide the correct information.

Supplier	Input	Process	Output	Customer
Project Managers Program Managers	Risk register Issue Register	Validate risks	Risk register	Project Managers Program Managers

How the PMO will measure the value of this service

This can be measured by reviewing how many data issues have been identified with the risk register. It can be measured by the feedback from the project or program manager.

Criteria when the PMO will use this service

- As part of a regular review of the project status
- As part of a gate review

Helpful hints for the PMO when delivering the service

- The PMO may offer to update the information in the register on behalf of the project or program manager
- The PMO may review the issue register to see if there are any issues which look, they are materialized risks, even if there is not a reference to indicate that it came from a particular risk in the first place

PMO Capabilities needed to fulfil this service

Competencies	Techniques and generic tools
Information Management Quality Management Reporting, Insights and Analysis Risk Management Assurance Relationships and engagement	Document Analysis Risk Register

Related services

Maintain the Risk Register Review the effectiveness of risk mitigation actions Develop the overall risk management framework Introduce tools for managing risks	Advise on risk mitigation and contingency planning Monitor assumptions register Establish and maintain an efficient flow of information regarding risk handling and escalation

Communicate with stakeholders affected either by the risk or the risk mitigations

Service description

The communication of information to and from the project or program to the individual or group responsible for managing a risk or dealing with one of the associated actions.

What the service provides for the customer

This ensures that all risks and related actions are communicated to their owners in accordance with the communication plan. Communication needs to be two-way to ensure that the individual or group know they have something assigned to them and to gain information from them about the current status of the risk or associated action.

Why is this service being offered to the customer?

Risk management is not something that is confined to the project or program manager. The people impacted by or who can impact a risk need to be communicated with to ensure that the risk can be successfully mitigated.

How PMO will apply this service

The PMO will review the risk register and the communications plan. When a new risk is assigned to a risk owner, who is not the project or program manager, the PMO will speak to the person concerned (as per the communication plan) to inform them that the risk has been assigned to them. They will provide them with an extract from the risk register along with any related actions.

Where a risk action has been assigned to an individual the PMO will inform the risk actionee what the action is, what the expected date of the action is. They will inform the individual about the risk, and any other related actions that would be of interest to the individual.

When there is an update required on a risk or on an action associated with that risk the PMO will speak to the individual concerned to get an update. If the action is closed, then the PMO will find out what was carried out. If the action has not been closed, then the PMO will obtain an update along with any new date when the action is expected to be delivered.

Having got the information from the individual then they will ensure the risk owner gets updated with the information alongside the risk register.

Supplier	Input	Process	Output	Customer
Project Manager Program Manager Portfolio Manager	Risk Register Communications plan	Manage risks	Communication	Stakeholders

How the PMO will measure the value of this service

This can be measured by checking to see which risks get updated. By the numbers of risks that turn into issues because actions were not performed.

Criteria when the PMO will use this service

- When a risk gets assigned an owner or an actionee
- As part of the regular review of the risk register
- When the owner or actionee on a risk change

Helpful hints for the PMO when delivering the service

- Consider having a regular point in the week/month where the risk register is reviewed, and updates are sought for all the risk actions
- Consider adding the risk actions into the regular progress meetings to get updates and ensure that risks are not forgotten about

PMO Capabilities needed to fulfil this service

Competencies	Techniques and generic tools
Information Management Risk Management Personal Integrity and reliability Personal Communication Relationships and engagement Teamwork	Risk Register

Related services

Maintain the Risk Register Review the effectiveness of risk mitigation actions Proactively look across Risk Registers identify common themes and mitigations Introduce tools for managing risks	Train the risk management framework Advise on risk mitigation and contingency planning Facilitate independent risk workshops Contribute to the identification of risks

Review the effectiveness of risk mitigation actions

Service description

A review of the risk registers to see which risks have been mitigated and which ones were not and subsequently turned into issues.

What the service provides for the customer

A review of the success, or otherwise, of risk mitigation leading to suggestions for improvement on how risks are handled within the PPM context. For systemic problems add these into an overall process improvement plan action log so that the process can be improved for future projects and programs.

Why is this service being offered to the customer?

By reviewing the effectiveness of risk management within the organization will lead to improvements in the risk management process. This can then be fed back into existing projects and programs to prevent risks turning into issues.

A periodic review of the risk register should identify which risks have turned into issues and which ones can be closed because they did not occur. For risks that turned into issues, identify whether there were any actions that could be taken to identify the risk earlier or prevent it from turning into an issue.

How PMO will apply this service

The PMO will obtain copies of this risk register and issue registers for the projects and programs. They will review these to see which risks turned into issues. For each of those risks they will review the actions that were taken to see whether the actions identified were carried out, and whether any other actions could or should have been taken to mitigate the risk and prevent it from becoming an issue.

They will review the risks which did not turn into issues. Did they close because the risk never materialized, or because the actions taken prevented the risk from occurring?

They will examine what made a mitigation action successful vs unsuccessful and see if they can gain some insight into the root causes of the successful actions. They will take those insights and add them into the help document about risk management. Where there are systemic problems that require an amendment to the risk management framework the PMO will add those into the process improvement plan for them to be managed alongside other improvements to the framework.

Supplier	Input	Process	Output	Customer
Project Manager Program Manager	Risk Register Issue Register	Review risks	Process Improvement Plan Risk Management help	Project Manager Program Manager Portfolio Manager PMO

How the PMO will measure the value of this service

This can be measured by an improvement in the risk management within the organization.

Criteria when the PMO will use this service

- As part of an annual review
- As part of the project or program closure process

Helpful hints for the PMO when delivering the service

- As well as looking at the documentation, ask the people managing those risks if, in hindsight, they what would they have done differently. If they had done that what change would that have made

PMO Capabilities needed to fulfil this service

Competencies	Techniques and generic tools
Issue Management Knowledge Management Reporting, Insights and Analysis Risk Management Resourcefulness	Root Cause Analysis 5 Whys Risk Register

Related services

Advise on risk mitigation and contingency planning Proactively look across Risk Registers identify common themes and mitigations Communicate with stakeholders affected either by the risk or the risk mitigations	Manage the Process Improvement Plan Enable sharing of good practice Monitor the Risk Register

Establish and maintain an efficient flow of information regarding risk handling and escalation

Service description

Ensure that the relevant risks are being escalated up to the next level of management to ensure they are successfully mitigated.

What the service provides for the customer

This provides a set of criteria for risks or their related actions to be escalated to a sufficient senior level to ensure that they get dealt with. This escalation is not just for information but is for action. By getting the relevant attention focused onto the risks will hopefully prevent them from becoming issues.

Why is this service being offered to the customer?

Not all risks require escalation, only the important ones. By defining what important is in the context of the program or portfolio (e.g. likelihood, impact, RAG) permits management by exception. This needs to be monitored to ensure that the process is being followed and amendments to the process documented in the risk management strategy.

How PMO will apply this service

The PMO will review the risk management strategy to see what the criteria, if any, is for the escalation of risks. Risks need to be escalated if they are important. This definition of important can vary depending on the project or program.

This importance of a risk could be based on:

- The risk assessment (the probability/impact rating)
- The Red, Amber, Green status of this risk – this will indicate how well the risk is being dealt with
- The proximity of the risk
- The number of outstanding actions
- The number of actions which are not getting a resolution

Having obtained the escalation criteria the PMO will review the risks in the risk register to see which ones of these should be escalated. They will look at the steering group packs to see which ones have been escalated. They will identify the risks which have not been escalated and challenge the project or program manager as to why they have not been. If necessary, the PMO can escalate these risks on behalf of the project or program.

The PMO should review to see what has actually happened as a result of the risks being escalated. Where actions taken, did escalating them actually help? If it did not, then the PMO should remind the sponsor and steering group of their responsibilities in dealing with risks. This is not just about the project or program manager; everyone has a role is dealing with risks.

Supplier	Input	Process	Output	Customer
Project Manager Program Manager	Risk Register Risk management strategy Communication plan Steering group pack	Escalate risks	Escalated risks	Project Manager Program Manager Portfolio Manager Sponsor

How the PMO will measure the value of this service

This can be measured by the numbers of risks which are escalated which have subsequently been successfully mitigated or otherwise dealt with. This can be measured by a reduction in the numbers of risks turning into issues.

Criteria when the PMO will use this service

- When a PMO is aligned with a project or program manager
- Where risks are not being escalated

Helpful hints for the PMO when delivering the service

- If there are no escalation criteria for risks within the risk management strategy the PMO should document this and get it added into the strategy
- If risks are not being escalated, then this can be a sign of underlying management issues for the project or program. The PMO should investigate further to see if there are any other issues that need attention
- The PMO should consider having sponsor training so they are aware of their responsibilities when being asked to sponsor a project or program. This should cover all their responsibilities not just those relating to risk management

PMO Capabilities needed to fulfil this service

Competencies	Techniques and generic tools
Issue Management Reporting, Insights and Analysis Risk Management Professionalism and ethics Personal Communication Relationships and engagement Negotiation Result Orientation	Risk Register Probability and impact matrix Swim-lane flowcharts Task responsibility matrix/RACI

Related services

Monitor the Risk Register Develop the overall risk management framework	Advise on risk mitigation and contingency planning Provide advice and guidance to prevent project or program failure

Proactively look across Risk Registers identify common themes and mitigations

Service description

The review of the risk registers of all projects within a program or all projects and programs within a portfolio to find common risks that would be better being managed at a higher level.

What the service provides for the customer

This ensures that risks are managed at the correct level to prevent time being wasted by individual projects all trying to mitigate and escalate the same risk when it could be handled better at a program level.

Why is this service being offered to the customer?

By looking across multiple projects or programs it is possible to see whether risks are appearing in lots of risk registers which means that these may be better managed at a higher level, so that a comprehensive mitigation action plan can be developed to reduce the risk across all the projects.

How PMO will apply this service

The PMO will obtain all the risk registers for projects within a program or projects and programs within a portfolio. They will review the risk register looking for risks, particularly ones which have been escalated that are in common. Where they find risks that are related, they will contact the program or portfolio manager with the information and suggest that these risks be managed at the program or portfolio level rather than by multiple people at the lower level.

If the program or portfolio manager agrees with the PMO''s assessment, then this will be added to the risk register at the program or portfolio level and removed from the other registers. The PMO will ensure that the relevant project and program managers are informed of the change to the risk. They will ensure that the lower-level managers get informed about the status of the risk as it gets dealt with.

Supplier	Input	Process	Output	Customer
Project Manager Program Manager	Risk Register	Review risks	Risk Register	Program Manager Portfolio Manager

How the PMO will measure the value of this service

This can be measured by looking at the numbers of risks which have been moved from project to program or program to portfolio level.

Criteria when the PMO will use this service

- When the PMO is aligned to a portfolio or program manager
- Where there are a number of related projects

Helpful hints for the PMO when delivering the service

- Rather than deleting the risk from the lower registers consider having a reference to the overarching risk. Using a tool could make this process easier

PMO Capabilities needed to fulfil this service

Competencies	Techniques and generic tools
Reporting, Insights and Analysis Risk Management Relationships and engagement Negotiation	Risk Register

Related services

Maintain the Risk Register Communicate with stakeholders affected either by the risk or the risk mitigations	Review the effectiveness of risk mitigation actions Advise on risk mitigation and contingency planning

Monitor the portfolio's total exposure to risk

Service description

A review of the risk registers within the portfolio to check the overall risk exposure.

What the service provides for the customer

This ensures that the overall risk exposure does not exceed the risk appetite of the portfolio or organization as a whole.

Why is this service being offered to the customer?

When seen individually the risks may not seem to have a particularly large impact to the portfolio. When looked at as a whole it may show that the individual risks add up to a greater exposure than the portfolio is willing to take.

How PMO will apply this service

The PMO will find copies of all the risk registers within the portfolio. They will review the impact and probability of all the risks and will see how many risks are in each category. They will consult with the portfolio manager to find out what the risk appetite is for the portfolio. They will then report what is actually occurring as opposed to what the expected risk assessment should be as a whole.

If the risk exposure is greater than desired, then the PMO will need to dig deeper into the risk register to find out what could be done to mitigate these risks. If there is a project which is particularly risky then the PMO could advise the portfolio manager to stop the project and thereby reduce the risk exposure as a whole. It this is split across lots of projects then then PMO will look to see whether there is a common theme for the high impact/probably. Is there something that could be dealt with at an overall portfolio level, rather than a lower level. That may therefore reduce the overall exposure as it has meant the same risk was being counted more than once.

Supplier	Input	Process	Output	Customer
Project Manager Program Manager	Risk Register	Review risk exposure	Advice	Portfolio Manager

How the PMO will measure the value of this service

This can be measured by in a reduction in the risk exposure across all the projects and programs within the portfolio.

Criteria when the PMO will use this service

- When the PMO is aligned to a portfolio manager
- Where there is a perception of a high level of risk across the portfolio

Helpful hints for the PMO when delivering the service

- Consider reviewing the risks for commonality before delivering this service
- Having a tool to access all the risks would make this reporting easier
- This should not be a one off, but will need to be performed on a regular basis, especially after decisions have been made the PMO will need to perform this service again to confirm that the decisions have been effective

PMO Capabilities needed to fulfil this service

Competencies	Techniques and generic tools
Reporting, Insights and Analysis Risk Management P3M Tools Relationships and engagement Teamwork	Risk Register Categorized frequency analysis (Frequency plot, bar chart)

Related services

Proactively look across Risk Registers identify common themes and mitigations Monitor the Risk Register	Strategic Risk Assessment Develop the overall risk management framework

Rollup Reporting

Rollup reporting

Description

This service area covers the roll up of information from projects to programs, from programs to the portfolio level. It can describe the consolidation of multiple projects information into a single view. This is more than just consolidation of the information and is about applying some knowledge of the project or program to know what information is useful to combine and what can be left out without losing the essence of the information.

What the services within the area provide for the customer

These services provide the program or portfolio manager with an overview of what is going on within the projects or programs. The PMO will highlight any areas of concern that the program or portfolio manager will need to focus on and deal with.

Helpful hints for when the PMO is delivering this service area

When rolling up information ensure you read the detail carefully to ensure you understand what is really being said. Perhaps there is a better way the information can be presented to make the decisions or actions required more visible or apparent.

Reporting Operations

Service group description

The creation of an overview of project status reports to a higher level to allow for further analysis and scrutiny.

Why have these services been grouped together?

These services relate to the rollup of individual project reports up to a higher level.

List of related services described in other areas

Maintain a release schedule

Responsibility Assignment Matrix

Service	Executive	Portfolio Manager	Program Manager	Project Manager	PMO	Sponsor	Other Stakeholder
Collate individual progress reports		I	I	C	A, R		
Make constructive challenge and recommendations on collated progress reports		I	I		A, R		
Combine individual progress reports		I	I	C	A, R		
Make constructive challenge and recommendations on combined progress reports		I	I		A, R		
Provision of Management Dashboards	I	I	I	C	A, R	I	

Helpful hints for when the PMO is delivering this service group

Understand that there is a difference between just collating individual progress reports and combining those progress reports to provide an overview of the entire program or portfolio. Depending on the way the PMO is setup there may be different people producing the reports versus analysing these reports. These services have been split out to cover each of these options.

It may be possible that the PMO will perform all these functions and will provide not only collated reports by combined reports to the same recipient.

Collate individual progress reports

Service description

The collation of individual progress reports into a single report for the program or portfolio. A collated summary report will list each project or program out separately as one line of information.

What the service provides for the customer

This provides the program or portfolio manager with a single summarized report of all the individual projects within their area.

Why is this service being offered to the customer?

Rather than have the individual reports sent separately to the program or portfolio manager they are sent through to the PMO who will collate these together and produce a summary view that focusses the reader on the important items that need management attention.

How PMO will apply this service

The PMO will speak to the program and portfolio manager to confirm how they would like their information reported. They will discuss with them what they would like in the summary report and produce a draft version. Once there is agreement on the content, they can confirm the frequency of the summary report. The PMO will provide the project and program managers with the timetable by which they need to have provided the progress reports through to the PMO.

According to the timetable the PMO will receive the individual progress reports from the project and program managers. They will then collate all these into a summary report. The PMO will then send the summary report, and the related detailed progress reports on to the program or portfolio manager.

Supplier	Input	Process	Output	Customer
Project Manager Program Manager	Progress report	Produce collated report	Collated report	Program Manager Portfolio Manager

Examples of collated reports

RAG progress report

	Overall		Plan		Scope		Resource		Risks/Issues	
Workstream	This Period	Last Period	This Period	Last Period	This Period	Last Period	This Period	Last Period	This Period	Last Period
Workstream 1a: Business Requirements Planning	A	G	G	G	G	G	A	G	A	A
Workstream 1b: Translate SC req'ts to Detailed Design	A	A	A	A	G	G	G	G	A	R
Workstream 4: Transition Planning	A	A	A	A	G	G	G	G	A	A

Milestone Gantt chart view

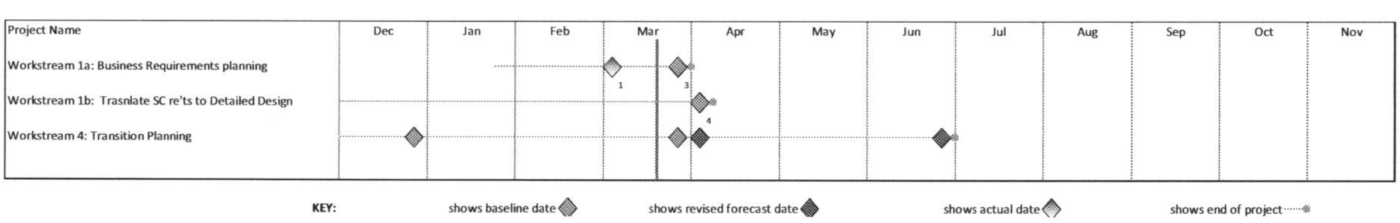

How the PMO will measure the value of this service

This can be measured by the portfolio or program manager asking for this information or suggesting other ways the information can be displayed. This proves they are reading it and finding it useful.

Criteria when the PMO will use this service

- When the PMO is supporting a group of projects
- When there is a need for a summary report of all the projects

Helpful hints for the PMO when delivering the service

- Understand the difference between collating the progress reports and combining the progress reports
- Ensure that there is a summary report which lists all the pertinent points of each progress report to enable easy viewing of the collated data
- Ensure that the summary report is kept to a single page (width) if possible
- Consider the use of technology to allow for drill down from the summary report to the detailed report
- Consult with the program or portfolio manager to see what they would like to see on their summary pages
- Provide a timetable for the report providers so they know what the deadlines are for providing information
- Consider using automation/canned reports to produce the summary reports
- The PMO may provide the report providers with reminders that their reports are due
- Decide what will happen when no information is available. Will the previous report be used, will it go in with no information, will it be omitted?
- There may be different summary reports depending on the audience

PMO Capabilities needed to fulfil this service

Competencies	Techniques and generic tools
Information Management Reporting, Insights and Analysis P3M Tools Personal Communication Relationships and engagement Negotiation	Project Management Information System

Related services

Make constructive challenge and recommendations on collated progress reports Combine individual progress reports Define, maintain, and implement reporting framework	Monitor and report on financial spend Prepare monthly financial reports Provision of Management Dashboards Automate Processes

Make constructive challenge and recommendations on collated progress reports

Service description

The critical review of the collated progress reports to provide insight and analysis. The recommendations drill into the detail of the available reports to provide areas of focus for the program or portfolio manager.

What the service provides for the customer

The program or portfolio manager will get some targeted insights into the status of the projects and programs. This will enable them to focus on the corrective actions required to bring the program or portfolio back on track.

Why is this service being offered to the customer?

The PMO are able to drill down into the detail of the individual progress reports to see any anomalies. They can provide trending information to see if there are common themes developing. The PMO are closer to the source of the information so can check for accuracy.

How PMO will apply this service

The PMO will receive the collated progress report. They will find the previous report and check for issues and recommend potential solutions. The areas that the PMO would look at would include:

- RAG Status – does the RAG status meet the guidance? If not, why not? Is there a desire to report everything green, or is this hiding a wider issue?
- Progress slippage – are there items which should have been delivered but are not
- Missing risks/issues – are there items referred to in the progress commentary that reflect risks or issues that are not shown. Does this mean they are not being managed?
- Financial issues – an underspend can be as problematic as an overspend. Does it mean that the funds can be moved elsewhere? Does it mean the project is not progressing as quickly as expected?
- Velocity – for agile projects is progress as expected?
- Milestone slippage – are milestones moving at the last moment. This could be a sign of poor control. Is only the next milestone moving and not the final one, is the project being squashed for time?
- Resources – are there enough of the right type, are they being worked too hard?
- Third parties – are things working out with third parties, could this have an impact on delivery?
- Change – is there are large volume of change on the project, compared with similar projects? This can be a sign of underlying problems
- Is everything perfect? Most projects will deviate at some point. If the progress report shows up as perfect, then either the project just started, or the report is hiding some issues that are not being surfaced. The PMO will need to dig deeper to find out which one.

In the first instance the PMO should check with the report author to verify whether the data contained in the report is accurate and give the individual chance to change this. If the report is accurate or the individual does not want to change anything then the PMO can submit their recommendations to the program or portfolio manager.

There will be a range of recommendation that the PMO can find when performing this analysis. The PMO needs to focus these so the more important or critical items get dealt with first

Supplier	Input	Process	Output	Customer
PMO	Collated progress report	Progress report assurance	Insight Recommendations	Program Manager Portfolio Manager

How the PMO will measure the value of this service

The PMO can measure this by seeing the numbers of recommendations suggested get acted upon.

Criteria when the PMO will use this service

- Where there is a collated report produced

Helpful hints for the PMO when delivering the service

- The PMO may consider looking at trends for progress reports e.g. milestone slippage reports
- They may provide an assurance report which will look for data anomalies such as risks being closed prior to a report being produced and then re-opened afterwards.
- The PMO should look for where the declared RAG status of the project does not match the rules for defining RAG status e.g. significant deviance from schedule or budget but being reported as Green.
- When reading the commentary check for items that should have been delivered according the previous report that have not been, yet not reported as slipped.
- Validate that the report has been updated prior to looking for detailed insights
- Find out what the major concerns are of the recipient of this service, so the checks can be focused in those areas

PMO Capabilities needed to fulfil this service

Competencies	Techniques and generic tools
Change Control Financial Management Issue Management Planning and Scheduling Reporting, Insights and Analysis Risk Management Assurance Personal Communication	Document Analysis Trend Analysis Performance variance report

Related services

Collate individual progress reports Provision of Management Dashboards	Provide advice and guidance to prevent project or program failure

Combine individual progress reports

Service Description

The combining and integration of multiple progress reports into a single progress report. Unlike a collated report which will show the individual progress reports a combined one gives a single report showing the general health of the portfolio or program.

What the service provides for the customer

This provides the portfolio manager with a view of the health/progress of the portfolio in a single report. For the program manager it would provide them a draft of the program level report they would then be able to revise before issuing.

Why is this service being offered to the customer?

For the program manager it saves them the effort in collating the data and provides them with a draft report they can edit.

For the portfolio manager it provides them with a single report to review the health of the portfolio in order that they can make decisions based on this information.

How PMO will apply this service

The PMO will speak with the program or portfolio manager to get their requirements for what information they wish to see in the report. The PMO will review where the best place to source this information from. It may require additional information not available in the progress report (e.g. report showing alignment to strategy would require the strategy as well as current project information).

Having worked out where the information can be sourced from the PMO will speak with the relevant providers and let them know the timetable by which data needs to be available.

According to the timetable the PMO will get the information and collate this into a single report for presentation to the program or portfolio manager.

Supplier	Input	Process	Output	Customer
Project Manager Program Manager	Progress reports	Collating progress reports	Collated report	Program Manager Portfolio Manager

Combined report examples

Financial summary

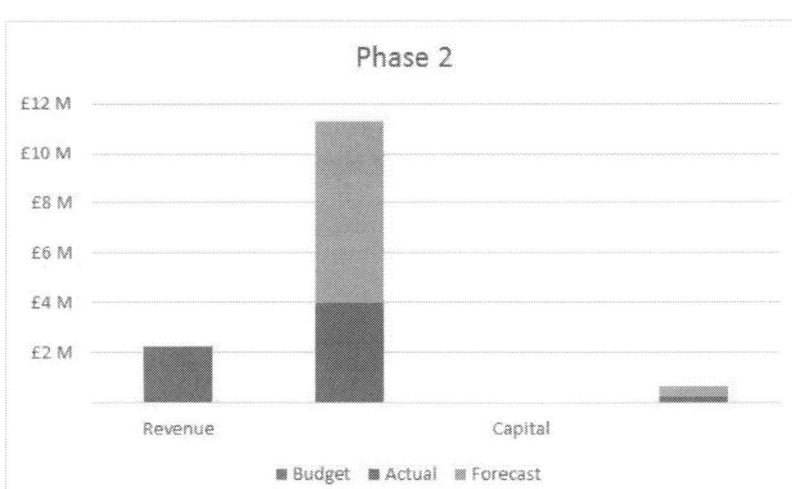

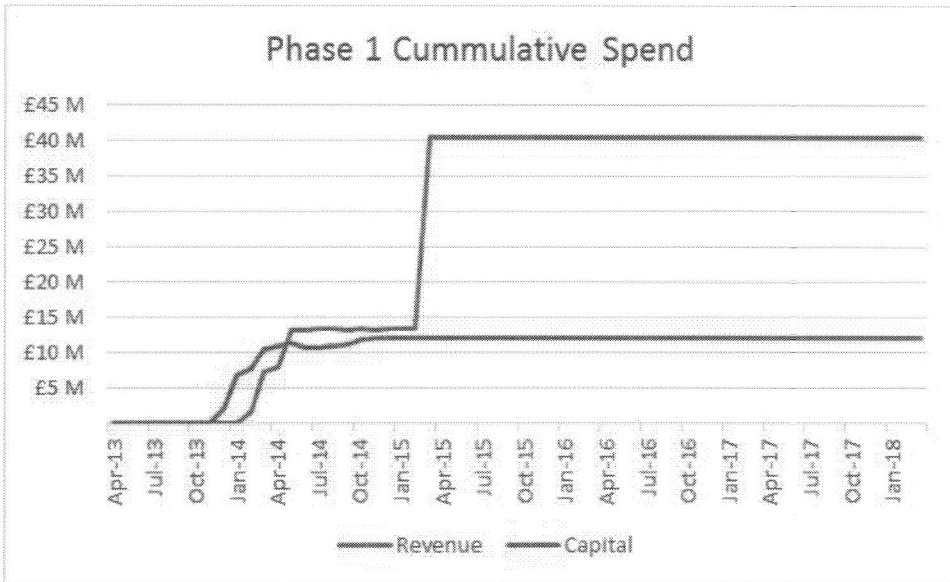

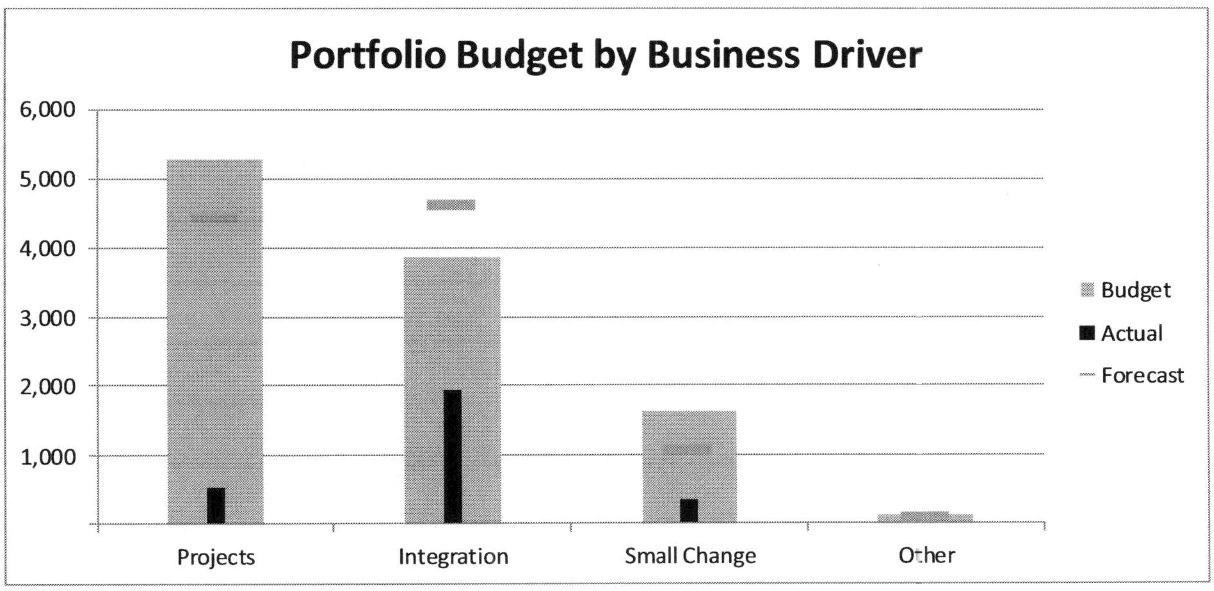

Project status

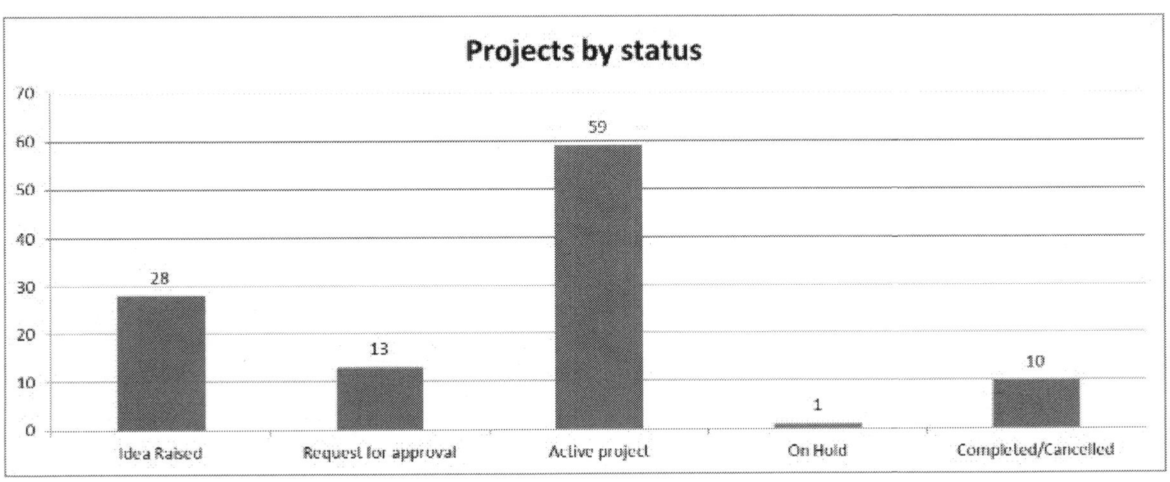

Rollup Reporting

Progress summary

Project Name | **Reporting Period** | **Report Date**

Progress to Date	Main Stream	Status Update	Prior	Trend	Now
An explanation of what the project is doing and why the status is what it is	Overall	Overall review of what the project has done so far#			Red
	Cost	Explaination of the cost etc.			Red
	Timescale				Red
	Resource				Amber
	Scope				Red
	Benefits				Amber

Risk/Issue	Mitigation / Action	RAG
Risk: Resource Business Resource - Subject Matter Expert availability	Sponsor is to participate at a more detailed level. May need to add high contingency for Define phase.	Amber
Issue: Documentation Documentation for Schedule, Statement of Fact etc pending business finalisation	Escalated with the Business sponors	Red

Focus for Next Period	Upcoming Milestones
This information is all about what is coming up for the next reporting period. This helps explain to people about what is likely to be expected for the future	Details on any milestones that will be delivered in the next few months

Status Indicator Definitions

●(Green) On schedule, no significant issues or risks that will impact transition
●(Amber) On schedule or slightly behind (1-2 weeks), some minor issues or risks that will impact transition
●(Red) Behind schedule by +2 weeks, major issues or risks will impact transition

How the PMO will measure the value of this service

This can be measured by the portfolio or program manager asking for this information or suggesting other ways the information can be displayed. This proves they are reading it and finding it useful.

Criteria when the PMO will use this service

- When the PMO is aligned to a single program
- When the PMO is performing a portfolio office role
- When the program or portfolio manager has asked for a report on the overall program or portfolio

Helpful hints for the PMO when delivering the service

- Ask the report recipient 'what decisions are you going to make based on this report'. This will enable the PMO to decide what is the relevant data that needs to be displayed and how it can be displayed to best help make those decisions.
- The PMO may provide the report providers with reminders that their reports are due
- Do not wait for the information provided to be 100% accurate before publishing, it never will be. The recipient will still find the report useful as it provides information, they can use to make decisions

PMO Capabilities needed to fulfil this service

Competencies	Techniques and generic tools
Information Management Reporting, Insights and Analysis P3M Tools Personal Communication Relationships and engagement Negotiation	Project Management Information System

Related services

Collate individual progress reports Make constructive challenge and recommendations on combined progress reports	Define, maintain, and implement reporting framework Monitor and report on financial spend Prepare monthly financial reports

Make constructive challenge and recommendations on combined progress reports

Service Description

The critical review of the combined progress reports to provide insight and analysis. The recommendations give an overview of the state of the program or portfolio as a whole.

What the service provides for the customer

The program or portfolio manager will get an overview of the status of the entire program or portfolio, focusing on the big picture. This will allow them to see how this is performing as a whole.

Why is this service being offered to the customer?

The PMO are able to take a view of how the portfolio or program is performing against expectations.

The PMO can relate the portfolio report back to the strategy and see how well the portfolio is set to deliver against that.

The PMO can relate the program back to the original context for the program and see how well this is being managed and the potential success of the delivery.

How PMO will apply this service

The PMO will receive the combined report, either for the portfolio level or for the program level.

At the portfolio level the PMO will find a current copy of the strategy for the organization. The PMO will review how well the portfolio is shaping up to achieve the strategic goals. They will provide recommendations about the balance and overall achievability of the portfolio. They will look at whether the balance of projects is right to fit in with overall strategy. They will look for whether the portfolio is over or underspending, both for the current year and over the next one to see whether there are changes to be made in the scheduling of the projects and programs within the portfolio. They will perform some what if review on the portfolio to see what the likely impacts are of items moving, considering hard deadlines for project delivery.

For a program level report, the PMO will look and see how this program compares with others that are being run inside the company. Is the program likely to achieve its overall goals, or are their issues that need dealing with? The PMO will concern themselves with the overall delivery and achievability of the program. They may highlight a few individual areas that need looking at, as examples of the concerns or recommendations the PMO has.

The PMO will provide their insight and recommendations through to the portfolio or program manager for them to action as they see fit.

Supplier	Input	Process	Output	Customer
PMO	Combined progress report	Review combined report	Insight Recommendations	Program Manager Portfolio Manager

How the PMO will measure the value of this service

The PMO can measure this by seeing the numbers of recommendations suggested get acted upon

Criteria when the PMO will use this service

- When there is a combined report produced
- When the program or portfolio manager requires insights based on the combined report

Helpful hints for the PMO when delivering the service

- Understand that this is about the overall, big picture view, rather than a detailed assessment of the projects within the report

PMO Capabilities needed to fulfil this service

Competencies	Techniques and generic tools
Change Control Financial Management Issue Management Planning and Scheduling Reporting, Insights and Analysis Risk Management Assurance Personal Communication	Document Analysis Trend Analysis Performance variance report

Related services

Combine individual progress reports	Provide advice and guidance to prevent project or program failure

Provision of Management Dashboards

Service Description

The provision of summarised information about projects, programs, and portfolios in a visual manner

What the service provides for the customer

An easy-to-understand way of identifying whether the projects, programs and portfolios are on track, highlighting issues that will need to be dealt with.

Why is this service being offered to the customer?

The PMO are best positioned to have access to the data that will be required to be provided for the dashboard.

Having an easy, visual way of identifying issues leads to a faster resolution of those issues. Being able to see quickly that everything is on track saves time and effort from the person reviewing the dashboard. The time that is saved will be available to focus on other things.

How PMO will apply this service

The PMO should review the decisions that are made by the customer of this service and work out which ones of those would be aided by the production of a visual overview report. Once the PMO understands what decisions need to be made they will need to have a look and see what information is required to make a good decision. The PMO should then look to source this information.

Once the information is available the PMO should collate this information together and display this in a suitable visual manner to enable the decisions to be made. Once an initial version of the dashboard is available the PMO should review this with the customers of the report and ensure they can interpret the information without need for an explanation. The PMO should be prepared to make changes to the dashboard based on feedback provided

The PMO should agree the frequency of the data provision to ensure the dashboard can be produced in a timely manner.

Supplier	Input	Process	Output	Customer
Project Managers Program Managers Portfolio Managers	Progress Reports Change registers Issue registers Risk registers Management Information tool	Produce Management Dashboard	Management Dashboard	Program Managers Portfolio Managers Senior Managers

How the PMO will measure the value of this service

- Reduction in time to make decisions
- Lack of queries on how to interpret the dashboard

Criteria when the PMO will use this service

- When needing to report on Key Performance Indicators to senior management
- When a simplified report is required to enable decision making

Tips and tricks for the PMO when delivering the service

- Consider adding the date that the data was extracted to go onto the report so that questions are not asked about how up to date the information provided is
- The use of a dedicated management information tool allows the separation between data provision and data visualisation, which means once setup all the PMO needs to do is to ensure the data is provided in a timely manner
- A dedicated management information tool can allow for the dashboard user to drill into more detailed information if they require
- Do not overcrowd the dashboard. It is better to use multiple dashboard pages which focus on a single decision each rather than one dashboard page to show all the data in one place
- If the individuals reading the dashboard are in a single place consider whether a lo-tech solution, such as a whiteboard in a prominent place, could be used to present simple information such as days to go live, number of defects, items outstanding
- Do not underestimate the need for data quality, it should be part of the checks to ensure that information provided is complete and where it is not the individual providing the data is aware of the consequences of partial information
- Make the people providing the data aware of where and how their information is used
- Consider whether you need to make the dashboard a push service (sent out to the customer), or a pull service (the customer to look when they need), or both

PMO Capabilities needed to fulfil this service

Competencies	Techniques and generic tools
Benefits and Value Management	Iteration burndown chart
Change Control	Run chart table
Financial Management	Tornado diagram
Information Management	Categorized frequency analysis (Frequency plot, bar chart)
Issue Management	Hierarchical charts
Planning and Scheduling	Matrix based charts
Quality Management	Matrix diagrams
Reporting, Insights and Analysis	Project Management Information System
Resource Management	Scheduling tool
Risk Management	Time series plots
Assurance	Time Value Map and Value-add Chart
Governance Frameworks	
P3M Tools	
Personal Communication	
Relationships and engagement	
Negotiation	
Result Orientation	

Related services

Track and report on benefit realization	Define, maintain, and implement reporting framework
Develop information management policy	Advise on PPM tools and software
Monitor and report on financial spend	Make constructive challenge and recommendations on collated progress reports
Automate Processes	Collate individual progress reports

Schedule Management

Schedule Management

Description

Facilitating the development and maintenance of the portfolio, program, or project schedules, estimating databases and dependency registers.

What the services within the domain provide for the customer

By providing dedicated schedule support the project or program manager gets expertise they may not have themselves.

Having a standard approach to schedule management allows for ease of rollup and integration across projects within a program.

Using an estimating database provides access to more accurate estimates for the project and program.

Helpful hints for when the PMO is delivering this service domain

On the larger projects and programs consider having a dedicated planner resource available to assist the development and maintenance of the schedule.

Scheduling Design

Service group description

The development of the standards and templates associated with scheduling of projects and programs.

Why have these services been grouped together?

This service is related to the setup of the standard way to organize a schedule. This enables the easier rollup, linking and comparison of schedules.

List of related services described in other areas

Automate Processes

Responsibility Assignment Matrix

Service	Executive	Portfolio Manager	Program Manager	Project Manager	PMO	Sponsor	Other Stakeholder
Define planning standards and templates		C	C	C	A, R		
Develop and maintain an estimating framework		C	C	C	A, R		C (Team managers)

Helpful hints for when the PMO is delivering this service group

Ensure that the estimating framework is aligned to and incorporated into the planning guidance.

Define planning standards and templates

Service description

The creation of template schedules, scheduling standards and advice for use in projects and programs.

What the service provides for the customer

This provides a set of guidance and templates on putting a schedule together. Having these standards ensures that project schedules can be rolled up to program level. It allows for standard ways to deal with contingency, tolerance, effort to allow for comparison across different project schedules.

Having a template provides a starter for projects and programs to ensure they cover the relevant parts and there is a linkage to the deliverables list.

Why is this service being offered to the customer?

As writers of the methodology the PMO can produce an outline schedule which will show the tasks required to deliver each of the deliverables. The PMO can be experts in scheduling and therefore can provide that advice to the project and program managers.

Providing standard milestones ensures that progress across different project types can be compared.

How PMO will apply this service

The PMO will review the PPM framework, in particular the deliverables list to see whether this would benefit from the production of a standard set of tasks linked into the deliverables list. They will look to see what planning tool(s) are in place in the organization and look to create the scheduling template in the appropriate tool(s).

The PMO will look to create a standard for how schedules are to be constructed and used. The standard includes:

- How to use the standard template (if there is one) – this will include guidance on how the standard template can be tailored for the particular project or program
- How resources are assigned – this will link to the resource capacity management information and will cover generic resources, group resources, non-people resources
- Tracking of resources – how actuals are captured, and at what level of detail
- Estimating – this will cover the linkage between the estimate for the project/stage and how those are to be entered within the schedule
- Baselining – how this will be done and under what circumstances can it be changed. This will have linkage to gate reviews and change control
- Progress reporting – any linkage between deviances in the schedule and how this is reported on the progress report e.g. RAG statuses

The PMO will look to create some help or guidance documentation on how to create and maintain a schedule for project managers. This guidance includes:

- Scheduling tool information – this will include a description of the tool(s) in place, how to obtain the tool, what the standard options are for the tool e.g. views used, calendar options
- Dealing with tasks/milestones – this will cover to add tasks or milestones into the schedule, how to move them around, how to remove them (this will include the impact of deleting them on any actuals recorded)
- Different views – this will cover the suggested views of the schedule to create tasks, dealing with resources, reporting the schedule, reviewing the progress
- Dependency management – this will deal with adding and removing dependencies, both internal to the project, but external to other projects
- Resource allocation – how resources are assigned. This will link into any resource allocation process and will include the roles of the resource manager and project manager
- Resource availability – how resource availability will be managed, is this a generic percentage, will individual calendars be used, will tasks be added for time spent on meetings, absence etc.?
- Change and risk budgets – how these are dealt with in conjunction with the schedule
- Contingency – how to deal with contingency in the schedule, will it be added to each task, a specific task created, is this done by project, phase, or activity?
- Baselining – how to perform this, linking back to the standards about when this is OK to do
- Reviewing the schedule – how and when actuals are entered, whose responsibility it is to do this. How to deal with the estimates. How to update the task and milestone information, including the use of any auto schedule options
- Linking schedules – hints and tips about how schedules can be combined, either for rollup purposes or seeing the capacity/demand across the program
- Reporting – how to roll up information so it can be reported for the progress report, steering group packs etc.

Supplier	Input	Process	Output	Customer
PMO	Standards template Scheduling tool PPM Framework	Develop Standard Develop Templates	Scheduling standard Scheduling template(s) Scheduling help	Project Manager Program Manager Team Manager PMO

How the PMO will measure the value of this service

The PMO can measure this by reviewing how easy it is to roll up projects to programs.

Criteria when the PMO will use this service

- When there is a need for a consistent approach to scheduling
- Where schedules are being rolled up to higher levels
- Where standard milestones are required for reporting

Helpful hints for the PMO when delivering the service

- Consideration should be given for allowing the schedule template to be added to in sections. The high-level schedule is available for the entire project, but each stage/timebox is planned in detail at the end of the previous stage. The template for the next section of the plan should be generated when the detailed planning is being done
- If there is more than one scheduling tool in place the guidance will include how to choose the best tool for the job. This can depend on the type of project being run as well as the experience of the project manager
- If a scheduling tool is in place the PMO may consider developing some training material such as videos or full courses to assist the individuals in the use of the tool

PMO Capabilities needed to fulfil this service

Competencies	Techniques and generic tools
Planning and Scheduling Reporting, Insights and Analysis Resource Management Delivery Methods Governance Frameworks P3M Tools Professionalism and ethics Personal Communication Relationships and engagement Teamwork	Communication requirements analysis Stakeholder checklist Stakeholder engagement assessment matrix Work Breakdown Structure

Related services

Provide planning assistance to portfolio, programs, or projects Define, maintain, and implement standard PPM framework Develop and maintain schedules for the portfolio, program, or project	Review of delivery schedules against Business as Usual Review cross project and program dependencies

Develop and maintain an estimating framework

Service description

The development and maintenance of a series of estimating templates, alongside some guidance in their use. This may contain linkages to an estimate database which uses past experience to verify the current estimates.

What the service provides for the customer

This provides a standard way that individual areas can provide an estimate allowing overall rollup to the project or program level. This may provide access to a database which will utilize previous experience around estimating to offset any bias in the production of current estimates.

Why is this service being offered to the customer?

Having all the detailed estimates in a consistent format will save time for the person collating them. Being able to collate the individual estimates into a single template will provide the project or program manager with an overview of the entire estimate in one place. This information can then be used to update the schedule.

It provides the PMO with a consistent set of information to refer back to when verifying the accuracy of the estimate and its changes as the project or program has progressed. It will provide input from this template into the estimating database (if this exists) to help verify the estimate accuracy.

How PMO will apply this service

The PMO will look at the PPM framework and see where an estimate is required. They will look to develop 2 levels of template. They will have a lower level (team) template which will be used by individual teams who have been asked for an estimate. They will then provide an overall project level template. The PMO should ensure that the estimate from the lower-level template can be quickly copied into the overall template. The PMO may consider providing a third level template which can incorporate the individual project estimates into an overall program level estimate.

For each of the templates the PMO will make some guidance available which explains how the templates are to be used and under what circumstances.

The PMO will ensure that the templates can not only be used at the start of a project but can be updated as the project progresses, and further estimates are required.

The PMO should look to create an estimating checklist to guide people through the necessary steps for providing an estimate. The checklist could include:

- Have the necessary people been spoken to
- Has more than one estimating technique been used?
- Are the correct rates /resource types been used?
- Has contingency been applied correctly?
- Has the estimate factored in risk/project complexity/resource experience?

The PMO should provide guidance on the different types of estimating techniques available such as:

- Top-down estimating
- Bottom-up estimating
- Delphi technique
- Parametric Estimation
- Comparative/Analogy Estimation
- Three-point Estimation

To support the comparative or parametric estimation techniques the PMO can look to provide an estimation database. If they are looking to support the comparative technique, then they can load the actuals from prior projects. The PMO should ensure that the database performs as expected by asking one of the more expert estimators to verify this and suggest improvements before issuing.

Supplier	Input	Process	Output	Customer
PMO	PPM Framework	Develop Templates	Estimating template Estimating checklist Estimating Guidance Estimating Database	Project Manager Program Manager PMO

How the PMO will measure the value of this service

The PMO can seek feedback from the project or program manager on how easy it is to obtain the estimates now, compared to what they used to use in the past.

Criteria when the PMO will use this service

- Where there is a desire to improve the accuracy of estimating
- Where there is a need to get consistency in the gathering of estimates
- Where there is the need to upskill individuals in the estimating process
- Where there have been enough similar projects run (and finished) to justify the building of an estimating database
- Where the lessons learned have provided feedback to improvements to the estimating framework

Helpful hints for the PMO when delivering the service

- Do not look to create an estimating database without having got feedback from how this organization has run estimates in the past if the estimating is variable e.g. software estimating
- For construction projects look to invest in a subscription to a cost estimating tool, which can provide detailed estimates of standard construction activities e.g. drying time of concrete
- Look to provide factoring into the estimate's dependent on the expertise of staff expected to perform the role. Do not always assume that this will be done by an expert
- Look to include contingency, tolerance, risk, and change budgets into the estimates
- Consider including the cost of support into the estimating template/guidance
- When inserting the actuals from prior projects into the estimating database, ensure you understand about the level of expertise of the individuals involved
- When estimates are updated the template should ensure that contingency (if used) is only applied to the remaining estimate, and not to any actual that may have been included in the template)
- If creating an estimating database, then ensure this gets updated with actuals from closed project. Probably best to build this in as one of the activities as part of project closure

PMO Capabilities needed to fulfil this service

Competencies	Techniques and generic tools
Planning and Scheduling Delivery Methods	Scenario analysis Communication requirements analysis Stakeholder checklist Stakeholder engagement assessment matrix

Related services

Provide estimating support Forecast portfolio, program or project spend	Manage the Process Improvement Plan

Scheduling Operations

Service group description

The creation and updating of schedules on behalf of the project, program, or portfolio manager. The assistance and provision of estimates to enable resource capacity planning and more accurate schedules.

Why have these services been grouped together?

These services relate to the day to day updating and review of the schedules on behalf of the project, program, or portfolio manager.

List of related services described in other areas

Business strategy and roadmap maintenance

Responsibility Assignment Matrix

Service	Executive	Portfolio Manager	Program Manager	Project Manager	PMO	Sponsor	Other Stakeholder
Develop resource plans to underpin the portfolio plan		A	C	C	R		
Provide planning assistance to portfolio, programs, or projects		C	C	C	A, R		
Provide estimating support		I	A	A	R		C (Team Manager)
Develop and maintain schedules for the portfolio, program, or project		A, C	A, C	A, C	R		
Maintain a release schedule		A	C	C	R		

Helpful hints for when the PMO is delivering this service group

- Work with the project or program manager to decide the how involved the PMO will be in assisting them. Will they be involved in providing advice, or is the PMO expected to run the schedule updates on behalf of the project or program manager

Develop resource plans to underpin the portfolio plan

Service description

The development of resourced project and program level schedules to enable the portfolio manager to review the overall demand vs capacity of the portfolio.

What the service provides for the customer

By ensuring that each of the projects and programs are correctly resourced the portfolio manager is able to calculate the resource capacity/capability requirements for the entire portfolio. Without having the detailed resource demand information, the portfolio manager will not be able to deliver their view across the portfolio.

Why is this service being offered to the customer?

The PMO can help the project and program managers by ensuring the schedules are correctly resourced, either at a generic level or named resource level. By having the detailed projects and program schedules resourced, the information is available for the portfolio manager to be able to review the overall demand across the portfolio. This will enable the portfolio manager to ensure the resources are being assigned to the most valuable projects and programs.

How PMO will apply this service

The PMO will speak with the program or project manager who is accountable for managing the schedule and will discuss the level of involvement that the PMO will have in the building of the schedule. Will the PMO be directly responsible for this or will they monitor what the program or project manager will be doing. If the PMO is directly responsible then this task will be easier to do, however it will take more time and involvement to deliver.

For each of the schedules the PMO will find out what the total labour estimate is. If this is a cost estimate, then they will convert that into an effort estimate using the standard labour costs.

They will speak to the project or program manager to find out whether they have been given a detailed breakdown of the different resource types against their project. If they have not been given that then the PMO can use the typical resource profile for this type/duration of project.

The PMO will then get this resource profile applied to the project. Where individual named resources are not known then this can be profiled out as a series of generic resources.

For the current stage, the schedule should contain named resources if possible.

The PMO will need to review these schedules on a regular basis to ensure the information remains current.

Supplier	Input	Process	Output	Customer
Project Manager Program Manager Resource Manager	Resource demand Role categories	Updating a schedule	Resourced schedule	Portfolio Manager Program Manager

How the PMO will measure the value of this service

This service can be measured by the ease of which the demand/capacity of the entire portfolio can be calculated.

Criteria when the PMO will use this service

- Where the PMO is responsible for updating the schedule on behalf of the project or program manager
- Where the portfolio manager has asked the PMO to assist with the gathering of resource demand information

Helpful hints for the PMO when delivering the service

- Use historical actuals booked on projects to calculate a typical resource profile for a project
- When profiling out generic resources ensure that this is done by resource type (i.e. skill, role, or contractual status) to enable the capacity management to be done at the portfolio level
- Only commit to profiling out the resource demand for the schedule if you are prepared to keep this information updated

PMO Capabilities needed to fulfil this service

Competencies	Techniques and generic tools
Planning and Scheduling Resource Management P3M Tools Teamwork	Resource breakdown structure Scheduling tool

Related services

Maintain resource database Provide resource tracking and capacity reports	Forecast future resource needs Provide planning assistance to portfolio, programs, or projects

Provide planning assistance to portfolio, programs, or projects

Service description

Provide support and advice for the project, program, or portfolio managers in how to plan and schedule the projects or programs within the portfolio.

What the service provides for the customer

This service provides support and guidance for the person putting together the schedule on the best approach given the particular circumstances of the project or program. It provides education for the individual in order that they are able to enhance and maintain the schedule for themselves rather than rely on others.

Why is this service being offered to the customer?

As the author of the schedule standard and guidance the PMO are best placed to offer this guidance. By training and coaching the person putting together the schedule it enables them to perform the role for themselves. It provides the individual with the knowledge and confidence to update the schedule.

How PMO will apply this service

Having identified that an individual needs assistance with their schedule, the PMO will arrange for some time to sit with the individual concerned.

The PMO needs to listen to the issues that the person is facing before they can offer advice. Having understood the issues involved the PMO will then look to offer advice to the individual. They may decide to show the individual how to perform a task or explain why updating information is important and the impact of not doing so.

The PMO needs to ensure that the person receiving the guidance understands how they can be using this for themselves once the PMO is no longer at hand to offer this advice.

Supplier	Input	Process	Output	Customer
PMO	Planning standard Planning templates Planning guidance	Scheduling a project	Project schedule Program schedule	Project Manager Program Manager Portfolio Manager

How the PMO will measure the value of this service

The PMO can measure this by looking at improvement in the quality of the schedules being built.

Criteria when the PMO will use this service

- When the person producing the schedule asks for advice
- When the PMO notices that the individual producing the schedule could require some help
- When the skills review for the individual indicates that the person requires training in scheduling

Helpful hints for the PMO when delivering the service

- Have some standard training that the PMO can deliver, linked into the scheduling tool and PPM framework in use within the organization
- Leave the person being advised with a crib sheet of useful tips for them to refer to
- Understand the context of the project before offering advice on the schedule
- Understand what problems the PMO is there to advise on. Is it details about scheduling, use of the tool, PPM framework or project context?
- Putting a schedule together is a combination of an art and a science. When you are looking into the future then this is guaranteed to be inaccurate. By asking the right questions the PMO can enable the scheduler to understand what is important and what is worth controlling
- Ensure that a balance in maintained between the detail required to have control and the frequency of update

PMO Capabilities needed to fulfil this service

Competencies	Techniques and generic tools
Planning and Scheduling Resource Management P3M Tools Personal Communication Relationships and engagement Result Orientation	Scheduling tool Work Breakdown Structure

Related services

Develop resource plans to underpin the portfolio plan Provide estimating support Develop and maintain schedules for the portfolio, program, or project	Perform coaching of portfolio, program, or project managers Define planning standards and templates

Provide estimating support

Service description

The provision of support for project and program managers in obtaining and collating an estimate for their project or program.

What the service provides for the customer

This ensures that a project or program manager gets the estimate they need. They will have the assurance that it is in the correct format (i.e. it uses the estimating template) so that it can be applied to their project or program.

Why is this service being offered to the customer?

Having the PMO chase up the estimate on their behalf will not only save the time of the project or program manager, but it will also ensure that estimate has been checked and collated according the estimating framework.

How PMO will apply this service

The PMO will receive a request to collate a project or program estimate. The PMO will speak to the project or program manager to confirm each of the areas that is expected to provide an estimate. The PMO will speak with the team manager or individual who is responsible for providing an estimate. They will ensure they have the necessary documentation (e.g. requirements, estimating template) to enable them to build a team level estimate.

The PMO may provide additional support for the team members in their use of the estimating template, being available to answer any questions that may be asked about the use of the template or the associated guidance.

Once each of the individual estimates have been provided, the PMO will confirm they are in the correct format and that all assumptions have been included. The PMO will combine each of the estimates into an overall estimate for the project or program (using the template provided). The PMO will then provide the estimate to the project or program manager.

Supplier	Input	Process	Output	Customer
PMO Team Managers	Estimating template Estimating checklist	Estimating a project or program	Project or program estimate	Project Managers Program Managers

How the PMO will measure the value of this service

The PMO can measure this from the feedback from the project or program manager. When doing an audit, they can measure the number of estimates using the correct template.

Criteria when the PMO will use this service

- Where the PMO is dedicated to a single project or program
- Where an estimate is required

Helpful hints for the PMO when delivering the service

- PMO should look to ensure that the estimate is provided in the correct template
- If there is one available, the PMO should use the estimating checklist to ensure the estimate has been correctly produced

PMO Capabilities needed to fulfil this service

Competencies	Techniques and generic tools
Planning and Scheduling Personal Communication Relationships and engagement Teamwork Negotiation Result Orientation	Capability and Capacity analysis Assumption and constraint analysis Resource breakdown structure

Related services

Develop and maintain an estimating framework	Provide planning assistance to portfolio, programs, or projects

Develop and maintain schedules for the portfolio, program, or project

Service description

The creation and regular maintenance of the schedule on behalf of the project, program, or portfolio manager.

What the service provides for the customer

An up-to-date schedule for them to be able to track against. They know that the information contained within the schedule will be an accurate representation of the status of the project, program, or portfolio.

Why is this service being offered to the customer?

The person responsible for the schedule may be too busy or not skilled enough in the use of the scheduling tool to update it themselves. By providing this service it allows the manager to focus on what the plan is telling them about the delivery of the change, rather than getting involved with the detail of how the planning tool operates.

How PMO will apply this service

Having received a request to create or update a schedule, the PMO will ascertain the scheduling tool to be used. If they are creating a schedule, they will look to find the appropriate scheduling template as a starter. They will speak to the project, program, or portfolio manager to get an overview of the schedule to be created and the level of detail that will be required. They will speak with the team managers to get the tasks/estimates for their pieces of work. The PMO will then put all this together into the schedule. The PMO will ensure that the necessary dependencies have been added and there are milestones to denote progress. They will use the levels within the scheduling tool to provide a structure to the schedule.

Once all the information has been added then the PMO will look to see what the possible outcomes are given both with and without resource constraints. This will allow the PMO to see whether the schedule is achievable. If it is not then they will speak with the project, program, or portfolio manager to discuss the possible options to deal with the issue. Some of the options to be considered include:

- Could items be delivered in parallel?
- Would adding more resources help?
- Could we remove activities, without affecting the scope?
- Could we re-schedule activities?
- Do we need a change request to accept we need a new date?

Once the appropriate option(s) have been chosen the PMO will apply the changes to the schedule.

On a regular basis the PMO will look to update the schedule. These updates include:

- Adding in new tasks
- Changing the status of existing tasks/milestones
- Adding in new dependencies
- Updating the schedule with actuals
- Revising estimates
- Updating the start/finish/duration of tasks

To update the schedule, the PMO will need to speak to the team members to get their information as to the progress of their activities. They will need to speak to the project, program, or portfolio manager to review the impact of the schedule updates.

Supplier	Input	Process	Output	Customer
Team members Team managers Project Managers Program Managers	Schedules containing milestones & dependencies Scheduling help Schedule templates Scheduling standard	Updating a schedule	Updated schedule	Project Managers Program Managers Portfolio Managers

How the PMO will measure the value of this service

This can be measured by the feedback from the person using the schedule. It can be monitored by the usefulness of the schedule to make decisions about the direction of the project.

Criteria when the PMO will use this service

- Where the PMO is dedicated to a single project, program, or portfolio manager
- Where the PMO has been asked to look after the schedule
- Where there is a dedicated planner role in the team

Helpful hints for the PMO when delivering the service

- Provide a regular cadence for the updates so people providing the updates know when to expect the request to come through
- Do not make the schedule overly complex as others may need to maintain it in your absence
- Ensure the reporting from the schedule is easily understood so that decisions can be made based on the information

PMO Capabilities needed to fulfil this service

Competencies	Techniques and generic tools
P3M Administration Change Control Planning and Scheduling Reporting, Insights and Analysis Resource Management P3M Tools Personal Integrity and reliability Personal Communication Relationships and engagement Resourcefulness Result Orientation	Component milestones Resource breakdown structure Scheduling tool Work Breakdown Structure

Related services

Provide planning assistance to portfolio, programs, or projects Define planning standards and templates Maintain a release schedule Review of delivery schedules against Business as Usual	Review cross project and program dependencies Liaise with procurement teams on new in initiatives to ensure early engagement Support contracts monitoring and management

Maintain a release schedule

Service description

Maintain a release or product schedule on behalf of the project, program, or portfolio manager. A release or product schedule is a high-level view of which products or functionality will be released over time.

What the service provides for the customer

This provides the business area or portfolio manager with a list of what products or functionality (for an IT system) will be available at what time. This allows the business area to focus on selling those products at the appropriate time. It allows training/education to be available at the right time when the products will be released.

Why is this service being offered to the customer?

This is a consolidation role where the detailed list of requirements is bunched together to release functionality that can then be used. The PMO can maintain this on behalf of the product owner, allowing them to focus on impact of those product deliveries.

How PMO will apply this service

Having been asked to produce a release schedule or product roadmap the PMO will speak to all the project and program managers to get their delivery schedules. With an agile environment this may involve looking at their backlog and seeing what functionality is scheduled for which sprint.

The PMO will collate all this together to provide an expected timeline of delivery. The release schedule or product roadmap will be shared with the portfolio manager or product owner. The PMO will perform this review and update on a regular basis in order that the release schedule or product roadmap remains current.

Supplier	Input	Process	Output	Customer
Program manager Project manager	Detailed requirements	Update a schedule	Release schedule Product roadmap	Portfolio Manager Product Owner Business area

How the PMO will measure the value of this service

This service can be measured by seeing how many people find the release schedule/product roadmap useful.

Criteria when the PMO will use this service

- When the PMO is working in a product based agile environment
- When the PMO is supporting a product manager

Helpful hints for the PMO when delivering the service

- If not done by the PMO then this would normally be done by a product owner
- The exact format of the release schedule/product roadmap will depend on why this is being collated and who is going to use the information
- Consider the use of a common tool to make the gathering of this information easier and more timely
- Speak to the individuals providing the data to explain why this is being collated, and offer to provide access to the collated report so they can see how the information has been used and the assistance it will provide

PMO Capabilities needed to fulfil this service

Competencies	Techniques and generic tools
Planning and Scheduling Reporting, Insights and Analysis Relationships and engagement Teamwork Resourcefulness	Component milestones Scheduling tool

Related services

Review progress of agile deliveries Develop and maintain schedules for the portfolio, program, or project	Business strategy and roadmap maintenance

Scheduling Monitoring

Service group description

The review of dependencies across projects and programs as well as the impact on Business as Usual of project delivery.

Why have these services been grouped together?

These services relate to the monitoring of the schedules within a portfolio or program.

Responsibility Assignment Matrix

Service	Executive	Portfolio Manager	Program Manager	Project Manager	PMO	Sponsor	Other Stakeholder
Review of delivery schedules against Business as Usual		A	C	C	R		C (Business areas)
Review cross project and program dependencies			A		R		
Review progress of agile deliveries				A	R		C (Agile team)

Helpful hints for when the PMO is delivering this service group

- This can be made easier if a central PPM tool is used for storing the schedules. This will make the job of finding the schedules to review and combine
- It helps if the schedules are following the standards and guidelines laid down, as that will make it easier to compare the schedules from different projects

Review of delivery schedules against Business as Usual

Service description

The combination of the detailed delivery schedules aligned to each business area.

What the service provides for the customer

This schedule allows for balancing of the portfolio so that business areas are not hit by change fatigue and are able to absorb the changes that are due. Used to help avoid changes occurring during peak times within the business. Assists with the training requirements of the business area.

Why is this service being offered to the customer?

The PMO are able to access the detailed schedules for all the projects and programs within a portfolio. They can then summarize this and display it in a way that will allow the portfolio manager to balance the portfolio across the business areas and avoid the delivery.

How PMO will apply this service

The PMO will review the delivery schedules of each of the constituent projects and programs within the portfolio. From these schedules they will extract the information about when the project or program will deliver into which business area. They will then collate this information to display by business area what releases are due.

The portfolio manager can then use this information to review the impact against the business area. Will they be delivering during peak periods for that business area? If so, the portfolio manager made decide to change the delivery date. The PMO may be responsible for providing that communication back to the project or program concerned.

Supplier	Input	Process	Output	Customer
Project Managers Program Managers	Schedules containing milestones and dependencies	Collating schedules	Portfolio delivery plan	Portfolio managers Project Approval Board Senior Management

How the PMO will measure the value of this service

This can be measured by the use of the finished report by the portfolio manager. Is this used to make decisions against, or is it just seen as a pretty picture?

Criteria when the PMO will use this service

- When the PMO supports a portfolio manager
- When the portfolio manager is trying to understand the impact of the portfolio on the business areas

Helpful hints for the PMO when delivering the service

- A single project may deliver into multiple business areas. For example, a new insurance product may deliver into the marketing department to advertise the product, the sales department to sell the product, the customer service team for any claims, the finance department to track the sales
- Each different business area may have peak times they are unavailable to accept change e.g. year end, peak business trading etc.
- It may be useful to display peak times on the summarized report to enable decisions to be made quickly and easily

PMO Capabilities needed to fulfil this service

Competencies	Techniques and generic tools
Change Management Planning and Scheduling Reporting, Insights and Analysis P3M Tools Relationships and engagement	Scheduling tool

Related services

Develop and maintain schedules for the portfolio, program, or project Define planning standards and templates	Establish a portfolio management framework

Review cross project and program dependencies

Service description

A review of the dependencies between projects within a program and the dependencies between programs within a portfolio to see whether there are any issues or risks with the delivery. This helps identify where the portfolio manager may want to focus their attention in assisting the project or program manager with delivery options.

What the service provides for the customer

It provides the portfolio manager with information to enable them to focus on the parts of the portfolio which may be in greater trouble of delivery. It helps identify when dependencies have been missed.

It provides a way that projects and programs can be connected. It allows the actual dependencies to be identified along with the drop-dead dates for delivery.

Why is this service being offered to the customer?

The PMO can get down into the detail of all the projects and programs to provide a detailed analytical view of the dependencies between each of the projects and programs. By getting into the detail and providing the analysis this allows the portfolio manager to retain the overview that is required for the role.

How PMO will apply this service

The PMO will examine in detail each of the schedules and the dependency register for each of the projects and programs to identify the cross project and program dependencies. They will identify dependencies which are only listed as one way (i.e. those where a project has listed a dependency on another project, but this has not been identified by the corresponding project) and inform the relevant project or program manager.

The PMO will identify the dependencies which are at risk (i.e. an issue has been created) and may be at risk (only a risk exists). They will flag these dependencies through to the portfolio manager, along with a set of suggested actions.

The portfolio manager will come up with some recommendations and the PMO may be asked to provide this feedback directly through to the project or program manager. If no suggestions are forthcoming, then the PMO may be asked to setup some workshops for these dependencies to be discussed and resolved.

Supplier	Input	Process	Output	Customer
Project Managers Program Managers	Schedules containing milestones & dependencies	Portfolio planning	Portfolio plan Dependency mapping	Portfolio managers Project Approval Board Senior Management

How the PMO will measure the value of this service

This can be measured by seeing a reduction in issues in the portfolio due to poor dependency management.

Criteria when the PMO will use this service

- When the PMO is aligned to a portfolio manager
- When the portfolio is complex and there are lots of interdependencies

Helpful hints for the PMO when delivering the service

- Look to display this information in a way that it is clear what actions are required, and by whom
- By identifying dependencies which are only listed as one way the PMO may undercover that this is not actually a valid dependency and the source project needs to be identified.
- By a detailed examination of the schedules and the dependency register the PMO may uncover a few new dependencies which will need to be added to the registers and dealt with appropriately
- Consider whether it is worth escalating dependency issues with the portfolio manager or whether this could be dealt with by the PMO having a conversation/meeting with the 2 projects/programs impacted
- Although this text talks about portfolio, the same can be applied at program level by looking at the constituent projects

PMO Capabilities needed to fulfil this service

Competencies	Techniques and generic tools
Issue Management Planning and Scheduling Reporting, Insights and Analysis Risk Management P3M Tools Relationships and engagement Teamwork Negotiation	Scheduling tool Work Breakdown Structure

Related services

Define planning standards and templates Develop and maintain schedules for the portfolio, program, or project Monitor dependency register	Provide dependency analysis Provide facilitation service

Review progress of agile deliveries

Service description

The monitoring and review of agile deliveries. Checking against the Kanban board to update burndown and burnup charts on behalf of the scrum master.

What the service provides for the customer

This provides an administrative function for the scrum master by ensuring that the Kanban board adequately reflects the progress within the sprint. It enables them to review this in the form of a burndown or burnup chart.

Why is this service being offered to the customer?

This offers the scrum master some assurance that the information they are using to control the sprint is accurate as it has been validated by the PMO.

How PMO will apply this service

The PMO will attend the daily stand-up. At the stand-up they will be informed of the progress that has been made. The PMO will use that information to update the Kanban board (or at least to verify that it reflects the information that has been said).

The PMO can then use the information from the Kanban board to update the burnup/burndown charts (if the software being used does not do this automatically). These can then be provided to the scrum master for them to understand whether the deliveries are happening at the correct rate (i.e. is the velocity of the sprint as expected).

Supplier	Input	Process	Output	Customer
PPM team	Progress update	Update Kanban board	Updated Kanban board Burndown chart	Scrum master

How the PMO will measure the value of this service

The PMO can measure this based on the feedback from the scrum master.

Criteria when the PMO will use this service

- When the PMO is working assigned to a single project
- Where the scrum master needs administrative support
- Where the project is working in an agile way

Helpful hints for the PMO when delivering the service

- If this service is not done by the PMO it will be performed by the scrum master
- The velocity is easier to see in a burn-up chart as that has the expected rate shown on it as well as the actual rate. The burndown chart only has the number of items left to be done

PMO Capabilities needed to fulfil this service

Competencies	Techniques and generic tools
P3M Administration Planning and Scheduling Reporting, Insights and Analysis P3M Tools	Iteration burndown chart

Related services

Maintain a release schedule

Stakeholder Management

Stakeholder Management

Description

Stakeholder Management is the collective tasks concerning with the identification and handling of relevant stakeholders.

What the services within the domain provide for the customer

You need identify, handle, and communicate with all relevant stakeholders in relation to your PMO work and you need to have a strategy for doing this. The stakeholders are your customers and input providers to PMO work, and it is therefore essential that you have adequate services tools and techniques to cover this area. Identifying and handling your stakeholders provide significant value and without this it does not make sense.

Helpful hints for when the PMO is delivering this service domain

The stakeholder management area requires the project or program manager to involve their team members is all steps of the service to spread the work and to make sure that the identifying and handling is done at a sufficiently deep level. At different time points in the project/program lifecycle senior management will be invited to contribute whenever a project/program stakeholder handling requires this.

Stakeholder Management Design

Service group description

The development of the standards and templates associated with stakeholder management on project, programs, and the portfolio.

Why have these services been grouped together?

The stakeholder design group of activities are essential to have a structured approach to the stakeholder management discipline. The collective group of services will ensure a holistic 360 view on stakeholders in projects and program. The foundation is designed and the "how to do" is developed and is providing the project/program manager with important tools to handle stakeholders.

Responsibility Assignment Matrix

Service	Executive	Portfolio Manager	Program Manager	Project Manager	PMO	Sponsor	Other Stakeholder
Develop and maintain the stakeholder engagement framework	A	C	C	C	R		
Facilitate the formulation of stakeholder engagement strategies		A	A	A	R		

Develop and maintain the stakeholder engagement framework

Service description

The development and maintenance of the process, templates, and standard to enable the management of stakeholders.

What the service provides for the customer

This provides the project, program, and portfolio managers with the templates to enable them to identify, track and manage their stakeholders.

Why is this service being offered to the customer?

By having a set of standard templates, good practice can be embedded from lessons identified on other projects. It enables the roll-up and comparison of plans and matrices on multiple projects, helping to identify overlaps and commonalities.

How PMO will apply this service

The PMO will review the external guidance on stakeholder management, including the usage of various techniques to enable the identification of stakeholders. They will check to see what templates are available externally and how these can be adapted (if required) for use within this organization.

As well as providing the template they will provide guidance on the approach to stakeholder engagement within the organization using feedback from lessons learnt on how the different stakeholders prefer to be engaged.

Supplier	Input	Process	Output	Customer
PMO	Existing process and templates Lessons register Improvement suggestions	Develop standard Develop templates	Stakeholder Plans Stakeholder profile Stakeholder matrix	Project Managers Program Managers Portfolio Managers

How the PMO will measure the value of this service

This can be measured by the numbers of people using the templates provided.

Criteria when the PMO will use this service

- Where consistency is needed in stakeholder management and engagement
- Where there is a need to roll up information across a program or portfolio

Helpful hints for the PMO when delivering the service

- Ensure that the stakeholder templates align with the communications plan template to ensure that information can be copied from one to the other
- Ensure that the framework is communicated to the project, program, and portfolio managers

PMO Capabilities needed to fulfil this service

Competencies	Techniques and generic tools
Stakeholder Engagement Delivery Methods Personal Communication	Salience model Stakeholder checklist Stakeholder engagement assessment matrix

Related services

Develop and maintain the communication framework Facilitate the formulation of stakeholder engagement strategies Develop stakeholder plans, profiles, and matrices	Facilitate stakeholder identification and communication workshops Be aware of stakeholders with an interest in the organization's delivery portfolio Map key value streams and processes

Facilitate the formulation of stakeholder engagement strategies

Service description

Defining a stakeholder engagement strategy and relevant communication tools are the collective services concerning how to identify stakeholders, define how to interact with them and designing the tools and templates as the framework for how to document the interaction and communication with stakeholders.

What the service provides for the customer

This provides the project or program manager with an approach to dealing with stakeholders in the project or program.

Why is this service being offered to the customer?

This service is being offered because projects or program need to have a structured and comprehensive approach to identifying, engagement and communicating with stakeholders.

How PMO will apply this service

The PMO will meet with the project or program manager to get an overview of all the input including: the scope of the project or program; the PESTEL factors impacting the project or program; previous stakeholder engagement plans and communications plans; feedback from previous engagements.

Using the relevant techniques, the PMO will ensure that the stakeholder strategy gets documented. They will advise the project or program manager on the stakeholder engagement activities. Once the strategy has been documented it will then be the responsibility of the project or program manager for carrying out the stakeholder engagement activities. Some stakeholder activities may be delegated to senior management.

Supplier	Input	Process	Output	Customer
Project Manager Program Manager Portfolio Manager	Project /program scope PESTEL elements Previous history regarding this stakeholder group, budget, and resource constraints Stakeholder templates	Develop stakeholder strategy	Stakeholder Strategy	Project Manager Program Manager Portfolio Manager

How the PMO will measure the value of this service

Customer satisfaction measurement on a scale e.g. The project/program manager + team, stakeholder satisfaction levels with KPI % of customer who are satisfied or very satisfied, %Number of complaints from project/program members customer compared to last project/program or compared to a previous measurement during the project/program.

Criteria when the PMO will use this service

- When a project or program is of significant importance
- When the stakeholder analysis shows complex structures and communication lines
- If the outcome of the project or program has a large component of change to it
- When the project or program manager does not have sufficiently experience within the relevant area

Helpful hints for the PMO when delivering the service

- Important to invite a large team to contribute to identify all stakeholders
- Take time to clarify PESTEL and what is really impacting the customers of the PM
- The engagement activities selected should be tested on a smaller group until rolled out in large scale
- If you do not develop an engagement strategy and identify the needed engagement activities the benefit of the project/program may be jeopardized
- Remember to put all stakeholder engagement activities in your project plan and be proactive in your communication with them so the stakeholders are not surprised

PMO Capabilities needed to fulfil this service

Competencies	Techniques and generic tools
Stakeholder Engagement Professionalism and ethics Relationships and engagement Negotiation	Salience model Stakeholder checklist Stakeholder engagement assessment matrix

Related services

Develop and maintain the stakeholder engagement framework Develop stakeholder plans, profiles, and matrices Facilitate stakeholder identification and communication workshops Advise on key stakeholders and influencing strategies	Enable the formulation of communication plans Provide facilitation service Manage Customer Interfaces Clearly communicates the PMO vision and objectives Be aware of stakeholders with an interest in the organization's delivery portfolio

Stakeholder Management Operations

Service group description

The identification and management of stakeholders for a project, program, or portfolio.

Why have these services been grouped together?

These services relate to the day-to-day identification and management of stakeholders on a project, program, or portfolio.

Responsibility Assignment Matrix

Service	Executive	Portfolio Manager	Program Manager	Project Manager	PMO	Sponsor	Other Stakeholder
Develop stakeholder plans, profiles, and matrices		A	A	A	R		
Facilitate stakeholder identification and communication workshops		A	A	A	R		
Advise on key stakeholders and influencing strategies		C	C	C	A, R		
Be aware of stakeholders with an interest in the organization's delivery portfolio		A	C	C	R		

Helpful hints for when the PMO is delivering this service group

Having identified the stakeholders, ensure that they are covered in the communications plan.

Develop stakeholder plans, profiles, and matrices

Service description

The creation and maintenance of stakeholder plans, profiles, and matrices on behalf of the project, program, or portfolio manager.

What the service provides for the customer

It ensures that stakeholder management is documented allowing assessment of the best way to interact with those stakeholders. It allows for an understanding of their needs and wants in relation to the project, program, or portfolio.

Why is this service being offered to the customer?

As the PMO sees across the projects within the organization and sees the feedback from the post implementation review and lessons registers they can see the best way to interact with the internal stakeholders within the organization. They can then document this in a consistent manner using the templates provided.

How PMO will apply this service

The PMO will receive a request for assistance with constructing stakeholder plans. They will arrange for a time to discuss this with the manager concerned. They will obtain a copy of the scope of the change along with the latest version of the templates. The manager and the PMO will identify the stakeholders of the change and look to group those together (if possible).

The PMO may book a workshop to enable a wider discussion of the possible stakeholders. The PMO will consider:

- Who the stakeholders are?
- What their involvement will be
- What their interest is in the project, program, or portfolio
- What their engagement will be
- The power the stakeholder has to impact the change
- Who 'owns' the relationship with the stakeholder?
- What do we want their interest/engagement to be?
- What needs to happen to move them from where they are to where we need them to do (if anything)

The PMO will document the information about the stakeholders and how they will be dealt with within the stakeholder templates.

Supplier	Input	Process	Output	Customer
Project Managers Program Managers Portfolio Managers PMO	Scoping statement Stakeholder templates	Creating stakeholder plans	Stakeholder plans Stakeholder profile Stakeholder matrix	Project Managers Program Managers Portfolio Managers

How the PMO will measure the value of this service

This can be measured by the development of the stakeholder documentation. I can be measured by seeing how successful stakeholder management has been for the project, program, or portfolio.

Criteria when the PMO will use this service

- When the PMO is aligned to the project, program, or portfolio manager
- Where the manager does not have the ability to do this service themselves
- When the project or program is starting up or moving into a new phase

Helpful hints for the PMO when delivering the service

- Ensure once the stakeholders are identified that this information is copied into the communication plan to enable those stakeholders to be suitable engaged
- Consider reviewing the central lessons register to find examples of what went well when dealing with particular groups of stakeholders within the organization
- When reviewing where stakeholders are versus where we want them to be, consider the amount of effort required to move people all the way
- As the project or program enters the next phase look to review the stakeholder information as new stakeholders may be identified, and the relationship with existing stakeholders may change
- Look to review the stakeholder matrices based on feedback from the communications effectiveness

PMO Capabilities needed to fulfil this service

Competencies	Techniques and generic tools
Knowledge Management	Salience model
Stakeholder Engagement	Stakeholder checklist
Personal Communication	Stakeholder engagement assessment matrix
Relationships and engagement	
Teamwork	
Negotiation	

Related services

Enable the formulation of communication plans Monitor the effectiveness of communications Develop and maintain the stakeholder engagement framework Facilitate stakeholder identification and communication workshops Advise on key stakeholders and influencing strategies Be aware of stakeholders with an interest in the organization's delivery portfolio Support supplier liaison across portfolio, program, or project	Manage Customer Interfaces Clearly communicates the PMO vision and objectives Develop and maintain the communication framework Facilitate the formulation of stakeholder engagement strategies Be aware of stakeholders with an interest in the organization's delivery portfolio

Facilitate stakeholder identification and communication workshops

Service description

Provision of an independent facilitation service to identify the stakeholders for a project, program, or portfolio.

What the service provides for the customer

A facilitated workshop to enable the development of a stakeholder engagement plan or communications plan.

Why is this service being offered to the customer?

By having a facilitated workshop in ensures that all voices are heard when it comes to identifying and classifying stakeholders. This ensures that different methods of engaging each of those stakeholder or stakeholder groups is considered and the best one chosen.

How PMO will apply this service

Having identified the need for a facilitated workshop the PMO will liaise with the project, program, or portfolio manager to work out who needs to attend the workshop. The PMO will then book the meeting and invite all the attendees. The purpose of the workshop will be clearly stated prior to the workshop commencing. Any background documentation (e.g. scoping documentation) should be sent to the participants in advance to give them time to read the materials prior to the meeting.

In the meeting the PMO will set the ground rules and re-state the objective of the meeting to ensure everyone has a clear understanding of what they are being expected to do. During the meeting, the PMO, as facilitator, will ensure that everyone gets a chance to speak and put forward their views.

The PMO should ensure each of the stakeholders are identified. For each of the stakeholders the participants should review where the stakeholder is perceived to be in relation to the project, program, or portfolio and where they would like the stakeholder to be. They will list out all the actions that will be required to change the stakeholder's position along with the responsibilities for doing so.

After the meeting, the PMO will ensure that all the information is captured and documented in the stakeholder plan and communications plan. This can then be passed to the PPM manager for them to manage.

Supplier	Input	Process	Output	Customer
Project Manager Program Manager Portfolio Manager PMO	Scoping document Stakeholder documentation templates Facilitation request	Facilitating a meeting	Stakeholder Plans Communications plan	Project Manager Program Manager Portfolio Manager

How the PMO will measure the value of this service

This can be measured by checking the number of stakeholder and communication plans that are used by the project, program, or portfolio manager. It can be measured by asking for feedback on the facilitation service.

Criteria when the PMO will use this service

- Where it is not obvious who the stakeholders are
- Where a stakeholder or communications plan needs to be created
- Where the PPM manager requires an independent person to facilitate the workshop

Helpful hints for the PMO when delivering the service

- Consider having a facilitation/workshop kit (pens, post-its, blue-tac, flipchart paper etc.)
- Assign one of the flipcharts as a parking lot to avoid wasting time discussing an intractable issue
- Consider training individuals within the PMO to deliver this service
- Consider reviewing the success of previous stakeholder/communication plans and bring those suggestions into the workshop

PMO Capabilities needed to fulfil this service

Competencies	Techniques and generic tools
Reporting, Insights and Analysis Stakeholder Engagement Personal Communication Relationships and engagement Negotiation	Diagramming techniques Matrix diagrams Salience model Stakeholder checklist Stakeholder engagement assessment matrix

Related services

Develop and maintain the stakeholder engagement framework Develop stakeholder plans, profiles, and matrices Enable the formulation of communication plans Provide facilitation service Provide a secretariat service for meetings	Manage Customer Interfaces Develop and maintain the communication framework Facilitate the formulation of stakeholder engagement strategies Advise on key stakeholders and influencing strategies

Advise on key stakeholders and influencing strategies

Service description

The provision of advice and guidance on the key stakeholders for a project, program or portfolio and the preferred ways of influencing them.

What the service provides for the customer

Provides a voice of experience on effective ways of dealing with stakeholders. Suggests alternative ways of approaching situations if the communication process is deemed to be unsuccessful.

Why is this service being offered to the customer?

The PMO has the feedback from the post implementation reviews and the lessons registers and is able to see what works and what does not work for when engaging the different stakeholder groups. They are able to identify who the key individuals are in a particular department based on feedback from other projects and programs being run.

How PMO will apply this service

The PMO will obtain a copy of the stakeholder plan. For each of the stakeholders listed they will review the lessons register to see whether there are any hints and tips which can be gleaned about how to deal with them successfully, or what to avoid. The PMO will review the stakeholder plans of other projects and programs to see whether they are engaging the same stakeholders. They will take the information from those plans and compare this against this stakeholder plan to see if there are any suggestions they can find.

Where the project or program is engaging a particular area of the business the PMO will review to see who the key stakeholders are within the area. They will check this against the stakeholder plan to see if there are any missing stakeholders.

Having reviewed all the related stakeholder material the PMO will then make some suggestions as to who the relevant stakeholders should be and how best to engage with them.

Supplier	Input	Process	Output	Customer
PMO	Lessons Register Stakeholder plan Communications plan	Provide guidance	PMO Advice and suggestions	Project Managers Program Managers Portfolio Managers

How the PMO will measure the value of this service

This can be measured by an increase in the successful engagement of stakeholders for a particular change. If can be measured by the number of suggestions that get incorporated in the stakeholder/communication plan.

Criteria when the PMO will use this service

- When the stakeholder engagement is not particularly successful
- When the stakeholder and communication plans are being created

Helpful hints for the PMO when delivering the service

- A key stakeholder is not necessarily the most senior person. It can be the individual who has the best connections within that department
- Consider doing this as part of a facilitated workshop to ensure that all parties get a change to add in their views

PMO Capabilities needed to fulfil this service

Competencies	Techniques and generic tools
Knowledge Management Stakeholder Engagement Personal Communication Relationships and engagement	Salience model Stakeholder checklist Stakeholder engagement assessment matrix

Related services

Develop stakeholder plans, profiles, and matrices Facilitate stakeholder identification and communication workshops Enable the formulation of communication plans Support supplier liaison across portfolio, program, or project	Manage Customer Interfaces Clearly communicates the PMO vision and objectives Facilitate the formulation of stakeholder engagement strategies Be aware of stakeholders with an interest in the organization's delivery portfolio

Be aware of stakeholders with an interest in the organization's delivery portfolio

Service description

The provision of a stakeholder identification service analysis on the portfolio as a whole on behalf of the portfolio manager and the Project Approval Board.

What the service provides for the customer

This provides the portfolio manager with a stakeholder engagement plan that can be used to work with stakeholders of the portfolio.

Why is this service being offered to the customer?

Portfolios have stakeholders as do projects and programs. The portfolio level PMO will interact with the stakeholders on a regular basis so are well placed to offer advice as to how to interact with them for the benefit of the portfolio as a whole.

How PMO will apply this service

The PMO will review the potential stakeholders for the portfolio based on the people who are coming to the PMO to ask questions on the portfolio. The PMO will note who the individuals are and the sort of information they are requesting, and the frequency they want the information. The PMO will note who uses and accesses the information about the portfolio that the PMO publish on a regular basis.

They will use the service 'Develop stakeholder plans, profiles and matrices' to develop the stakeholder plan and discuss this with the portfolio manager.

Supplier	Input	Process	Output	Customer
PMO	Project Register	Stakeholder identification	Stakeholder engagement plan	Portfolio Managers Project Approval Board

How the PMO will measure the value of this service

This can be measured by reviewing how successful the stakeholder engagement is for the portfolio. It can be measured by getting feedback from the portfolio manager.

Criteria when the PMO will use this service

- When the PMO is aligned to a portfolio manager
- When there is no existing stakeholder engagement plan for the portfolio

Helpful hints for the PMO when delivering the service

- Anyone who has an interest in or uses the information from the portfolio can be considered as a stakeholder
- Before suggesting portfolio stakeholders, check they are not already included in the stakeholder management plan

PMO Capabilities needed to fulfil this service

Competencies	Techniques and generic tools
Stakeholder Engagement Relationships and engagement Teamwork	Communication requirements analysis Salience model Stakeholder checklist Stakeholder engagement assessment matrix

Related services

Develop stakeholder plans, profiles, and matrices Facilitate the formulation of stakeholder engagement strategies Advise on key stakeholders and influencing strategies	Develop and maintain the stakeholder engagement framework Support the Project Approval Board Manage Customer Interfaces

Supplier Management

Description

Ensure the organization carries out the role of informed customer and all commercial/procurement practices and decisions meet designated standards and offer the organization 'value for money'.

What the services within the area provide for the customer

These services provide a way for suppliers to be dealt with in a consistent manner. The PMO can act as liaison between procurement and the PPM teams to be able to get contracts in place that will flex and will allow the project or program manager to deliver successfully.

Helpful hints for when the PMO is delivering this service area

Build a good working relationship with the procurement department to ensure you understand their timescales, standards, and tools.

Understand that a contract for project delivery is very different from a contract for provision of a set of goods. If all does not go well with the supplier you may be forced to work with the supplier to resolve the issue, rather than just default to looking at the legal issues about contract non-delivery.

Ensure the person looking at the contract has clearly included the circumstances where payment should occur and linked this into a working product that satisfies particular quality criteria.

Supplier Management Design

Service group description

The setup and communication of the procurement strategy, standards, templates, and tool documentation.

Why have these services been grouped together?

These services relate to the creation and maintenance of the approach to procurement within the PPM environment.

Responsibility Assignment Matrix

Service	Executive	Portfolio Manager	Program Manager	Project Manager	PMO	Sponsor	Other Stakeholder
Work with Procurement teams to agree PPM purchasing Framework					R		A (Procurement)
Communicate PPM purchasing Framework		I	I	I	A, R		

Helpful hints for when the PMO is delivering this service group

Ensure that you take the lead from procurement in the development of this framework. They will have some existing tools and standards the PMO needs to ensure whatever is come up with fits in with those existing items.

Work with Procurement teams to agree PPM purchasing Framework

Service description

To work with the procurement teams to develop a set of templates, standards, and guidance in how to purchase items for use in projects.

What the service provides for the customer

This provides the program and project manager with a set of guidance on how to work with procurement to purchase items. This includes:

- How any procurement tools work
- Responsibilities for ordering including when to involve procurement or legal
- Any templates that need to be used, and when
- Whether individual contracts need to be raised or whether items can be raised as part of existing relationships with suppliers
- Likely timescales for ordering items
- Coding advice when using the templates/tools
- Help on how any procurement tools can be used to raise an order, track an order
- How to get access to any tools or templates

Why is this service being offered to the customer?

Having a central framework prevents each project and program manager having to work out the rules themselves each time and therefore wasting effort in doing so. Having a simplified set of rules to follow will cut down the time taken to get items brought for the project.

How PMO will apply this service

The PMO will speak to procurement and find out their standards and guidelines about how they go about purchasing items. They will look at any purchasing tools that may be in place and how they can get access to them. If there are any tools in use, they will discuss how this can be tracked into finance to ensure that the project (or program) is correctly charged for the item.

There are a range of items that can be brought for a project, for example: licenses, people, machinery. Some of those are a one-off purchase, however others may require a support contract to be purchased as well. The PMO need to identify the typical items that are purchased by projects and programs and include in their guidance how to deal with each of these items.

For larger purchases it may be necessary to have a bidding process e.g. Request for Information, Request to Tender, contract. For these procurement, maybe legal and finance departments will want to be involved in this process. They may offer to lead those on behalf of the organization. The PMO needs to include the guidance the circumstances by which this process is required, and how procurement need to be engaged.

For other items it may be an amendment to an existing contract or just a Statement of Work will be required. The PMO need to show which one of these is required.

If a procurement tool is in place the PMO will need to offer some training/help guides in how this is to be used. This should cover creating an initial request, approvals for the request, receipting the goods, tracking payment of the goods, how to gain relevant access to the tool, where to go for further help. The PMO need to know how to ensure all projects (that will need the tool) are loaded into the system, with the appropriate access for people to raise items against the project and get the items approved. How additional vendors get added in.

The PMO need to provide the links between purchasing and finance as there will be rules around who is able to approve purchases of a certain type and amount. The PMO should look to include those, or reference to those rules within this guidance.

Supplier	Input	Process	Output	Customer
Procurement	Procurement standards	Develop Standard Develop Templates	PPM procurement standards PPM procurement guidance PPM procurement templates	Program Manager Project Manager Procurement

How the PMO will measure the value of this service

This can be measured by feedback from the project and program manager about the smoothness of the service and the easy of getting the information they required. It can be measured by looking at the reduction in time wasted understanding the procurement process.

Criteria when the PMO will use this service

- Where there is a need to purchase goods for a project or program
- Where the procurement standards have changed
- Where the finance approval rules have changed
- If procurement introduce a new tool for purchasing items

Helpful hints for the PMO when delivering the service

- Not every project or program will need to purchase external items. Those that do will want to make the process as easy and as pain free as possible
- As there are many variations about what is required to be purchased on a project consider releasing early versions of the guidance and then updating this as new examples of purchases come along
- Put this guidance somewhere central that people can come back and refer to

PMO Capabilities needed to fulfil this service

Competencies	Techniques and generic tools
Financial Management Supplier Management Governance Frameworks P3M Tools Relationships and engagement Teamwork Resourcefulness Negotiation	Process Analysis Swim-lane flowcharts Task responsibility matrix/RACI

Related services

Communicate PPM purchasing Framework Support contracts monitoring and management Liaise with procurement teams on new in initiatives to ensure early engagement Map key value streams and processes	Place and track small orders for portfolio, program, or project Work with Procurement teams to select 3rd party vendors Manage the Process Improvement Plan

Communicate PPM purchasing Framework

Service description

Ensure all the individuals who need to purchase something for a project or program are aware of the PPM purchasing framework.

What the service provides for the customer

This ensures that the people needing to purchase items for a project or program know how to do so.

Why is this service being offered to the customer?

As the PMO have written the PPM purchasing framework they will be best placed to offer training on it. They will see lots of items being purchased and can offer advice and guidance on how particular purchases should be made.

How PMO will apply this service

The PMO will identify everyone who will be responsible for purchasing or tracking the purchases of items on a project or program. This will be the project manager, the team managers, but may include individuals within the project team.

The PMO will need to decide whether it is best to organize a full training course, individual sessions (as each person's need will be different) or just communicate the framework via email (as only minor updates have been made).

If the PMO decide to organize a full training session they will need to write the materials, book the meeting spaces, invite the individuals. They can then check that all people have attended and gain feedback from those who have attended.

If they organize individual sessions, then these can be tailored to the need of the individual and the circumstances of the project or program. They can be aligned to when the people are likely to use the process and therefore these may be more effective.

Supplier	Input	Process	Output	Customer
PMO	PPM Purchasing Framework	Deliver training	Informed people	PPM team

How the PMO will measure the value of this service

This can be measured by numbers of people trained and the satisfaction with the training.

Criteria when the PMO will use this service

- When there is a change to the PPM purchasing framework
- When new people are added into the teams

Helpful hints for the PMO when delivering the service

- If organizing a training session, it may help to have support from the procurement department in order that they can answer some of the more difficult or technical questions
- If organizing a full training course be aware you may have to schedule some extra sessions for those people who missed the original set
- If doing individual session have a standard checklist of items that you wish to cover to ensure that there is consistency in the training
- Leverage the training sessions (full or individual) to help find out where people are struggling and look to incorporate more help around those points
- If there is a tool used ensure you can demonstrate the use of that in the training. Use of a training environment or ID would be useful to ensure that items are not actually purchased in error as a result of the training course

PMO Capabilities needed to fulfil this service

Competencies	Techniques and generic tools
Financial Management Supplier Management Governance Frameworks P3M Tools Personal Communication Relationships and engagement	Communication requirements analysis Stakeholder checklist Stakeholder engagement assessment matrix

Related services

Work with Procurement teams to agree PPM purchasing Framework Place and track small orders for portfolio, program, or project Work with Procurement teams to select 3rd party vendors Liaise with procurement teams on new in initiatives to ensure early engagement	Manage the Process Improvement Plan Provide PPM training Provide training logistics support

Supplier Management Operations

Service group description

Dealing with suppliers and procurement directly, either ordering items, paying invoices, or ensuring handovers happen prior to contract closure.

Why have these services been grouped together?

These services relate to working day-to-day with suppliers, procurement, finance and the project and program managers.

List of related services described in other areas

Manage invoicing processing for portfolio, programs, and projects
Facilitate timely calculation of accruals, forecasts, and anticipated cash flow

Responsibility Assignment Matrix

Service	Executive	Portfolio Manager	Program Manager	Project Manager	PMO	Sponsor	Other Stakeholder
Liaise with procurement teams on new in initiatives to ensure early engagement		A	A	A	R		C (Procurement)
Support supplier liaison across portfolio, program, or project		A	A	A	R		C (Supplier)
Place and track small orders for portfolio, program, or project		A	A	A	R		C (Procurement)
Ensure program and project supplier relationships are embedded in Business as Usual			A	A	R	I	C (Procurement) C (BAU team)
Work with Procurement teams to select 3rd party vendors		A	A	A	R		C (Procurement)
Ensure invoices are paid according to the contract terms		A	A	A	R		C (Procurement) C (Legal) C (Finance)

Helpful hints for when the PMO is delivering this service group

Ensure that there is a general understanding of the roles and responsibilities connected with dealing with suppliers. Understand what, if any, role procurement, legal and finance teams will have in the day-to-day dealings with suppliers. Understand whether different contract will be required once the project hands over to support teams.

Liaise with procurement teams on new in initiatives to ensure early engagement

Service description

In accordance with the PPM procurement framework ensure that procurement have early involvement with any project or program that will require their involvement to get a deal organized with a supplier, even if the actual supplier is unknown.

What the service provides for the customer

It provides procurement with early warning of their involvement in a project or program to establish a contract with a new or existing supplier.

It provides the project or program manager with procurement experience to ensure that the correct processes are followed in engaging a new or existing supplier for the project or program. It will ensure that the contract is suitable for delivery and that due diligence is done on any potential suppliers.

Why is this service being offered to the customer?

Both the project or program and procurement need to work together to get a supplier on board. This can be a lengthy process, so the more warning that is provided the better for both parties.

How PMO will apply this service

Where the PMO is aligned to a project or program that will require external purchases the PMO will look at the PPM purchasing framework to find out whether procurement need to be engaged. If procurement need to be involved the PMO will speak to the appropriate person. The PMO will discuss the necessary steps, and timescale to get procurement involved and the supplier onboarded. The PMO will ensure this information is fed back to the project or program manager and incorporated into the schedule.

The PMO will liaise with procurement to find out any additional department that may need to be involved including legal and finance. The PMO will agree who will be responsible for the different actions and whether procurement or the project/program manager will be taking the lead role in these activities.

Supplier	Input	Process	Output	Customer
Program Manager Project Manager	Project Initiation Document PPM Purchasing Framework	Engaging a supplier	Request for Information Request for Tender	Program Manager Project Manager Procurement Legal Finance

How the PMO will measure the value of this service

This can be measured by asking for feedback from procurement and the project/program manager. It can be measured by looking at the feedback from the lessons learned around procurement.

Criteria when the PMO will use this service

- Where a PMO is aligned to an individual project or program
- Where the project or program will be engaging an external supplier

Helpful hints for the PMO when delivering the service

- Look to engage with procurement even if the supplier is unknown as procurement can help with the supplier selection process
- Work with procurement to get a workable contract in place. Getting into a contractual conflict will not help the project delivery. Ensure the contract had flexibility for work to continue even if there is a dispute in process
- The steps taken to onboard a supplier will differ depending on whether the supplier is known or if there is a need for bids to be submitted
- Once the supplier is known the steps taken may differ if there is a new contract required versus an amendment to an existing one

PMO Capabilities needed to fulfil this service

Competencies	Techniques and generic tools
Financial Management Planning and Scheduling Stakeholder Engagement Supplier Management Delivery Methods Governance Frameworks Personal Communication Relationships and engagement Teamwork	Market / Competitor Analysis Complexity Matrix

Related services

Work with Procurement teams to agree PPM purchasing Framework Communicate PPM purchasing Framework	Develop and maintain schedules for the portfolio, program, or project Work with Procurement teams to select 3rd party vendors

Support supplier liaison across portfolio, program, or project

Service description

Ensure that there is a 2-way communication between the internal resources and external suppliers (or between external suppliers). To ensure confidentiality is kept the PMO will control the flow of information to limit access to only those who are authorized to see it.

What the service provides for the customer

By ensuring there is a 2-way communication the PMO can help prevent a them and us culture developing in the project, program, or portfolio.

Why is this service being offered to the customer?

This provides a brokerage mechanism to ensure that communications can still flow between the internal and external resources, or between different external suppliers. Even when things may be not going well the PMO can keep the communications flowing in order that the project, program, or portfolio is able to deliver.

How PMO will apply this service

Where there are external suppliers working on the project, program, or portfolio the PMO will identify what they are working on and who they are working with. They will look at the stakeholder map and the communication required between the PPM team and the external supplier. The PMO will offer to be a broker for that information if they feel that the communication lines are not working.

To increase the morale of the team and the interaction between the team and the supplier the PMO can look to organize some events. These may be formal such as kick-off workshops or may be informal such as social events.

The PMO can ensure that the supplier and the PPM team have access to the necessary documentation to do their work. The PMO can assist the supplier by providing some background about the style of working within the organization and the culture to be expected.

Supplier	Input	Process	Output	Customer
PPM teams External Suppliers	Documentation	Communication	Informed team	PPM teams External Suppliers

How the PMO will measure the value of this service

This service can be measured by looking at the morale of the team as a whole.

Criteria when the PMO will use this service

- Where there are external resources working on a project, program, or portfolio
- Where there is potential for dispute
- Where the PMO is aligned to a single project or program
- Where the PMO is aligned to a portfolio manager

Helpful hints for the PMO when delivering the service

- Consider speaking with the senior management and get the supplier and PPM teams co-located
- Consider taking it in turns to organize events between the supplier and the PPM team
- Consider starting events/meetings with food to entice people to attend

PMO Capabilities needed to fulfil this service

Competencies	Techniques and generic tools
Information Management Stakeholder Engagement Supplier Management Professionalism and ethics Personal Communication Relationships and engagement Teamwork Conflict and Crisis Resourcefulness Negotiation	Organization charts & position descriptions Resource breakdown structure Scheduling tool Stakeholder engagement assessment matrix Swim-lane flowcharts Task responsibility matrix/RACI

Related services

Events management Monitor supplier performance Develop stakeholder plans, profiles, and matrices	Advise on key stakeholders and influencing strategies Coordinate the internal communication Monitor the effectiveness of communications

Place and track small orders for portfolio, program, or project

Service description

The procurement of goods and services on behalf of a portfolio, program, or project manager.

What the service provides for the customer

It provides a way that orders can be processed and tracked through using the organizations procurement processes and tools. It provides a way of ordering items where the person initiating the order does not have access to the purchasing tool.

Why is this service being offered to the customer?

It ensures that as orders are raised these are linked into the finances for the initiative as accruals would be raised. Having a central contact to process orders can assist the project or program manager control costs.

How PMO will apply this service

Having received a request to order some goods and services the PMO will need to find the details including:

- Vendor – who are you buying the items from
- The detail of the goods/services required – exact details of items being brought. Rather than just purchasing pens, you would need to specify blue micron ballpoint pens
- Amount – the number required
- Financial details – What are the codes needed to ensure these are charged back correctly

They will then follow the PPM procurement framework to order the items. When the items have been delivered then the PMO will ensure the goods are receipted. The PMO will then deal with the invoice when it comes in ensuring it gets paid.

Supplier	Input	Process	Output	Customer
Portfolio Manager Program Manager Project Manager	Procurement request PPM Procurement Framework	Purchasing items	Purchase order Invoice	PPM Team

How the PMO will measure the value of this service

This service can be measured by asking for feedback from the person requesting the order. It can be measured by looking at the number of orders which are successfully included within the financials for the project or program.

Criteria when the PMO will use this service

- When the PMO is assigned to a single project or program
- Where the PMO supports a portfolio manager
- Where the person needing to raise the order does not have access to the tools to order the goods or service
- Where the PMO needs to track the finances for the project or program

Helpful hints for the PMO when delivering the service

- After raising the order, ensure that accruals are raised for the items procured
- Ensure that the goods are tracked through to invoice and eventual payment

PMO Capabilities needed to fulfil this service

Competencies	Techniques and generic tools
P3M Administration Financial Management Supplier Management P3M Tools Relationships and engagement	Prompt Lists Check sheets

Related services

Communicate PPM purchasing Framework Work with Procurement teams to agree PPM purchasing Framework Order office equipment and stationery	Control adherence to accounting procedures Ensure program and project supplier relationships are embedded in Business as Usual

Ensure program and project supplier relationships are embedded in Business as Usual

Service description

Ensures that any contracts created as part of a project or program are successfully transferred over into the Business-as-Usual environment.

What the service provides for the customer

Information on the contracts that are created as part of the project or program that will need to be transferred across to Business as Usual.

Why is this service being offered to the customer?

As the PMO have been monitoring the contracts during the life of the project/program they are ideally positioned to warn of any potential issues once this moves into BAU. By ensuring this is considered as part of the handover, along with the setting up of contract reporting and regular meetings with suppliers the PMO can make the transition process smoother.

How PMO will apply this service

When the project or program is coming to an end and there have been external contracts created the PMO will review these to see whether any need to be transferred into Business as Usual. It may be that a separate contract will need to be created for the support. For example, if equipment has been purchased there may need to be a support contract to ensure this maintained.

If a separate contract is required, then the PMO will ensure that procurement is informed and that the Business-as-Usual area responsible will raise the contract.

If a contract is likely to continue, then the PMO will ensure the contract details are transferred over to the Business-as-Usual manager.

Supplier	Input	Process	Output	Customer
Project Manager Program Manager	Contract	Project closure Program closure	Handover document	Business as Usual team Supplier

How the PMO will measure the value of this service

This can be measured by the number of contracts that get correctly moved over to Business as Usual

Criteria when the PMO will use this service

- Where the PMO is assigned to a single project or program
- Where a project or program is closing
- Where external suppliers have been engaged

Helpful hints for the PMO when delivering the service

- If transferring a contract over to Business as Usual, ensure the financial details are transferred as well. Need to ensure that project or program does not pay for business-as-usual costs. Need to ensure that person receipting the goods is in the business-as-usual department
- Add information about contract handover into project or program closure checklist

PMO Capabilities needed to fulfil this service

Competencies	Techniques and generic tools
Stakeholder Engagement Supplier Management Delivery Methods Governance Frameworks Relationships and engagement Teamwork	Communication requirements analysis

Related services

Place and track small orders for portfolio, program, or project	Support closure process

Work with Procurement teams to select 3rd party vendors

Service description

The selection of a third-party supplier to deliver part of a project or program.

What the service provides for the customer

This ensures that the project or program follows the correct process of engaging a supplier. This means that due diligence is followed, and the necessary procurement and legal steps have been undertaken.

Why is this service being offered to the customer?

As the PMO has been involved with creating the PPM procurement framework they will know the necessary steps to be taken. They will have the contacts with the procurement department and can make it easier for the project or program manager to engage the third party.

How PMO will apply this service

The PMO will identify the need to engage a third-party supplier. The PMO will speak with the project or program manager to see whether they need assistance with the process. If they do then the PMO will speak with the procurement team to find out whether they need to go through the Request for Information, Request for Tender, Contract steps.

The PMO will support the project or program manager in getting the Request for Information prepared. They will collate the responses to the Request for Information. They will present this in a way that makes it easier to work out which of the initial long list of suppliers can be reduced to a short list of suppliers.

From the short list of suppliers, the PMO can ensure the Request for Tender is send out to them. They will collate the responses and ensure that answers are obtained to any questions or clarifications. They will present the collated responses back to the project or program manager can get the decision made as to whom to award the contract.

Once the finial supplier has been chosen the PMO will work with the procurement, legal and finance departments playing a coordinating role on behalf of the project or program manager. They may assist with getting the contract signed by the appropriate people.

Supplier	Input	Process	Output	Customer
Project Manager Program Manager	Requirements	Engaging a supplier	Request for Information Request for Tender Contract	Project Manager Program Manager Procurement

How the PMO will measure the value of this service

This can be measured by the ease with which third-parties are engaged. This can be measured by feedback from the project or program manager.

Criteria when the PMO will use this service

- Where a PMO is aligned to an individual project or program
- Where the project or program will be engaging an external supplier

Helpful hints for the PMO when delivering the service

- It may be possible to skip some of the steps if the organization already has dealing with the particular third-party supplier that is being engaged

PMO Capabilities needed to fulfil this service

Competencies	Techniques and generic tools
Stakeholder Engagement Supplier Management Assurance Personal Communication Relationships and engagement Teamwork Resourcefulness Negotiation Result Orientation	Market / Competitor Analysis Complexity Matrix Proposal evaluation system

Related services

Liaise with procurement teams on new in initiatives to ensure early engagement Work with Procurement teams to agree PPM purchasing Framework	Communicate PPM purchasing Framework Ensure invoices are paid according to the contract terms

Ensure invoices are paid according to the contract terms

Service description

On behalf of the project or program ensure that invoices are tracked, accrued, and paid according to the accounting procedures and approved contracts.

What the service provides for the customer

Ensures that only valid invoices are paid. Inappropriate invoices are challenged. Invoices are held under configuration management. Provides a linkage between unpaid invoices and accruals raised.

Why is this service being offered to the customer?

The PMO is likely to have access to the purchasing system and may be the individual who is receipting the goods. They will have access to the contract and know what invoices should be due, under what circumstances. They will have links to the financials and be able to account correctly for the invoice to ensure it gets paid according the accounting procedures.

How PMO will apply this service

The PMO will receive an invoice from the supplier. They will find and check the terms of the contract. If the invoice does not meet the terms of the contract, they will contact the supplier and inform them of the changes required. If the invoice does meet the contract terms, then they will arrange for this invoice to be paid.

Supplier	Input	Process	Output	Customer
Suppliers	Invoices Contracts	Paying an invoice	Invoice Payment	Project Manager Program Manager Supplier

How the PMO will measure the value of this service

This can be measured by the reduction in the number of incorrectly paid invoices. It can be measured by the reduction in time taken to authorize an invoice for payment.

Criteria when the PMO will use this service

- When the PMO is aligned to a single project or program
- Where there are third-party suppliers engaged via a contract

Helpful hints for the PMO when delivering the service

- Payments are likely to be triggered based on deliveries. By viewing the schedule, the PMO can see when the invoices are likely to be received

PMO Capabilities needed to fulfil this service

Competencies	Techniques and generic tools
P3M Administration Financial Management Information Management Supplier Management Professionalism and ethics Personal Integrity and reliability Relationships and engagement Teamwork Negotiation Result Orientation	Cash flow analysis

Related services

Support contracts monitoring and management Control adherence to accounting procedures Manage invoicing processing for portfolio, programs, and projects	Facilitate timely calculation of accruals, forecasts, and anticipated cash flow Work with Procurement teams to select 3rd party vendors Oversee the quality review process for contractual supplier deliverables

Supplier Management Monitoring

Service group description

The review of how well suppliers are performing their role. Ensuring that contracts are being adhered to.

Why have these services been grouped together?

These services are concerned with monitoring supplier performance against the agreed standards.

Responsibility Assignment Matrix

Service	Executive	Portfolio Manager	Program Manager	Project Manager	PMO	Sponsor	Other Stakeholder
Support contracts monitoring and management			A	A	R	I	
Monitor supplier performance			A	A	R	I	

Helpful hints for when the PMO is delivering this service group

Need to ensure that the PMO has the latest version of the contract together with any agreed changes.

Support contracts monitoring and management

Service description

Ensures that the delivery of products by the supplier is in accordance with the contracts. Ensures that any pre-requisites from any party have been met.

What the service provides for the customer

Prevents any conflicts developing due to contract disputes. If this were to be the case, then this to be escalated at the earliest possible point.

Why is this service being offered to the customer?

The PMO may have assisted in the contract development. They may be acting as configuration manager and would have access to the contract. They monitor progress against schedule and can tie that back to the contract delivery terms.

How PMO will apply this service

The PMO will obtain and read the contract. They will look to see what is needed to be provided by all parties. They will verify that these items have been supplied. They will examine the schedule to see whether all the contractual deliverables have been incorporated. If there are any missing, then they will look to see that they can be included

If there are any issues with the provision of information as specified in the contract, then the PMO will alert the project or program manager of the omission in order they can rectify the matter.

If there are any issues with the delivery of the deliverables as specified in the contract the PMO should discuss this with the supplier to find out further information as to any root causes of the issue. This may be related to an existing known issue, or it may uncover something new which will need to be dealt with by the project or program.

Supplier	Input	Process	Output	Customer
Legal Procurement	Contract Deliverables Schedule	Assurance review	Contract confirmation Escalations	Project Manager Program Manager Supplier

How the PMO will measure the value of this service

This can be measured as adherence to the contract terms.

Criteria when the PMO will use this service

- When the PMO is aligned to a single project or program
- Where there is a third-party supplier being used under contract

Helpful hints for the PMO when delivering the service

- If this is not done by the PMO then the project or program manager will perform this task
- It may be pertinent to offer some flexibility with the terms written into the contract to allow for better working relations between the supplier and the organization
- The PMO should look to perform this service on a regular basis, perhaps as part of a monthly review cycle
- Any escalations should be dealt with informally in the first basis to ensure speedy resolution. If this does not occur, then the PMO may consider escalating this to a higher level e.g. the steering group

PMO Capabilities needed to fulfil this service

Competencies	Techniques and generic tools
Change Control Information Management Issue Management Supplier Management Professionalism and ethics Personal Communication Relationships and engagement Teamwork Conflict and Crisis Negotiation	Prompt Lists Check sheets Performance variance report

Related services

Monitor supplier performance Perform logging and tracking to resolution of issues Control escalation of issues to higher authority Maintain the change control register	Develop and maintain schedules for the portfolio, program, or project Work with Procurement teams to agree PPM purchasing Framework Ensure invoices are paid according to the contract terms Oversee the quality review process for contractual supplier deliverables

Monitor supplier performance

Service description

The review of supplier activities against the expected level.

What the service provides for the customer

This provides the project or program manager, along with procurement an independent view of the performance of the supplier.

Why is this service being offered to the customer?

As the PMO is independent of the project or program manager and the supplier but close to the work being performed. They can be involved as an arbitrator to review the performance of the supplier against the expected levels.

How PMO will apply this service

Having been asked to monitor the performance of a supplier the PMO will have a look at the contract to see what has been formally agreed as to what the supplier must deliver. They will review the progress reports; any milestone slippage reports; assurance reports available. Based on the background information they will perform an assessment of the supplier's performance.

If there are current issues with the supplier's performance, then the PMO need to bring that to the attention of the project or program manager. If there are potential issues that the project or program based on the supplier's performance that should be highlighted and the relevant risks raised.

Supplier	Input	Process	Output	Customer
Third-Party supplier	Contract	Monitor Supplier	Supplier Assessment	Project Manager Program Manager Procurement

How the PMO will measure the value of this service

This can be measured using feedback from the project or program manager.

Criteria when the PMO will use this service

- When the PMO is aligned to a specific project or program
- Where there are third-party suppliers
- Where an independent review of performance is requested

Helpful hints for the PMO when delivering the service

- This is not intended to catch the supplier out. Good and excellence performance should be noted as well as any poor performance
- If the supplier has been used before then that can be used as a baseline for the performance within this project or program
- The level of performance can be judged against the standard expected of internal staff
- It may be worth speaking to a few of the PPM team, including from the supplier to gain first-hand feedback on people's perception of the performance of the supplier
- If raising an issue to the project or program manager, the PMO should provide some choices as to the potential actions that can be performed to get the performance back to expected levels

PMO Capabilities needed to fulfil this service

Competencies	Techniques and generic tools
Reporting, Insights and Analysis Stakeholder Engagement Supplier Management Assurance Professionalism and ethics Relationships and engagement Conflict and Crisis	Check sheets

Related services

Support supplier liaison across portfolio, program, or project Support contracts monitoring and management	Oversee the quality review process for contractual supplier deliverables

Index

Index

5

A

B

C

D

E

K

L

M

N

O

P

Q

R

Printed in Great Britain
by Amazon

69338924R00398